PHILIPPINES

GUIDE

BE A TRAVELER - NOT A TOURIST!

OPEN ROAD TRAVEL GUIDES SHOW YOU
HOW TO BE A TRAVELER – NOT A TOURIST!

*Whether you're going abroad or planning a trip in the United States, take Open Road along on your journey. Our books have been praised by **Travel & Leisure, The Los Angeles Times, Newsday, Booklist, US News & World Report, Endless Vacation, American Bookseller, Coast to Coast,** and many other magazines and newspapers!*

Don't just see the world – experience it with Open Road!

ABOUT THE AUTHORS

Jill Gale de Villa and her daughter, Rebecca Gale de Villa, are initimately familiar with The Philippines, having made it their home for many years now. Jill is both a travel writer and a development project consultant; Rebecca is a travel writer. They are the authors of *Philippine Vacations & Explorations*. They live in Manila.

BE A TRAVELER, NOT A TOURIST - WITH OPEN ROAD TRAVEL GUIDES!

Open Road Publishing has guide books to exciting, fun destinations on four continents. As veteran travelers, our goal is to bring you the best travel guides available anywhere!

No small task, but here's what we offer:

• All Open Road travel guides are written by authors with a distinct, opinionated point of view - not some sterile committee or team of writers. Our authors are experts in the areas covered and are polished writers.

• Our guides are geared to people who want to make their own travel choices. We'll show you how to discover the real destination - not just see some place from a tour bus window.

• We're strong on the basics, but we also provide terrific choices for those looking to get off the beaten path and *experience* the country or city - not just *see* it or pass through it.

• We give you the best, but we also tell you about the worst and what to avoid. Nobody should waste their time and money on their hard-earned vacation because of bad or inadequate travel advice.

• Our guides assume nothing. We tell you everything you need to know to have the trip of a lifetime - presented in a fun, literate, no-nonsense style.

• And, above all, we welcome your input, ideas, and suggestions to help us put out the best travel guides possible.

PHILIPPINES GUIDE

GUIDE

> BE A TRAVELER - NOT A TOURIST!

JILL GALE DE VILLA
& REBECCA GALE DE VILLA

OPEN ROAD PUBLISHING

1st Edition

TABLE OF CONTENTS

CONTENTS

CONTENTS

CONTENTS

CONTENTS

CONTENTS

CONTENTS

SIDEBARS

1. INTRODUCTION

In the past, most Americans who visited the Philippines came on a World War Two nostalgia trip or to see family and friends on assignment here. Yes, indeed, the Philippines contains a treasure trove of memorabilia, but there is much more to this wonderful island nation. It is an extraordinary place with beauty, diversity, genuine tropical charm, and the warm smiles for which Filipino people are well known.

The adventure seeker can climb and camp out on a mountain or volcano, and explore tropical forests and caves. If you gravitate to the shores, you can swim, snorkel, sail, scuba dive, windsurf, surf, or kayak in the azure waters off a beach with sand almost the consistency and color of powdered sugar. And, if you enjoy driving, take a road trip through farms, over mountains, and along panoramic seaside cliffs, admiring the intense hues of the fabled sunsets this nation has to offer.

The Philippines also caters to you if you expect the ultimate relaxation and pampering found only at an exclusive beach resort, hobnobbing with the rich, famous, and infamous who come here from all over the world.

We cover a variety of destinations so that you can find the perfect vacation suited to your tastes and budget. We include well-known major highlights and lesser known fascinating finds. We also introduce you to one of the country's outstanding features: its genuinely hospitable people. And we guide you to delicious meals, both fine dining and simple yet tasty fare.

The Philippines offers you a multitude of tropical delights. *Mabuhay* – welcome, and enjoy!

2. EXCITING PHILIPPINES! - OVERVIEW

This diverse tropical nation of over 7,000 islands offers you spectacular beaches and islets fringed with fine white and pink sand and crystal clear azure waters, some world-renowned and some that are still deserted and pristine; its enchanting underwater realm teeming with colorful marine life; coral gardens where brilliant fish and other creatures make their home; wrecks that include Chinese junks, Spanish galleons, and vessels sunk during the Second World War; trips down memory lane to World War Two sights and monuments; to an old Spanish walled city and to towns with impressive colonial churches, some of which are included in UNESCO's World Heritage List; one of the Eighth Wonders of the World – the famous and awe-inspiring rice terraces, which, if linked together, could circle the world; volcanoes such as Taal, where you may hike on one of the world's smallest active volcanoes; Mayon, the near perfect cone that is as treacherous as she is beautiful; and Pinatubo, famous for recent destruction that has buried towns and vast areas of farm lands and altered the earth's sunsets for many years; and much more.

Here is a taste of what the Philippines has in store for you:

METROPOLITAN MANILA

The country's capital is an eclectic study in contrasts. You can see remnants of the old colonial past in the medieval European-style walled city of **Intramuros**, or board a hydrofoil on a short ride to **Corregidor**, the island fortified by General MacArthur's troops. In **Manila**, the affluent are chauffeured around in darkly tinted expensive cars, of the latest models, while the poor live off the streets.

In Manila, you will see modern high-rise structures, and five minutes later you will be looking at a shanty (with a television antenna on an unstable roof). Here you can shop in sprawling malls or go bargain hunting in local markets. Metropolitan Manila, incorporating 17 cities and towns, is a multifaceted city with much to explore.

EXCURSIONS FROM THE METROPOLIS

Within a three-hour drive, and even as close as an hour from Manila, are a wide range of destinations for day outings. At **Tagaytay**, you can tee off at a world-class golf course or drive down the scenic ridge where you can hike around a volcano island that sits in the crater lake of what may once have been one of the world's largest volcanoes (at an estimated 4,340 meters or 14,000 feet tall). Journey to **Taal City** or to the towns around **Laguna de Bay** where colonial churches and ancestral houses still stand.

Beach-bound people can head either to **Anilao**, a popular haven for experienced divers as well as for those who want to learn; or to the **Calatagan Peninsula** for beaches, golf, and developed resorts. If you are looking for a challenge, climb **Mount Banahaw**, **Mount Makiling**, or **Mount Arayat**, all dormant volcanoes. Or, in an ultralight, soar over the desolate lahar fields created by **Mount Pinatubo**. Visit the former US bases, which are being transformed into special economic zones with factories, resorts, and a free port.

Collect a variety of souvenirs as you venture from town to town: *balisongs*, more commonly known as butterfly knives; embroidered cloth of *piña* or *jusi*, fine local fabrics; woodcarvings and intricate wood filigree; the list goes on and on. Admire the work of national artists in **Angono**, where houses also serve as studios and galleries.

If you are around in May, *the* month for fiestas, experience the unique colorful decor and processions of **Pahiyas**, honoring San Isidro Labrador, the patron saint of several towns in Quezon Province. There is also the **Carabao Festival**, a parade of decorated carabaos (water buffalo) that on other days are used for plowing farm lands.

NORTHERN LUZON

The northern part of the country's largest island is mountainous towards the center and has a panoramic coastline dotted with beaches. Play golf, relax, or hike around **Baguio**, the summer capital of the Philippines. This city was built at the turn of the century by Americans and used as an escape from the oppressive summer heat.

Go off the beaten track spelunking around the burial caves of **Sagada**, a picturesque mountain town with several interesting limestone formations, waterfalls, and pretty views of terraces. Continue to **Banaue's** famous rice terraces, a haven for hikers, trekkers, and photographers who often return to admire the beauty created both by nature and by the toil of men.

Go island hopping in a nature reserve: the **Hundred Islands**, a national park with many islands for you to explore; go caving, snorkeling, or simply relax on a deserted islet. Drive along the western coastline, through the province of **La Union** to **Ilocos Sur**. Stop in colonial-style **Vigan** and tour the streets of ancient ancestral mansions in a kalesa (horse-drawn carriage). Continue through tobacco country to **Ilocos Norte**, passing many towns that have remarkable centuries-old Spanish churches and ruins. Spend a day or two at **Pagudpud**, on one of the world's prettiest beaches (still relatively infrequented), located at the top of Luzon.

Venture into **Cagayan**, one of the less touristed provinces. This interesting area has an assortment of historic and scenic spots, and things to do that range from hiking, swimming, and fishing to spelunking in the breathtaking **Callao Caves**.

SOUTHERN LUZON

Sorsogon, **Albay**, and **Camarines Norte and Sur** make up the mainland provinces of the Bicol Region. **Mount Mayon**, soaring to its graceful peak of 2,462 meters, possesses a near perfect conic shape, and is the region's best known attraction.

ISLANDS AROUND LUZON

Luzon is surrounded by numerous islands and islets. We cover the four larger islands that offer you spectacular scenery and activities that include hiking, diving, relaxing on a beautiful beach, visiting tribes, and more: the distinctively beautiful and unique **Batanes Islands**; the seldom traveled and charming **Catanduanes**; heartshaped **Marinduque**, known best for its special Easter-week celebrations; and popular **Mindoro**, easily accessible from Manila but still a different world of precipitous mountains, primitive tribes, and nice beaches with dive spots nearby.

PALAWAN

Frequently referred to as the Philippines' last frontier, the flora and fauna you will find in this island group are more related to that of Borneo than to that of the rest of the Philippines. **Palawan** possesses numerous beautiful islands, with facilities that range from very simple and inexpensive cottages fronting a nice beach to the exclusive, luxurious hideaway of **Amanpulo**. Also an adventurer's paradise, there are many things to do, from hiking or island hopping on kayaks to cruising down a scenic eight-kilometer underground river, or diving into the deeps of fabled **Tubbataha Reef**, one of the best dive spots in the world.

VISAYAS

The numerous islands that make up this middle region are sandwiched between the Philippines' two largest islands. Here you will find the famous **Boracay**, stroll along its extensive beach with sand granules as fine and white as icing sugar, swim in the aquamarine waters, and partake of the tropical nightlife many travelers enjoy.

In **Iloilo**, enjoy the relaxed pace, clean and gracious city, delectable seafood, imposing churches and ancestral homes, and beach resorts on the nearby islands of **Guimaras**, an area also known for its prolific mango trees. **Bacolod** offers a variety of activities, from golfing and gambling to visiting the new wildlife sanctuary of **Danjugan Island**. Select from various tours: a five-day locomotive tour, a four-day climb up **Mount Canlaon**, a three-day island hopping tour, an eight-hour sugarmill and city tour, or a World War Two memorial tour. Visit **Dumaguete**, a lovely college town where you can snorkel, dive, dolphin and bird watch, and hike.

Spend days on **Cebu**, the center of Visayan activities. **Cebu City** is the Philippines' second busiest metropolis, and is popular for its hotels and nearby beach resorts that range from basic places catering to divers to exclusive high-end destinations. This is where the conquistador Magellan ended his circumnavigation of the globe when he was killed by the native chief, Lapu-Lapu. There are many fine sights here, from ancient churches to Chinese temples, from museums of religious and historical artifacts to one of butterfly wing mosaics.

Marvel at the **Chocolate Hills, Bohol's** best publicized asset. The island's other attractions include its cream sand beaches, reefs for diving, quaint towns, old churches, a river safari, and friendly people. They will entice you to linger.

In **Leyte** and **Samar** in the Eastern Visayas, World War Two enthusiasts will enjoy nostalgia trips. In **Tacloban**, capital of Leyte, General Douglas MacArthur fulfilled his famous promise – "I shall return." Aside from war monuments, this region also has several national parks, including one where you can cruise on a river and investigate caves with numerous chambers and interesting formations. The two provinces also offer a number of less frequented islands where you can relax in seclusion.

MINDANAO

The Philippines' second largest island is a meeting place of people from many cultural backgrounds. An adventurer's paradise, it is home to **Mount Apo**, at 2,945 meters, the tallest mountain in the country; spectacular beaches – do you prefer your sand the consistency and color of sugar? or how about a shade of pink? – exotic fruits and a variety of wildlife, on land and under water; warm smiles; and much more.

At industry-oriented **Cagayan de Oro**, where the downtown area bustles with shoppers and traffic, the harbor is filled with shipping activity. A few industries hug the coastline. Much of the surrounding area consists of grassed flatlands and forested canyons. Here you can wander around **Macahambus Cave and Gorge**, **Huluga Cave**, and **Catanico Falls**. Venture upland, just into **Bukidnon**, to the vast Del Monte plantation, or go off the beaten track on a canopy walk. Adventurous visitors will enjoy days exploring **Camiguin's** dormant volcanoes, pretty waterfalls, and springs. Or relax on its pretty crescent-shaped white sandbar.

Imagine yourself on fine white sand beaches that are among the best in the world, in breathtaking caves with limestone formations and lagoons; amid lush mangrove and tropical forests teeming with a variety of wildlife. These delights await you at one of the country's best kept secrets: **Siargao** – the powerful waves of its Cloud Nine are infamous in the international surfing community.

Pretty islands, fruit and souvenir markets, museums, shrines, plantations, an array of palate-pleasing cuisines, and friendly people can all be found in one city: **Davao** –the prettiest southern metropolis. Attractions range from islands in the bay to markets, museums, religious shrines, orchid and fruit plantations, golf and mountain climbing.

At **General Santos City**, the deep-sea fishing capital of the Philippines, you can feast on grilled fresh tuna and blue marlin. Visit the tribal areas to see the artistically rich cultural tradition of the reclusive and gentle **T'Boli**.

And last, but not least, we take you to **Zamboanga**, for superb beaches (one with pink sand), good diving, bazaar-like markets, weavers, antiques, and then to the southernmost islands of the country, including a town literally in the sea, as it was built over a reef.

PRICES IN US DOLLARS

In this book, prices are given in US dollars

3. SUGGESTED ITINERARIES

We provide five sample itineraries. The first is a Manila tour, and assumes that you will arrive in the Philippines through Manila. The day tours and rice terraces itineraries are "add-ons" to the first. If you intend to skip Manila, add the first and last day of that tour to your preferred itinerary, as you need at least a one-day stay in Manila at either end. It is safer to allow two days, because domestic flights are often canceled or delayed.

The fourth itinerary takes you to the Philippines' most popular beach destination. After reading beach sections of this book, you can construct similar itineraries for other beach destinations.

The last itinerary takes you to Mindanao, the Philippines' second largest island. The tour starts you off in Davao, which frequently receives tourists; then takes you to General Santos, which receives fewer tourists; continues to a remote area for a cultural experience with a hill tribe; returns to Davao for pampering at a top resort; and finishes in Cebu, in the central Philippines.

MANILA HIGHLIGHTS TOUR (4 DAYS)
Day 1

Arrive in Manila.

Check into the hotel of your choice: we especially recommend Pension Natividad (budget), Garden Plaza (moderate), and the Mandarin or Shangri-La (very expensive). Reservations are recommended at all hotels.

If you are billeted at Pension Natividad, walk over to Cosa Nostra for great home-style Italian cooking and wonderful ambiance, or Wok Inn for inexpensive Chinese fare. If you are at the Garden Plaza, try their Filipino or Swiss restaurant. And, if you are not jet lagged, get a taste of Malate's nightlife at one of the bars along Remedios or J Nakpil Streets.

If you have opted for top-end accommodation and are staying at the Mandarin, have a light dinner in the Cake Shop or a complete meal at the

Tivoli, followed by a drink at the Captain's Bar for good live music. If you've chosen Shangri-La, enjoy the variety of Asian fare its restaurants offer, then, if you still have energy, cap your evening at Zu or Conways (both in the hotel).

Day 2

Breakfast – try the fresh fruits that are in season. If you like a heavier meal, try the Filipino breakfast – fried rice, eggs, and *tapa* (meat) or *daing* (marinated milk fish) or *longanisa* (local sausage).

Morning: taxi to Nayong Pilipino, near the airport, for a walk (or a *calesa* or jeepney ride) around areas that represent the architecture of various regions of the Philippines. Buffet lunch (lots of Filipino food to chose from) at Nayong's restaurant.

Afternoon: taxi to Makati's shopping center. Visit Ayala Museum and walk through the dioramas depicting Philippine history – for insights into the way the country has evolved. Then taxi to the American Cemetery, a beautifully peaceful place where, amid trees, over 17,000 of the allied forces who died in the Pacific theater of World War Two are buried. The central memorial has mosaics of some of the important battles. Sit beneath the trees and meditate on the past and present. Visit Tesoro or Balikbayan for an introduction to the handicrafts the country has to offer.

In the evening, dine on good Filipino food at Nandau's – great blue marlin steak "a la pobre" (with garlic).

Day 3

Breakfast (see day 2).

Morning (for history buffs, this could be a full day): tour Intramuros (by foot or *calesa*). Take a taxi to Intramuros, and start at Fort Santiago, then move around the walls. Take a breather from the noon heat and enjoy a tasty meal at Café Ilustrado (do try the refreshing *sampaguita* [jasmine] ice cream for dessert).

Afternoon: Browse around El Amanecer's very good collection of souvenirs from all over the Philippines – reasonably priced. Taxi to Malacañang Palace, the seat of the Philippine Presidency. Tour parts of Malacañang that are now maintained as a museum.

Evening: End the day with (for up-market dining) a seafood dinner at the Manila Hotel's Cowrie Cove (the scallops are superb), or have a casual and inexpensive meal at Harbor View. If you arrive at the Manila Hotel early, and if the MacArthur Suite is not booked, take a look at what was once the General's residence – ask for permission at the guest relations desk.

Day 4
Depart Manila.

TOP SPOTS NEAR MANILA (FOUR OPTIONS)

Note: the Corregidor and Villa Escudero tours may require reservations.

Day 1: Corregidor

(book in advance; recheck departure time)

Arrive at the Cultural Center Complex before 8:00am for the boat to **Corregidor**. This World War Two memorabilia tour includes lunch. You return to Manila around 5:00pm. Head over to the nearby Philippine Plaza (a five-minute walk west, then south along the bay will get you to this hotel) for a fruit shake (with or without alcohol) and enjoy one of Manila Bay's fabled sunsets. Follow this with dinner in the walled city, Intramuros, at Ilustrado (order the Duck Ilustrado, it is not on the menu but is delicious).

Day 2: Pagsanjan

(book a standard tour through your hotel, or arrange to hire a car or taxi)

Note: Pagsanjan is not advisable during the rainy season (June through November or December).

Pack a change of clothes, a swim suit, and a plastic bag to protect anything you don't want to get wet. Depart early in the morning by bus, hire car, or taxi for Pagsanjan, Laguna. Go straight to the Pagsanjan Rapids Hotel, enjoying the countryside along the way. Take the river trip (be sure to have a life preserver if you don't swim). Enjoy lunch at the hotel (they have a good buffet) before heading back to Manila.

If you are doing this trip by hired car or taxi, you could stop on the way back to see the rice museum at the International Rice Research Institute in Los Baños (prior arrangements preferred).

Dinner at the Chinese restaurant Hua Ting in the Heritage Hotel, and if you enjoy gambling, you may hit the casino after.

Day 3: Volcano

Pack 2-3 liters of water and, if you're a hiker, include lunch (enough for you and a guide) and a swim suit. Depart very early by hired car or taxi for Tanauan, Batangas. Turn right at the main intersection in Tanauan, and continue through Talisay to *barangay* Leynes. Stop at Mrs. de Castro's and ask her to arrange a *banca* and guide. Cross to Volcano Island and hike up to overlook the new crater (about 20 minutes).

If you're a hiker, continue to the interior lake (1 to 1.5 hours) for a picnic lunch and swim. Return for an afternoon lunch of lake fish at Mrs.

de Castro's. Take the road up to Tagaytay for views of the lake, and possibly sunset at Taal Vista Lodge before returning to Manila.

If you're not a hiker, return to Mrs. de Castro's for a lunch of lake fish. Then continue to the Tagaytay Ridge for views of Taal Lake and volcano.

Continue to historic Taal town, and tour the market (embroideries), church, and nearby museums. Return to Manila via Lipa.

Casual dinner and good Indian cuisine at Kohinoor.

Day 4: Villa Escudero
Note: Reservations advisable.

Depart by hired car or taxi for a day at a functioning coconut plantation-cum-resort. Lunch is included in the tour.

Dinner at the Seafood Market – select your meal and how you prefer it cooked.

RICE TERRACES TOUR
(8 days, adjustable to 6 days if the 2-day trek is omitted)
Day 1
Have a very early breakfast then catch the bus or take a hired car to Banaue. If you have hired a vehicle, stop for a snack at Marquez Restaurant in San José, Nueva Ecija, and try the *puto*, a sweet rice-cake.

Arrive in Banaue and check into Spring Village Inn or Banaue View Inn.

Head over to Viewpoint, for photos of the terraces and, for a small fee, snaps of some older Ifugaos donning traditional garb. Return to the town center to Coolwinds for a drink and to make arrangements for guides and transport for the rest of your visit (ask the restaurant's owner, Percy, to send for her brother, Hygie); then have dinner at Las Vegas.

Day 2
Breakfast at Coolwinds (we recommend the omelets and garlic fried rice).

Morning: hike up through Bocus Village, across a bridge beside some waterfalls, and down through Matang-lag to see the bronze smiths.

Lunch at People's.

Afternoon: hike through Poitan (see the sacred stone) and across the terraces to Tam-an (weavers).

Dinner at Halfway or Stairway

Day 4 (start of a 2-day trek)
Breakfast at Coolwinds. Take a jeep to the Batad trailhead, then trek to the village. Along the way, photograph the amphitheater-shaped

terraces. Check into Simon's or Hillside. If time permits, carefully clamber down to the waterfall below the village for a refreshing swim. Have an early sunset dinner, take more photos. You will probably be tired and may want to sleep after an early dinner, especially if there's no folk singing to enjoy.

Day 5

If you are a photo buff, you may want to wake up early to get sunrise photos of the terraces and village.

After breakfast, head back to Banaue via Banga-an. Lunch at Family Inn above Banga-an, then take a side trip down to the village if you still have the energy.

Back in Banaue town, check out the shops for items to add to your collection of handicrafts. Dinner at Hidden Valley, just uphill from the driveway to the Banaue Hotel. If the Banaue Hotel has an evening cultural show scheduled, treat yourself to it.

Day 6

Grab some freshly baked sweet-breads at People's Bakery. Take the 7:00am jeepney to Sagada (leaves when full), or hire a jeep. Check in at one of the inns. Browse through Ganduyan Museum if it is open, and lunch at Shamrock.

Head over to the Log Cabin to order your dinner. In between, treat yourself to one of the two following activities:

• Walk through the church area and the cemetery to Echo Valley to admire the limestone formations (and your echo) and see hanging coffins. Make your way down into the valley, and come out on the road to Ambasing. Continue along this road until you come to the school. Turn right here to walk through the farmer's gardens (a guide is really helpful), and back to the road to town.

• Walk along the road to Bontoc, past the turn-off to Banga-an and the driveway to Mapiyaaw Pension. Take the next road left, and follow it (keeping straight at the x-junction) to the Kiltepan tower for a spectacular view of the terraced valley below and the mountains beyond. En-route back to town, stop in at the Sagada Weavers for the popular and useful backpacks and other attractive items.

Note: for serious caving, add 1 day.

Day 7

Take an early jeep to Bontoc.

Walk up to the Bontoc Museum to see its very good exhibits and photographs of mountain life, plus several traditional houses that are furnished with implements used in the traditional lifestyle. Have lunch in one of the small bakeries along the main road, or at the Pines Kitchenette. Take a mid-afternoon jeep to Banaue.

Browse through the Bayer Museum in the Banaue View Inn.

Early dinner at Coolwinds or Las Vegas.

Day 8

Take the bus to Manila, arriving at about 5:00pm.

Have dinner at Sakura for a scrumptious meal of *yakiniku* (thinly sliced and marinated pieces of prime rib that you grill at your table). Head over to Ciao for good dessert, drinks, and a live band, or Venezia to rub elbows with "high-society" types, then on to Giraffe for the after-midnight-crowd and Zu for dancing.

BORACAY

(4 days)
Day 1

Breakfast, then head off to the domestic airport area to catch your flight to Caticlan. Keep in mind that if you are taking AirAds or Pacific Air, the terminals are separate from the main domestic terminal.

Arrive at Caticlan, where you will be met by an agent who escorts you to some form of transport (usually an air conditioned coaster) that takes you to the "dock" where you board a *banca* for the short ride to Boracay Island.

Clamber off the boat and squeeze yourself and your luggage (hopefully you did not bring too much) into a tricycle. The first several minutes of the ride are on an unpaved road (hence bouncy). There is a portion where you may have to walk up a hill if the road is slippery and in bad condition, then reboard the tricycle at the top.

Check into Friday's or a suite room (not the regular rooms) of Pearl of the Pacific 2 (expensive); Willy's Place or Sandcastles (moderate); or VIP Lingau or Nigi-Nigi Nu-Noos (budget). Reservations are recommended at all resorts.

Change into beach clothes and have lunch at the place you are billeted. Take a few minutes to admire the fabled powder fine white sand beach.

Walk down towards the tourist information center. Make sure you have a big beach towel with you; if not, stop in any of the and purchase a beach mat, blanket, or towel.

When you see a woman in a green vest with "massage" on the back, ask her for a massage, and don't forget to bargain (in 1997, the standard price for 30 minutes was $8-10). The massage should feel great after your trip over here.

Get a map at the tourist center or in the Boracay Shopping Center, where you can buy sunblock, film, and other necessities.

Head over to Willy's Place for a terrific fresh fruit shake, before or after a refreshing dip in crystal clear waters off White Beach.

Treat yourself to dinner at Titay's Theater Garden for good seafood and local dishes and sometimes an evening cultural show.

If you enjoy the party scene – Moondogs is the place to be in the evenings.

Day 2

After breakfast, head to the tourist center where several places nearby and along the way rent bicycles and/or motorcycles. Book either for the afternoon.

If you do not have snorkeling gear, rent it from one of the dive operators recommended in the Boracay section of the PANAY chapter. If you are a diver, arrange for a dive at one of the dive centers and enjoy the pretty underwater tapestry of coral and other colorful marine life. If you do not dive, rent a *banca* and go to Lapuz-Lapuz or other snorkeling points.

In the afternoon, bike (motor or peddle) around the island to see the sights and other pretty (and much less crowded) beaches.

Return the rented bike and browse through the Talipapa Flea Market for handicrafts and postcards.

Head along the beach over to Diniwid and climb up several steps for a sundowner and great views at the cliffside Sundance.

Dinner at Severo de Boracay – great Italian food.

If you are a "creature of the night," go bar hopping.

Day 3

After breakfast, head over to Green Yard Seasport Center or Richie's Mistral for an hour of windsurfing (and lessons if needed). Or, check if there are any sea-kayak trips scheduled.

As this is your last day here, spend the afternoon at your leisure.

Late afternoon fruit shake at Willy's.

Have an excellent dinner at Friday's; don't forget to top off your meal with the delicious *leche flan* (caramel custard).

Day 4

Breakfast and last minute shopping at the flea market and other stores. Perhaps a last massage on the beach.

Early lunch.

Tricycle then *banca* back to Caticlan and bus to the airstrip where you board your flight back to Manila.

Arrive in Manila in the latter part of the afternoon.

Dinner at Nandau for the excellent blue marlin steak "a la pobre" (with garlic).

DAVAO-GENSAN (GENERAL SANTOS) ADVENTURE

(10 days)

Day 1

Depart Manila for Cebu.

Check in at (i) the luxurious Shangri-La and be pampered for the rest of the day, and enjoy a delectable grilled seafood dinner at the Poolside Grill; (ii) for less-expensive but first-rate service and rooms – the Cebu Plaza, with its great views and service, and you can feast on fresh seafood at the Lantaw; or (iii) for budget lodging, the Kukuk's Nest. Reservations are recommended at all hotels.

Day 2

After a great breakfast, including fresh fruit – order mangoes if they are in season. Depart for Davao by air (take the 10:40 Cebu Pacific flight, or forgo breakfast and take Philippine Airlines' early morning flight).

Check in at Insular Century (expensive), Casa Leticia (moderate, and one of our favorites),or Elle's Pension (budget). Reservations are recommended at all hotels.

Take a taxi to the Magsaysay Park, or, walk – stop by the Madrazo fruit market for a snack to tide you over. If you are staying at Casa Leticia or Elle's and want to walk, head down J Camus to E Quirino Avenue, where you turn right and continue to Ramon Magsaysay Avenue. Turn right to Magsaysay Park. This walk should take 30 minutes.

Enjoy lunch either at Luz Kinilaw, just down Quezon Boulevard from the park, or at Kanaway, beside the park, for a taste of the wonderful local cuisine. At Luz Kinilaw, order *kinilaw* (tuna sashimi marinated in vinegar and spices), and the barbeque *bariles pangga* (tuna jaw) and *pusit* (squid). Kanaway offers the same delicacies and is known for its great *lechon kawali* (roast pig, sliced and served with a special sauce).

After feasting on native food, stop by the DOT office in the Magsaysay Park for free maps, brochures, and information. The office is staffed with helpful people – ask for Frank Villaraiz.

Walk (or taxi) to Jones Circle (along Ramon Magsaysay Avenue), and venture through the stores of the Aldevinco shopping center. Remember to bargain for the wonderful fabrics and other handicrafts from Mindanao, Indonesia, and Malaysia.

Rest for a couple of hours at your lodging, then head to Claude's for an excellent French meal – the chicken in red wine is superb.

In the evening, have your hotel arrange for a rental car for the next day.

Day 3

This adventure could be done by public transport, but is much easier if you have a hired vehicle.

Breakfast at the Top of the Apo in the Apo Hotel, for the great view of the city and Mount Apo.

Head off to the Philippine Eagle Nature Center, in Malagos, to see the endangered and largest eagle in the world, and other Philippine birds.

Lunch at the Malagos Garden Resort nearby. Stick to Philippine food. Browse through the huge, manicured orchard.

Head back to the city and, if you are interested in seeing more orchids, a cave used by the Japanese during World War Two, and a large cement sculpture of a *carabao* (water buffalo) relieving itself, stop by the Gap Farm Resort along the way.

Tour the Dabaw Museum, in Insular Village 1, then walk through the grounds of the Davao Century Insular Hotel to Dabaw Etnica to admire final products (bags, table runners, pillow cases, etc.) of the *dagmay* fabric as you watch Mandaya women preparing various stages of the attractive fabric.

Have dinner at Harana 1 & 2 or Sarungbangi, then a nightcap at Toto's, on the top floor of Casa Leticia.

Day 4

Breakfast buffet at the coffee shop of Casa Leticia or the Insular.

Take the morning bus or flight to General Santos City.

Check in at a hotel (try Sydney or Anchor 2).

After lunch, head to Gumasa, Glan, in Sarangani. If you dive, make arrangements with Mike or Steve Kingery of the Sarangani Divers. Rent a jeepney (ask assistance from your hotel or the City Tourism Office) for a round trip, or risk the infrequent schedules of public transport.

Spend a relaxing afternoon strolling on the extremely fine white sand of the neighboring coves of Gumasa.

Note: call Sarangani Divers or the City Tourism Office in advance, the telephone numbers are given in the *Southern Mindanao: Gensan* chapter.

Dinner at Lola Sisay's or Fiesta Sa Barrio. You *must* order the very fresh blue marlin or (and) tuna steaks – barbequed – or tuna sashimi.

Day 5

Head off to Lake Sebu. If you chose not to rent a vehicle for two days, then take an early bus to Koronadal (Marbel) then a jeepney to Lake Sebu.

While waiting for the jeepney departure, have a tasty fruit shake at the Breeze Restaurant in Marbel.

At Lake Sebu, check in at Estares.

Cruise the lake on a *banca* and take numerous photographs.

Back at Estares, enjoy a fresh dinner of lake fish at one of the tables in a nipa hut over the lake.

Day 6

Breakfast, and arrange for a guide and a packed lunch for yourself and the guide, for the hike to "Hikong Bente" or the Second Falls.

Picnic lunch.

In the afternoon, explore the hauntingly beautiful buildings, sadly, all that remains of the Sta Cruz Mission.

Hike to a nearby T'Boli village and be treated to their music.

Dinner back at Estares.

Day 7

Return to GenSan, and catch a flight or bus to Davao.

At the Davao Century Insular, you will be met by a guest relations officer who will then escort you to the Pearl Farm (very expensive). Reservations are recommended.

Settle into your well-appointed room.

Sundowners (drinks) in the Parola Bar, followed by a scrumptious dinner.

Day 8

Breakfast, lunch, dinner at your leisure.

If you dive, make arrangements at the dive center.

Relax by the beautiful pool, or on one of the natural beaches of nearby Talicud.

Day 9

Depart Pearl Farm; catch a flight to Cebu.

Visit Fort San Pedro, Magellan's Cross, the Basilica, and Casa Gorordo.

Sundowner at the Cebu Plaza.

If you want a casual setting: have a hearty dinner and good wine and company at the Kukuk's Nest.

If you enjoy gambling, check out the floating casino at the Delta Philippine Dream or the casinos at the Waterfront Hotel adjacent to the airport.

Day 10

Depart Cebu.

4. LAND & PEOPLE

THE LAND

The Philippines is located in Southeast Asia, with the Pacific Ocean to its east and the South China Sea on its west. The total land area is 299,404 square kilometers (slightly larger than the state of Arizona). It extends 1,850 kilometers north to south, and 1,100 kilometers east to west. Although there are officially 7,107 islands, only 2,000 are inhabited.

The islands were formed by faulting and folding along major fault lines and by volcanic processes. The country has several major volcanoes, and some of them are important attractions.

Mount Apo, a dormant volcano south of Davao City in Mindanao, is the country's tallest mountain, at 2,945 meters. **Mount Pulog**, the country's second highest peak (located in Northern Luzon), is just a few meters shorter and was formed through crustal uplift.

Philippine highlands are of fairly recent formation, and tend to be precipitous. Much of the forest that once carpeted the land has been logged, with farms taking over arable land even on steep slopes.

The mountains have also played an important part in Filipino history. Being more difficult to penetrate, they have served as a shelter for tribes pushed back by waves of immigration; for revolutionaries against the Spanish, American, and Japanese colonizers; and (in the more recent past) for communist and other insurgents.

Much of the valleys and lowlands are dotted with farms that grow coconuts, rice, sugar, corn, vegetables, fruits, tobacco, and a wide variety of livestock. Although you will see a lot of rice fields during your travels, there are times when rice has to be imported, as the amount produced locally is not enough to support the rapidly growing (over) population. Little swampland remains in the country, as most wetlands have been converted to prawn and fish ponds.

The Philippine shores and offshore reefs, when not damaged, are the breeding grounds for an incredible wealth of marine life that helps to feed a large portion of the population and delight both the scuba diver and the gourmet. Coastal areas are usually fringed with coconut trees.

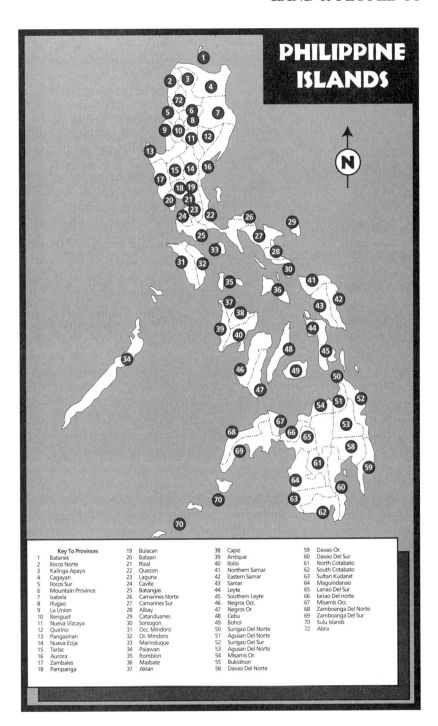

PHILIPPINE ISLANDS

Key To Provinces			
	19 Bulacan	38 Capiz	59 Davao Or.
1 Batanes	20 Bataan	39 Antique	60 Davao Del Sur
2 Ilocos Norte	21 Rizal	40 Iloilo	61 North Cotabato
3 Kalinga Apayo	22 Quezon	41 Northern Samar	62 South Cotabato
4 Cagayan	23 Laguna	42 Eastern Samar	63 Sultan Kudarat
5 Ilocos Sur	24 Cavite	43 Samar	64 Maguindanao
6 Mountain Province	25 Batangas	44 Leyte	65 Lanao Del Sur
7 Isabela	26 Camarines Norte	45 Southern Leyte	66 Ianao Del norte
8 Ifugao	27 Camarines Sur	46 Negros Occ.	67 Misamis Occ.
9 La Union	28 Albay	47 Negros Or.	68 Zamboanga Del Norte
10 Benguet	29 Catanduanes	48 Cebu	69 Zamboanga Del Sur
11 Nueva Vizcaya	30 Sorsogon	49 Bohol	70 Sulu Islands
12 Quirino	31 Occ. Mindoro	50 Surigao Del Norte	72 Abra
13 Pangasinan	32 Or. Mindoro	51 Agusan Del Norte	
14 Nueva Ecija	33 Marinduque	52 Surigao Del Sur	
15 Tarlac	34 Palawan	53 Agusan Del Norte	
16 Aurora	35 Romblon	54 Misamis Or.	
17 Zambales	36 Masbate	55 Bukidnon	
18 Pampanga	37 Aklan	58 Davao Del Norte	

Architecture

Much of the center of the country, from Luzon through the Visayas, has modest houses of nipa, bamboo, and cogon grass, often with tin roofing; wealthier people live in houses of brick, wood, and more durable materials. Around most of the country, impressive, imposing churches with their *conventos* are durable signs of the Spanish influence.

In the far northern Batanes, people combat six months of strong winds by building houses with meter-thick stone walls. And in Mindanao, the graceful spires of mosques pierce through the skylines of the Muslim villages, where some houses have steep, curved roofs reminiscent of the famed Moro *vinta*.

Flora & Fauna

Coconut trees are almost everywhere, constant reminders that you are in the tropics. Unquestionably the Philippines' most important tree, it has many uses: coconut milk to drink, meat to eat, wine to imbibe, heart of coconut for salad and *lumpia* (egg roll), coconut oil for tanning and cooking, and cocowood for building.

Other plants used for building and furniture include nipa palms, (important for roofing); rattan (for furniture); mahogany (for building and carving); bamboo (for housing and furniture); and the now scarce beautiful narra (for building and furniture).

Mountains and lowlands that are not farmed often have a thick covering of cogon — a tough grass with razor sharp edges. Many flowering plants, including *sampaguita* (jasmine), *gumamela* (hibiscus), bougainvillea, *kalachuchi* (frangipani), water lilies, and water hyacinth enhance the beauty of rural Philippines. Wild orchids grow in mountainside rain forests, especially in Mindanao. The land also produces a bounty of delicious fruits.

And there is a variety of fauna, too. Each September, migratory birds stop over on their way south from a chilling China. The Philippines is home to several indigenous birds and animals: the tamaraw (a small water buffalo-like animal), sea turtles, mouse deer, tarsiers, and the Philippine eagle to name a few. Sadly, most of these animals face extinction. Their habitats are being rapidly destroyed, primarily because of pressure from the incessantly over-expanding human population.

The strong domesticated *carabao* (water buffalo) is widely used in farms — as a form of transport and for tilling the soil. The *carabao* have no sweat glands and they cannot work in intense heat. In areas where it is too hot for *carabao*, farmers use *zebu* (Brahma cattle). In many places you will see ponies providing transportation.

THE FILIPINO PEOPLE

The Philippines' most outstanding feature is its people. Filipinos are Asian of Malay-Polynesian origin, with mixtures of Chinese, Spanish, American, Japanese, Arab, Indian, Portuguese, English, French, and many other nationalities whose peoples have found their way here, been welcomed, and stayed to add to the richly diverse cultures they found. The mixture has worked well — Filipinos in general are very attractive people.

Before the Spaniards arrived, the Filipinos divided themselves into approximately three classes: the upper, ruling class; the middle class, which owed some allegiance to the upper class; and the serfs or slaves, who were to varying degrees owned by the ruling class. (There were regional variations on this theme.) The upper class had duties and responsibilities to the lower classes, and unpopular rulers might be abandoned by their followers.

The Spanish installed themselves and their emissaries on the top rung. They prohibited some forms of abuse of the lower classes, but their rule widened the distances between the classes and removed the social responsibility the upper level had once had for the lower ones.

The Americans attempted to introduce democratic institutions and expanded educational opportunities while still trying to maintain control, hence perpetuating the gulf between the rich and poor. The lowland Filipino was unavoidably altered by the colonial experience. He developed a sense that, because he was ruled by outsiders, his fate was not his own. Thus, the post-American attempt at democracy easily gave way to dictatorship.

The "**People Power**" revolution of February 1986 began to change the feeling of impotence. Millions of unarmed citizens took to the streets and used Filipino behavioral principles to stop armed soldiers and tanks. With almost no violence, they rejected the increasingly unpopular Marcos regime and brought in a new one led by Cory Aquino, the wife of a popular opposition figure who was slain upon returning to the Philippines. Nuns knelt in front of tanks, which ground to a halt, as people offered food and flowers to the soldiers. The revolution was won peacefully. The world was amazed. So were the Filipinos, who began to regain the pride buried for so long under domination.

Filipino Culture

Make an effort to understand Filipino culture and you will find your stay greatly enriched. Filipinos genuinely want visitors to have a good time. Most of them are pleased to pose for photographs — you may find it difficult to take candid shots. Visitors who learn to understand the people are seldom disappointed.

Filipinos may be the world's most hospitable people. Guests are honored, their idiosyncrasies tolerated even when found offensive – but this should not be used as an excuse for inconsiderate behavior. If you arrive around mealtime, you will always be asked to stay and share the repast, no matter how meager. Even a beggar will offer you a bite of his food before he starts to eat. Hence you should not arrive uninvited at mealtimes. When an invitation is offered, you should tactfully decline a couple of times before accepting—only when the offer is repeated can you be sure it was genuinely intended.

Filipinos have a refined sense of *delicadeza* – a sensitivity to the feelings of others. Individualism is not valued highly. They prefer getting along: the group will is all important. It is not nice to "rock the boat," and Filipinos avoid direct confrontations. They often deliver negative messages through a third party. Efforts are made to keep communications smooth and courteous.

Consequently, if you ask a question, you may be told "yes" or "maybe" when in fact the correct answer should have been "no." If you are observant, you can tell the difference between a genuine "yes," which is offered unreservedly, and a "yes" that essentially means "no," and is offered with averted eyes and lack of enthusiasm. If you are unsure, repeat the same question, or ask a similar one, or ask if the particular request is a difficult one. Should the answer then be, "Yes, it is difficult," you know the response intended is "no."

The giving and receiving of favors comprise part of a network of debts of gratitude – *utang na loob* – which is at the heart of most relationships. A favor given is to be reciprocated.

Roots

Filipinos are divided into many ethnic groups: **Ilocanos** are the frugal, hard-working people of Northern Luzon's coasts and valleys; **Tagalogs** are pragmatic people from the middle of Luzon; **Bicolanos** are from southern Luzon; **Visayans** are refined folk from the central islands.

All are subdivided into smaller groups. Many have emigrated to and mingled in other islands. These major groups may be descendants of later immigrants who displaced original peoples that are now known as tribal minorities. The tribal groups, hidden in the interiors of some of the larger islands, escaped the impact of colonialism, but recently have been affected by the in-migration of lowland Filipinos.

Attitudes of most Filipinos towards their tribal minorities range from abusive to benign neglect to microscopic inspection. Often looked down upon by the lowlanders as inferior beings, some minority people have adapted and become assimilated. Others remain true to the tribe, clan, custom, and law of their forebears.

The minority groups produce superb handicrafts, both useful and beautiful. Interpretations of their crafts (especially basketry and weaving) are exported. Individual pieces are prized as collectors' items. The remoteness of their communities, the exotic appeal of their spirit, and the uniqueness of their culture are an enticement to many travelers.

Cordilleran Tribes

Ethnic groups of Luzon's central mountains include the **Bontok, Ibaloi, Ifugao, Gaddang, Kalinga, Kankana-ey** and **Tinguian**. These groups have a highly developed agricultural economy. Being animists, they have numerous rites pertaining to their crops. They also created extensive terracing in which they grow crops, and maintain a fierce independence. Superb utilitarian baskets and excellent woven products are among the crafts in which they excel.

In the past, these tribes had a community in which married couples and young children lived together in a one-room abode, and older children had to move to separate housing for males and females until they were married.

These tribes were not as quiescent as lowland peoples, and in the past practiced headhunting to settle disputes between groups. The missionaries and "liberators" found this practice most appalling, yet the colonizers themselves practiced horrific methods of torture during Christianization and the Second World War.

Mangyan

The Mangyan, the term used to describe descendants of Mindoro's original inhabitants, consist of several groups: **Alangan, Buid, Iraya, Hanunoo, Tagaydan** and **Tatagnon**. Highly literate, they inscribe script on bamboo, telling of ancestral songs and poems known as *Ambahan*, which stretch back hundreds of years. They compose and play music on the *git-git*, a small violin-like instrument with strings made of human hair. They weave sturdy cloth from nito, bamboo, buri, and other forest plants.

Once a friendly people, many Mangyan, fearing persecution by lowlanders, now disappear when they see strangers. It was the immigrant lowlanders who pushed them back, away from their original lands. In an effort to help the tribes retain some ancestral lands, the government has set aside limited reservation areas.

Tribes of Mindanao

Non-Muslim tribes inhabit the mountainous areas. The **Bukidnon** (people of the forest) of eastern Lanao are known to be fierce and independent. In the highlands of Bukidnon and Agusan are the **Manobo**, a tribe respected for their prowess as warriors and for their rich artistic tradition. The **Mandaya** of Davao Oriental are famous for their colorful abaca fiber weaves embroidered with tribal designs, and are also respected for their silvercraft and for being highly musical. The **Bagobos**, of Mount Apo's foothills, are considered to have the most stunning costumes of all the tribes in Davao; their traditional costume is of woven abaca heavily adorned with beads, shells, metals, and bright embroidery.

The **T'Boli** and the **Tiruray** are found in the area known as the Tiruray Highlands of Sarangani and South Cotobato. The T'Boli are a reclusive and gentle people of an artistically rich cultural tradition that dates back more than 2,000 years. They weave beautiful T'Nalak cloth, forge attractive brass-bronze ware, and compose hauntingly serene music. The **Subanon** were among the earliest settlers of Zamboanga and live in small family farming units.

The Muslims of the south are considered the largest cultural minority. Some seek autonomy for Mindanao, which is now predominantly Christian. The largest ethnic group of Zamboanga are the **Tausug**, who tend to be more aggressive and wealthier than the others. The **Sama** (also called Samal) inhabit the coastal regions of Zamboanga, Jolo, and Tawi-Tawi. A generally peaceful people, they tend to live in dense settlements of houses on stilts or in houseboats. Their livelihood is based on fishing and diving for pearls and shells. The **Badjao** are sea nomads. Many live in houseboats and come to shore only to be buried.

The **Yakan**, found in the uplands of Basilan, are master weavers and farmers. Although the Yakan are predominantly Muslim, there is a small settlement of Christian Yakan living on the outskirts of Zamboanga City. Inhabiting the area around Lake Lanao in Lanao del Sur are the **Maranaw**, known for being skilled artisans and traders. This tribe, the last to convert to Islam, was successful at resisting both Spanish and American attempts of colonizing. The **Maguindanao** are culturally similar to the Maranao, and make up 60% of the people of Maguindanao Province. They specialize in brass making, mat weaving, and making *malong* (a tube of material used as clothing).

Negritoes

The Negritoes, also called **Aeta**, **Ati**, **Eta**, **Ito** and **Batak**, live in small groups in remote areas throughout the Philippines. Sometimes timid, they are distinguished by short stature, dark skin, and kinky hair. Masters of life in tropical rain forests, when the Americans still had military bases in the Philippines, some Negritoes were regularly employed teaching US army soldiers how to survive in the jungle. Considered the original owners of at least one island, they are the object of the Philippines' most famous festival, the **Ati-atihan**.

LANGUAGE

Most Filipinos are multilingual, speaking at least the national language (**Filipino** or **Tagalog**) and their own regional dialect (of which there are a profusion). Many also speak some **Spanish** and a version of **American-English**. In some areas of Luzon's central mountains, English is as widely spoken as the national language. The literacy rate in the Philippines is high, as Filipinos value education highly.

In Filipino, the b and v, f and p are interchangeably pronounced and used. Vowel sounds blend into one another: a and e, e and i, o and u may be indistinguishable. Communications are enhanced if you will speak slowly and distinctly.

Double vowels are pronounced separately, for example Ta-al Volcano. I is pronounced "ee." Ay is pronounced as the "y" in by. And j is pronounced as "h."

While you do not have to speak Filipino to get along, a few words will be much appreciated, even if you can not pronounce them like a native speaker. The honorific *po* or *ho*, meaning "sir" or "ma'am," should be used whenever talking with an older person, or someone in a position of authority or respect.

HANDY TAGALOG WORDS & PHRASES

English	Tagalog
Hello, how are you	*kumusta ka* or *kumusta po kayo*
I am fine	*mabuti (po)*
Thank you very much	*maraming salamat (po)*
Yes/no	*o-o/hindi*
Good morning/afternoon/ evening	*magandang umaga/hapon/ gabi (po)*
May I ask (the correct way to start a conversation asking for assistance or information)	*puede (po) magtanong?*
Where is the ...	*nasaan (po) ang ...*
Toilet	*CR* (comfort room)
City hall	*municipio*
Bus or jeepney to	*bus o djipney sa*
Where is (a person)	*saan (po) ba si (na*me)
What time is it now?	*anong oras na ba?*
What time does the (bus, jeep) leave for (destination)? *para sa*	*anong oras aalis ang (bus, djip)* (destination)?

How much is this?	*magkano (po) ito?*
It is too expensive	*masyadong mahal naman*
Time to eat	*kumain na (po)*
Delicious	*masarap*
Water	*tubig*
Large/small	*malaki/maliit*
Hot/cold	*mainit/malamig*
Good or kind/bad	*mabait/masama*
Man/woman/child	*lalake/babae/bata*
Okay	*sigue*
Good-bye	*pa-alam*
How many minutes/hours/ kilometers to?	*ilan minutos/oras/kilometro hanggang?*
What time is it?	*anong oras na?*
Is there any discount?	*may (mayroon po) tawad?*

More Tagalog

How many trips/km?	*Ilan ang biyahe/kilometro?*
Boat	*banca*
Ship	*barko*
There	*doon*
Here	*dito*
Station (bus/jeep)	*istasyon (bus/djip)*
Stop	*tigil; para* (used for stopping a vehicle to ride or get off)
Enough	*tama na*
Money	*pera*
Dark	*madilim*
River	*ilog*
Sea	*dagat*
Seashore	*tabing dagat/pampang*
Beach	*dalampasigan/ baybay*
Island	*pulo*
Lake	*lawa*
Waterfall	*talon*
Mountain	*bundok (adopted into American English as boondock)*
Road	*kalye/daan*
Food	*pagkain*
Fruit	*prutas*

Clean	*malinis*
Dirty	*madumi*
Right	*kanan*
Left	*kaliwa*
Straight	*diretso*
Half	*kalahati*

Numbers

1	*isa*
2	*dalawa*
3	*tatlo*
4	*apat*
5	*lima*
6	*anim*
7	*pito*
8	*walo*
9	*siyam*
10	*sampo*
20	*dalawampu*
50	*limanapu*
100	*isang daan*
500	*limangdaan*
1000	*isang libo*
5000	*limang libo*

Months

January	*Enero*
February	*Pebrero*
March	*Marso*
April	*Abril*
May	*Mayo*
June	*Hunyo*
July	*Hulyo*
August	*Agosto*
September	*Setyembre*
October	*Oktubre*
November	*Nobyembre*
December	*Disyembre*

Days

Monday	*Lunes*
Tuesday	*Martes*
Wednesday	*Miyerkoles*
Thursday	*Huwebes*
Friday	*Biyernes*
Saturday	*Sabadao*
Sunday	*Linggo*

SANTA & SANTO

Throughout this book, you'll see two abbreviations you may not have seen before: **Sta** *and* **Sto**. *"Sta" is short for* **Santa**, *and "Sto" is short for* **Santo**.

5. A SHORT HISTORY

There are several theories on the geological origin of the Philippines. One suggests that the territory was once a part of mainland Asia, and was lush land with volcanoes and towering mountains. After the Ice Age, parts of the mainland rim sank, and the peaks that remained, surrounded by the waters of the China Sea, are the Philippine archipelago. Another theory is that the country was once part of a massive continent. The vast landmass was destroyed by massive earthquakes and volcanic eruptions, leaving what is today the Philippines, Borneo, Java, Sumatra, the Moluccas, the Marianas, the Carolines, Guam and Hawaii.

The Philippines is a young nation. For most of its recorded history, the territory has been ruled by various Asian and western empires. The first signs of man in the Philippines date back to over half a million years ago. Artifacts older than 200 millennia suggest that hunter-gatherers were among the very early settlers.

Trade with Indonesia, Borneo, mainland Southeast Asia, Japan, Persia and India developed shortly after the Ice Age – and many merchants made the Philippines their base.

PREHISPANIC RELATIONS

Between 1500 BC and 1440 AD, the Philippines traded with several Asian empires. And, from 200 to 1565, parts of the Philippines may have been ruled by Hindu-Malay empires, the Javanese Madjapahit empire, and the Ming Dynasty of China. From 1440 to 1565, Japan controlled northern Luzon, while Borneo and Brunei controlled the south.

Indian-Philippine Relations

Indian influence probably filtered into the Philippines indirectly, through Sumatra and Java. The first contact is believed by some historians to date back to 800 BC, while others believe that 10 AD is more likely. Evidence of contact is seen in beads, glass, and metal work. Some historians say that the name Visayas was derived from Swirijaya, the Indo-Malay Empire that ruled Sumatra from the 7th to 13th centuries.

Chinese-Philippine Relations

The earliest known trade with China occurred during the T'ang Dynasty (618 to 906 AD), although contacts did not become extensive until the Sung (960 to 1279), Yuan (1260 to 1368), and Ming (14th to 16th centuries) dynasties. Records show that the Chinese named the Philippines' largest island "Liu sung:" it is now called Luzon.

Arab-Philippine Relations

Trade with the Arabs, which started around the 9th century, resulted when the Arabs were denied access to China by authorities of the T'ang Dynasty.

Japanese-Philippine Relations

By the 1400s, Japanese traders settled around the areas of the Cagayan River Delta, Davao, Manila, and along the western coast of northern Luzon.

Bornean-Philippine Relations

Ties with Borneo date to 1212, when *datus* (chiefs) fled the tyranny in Sabah and settled on Panay Island. Some of the *datus* later moved north to Batangas.

SPANISH RULE

Spanish contact began when the Portuguese explorer, **Ferdinand Magellan**, was sent by the king of Spain to find a new trade route. Magellan first landed on March 16, 1521, on the uninhabited Homonhon Island off southern Leyte. Magellan and his crew continued to Cebu, where, on April 8, he claimed the islands for Spain. Twenty days later, Magellan was killed by **Lapu-Lapu**, a local chieftain.

The next conquistador who attempted to claim the area for Spain was **Ruy Lopez de Villalobos**. Upon reaching the islands in 1543, he named the archipelago "Filipinas" after Spain's king, **Philip the Second**. However, it was not until 1565 that the archipelago was firmly under the realm of Spain. In November 1565, **Miguel Lopez de Legazpi** landed in Bohol and sealed a blood compact with **Rajah Sikatuna**. Legazpi then conquered Cebu, where the first Spanish fort was built. In 1571, Legazpi defeated **Rajah Sulayman**, Manila's Muslim ruler. Within a year, with the help of his grandson **Juan de Salcedo**, Legazpi had almost the whole country under Spanish rule, with the exception of the Sulu islands and parts of Mindanao and interior Luzon.

Manila, being better positioned than Cebu for trade with China, was made the capital. Here the colonizers built **Intramuros**, a European-style walled city, which was the seat of Spanish rule. Initially, only Spaniards were permitted within the confines of the walls. Natives were moved elsewhere, while the Chinese, necessary for financial matters, trade, and menial jobs "not good enough for a Spaniard," were moved outside the walls, but within canon range.

The importance of the Philippines was as a port, because the Spaniards found that the islands had little gold or spices. Galleons brought gold and silver from Acapulco to be traded for porcelain, jade, bronze, silk and velvet, mainly from China. Until 1821, the Philippines was administered by the Viceroy of Mexico; direct rule by Spain only started in 1821.

The "introduction" of Catholicism arrived with Magellan. Friars were dispersed throughout the entire country to convert and "enlighten" the natives. Many formidable churches and convents were built, and a majority of the people converted to Christianity. Today, over 80% of the population is Roman Catholic.

Community life became centered around the **church**. As a result, the priests were closer to the people than were the Spanish government officials. Church and state wrestled for power, and, as both committed many mistakes and abuses, the locals suffered most. Regional officials gained autonomy, and were often corrupt and abusive. In most places, real power was held by the parish priest, while little authority was left to the *gobernadorcillos* (mayors), the officials appointed by Spain. After the *gobernadorcillos* came the *barangay* (village) heads, who collected taxes from everyone in their village. Filipinos were allowed only minimal participation in the government; this resulted in a widening gap between the lower and upper classes. The hierarchical system set up by the Spaniards enabled the hereditary elite to amass land and wealth, forming the oligarchy that to some extent still exists.

Wrestling with Outside Forces

Although Spain ruled much of the time until 1898, the Spanish had to fight off other powers. Dutch fleets attacked Manila several times between 1600 and 1647. The British led a joint expeditionary force with the Indians in 1762, and succeeded in gaining control of Manila and the surrounding areas for 20 months. Manila was returned to Spain under the Treaty of Paris in 1763.

In Mindanao, the Spanish never succeeded at subduing the Muslims, and were frequently at war. The Muslims declared Jihad (Holy War), which gave them the fervor that enabled them to resist domination under Spain. The Spanish made Christian Filipinos the dominant group in the country.

Rebellion & Revolution

During the Spanish era, Filipinos were permitted to study in Europe. Many who returned brought with them ideas of freedom. This, and the prevalent corruption, laid the basis for years of rebellion. In 1872, Filipino soldiers revolted against their Spanish superiors. The government quickly suppressed the revolution, and used it as an excuse to execute its powerful enemies. Among those executed were **Father José Burgos** and Fathers Gomez and Zamora, all outspoken opponents of racial discrimination against local priests. The three priests became the first martyrs of the revolution.

The execution was followed by persecution of Filipino intellectuals, some of whom fled to Europe. Among them was **José Rizal**, whose writings on the abuses of the government and church galvanized his generation. When Rizal returned to Manila, he was arrested, then exiled to Dapitan (in Mindanao) on July 17, 1892. The **Katipunan**, an underground revolutionary organization, was created by **Andres Bonifacio** and others as a reaction to Rizal's arrest. When the Spanish authorities were informed about this society in 1896, arbitrary arrests were made and Rizal and hundreds of others were executed. Fighting erupted into a full-fledged rebellion.

Within the revolutionaries, a rift occurred between Bonifacio and **Emilio Aguinaldo**, and Aguinaldo was the more successful in the battlefield. In 1897, the Katipunan was replaced by a new revolutionary government, with Aguinaldo as the leader. Shortly after, Bonifacio was tried for sedition and executed. The fighting continued, but the revolutionaries were not able to overpower the Spanish military. Aguinaldo was captured, signed a pact that gave him a monetary settlement, and was exiled to Hong Kong.

THE AMERICAN PERIOD

The **Spanish-American War** ended Spanish rule over the Philippines. In 1898, **George Dewey** led a fleet of American ships into Manila Bay and easily defeated the Spanish warships at anchor there. Aguinaldo agreed to help the Americans fight, because Dewey promised to support Philippine independence. On land, the Filipino army succeeded in beating the Spanish troops. However, independence was not granted; the **Treaty of Paris** (December 1898) awarded the Philippines to the United States, and Aguinaldo and his army were barred from entering Manila to complete their victory.

Until this time, little was known in the United States about the Philippines. Originally, **President McKinley** had no plans to colonize the country. After Dewey's victory over the Spaniards, he had to decide what to do with the islands. Under pressure from expansionists, McKinley decided to retain control of the country. He thought this would benefit the Filipinos, as they would become educated, civilized, and Christianized — he was unaware that most of the country had been Catholic for centuries.

The Philippine-American War (1899-1901)

After being exiled from Manila, Aguinaldo resumed his rebellion, this time against the American imperialists. Brutal guerrilla warfare ensued until Aguinaldo was captured in 1901. The fighting did not completely stop until mid-1902.

American Influence

The Americans introduced their system of education, style of government, and commercial products. Although sanitation was greatly improved and education expanded, the Americans perpetuated the governing practices that had allowed Spain to control the country, and thus maintained the gap between the elite and the poor. With the introduction of large-scale agricultural production, land reform was inhibited, prolonging ill feelings. Elite Filipinos had positions of authority under the American governor; political parties were based on personal followings and not ideas — this resulted in favoritism and long tenure.

The most important contributions that the Americans made were installing an education system; introducing ideas of democracy; separating church and state; improving public health; and improving roads, transportation, and communication.

The United States began moving towards granting the Philippines independence. In 1934, Philippine President **Manuel Quezon** was promised commonwealth status by 1936, and independence in 1946.

WORLD WAR TWO

Japan invaded the Philippines three days after bombing **Pearl Harbor** (December 7, 1941); dozens of the 277 aircraft at Clark Air Base were destroyed. The Japanese landed on the 22nd of December at Lingayen Gulf and on the 24th at Lamon Bay. From these two points they moved towards Manila.

General Douglas MacArthur, with Filipino and American troops, retreated to **Bataan** in order to avert the destruction of Manila. For four months, Americans and Filipinos fought side by side. On March 11, 1942, MacArthur was ordered to leave by **President Franklin D. Roosevelt**. MacArthur departed Corregidor for Australia, where he made his famous promise — "I shall return."

The 76,000 soldiers on Bataan surrendered on April 9. Because the Japanese believed in fighting to the end and considered surrendering disgraceful, they assumed their opponents would behave accordingly and did not have the logistics to deal with the captives. Consequently, the Japanese force-marched all 76,000 prisoners 184 kilometers to internment facilities in San Fernando, Pampanga. The **Death March**, which started on April 9, took place during the hottest season and claimed the lives of 7,000 to 10,000 soldiers, about 2,600 of which were American. Many more died during the subsequent internment.

Troops on Corregidor, "The Rock," held out for a while longer. Thirteen thousand people had retreated into the **Malinta Tunnel**, a one-kilometer long tunnel with four kilometers of side tunnels. They lived here for nearly five months, starting from the time the Japanese shelled the island on December 29, 1941. In May, General Wainwright surrendered — he had no choice, as they had run out of water, food, medicine, and ammunition.

Japanese Occupation

Under the Japanese, freedom of Filipinos was severely curtailed and labor was often forced. Japan had plans of making the Philippines its territory. In the meantime, over 250,000 Filipinos resorted to guerrilla warfare against the Japanese, and in Washington DC, a Philippine government-in-exile was set up.

The country was in a state of crisis: the economy was a mess, food was in short supply, and cases of Japanese brutality were increasing. Despite the ongoing fighting, nightclubs flourished: the clientele were ruthless businessmen making fortunes from selling war materials to the Japanese. When the war ended, these same unscrupulous people handled the distribution of relief goods; as their wealth continued to grow, they became the new rich.

Liberation

Because of its strategic location, the Philippines was the main battleground in the Pacific War. While the Japanese were occupied with the resistance in Bataan and Corregidor, the Allied Forces had time to recover and begin to plan.

On October 20, 1944, MacArthur fulfilled his promise and returned. With 700 ships and 174,000 soldiers, he landed along the coastline of Leyte. With him was Carlos P. Romulo. President Quezon had died in the United States during the war.

Not until late December did American forces control Leyte. The **Battle of Leyte Gulf** — one of the greatest naval battles in history — involved 64 Japanese and 216 US warships and took place near Cape

Engaño (off Samar) and in the Surigao Strait. This three-day battle ended with the decimation of the Japanese fleet. During this battle, Japanese pilots first used their fabled *kamikaze* tactics — the suicidal method of dive-bombing their rivals.

KAMIKAZE

Kamikaze, meaning "divine wind," refers to a typhoon in 1281 that blew away a Mongol fleet that was threatening Japan. In hopes of ending the war (in their favor), the Japanese planned on "blowing away" the Allied Forces by loading planes with bombs and extra gasoline. These planes, called kamikaze, were flown deliberately to crash into their targets.

The US troops and the Filipino guerrillas fought together against the Japanese. On January 9, 1945, US troops landed at Lingayen Gulf and proceeded to Manila. Manila was finally liberated, after 20 days of intense fighting in the city, on the 23rd of February. Japanese troops were trapped by Filipinos and Americans advancing from the north and the south. Many Japanese turned to random rape, murder, torture, and massive destruction; thousands of civilian Filipinos died.

The last hold of the Japanese in the city was Intramuros. Hand-to-hand combat ensued for many days, and bombs leveled the city. Manila was the second most devastated city of the Second World War.

The last resistance of the Japanese ended in Baguio, where **General Yamashita** surrendered on September 3. Yamashita, who is still respected as a true soldier, a top general, and a humanitarian who tried to avert destruction where possible, was executed in disgrace.

INDEPENDENCE

The United States granted the Philippines independence, and the first president of the Philippine Republic, **Manuel Roxas**, was sworn in on July 4, 1946. With the city smashed, and much of the country's infrastructure in shambles, rebuilding drained the treasury. Some financial aid was provided by the United States, but most American aid went to Japan.

Corruption and the use of power to gain official positions was standard operating procedure. Politics, as in the Spanish era, remained dominated by the wealthy elite. The feudal landlord-tenant relationship continued in most of the country. Discontent was inevitable. The Hukbalahaps (Huks) who led the Luzon resistance against the Japanese turned their efforts against the government. However, **President Ramon Magsaysay**, who was honest and responsive to the needs of the masses, was able to defeat the Huks. A treaty was signed and the insurgents were granted amnesty. Shortly thereafter, Magsaysay was killed in a plane crash.

Political deterioration resumed under Magsaysay's successors, Carlos Garcia (1957-1961), and Diosdado Macapagal (1961-1965). In 1965, **Ferdinand Marcos**, a young Congressman from Ilocos, ran against Macapagal for the presidency. Marcos had successfully appealed a conviction for killing his father's opponent in an election.

MARCOS

While running for the presidency, Ferdinand Marcos and his wife, the beauty queen Imelda Romualdez, sang campaign duets as part of his strategy to win votes. During his first term, he achieved considerable improvement in the infrastructure and increased rice production. The country was ranked second in Asia in terms of economic standings.

In 1969, Marcos became the first president to be reelected. After '69, the economy, which had already started to decline, worsened. The administration was faced with opposition as it attempted to draft a new constitution. The **New People's Army** (NPA), an armed wing of the banned communist party, was formed and resorted to terrorism around the country, with bases in the mountains. In Mindanao, the **Moro National Liberation Front** (MNLF) was fighting for sovereignty over that southern island; this exacerbated the existing tension between Christians and Muslims in the south.

In 1972, Marcos declared Martial Law "to handle the economic crisis and the peace-and-order situation." The constitution was revamped. Marcos gained complete control of the National Assembly along with major businesses and the media, and he jailed his opponents.

The Muslim rebellion in the south had claimed 50,000 lives. It finally ended in 1976, when a treaty was signed and limited autonomy was granted. The political and economic situation never recovered. The Marcoses and their associates controlled the monopolies that made up most of the successful industries. The military became corrupt and was used as a tool to control opposition and to settle personal vendettas. During this time, Imelda chaired 24 agencies, councils, and corporations, giving her control of budgets that amounted to more than $500 million annually.

PEOPLE POWER

Benigno "Ninoy" Aquino was Marcos' main political opponent. Marcos had him jailed for eight years. Aquino was permitted to leave for the United States for heart surgery and remained there in exile for three years.

Ninoy Aquino returned in August 1983, and, as he stepped onto the tarmac, he was assassinated. In reaction, many Filipinos turned against their government, separatist movements surfaced in the military, and confidence in the government plummeted. The economy collapsed and Marcos was forced to hold an election; Aquino's widow, **Corazon "Cory" Cojuanco Aquino**, was his opponent.

Marcos was declared "winner" of the fraudulent election. On February 25th, 1986, both Marcos and Cory Aquino were sworn in as president, during separate ceremonies. Cory and the Catholic Church called for civil disobedience. Defense Minister Juan Ponce Enrile and Vice Chief of Staff General Fidel Ramos defected along with most of the military and joined Aquino. Thousands of civilians protected Aquino and her party as they blockaded the military that remained loyal to Marcos.

The United States withdrew support from Marcos and convinced him to leave. The Marcoses were flown to Hawaii, where he died in 1989. His eccentric widow, Imelda, is currently a congresswoman from her home province, Leyte.

Cory restored democracy and the political institutions of a democratic parliament, and reinstituted the supreme court. However, the economy did not recuperate and social unrest persisted. During her six-year period as President, she survived seven coup attempts. Also during her term, the country suffered two major natural disaster: in 1989, a severe earthquake destroyed most of Baguio, Cabanatuan City, and the hills around the Balete (Dalton) Pass; in 1990, **Mount Pinatubo** erupted, spewing tremendous amounts of ash into the atmosphere, blanketing villages and farmlands in lahar, and changing the world's atmosphere and climate for many years. Sunsets were deepened worldwide for several years. The lahar deposited on the volcano's slopes will continue to flow downhill for over a decade; the vast desert of lahar will continue to expand, clogging waterways and altering the lives of hundreds of thousands of people and the floor of Manila Bay.

ROAD TO RECOVERY

Fidel V. Ramos, chosen by Cory as her successor, narrowly won the election in 1992 (being a Protestant, he did not have the backing of the Catholic Church's Philippine Primate, Cardinal Sin). President Ramos was sworn in on July 1. Ramos furthered democratic reform, sealed the peace negotiations with the MNLF, and has succeeded in turning the economy around—he gained global confidence in the Philippine economy. Many nations and companies have new investments in the country. Ramos has received recognition worldwide for his success, and was named by Time Magazine as the Asian Newsmaker in 1996.

If the next president is able to continue the progress that Ramos' administration has achieved, the country will have a bright future and will continue to be a stable emerging market. This depends on the outcome of the 1998 elections.

GOVERNMENT

The 1987 constitution reestablished the American-style legislature that existed before Marcos changed the constitution in 1971. There are 24 senators elected nationally and 250 congressmen elected by district. The president is only allowed a single six-year term.

The president is advised by a cabinet of members who he appoints to serve him. The country is divided into regions, then provinces, and each province is under the jurisdiction of its elected governor. Provinces are divided by municipalities that are headed by the elected mayor. These municipalities are made up of *barangays* (villages or districts) and the elected *barangay* captains report to their mayor.

UNITED STATES BASES

In September 1991, the **Military Bases Agreement** *expired and Aquino did not grant an extension. The agreement had been signed in 1966 and allowed the United States to maintain military bases in the Philippines. Clark Air Base in Angeles and Subic Naval Base in Subic were by far the most important in the country. During the cold war, these bases were considered of high strategic importance, vital to preserving American and allied interests in the Pacific. The bases also were the country's third largest employer, as 68,500 Filipinos worked on the two bases. Many more derived their income from industries such as construction, housing, and of course the nightclubs and bars that popped up right outside the bases. American aid for the use of the bases, local payrolls and contracts, and the servicemen spending money outside the bases pumped about $1.4 million a day into the Philippine economy.*

However, the other implications for the country included continued presence of an autonomous foreign-controlled area on Filipino soil, and the moral problems associated with a large collection of troops, including prostitution and drugs. Consequently, the Philippines chose to terminate the agreement.

Today, there is a world-class golf resort (with a hotel managed by Holiday Inn) and casino at the former Clark Air Base. Subic has become a free port with several industries, hotels, and a casino.

6. PLANNING YOUR TRIP

WHEN TO VISIT - CLIMATE & WEATHER

The Philippines has four climatic zones:

• **Rainy, June-November; mostly dry, November-May**. Areas included are most of the center of northern Luzon; Masbate; eastern part of central Palawan; in the Visayas: Romblon, Aklan, Capiz, northern Iloilo, Negros Oriental, northern Negros Occidental, most of Cebu, and Siquijor; and in Mindanao: Misamis Oriental, parts of Bukidnon, and the southern region of the Zamboanga peninsula.

• **Pronounced rainy season, June-November; dry, November-April**. Western regions of northern Luzon, Manila and most of central Luzon, Mindoro Occidental, most of Palawan, Antique, southern Iloilo, Guimaras, and Negros Occidental.

• **Rainfall evenly distributed year round**. Eastern region of Northern Luzon, Quezon and southern Bicol region, Marinduque, Mindoro Oriental, northwest parts of Samar Province, west coast of Leyte, northern tip of Cebu, Bohol, most of southern Mindanao, and the southernmost islands of Basilan and Tawi-Tawi.

• **Most rainfall, November-January; no distinct dry season**. East coast of Southern Luzon, Catanduanes, both Northern and Eastern Samar, southern region of Samar province, Camiguin, much of the northern and eastern coast of Mindanao, Davao Oriental, parts of Davao del Norte, and Agusan del Sur.

The best time to vist most of the north and central Philippines is December through May. December through January is cool; from February on, the country becomes increasingly hot. Humidity is usually high except in December and January, and temperatures are generally 75-95°Fahrenheit or 24-35°Celsius, with mid-day summer highs over 100°F and 37°C. Southern Mindanao has fairly even climate and temperature year round.

Much of the Philippines is in the "typhoon belt," and the country experiences several storms from June through November. During the height of rainy season, as much as 18 inches (46 centimeters) of rain may fall in one day, and land and sea travel in many places is very difficult.

WHAT TO WEAR & PACK

General Clothes

Light, natural fiber, loose fitting garments are most comfortable. Have a jacket or sweater for the mountain areas, especially during December through February. If you plan on walking, wear sneakers or other comfortable shoes.

Do not wear shorts and skimpy tops when visiting churches or mosques. Do not bathe nude — or, for women, topless — on public beaches.

Business & Formal Wear

If you are a man and attend a formal occasion, you may wear the *barong Tagalog* — a long-sleeve shirt of light fabric. The more formal *barong* has intricate embroidery. The *barong* is worn outside the pants and without a tie, and may be worn instead of a suit, which is very hot in the Philippine climate. In more casual meetings and general office wear, a shirt and tie is fine.

If you are a woman, a cocktail dress or formal pantsuit is fine for formal occasions, and a blouse with tailored slacks or skirt are acceptable for office wear and meetings. Light suits or dresses are better for more formal meetings.

Other Personal Items

Hats and sunglasses provide helpful relief from the sun. Sun screen and block are essential; and do not forget your favorite sunburn remedy (aloe vera gel or vitamin E cream). Insect repellent helps keep evenings pleasant. Apply baby oil thickly to keep sand fleas (encountered on some beaches) from inflicting lasting, itchy bites. We have found that Avon's Skin So Soft works well against mosquitoes (it's the stuff the GIs used), although others prefer Cutters or Off.

You should also bring any medicines you normally need (aspirin, antihistamine, etc.). Although most medicines are available in the Philippines, you may not find your favorite brand names. Women may want to consider that tampons are not always available outside the major cities here.

Divers must bring their certification cards, and although scuba equipment is available for rent, most divers prefer using at least their own regulator, mask, and snorkel.

Camping equipment is not readily for rent, and can be expensive, so you may want to bring your own gear. Prices are higher than in the United Sates, as most of the camping gear is imported.

Bring your own **camera**. You can find film at most destinations, and it is not expensive. You should consider buying it in the several camera and film stores in the major cities, as film will cost more at tourist destinations, and in hotels. Bring extra **batteries** – the ones specifically for your camera may not be readily available outside Manila or Cebu (and even then, for one of our cameras, the nearest place that had a battery was Hong Kong – granted it is a collectors item ...). Developing photographs is inexpensive in the Philippines, but the colors are sometimes not good. Try Fuji, Kodak, or Island Photo in Manila.

MAKING RESERVATIONS IN THE US

• **SAF Travel World Inc.**, *201-A North 9th St., Philadelphia, PA 19107-1832. Tel. 215/440-7200, Fax 440 9602.*
• **Rajah Tours**, *Suite 901, 500 Sutter St., San Francisco, CA 94201. Tel. 415/ 397-0303, 397-0304*

GETTING TO THE PHILIPPINES

Air travel is basically the only way to get to the Philippines; there are no regular passenger shipping services to the country. A few cruise ships stop here, but not long enough to allow passengers much time to explore the country.

Most international flights come in through the **Ninoy Aquino International Airport** in Manila (NAIA). There are also international flights to Cebu (from Hong Kong, Singapore, Malaysia, and Japan), and a few to Davao (from Malaysia, and Indonesia).

From the US

Flying in from the US will take you, including stop-overs, approximately 24 hours from the East Coast, 14-18 hours from the West Coast. As you can see, it is not a short flight, and you cross the International Date Line. Thus, you will lose at least 12 hours going (the Philippines being ahead, time-wise) and upon returning to the United States you will arrive in Hawaii "before the time you left," something that always amazed a college roommate of mine.

Airlines with service to Manila include **NorthWest**, *Tel. 1-800/225-2525*; **United**, *Tel. 1-800/241-6255*; **Continental**, *Tel. 1-800/231-0856*; **Korean**, *Tel. 671/649-3301*; **Cathay Pacific**, *Tel. 1-800/233-2742*; **Japan Airlines**, *Tel. 1-800/525-3663*; **Philippine Airlines**, *Tel. 1-800/435-9725*; and most Asian airlines that serve the United States. The only airline that has a direct flight from the US (out of San Francisco or Los Angeles) is Philippine Airlines; most of the other airlines will have a layover in Japan or Korea.

Ticket prices (from the mainland) range from $700 to $1400 for economy, and $1,200 to $2,500 for business class. Prices fluctuate with the seasons: expect Christmas to be expensive, and summer as well. We have found that cheap tickets to the Philippines (and most parts of Asia) are available at travel agencies in the Chinatown districts of major cities in the United States; you may also try *1-800/FLYCHEAP*.

The Manila Airport

NAIA (still referred to as its former name — the **Manila International Airport** or MIA) is not as nice as the major airports you may be accustomed to in North America or Europe, but plans are on the way for its expansion and improvement. Its one runway (with two lanes) is just long enough and one end stops at a major highway.

However, immigration and customs staff are usually pleasant. You can never really tell how long it will take you to clear immigration and customs — allow 45 minutes to an hour. If your plane arrives at around the same time as four other international flights, the entry formalities may take a while. If you arrive during December, your checked-in baggage may take a long time to come out of the carousel, as many overseas workers are coming home for the holidays and bring a number of *balikbayan* boxes with them (see sidebar below).

A line of "airport taxis" (private companies that serve the airport) will be waiting to take you to your desired destination. Rates are fixed (around

---

WHAT'S A BALIKBAYAN?

Balikbayan is a word that you will hear and see when you are arriving at the airport in Manila. Balik means return, and bayan means country: balikbayan usually refers to a Filipino who is returning to the Philippines after having resided in another country for several years, and often having become a citizen of another country. Balikbayan boxes are cartons that are just within the allowable size limits for airline baggage and are frequently used by Filipino travelers to bring back as much as they can into the country. Filipinos are avid shoppers and when traveling usually amass more than can fit in the luggage they brought; instead of buying a new suitcase, most people will use balikbayan boxes. If you are checking into a Philippine Airlines flight in San Francisco or Los Angeles, you will see dozens of these cartons lined up.

$12 to Makati, $20 to Pasig), and are usually higher than regular taxis. This is probably the most hassle-free way to get to your accommodations unless your hotel provides an airport service. If you are going to the Malate and Ermita area, **Sunshine Bus Service** shuttles passengers to various hotels in the area, and costs $1.50 per person.

Aside from transportation services you will notice a mob of people hanging around outside in designated "greeters" areas, behind metal rails. No matter what time of day you arrive, there always seems to be greeters, as families of Filipinos arriving or departing congregate to meet their relatives or to see their kin off.

CUSTOMS, ENTRANCE, & EXIT REQUIREMENTS

Arriving in the Philippines

If you have a valid passport, you may enter the country and stay for a maximum of 21 days without a visa if you have a ticket out of the country. However, you must have a visa if you are a national of a country with which the Philippines has no diplomatic relations – People's Republic of China, Cambodia, North Korea, Tonga, Lebanon, Jordan, Iraq, and Belize. Palestinians also must acquire a visa.

Because it is both costly and time-consuming to extend the 21-day tourist visa, we advise you to get a 60-day multiple entry tourist visa. Visas are available from your nearest Philippine Consulate. Addresses of consulates in the United States are listed later in this chapter under *More Information*.

You may bring in the following duty-free: 400 sticks of cigarettes or two tins of tobacco, and two bottles of alcoholic beverage not to exceed 1 liter each. You must declare any amount over the $3,000 that you are allowed to bring into the country.

Returning to the US

Departure tax in the Philippines is $20 or P500. You should also change any leftover Philippine pesos: exchange rates for them outside the Philippines are bad.

If you are returning to the United States, you are allowed to bring in $400 worth of goods purchased in the Philippines. Duty-free items include 200 sticks of cigarettes or 100 cigars (no Cuban cigars, which you can buy in Manila); a liter of alcohol; and most handicraft goods from the Philippines. Fresh produce is not allowed, dried fruits (such as dried mangoes, which make nice gifts) are. Over $10,000 in currency must be declared.

GETTING AROUND THE PHILIPPINES

By Air

Air is the quickest and most efficient way to get around the Philippines (if the flight is not canceled or delayed...). Airfares range from inexpensive to pricey considering the distance covered. Flights do get canceled occasionally — due to weather, mechanical problems, not enough passengers, or strikes. Passengers will be booked on the next flight provided that there are unbooked seats. Thus, it is always safest to allow at least 36 hours in Manila or Cebu before your flight abroad.

As a rule, airlines should shoulder accommodations if the next flight they can book you on is the following day; however, the airlines do not always offer this, and you should ask for what you are entitled to.

Jeepneys and buses wait for passengers at provincial airports. Board promptly as they will leave when full and will not return until the next scheduled flight.

At the time of publication, there were seven airlines covering regularly scheduled domestic routes. Philippine Airlines, which has the greatest number of flights and serves the largest number of destinations, changes its schedule four times a year.

DOMESTIC AIRLINES

- *Air Ads Inc.*, Tel. 833-3264, 833-3278
- *Air Philippines*, Tel. 526-4741 to 50
- *Asian Spirit* ,Tel. 840-3811 to 18
- *Cebu Pacific*, Tel. 636-4938 to 45
- *Grand Air*, Tel. 833-8080, 833-8090
- *Pacific Air*, Tel. 812-1555, 812-1511
- *Philippine Airlines*, Tel. 816-6691

There are also reliable charter companies, including **Paradise Travel Service**, *Tel. 912/315-1835*, and **A. Soriano Aviation**, *Tel. 834-0371*. Both Air Ads and Pacific Air also offer charter flights.

By Bus, Jeepney, & Assorted Vehicles

Major roads surrounding Manila are usually in good condition; however, during and after rainy season, they are in need of repair. There is an extensive road system in Luzon. A national highway, most of which is well paved, goes through Luzon to Samar and Leyte in the Visayas and extends through southern Mindanao. Boats ferry cars between the islands.

Major towns have paved roads, but beyond, the roads are often unsurfaced. Road travel is often slow because of the volume of traffic, slow moving vehicles, and local events such as religious processions, which may wholly or partly block the way.

Buses operate to all Luzon provinces, and Philtranco continues through to Davao. Buses are either air conditioned (sometimes referred to as "first class"), or non-air conditioned ("ordinary" or "regular"). Express buses (usually aircon) have less stops. Store your baggage directly above your seat or in front of you. Street vendors will come on the buses at several stops offering snacks and refreshments. There are also designated meal stops, where the driver and conductor will get off and eat (usually for free: it's their commission from the passengers' meals). Sometimes, conductors will check tickets several times during long trips, so keep yours handy.

Connecting services, usually **jeepneys** and **minibuses**, cover shorter areas. These vehicles are less comfortable than large buses, cheaper, and not air conditioned. They also cover some of the same routes as their larger relatives, though they stop more often and pack very full; at times even the roof will have passengers. Some colorful jeepneys are decoratively and imaginatively painted.

UBIQUITOUS JEEPNEYS

The jeepney is an innovation from the American army jeeps. Filipinos have since personalized these jeeps to suit their needs, wants, and culture. These jeeps have been "stretched" and can fit 15 people in the passenger compartment.

You will see jeepneys wherever you go – they are all over the country (and all over the road). Despite several attempts to remove them from the streets – to improve traffic, safety, and efficiency – the jeepney is a cheap form of public transportation, and has stood its ground as an institution of Philippine daily life.

You may find some jeepneys elaborately decorated – mirrors, iron horses, and colored lights on the hood; and colorful patterns or landscapes painted on the sides. And inside many you will see a mini-altar, possibly along with a pin-up poster. Nowadays, most of the ones you will see are not as ornate as they once were.

Tricycles, which are motorcycles with a cab attached, are often the most convenient and inexpensive way to get around towns and to do short trips in the province. (We do not advise taking them within major cities, unless you enjoy breathing unhealthy amounts of carbon monoxide.) Do not be surprised if you see a tricycle go by with a dozen people attached. Some places will have variations on tricycles: in Cagayan de Oro, they are referred to as "motorelas" and are larger; in Camiguin, "multicabs" are a cross between tricycles and small jeepneys, but with the power of a tricycle.

Horse-drawn vehicles (*kalesas* and *karetelas*) are a relaxing way to get around, and they still operate in a few cities and provinces. In Manila, you would probably only want to ride one inside Intramuros, around Binondo, and at Nayong Filipino.

Transport schedules for various forms of land transportation are not usually fixed, vehicles may run late as they wait to fill up, or leave early when full. We suggest that you arrive early and be prepared to wait. Toilet facilities along the way vary from acceptable to primitive or nonexistent (e.g., the wall, shrub, or whatever.) Men, backs toward the road, urinating, are common road-side scenery throughout the Philippines. Women are more discrete.

By Car & Taxi

Several companies hire cars and drivers; most of them also have taxis. **Car rental** companies in Manila include:
• **Avis**, *Tel. 734-5851*
• **Budget**, *Tel. 818-7363*
• **Dollar**, *Tel. 844-3120*
• **Nissan Rent-a-Car** (desk at the airport), *Tel. 816-1808*
• **Transport 2000** (desk at the airport).

Check the yellow pages (under automobile rentals) for other companies.

Regular **taxis** serve most of the major cities, and are either airconditioned or non-air conditioned. Air conditioned taxis charge a small fee (60¢) to use the aircon. Most taxis have their company name and car number painted on the outside; some are not marked. These taxis, often called **PU's** (Public Utility Vehicles) can be rented by the hour, day, or for short trips. Rates are negotiable, so we suggest acquiring a leaflet from one of the rental companies (available at a stand in the airport, or at most hotels). The rates you pay should be comparable to or lower than the rental company rates.

As street signs are an oddity outside major cities, and if you cannot find a point of interest of a town or barangay, ask a local. Filipinos understand and speak English quite well, and are happy to help visitors out.

By Light Rail (LRT)

In Manila, the elevated **Light Rail Transit** provides the most painless, smogless way to cross the city. It runs from Monumento, Caloocan, in the north to Baclaran, Parañaque (a five- to ten-minute taxi ride from the airport) in the south. The LRT runs above Taft Avenue south of the Pasig River, and atop Rizal Avenue north of the river. No matter where your destination is, the fare is 40¢ (P10), except from Buendia to Baclaran, where it is 10¢ (P2). Construction of another elevated transit system down (EDSA) has begun.

By Sea

A vast network of boats sail the inter-island waters — within Luzon and the nearby islands; from Manila to the Visayas and Mindanao; and within the central and southern islands. The vessels vary in size, speed, and facilities:

• *Bancas* are motorized outrigger boats that carry from four to 40 people, depending on the boat's size.
• Ferries and ships, on the shorter journeys have regular seats and tourist class (in an air conditioned room with padded seats). On long journeys, passage on ships with facilities such as common cabin with bunk beds (the cheapest) costs approximately $10, and suite rooms can cost from $50 to $98 depending on the boat and length of the journey. In between are cabins with reserved bunks, private cabins for groups, and rooms of varying sizes. Meals are served; you will not be getting anything gourmet. The bathrooms in the common cabins are bearable, sometimes they may not flush well, and not everyone remembers to flush; bring a supply of toilet paper (called "tissue" in the Philippines). The ones in the private rooms are clean.
• High-speed catamarans and hydrofoils are the latest addition to the seafaring family. Their travel time is a lot less than that of the regular ferry, and seats are comfortable. Cebu is the main port of these vessels, and they ply the routes between Cebu and some Visayan ports and to Northern Mindanao. Passage is from $10 to $25, food and drinks can be purchased at a snack bar, and the toilets are clean.

By Train

We don't advise using trains in the Philippines because there are few of them, they are uncomfortable, and they are slower and less convenient than other means of land transport.

HOTEL RATES

In the Philippines, as in the United States, hotel prices vary according to season. The busy seasons in the Philippines are late November to mid-January, and March to May. If you are a travel agent, you can get discounted rates for most hotels and resorts. The **rack** or **list rate** is the official listed rate that hotels are charging for rooms; this is also the rate that walk-ins (people without reservations) are charged. Even in the expensive hotels, you can avail of special promotions, so ask your travel agent to inquire.

Particularly for highly touristed destinations such as Boracay, the cheapest way to get accommodations is usually through package deals that include airfare, transportation to and from resorts, rooms, and one meal (usually breakfast) a day. You can get these packages at a number of local travel agencies; local newspapers also have ads for such arrangements. However, if you are not going on a package tour, it is sometimes best to contact the resort directly, as the list rate includes a travel agent's commission, and when you make the reservation yourself you can ask for a discount or for a rate without the agents' commission.

Some of the higher-end resorts and hotels do give discounts for Philippine citizens or residents. The cheap ones do not have different rates.

Generally, we give the rack rates in this book.

MORE INFORMATION

In the United States, you can get information, maps, and brochures, as well as visas, from four Philippine consulates:
• **Los Angeles**, *Philippine Consulate General, 3660 Wilshire Blvd., Suite 825, Los Angeles, CA, 90010. Tel. 213/487-4527, Fax 386-4063.*
• **New York**, *Philippine Center, 556 Fifth Avenue, New York, NY, 10036. Tel. 212/575-7915, Fax 302-6759.*
• **San Francisco**, *Philippine Consulate General, 447 Sutter Street, Suite 507, San Francisco, CA 94108. Tel. 415/956-4060, Fax 956-2093.*
• **Washington DC**, *Embassy of the Philippines, 1600 Massachusetts Ave., NW Washington DC, 20036. Tel. 202/467-9300.*

7. BASIC INFORMATION

BUSINESS HOURS

Both private and government offices are usually open from 8:00am to 5:00pm, although some may start at 9:00am and some may stay open until 6:00pm. A number of private companies open on Saturdays from 9:00am to noon, and some stay open the whole day.

Most shopping centers, stores, and supermarkets open at 10:00am and close at 7:00pm; during December, stores stay open until 10:00pm.

COST OF LIVING & TRAVEL

Generally, it costs less to live in the Philippines than in the United States if you live as a Filipino, but "imported lifestyles" cost more in the Philippines than at home. Most travelers will find the Philippines a relatively cheap country (excluding the first-class resorts and hotels). Almost everywhere you go, you will find inexpensive lodging that is in a reasonably good location and is clean. You can get a full meal for under $4 in the major cities and outside. Meals in five-star hotels and resorts, and pricey restaurants will cost around $25 per person.

Locally produced liquor is cheap — a bottle of rum will cost 76¢ — beer is the same price, or in some cases cheaper than sodas (more commonly called soft-drinks here) and cost 60¢; bottled water costs 70¢.

Imported items can cost considerably higher here. Do not come here to buy western name brands in the up-scale department stores; most will cost much more than in the US, even when on sale. Renting houses or apartments can also be very expensive; a small apartment in Manila will cost $1,000 a month, not furnished. Rents are lower outside the country's main metropolis. Gasoline and electricity also cost more here.

ELECTRICITY

Electricity is 220 volts, 60 cycles. Most hotels in Manila have outlets for 220 and 110 volts.

FEMALES TRAVELING ALONE

Jill and Rebecca, the authors of this guide, have found traveling around most of the country safe. We do advise that women travelers take extra precautions and travel during the day.

Some Filipino men consider themselves macho "Don Juans," but can also be gentlemen. They tend to shower females, especially foreign ones, with praise, and may address women as Ma'am, regardless of age.

Filipinos and Filipinas will be even more curious when a female is traveling alone or with a group of females. Typical questions will be: "Where are you from?" "What is your country?" "What is your name?" "How old are you?" Expect to be asked if you are married or have a boyfriend, or if you have children.

Avoid drunk people; some may become violent, and your friendliness may be interpreted as an "okay to get to know each other better."

See also *Staying Out Of Trouble* below.

FIESTAS

Filipinos love celebrating; they honor harvests, births, and everything else. The Spanish adapted traditional rituals by celebrating a saint's birthday on dates formerly associated with animistic rituals.

You will see festivals in every ethnic group, as people get together for essentially spiritual events. Drama, excitement, food, music, and renewal of relationships are shared extensively. Fiestas range from large, organized, regional events to small *barangay* happenings.

You will be most welcome at festivals and should make an effort to attend one when you are in the Philippines. Descriptions of some festivals are given in chapters covering the area where they are held. Activities usually center around the church, and from there, proceed into the community.

JANUARY

1	**New Year's Day** — people attend mass after a night's revelry.
1st Sunday	**Three Kings** — last day of Christmas celebrations and gift giving.
2nd Tuesday	**Black Nazarene**, Quiapo, Metro Manila (MM) — the black Christ is brought out from Quiapo church in a huge procession. People try to touch his carriage in hopes of having their sins forgiven.
movable	**Appey**, Bontoc, Mountain Province — planting rites.
3rd weekend	**Ati-atihan**, Kalibo, Aklan — during this spectacular festival, centered around the reenactment of the legend of the Negritoes selling Panay to Bornean chiefs, people

paint their faces black (to look like the Negritoes) and parade and dance around in costumes that range from very artistic to outrageous.

Santo Niño de Cebu (Sinulog), Cebu City — the highlight of Cebu's biggest annual festival is a long parade and contest of groups of people dressed in costumes, marching or dancing their way to the basilica. Various cities from other provinces send representatives to compete and join in the revelry.

4th weekend   **Dinagyang**, Iloilo — A choreographed version of Ati-atihan, activities include a Mardi-Gras-like celebration and parades of costumed "tribes" that are painted black to resemble the Negritoes.

FEBRUARY

movable   **Hariraya Hadji** — pilgrimage of Moslems to Mecca.

International Bamboo Organ Festival, Las Piñas MM church — A week-long series of evening concerts featuring very good local and international musicians.

1-3   **Feast of Our Lady of Candles** — blessing of candles, which people then take home to protect their house against danger.

11   **Feast of Our Lady of Lourdes**, Quezon City.

22-26   **People Power Anniversary** MM — commemorates the end of the Marcos era.

MARCH & APRIL

movable   **Hari Raya Poasa** — festival week celebrating the end of Ramadan. (Sometimes held in February.)

Sarangolahan — Kite-flying contests.

Ulpi, Banaue, Ifugao — thanksgiving rites.

Friday before   **Feast of the Virgin de Turumba**, Pakil, Laguna — a throwback to ancient rites.

Palm Sunday   Vigan, Ilocos Sur — a procession makes 14 stops following the stations of the cross.

Holy Monday   Paete, Laguna — a procession in which images of Christ and saints are moved and worked to appear life-like.

Holy Thursday Navotas & Malabon, MM; Arayat & Floridablanca, Pampanga; Bocaue, Bulacan; Bagac, Bataan — flagellants and penitents move down the roads to churches.

Good Friday   Processions for the dead Christ.

Easter Sunday   Dramatizations of Mary's meeting with the risen Christ, processions, flagellants, and penitents.

Holy Week	**Moriones Festival**, Marinduque — Week-long festivities centered on the reenactment of Longinus' conversion to Christianity. Longinus was a Roman Centurion who ended Christ's agony. The conversion resulted in his persecution and decapitation. Participants wear colorful costumes and artistic masks resembling Roman warriors.
March 10-16	**Araw ng Dabaw** — Davao City fiesta in honor of the founding of Davao, tournaments between schools and organizations, tribal presentations, awards, beauty contests, and a parade.
April 9	**Bataan Death March** — reenactment in Bataan & Tarlac.
MAY	THE month for festivals
whole month	**Santacruzan** — processions in honor of Sta Helena of Constantinople
	Flores de Mayo — floral processions
1	**Labor Day**
6	Pilgrimages to Corregidor
8	**San Miguel de Mayumo**, San Miguel, Bulacan — folk art decor, local food and confectionery, procession.
14-15	**Carabao Festival**, Pulilan, Bulacan & Angono, Rizal — decorated *carabao* and oxen parade into town, some pulling carts with people, produce, and saints. A few of the animals are made to kneel in front of the church.
15	**Pahiyas**, Lukban & Sariaya, Quezon — fabulous folk art decor adorn the houses along the route of the procession in honor of San Isidro Labrador, the patron saint of Lucban, Lucena, Sariaya, and Tayabas.
17-19	**Kasilonawan**, Obando, Bulacan — fertility rites.
21-22	**Manggohan sa Guimaras** — parades, contests, exhibits featuring mangoes.
24-25	**Bale Zamboanga** — Zamboanga City festival.
JUNE	
12	**Independence Day**
24	**St. John the Baptist**, San Juan, Rizal — everywhere, water throwing is possible; Balayan, Batangas — parade of roast pigs.
28-30	**Fluvial Parade**, Apalit, Pampanga — Saints Peter & Paul are borne down the Apalit River.
30	**Santo Niño de Tacloban**, Tacloban, Leyte — Feast of the patron saint of Tacloban, celebration of the recovery of

the image of the Sto. Niño that was lost at sea; parade, sailboat races, and other festivities.

JULY

movable	**Apuy**, Banaue, Ifugao — harvest rituals.
	Pisit, Bontoc, Mountain Province — harvest rituals.
1st Sunday	**Bocaue Fluvial Festival**, Bocaue, Bulacan.
24-25	**Kinabayo**, Dapitan, Zamboanga del Norte — two days of dancing, a pageant depicting the Spanish-Moorish wars.
4th week	**Sandogo**, Tagbilaran, Bohol — commemorates the blood compact between Datu Sikatuna and Legazpi.
	Sinulog sa Tanjay, Tanjay, Negros Occidental — two-day festival with costume ball, horse fighting, serenading of visitors.
	Kahimonan Abayan, Butuan, Agusan del Norte — honoring Sta Ana for protecting the people from crocodiles
29	**Fiesta of St. Martha**, Pateros, Rizal — in memory of the occasion when the apparition of St. Martha saved the town's ducks from a crocodile.

AUGUST

movable	**Kadayawan sa Davao**, Davao City — Rituals in the form of rhythmic dances and music, floral demonstrations and contests, fruit contests, and a floral parade are all part of this vibrant festival.
	Lesles & Fagfagto, Bontoc, Mountain Province — harvest rituals
26	**Cry of Pugad Lawin** — commemorating the first uprisings against Spain.

SEPTEMBER

first week	**Kaamulan**, Malyabalay, Bukidnon — tribes adorned in their traditional dress parade and perform dances.
9-10	**Maradjao Karadjao**, Surigao City, Surigao del Norte — in honor of the patron saint, San Nicolas de Tolentino; parade, colorful street dancing, and other festivities.
10	**Sunduan**, La Huerta, Parañaque — bachelors escort formally dressed young ladies around; bands play.
3rd weekend	**Peñafrancia Festival**, Naga, Camarines Sur — Virgin of Peñafrancia rides down the Naga River accompanied by many decorated boats.
3rd week	**T'Boli Festival**, Lake Sebu, South Cotabato — tribal gathering and festival.

23 to 29	**San Miguel**, Iligan City — in honor of the city's warrior patron saint, ritual dances and reenactments of fights that occurred during the process of Christianization.
4th week	**Lanzones Festival**, Camiguin Island — parades and festivities honoring the fruits' abundance on the island.

OCTOBER

5	**Feast of Our Lady of Solitude**, Porta Vaga, Cavite City — commemorates finding the image floating at sea.
2nd Sunday	**La Naval de Manila**, Sto. Domingo Church, QC — commemorates the defeat of the Dutch fleet in 1646.
3rd week	**Zamboanga Hermosa**, Zamboanga City festival.
4th week	**Masskara**, Bacolod City festival — Bacolod's Mardi Gras-like festival.
last Sunday	**Christ the King** — all male processions.

NOVEMBER

1	**All Saints Day** — during the preceding week, people clean and paint the graves of their ancestors. On the 1st, they hold a 24-hour vigil and leave offerings of flowers and candies at the graves.
2nd week	**Baguio Arts Festival**, Baguio City.
15-30	**Yakan Harvest Festival**, Basilan.
23	**Feast of San Clemente**, Angono, Rizal — fluvial parade.

DECEMBER

	Christmas lasts from December 1 through the second Sunday of January, except in Vigan, where it starts a week earlier.
8	**Feast of Our Lady of Immaculate Conception**, Malabon MM & Vigan, Ilocos Sur — in Malabon, a fluvial parade along the Malabon River.
8-9	**Feast of Our Lady of Caysasay**, Taal, Batangas — fluvial parade.
12	**Pagsanjan town festival**.
16-25	**Misas de Gallo** — literally, masses of the cock, as everyone wakes at dawn to go to church.
4th week	**Binirayan**, San José, Antique — commemorating the arrival of Malaysian datus on Panay Island.
moveable	**Lantern Festival**, Paskohan Village, San Fernando, Pampanga — judging of giant, gaily lit lanterns (*farol*).
24	**Maytinis**, Kawit, Cavite — reenactment of Joseph and Mary's search for a room.

last Sunday	**Bota de Flores**, Ermita Church, Manila — girls toss flowers to Nuestra Señora de Guia.
28	**Holy Innocents' Day** — a day of pranks.
30	**Rizal Day** — commemorating the national hero, Dr. José Rizal.
31	**New Year's Eve** — incredible noise.

HEALTH CONCERNS

Sidewalk vendors offer a tempting array of food, but it is safest to stick to delicacies that have just emerged steaming hot from the pot or barbecue.

Malaria is a problem in the interior of more remote islands, such as Palawan, Mindoro, and Mindanao. Start anti-malarials a couple of weeks prior to leaving for these destinations.

Should you become ill, seek medical advice before leaving the country. Philippine doctors may be more knowledgeable about tropical diseases than their counterparts in temperate areas.

Makati Medical Center in Manila has a good emergency room. Many embassies have a current listing of recommended physicians and dentists.

Medical care is inexpensive in the Philippines. Most medicines are available in cities, but under local brand names. Bring with you any medicines you anticipate needing, and a good comprehensive first aid kit. Medical facilities may be rudimentary or unavailable in remote areas.

Telephone Numbers of Manila Hospitals
• **Makati Medical Center**, *Tel. 815-9911*
• **Cardinal Santos Medical Center**, *Tel. 721-3361*
• **Medical City General Hospital**, *Tel. 631-8626*
• **Saint Lukes Medical Center**, *Tel. 722-0901*

MONEY & BANKING

Banks are open from 9:00am to 3:00pm weekdays except on holidays.

The Philippine unit of currency is the **peso**, denoted as "P," which is divided into 100 centavos.

DOLLAR-PESO EXCHANGE RATE
At the time of publication, US$1 was about P26.

In Manila, most foreign currencies and travelers checks can be exchanged at banks, major hotels, and authorized dealers. **PNB** (Philippine National Bank) branches are reputed to have the best rates. For travelers checks, bring the original receipt — you may be asked to show your proof of purchase.

Most currencies can be exchanged in Metro Manila. Boracay, Cebu, Davao, and a few other places change the yen, won, deutschmark, pound, and some other currencies. Beyond these destinations you may be able to change only US dollars, and at a disadvantageous rate.

Major credit cards are accepted at larger resorts, hotels, restaurants, and shops. Be aware that although some small shops out of Manila accept credit cards, they may add a 10% surcharge.

In Manila, Cebu, and Davao, Cirrus and Plus cards can be used to withdraw pesos from certain machines.

OWNING LAND

The Philippine Constitution prohibits foreigners from acquiring land except through inheritance. However, under current investment policies, subject to foreign equity restrictions, foreigners are allowed to invest in corporations registered with the Securities and Exchange Commission (SEC) and through such companies may own property.

POSTAL SERVICE

Airmail letters cost 30¢ to North America and Europe, and postcards cost 20¢. Send important documents by courier or by registered mail.

There are several courier companies in Manila: international companies with Philippine offices include **DHL**, *Tel. 895-0511;* **Federal Express**, *Tel. 833-3604 or 831-0109;* and **UPS**, *Tel. 832-1516;* local companies with domestic and international coverage include Aboitiz Express, JRS, LBC, OCS, and TNT. DHL, JRS, LBC, and TNT have outlets in many Philippine cities and towns.

If you must check your e-mail when you are on vacation, there are Internet cafes in Manila, Cebu, and Davao.

RECOMMENDED READING

Travelers who are staying in the Philippines for a long time will want to acquire *Luzon by Car, the Map* (and the book with the same name) — a beautifully illustrated map of the Philippines' largest island. The map locates and highlights points of interest.

Ins & Outs of Manila is a reasonably good book of maps. The *Metro Manila Landmarks Map* and the *Manila Survival Map* are good city maps.

Divers will want to get a copy of the latest dive book and maps by Gretchen Hutchinson and Edgar Ventura.

Families with young children should get a copy of *Fun in Manila, a Leisure Guide for Families*, published by the In Touch Foundation, and available from their office at the Holy Trinity Church compound on McKinley Road, Forbes Park, Makati City.

RETIRING IN THE PHILIPPINES

To retire in the Philippines, foreigners must be nationals of countries with diplomatic relations with the Philippines, physically healthy, have no criminal record, and at least 35 years old.

All those applying must make a time deposit of six months. For people ages 50 and older, the amount is $50,000; for 35 to 49 years it is $75,000; and for former Filipinos, $1,500. The requirement for retired military personnel of governments recognized by the Philippines, former members of the diplomatic corps, and retired employees of international organizations (United Nations and its affiliates, World Health Organization, World Bank, and similar organizations) is $50,000 if they are at least 35 years old.

Fees for retirement are:
- $1,300 for those ages 50 and above, and former Filipino citizens; $1,800 for others;
- $200 service fee;
- $85 to the Bureau of Immigration for each dependent;
- a visitors fee of 0.5% per year of the deposit converted into an actual investment; and
- $77 annual membership fee in the Philippine Retirement Authority Membership Association Foundation.

Benefits retirees are entitled to include:
- permanent non-immigrant status with multiple-entry privileges;
- exemption from customs duties and taxes for the importation of personal effects, appliances, and furniture worth $7,000;
- exemption from exit clearance and re-entry permits;
- conversion of the required deposits into active investments;
- ownership of condominium units;
- tax-free interest on foreign currency deposits; and
- no taxes on pensions and annuities remitted to the Philippines.

Forms and brochures on retiring in the Philippines are available from the office of the **Philippine Retirement Authority**, *second floor of the PDCP Bank Building, 371 Sen. Gil J. Puyat Avenue (Buendia), Makati City*. Information is also available from Philippine Embassies and Consulates.

SHOPPING

Shopping in the Philippines can be a delightful surprise. You can still find quality items that are inexpensive, and you can bring home a variety of neat handicraft items.

Places to shop range from large malls that are usually very crowded on the weekends and on weekdays from 5:00pm onwards; department stores (ShoeMart, Robinson's, Rustans, Gaisano, are some of the large ones); shops along Manila's tourist belt (Mabini Street in Malate); in the many markets that we mention; and several handicraft stores.

When poking around the various markets and in the malls, do watch your bags and wallets carefully. Men should avoid placing their wallet in a back pocket; women should make sure their handbags are in front of them at all times. A belt-bag is preferable, as you can strap it around your waist with both the buckle and the pouch in front of you.

SOCIAL ORGANIZTAIONS

• **American Chamber of Commerce (AMCHAM)**, *Sen. Gil J. Puyat Ave., Makati. Tel. 818-6955.*
• **American Women's Club of the Philippines**, *Ground Floor, Cathedral of the Holy Trinity, 48 McKinley Road, Forbes Park, Makati. Tel. 817-7587.*
• **In Touch Foundation**, *2nd Floor, Cathedral of the Holy Trinity, 48 McKinley Road, Forbes Park, Makati. Tel. 893-1893.* The only international counseling agency in the country.

STAYING OUT OF TROUBLE

In general, the Philippines is pleasantly safe for travel. However, as in most countries, you should take reasonable precautions and use common sense — do not display wads of money and expensive jewelry; do not go off with people who promise you they know a better place to shop, where things are cheaper, as you may be drugged or robbed; do not accept food or drink from strangers, it may be drugged; if you are approached by a drunk person, excuse yourself politely.

We do advise you to stay away from a few areas. Some portions of Mindanao, particularly the southern islands of Sulu and Jolo, were in this category when we wrote this book. A few less remote areas of Mindanao have periodic problems that make it advisable for you to ask before venturing afield. This is also true of some of the more remote mountain areas of Luzon. Caution must be exercised in and around public markets and transportation areas, where thieves traditionally operate.

When visiting a rural area for more than a few hours, you should introduce yourself to the *barangay* captain, mayor, or priest. Almost all will offer valuable assistance and advice, and many will take it upon themselves to look out for your welfare. Filipino hospitality is a wonderful thing indeed.

TAXES & SERVICE CHARGE

A 10% tip is generally expected for most services. Most hotels and restaurants include a 10% service charge on your bill; additional tipping is optional. Taxes on food and rooms are 10%.

TELEPHONE

You should have no problems finding a telephone in major cities and well-developed tourist destinations (e.g., Boracay, Mindoro, Banaue, etc.). Facilities include international direct dial, telex, facsimile, courier, and telegram services. There are also several cellular phone networks; coverage varies with companies. **Piltel**, a subsidiary of Philippine Long Distance Telephone (PLDT) company, has the greatest coverage. Check with your home server to see if they have "roaming" in the Philippines.

USEFUL TELEPHONE NUMBERS IN MANILA
- *US Embassy, Tel. 521-7116*
- *Police Assistance, Tel. 116*
- *International flight information, Tel. 832-1961*
- *Domestic flight information, Tel. 818-6757*
- *Directory Assistance, Tel. 114*
- *International calls, Tel. Direct dial 00+ country code operator assisted 108*
- *USA Direct, Tel. 105-11 (AT&T); Tel. 105-14 (MCI); Tel. 105-16 (Sprint)*

Domestic Area Codes

The country code for the Philippines is **63**, and the area code for Manila is **2**. If you are in the US and are calling a number in the Philippines (say Manila), dial 011-63-area code (2)-number. If you are in the Philippines making a domestic long distance call, dial 0-area code-number; to call the US from the Philippines, dial 00-1-area code-number.

The sidebar on the next page lists the area codes for the provinces of the Philippines.

PROVINCIAL AREA CODES

Abra: 74	Leyte: 53
Agusan del Norte: 85	Maguindanao: 64
Agusan del Sur: 85	Marinduque: 42
Aklan: 36	Masbate: 56
Albay: 52	Metro Manila: 2
Antique: 36	Mindoro Occidental: 43
Aurora: 42	Mindoro Oriental: 43
Basilan: 62	Misamis Occidental: 88
Bataan: 47	Misamis Oriental: 88
Batangas: 43	Mt. Province: 74
Benguet: 74	Negros Occidental: 34
Biliran: 53	Negros Oriental: 35
Bohol: 38	North Cotobato
Bukidnon: 88	& Lake Sebu: 64
Bulacan: 44	Nueva Ecija: 44
Cagayan: 78	Nueva Vizcaya: 78
Camarines Norte: 54	Palawan: 48
Camarines Sur: 54	Pampanga: 45
Camiguin: 88	Pangasinan: 75
Capiz: 36	Quezon: 42
Catanduanes: 52	Quirino: 78
Cavite: 46	Rizal: 2
Cebu: 32	Romblon: 42
Davao del Norte: 84	Samar: 55
Davao City & del Sur: 82	Sarangani: 83
Davao Oriental: 87	Siquijor: 35
Guimaras: 33	Sorsogon: 56
Ifugao: 74	South Cotobato: 83
Ilocos Norte: 77	Sultan Kudarat: 64
Ilocos Sur: 77	Sulu: 68
Iloilo: 33	Surigao del Norte: 86
Isabela: 78	Surigao del Sur: 86
Kalinga-Apayao: 74	Tarlac: 45
La Union: 72	Tawi-Tawi: 68
Laguna: 49	Zamboanga del Norte: 65
Lanao del Norte: 63	Zamboanga del Sur: 62
Lanao del Sur: 63	Zambales: 47

TIME ZONE

Philippine time is **GMT plus eight hours**. The time difference from the East Coast of the United States is 12 to 13 hours depending on daylight savings; from the West Coast it is 15 to 16 hours.

TOURIST OFFICES

Your best source of information will probably be a traveler who has been to the area recently, as he or she will have the latest rates and information. It is typical of the tropics that while some things stay constant, others change, grow, disappear.

The **Department of Tourism (DOT)** has several regional offices. Some places have terrific staff that are very helpful and friendly, and are a wealth of accurate information; others unfortunately fall short. We mention in the text the offices and people that can be useful sources of information and services for your travels. You should be able to get maps and simple brochures on the region from these offices. Some regional offices also offer good package tours.

The head office, *DOT Building, Rizal Park, Manila, Tel. 523-8411 (local 146 for tourist information),* has rate and schedule information throughout the country, and several nice looking brochures and maps that may come in handy. There is also a tourist assistance hotline that is 24-hours Mondays through Saturdays, *Tel. 524-1660.* In Cebu City, the 24-hour number is *Tel. 254-1136.* There is an information desk at the international airport in Manila, and at the international terminal of Cebu's Mactan Airport (look for Florentino "Bebot" Estillore, who is very helpful).

Regional Offices
Asterisks indicate offices that were particularly helpful.
- **Baguio City, Benguet**,* *DOT Complex, Gov. Pack Road, Baguio City. Tel. 442-7014, 442-6708*
- **San Fernando, La Union**,* *Mabanag Building, Capitol Hills, San Fernando, La Union. Tel. 412-411*
- **Laoag, Ilocos Norte**, *Ilocano Heroes Hall, Laoag City. Tel. 712-0467*
- **Tuguegarao, Cagayan**,* *Second Floor, Tuguegarao Supermarket, Tuguegarao, Cagayan. Tel. 844-1621*
- **Legazpi City, Albay**, *Penaranda Park, Albay District, Legazpi City. Tel. 44-492, 44-026*
- **Iloilo City**,* *Provincial Capitol, Bonifacio Drive, Iloilo City. Tel. 75-411, 335-0145*
- **Bacolod City**,* *City Public Plaza Building, Bacolod City. Tel. 29-021*
- **Cebu City**,* *Third Floor GMC Plaza Building, across Plaza Independencia, Cebu City. Tel. 254-2811*

- **Tacloban City, Leyte**, *Children's Park, Senator Enage Street, Tacloban City. Tel. 321-2048*
- **Cagayan de Oro City**, *Pelaez Sports Center, Apolinar Velez Street, Cagayan de Oro. Tel. 726-394*
- **Butuan City**, *City Hall Compound, Butuan City. Tel. 82-041*
- **Davao City**,* *Magsaysay Park Complex, Door 7, Santa Ana, Davao City. Tel. 221-6798, 221-6955*
- **Zamboanga City**,* *Lantaka Hotel, Valderosa Street, Zamboanga City. Tel. 991-0218*

Other Tourism Associations

Some cities and towns have their own tourist information centers that can give you additional information or serve as an alternative to DOT offices. These "City Tourism Offices" and "Tourist Information Centers" are not directly under the DOT, but are managed by the office of the local mayor. Throughout this book, we mention the offices that have been helpful.

WATER

Water may not be potable. Therefore, stick to bottled water, canned beverages, coffee, tea, or hot water. You can buy water purification tablets in the large drugstores of major cities.

8. SPORTS & RECREATION

BASKETBALL

Although most Filipinos are much shorter on average than Americans, they are agile basketball players and avid fans. Many large companies have professional teams that often include an "import" or two from the US, and nearly every village has a basketball court.

BOWLING & BILLIARDS

Most major cities have bowling alleys, some with billiard tables as well. The prices are more or less the same at all establishments: $2 for one game of bowling; 40¢ for shoe rental (bring your own socks, some shoes can be squishy); and $4.60 for one hour of billiards.

See Chapter 11, *Metropolitan Manila*, for a list of bowling & billiards places in Manila.

CAVING

See *Spelunking* below.

COCK-FIGHTING

This gory spectator sport, locally called *sabong*, is not for animal lovers, nor the faint-hearted and squeamish. This ancient game is part of local culture, and one of the few activities where class distinctions are not recognized among the people involved, except that a few urban arenas have air conditioned seating. Almost every town in the Philippines has a *sabungan* or *galleria* (cockfighting arena), where crowds gather on Sundays, holidays, and during fiestas. Most people go to gamble. Even in very small rural towns, you will see bets reaching several thousand Philippine pesos. Good fighting birds are very valuable.

As the action gets under way, the birds are paired off to fight the same way boxers are — by weight. A razor-sharp spur of equal length is attached to each opposing cock. The birds are then brought to the center of the circular arena, and the fight begins as soon as the protective sheaths of the spurs are removed. Fights may last from a few seconds to minutes, and end when one bird is killed, severely maimed, or runs away. The *sentenciador* ("he who gives the sentence") announces the winner, and his decision is never questioned.

Bets are taken and kept track of by *Kristos* (so named as they strike a Christ-like pose with extended arms as they move around the arena acknowledging bets). All records are kept mentally, and betting is done by word of honor — there is no need to prove that you have money to cover your bet. The betting is resolved as money passes between the *Kristos* and the bettors. Do not renege on your bet or try to lower the value you originally declared.

DIVING

See *Scuba Diving* below.

FISHING

The Philippines has very good spots for catching blue marlin and tuna. **General Santos City**, the tuna capital of the country, is where most of the tuna and marlin are brought in and bid off daily to buyers from Japan, Taiwan, Davao, and Manila.

There is supposed to be some decent game fishing — marlin and tuna — around Cape San Agustin. Fishing tours are offered by **Island Tour Transport Services**, *Ong Building, Bolton Street, Davao City, Tel. 224-2435, 224-1883*. Tours require a minimum of three people and the cost of $195 per person includes boat rental, food (for you to eat), as well as bait. Other places to fish for tuna and marlin include off **Siargao Island**, and in the **Maqueda Channel** off the Catanduanes.

Fishing boat charters are very expensive. Try **International Golden Horizon Cruise and Travel**, *Manila, Tel. 525-5698, Fax 524-1571*; **Excello Aquatic Charters International**, *Manila Tel. 785-225*; and **Starcraft Corporation**, *South Sea Dive and Travel Inc., 1501 Sto. Sepulcro Street, Paco, Tel. 524-2841, Fax 526-2511*.

FOOTBALL: RUGBY & SOCCER

Physically, Filipinos have the build for soccer more so than basketball and yet basketball is a much more popular sport here — perhaps because of the American influence. There is a small soccer league and in Manila, you may join pick-up-games at **Nomads** where there is also Rugby. See Chapter 11, *Metropolitan Manila*, for more details.

There is no American football.

GAMBLING

There are several casinos in Cebu City (including one on a cruise ship) and in Manila, and at least one each in Laoag, Ilocos Norte; Bacolod City; Davao; Angeles; and Subic. Some tours come just for the casinos, from Taiwan, Korea, and Japan.

GO-CARTS

Approximately an hour south of Manila is the **Carmona Race Track**, where you can rent go-carts by the hour or half hour. The go-carts are classified into separate groups: for ages nine to 15, for 16 and above, and for "professional executives" — ages 30 and up. The costs are $18 for half an hour, and $36 for an hour.

We recommend that you call in advance (there may be a race) and make reservations at: *Barrio Bangkal, Carmona, Cavite, Tel. 817-2241 (Manila); look for Johnny Tan.*

GOLF

The Philippines has a number of fine golf courses, some of international championship standard. Most of the courses are owned by private clubs, although some clubs will allow non-members to use the facilities on weekdays. We have included the rates for courses open to the public.

Manila has five courses (see Chapter 11). Near Manila, there are a number of courses in Antipolo and Tagaytay; and one course each at Canlubang, Calatangan, and Cavite. In the provinces, you can play golf in Baguio City; Laoag, Ilocos Norte; Legaspi City; Iloilo City; Bacolod City; Cebu; Davao (three courses); South Cotobato (in the Dole Plantation); Zamboanga City; Bukdinon (in the Del Monte Plantation); and near Cagayan de Oro.

GOTCHA! PAINTBALL WAR GAME

If you are a war enthusiast or just want to get rid of excess energy, you can spend a morning or afternoon at this game, where participants are divided into groups that will then go to war against each other; your ammunition is a paint gun. There are four different war game scenarios to go through. Wear rugged clothes, or (if you have any) camouflage gear. "Guns" and a helmet are supplied; direct paintball hits do bruise, so consider wearing long sleeves. The cost, including bullets and a helmet, is $10 for half a day.

The organizers prefer to handle large groups in the morning, and individuals in the afternoon. The easiest way to get to the game site is by car, although taxis and public transport are possible. The site is at the **Alpadi Compound**, *Sumulong Highway, Antipolo, Tel. 706-447, 703-489.*

HORSE RACING

The Philippines' first horse racing club was built in Manila 1867, and racing remains a popular sport for betting. See Chapter 11.

HORSEBACK RIDING

You can rent a horse and take lessons in Manila at **Pook Ligaya Stables**, a small family-run establishment. See Chapter 11 for details. You may also ride in Subic (see Chapter 12).

There is also riding in Makati at the **Manila Polo Club**, but you must be sponsored by a member. At the **Equestrian Promotions** inside Ayala Alabang Subdivision, the management, which is looking for competition riders; do not bother coming here if you just want to ride for fun.

ICE SKATING

Surprising as it is, there are facilities for ice skating in Manila — see Chapter 11.

KAYAKING

Kayaking is relatively new in this country, but is a great way to island hop. **Sea Canoe** runs tours around Coron, in northern Palawan. The itineraries take you around the island, to mangrove swamp inlets, lagoons, caves, and coral gardens and reefs. Day trips cost $40, including kayak, and the three-day trip costs $360 per person, and includes transfers, supplies for camping and food, and inflatable kayak. To make reservations, contact *Sea Canoe Thailand Co. Ltd., PO Box 276 Phuket 83000, Thailand, Tel. 6676-212-252, Fax. 212-172*; via Internet: *sea.canoe@phuket.com*; in Manila, inquiries can be made through the **Blue Horizon Travel Agency** in the *Shangri-La Hotel, Tel. 813-8888*.

You can also go kayaking in Northern Surigao del Norte, around Siargao and nearby islands. Here, day trips take you island hopping, through mangrove forests, and through a spectacular cave that opens into a beautiful blue lagoon. Tours are run by Nicolas or Florence Rambeau; write to them at: **Siargao Pension House**, *General Luna, Siargao, Surigao del Norte, Tel. 87268-204-1283, Fax 204-1284*. Tours cost around $40 per person, and the Rambeaus give priority to guests staying at Siargao Pension.

Kayak tours around Boracay and some parts of northern Visayas are run by Greg Hutchinson of **Tribal Holdings**, *c/o Sand Castles, Balabag, Boracay, Tel. 288-3207, Fax 288-3449; or in Manila at Tel. 823-2725*. Day tours cost $40 per person and overnight costs $100-200, depending on the destination.

MARTIAL ARTS

Karatedo and **Taekwondo** lessons are available in Manila. See Chapter 11.

MOUNTAIN CLIMBING

The Philippines has numerous mountains and volcanoes to climb, from easy little ones like **Taal Volcano** (a 20-minute uphill walk to overlook the new crater), to moderate one-day efforts (**Arayat** in Pampanga, and **Makiling** in Laguna, are two dormant volcanoes that are nice climbs); to three- or four-day climbs. The country's tallest peak is **Apo**, a 2,945-meter-high dormant volcano in Davao, Mindanao, and the second highest is **Mount Pulog** (not a volcano), which is barely 30 meters shorter, and is in the heart of the Cordillera Mountains of Central Luzon. Neither of these is really difficult, and you can start the climb about 1,500 meters or so above sea level. The main challenge is provisioning and, if you hire porters or guides, you will probably need an extra tent or space for them in yours, as they may not have a tent of their own.

Mount Mayon, a truly beautiful peak, is a difficult climb (lots of scree, and you have to avoid sulfur smoke when you reach the crater's rim). There are other challenging climbs in the country, such as **Halcon** on Mindoro and **Guiting-guiting** on Sibuyan Island in Romblon.

Guides are usually almost essential, as many trails cross-cross and local knowledge is very important. There are no marked trails. Most areas have local mountaineering clubs that can be helpful. Remember that mountain climbing in the tropics can be a very thirsty experience indeed – you will need up to six liters (six quarts) of water a day per person. For more information, see individual chapters and the "mountain and volcano" section of the index. Proper equipment can be difficult to find and expensive to acquire, so if you intend to do any serious climbing, bring your own gear.

NATIONAL PARKS

Surprising to many residents of the country, the Philippines has a number of national parks and areas proclaimed as "national reserves." However, these areas often do not seem like national parks: partly due to lack of funding, they are often encroached upon, forests or reefs are damaged, etc. A number of dive sites are classified as protected areas. The following are among the country's parks and reserves (an asterisk indicates parks covered in this guide):

• **Mount Makiling Forest Reserve**, *Luzon*
• **Quezon National Recreation Area**, *Luzon*
• **Hundred Islands National Park**, *Luzon**

• **Mount Pulog National Park**, *Luzon**
• **Mount Ilig-Mt Baco National Wildlife Sanctuary**, *Mindoro*
• **Mount Manunggal National Park**, *Cebu*
• **Mount Kanlaon National Park**, *Negros Occidental**
• **Danjugan Wildlife Sanctuary**, *Negros Occidental**
• **Leyte National Park and Mahagnao Volcano**, *Leyte**
• **Sohoton Natural Bridge National Park**, *Western Samar**
• **Saint Paul Subterranean National Park**, *Palawan**
• **Mount Apo National Park**, *Mindanao**

PARASAILING

The one place that you can go parasailing is in the **Hilutungan Channel** off Mactan Island, Cebu. The A**dvance Marine Sports**, *Shangri-La's Mactan Island Resort, Cebu, Tel. 231-5060, Fax 231-5061*, offers parasailing daily; you will need to make reservations a day in advance. The company, run by Americans, is licensed by the International Parasail Boating Association and by the US Coast Guard. Cost per flight for guests (single or tandem) is $50, and because of limited space on the accompanying boat, observers are charged $19.

POLO

You can watch this exclusive "game of kings" at the **Manila Polo Club** on Sundays during January to May. To play polo, you will have to be sponsored by a member of the club. See Chapter 11.

SAILING

Every other year (even-numbered years), during Easter, the **China Sea Race** starts in Hong Kong and finishes in the Philippines. Boats take 4-7 days to complete this 1,200-kilometer international regatta. Spectators come mainly from Manila and Hong Kong, but the race includes fans and participants from other countries.

Sailing lessons are available at the **Manila Yacht Club (MYC)**, *Roxas Boulevard, Tel. 521-4457*. There are also yacht clubs in Cebu, Puerto Galera, and Subic.

SCUBA DIVING

If you are a diver, or want to learn to dive, you will be pleased to know that the Philippines has a number of the world's top diving destinations. The country is home to extensive reefs, colorful marine life, and warm tropical water (77-79°F or 25-26°C). Even though dynamite and cyanide fishing have taken a serious toll, recent protection has encouraged new growth in some of the affected areas.

FIVE REEF TYPES FOUND IN THE PHILIPPINES
- *fringing reefs* surround islands and land
- *barrier reefs* are platforms separated by a lagoon from land
- *atolls* are circular shaped with a lagoon in the center and rest on the top of a submerged volcano
- *small patch reefs* usually rise up from the floors of lagoons
- *table reefs* are small reefs in the open sea

According to professional divers, the marine life here is one of the most diverse in the world — over 2,000 species of fish and even more invertebrates. Hundreds of differently patterned and colored nudibranchs; tridacna clams; numerous sea stars; eagle, marble, leopard, and manta rays; white tip, black tip, grey reef, leopard, and nurse sharks; moray eels; angel fish; parrot fish; jack fish; squirrel fish; hawksbill and green sea turtles; whales; dolphins; and (if you are lucky) a rare sea cow — these are a tiny sampling of what is in store for you.

Probably the best place to dive in the country is around the area of **Tubbataha Reef** in the Sulu Sea. As the area is remote, it serves as a breeding ground and home to hundreds of species of fish, and the reefs are mostly intact. Access is by live-aboards. Other destinations with dive operations include **Anilao** (the nearest to Manila — three to four hours away by land); parts of **Mindoro**; around **Palawan, Cebu, Bohol, Dumaguete, Boracay**, around **Davao**; in **Sarrangani Bay**; and parts of **Zamboanga**. Refer to the appropriate chapters for details on each place.

The Philippines also has numerous sites for **wreck diving**. The destinations closest to Manila for wreck diving are **Subic Bay** and **Batangas**. Probably the most exciting place for wreck diving is around **Palawan**, where there are vessels from World War Two, ancient Chinese junks, and Spanish galleons. There are also wrecks around the bay in **Davao**, and off **Poro Point** in La Union.

As the Philippines was a major naval battleground during World War Two, particularly off **Leyte Gulf**, a number of areas are littered with sunken ships. Several of these areas are unsafe to dive — the currents are extremely dangerous.

There are many excellent instructors and divemasters in the Philippines. But there are also some that are not competent and are not truly certified. You should always ask your instructor or divemaster to show his international C-card and certification. In the various chapters that include diving, we recommend a number of reputable dive operators. Also, we strongly suggest that you get a copy of the latest dive book by veteran divers Gretchen Hutchinson and Edgar "Bong" Ventura, for more details on diving and dive operators in the Philippines. Gretchen and Bong have extensive and up-to-date underwater experience in the Philippines, and know the ins and outs of diving in the country. They have provided most of the diving information for this book.

Keep in mind that you are a visitor in the underwater realm. Most marine animals will avoid contact with humans, and will not attack unless provoked and they feel threatened. Exercise general common sense — it is best not to handle the animals, especially when you are not sure what they are; if a fish is acting aggressively, go elsewhere; do not act aggressively; watch where you grab or kneel, you may end up touching a scorpion or stone fish — scorpion fish have very painful stings and stonefish stings can be fatal. Always inquire about the currents of the area.

If you are bringing most of your equipment with you, then acquire a **Flying Sportsman Card** from Philippine Airlines. This enables scubadivers and golfers to carry excess baggage (gear and equipment) on flights without having to pay excess baggage fees. To obtain a card, write or go to the *Tours and Promotions Office, Marketing and Sales Department, PAL Building 1, Legaspi Street, Makati, Tel. 818-0111.* You will need to submit your application with a passport sized photo and a photocopy of your certification card.

Weather Conditions

The weather is best from November to mid-June, and expect the rates to be highest during this time. Although you may get landed for a few days from June to October, you can avail of off season rates and dive sites will not be crowded nor tours fully booked.

Dive Shops in Manila

- **Aqua Tropical Sports**, *Suite 201, Manila Midtown Hotel, P Gil Street, Ermita, Tel. 523-1842, Fax 522-2536*
- **Aquaventure**, *Almeda Building, 2150 Pasong Tamo Street, Makati City, Tel. 844-1996, 844-1492*
- **Asia Divers**, *Swagman Travel, 1133 Guerrero Street, Ermita, Manila, Tel. 522-3663, Fax 522-3650*
- **Dive Buddies**, *Ground Floor, L & S Building, 1414 Roxas Blvd., Manila, Tel. 524-0838, 524-0867, Fax 521-9170*
- **Divemate**, *2172C Pasong Tamo, Makati City, Tel. 816-0366, Fax 816-0598*
- **Scubaworld**, *7246 Malugay Street, Makati City, Tel. 843-2710, Fax 817-4504*
- **Southsea Dive**, *1501 Sto. Sepulcro Street Paco, Tel. 524-2841, Fax 523-3237*
- **Whitetip Divers**, *Unit 206-209, 1362 A Mabini Street, Ermita, Tel. 526-2629, 526-8190, 526-8191*

Certification

Do not dive without being certified. This is one of the cheapest countries to take a full course and get your certification. Many dive shops, camps, and resorts offer introductory and advanced classes. An intensive basic course can be completed in a few days and can cost $250 to $400, including equipment and boat rentals, etc. The most common certification agencies are SSI, PADI, NAUI, NASDS, VIT, BSAC, and CMAS.

Live-Aboards

To explore the more remote reefs with abundant marine life, the best way is by **live-aboards**. The popular areas for live-aboard cruises are between the islands of Cebu and Palawan. Some of the recommended live-aboards currently operating are:

• **Tristar Sea Ventures Corporations**, *2038 Kalamansi Street, Damariñas Village, Makati, Tel. 843-5453, Fax 810-9180.* Tristar schedules trips from March to June – Tuabbataha, Sulu Sea; June to October – Cebu and Bohol; and October to February – Northern Palawan. Approximate cost: $150 to 200 per person per day.

• **Svetlana**, *Dakak Aqua Sports Inc., Ground Floor, Makati Tuscany Building, 6751 Ayala Avenue, Makati City, Tel. 844-5970, Fax 844-5971.* Trips are schedule: April to May — Sulu Sea; and July to October — Visayas. Approximate cost: $140 to $200 per person per day.

• **Aquastar**, *312 Sarmiento Building, 2316 Pasong Tamo Extension, Makati, Tel. 816-7233, Fax 813-1967.* Trips are scheduled year-round — Sulu Sea, Boracay, Cebu, Dumaguete, Anilao. Approximate cost: $200 to $250 per person/day.

• **Black Fin**, *Maris Chartering Inc., Room 8 Upper Penthouse, 107 Paseo De Roxas, Legaspi Village, Makati, Tel. 812-7027, Fax 819-1157.* Cost: $200 per person per day.

• **Island Explorer**, *Cruise Island Adventures Inc., 7246 Malugay St., MCPO Box 2815, Makati City, Tel-Fax 817-4504.* Cost: $200 per person/day.

• **Nautica**, *Eagle Trek Adventures, Ground Floor, L & S Bldg., 1414 Roxas Boulevard, Ermita, Tel. 524-0838, 524-0867, Fax 521-9170.* Cost: $150 to $200 per person/day.

SNORKELING

The Philippines is one of the world's best places for scuba diving, and snorkeling here is equally as fascinating. Shallow reefs and coral-fringed beaches and islands are great places for non-divers to enjoy the colorful marine life here. If you do not bring a snorkel and mask, you can rent or buy them at dive shops (see above) or buy them at some sports stores, and at the American Discount Store in MegaMall.

We advise wearing booties or a form of protection for your feet. Don't touch coral at all, to avoid damaging it, and certainly not without gloves: you may get cut or stung by a poisonous fish or shellfish. Even coral can give you a nasty infection.

Many of the better snorkeling areas will be away from the shore, too far to swim to. Consider renting a *banca* for several hours. When you are tired, you can rest by hanging on to the outriggers of these boats – in many areas, you can snorkel while floating with an arm wrapped around an outrigger. If you want company, ask around at dive centers: dive groups may allow you to tag along for a small fee (usually to chip in for boat rental).

The nearest place to snorkel is in **Anilao**, **Batangas**; refer to Chapter 11, *Excursions & Day Trips From Manila*, for more information. Other places include the **Hundred Islands** in Pangasinan; many areas of **Palawan**; parts of **Mindoro**, **Marinduque**, **Bohol**, and **Cebu**; **Apo Island** in Dumaguete; and **Samal** and **Talicud islands** off Davao City.

SPELUNKING

There are hundreds, probably thousands of caves in the Philippines. Several have been explored, but few are frequented. During World War Two, the Japanese purportedly hid gold and other precious stones in over a hundred caves throughout the country. In the '60s and '70s, teams searched and excavated areas in the hopes of finding a fortune. President Marcos claimed that his fortune came from finding a golden Buddha in a cave in Baguio City. To this day, some people are still searching for the fabled "Yamashita treasure," the gold and silver that the Japanese took from central banks in many countries that has not been recovered.

The accessible caves of **Sagada** in Mountain Province have been used for centuries as burial grounds. This is a popular "off-the-beaten-track" destination; unfortunately some visitors have taken bones from the caves as "souvenirs." This is a desecration. Another of Luzon's notable caves is the **Callao Cave** of Peñablanca, Cagayan. You may also visit **Hoyop-hoyopan and Calabidongan** caves near Legazpi.

The **Sohoton National Park** in Western Samar is a great place for spelunkers. It has a labyrinth of caves and underground waterways. The beautiful Sohoton Cave has brilliant stalactite and stalagmite formations. At Palawan's **St. Paul's Subterranean National Park's Underground River** you can enjoy a scenic and relaxing *banca* ride through most of the river. And, over to the southeast region of the Philippines, paddle your own kayak through Surigao del Norte's **Suhoton Cave**, on Bucas Grande Island, to the breath-taking blue lagoon on the other side.

There are numerous other caves for you to explore, and we cover some of the better ones in the destination chapters.

SURFING

Most Filipinos are not familiar with surfing, so not much information is readily available, even though the country hosts an international surfing competition in **Siargao** annually. A good part of the country's 18,000-kilometer coastline faces the open Pacific Ocean, and there are numerous spots around the country. If there are a lot of people out surfing, your quality time is minimized; so, the hardcore surfers like to keep a number of places secret.

The few places that we have been told about, by surfers, are:
- **Cape Encanto** at Baler Bay in Aurora
- **Puraran** (**Mystic**) in Catanduanes
- **Tandag** in Surigao del Sur
- **Bagasbas Beach** near Daet in Camarines Sur
- **Mona Lisa** in La Union

TENNIS

Most high-end hotels in the major cities have tennis courts open to non-guests for a fee. Many cities have public tennis courts and locals often welcome visitors. When available, tennis trainers are inexpensive — and you may be able to have a ballboy as well. See Chapter 11 for a list of courts in Manila.

WINDSURFING

You may windsurf and take windsurfing lessons at **Lake Caliraya**; **Anilao**; **Boracay**, where there is an annual windsurf competition; and at most up-scale resorts on **Mactan Island** in Cebu.

9. FOOD & DRINK

FOOD

Dining in the Philippines is an experience you will enjoy — from international cuisine to local delights — no matter what your budget is. In major cities, you will enjoy the profusion of restaurants that have recently emerged: European, Chinese, and Japanese are most common, and you will also see a number of restaurants that specialize in Indian, Korean, Thai, Vietnamese and other cuisines.

If you find yourself craving for a good-ol'-American meal, in Manila you can chose from Friday's, Hard Rock Café, Tony Roma's, Chilli's, and Fashion Café. Throughout the country, American and American-influenced fast-food chains have cropped up. McDonalds, Shakeys, Wendys, Kentucky Fried Chicken, and Kenny Rogers Roaster (to name a few), compete with the local burger giant Jollybee and with Chinese dim sum for the meal-on-the-run business, while sidewalk barbecue stalls and *turo-turo* (the Filipino version of a canteen) are inexpensive ($1.15) and can be a great experience, as long as the food is fresh and newly cooked.

We list a number of restaurants, from *turo-turo* to formal establishments, from local and Asian to Western, in each of the chapters. If we have referred to a restaurant in the provinces (outside Manila and Cebu) as "finer dining," we advise you not to appear in grubby clothes — jeans and a shirt or nice shorts and a shirt and shoes (not slippers) are acceptable; and expect the prices to be higher than most eating places in the area. These "finer" restaurants would still be considered casual dining places in New York, San Francisco, Manila, etc. In the provinces, a full meal at a simple restaurant will cost you from $3 to $6, and in the "finer dining" establishments, from $8 to $16.

Restaurants of the major hotels are frequented by local and expat business people and the well-to-do of Philippine society. Several of these hotels do have one or two very good restaurants. A meal in one of these restaurants will probably cost you around $25 (in the US you may spend $10 more), plus drinks; many have lunch buffet specials that go for $20.

Filipino cooking is an experience you must try. Some of it is very good. The seafood (except of course into the mountains) is so fresh and delicious — not to mention much cheaper than in the US — that many westerners who did not particularly like fish are converted. Filipino cooking, unlike most Asian cuisine, is generally not spicy, although you will find a few dishes that are usually prepared or served with a lot of chilies.

If you are an adventurous eater, you may want to try:

• *bagoong* (dried, fermented tiny shrimp or fish); it is on the salty side, is used to flavor some dishes, and is eaten with mango slices; and

• *balut*, which is unhatched duck embryo.

While you are here, do treat yourself to the fruits in season — mangoes, pomelo (*suha*), papaya, avocado, and guava are among the well-known ones; lesser known delights include *lanzones* (beige clusters of fruit), *chico* (brown fruits), *langka* (jackfruit), *atis* (custard apple or sweet sop), *santol, caimito* (star apple), mangosteen, *mabolo*, rambutan, the smelly durian, and the less odiferous *marang*.

Several establishments offer fruit shakes or juices. Green mango, *buco* (young coconut), and *calamansi* (small green lemon-lime fruit) juices are among the favorites. Specify little or no sugar if you don't want the drink to come very sweet.

Rice is a staple here and is present at just about every meal. Filipinos eat hearty breakfasts that are often a combination of a western breakfast with plain or fried rice and anything left over from yesterday's meals. Meals are often multi-dish affairs. Snacks (*merienda*) are eaten between meals. Dinner is served around 7:00pm. Several dishes and foods that you might like to try are listed below.

Main Dishes

adobo — dishes cooked with vinegar and soy sauce, including *baboy* (pork) and/or *manok* (chicken), *pusit* (squid), *isda* (fish), *kangkong* (vegetable similar to spinach, grown in water)

alimango — large shore-line crab

alimasag — the slender deep-sea crab

bangus — milk fish served stuffed, grilled, or fried; specify boneless if you don't want to deal with many tiny bones

beefsteak *Tagalog* — thin slices of beef cooked with soy sauce and onions

calamares — fried squid rings

camote — sweet potatoes/yams

chop suey — (transplanted American food): stir-fried vegetables in a sauce

crispy pata — pork leg, boiled then roasted or fried

dinuguan — pork tripe stewed in blood

guinataan — cooked in coconut milk (vegetables, shrimp, chicken, or fish for a main course; see also sweets and snacks)

gulay — vegetables

inihaw or *ihaw-ihaw* — barbeque

kare kare — beef tripe

kambing — goat

kilawen — raw fish (or oysters, etc.) soaked in vinegar, garlic, etc.

la Paz batchoy — noodle soup with meat

lechon — whole roast pig

lapu lapu — grouper

lumpia — egg roll; fillings include *shanghai* (meat); *sariwa* (fresh vegetables); *ubod* (heart of palm); *gulay* (vegetables)

mechado — stewed beef roll

nilaga — stewed

pakbet or *pinakbet* — Ilocano vegetable dish with pork, shrimps, and *bagoong*

pancit — noodles, which come in many varieties: *pancit* Malabon has a mixture of seafood, vegetables, and pork; *pancit bihon* is similar but made with thin noodles; *pancit guisado* is fried noodles with meat and vegetables; *pancit Canton* is similar

singkamas — turnip (jicama), good peeled and eaten raw

sinigang — a delicious sour tamarind-based soup

talaba — oysters

tahong — mussels; very good baked

tapa — dried or marinated meat

tinola — chicken vegetable soup with lemon grass

Sweets & Snacks

bibingka — rice cake, many varieties, some used as a sweet, others as a bread

guinatan or guinataan — fruits boiled in sugar and coconut milk; *guinatan* refers to the method of cooking, as it is also served as a main dish.

halo-halo — sweet beans and preserved fruits with ice, milk, and ice cream

leche flan — custard

maja blanca — coconut milk and milk

pulutan — finger foods with drinks

puto — rice cake

siopao — dim sum with meat and gravy filling in a steamed bun

DRINK

Soft drinks are sold everywhere in the Philippines, and, so is beer. Bottled water is also found in many places around the country, but not as extensively as soft drinks and beer. You should stick to drinking bottled water, soft drinks, hot tea, or coffee, as the local water may not be boiled or clean. The major brands of soft drinks you will find here are Coke, Pepsi, Sarsi, Sprite, Seven Up, Royal Tru Orange (not a spelling error), and Mountain Dew; in the major cities, you will be able to find the diet line of sodas.

The Philippines also carries the American beers Budweiser and Miller in major cities only. The local beer brands can be found practically everywhere: world-renowned **San Miguel** beer (contrary to many people's belief, this beer originated here, not Spain). Do try San Miguel here: the version available in the United States has been watered down to meet US government standards. Other local beers include **Red Horse** (very strong for a beer) and **Beer na Beer**. When you are in the provinces, you will sometimes find that the cheapest beverage is beer! Bottled water is more costly than beer or softdrinks. In general, beer and soft drinks cost the same, 35¢; bottled water will cost 50¢.

A number of local spirits are also available cheaply. A small bottle of **Tanduay Rhum**, popular with many foreigners, will cost 80¢; the gin, ginebra, is not that popular and can taste and smell like rubbing alcohol. If you enjoy trying different alcoholic drinks, taste *tuba* (made from the juice of coconut palms) and *lambanog* (distilled *tuba* — it is very strong); *tapuy* ("rice wine" — this beer can be sweet when newly brewed); and *basi* (liquor made from sugarcane).

Most of the bars and restaurants in the major cities and frequently touristed destinations will have imported alcohol available.

10. BEST PLACES TO STAY

AMANPULO, *Pamalican Island, Cuyo. Manila reservations: Tel. 532-4044. 40 cottages. $300-610 per cottage. Visa, Master Card, American Express, Diners.*

Amanpulo means peaceful island, and not only is it peaceful, but breathtakingly beautiful. It is a private island you may visit only if you are staying at the resort. The island is fringed with fine white sand, aquamarine water, and a coral reef that abounds with life. The beaches are indescribably beautiful.

The cottages, called *casitas*, are well spaced, affording guests privacy. All casitas are attractively designed and are the same size. Prices vary with season, and casitas 39 & 40 are the most expensive as they are on "their private beach." All have air conditioning, cable TV, laser disc players, are lavishly and tastefully furnished, and have nice views. The casitas are spacious, have king-sized beds, and a large bathroom and dressing area. Each casita is provided with a personal motorized cart so you can tour the island on your own time and pace.

The architecture of the main areas gives the resort an expensive yet refreshingly airy feel. The attention given to details is obvious. Aside from its beautiful swimming pool, facilities and services include tennis, a library with a good selection of Filipiniana and international material, small art gallery, jogging and walking paths, and massage services (in the privacy of your casita). Aquasports are ample: sailing (hobiecats, lasers, windsurfs), rowing, fishing, snorkeling, and diving. The dive center is complete and courses are offered from introductory to advanced levels. An open water course costs $480, boat fees not included.

Dine in the privacy of your casita or select from one of the three outlets, each with a pretty view.

As one expects from an exclusive resort, service and staff are first-rate. This is a well-managed resort, you get top-of-the-line facilities, views, and service, for top dollars. Note that the flight to the island from Manila is an additional $350 per person.

Amanpulo's memorable features are its gorgeous beaches, first-class facilities, and attentive staff who pamper you and yet do not infringe upon the utmost privacy you can possibly get — save for being on a secluded island. See the"Distant Islands" section of Chapter 19, *Palawan*.

SHANGRI-LA'S MACTAN ISLAND RESORT, *Punta Engaño Road, Lapu-Lapu City. Tel. 231-0288, Fax 231-1688. Manila reservations: Tel. 813-8888. US reservations: 1-800/942-5050. 547 rooms. $224-430 per single ($290 for ocean view), $245-450 per double ($310 for ocean view), $390-1,126 per suite, $40 per extra bed. Visa, Master Card, American Express, Diners.*

Mactan's top-of-the-line resort is indeed luxurious. The lobby is very pretty and airy. You are greeted warmly at the reception then whisked away to the comfort of your well-appointed and tastefully designed room. All rooms have a private balcony and complete amenities.

"Bayview" rooms overlook the Bay of Cebu; "oceanview" rooms overlook the beautiful pool and gardens and the ocean, and cost more because of the view. The "terrace" rooms have a large terrace, perfect for private sunbathing.

The staff are warm and friendly. The many places to dine here include the Pool Bar where you can feast on fresh seafood, which you grill or have grilled right by your table; the Cowrie Cove, for more delectable seafood, overlooking the ocean; Asiatica for a selection of Asian cuisines; Shang Palace for good Chinese dishes; the Garden Patio, for buffet and continental fare; and the Lobby Lounge for snacks while listening to the piano.

The pool is impressive. Other facilities include a business center, complete gym, an extensive aquasport center that has parasailing, and a very good scuba center.

If you are looking for a weekend of complete relaxation with first-class amenities and comfort, friendly service, refreshing landscaping and design, and easily accessed — the Shangri-La's Mactan Island resort is a great escape.

MANDARIN ORIENTAL MANILA, *Intersection of Paseo de Roxas and Makati Avenue, Manila. Tel. 750-8888, Fax 817-2472. US reservations: 1-310/ 649-1634. 468 rooms. $210-350 per single, $235-373.50 per double, $410 per suite. Visa, Master Card, American Express, Diners.*

This hotel is good value — Mandarin's quality is at par with all the top hotels. It has an extremely loyal clientele of business executives who will only stay at the Mandarin because of its unwavering service. The staff are superb.

White- or red-clad employees warmly welcome you through glass doors to the small lobby of wood-paneled front desks, marble floor. A few steps up a red carpet lead you to the elevators or stairs. The rooms are spacious and tastefully furnished including a good desk with ample space, and all the amenities of a first-class hotel.

Facilities include a business center, gym, swimming pool, and a salon for men and women. The Mandarin also has several good eating establishments.

The Mandarin ranks among our most memorables because it always receives high praise from our friends that have been billeted here. As we live in Manila, we admit that we have not stayed at this hotel; we do, however, enjoy its bakeshop, coffee, and food. See Chapter 11, *Metropolitan Manila*.

PEARL FARM BEACH RESORT, *Samal Island. Tel. 221-9970. Manila reservations: Tel. 526-1555. $191-219 per single, $202-251 per double, $362 per suite, $612-721 per villa. Visa, Master Card, American Express, Diners.*

This former pearl farm has been transformed into a resort with a unique blend of western and ethnic styles. The beach is nothing to rave about, but the resort more than makes up for it. The resort was designed by one of the country's top architects — Bobby Mañosa — who incorporated the pool into the landscape: it appears to flow into the South China Sea. Beside the pool, a waterfall flows into a pond, home to turtles and starfish. The dining room, behind the pool, resembles a ski chalet, but is made with bamboo. And by the beach, an old watch tower has been converted into the Parola Bar, a nice place to have a drink as the sun sets. Landward, the resort is encased in lush flora and tall coconut trees.

The Samal suites and cottages, built over the water, take their design from the stilt houses of the Sama tribe found around the Sulu Islands. As you walk out onto the verandah of your cottage, imbibe the spectacular view of the sea, the marine life right below you, and Isla Malipano in front. The interiors are decorated with tribal handicrafts and materials with ethnic designs, and the furniture is mostly bamboo.

The Mandaya cottages, more expensive rooms, are on the other side of the resort. Built beside the shore, these attractive cottages are more spacious than the other rooms (price varies with space).

Isla Malipano is a small island right in front of the Pearl Farm, and is part of the resort. The beach on the island is better than that of the main area. This is where the "Luxury Villas" are located. These spacious cabins have three or four bedrooms, ideal for a group of people seeking privacy.

The resort also has a complete dive center where you could take an intensive course and be certified in three days. The cost will be $400, including equipment, boat rental, and certification. There are also jet skis for rent at $100 per hour.

When the Pearl Farm isn't full, this is a great place to spend a weekend. We really like the native touches that blend perfectly with modern comforts to make the resort, from the main pavilion and pool to the confines of your well-appointed room, very attractive. See Chapter 25, *Mindanao*, for more details.

CEBU PLAZA HOTEL, *Nivel Hills, Lahug. Tel. 231-1231 to 59, Fax 231-2071. Manila reservations: Tel. 634-7505 to 08, Fax 634-7509. US reservations: 1-800/44-UTELL. 385 rooms. $110-150 per single, $140-198 per double, $224-437 per single or double "Presidents Club" floors, $377-1,192 per suite, $30 per extra person. Visa, Master Card, American Express, Diners.*

The Plaza is superbly managed and staffed — you are made to feel at home in the city's top hotel — and commands wonderful views, especially at night, of the city; request a city-view room. The rooms on the regular floors are a mix of European and native styles. The furniture is wood and nicely varnished bamboo, and all rooms have the usual amenities you expect from a first-class hotel (carpeting, air conditioning, cable TV, minibar, etc.). If you are staying at the "Presidents Club," you can enjoy the 24-hour butler service, business center, complementary breakfast, and 6:00pm cocktails. The spacious rooms have been elegantly decorated. The furnishing is European and the solid dark wood door with faint light brown streaks is very striking.

Facilities include two swimming pools, two tennis courts, a shooting range, minigolf, sauna, salon, and business center. The hotel also offers car rental, travel and tour arrangements, and massage. You will not be disappointed with the food — the Lantaw offers delectable seafood and Asian dishes and Café Tartanilla's buffet has a wide variety of dishes. For evening entertainment, the popular Pards Restaurant and Bar has tasty food, and the Bai Disco and Raquets Karaoke Bar are equally popular.

The staff, from the doormen and the room staff through management, are terrific. You will definitely feel welcome with the genuine hospitality we always experience at the Cebu Plaza. The great views and comfortable rooms are other stand-outs of this hotel.

CASA LETICIA, *J Camus Street, Davao. Tel. 224-0501, Fax 221-3585. 41 rooms. $35-53 per single, $51-65 per double, $85-135 per suite. Visa, Master Card, American Express, Diners. E-mail address: casalet@interasia.com.ph*

This very charming hotel is in an attractive Spanish-style dusty rose-colored building. The friendly staff are very efficient, and the hotel is well-managed and family run. The rooms are very clean, and all are painted a light pastel green. The "studios," the cheapest of the single rooms, are narrow but long. All other rooms have sufficient space and are very comfortable. In the bathrooms you will find a note on tips for water conservation, which is impressive for the Philippines, as you usually see this only in the five-star hotels. Ask for a room facing J Camus street for a better view, and adjoining rooms are available upon request. All rooms are air conditioned and have cable TV. The suites include a hairdryer, refrigerator, and an extension phone in the bathroom. Daily newspapers are provided in all rooms.

Facilities include business center services, safe deposit boxes, and function rooms. The lobby coffee shop specializes in local cuisine, has some western dishes, and is open 24 hours a day. On the sixth floor is the popular bar, Toto's.

Included among the regular guests of this hotel are people working with the US Agency for International Development. The staff is also very honest and guests who are going out of the city for a few days have left their baggage with the staff to watch. Everyone here, from the manager to the reception, concierge, bellboys, guards, waiters, and room staff, is hospitable, and this makes you feel almost at home.

Casa Leticia's superb service makes it one of our all-time favorites. We recommend this place to all our friends that are headed for Davao City. The genuine warmth is very nice — all staff, from the manger through the concierge, guard, and room staff look out for guests. See Chapter 25, *Mindanao*, for more details.

BANAUE VIEW INN, *Banaue. Tel. 386-4078. 11 rooms, $15-20 per single or double, $5 per person per dorm;* and **SPRING VILLAGE INN**, *Banaue. Tel. 386-4087. 9 rooms, $10-30 per single or double.*

These family-run inns have large central areas. The phone is at the desk in the lobby. All rooms are clean, nice, and homey. And both inns are within walking distance to restaurants.

At Spring Village, the three more expensive rooms have private bathrooms and are in the back. The other rooms face the main road, have a surrounding balcony, and are quiet at night. The two common bathrooms are kept very clean.

Banaue View has rooms with a good view. Some rooms have private bathrooms, others are shared. Run by the progeny of Otley Beyer, the American anthropologist who made Banaue famous, the inn also has a small museum of antiques and artifacts that provide a good introduction to the area. Banaue View has ample parking and is popular with consultants: this inn is often booked.

We frequent Banaue and recommend these places for their homey feeling, security, and good value. See the "Banaue" section of Chapter 15, *The Cordilleras.*

SIARGAO PENSION HOUSE, *center of General Luna, on the main road. Tel. 87268-204-1283 (this is a satellite phone, so wherever you are, dial the country's international prefix and then this number, e.g. in the US dial 011, then 87...), Fax 87268-204-1284. 4 rooms. $20 per person, all meals included.*

This is a charming pension, run by a French couple — Nicolas and Florence Rambeau. Each room is named after one of the nearby islands. Pictures of guests are posted along the staircase that leads up to the rooms on the second floor. The clean rooms are small but can accommodate two people comfortably; they are cozy, and the decor is tastefully done with a beach theme. You do feel "at the beach" here. Bathrooms are common and are kept clean; hot water is available for showers.

The Rambeaus are a nice couple with a serious demeanor and run the pension very well. The staff are friendly. You will not be disappointed with the food here. Florence arranges the daily meals, which may include excellent crêpes for breakfast. If you are interested in kayaking, this is where you go. Priority is of course given to in-house guests.

Perhaps what makes this place very dear is that your days will be filled with activities: island hopping (and there are several to see); kayaking through mangroves, or through Suhoton Cave to the breathtakingly beautiful lagoon; exploring quaint villages; and more. You can stay for many days, and you still won't run out of things to do. At the Siargao Pension House, you won't have to spend time organizing your activities; the owners have everything set up for you — all you have to do is get there. See Chapter 25, *Mindanao*, section on "Siargao".

SIMON'S INN or **HILLSIDE INN**, *Batad, Banaue, overlooking the village. 13 rooms each. $1-1.25 per person.*

Both places have fabulous views, great food, and good clean rooms (plywood walls), but don't leave belongings near open windows beside the balcony. Bathrooms are outside and are very basic. The menu includes Israeli food. Very friendly, helpful owners.

Waking up to the the spectacular (especially at dawn) view of Batad's amphitheater terraces is what makes these places very memorable. See the "Banaue" section of Chapter 15, *The Cordilleras*.

11. METROPOLITAN MANILA

Manila, the country's capital, is an eclectic study in contrasts. You can see remnants of the old colonial past in the medieval European-style walled city of **Intramuros**, or board a hydrofoil on a short ride to **Corregidor**, the island fort. In Manila, the affluent are chauffeured around in darkly tinted expensive cars of the latest models, while the poor live off the streets. In the city, you will see modern high-rise structures, and five minutes later you will be looking at shanties (with television antennae on an unstable rooftop). You can shop in sprawling malls or go bargain hunting in local markets. What began as a small settlement on the eastern shores of **Manila Bay** has grown into a multifaceted metropolis incorporating 17 cities and towns, with a steadily increasing population of over 10 million.

Once called "The Pearl of the Orient," Manila is now often referred to as a "tarnished pearl." Demolished during the Second World War, it recovered and was rebuilt into a glitzy city, but only for a while. Its coffers were pilferaged, and Manila once again suffered a downturn. However, during the decline, few of the city's resident expatriates wanted to be transferred to Hong Kong — where respite is almost an alien word; or Singapore — too clean and regulated; or Tokyo — where almost everything is very expensive and living space is small; and so on. Although parts of Manila are desperately in need of a face lift, beneath its scratchy surface lies a vibrant, alive, and fascinating city. Now en route to recovery, the country is seen as an emerging market with a favorable future.

HISTORY

Manila had been named long before the coming of the Spanish. "Maynilad," its native name, comes from the Tagalog words *may* — there is — and *nilad* — the water lily that once flourished along the shores of Manila Bay.

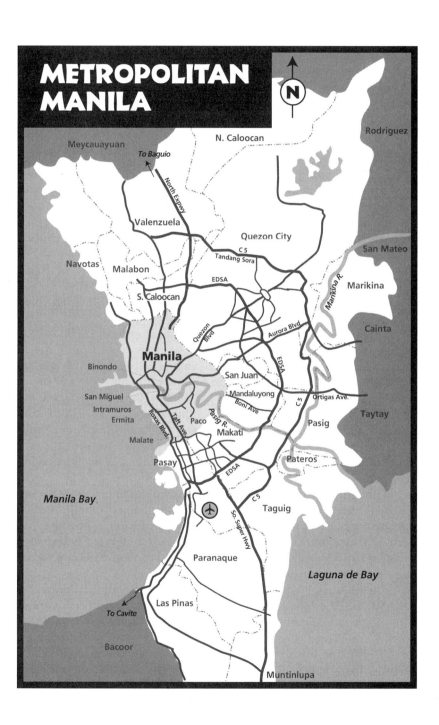

Among the city's earlier residents were the Malays, who were Muslim. They came in groups from the Malay Peninsula and Indonesia in sailing vessels called *barangays*. *Barangay* evolved into the term for small communities; the word is used today to describe subunits of towns. Some *barangays* joined together into kingdoms ruled by rajas.

Manila's largest settlement was Tundo; the political center was the community of Maynilad; and a few kilometers inland from the Pasig River was one of the oldest settlements, a kingdom known as Namayan. Namayan was large and encompassed what is today Quiapo, San Miguel, Sampaloc, Pandacan, Paco, Ermita, Malate, Pasay, Makati, and Mandaluyong. Settlements along the Pasig River and Manila Bay frequently traded with merchants from China, Japan, and other countries.

Martin de Goiti and **Juan de Salcedo** attempted but failed to take possession of the city in 1570. What was meant to be a peaceful process ended in bloodshed and the burning of much of Maynilad. The start of the Spanish reign in Manila began in 1571 with the end of **Rajah Sulayman**'s rule of Maynilad, when **Miguel Lopez de Legazpi** and his men arrived and overcame the little resistance the Rajah and his men could muster.

A medieval European-style walled city was eventually built, and the seat of the Spanish empire in the east was transferred from Cebu to Manila. Before the walls and their fortifications were erected, Manila was attacked by the Chinese corsair, **Lim Ah Hong** and his fleet of 62 junks. That invasion was nearly successful, and the Spaniards had to be wary of attacks from the Portuguese, Muslims, Japanese, Chinese, Dutch and English, and from the natives (who were unhappy with the unjust treatment by the Spaniards). Therefore, the Spanish fortified the city. They built massive tuffa walls to replace the original wooden palisades, and in 1609 added a moat.

Within the confines of the walls were imposing churches, convents, a hospital, schools, grand government offices, barracks, and over 600 opulent houses that only the Spanish and their m*estizo* offspring could occupy. Natives were moved to other areas, and immigrant Chinese were required to live outside, but within the range of cannons. The city's seven gates were closed by drawbridges at night.

Life inside the city reflected the flourishing trade with China and the New World. The Spaniards were adorned in silk and other luxurious trimmings; the Filipinos wore their intricately embroidered native apparel with gold jewelry and crosses. Balls and parties were held frequently.

In 1762, the British took Manila and the surrounding areas for 20 months, then returned it to Spain under the 1763 Treaty of Paris. Realizing that Intramuros was not unconquerable, the Spaniards began to move beyond the walls. After the Governor's Palace was destroyed by an earthquake in 1863, the seat of the government was transferred to Malacañang.

Another Treaty of Paris, this one in 1898 following the Spanish-American War, marked the beginning of the American reign. A number of changes were made. The Americans emphasized secular matters, which expanded commerce and focused on education, urban development, and sanitation. One of the first projects was filling the moat around Intramuros because it was a breeding ground for diseases.

Massive development modernized and expanded Manila. Business and residential areas sprouted up all over the city. However, progress and growth came to a halt with World War Two. The Japanese occupied the city from 1942 to 1945. Many civilians died; some were placed in the dungeons of old Manila, where many of them perished. In an attempt to spare Manila from the ravages of war, General MacArthur moved to Corregidor. However, during the liberation of Manila, bombs and hand-to-hand combat damaged most of the structures and reduced many parts of the city to rubble.

Some aid from the US helped to rebuild Manila (more aid went to Japan than the Philippines). Slowly Manila has re-emerged, surviving both natural and political disasters.

ARRIVALS & DEPARTURES

By Air

Domestic and international flights share the same two-lane runway. The domestic terminal is a two- to 10-minute ride from the international airport. See Chapter 6, *Planning Your Trip*, for more information on the international airport, and entrance and exit requirements.

NAIA (still referred to as its former name – the **Manila International Airport** or MIA) is not as nice as the major airports you may be accustomed to in North America or Europe, but plans are on the way for its expansion and improvement. Its one runway (with two lanes) is just long enough and one end stops at a major highway.

Getting to Town from the International Airport

Transportation from the airport is by "**airport taxi**" (rates are fixed: $12-20 depending on your destination) or **Sunshine Bus Service** which shuttles passengers to a number of hotels in the Ermita-Malate area ($41.50 per person).

The Domestic Airport

Some domestic flights leave from the international terminal. Most leave from the terminals on **Domestic Road**. The Domestic Airport is significantly smaller than the current international one. There are two waiting areas for domestic flights leaving from the terminal: ask on arrival which area serves your flight. Food, drinks, magazines, books, newspapers, and film (expensive) are sold inside the waiting areas.

The terminal for **Pacific Air** is half a block from the main domestic terminal, and the terminal for **Grand Air** is inside the Philippine Village Hotel grounds, between the domestic and international terminals. Minimal airport taxes are included in the price of all domestic tickets. You should arrive an hour ahead of your departure time. When arriving at domestic terminals, baggage delivery is usually punctual.

Getting to Town from the Domestic Airport

Taxis outside the arrivals gate may charge high prices ($12-20). If so, walk out to the street in front, where you may get a taxi at normal prices (about half price).

ORIENTATION

The **Pasig River**, which flows between the interior lake, Laguna de Bay, and Manila Bay, divides the metropolis. On its northwest are (1) **Binondo**, Manila's Chinatown; (2) **Malacañang**, the seat and residence of the Philippine President, in San Miguel District; (3) the fishing towns of **Navotas** and **Malabon**; and (4) industrial **Caloocan**. To the northeast is **Quezon City**, which has many government and education institutions; **Marikina**, which is an industrial area; and Pasig, an industrial town and a relatively new financial area.

South of the Pasig River, near Manila Bay, is most of **Old Manila**, the "tourist belt" area of Ermita and Malate, Pasay City, and parts of Parañaque. Southeast of the river is **Makati**, the major financial center.

Most tourists will be interested in the areas just southwest and immediately northwest of the Pasig River. This is where you will find the walled city, many souvenir shops, quaint restaurants, and Malacañang; and the departure point of boats to Corregidor.

Filipino politicians often rename streets and landmarks, a practice met with passive resistance by the general population, who usually continue to use the old name for years (sometimes decades) beyond the change. Destination signs on jeepneys and buses will often refer to the old name — do ask Filipino travelers if you are confused about those signs.

Climate & Weather

The best time to be in Manila is November through early February, when the temperature is mild (mid-70s to mid-80s during the day; upper 60s to lower 70s in the evenings) and humidity is lower than at other times of the year. The heat and humidity during summer months (March through June) can be high (upper 80s to upper 90s, and near 100%

humidity as rainy season approaches), and with the pollution it can be oppressive. This is one reason that the malls, which are air conditioned, are usually full.

GETTING AROUND TOWN

Once you have a good map and some directions, it is fairly easy to get around the city. Public transport is cheap, and people can help with information on which bus, jeepney, etc. to take.

• **Hire Cars** are available at major hotels and at the airport, or contact them by phone: **Avis**, *Tel. 734-5851*, **Budget**, *Tel. 818-7363*, **Dollar**, *Tel. 844-3120*, and **Nissan**, *Tel. 816-1808*; check the yellow pages (under automobile rentals) for other companies.

• **Taxis** are practically everywhere, except you may have problems flagging one down during the height of rush hour, and even then, they may not be willing to go to your destination. Doormen at hotels take down the license plates of taxis, providing added protection. Taxis charge a small fee (P12.50, about 50¢ in 1997) for use of the aircon.

• **Buses** ply (or fly) most of Manila's major thoroughfares. Signs on the front windows of the buses give the final destination; for points in between, ask people at the bus stops.

• **Jeepneys** and **tricycles** serve most of the smaller streets not accessed by buses.

• **Light Rail Transit (LRT)** is the most painless and smogless way to get from Monumento (Caloocan) to Baclaran, Parañaque. Rides are P10 (40¢). Know your departure terminals – there are maps in all stations. An LRT is currently being built down EDSA, and will be functional in 1999 at the earliest.

MANILA STREET CAUTION

Buses and jeepneys often pick up and discharge passengers in the middle of the road – take care when alighting. Manilans often use handkerchiefs to filter out some of the smoke that many vehicles belch.

Manila's Main Streets

Because Manila's streets do not follow a grid or any simple pattern, you should get a good map of the city, especially if you are staying for a while. Manila's roads are congested (less so on Sundays), especially heavy during rush hours, which may extend from 7:00am to 10:00am and 4:15pm to 7:30pm.

Manila's main thoroughfares are listed below:

• **Roxas Boulevard**. (formerly Dewey Boulevard) starts at **M Roxas**, which spans the Pasig closest to the bay. This bridge is still referred to by its previous name — **Del Pan** Bridge. Roxas continues along the coast of Manila Bay through Ermita, Malate, Pasay City, and Parañaque, and extends to Cavite.

• **Epifanio de los Santos Avenue** (mercifully shortened to **EDSA**, pronounced Ed-sa) is a semi-circular highway that runs from Caloocan through Quezon City and Cubao shopping area, divides the military camps Aguinaldo and Crame (pronounced crah-may), passes through Makati, and ends on Roxas Boulevard.

• **C5**, a new circumferential road, goes from the South Expressway in Taguig to Quezon City. It was developed to lessen the traffic on EDSA.

• The **South Expressway** (frequently called **South Superhighway**) starts at Paco, runs through Makati's southern fringe, passes under EDSA, and continues to points south.

WHERE TO STAY

The hotels are grouped together by location and price, and are arranged solely on the basis of price starting with the most expensive and ending with the cheapest. (Note: [#n] corresponds to the location on either the Near Manila Bay, Makati, or Ortigas Center map.)

For rates in the "very expensive" and "expensive" categories, inquire with your travel agent, or, if you make the booking yourself, ask the hotel if you may avail of a corporate rate (you will have to give them the name of the company you are associated with). Assume that rooms in all "very expensive," "expensive," and "moderate" hotels are air conditioned and have cable TV.

Near Manila Bay — Very Expensive

MANILA DIAMOND, *Roxas Boulevard corner Quintos Street, Malate, Tel. 526-2211, Fax 526-2255. 500 rooms. $296-324 per single, $332-360 per double, $500 per suite. Visa, Master Card, American Express, Diners.* [#16]

Rooms are the average size for hotels in this price level. On the higher, executive club floors, there are wonderful rooms with floor-to-ceiling, wall-to-wall glass windows, affording you a spectacular sunset or night view of Manila Bay. The staff are efficient and friendly.

On the top floor, you may have a great view dining at either Yurakeun (good Japanese food) or the Bellevue (French cuisine). There is also a pleasant lobby coffee shop. Facilities include a swimming pool and a business center.

CENTURY PARK HOTEL, *Vito Cruz Street beside Harrison Plaza, Malate, Tel. 522-1011, Fax 521-3141. 500 rooms. $289 per single, $313 per double, $506-578 per suite. Visa, Master Card, American Express, Diners.* [#33]

This hotel has several restaurants and a very good delicatessen. There is also a pool. Rooms are average size but, along with most of the hotel, could use a renovation.

WESTIN PHILIPPINE PLAZA, *CCP Complex, Malate, Tel. 551-5555, Fax 551-5610. 670 rooms. $271-295 per single, $299-323 per double, $455-3,128 per suite. Visa, Master Card, American Express, Diners.* [#35]

You can enjoy the fabled sunsets of Manila as the hotel is right beside the bay. The Philippine Plaza is more like a resort than a hotel. It has a wonderful garden pool that winds around water slides and an island bar. And, if you want to practice your swing — for golfers, there is a putting green. For tennis players, there are courts.

For great views of Manila Bay and the pool, request a "pool-view" room, which costs $20 more. On the other side, rooms have a view of the city, which actually looks interesting at night. Inside the rooms you will find all the amenities of a five-star hotel. The Philippine Plaza also has several good restaurants and a bar.

HYATT REGENCY, *2702 Roxas Boulevard, Pasay, Tel. 833-1234, Fax 831-8303. 265 rooms. $265-295 per single or double, $355-542 per suite. Visa, Master Card, American Express, Diners.* [#37]

This pleasant establishment has the good service the Hyatt chain is known for; the staff are very efficient and hospitable. The rooms are comfortable and are typical of hotels in this range. Facilities include a swimming pool and business center. The Hyatt has a music lounge and a number of restaurants; the best-known is Tempura Misono, where you may have your fortune told and enjoy good Japanese food.

MANILA HOTEL, *Rizal Park, Manila, Tel. 527-0111, Fax 527-0023. 510 rooms. $241-277 per single, $271-307 per double, $360-2,410 per suite. Visa, Master Card, American Express, Diners.* [#2]

This is without a doubt Manila's most famous hotel. Its beautiful spacious lobby radiates the elegance you expect from a grand old hotel — nice wood paneling, chandeliers hanging gracefully from the ceiling, and marble floors and imposing columns.

Since its opening in 1912, it has hosted a number of famous people. General MacArthur lived here for six years; his suite has been recreated and named after him (you may stay there for $1,807.50 per night). Other notable guests include the Beatles, the Duke of Windsor, Ernest Hemmingway, Robert Kennedy, Richard Nixon, John Wayne, and, more recently, President Clinton.

Rooms in the initial structure are slightly larger (and cost just a bit more) than those in the 18-story wing, which was added in 1970. The

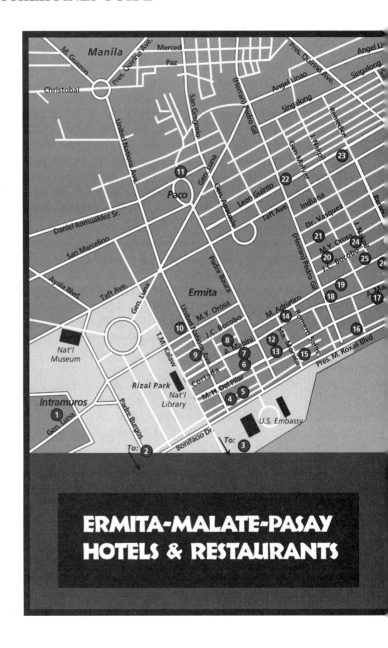

ERMITA-MALATE-PASAY HOTELS & RESTAURANTS

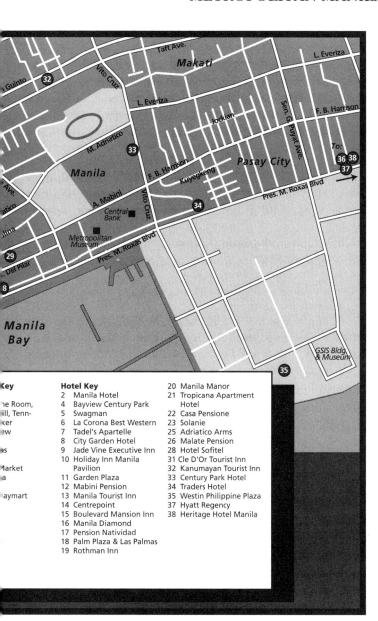

Key

- ne Room,
- ill, Tenn-
- ker
- ew

- is

- Market
- a

- aymart

Hotel Key

- 2 Manila Hotel
- 4 Bayview Century Park
- 5 Swagman
- 6 La Corona Best Western
- 7 Tadel's Apartelle
- 8 City Garden Hotel
- 9 Jade Vine Executive Inn
- 10 Holiday Inn Manila Pavilion
- 11 Garden Plaza
- 12 Mabini Pension
- 13 Manila Tourist Inn
- 14 Centrepoint
- 15 Boulevard Mansion Inn
- 16 Manila Diamond
- 17 Pension Natividad
- 18 Palm Plaza & Las Palmas
- 19 Rothman Inn

- 20 Manila Manor
- 21 Tropicana Apartment Hotel
- 22 Casa Pensione
- 23 Solanie
- 25 Adriatico Arms
- 26 Malate Pension
- 28 Hotel Sofitel
- 31 Cle D'Or Tourist Inn
- 32 Kanumayan Tourist Inn
- 33 Century Park Hotel
- 34 Traders Hotel
- 35 Westin Philippine Plaza
- 37 Hyatt Regency
- 38 Heritage Hotel Manila

rooms come with all the standard amenities of a first-class hotel. Facilities include tennis courts, swimming pool, putting green, and a business center. There are a number of good restaurants where you may feast; among them, the Champagne Room and Cowrie Grill (see *Where to Eat*).

HERITAGE HOTEL MANILA, *Roxas Boulevard corner EDSA, Pasay, Tel. 891-8888, Fax 891-7848. 467 rooms. $241-265 per single, $265-289 per double, $337-482 per suite. Visa, Master Card, American Express, Diners.* [#38]

Many guests have commented on the excellent service they receive from the Heritage. The rooms are comfortable and the size and amenities are typical of high-priced hotels. Facilities here include a nice swimming pool, business center, and a casino. There are a number of restaurants, including the very good Hua Ting (see *Where to Eat*), and a bar and music lounge.

HOTEL SOFITEL, *1990 Roxas Boulevard, Malate, Tel. 526-8588, Fax 524-2526. 500 rooms. $230 per single, $265 per double, $482 per suite. Visa, Master Card, American Express, Diners.* [#28]

The pleasant lobby softens the exterior of the hotel. Rooms are the average size of hotels in this range, and have the standard air conditioning, cable television, carpeting, and marble bathroom. From the rooms, you may have nice evening views of either the bay or Malate and, if you are high enough, of Makati and beyond. Facilities include a nice swimming pool, business center, and a casino. There are several restaurants and a good music lounge.

Near Manila Bay — Expensive

PHILIPPINE VILLAGE AIRPORT HOTEL, *Nayong Pilipino Park, NAIA Road, near the airport. Pasay, Tel. 833-8080, Fax 833-8248. 444 rooms. $181 per single, $205 per double, $289-578 per suite. Visa, Master Card, American Express, Diners.*

This hotel has several restaurants, a pool, and a gym. Rooms are average size and have the standard amenities for this price level. The departure and arrival area for Grand Air is beside the hotel.

TRADERS HOTEL MANILA, *3001 Roxas Boulevard corner of Vito Cruz Street, Malate, Tel. 523-7011, Fax 522-3985. 334 rooms. $168-192 per single, $192-217 per double, $295 per suite. Visa, Master Card, American Express, Diners.* [#34]

Popular with local and foreign business people who are looking for value and quality, you will find the Traders Hotel very comfortable and the staff efficient and friendly. Rooms are cozy and have the standard amenities for this price range; some may afford you a nice view of Manila Bay. There is a business center, a swimming pool, a few restaurants, and a bar.

BAYVIEW PARK CENTURY HOTEL, *118 Roxas Boulevard, Ermita, Tel. 526-1555, Fax 522-3040. 276 rooms. $162.50-241 per single, $180-241 per double, $300-361.50 per suite. Visa, Master Card, American Express, Diners.* [#4]
    You will find several restaurants, a pool, and a fitness center at the Bayview. Room size and amenities are standard for this price level. The staff are quite hospitable.

HOLIDAY INN MANILA PAVILION, *UN Avenue corner Maria Orosa Street, Ermita, Tel. 526-1212, Fax 522-3531. US reservations: 1-800/465-4329. 590 rooms. $154-202 per single, $167-215 per double, $340 per suite. Visa, Master Card, American Express, Diners.* [#10]
    Simple comfort and uncompromising warm hospitality await you at the Holiday Inn. The rooms are comfortable and have the usual amenities of establishments in this price level. The Holiday Inn attracts business people who are looking for quality and value. It is a festive hotel with monthly promotions that may serve a national cuisine, celebrate the Oktoberfest, and reenact various holidays. Facilities include a pool and a business center. You may dine at the Rotisserie for good continental dining and an extensive wine list; Pavilion Court for Chinese cuisine; and Café Coquilla for both Asian and continental fare.

Near Manila Bay — Moderate
HOTEL LA CORONA BEST WESTERN, *1166 MH del Pilar corner Arquiza Street, Malate, Tel. 521-3906, Fax 521-3909. 54 rooms. $80-85 single or double. Visa, Master Card, American Express, Diners.* [#6]
    The rooms in this old-style white building are nice and very clean. You may want to request a room facing Arquiza Street — for less noise; MH del Pilar can stay noisy late into the evenings. The hotel is well managed and staff is friendly.

PALM PLAZA & LAS PALMAS, *P Gil Street between Mabini Street and M Adriatico Street, Malate, Tel. 521-3502 (Plaza), 506-661 (Palmas), Fax 509-384 (Plaza), 522-1699 (Palmas). 200 rooms. $60-90 per single, $66-110 per double, $156-180 per suite. Visa, Master Card, American Express, Diners.* [#18]
    Two well-managed adjoining hotels staffed with friendly people. All rooms are simply furnished and clean. Rooms in Palm Plaza are $15 more expensive (slightly larger) and all the suite rooms are in the Plaza; Las Palmas has a few rooms that face Manila Bay. The common facilities include a small pool, business center, tours and travel services, and laundry. Each hotel has a restaurant and a coffee shop.

CENTREPOINT (formerly Sundowner Hotel), *1430 A Mabini Street, Ermita, Tel. 521-2751, Fax 521-5331. 104 rooms. $60.25-72.30. Visa, Master Card, American Express, Diners.* [#14]

You will find the staff here very charming and eager to please guests. All rooms are carpeted and have a mini-bar. Dimly lit hallways lead to the rooms, which are average sized for a moderately priced simple, and clean hotel. The restaurant serves continental fare.

TROPICANA APARTMENT HOTEL, *1630 LM Guerrero Street, Malate, Tel. 536-1590, Fax 522-3208. 100 rooms. $46 per single or double, $60-100 per single or double with kitchenette. Visa, Master Card, American Express.* [#21]

The rooms are spacious, simply furnished, and clean. Inside your room, you will find very nice Chinese brush paintings hanging on a wall, and at least one potted plant. Facilities include a nice medium size pool and a small boutique. The staff is very friendly and attentive. The restaurant serves continental food, with Chinese specialties.

THE GARDEN PLAZA, *1030 Belen Street,, Paco, Tel. 522-4835, Fax 522-4840. 125 rooms. $58-73 per single or double, $110-205 per suite. Visa, Master Card, American Express, Diners.* [#11]

This is a very delightful hotel. This hotel maintains the old-style charm of its building. Marble floors will lead you from the reception up the stairs with wrought iron railings, and through refreshing airy hallways to your room. All rooms are nice and come with a mini-bar, in-room safe, and a hairdryer. The superior and deluxe rooms have a kitchenette.

Facilities include a swimming pool, business center, laundry service, and foreign exchange. You may feast at Isidro's for Filipino food, or at the spacious and charmingly decorated Old Swiss Inn for Swiss, German, French, and Italian dishes.

BOULEVARD MANSION APARTMENT INN, *1440 Roxas Boulevard, Ermita, Tel. 521-8888, Fax 521-5829. 184 rooms with kitchenette. $50-55 per single or double, $70-175 per suite. Visa, Master Card, American Express, Diners.* [#15]

The staff is very nice and efficient. Rooms are simply furnished, of pastel hues, very clean, and spacious, air conditioned, and have cable television. Request a boulevard-side room for a great view of Manila Bay. There is a restaurant that serves Chinese food, and a coffee shop. Dry cleaning and laundry services are available. You may also try the sister apartment inns: **Dakota Mansion**, *Gen Malvar St. corner M Adriatico St., Malate*, and **Mabini Mansion**, *1011 A Mabini St. near UN Ave., Ermita.*

CITY GARDEN HOTEL, *1158 A. Mabini Street, Ermita, Tel. 536-1451, Fax 504-844. 92 rooms. $55-78 per single, $66-85. Visa, Master Card, American Express, Diners. Email: garden@iconn.com.ph* [#8]

This simple, friendly hotel has clean rooms. There is a coffee shop offering a variety of international dishes, and a small business center.

MANILA MANOR, *1660 J Bocobo Street, Malate, Tel. 574-716, Fax 521-8996. 67 rooms. $51 per single, $58 per double, $82-109 per suite. Visa, Master Card, American Express.* [#20]

This place has a charming art gallery where you may see some very good works of local artists. Although the Manila Manor is near Remedios Circle, it is very quiet inside. The rooms are simple and clean. Suites have a kitchenette. Services include laundry, car rental, tour and travel arrangements, foreign exchange, and use of the fax machine.

ADRIATICO ARMS HOTEL, *561 J Nakpil Street, Malate, Tel. 521-0736, Fax 588-014. 28 rooms. $45-60 per single or double. Visa, Master Card, American Express.* [#25]

This is a quaint family run hotel. The rooms are pleasant, cozy, and clean. All are carpeted and the bathrooms have marble flooring. The restaurant-bar serves good continental dishes, with highly recommended specialties such as Cajun dishes and the superb Iberian chicken – it's Mrs. Gonzalez' specialty, but you must order it at least five hours in advance. The staff is friendly.

SOLANIE HOTEL, *1811 Leon Guinto Street, Malate, Tel. 508-641, Fax 508-647. 53 rooms. $45-68 per single or double, $64 with kitchenette, $78 per suite. Visa, Master Card, American Express, Diners.* [#23]

The Solanie has some nice cozy rooms that are carpeted and clean. It is just outside the tourist belt, in a more quiet area. The coffee shop serves a variety of international dishes.

SWAGMAN HOTEL, *411 A. Flores Street between Roxas Boulevard and MH del Pilar Street, Tel. 599-881, Fax 521-9731. 57 rooms. $42-57 single or double. Visa, Master Card, American Express.* [#5]

The Swagman has cornered the market of the Australian male budget tourists. An in-house travel agency has a few local tours. The bathroom in the coffee shop is dirty.

ROTHMAN INN HOTEL, *1633 M Adriatico Street, Ermita, Tel. 521-9251, Fax 522-2606. 100 rooms. $36-44 per single or double, $56 per suite. Visa, Master Card, American Express, Diners.* [#19]

All rooms are fully carpeted, clean, and were in good condition in 1997. The suite rooms have a kitchenette. Staff is friendly and helpful. The restaurant serves Filipino, Japanese, and Arabian food; and there is a coffee shop-piano bar.

Near Manila Bay — Budget

KANUMAYAN TOURIST INN, *2317 Leon Guinto Street & 2284 Taft Avenue, Malate, Tel. 521-1161, Fax 521-7323. 50 rooms. $40-55 per single or double, $93.50 per suite. Visa, Master Card, American Express.* [#32]

You will find this place cozy, and the staff looks after their guests. The rooms are simply furnished; all are clean, air conditioned, and come with a television that shows in-house movies and a mini-bar. There is a pleasant pool in the courtyard garden. The restaurant is open 24 hours and serves mainly European dishes.

CLÉ D' OR TOURIST INN, *612 Remedios Street, Malate, Tel. 500-474, 500-0495. $37-55 per single or double. Visa, Master Card, American Express, Diners.* [#31]

The inside of this inn is homey and pleasant. The simply furnished and cozy rooms are air conditioned, carpeted, clean, and have a television. Located right off Remedios Circle, you are near an array of restaurants.

JADE VINE EXECUTIVE INN, *533 UN Avenue corner J Bocobo Street, Ermita, Tel. 508-601, Fax 598-432. 38 rooms. $35-70 per single, $43-70 per double. Visa, Master Card, American Express.* [#9]

For a budget-priced establishment, you get good sized rooms that are very clean and nice — comparable to a lower-moderate-priced hotel. All rooms have air conditioning and cable television. The restaurant serves continental food, with a buffet for $6 per person. You may also rent cars at the hotel.

PENSION NATIVIDAD, *1690 MH del Pilar, Malate, Tel. 526-0992, Fax 522-3759. 48 rooms. $30 per room w aircon, $22 per room w fan, $18 per room with fan and common bathroom, $6 per person per dorm. Visa, Master Card.* [#17]

This very charming and homey pension is well managed and very safe. You will be well cared for here; the staff is friendly and helpful. All rooms are clean and simply furnished. Simple meals can be prepared — even at odd hours, someone will whip up a meal for you. There are lockers for valuables; you may bring your own lock or rent one (ideal if you are going out of town and do not want to lug everything with you). This place is popular with non-governmental organizationss, which frequently book their people here. Guests are not allowed to bring "escorts" here.

MALATE PENSION, *1771 M Adriatico Street, Malate, Tel. 596-672, Fax 597-119. 45 rooms & 48 dorm beds. $31-38 per room with aircon, $22 per room with fan and private bath, $13-15 per room with fan and common bath, $6 per person in dorm with fan, $5 per person in dorm with fan. American Express.* [#26]

The cozy atmosphere here is complemented by lovely antique furniture in the rooms. All the rooms are clean and nice. The common bathrooms are kept clean. The staff is very friendly. There is also a small business center. There restaurant serves good continental food, as does the charming café, where you may choose to sit at a table in the garden.

CASA PENSIONNE, *1602 Leon Guinto Street corner P Gil Street, Malate, Tel. 522-1375, 522-1740. 20 rooms (2 with aircon). $28 per room with aircon, $13 per room with fan and common bath, $4 per extra person.* [#22]

The rooms are clean, secure, and spacious (for its category). The staff is friendly and helpful.

SAN CARLOS MANSION, *777 San Carlos Street, Ermita, Tel. 523-8110, Fax 521-3768. 61 rooms. $25 per single or double, $27.50-30 per single or double with kitchenette, $34-40 per suite.*

All rooms are air conditioned, simply furnished, clean, and have television. The restaurant has local and continental dishes.

MANILA TOURIST INN, *487 Sta. Monica Street between Mabini and MH del Pilar, Tel. 597-721, 507-772. 21 rooms. $23 per single or double.* [#13]

Inside this red and grey brick building you will also find brick walls in the lobby, corridors, and rooms. It is a cozy place, all rooms are clean, air conditioned, carpeted, and with bathtubs in the bathrooms. The lobby is furnished with local antique furniture, and has paintings by Filipino artists. The coffee shop serves simple local and continental dishes.

TADEL'S APARTELLE, *Arquiza Street near A Mabini Street, Tel. 521-9766. 8 rooms. $21-25 per single or double with aircon, $29 room with aircon and TV, $13 per room with fan.* [#7]

Although the hallway is dimly lit, all rooms in this simple pension are clean and simple with adequate lighting. The bathrooms do not have shower curtains, so expect the toilet to get wet when showering. The staff is very friendly, and there is a small area where coffee and breakfast is served.

MABINI PENSION, *1337 A Mabini Street, Ermita, Tel. 594-853, 505-404. $25-28 per single or double with aircon, $19 per single or double with fan & bath, $13.50 per single or double with fan & common bath.* [#12]

The rooms are simple and clean. Laundry service is available.

Makati — Very Expensive

SHANGRI-LA HOTEL MANILA, *Ayala Avenue corner Makati Avenue, Tel. 813-8888, Fax 813-5499. US reservations: Tel. 800/942-5050. 703 rooms. $331-415 per single, $361-444 per double, $444-3,500 per suite. Visa, Master Card, American Express, Diners.* [#61]

Shangri-La is one of the premier Asian hotel chains. You will be pampered with world-class ambiance, facilities, and service. A perfect blend of east and west is noticeable almost everywhere — in the decor, service, and food. After walking through the palatial lobby, the wonderful Filipino hospitality of the staff combined with Shangri-La's personalized service will make you feel at home and important in a grand hotel. Beyond the lobby is the lounge, backed by glass windows and tropical greenery, where many of Manila's notables sit comfortably in the plush club chairs while having an early morning breakfast meeting.

The spacious rooms have fine furniture and decor. All rooms have the complete amenities of a top hotel, among them: cable television, tea and coffee-making facilities, and in the roomy marble bathroom, a separate bath and shower area. You may choose from a view of Makati's main shopping center, or of the financial district including a small park where the international airport and terminal once were. Floors 19-24 are non-smoking.

Check into your own world in one of the luxurious suites. The "Specialty Suites" have a foyer, master bedroom and bathroom, living room and guest bathroom, and a room that may be used for dining, or as a study. The soothing colors complement the timeless furniture – marble, wrought iron, select wood, and highlights of gold radiate a truly sophisticated ambiance. The presidential suite is opulent. It is meticulously designed and decorated, perhaps for Spanish royalty, with the obvious Hispanic influence in the decor. This suite features a foyer, a large living room with two crystal chandeliers, a dining room, master bedroom and bathroom, guest bedroom, two guest bathrooms, a study, and a sitting area that is a perfect place for breakfast.

The Shangri-La has several good restaurants featuring cuisines from east to west, among them the Garden Café (see *Where to Eat*). If you are here on business, you will appreciate the terrific business center with professional staff, computers, fax and courier services, and a number of meeting rooms equipped with audio-visual, lighting, and simultaneous interpretation facilities including closed-circuit television. Other facilities include a complete fitness center with a gym, tennis courts, and a large swimming pool; a health club with sauna, jacuzzis, and masseuse; a parlor; a good florist; and a kiosk. Evening entertainment is provided at Conways (live bands play in the evenings) and the city's most frequented disco, Zu (see *Nightlife*).

MANILA PENINSULA, *Makati Avenue corner Ayala Avenue, Tel. 812-3456, Fax 815-3402. US reservations: Tel. -800/262-9467. 525 rooms. $319-406 per single or double, $494-3,253.50 per suite. Visa, Master Card, American Express, Diners.* [#60]

After passing the two huge white marble lions (symbolizing prosperity) at the main entrance of the Peninsula, you will find what many consider the nicest lobby of all the Makati Hotels. It is elegant and bright, with soaring glass windows complemented with graceful arched windows and balustrades. On the ceiling is a large metal sun sculpture (with a slight resemblance to the Versace emblem) created by renowned Philippine national artist Napoleon Abueva. On each side of the lobby is a large tapestry – one depicts Mount Mayon, the other, the Sierra Madre range. Beside the tapestries, wide cream marble staircases curl up to a continuation of the lobby lounge, where you may sit and have a drink or snack while listening to the band (relaxing music, local folk songs, classical, or Latin sounds) or, during Christmas, a choir. The Conservatory bar and lounge is just behind.

Your room will be in the Ayala wing – with views of the commercial center or a posh residential village; or the Makati Avenue wing – overlooking Makati's business district or the village and the hotel's pretty swimming pool below. The rooms are spacious and very comfortable.

Each room has a spacious wooden desk and a fax machine; a wooden cabinet containing a television, coffee and tea amenities, and the minibar. On a wall is a nice black-and-white sketch of a prewar Philippine structure. The bathrooms are nice and big, with separate areas for the shower, toilet, and bath. Room rates vary with size and view (the most expensive being the corner rooms). Each wing has three non-smoking floors, and there are handicapped rooms as well.

You may please your palate at a number of outlets: Old Manila (fine dining and good food); Spices (a variety of Asian cuisines); Mi Piace (Italian) and (adjacent to it) The Bar (very cozy); Nielsen's (24-hour coffee shop); the Conservatory (for high tea and music); the Cake Shop and Delicatessen; and, of coarse, the Lobby (popular with high society and politicians for afternoon or late-night snacks).

Facilities include the pretty pool area with an L-shaped swimming pool among landscaped terraces, a health and fitness center, business center, limousine services, helicopter rental, laundry and dry cleaner, flower shop, gift stand, and a cigar store.

INTER-CONTINENTAL MANILA, *1 Ayala Avenue, near EDSA, Tel. 815-9711, Fax 817-1330. US reservations: Tel. 212/755-5900. 343 rooms. $301-361.50 per single, $325-361.50 per double, $421-566 per suite. Visa, Master Card, American Express, Diners.* [#63]

The Inter-Con has a pleasant and bright lobby of marble and predominantly pastel hues. You will find the staff very cordial. Rooms have the usual amenities of hotels in this price range, and appear slightly smaller than its counterparts. Views from the rooms are either of the commercial center — which is very nice in the evenings from higher floors; or, on the pool-side, of EDSA and three plush residential villages.

The Inter-Con has a very nice pool in a landscaped garden — definitely a refreshing oasis in the city. Other facilities include a good gym and a business center. The several restaurants include the Jeepney Coffee Shop (popular for coffee and breakfast with the political elite) and the Prince Albert (mentioned in *Where to Eat*). For evening entertainment try the music lounge and the Euphoria disco.

DUSIT HOTEL NIKKO, *Arnaiz Avenue corner EDSA, Tel. 867-3333, Fax 867-3888. 549 rooms. $289-361.50 per single, $313-385 per double, $506-1,687 per suite. Visa, Master Card, American Express, Diners.* [#68]

As you enter the spacious yet comfortable lobby, the staff greet you warmly. There is an obvious Asian feel to the Dusit that goes beyond the name (Dusit is a Thai hotel and resort chain and Nikko is a Japanese chain) — receptionists don an elegant Thai-styled uniform. To the right of the lobby, a wide, curving staircase takes you above Paulaner Brauhaus, a German brewery, to the second floor for Benjarong (super Thai cuisine) and Ciao (great dessert and pizza).

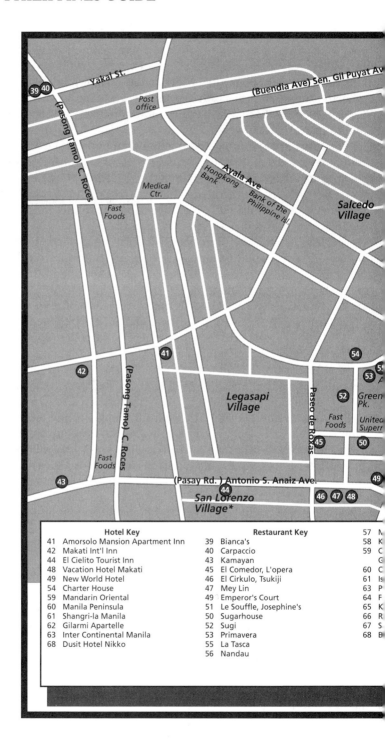

Hotel Key		Restaurant Key			
41	Amorsolo Mansion Apartment Inn	39	Bianca's	57	M
42	Makati Int'l Inn	40	Carpaccio	58	K
44	El Cielito Tourist Inn	43	Kamayan	59	C
48	Vacation Hotel Makati	45	El Comedor, L'opera		G
49	New World Hotel	46	El Cirkulo, Tsukiji	60	C
54	Charter House	47	Mey Lin	61	Is
59	Mandarin Oriental	49	Emperor's Court	63	P
60	Manila Peninsula	51	Le Souffle, Josephine's	64	F
61	Shangri-la Manila	50	Sugarhouse	65	K
62	Gilarmi Apartelle	52	Sugi	66	R
63	Inter Continental Manila	53	Primavera	67	S
68	Dusit Hotel Nikko	55	La Tasca	68	B
		56	Nandau		

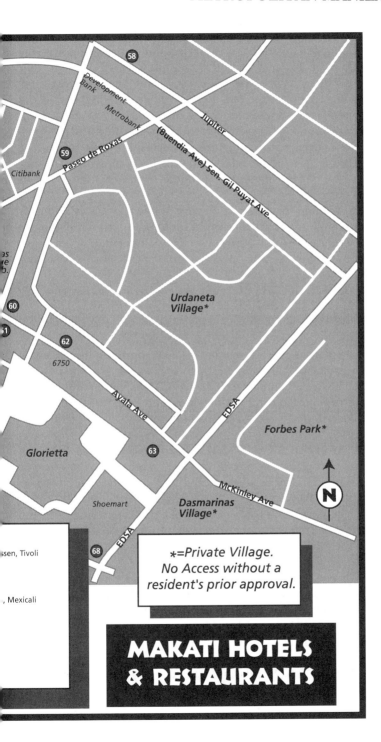

58

Development Bank

Metrobank

Jupiter

59

Paseo de Roxas

(Buendia Ave) Sen. Gil Puyat Ave

Citibank

as ve b.

60

1

62

6750

Urdaneta Village*

Ayala Ave

EDSA

Forbes Park*

Glorietta

63

McKinley Ave

N

Shoemart

Dasmarinas Village*

EDSA

ssen, Tivoli

68

*=Private Village.
No Access without a
resident's prior approval.

, Mexicali

MAKATI HOTELS & RESTAURANTS

Stepping out of the elevator onto a residential floor, you are greeted by a cheerful guard. The well lit corridors lead you to the rooms, with the views of either the commercial center, a southward EDSA view, or a northward EDSA view with the pool below. The hotel has two non-smoking floors. Rooms for the disabled have guide bars on the walls and in the bathrooms, and rooms and bathrooms are slightly larger than the regular rooms. The brightness of the rooms is refreshing; the predominant color is a soothing cream complemented nicely by the Victorian-style floral bedspreads. All rooms come with either a complementary fruit basket or a box of chocolates, and a bottle of mineral water that is replenished daily.

Additional dining places are a 24-hour coffee shop, a deli, Benkay (Japanese cuisine), and a Chinese restaurant. Among the facilities and services are a swimming pool, fitness center, business center, salon, flower and gift shop, laundry and dry cleaning, limo and airport service, and babysitting services.

NEW WORLD HOTEL, *Makati Avenue between Arnaiz Avenue and Esperanza Street, Tel. 811-6888, Fax 811-6777. 588 rooms. $289-313 per single or double, $325.25-1,084.50 per suite. Visa, Master Card, American Express, Diners.* [#49]

This nice hotel has good service and pleasant comfortable rooms with the usual furnishings of high-priced establishments. The gym and pool are nice, and the business center is well managed. The New World has two popular and good restaurants — Bocarinos, and Emperor's Court (described in *Where to Eat*), and a coffee shop. And for evening entertainment, Cats.

MANDARIN ORIENTAL MANILA, *Intersection of Paseo de Roxas and Makati Avenue, Tel. 750-8888, Fax 817-2472. US reservations: Tel. 310/649-1634. 468 rooms. $210-350 per single, $235-373.50 per double, $410 per suite. Visa, Master Card, American Express, Diners.* [#59]

This hotel is good value — Mandarin's quality is at par with all the top hotels. It has an extremely loyal clientele of business executives who will only stay at the Mandarin because of its unwavering service. The staff is superb.

White- or red-clad employees warmly welcome you through glass doors to the small lobby of wood-paneled front desks, and a marble floor. A few steps up a red carpet lead you to the elevators or stairs. The rooms are spacious and tastefully furnished including a good desk with ample space, and all the amenities of a first-class hotel.

Facilities include a business center, gym, swimming pool, and a salon for men and women. The Mandarin also has several good eating establishments, two of which are mentioned in *Where to Eat*.

Moderate Hotels-Makati

MERCURE MILLENNIUM PLAZA, *Makati Avenue corner Eduque Street, Tel. 899-4718, Fax 899-4746. 114 rooms with kitchenette. $106-126 per single, $120-132 per double, $156-170 per suite. Visa, Master Card, American Express, Diners.*

This tall, skinny hotel is geared to long-staying business travelers. The rooms are pleasant and facilities include a swimming pool, sauna, and jacuzzi. The coffee shop serves continental fare.

AMORSOLO MANSION APARTMENT INN, *130 Amorsolo Street corner Herrera Street, Tel. 818-6811, Fax 818-5993. 100 rooms with kitchenette. $90-130 per single, $110-150 per double. Visa, Master Card, American Express, Diners.* [#41]

Rooms are simple and clean. Guests may use the facilities of the Gillarmi Apartelle (see below).

CENTURY CITADEL INN, *5007 P. Burgos Street, Tel. 897-2370, Fax 897-2666. 162 rooms with kitchenette. $64 96 per single or double, $105 per suite. Visa, Master Card, American Express.*

Another tall skinny hotel catering to business travelers. The rooms are nice and comfortable. Facilities include a pool and a small gym. There is a restaurant and a coffee shop. The staff is very friendly.

VACATION HOTEL MAKATI, *914 Arnaiz Avenue (Pasay Road), Tel. 843-7936, Fax 818-7756. 40 rooms. $69 per single $79 per double. Visa, Master Card, American Express, Diners.*

This hotel is conveniently located near the malls, several bars, and restaurants. The rooms are clean, but are a bit small. The restaurant serves continental food. [#48]

GILARMI APARTELLE, *6749 Ayala Avenue, Tel. 812-9311, Fax 818-3848. 100 Rooms with kitchenette. $50 per single, $65 per double. Visa, Master Card, American Express, Diners.*

This is also a residential condominium. The rooms here are clean, cozy, and spacious; some have a balcony. Views are either of Ayala Ave., or facing one of the residential villages. There is a pool and a coffee shop with good food. [#62]

CHARTER HOUSE, *114 Legaspi Street, Tel. 844-3461, Fax 817-7071. 50 Rooms. $51 per single, $68 per double. Visa, Master Card, American Express, Diners.*

This apartelle is frequented by long-staying business travelers. The staff is very efficient and friendly. Rooms are comfortable; some face the Greenbelt Commercial Center. There is a small roof-top swimming pool. The coffee shop, open 24 hours, serves continental fare. [#54]

ROBELLE PENSION HOUSE, *4402 Valdez Street, near the International School, Tel. 899-8209, Fax 899-3064. $45 per single, $49 per double. Visa, Master Card, American Express.*

This pleasant hotel with clean and simple rooms has a small pool and a restaurant. The staff is very friendly.

MAKATI INTERNATIONAL INN, *2178 C. Roces (Pasong Tamo) Avenue, near Makati Cinema Square, Tel. 892-5989, Fax 819-5722. 50 rooms. $42-51 per single, $50-57 per double. Visa, Master Card, American Express, Diners.* [#42]

This charming inn has nice rooms that have minibars. The staff is wonderful — friendly and attentive. The restaurant and coffee shop are open 24 hours. Pamper yourself in the spa on the ground floor — services include Shiatsu, Swedish, or combination massages; aromatherapy; sauna; and jacuzzi.

OKA HOTEL, *8459 Kalayaan Avenue corner Don Pedro Street, Tel. 894-4408, Fax 895-4395. $41 per single, $46 per double. Visa, Master Card, American Express.*

All rooms are clean and have a small refrigerator. Breakfast is included in the price of the room. The restaurant serves Japanese, Filipino, and continental food.

EL CIELITO TOURIST INN, *804 Arnaiz Avenue (Pasay Road), Tel. 815-8951, Fax 817-9610. 30 rooms. $40 per single, $50 per double, $70 per suite. Visa, Master Card.* [#44]

This pleasant place has comfortable, clean rooms; a good coffee shop; and a beauty salon. The staff is very friendly.

YMCA, *7 Dao Street, San Antonio Village, near the Makati Central Post Office, Tel. 899-6101, Fax 899-6097. $35 per single, $46 per double. Visa, Master Card, American Express, Diners.*

Rooms are very clean and simple. You will get good value here! Facilities include a pool, small gym, tennis court, and basketball court. The restaurant has good local and continental dishes.

Ortigas Center

SHANGRI-LA'S EDSA PLAZA HOTEL, *1 Garden Way, Ortigas Center, Mandaluyong. Tel. 633-8888, Fax 631-1067. 440 rooms. US reservations: Tel. 800/942-5050. $277-380 per single, $307-410 per double, $718-1988 per suite. Visa, Master Card, American Express, Diners.* [#70]

The EDSA Plaza, part of the well-known Asian Shangri-La chain, has a traditional elegant appearance. The lobby has white marble floors and soaring glass windows behind the lobby lounge afford a soothing view of the lush pool area beyond. The lobby lounge is a great place to relax and enjoy a light snack, coffee, or tea. The rooms are a nice size and have good carpeting, comfortable beds with plush spreads, wood furniture including a desk with adequate work space, and a minibar. The marble bathrooms are spacious. Your view will either be northward — the Ortigas Center (higher floors will have a view of mountainous Antipolo beyond);

ORTIGAS HOTELS & RESTAURANTS

Hotel Key:	Restaurant Key:	
		House, S'Barro, Vietnam Food
70 Shangri-La's EDSA	69 Figaro	House, Almon
Plaza Hotel	70 Paparazzi	Marina, Mexicali,
75 Manila Galleria	71 Grassi's	Sugarhouse
Suites	72 Area Cafe, Bacolod's	73 Mario's
	Finest, Koffee	74 Primavera
	Kalifornia, Koryo	

or south — the upscale mall, with the pool area below (higher floors have a nice evening view of Makati's skyline). The room staff and the concierge are delightful.

Aside from the pretty swimming pool, the EDSA Plaza has a good gym, spa, and fitness center, and hardcourts for tennis. Business people may avail of the 24-hour fully equipped business center. Enjoy a good meal at any of the several outlets: Paparazzi (see *Where to Eat*); Summer Palace (good Chinese cuisine); Coffee Shop (continental food with a good breakfast buffet and some Asian a-la-carte dishes); the lobby lounge; and Inaho Tei (Japanese food — pricey).

MANILA GALLERIA SUITES, *1 ADB Avenue, Ortigas Center, Pasig, Tel. 633-7111, Fax 633-2824. 387 rooms. $150 per single, $161 per double, $171-$480 per suite.* [#75]

Great value! The rooms are very nice and spacious, with tasteful conservative decor (most clients are business people). The beds and cabinets are of a nice solid wood, varnished in a medium brown, and are complemented with soft pastel hues on the walls and bedspreads, giving the rooms a comfortable feel. You may request a room on a non-smoking floor. The staff is friendly.

Facilities include a business center, swimming pool, gym, jacuzzi, and sauna rooms. There are a number of restaurants and a music lounge. The hotel has direct access to the mall.

WHERE TO EAT

Manila has a wide variety of restaurants. There is something for almost everyone — whether you are looking for gourmet dining or a quick, cheap, but tasty meal.

If you have a craving for American food, there are several franchises in Manila — **Friday's** (Glorietta, Makati and Ortigas Center); **Hard Rock** (Glorietta, Makati); **Fashion Café** (Glorietta, Makati); **Chili's** (Greenbelt, Makati); **Tony Roma's** (Greenbelt, Makati); **Italiani's** (Greenbelt, Makati), and **Benihana** (Ortigas Center). American fast food chains sprinkled around the metropolis include **McDonalds, Wendy's, Dominos, Pizza Hut, Shakey's, Kentucky Fried Chicken, Kenny Roger's Roaster; Pollo Loco**, and **Texas Chicken**. For local hamburgers, try **Jollybee**; and for fried chicken try **Max's** or **Rack's**. All the malls have food courts where you may find a variety of snacks and meals.

We have arranged this section starting with the restaurants of first class hotels, then those around the Manila Bay area, followed by Makati; and finally Ortigas Center and San Juan. (Note: **[#n]** corresponds to the location on either the Near Manila Bay, Makati, or Ortigas Center map.)

The type of cuisine is described for each restaurant; it's the item just before the map locator in the italicized part of each entry.

First Class Hotels

Manila's first class hotels all have a number of restaurants; most have at least one that is particularly good. We have listed our favorites for you to try. Except in the delis and bakeries, a meal (appetizer, main course, and one non-alcoholic beverage) in one of the hotel restaurants may cost $20-50; a cup of brewed coffee costs about $3. The restaurants appear in order of location, starting at the Old Manila area, then Makati, and finishing in the Ortigas Center.

CHAMPAGNE ROOM, *Manila Hotel, Rizal Park, Manila, Tel. 527-0011; Visa, Master Card, American Express, Diners. European cuisine.* [#2]

The decor and ambiance is in keeping with the elegance expected from the Manila Hotel. There is also a cozy feel to the restaurant, it is dimly lit but not too dark, good size tables, and comfortable chairs. The food is quite good.

Also at the Manila Hotel is the **COWRIE GRILL**, where you can enjoy excellent seafood dishes and steaks. The service is superb.

YURAKUEN, *Manila Diamond Hotel, Roxas Boulevard, Ermita, Tel. 526-2211; Visa, Master Card, American Express, Diners. Japanese cuisine.* [#16]

Being a Japanese-managed hotel, it is not surprising that Yurakuen is well liked. The food is good — very fresh sushi and sashimi, and the shabu-shabu, which you cook in a pot set up in front of you and dip into their tasty sauce with a hint of peanut, is great.

HUA TING, *Heritage Hotel, Roxas Boulevard corner EDSA, Pasay, Tel. 891-8888; Visa, Master Card, American Express, Diners. Chinese cuisine.* [#38]
Good Cantonese cuisine – the roast duck is superb. Because of its location, Hua Ting is not often frequented, but, it is one of the best Chinese restaurants in the country. The decor is contemporary Chinese.

DELI SNACK, *Century Park Hotel, beside Harrison Plaza, Pablo Ocampo Street corner M. Adriatico Street, Malate, Tel. 522-1011; Visa, Master Card, American Express, Diners. Deli & Bake Shop.* [#34]
At this nice cozy deli, you can enjoy a good sandwich on fresh bread of your choice. Try the smoked tang*uige* (a large mackerel) with dill sauce. There are only a few tables; to be sure of a seat during lunch, come early or late. The staff is very nice. Expect to spend about $12 for a sandwich and drink.

ISLAND CAFÉ, *Shangri-La Manila, Ayala Avenue corner Makati Avenue, Makati, Tel. 813-8888; Visa, Master Card, American Express, Diners.* [#61]
Partake of the extensive buffet or the a la carte menu, both offering continental fare and a variety of delectable Asian dishes. In the evenings, feast on a hearty cut of prime US steak, grilled perfectly to suit your preference. The casual decor and lighting of the café lend a relaxing atmosphere, and service is prompt and friendly.

CAKE SHOP & DELICATESSEN, *Mandarin Oriental Manila, intersection of Makati Avenue and Paseo de Roxas, Makati, Tel. 750-8888; Visa, Master Card, American Express, Diners. Deli & Bake Shop.* [#59]
The sandwiches and bread are very good and the brewed coffee is about the best you can get here: it is also quite strong. Try the chicken tandoori pocket: it is excellent. Go early for lunch or you may have to wait a while. The non-sandwich dishes are also good. The place is bright and cheerful, and the staff efficient and friendly. A sandwich and drink or coffee will cost around $15.
Also at the Mandarin is **THE TIVOLI GRILL**, where you may enjoy California cuisine complemented with Asian spices and ingredients. The grilled dishes are delectable.

OLD MANILA, *The Peninsula Manila, Ayala Avenue corner Makati Avenue, Makati, Tel. 812-3456; Visa, Master Card, American Express, Diners. European cuisine.* [#60]
You enter through iron grill gates to a simple and elegant dining room. The food is very good – especially the seafood. The grilled prawns with lemon butter are succulent. And they have a good wine list.

PRINCE ALBERT, *Hotel Inter-Continental Manila, Ayala Avenue near EDSA, Makati, Tel. 815-9711; Visa, Master Card, American Express, Diners. Steaks.* [#63]
This is one of Manila's most formal restaurants. It is dimly lit and the furnishing is mostly wood. The food is superb and the service impeccable.

Prince Albert has the reputation for having the best steaks in the country — excellent prime rib.

BENJARANG, *Dusit Hotel Nikko, Arnaiz Avenue corner EDSA, Makati. Tel. 867-3333; Visa, Master Card, American Express, Diners. Thai cuisine.* [#68]

This is probably the best Thai restaurant in Manila, which is not surprising as Dusit is a Thai hotel chain. The ambiance is very pleasant and Asian. You can have your dishes prepared mild, medium, or very hot (spicy). The main dishes are very good, and are served with genuine aromatic rice from Thailand.

CIAO, *Dusit Hotel Nikko, Arnaiz Avenue, corner EDSA, Makati. Tel. 867-3333; Visa, Master Card, American Express, Diners. Italian cuisine.* [#68]

The decor of this large restaurant is very modern — hanging metal stars and moons — and tastefully done. Order the pizza; its thin crust has a flavorful sauce with just the right amount of herbs. The desserts are very good. Try the Latte Cotto, a light pudding of milk, honey, and cinnamon; it is superb! The coffee here is pretty good and is strong.

EMPEROR'S COURT, *New World Hotel, Makati Avenue between Arnaiz Avenue and Esperanza Street. Tel. 811-6888; Visa, Master Card, American Express, Diners. Chinese cuisine.* [#49]

Come for tasty Chinese food; this is one of the best places to go for dim sum. The decor is simple and the restaurant is spacious.

PAPARAZZI, *Shangri-La's EDSA Plaza, 1 Garden Way, Ortigas Center. Tel. 633-8888; Visa, Master Card, American Express, Diners. Italian cuisine.* [#70]

In a comfortable-modernish setting with a relaxing atmosphere, you can enjoy tasty Italian dishes and a good wine list. The service is efficient and friendly.

Near Manila Bay

ILUSTRADO, *El Amanecer Compound, along General Luna Street, Intramuros. Tel. 527-3674. $10-23. Visa, Master Card, American Express. Spanish-European cuisine.* [#1]

Located in Old Manila, the ambiance in the main dining room is wonderful — candle lit, plush seats, a view into the old Spanish-style garden with tiled walkways, and a good pianist who will play your requests. The food is pretty good. The Duck Ilustrado — roasted in an orange, plum, and brandy sauce — is delicious. Another good reason to come here is the homemade *sampaguita* ice cream, made from the fragrant jasmine flower; it is refreshing and tastes like the scent of the flower.

The coffee shop, for informal dining offering Filipino-Spanish cuisine, is open from breakfast through dinner. The decor is charming, the chairs and tables are iron, and there are some interesting posters of various important displays of Filipino artists. They have good breakfasts, sandwiches, and ice cream.

TENNESSEE WALKER, *departs from the Manila Hotel, Rizal Park. Tel. 527-0011. $25. Visa, Master Card, American Express, Diners. Continental cuisine.* [#2]

This is a nice alternative to the usual city dining. The dining room, in the main cabin of this boat, is air conditioned and has red carpeting. The buffet is served as soon as the boat leaves the dock. The garlic pasta is good. After your meal, proceed to the upstairs deck for music and drinks. The cruise takes about an hour and 30 minutes.

SEAFOOD MARKET, *Ambassador Hotel, Mabini Street, Malate, Tel. 524-7756. $15-35. Visa, Master Card, American Express, Diners. Seafood.* [#29]

Take a cart or basket, and choose your meal from a selection of seafood and fresh vegetables. Pay at the cashier, then proceed to your table, where a waiter asks how you want your selection cooked.

COSA NOSTRA, *Adriatico Street between Remedios Street and San Andres Street, Tel. 523-7889. $10-15. Italian cuisine.* [#30]

A charming, dimly lit place that resembles small restaurants in Italy. Antiques and pictures adorn the walls. Enjoy the ambiance and the excellent home cooking. The pesto pizza is very tasty and the pasta sauces are flavorful. The staff is cordial and efficient.

CASA ARMAS, *J Nakpil Street, Malate; $10-20. Spanish cuisine.* [#24]

This small restaurant with an elegant Spanish ambiance makes very good paella, and service is friendly.

HARBOR VIEW, *at the waterfront of Manila Bay by Rizal Park. $5-10. Filipino cuisine.* [#3]

Come for the wharf atmosphere and local fare.

WOK INN, *Remedios Street near Malate Church, Malate; and Arkansas Street, Ermita. $3.50-6. Chinese Fast food.* [#27]

This is a good place for a quick, tasty, and inexpensive Chinese meal. Customers range from blue collar workers to wealthy businessmen and politicians. Choose from an array of fresh seafood, meats, vegetables, and watch the cooks stir-fry your meal.

PEKING PARK, *San Juan Street between Taft Ave. and Leveriza St. $2-4. Chinese Fast food.*

This place is patterned after Hong Kong's street-side eateries, and the chef, Rommie Ofiaza, trained in Hong Kong. The food is tasty and cheap. It is small and is packed during lunch — come early or do not expect a seat.

JOSEPH & JAYMART, *right beside the Cuneta Astrodome (on Roxas Boulevard), Pasay; and along Katipunan in Quezon City. $1.50-4. Grilled Seafood.* [#36]

Do not be put off by this hole-in-the-wall in Pasay; they do great grilled seafood, including tuna and marlin, steaks or jaws. The food is cooked just right (tasty and juicy), is safe, and surprisingly clean. They have a slightly larger outlet, with "more respectable" facilities in Quezon City.

Makati

EL COMEDOR, *Anson Arcade, along Paseo de Roxas. Tel. 892-5071. $12-27. Visa, Master Card, American Express, Diners. Spanish cuisine.* [#45]

This place serves pretty good classic Spanish food. It is popular for its roast baby pig. The decor resembles a typical restaurant in Spain, with hand-painted plates on the walls. The staff is very well trained.

L'OPERA, *Anson Arcade, Paseo de Roxas corner Esperanza. Tel. 844-3283. $12-25. Visa, Master Card, American Express, Diners. Italian cuisine.* [#45]

Most of the dishes here are very good, rich in flavor, and heavy. The lighting is perfect: not too dark, nor too bright. Service is usually good. Some of the tables, for two, are small, but there are large tables for big groups. Chairs are comfortable and the atmosphere is cozy.

EL CIRKULO, *900 Arnaiz Avenue where Paseo de Roxas ends. Tel. 892-5071. $11.50-25. Visa, Master Card, American Express, Diners. Nouveau Spanish cuisine.* [#46]

This semi-circular restaurant was designed to resemble a bull ring. The staff is friendly, and the restaurant is managed well. The salads are large, very fresh, and topped with tasty dressings. You get a variety of dishes, from light and small to heavy. The appetizers are pretty good.

TSUKIJI, *900 Arnaiz Avenue where Paseo de Roxas ends. Tel. 843-4285. $15-40. Visa, Master Card, American Express, Diners. Japanese cuisine.* [#46]

The sushi and sashimi here are very fresh. During lunch, the restaurant is very bright. The walls are white and most of the furniture is dark wood. There are several *tatami* rooms (where you must remove your shoes and sit on cushions on the floor with your feet under the table).

MEY LIN, *Charter House Building, Arnaiz Avenue. Tel. 844 1074; and MegaMall, Ortigas Center. $10-25. Chinese cuisine.* [#47]

Great food, most of it quite cheap. The garlic crabs are very good.

KOHINOOR, *1006 Arnaiz Avenue. Tel. 892-4227. $12-25. Visa, Master Card. Indian cuisine.* [#65]

This simple restaurant has pretty good food, as close to authentic as you can get here. The tandoori chicken is very tender and succulent; you can ask for your curries mild, medium, or spicy. You will enjoy the garlic nan if you like garlic; it goes well with their curries.

RAMEN TEI, *Tesoro Building, Arnaiz Avenue. $8-20. Japanese cuisine, 24-hour dining.* [#66]

You can come here for a decent, inexpensive meal. It is frequented by Japanese men during lunch or late at night. The fried gyozas are tasty.

SAKURA, *Arnaiz Avenue across the street from Park Square. $15-35. Japanese cuisine.* [#67]

Excellent yakiniku (marinated seafood or meat that you grill yourself); the success of the dish is in the marinade and the dipping sauce.

Upon arrival and departure, you are greeted by almost the entire staff in Japanese. This place gets packed during dinner, and most of its clients are Japanese. You may smell like food after your meal, so if you are going somewhere else after, you may want to consider changing first.

LE SOUFFLÉ, *Josephine's Building in Greenbelt Center near Makati Avenue. Tel. 812-3278. $17-30. Visa, Master Card, American Express, Diners. French-European cuisine.* [#51]

This large restaurant doubles as a classy bar. It is very popular with expatriates. As expected, it is known for good soufflés; the other dishes are also quite tasty. The chocolate soufflé is yummy.

JOSEPHINE'S, *Josephine's Building, Greenbelt Center. Tel. 892-6595. $10-20. Visa, Master Card, American Express, Diners. Filipino-Seafood cuisine.* [#51]

A casual well-known restaurant where you can have a nice native meal. The menu is extensive. The building resembles a traditional ancestral house, and the interior is mostly wood.

SUGI, *Greenbelt Mall. Tel. 816-3885. $15-38. Visa, Master Card, American Express, Diners. Japanese cuisine.* [#52]

Very good food in a cozy atmosphere. Service is also good.

PRIMAVERA, *Greenbelt Park, along Legaspi Street, Tel. 843-7286; and El Pueblo Complex, corner ADB Avenue and J. Vargas Street, Ortigas Center. Tel. 632-7117. $15-30. Visa, Master Card, American Express, Diners. Italian cuisine.* [#53, 74]

The pastas are pretty tasty; you can choose from light, tomato-based sauces or heavier cream sauces. They also have a good selection of wine: even by the glass, you may choose from four reds or four whites. If you prefer white, it is served perfectly chilled. Both branches are lit softly, affording a romantic atmosphere. We prefer the outlet in Ortigas: it is newer, and the interior is simple and elegant.

LA TASCA, *Greenbelt Park, along Legaspi Street. Tel. 893-8586. $15-35. Visa, Master Card, American Express, Diners. European-Spanish cuisine.* [#55]

The setting is definitely Spanish, with white walls, dark wood windows, banisters, and chairs, and red carpeting and cushions. The food is mostly heavy but good. They also serve beef, cheese, seafood, and chocolate fondue. You may cook your seafood fondue in oil or water. A variety of sauces is served with the fondue.

NANDAU, *Greenbelt Park, along Legaspi Street. Tel. 818-3388; and Roxas Boulevard, Pasay. Tel. 521-8007. $10-23. Visa, Master Card. Filipino Seafood cuisine.* [#56]

This restaurant is known for its good seafood dishes. The grilled blue marlin is usually superb, and the *adobong kangkong* (a vegetable dish with a garlic sauce) is very good.

MARIO'S, *de la Rosa Street near Makati Avenue, Tel. 899-3377; and St. Francis Square, Bank Drive across from MegaMall, Ortigas Center, Tel. 634-3417. $15-27. Visa, Master Card, American Express, Diners. Continental-Filipino cuisine.* [#57, 73]

This restaurant is cozy and elegant. The chairs are very comfortable. Most of the dishes are tasty, and the Ceasar salad is quite hearty. It is a nice place to relax, chat, and have coffee after a meal.

CARPACCIO, *7431 Yakal Street near Makati Central Post Office. Tel. 843-7286. $12.50-23. Visa, Master Card. Italian cuisine.* [#40]

Our visiting Italian friend says that the food here is pretty authentic; he really likes it and so do we. The sauces are flavorful, and they serve a good rib eye too. The wine list is extensive, including a selection by the glass. The ambiance is casual. A bar curves around the center.

BIANCA'S, *7431 Yakal Street near Makati Central Post Office. Tel. 815-1359. $12.50-20. European cuisine.* [#39]

This is a great place for a quick gourmet lunch. It gets packed, but turnover is faster than most places here. There is a set menu for lunch: you choose from two dishes that change daily or select from the sausages. The food is usually very good, as is the coffee.

KAMAYAN, *47 Arnaiz Avenue near the South Superhighway. Tel. 843-3604. $10-23. Visa, Master Card, American Express, Diners. Filipino cuisine.* [#43]

Kamay is Tagalog for hands: experience eating "Filipino-style" with your hands (cutlery is available as well). The menu is extensive, and the food is relatively good.

KAYA, *Jupiter Street. Tel. 895-0404. $15-25. Visa, Master Card, American Express, Diners. Korean cuisine.* [#58]

The bulgogi (marinated beef), kalbi (marinated short ribs), and dak-bulgogi (chicken), all served on sizzling plates, are very tasty. A number of the other dishes are pretty good; it is frequented by Koreans. You are greeted by the staff in Korean when you enter, and once again when you leave. You may end up smelling like food after your meal, so if you are going somewhere else after, you may want to consider changing first.

LA TIENDA, *corner of Kalayaan Street and Burgos Street. $12-23. Spanish cuisine.*

This very casual, small, and charming restaurant is frequented by a number of Manila's Spaniards and Spanish-mestizos. On Fridays, they have very good paella.

SUGARHOUSE, *Greenbelt Center in the Esperanza Arcade. Tel. 844-3522; and in MegaMall, Ortigas Center. Tel. 634-0610. $5-15. Bakeshop.* [#50, 72]

At this chain of bakeries, you may select from a variety of cakes, baked daily. Most of the cakes are moist and tasty. They also serve snacks and pastas.

FIGARO, *Glorietta; and Shangri-La Mall. Coffee Shop.* [#64, 69]
If you are looking for an American-style coffee shop, this is probably the closest you can find. It has the largest selection of imported coffee beans and local blends to chose from. You may order your coffee hot or iced. They have a selection of teas as well. The rum cake is very good.

ALMON MARINA, *Glorietta; and MegaMall, Ortigas Center. $5-16. Deli.* [#64, 72]
They serve some pretty good gourmet sandwiches here. One of the favorites is the smoked San Francisco chicken served on French bread with a tangy mayonnaise dressing and a few slices of mango. They also serve good salads.

MEXICALI, *Glorietta; and MegaMall, Ortigas Center. $3-8. Mexican Fast food.* [#64, 72]
They serve good "Mexican" fast food — tacos, burritos, cnchiladas, with an assortment of fillings to chose from.

Ortigas Center & San Juan

See Makati restaurants above for descriptions of Mario's [#73]; Primavera [#74]; Figaro [#69]; and Mey Lin, Almon Marina, Mexicali, Sugarhouse [#72].

GRASSI'S, *5th floor Benpres Building, Tektite Road corner Meralco Avenue, Ortigas Center Tel. 632-1204. $16-40. Visa, Master Card, American Express, Diners. French cuisine.* [#71]
This is the most formal dining in the Ortigas Center. One of its outstanding features is the innovative menu that puts a European twist into local food; the ingredients are very fresh. They also have a good set lunch — for $10 you may have a starter, salad, and main dish (usually fish), and for an extra $2, dessert. The ambiance is geared to business people. During lunch, it is frequented by top executives from the offices nearby.

CAFE YSABEL, *655 P Guevarra Street near Wilson Street, San Juan. Tel. 722-0349. $12.50-25. Continental-Spanish-Filipino cuisine.*
Set inside an old house, the ambiance keeps people coming back. It is romantic but not overly so; the lighting is dim, and there is a candle on every table. Seating is inside one of the two rooms, or by the window along a corridor. They also have an extensive coffee menu with mixtures containing different liquor.

AREA CAFE, *MegaMall, Ortigas Center. $10-15. Cafe-style cuisine.* [#72]
Excellent gourmet sandwiches, soups, and pastas. They also have a selection of tea, and serve coffee.

KORYO HOUSE, *MegaMall, Ortigas Center. $7-20. Korean cuisine.* [#72]
You can get a variety of tasty and inexpensive dishes here.

BACOLOD'S FINEST (BALAY 21), *MegaMall, Ortigas Center. Tel. 635-7814. $4-15. Filipino cuisine.* [#72]

This is our favorite place for casual Filipino food in Manila. The Bacolod-style chicken is superb. They also have a number of tasty seafood dishes.

VIETNAM FOOD HOUSE, *MegaMall, Ortigas Center. Tel. 633-1702. $4-15. Vietnamese cuisine.* [#72]

You can get some good Vietnamese dishes here. The restaurant is small, and there isn't much room as the tables are close together.

S'BARRO, *MegaMall, Ortigas Center. $4-10. Italian fast food.* [#72]

This fast food franchise from the US serves a good big slice of pizza. They also have a small selection of good pastas, and tasty garlic bread.

KOFFEE KALIFORNIA, *MegaMall, Ortigas Center. Coffee Shop.* [#72]

The ambiance here is great if you are looking for a laid-back place to have a cup (or glass) of coffee, read a magazine, or just hang out and listen to the music. The friendly staff wear Hawaiian-style flowered shirts. It is a small and cheerful place; seating is at the bar, along a table on the wall, or at one of the three tables. Along the back wall is a supply of magazines. Choose from a wide selection of coffee concoctions, all made with local beans, and have it served hot or on ice. The pleasant manager is nice to chat with.

SEEING THE SIGHTS

You may join guided tours that leave from some hotels; inquire at your hotel's desk. Most of the higher priced hotels have chauffeured car rental services. (Chauffeurs in the Philippines are called drivers, or *tsupers*). Street signs do not always exist, so if you are not familiar with the streets, a driver is a good idea, and isn't very costly.

If you are going to be here for some time, you may eventually want to get out and about on your own for a first-hand experience of the city at your own pace.

OLD MANILA – INTRAMUROS

The tremendous task of restoring the old walled city as close as possible to its previous grandeur began in the 1970s. Slowly, the rehabilitation is progressing. **Intramuros** is a wonderful place to walk around while discovering its fortifications and structures. Or, by **Fort Santiago**, you can board a *calesa* and tour the city.

Around the Plaza

Begin your stroll at the **Governor General's Palace**. Drop by the Intramuros Administration offices on the 5th floor. Here you can get information and attractive brochures, and see a scale model of Intramuros.

Fronting the Palace is **Plaza Royal**, where, during the Spanish era, concerts were held amid its gardens and fountains. The **Manila Cathedral**, rebuilt shortly after the war, faces the plaza.

Fort Santiago

North of the Plaza, along General Luna Street, is **Fort Santiago**. The fort was built on the original site of Rajah Sulayman's settlement and was used to control traffic along the Pasig River. Two centuries ago, passage to Laguna de Bay's coastal towns was by water.

The fort served as headquarters to several occupying armies. Many atrocities have been committed here — prisoners were left to drown as the tide rose and filled the lower dungeons; when the Japanese left, 600 bodies were found in the powder magazine chamber.

Today, the fort is an attractive park. Its barracks have been converted to the **Rajah Sulayman Theater** where performances are held. Historic cars and an old wood-burning railroad engine are kept in niches in the walls. Signs name and describe the dungeons, and from the walls above, you can view Binondo across the Pasig River.

The **Rizal Museum** occupies rooms where the country's national hero, Dr. José P. Rizal, was imprisoned before he was executed. His memorabilia are displayed: he was a nonmilitant poet, physician, artist, and intellectual. He wrote two novels that denounced the abuses of the Spanish friars, and founded a society that pressured for reforms.

December is a wonderful time to visit the fort — you can sit by the fountains and enjoy the Christmas music piped in through speakers hidden in trees and shrubs aglow with lights.

San Agustin & Barrio San Luis

San Agustin Church, two blocks south from the Cathedral along General Luna Street, was built between 1587 and 1607. Enter the church to see its beautifully painted ceilings. For $1.20, you can browse through the museum's impressive collection of religious art and artifacts; it is open daily from 9:00am to noon and 1:00pm to 5:00pm.

In **Barrio San Luis**, across from San Agustin Church, you can look through a nicely reconstructed 18th-century building. Inside is the **Casa Manila Museum**, open Tuesday through Sunday, from 9:00am to 6:00pm; admission is 60¢. Casa Manila is a replica of the typical home of a wealthy 18th century family. You will see furnishings and paraphernalia they may have used, including a 2-seater toilet with a chess board in between. Within the complex is a small restaurant, and several curio and antique shops.

Shop Stop

For shopping and looking, around you will enjoy **El Amanecer**, General Luna Street, two blocks from Barrio San Luis. This attractive four-story building has a fine collection of handicrafts at good prices, and a good restaurant, the Ilustrado, behind it.

The Walls

At the end of General Luna is **Puerta Real**, which was formerly the main entrance used by officials during ceremonies. From December through the beginning of March, open air performances are held here.

If you turn right on Fundicion Street and follow the wall, you will get to **Bastion San Diego**. To the left of Puerta Real, you will find **Bastion San Andres** (corner of Fundicion and Muralla Streets), **Aurora Gardens**, and the ruins of **Bastion de San Fernando Dilao**.

Puerta del Parian, along Muralla Street, was used as the exit to the Chinese settlement (called Parian).The next fortification you will pass is **Bastion San Gabriel**. Here the Spaniards trained Intramuros' guns in silent threat at the Parian, in an attempt to keep the Chinese submissive. Take the stairs and climb to the top of San Gabriel for a view of the area. If you look diagonally towards the Pasig River, you will see the art-deco **Metropolitan Theatre**, built in 1935. The Met was formerly the venue for many plays, concerts, and other performances; sadly it is no longer used regularly.

Inside the walls, behind San Gabriel, you will see **San Juan de Letran** College, founded in 1639. This is one of few establishments that has remained on its original site. Just outside **Puerta Isabel**, at the corner of Muralla and Maestranza, is a statue of Queen Isabel II. Across the street is the **Commission on Immigration**, where you will need to go for visa extensions.

JUST OUTSIDE THE WALLS

West of Intramuros is **South Harbor**, where most cargo ships arrive from abroad. Southeast of the walled city is Manila's **City Hall** and other government offices near the LRT's Central Station.

RIZAL & LUNETA PARK

The Spanish first relocated the natives from Intramuros to **Bagumbayan** ("new town"). For security, the Spaniards then moved them further away, and the area was converted into a park named **Luneta**. Here, Manila's society came in carriages, dressed in their finery. It was "the" place to be seen.

The Spanish executed José Rizal in 1869 at the Luneta, in hopes that his death would deter rebellion. Rizal's body was placed in a mismarked grave in Paco Cemetery, then moved to his mother's house, and finally was laid to rest under the **Rizal Monument**. The Monument faces the parade ground. Today, you will see crowds gathering at the park on Sundays and holidays, or attending political or religious rallies.

The **Manila Hotel**, which served as **MacArthur's headquarters**, is at the northwest end of the park. It has been a landmark since its 1912 inauguration. Beside the bay are the huge Quirino Grandstand, restaurants, and boats for sunset cruises. The new **Children's Museum** is near the southeast border.

Along the southern fringes of the park are the **National Library**, open Monday through Friday from 8:00am to 5:00pm, and on Saturday from 8:00am to noon. Inside the library is the **Museum of the National Historical Institute**, open Tuesday through Saturday, from 9:00am to noon, and 1:00pm to 5:00pm. Nearby, you can get snacks from a café run by and for the deaf. Further east are several government offices and the **Department of Tourism**. You will find a large relief map of the Philippines and a children's playground near the tourism offices.

The **National Museum**, along P Burgos Street just north east of the park, has interesting exhibits and a good gift shop. It is open Tuesday through Saturday, from 9:00am to noon, and from 1:00pm till 5:00pm.

NORTHWEST OF THE PASIG – SAN NICHOLAS

San Nicholas was Manila's commercial center during the galleon trade. You will still find warehouses lining the riverbank. Although a few colonial-era houses were not damaged during the war; sadly, they are falling apart.

North Harbor is where you will board inter-island vessels headed to Philippine points.

At **Divisoria**, a vast, bustling market, anything and everything is wholesaled and retailed. Do not wear anything fancy here, as bargaining will not be effective, and you do not want to attract pickpockets.

Across the market is the elegant 19th century **Tutuban Station**, now a shopping mall. Above the buildings, you will see the golden stupa of The **Seng Guan Buddhist Temple** where 10,000 Buddhas line the dome.

Tondo, just north, was where many artisans and craftsmen once lived. It is now a big steaming slum, home to many who came from the provinces to the city, hoping for a better life.

BINONDO

Binondo is the heart of Chinatown, and **Escolta** is the older of Manila's business centers. The Chinese moved here when the Parian district burned in the 16th century. During the 18th century, the Spaniards built warehouses and mansions here. Binondo was severely damaged during World War Two, the Spanish-Filipino residents moved elsewhere, and eventually Binondo reverted to being a predominantly Chinese area and a business hub.

The streets of Binondo are narrow, full of parked trucks, *calesas*, cars, and people that speak Tagalog, Fukien, Cantonese, Shanghaienese, Mandarin, and English. You will find almost anything available here, in an assortment of hardware shops (**Gandara area**), Chinese apothecaries and groceries, clothing and material shops, and jewelry. You can tour Binondo by hired *calesa* – flag them down anywhere.

Jones Bridge will take you to Binondo from old Manila. The first thing that you will see is the imposing **Filipino-Chinese Friendship Arch** on Quintin Paredes Street. It also marks the heart of Manila's banking area. Continue to Plaza Calderon de la Barca and **Binondo Church**. The church was originally built in 1596 and has been damaged several times. The octagonal bell tower is the only surviving element from the first structure. As you look directly across from the church, you will see a distinctly Chinese-style bridge – cross it to get to a pagoda-style fire station.

Ongpin Street is known as "24-karat street." You will find a number of jewelry stores here, and most of the gold jewelry they have is 18-karat and up. Along Ongpin and the streets that lead off it, you can feast at a number of Chinese restaurants. The **Mandarin**, **President**, **Shui Hing** (in the Lai-Lai Hotel), and **Ocean Dragon** all serve delicious meals. If you want a casual place, try the *estero* (canal) eateries by the canal, where the Pasig forks into Binondo. Here you will find 21 stalls where food is cooked mostly by Cantonese and Fukienese immigrants. You can also find tasty snacks, sweet breads, and pastries in the bakeries around Binondo.

SANTA CRUZ & LA LOMA
The district of **Santa Cruz**, a farm in 1640, is large and has markets, hospitals, a church, and two fascinating cemeteries. **Sta Cruz Church** was first built in 1608 by the Jesuits for Chinese converts. However, the structure you see was built in 1957; the original was damaged twice by quake and then destroyed during the Second World War. Fronting the church is **Plaza Locsin**. The bridge that spans the Pasig near the church is MacArthur Bridge, and on the other side is City Hall.

Bilibid Viejo, once the national penitentiary, lies unused. **Central Market**, on Mendoza Street, spills its textiles, clothes, and dry goods onto the streets.

North Cemetery (**La Loma**), the resting place of many rich and famous Filipinos and Spaniards, contains some extraordinary mausoleums. You will find two pyramids and a sphinx, complete with kitchens and bathrooms. Do not visit alone, as it is home to many squatters.

Because the Chinese were forbidden from burying their dead at La Loma and other Spanish cemeteries, **Lim Ong** and **Tan Quien Sien** (Don Carlos Palanca) founded the **Chinese Cemetery**. You will find several mausoleums that are as interesting and elaborate as those in North Cemetery. Pictures of Christ, Buddha, the Virgin Mary, and Kuan Yin may decorate one mausoleum — the flexible Chinese turn to whatever proves useful and advantageous. The cemetery is well guarded. To enter, you pay $2, and the guard at the entrance may be able to arrange for a guide. A complete tour may cost around $12.

QUIAPO

Churches and markets are the highlights of **Quiapo**. Geographically at the center of Manila, the area was named after the water lily (*kiyapo*). From south of the Pasig River, you will get to Quiapo either via the Quezon Bridge or the Ayala Bridge.

Midway over the Ayala Bridge is a turn-off that takes you to **Isla de la Convalencia**, formerly a rest area for Spanish Soldiers. The **Hospicio de San Jose** was built on the island in 1782 and is used as a home for orphans and the aged. It has a turncradle for unwanted babies.

You will find **Quiapo Market** and **Ilalim ng Tulay** (literally "under the bridge") beneath Quezon Bridge. Shop for handicrafts, bird cages, fish traps, and an assortment of other things. Do not bring valuables, and be aware that the area is notorious for pickpockets. If you are looking for brass and Muslim crafts, you will find them nearby at the **Rajah Sulayman Market**, next to the gold-domed **Globo de Oro mosque**.

Facing **Plaza Miranda** is **Quiapo Church**. Formerly a Mexican baroque cathedral, it was gutted by fire in 1928. In the church, you will find the 17th century life-size *Black Nazarene* (Padre Señor Jesus de Nazareno) that came from Mexico by galleon. Every January 9, the figure is paraded on a carriage through the streets of Quiapo as people reach out to touch it in hopes that the past year's sins will be forgiven. Every Friday, hordes of people flock to the church; many crawl to the altar for penance, some asking for cures. Vendors outside sell medicinal herbs and potions, amulets, and an assortment of other things. You may also have your fortune told by a *manghuhula* (fortune teller).

San Sebastian Church, on Plaza del Carmen, is very pretty. A church has been on this site since 1621. Three former churches were destroyed by earthquakes. The current structure was built completely of prefabricated steel, imported on eight ships (between 1888 and 1891) from Belgium. Go inside the "jewel box church" so you can see the iron chandeliers that hang from steel rafters, beautiful stained glass windows, and the exquisite interior work.

MALACAÑANG

The offices and residence of the President are at **Malacañang Palace** in San Miguel. This district was formerly the summer home area of wealthy families. Malacañang was the family home of Don Luis Rocha, who built it in 1802. The Spanish government bought it in 1825 for $5,000. The name Malacañang comes from "*may lakan diyan,*" the Tagalog phrase for "there are powerful people there."

You can tour parts of Malacañang that are maintained as a museum; one hall displays rotating exhibits. Guided tours are $10 per person and are run on Tuesday and Wednesday from 9:00am until 3:30 pm, on Thursday from 9:00am until noon, and on Friday from 1:00pm until 3:00pm.

While in San Miguel, take a look at the pretty **San Beda Chapel**, not far from Malacañang. Ring the bell on the door to the right of the chapel to enter so you can see the impressive paintings, murals, and gothic pews.

The **Mabini Shrine** is found near Malacañang's grounds on the south side of the Pasig River. Apolinario Mabini, the brains of the revolution against Spain, lived in this house (originally located on the north side of the river).

UNIVERSITY OF SANTO TOMAS

The **University of Santo Tomas** is the oldest university in Asia. Founded by the Dominicans in 1611, it was moved here in 1927 from its original site in Intramuros. If you look at the top of the main building, you will see a huge clock and statues of Faith, Hope, Charity, St. Vincent, St. Agustin, St. Raymond, Aristotle, St. Albert, Plato, de la Barca, Sophocles, Shakespeare, Lope de Vega, Aristophanes and Molière.

Prior to the 19th century, only Spaniards and Spanish *mestizos* were allowed to attend the university; women were admitted first in 1927. During World War Two, the campus was used for three years as an internment camp for allied nationals. Many famous national figures were educated at UST.

The university houses extensive archives and relics. You may browse through its interesting museum, although its space continues to shrink as the student body expands. Originally designed for 5,000 students, there are now over 40,000.

MANILA BAY & NEARBY
Paco

Plaza Dilao (yellow), on Quirino Avenue just north of the South Superhighway, was so named by the Spaniards because they found some 3,000 Japanese living there when they first arrived. The statue at the center is of **Lord Ukon Takayama**, a Christian Samurai who was exiled to the Philippines in 1614 because he refused to renounce Christianity. Across the street is the Paco Post Office and Train Station.

Paco Park, a block from the corner of UN Avenue and Taft, is a small park surrounded by a double-walled circular cemetery. For a small fee you can enter the park, an oasis where you can relax on green grass under shady trees, surrounded by ancient walls. It was built in 1822 for those who perished during the cholera epidemic. The outer wall was added in 1859 for victims of other epidemics. When Rizal was executed, his body was placed here, under a headstone that had his initials written backwards. A white cross marks the spot where he was first buried; his remains are now at the Rizal Monument, just outside Intramuros. At the central chapel, many rich and famous Spaniards were laid to rest. Today only the remains of Governor General Roman Solano remain inside the Chapel of San Pancratius. Behind the park, you will find the **Paco Hong Giam Taoist Temple**. If you wish to enter and see the ornately decorated main temple, fishponds, and fountains, ring the bell at the gate.

If you are interested in seeing how cigars are made, the **Tabacalera Factory**, on Romualdez Street, *Tel. 524-8026*, allows visitors to browse and watch cigars being rolled, cut, and packed. Cigars are for sale, and for an extra charge you can order a box with your name engraved on it. The factory is open to visitors Monday through Friday, from 8:00am until noon, and again from 1:30 pm until 5:00pm.

Ermita

This district takes its name from a hermit who moved here to get away from city life. Today you will find several bars, handicraft and antique stores, art galleries, several money changers and travel agencies, a range of hotels, and a number of restaurants.

The **US Embassy** is along Roxas Boulevard fronting Manila Bay. The older, more pleasing structure is nestled in the trees behind the newer building. Every weekday, you will see a line of visa applicants that extends outside the gates.

Many handicraft and antique stores line the streets of Mabini and MH del Pilar. You can also get fine local material, *jusi* and *piña*, here. There are several souvenir shops inside **Discovery Plaza**.

Inside the **Ermita Church** is the icon of **Nuestra Señora de Guia**. On the last Sunday in December, single girls hoping to wed come and toss flowers at the statue, asking for the saint's assistance with their pursuit.

Malate

Like Ermita, you will find stores, bars, and restaurants along the streets of Malate. This is Manila's artsy area. Its night crowd, more laid-back than Makati's, includes people from all walks of life.

Malate Church is an interesting mixture of Mexican, baroque, Muslim, Spanish, and Romanesque motifs. Its first structure was built in 1588 and was dedicated to Nuestra Señora de Remedios (Our Lady of Remedies). The current structure dates to the latter 19th century.

In front of the church is the very run-down **Rajah Sulayman Park**. There is a statue of Maynila's Muslim ruler pointing his sword towards the bay from which the Spaniards appeared. Around the park you will find a number of places to snack. Wok Inn is a popular place for inexpensive, quick, and tasty Chinese food.

If you continue southwards down Roxas Boulevard, you will get to the Central Bank complex. **Fort San Antonio Abad**, built in 1584 on the water's edge, is in the back of the grounds. It was occupied by several imperial forces: the Spaniards, who built it; the British when they took over the city in 1762; the Americans in 1898; and the Japanese during World War Two. You can still see the original powder room and many of its battle scars.

In front of the fort is the **Metropolitan Museum**. Browse through several excellent galleries, and the Central Bank's extensive coin collection. There is also a good shop, and café. Across the Boulevard are the **Manila Yacht Club** and the **Philippine Coast Guard**.

You will find fresh fruits in a delicious display in the stalls of the **San Andres Market**. It has one of the best selection of fruit available, but is not the cheapest. Nearby are a few antique shops that sell *santos* and other icons; not all are genuine.

Across from **Harrison Plaza**, a shopping mall, is the **Rizal Coliseum**. Many sports events are held here. There is an LRT stop on Taft Avenue, just down the street from the coliseum.

PASAY

The more interesting and wholesome sights of Pasay are on the bay side of Roxas Boulevard.

The sprawling **Cultural Center Complex** was built on reclaimed land and has many structures that were built in a hurry under the orders of Imelda Marcos, regardless of the of the time the refilled land beneath needed to settle.

The most imposing structure Imelda built is the **Cultural Center of the Philippines** (**CCP**), offering ballet, concerts, and various performances in either the main theater upstairs or the little theater below. It also has a museum and art gallery. Beside the CCP is the wharf where you may catch the boats to Corregidor.

Further west is the **Folk Arts Theater**, used for concerts and performances that attract large crowds. Beside the Folk Arts you will find the **Coconut Palace**, built by Imelda for the 1981 visit of Pope John Paul. The

Pope firmly declined to stay there, and advised her to spend her money on the poor. For $4 you may enter and see the palace, which is almost entirely built of coconut products.

Behind the CCP, the **Design Center of the Philippines** was erected to foster product design improvements; sometimes you may see some interesting displays. The **Philippine International Convention Center** is nearby. Next to the PICC is the **Philippine Plaza Hotel**, a nice place to watch Manila's fabled sunsets.

Southward is the **Manila Film Center**, a small copy of the Parthenon. Many believe it is haunted. Within its cement are the bodies of workers who perished in an accident that occurred during the rushed construction. You will notice that its once straight steps are wavy — suffering from continued subsidence of the fill beneath.

At the corner of Roxas Boulevard and Buendia is the **Philtrade** building and **Golden Shell Pavilion**, where many export-oriented businesses display their products. Further south and by the bay is the **GSIS** building. You may investigate the **GSIS Museum**, which occupies two floors and displays the works of local artists, including world-renown Luna and Amorsolo, and foreign artists. The museum is open Tuesday through Saturday, from 8:00am until 4:00pm.

If you continue south down the boulevard, you will pass the Department of Foreign Affairs, a few handicraft stores, restaurants, the **Cuneta Astrodome** (where concerts and Philippine Basketball Association games are held), and the Embassy of Japan.

CORREGIDOR

If you are into World War Two memorabilia, or are looking for a rainforest to hike through, hop on a boat to **Corregidor**. This small, tadpole-shaped island, only about 15 square kilometers, lies at the entrance of Manila Bay.

The island was used by the Chinese corsair Lim Ah Hong before he entered Manila in 1574; then as a hiding place for Moro Pirates waiting for ships during the galleon trade. Corregidor was first fortified in 1795 by the Spaniards, then further fortified by the Americans — who called it **"the Rock."**

The Americans developed it as a military reservation, believing that its fortifications rendered it impregnable to seaward attacks. Corregidor also had a street lined with shops, a golf course, tennis courts, schools, a movie theater, a church, and a cable car that took people around the island.

General Douglas MacArthur, Philippine President Manuel Quezon, Carlos P. Romulo, and a few other officials were taken off Corregidor by submarine prior to the final surrender of the remaining troops in the

Philippines. Corregidor, not invulnerable to air raids, was saturated by bombs from Japanese planes and its topography was altered.

A light and sound tour inside the **Malinta Tunnel** brings the Corregidor war experience to you. The tunnel, which is almost a kilometer long and has side tunnels adding up to nearly another four kilometers, served as home to the 12,000-man combined American and Filipino resistance forces for nearly five months.

Towards the west-end of the island you can see huge cannons on **Battery Hearn & Battery Way**, and walk through the nearby ruins of **Topside Barracks**. If you walk south, you will come across the old Spanish lighthouse that has been rehabilitated and is used today. The **Pacific War Memorial**, nearby, was built by Americans in 1968 and dedicated to the allied forces. The small **museum** houses old pictures and artifacts from the war. At **Suicide Cliff**, a Buddhist shrine was built in memory of the Japanese soldiers that chose to jump to an honorable death in the sea below rather than surrender.

If you enjoy hiking, a number of trails will lead you through the small rainforest on the island.

Getting There

At the wharf beside the Cultural Center, you can board a boat run by **Sun Cruises**, *Tel. 831-8140*. Your day will include a guided tour of the island and a small lunch; about $35 per person. You should book a seat in advance.

Where to Stay

Facilities on the island include a very nice small hotel, a hostel, campgrounds, and golf.

CORREGIDOR INN, *Tel. 831-8140, $115 per person (including tour) or $68 per person*. The inn is simple and pleasant. Rooms are clean, and cozy. You will find the staff friendly and accommodating. The restaurant serves western and local dishes.

PARAÑAQUE

Back along Roxas Boulevard on the mainland, **Baclaran Church** and **Market** are at the boundary of Parañaque and Pasay. Every Wednesday, thousands of people flock to the church to worship the icon of Our Lady of Perpetual Help. You will find excellent bargains at the many stalls surrounding the church. Be aware of pickpockets.

Shortly after Baclaran, a road exits Roxas Boulevard, and heads towards the **airports**. Across from the international terminal is the **Duty Free Building**, where you can buy tax-free goods for up to 48 hours after your arrival.

Between the two airports, you will find **Nayong Filipino**. The complex, open daily, is a mini-Philippines where you may see a bit of all the provinces. Entrance is $1 per person. There is enough to keep you occupied here for at least two hours — several provincial-style buildings, many shops, jeepneys to ride around in, a mock Mayon Volcano and Chocolate Hills, a restaurant, and two museums.

The **Museum of Ethnology** displays artifacts from various ethnic groups, and in **Museo ng Buhay Pilipino** (Museum of Philippine Life), you will see what rooms of a typical rural landowner's house looked like in the early 1900s.

MANILA'S CURRENT FINANCIAL CENTER – MAKATI

The face of **Makati** that you, as a traveler, will see is the high-rise buildings, malls, banks, restaurants, and hotels. Makati also has a number of posh villages; all are guarded.

During the Spanish reign, the entire area was owned by Agustinian Friars, who later sold it. In the 1950s, the MacMiking and Zobel de Ayala family began construction of a new city. They leased the land out; it returned to them in a decade or two, with vast improvements. Today, Makati's business district bustles with as much activity as Binondo and Escolta. It has its own stock exchange, and is littered with banks.

At **Makati's Commercial Center** (now called the **Ayala Center**) you may shop in air conditioned malls and stores, a world apart from Manila's markets. The stock exchange is along Ayala Avenue, at the triangle.

The **Filipinas Heritage Library**, formerly Neilson Tower, was once the terminal of Manila International Airport. Part of Makati Avenue was the runway. In the **Ayala Museum**, further down Makati Avenue, you can stroll past dioramas depicting Philippine history; the museum also has changing displays of various artists, a good gift shop, and a small café.

Ayala Avenue narrows into McKinley Road, where you find Makati's two exclusive clubs — **Manila Polo** and **Manila Golf**. The road continues to what was once **Fort Bonifacio**. Here you will find the **American Cemetery**, the resting place of more than 17,000 allied soldiers who died in Asia during the Second World War. After passing through security at the entrance, you go to the reception area immediately inside the gate, then walk or drive past picturesque concentric circles and undulating lines of white grave markers. On the walls of the memorial in the center, you may read the names and states of 36,000 people who were killed in action, and on the ends are mosaics of the battle areas.

This is a wonderful place to walk under the shade of the few remaining large acacia and flame trees. Sadly, those outside the cemetery grounds have recently been demolished to give way to more "development."

If you venture southward down Makati Avenue, you will start to see a different Makati. After passing an area of restaurants, nightclubs, and girlie bars, head off a block eastward to the **Church of Saints Peter and Paul**, along P Burgos Street. This pretty stone church has a small acacia-shaded plaza. Turn west on Rizal Avenue if you want to get to **Santa Ana Race Course**, where horse races are held on Tuesday, Wednesday, and weekends.

Head towards EDSA to **Our Lady of Grace Church** in **Guadalupe**. The original structure was built in 1601. The church was a sanctuary for Chinese who were escaping punishment after an uprising in 1893.

NORTHEAST OF THE PASIG – MANDALUYONG & SAN JUAN

On the west of EDSA is San Juan, where you will find two historical points: the **San Juan del Monte Church**, which served as a meeting place for the *katipuneros* rebelling against Spain; and the **Pinaglabanan Shrine**, built on the site of one of the 1896 battles against Spain. The church is interesting to visit; the shrine is not well kept.

Cross EDSA to get to the **Ortigas Center**, one of the newer financial and shopping sectors of the metropolis. You will find three large malls along EDSA: **Shangri-La**, **SM MegaMall**, and **Robinson's Galleria**; and several restaurants in the malls and at **St. Francis Square** and **El Pueblo**. The city's other stock exchange is inside the Tektite Towers, on Tektite Road. Beside it you will find the **Lopez Memorial Museum** in the Benpres Building. The museum has paintings and sculptures of local artists, including a collection of works by two famous Filipino artists – Juan Luna and Felix Hidalgo – and back issues of the Bulletin newspaper. The museum is open Tuesday through Saturday, from 9:00am until 6:00pm; entrance costs $1.

The Ortigas Center is bordered on one end by Ortigas Avenue. Follow this street back over EDSA to the **Greenhills Shopping Center**. This large mall has many shops with a wide range of items – some offer discounted designer and imitation name-brand products, CDs, computers and programs, and handmade wood furniture brought in from the provinces. In and around this shopping complex you will find several restaurants.

QUEZON CITY

In **Quezon City** you will find two military camps, large shopping centers, several universities, a few galleries, and a number of government offices. At **Cubao** you will find a large shopping center and the **Araneta Coliseum**, host to circuses, cockfights, boxing matches, and pageants.

Many government offices are near the elliptical road that goes around the **Quezon Monument**. Beneath the monument are the remains of

President Quezon, and two museums — one houses his memorabilia, the other is of Quezon City.

You will find the main campus of the **University of the Philippines** at Diliman, Quezon City, eastward from EDSA. The UP's **Vargas Museum** has an extensive collection of Filipiniana.

NIGHTLIFE & ENTERTAINMENT

Manila's society bores easily. The popularity of a night spot will rise and fall fairly rapidly. Most places with live bands have a cover charge on weekends, none on weekdays. The clubs' main activities will be during cocktail hours, and then after dinner, which will mean around 10:00pm, sometimes 11:00pm. Dance clubs do not get full until after 1:00am (unless there is a fashion show or product launch), and may remain open until dawn or when the last people leave (which ever comes first).

A glass of wine or a mixed drink with imported alcohol will cost $3.50 and up. Local beer will be $1-2, and imported beer costs $2.80 and up.

Live Music

All of the major hotels have live music, usually jazz and light rock, in the evenings. During the "cooler and dry months" (December to February), bands play at the center of the Remedios Circle in Malate, a very relaxed and friendly atmosphere.

- **Captain's Bar**, *Mandarin Oriental Hotel, Makati*, usually has popular local singers. The regular bands are also good, with music from jazz to soft rock. Seats are plush and comfortably big.
- **Ciao**, *Dusit Hotel Nikko*, features mostly light rock and top 40s music in a nice modernish atmosphere. It is attached to the restaurant (same name), so order the pizza if you get hungry, it's good. You can sit close to the band in a small area or, if you don't like it loud, in the spacious main area.
- **Conservatory**, *Manila Peninsula Hotel*, has jazz and light rock, and visiting artists sometimes. The ambiance is elegant, with high ceilings near the stage and both the bar areas, and glass windows behind the stage.
- **Conways**, *Shangri-La Hotel, Makati*, has jazz and groovy '60s and '70s music, and a good snack menu.
- **Guernicas**, *Remedios Circle, Malate*, has piano music and dim lights.
- **Hobbit House**, *Mabini Street, Malate*, is a unique bar for folk music; your waiters are dwarfs.
- **Bistro RJ**, *Atrium Building, Makati Avenue, Makati; and 28 Timog Avenue, Quezon City*, is for the older crowd that enjoys rock music of the '60s. RJ and the Riots is a favorite of many (RJ is the owner, too).

- **Hard Rock Café**, *Glorietta, Ayala Center, Makati*. Yup, it's the franchise from the US. There are two stories with an opening on the second floor so you can see and hear the band playing on the first. It's your typical hard rock with memorabilia from famous people, some visiting bands, and good local rock bands.
- **News Bar Café**, *Jupiter Street, Makati*, has local bands ranging from light to hard rock. The place is small; it can get cramped inside.
- **Strumms**, *Makati Avenue, Makati; and El Pueblo Complex, Ortigas Center, Pasig*, is popular with yuppies. It has modern-type music, some decent local bands, a good comedian (usually on Thursday), and (sometimes) popular visiting bands.
- **Café New Orleans**, *Shangri-La Mall Complex, Ortigas Center, Pasig*, serves Cajun cooking and good jazz music.
- **Music Hall**, *Annapolis Street, Greenhills, Mandaluyong*, has adequate space and local bands, some are good.
- **Music Museum**, *Virra Mall, Greenhills Shopping Center, Mandaluyong*, has ample space in a stage-type seating where you can order drinks and food, and listen to local bands and (sometimes) popular local singers. They also host musicals and plays.
- **Club Dred**, *EDSA, Cubao, Quezon City*, is where you go for head-banging music.
- **Club 690**, *T Morato Avenue, Quezon City*, for jazz.

Regular Bars

Most bars in the metropolis play music, and loud. You will get your range of music from the '60s to the latest sounds from the US and Europe. Places in Malate have a more laid-back atmosphere and are popular with the arts crowd.

- **Blue Café**, *J Nakpil Street, Malate*, is frequented by members of all sexes. The atmosphere is relaxed.
- **Café Adriatico**, *Remedios Circle, Malate*, is a nice place to go after the theater. It serves food into the morning hours. The antique-style decor enhances the ambiance of the old house it is in. Music is played very softly.
- **Café Iguana**, *J Nakpil Street, Malate*, has 80s and 90s music, and serves good *chicharon manok* (fried chicken skin).
- **Insomnia**, *J Nakpil Street, Malate*, is sometimes frequented by Makati's social crowd, and plays '90s music.
- **Larry's Bar**, *Adriatico Street, Malate*, has '90s music and good food.
- **Penguins**, *Remedios Street, Malate*, is frequented by the arts crowd. This cool place exhibits works of budding local artists. Dare to try the "super submarine," a powerful drink made with Red Horse (a local

strong beer) and a shot of *lambanog* (very strong alcohol distilled from coconut liquor).

- **Ten Years After**, *Adriatico Street, Malate*, known as Hard Rock until the real franchise arrived, this place remains popular because they play your request and have an extensive collection of discs from the '70s through the '90s. A branch with a smaller collection of discs is at *St Francis Square, Ortigas Center, Pasig*.
- **Cable Car**, *Arnaiz Avenue, Makati*, is open 24 hours. It enjoys cyclical popularity with the stockbrokers during cocktail hours, and serves good burgers and finger foods. Try the Jell-O shots, but not too many.
- **Friday's**, *Glorietta, Makati; and El Pueblo Complex, Ortigas Center, Pasig*, is what you expect from the American chain. Patrons are mostly college age crowd on the weekends. The oreo, baileys, and khalua shake is delicious (it comes with mint liquor if you like it that way).
- **Giraffe**, *6750 Ayala Avenue, facing the Glorietta Circle, Makati*, is frequently an "in" bar. It attracts the cocktail crowd of Manila's younger power people, and the evening crowd (which doesn't pour in during the weekends until midnight). Locals come to see and be seen, and it is also popular with expatriates (late 20s to late 30s). The bar is managed well, and waiters are cheerful even when very busy. It can get very full, and sometimes has theme nights for various fund-raisers for charity.
- **San Mig Pub**, *Legaspi Street, under La Tasca Restaurant*, is set up like a *meson* (bar in Spain) — dimly lit, white walls, plush red sofas, bar with wooden stools, and banisters. The crowd is composed mostly of the Spanish *mestizos* of Makati's society, aged 18 to mid-30s. Music varies mostly from '80s to '90s, mellow to hard rock. You can order good bar food here, and they are open until early in the morning.
- **The Bar**, *Manila Peninsula Hotel, Makati*, is quiet, very cozy; you sit at the bar or in a comfortable seat at one of the tables. Music by an Italian singer (Eros Ramazotti) plays softly.
- **Tipsy's**, *Creekside, Along Amorsolo Street, Makati*, attracts Makati's younger working crowd. Music is usually from the '80s. There is a medium-size tank with a baby shark (they set the shark free — far from Manila — when it grows too big for the space).
- **Travessia**, *Arnaiz Avenue, Makati*, gets packed on Saturday nights. It features '80s and '90s music and a modern-style bar, and is one of few places that has cranberry juice to mix with vodka and orange juice. If you get hungry, stick to the squid balls; they are tasty.
- **Peps**, *Arnaiz Avenue, Makati*, is popular with the college-age crowd.
- **Prince of Wales Pub**, *Greenbelt Center, Makati*, is very popular with the working expatriate community, usually ages 30 and up. It is dark, typical of a pub, and the food (including items like fish and chips, and cottage pie) is pretty good.

• **Venezia**, *Glorietta, Makati*, is one of the more recent bars put up by a group of Manila's (very) high-society men; it is a place "to see and be seen." The bar is spacious and tastefully decorated. Music varies from mellow to the latest sounds from the dance club scenes. Venezia offers a good selection of wines and cigars.

• **Vincent's San Mig**, *Jupiter Street, Makati*, is the newest franchise of the San Mig pub. It is much larger than the original, but with similar decor. The crowed here is mixed. There is also another outlet of "Vincent's San Mig" at *Shangri-La Mall, Ortigas Center, Pasig*.

• **Capers**, *St. Francis Square, Ortigas Center, Pasig*, is a small resto-bar with charming wooden figurines of hot air balloons hang from the ceiling and a unicycle hanging by the window. Music is mostly '80s, waiters are friendly, the crowd is mixed. If you are hungry, order the chicken-teriyaki pizza — it is very good. Also open for lunch.

• **Side Bar**, *El Pueblo Complex, Ortigas Center, Pasig*, has loud music from the '80s and '90s. The bar food is okay.

• **Tribeca**, *Shangri-La Mall, Ortigas Center, Pasig*, is no relation to the one in California. This resto-bar has modern interior design, and plays modern music. An interesting and unique sink in the ladies' bathroom has a bronze metal bowl with the faucet relatively high above it — stand back or get wet. Also open for lunch.

• **Roofdeck**, *Makati Avenue, above Max's, Makati*, has a high ceiling with a canopy hanging from it. The chairs are not comfortable, but the food is good (Bacolod food). '80s and '90s music plays to a teenage to mid-30s crowd. The place is very casual, and warm when full.

Dance Clubs (Discos)

• **Zu**, *Shangri-La Hotel, Makati*. Zu is now the most popular dance club. People start strolling in after 1:00am. There are a few interesting shows every night — transvestites do good impersonations of singers such as Madonna and Tina Turner; though looks are far off, Tina's impersonator also has sexy legs. The interior looks like an Aztec or Mayan temple — unique for Manila. Bartenders do some cool tricks with bottles, and the staff is friendly. You get people from all walks of life here: from teenagers to DOMs, high-society people to local celebrities, hotel guests, and some of the Giraffe crowd. There are also four KTV rooms near the back.

• **Euphoria**, *Hotel Intercontinental, Makati*. The main decor seems to be tiles. This is the place for after-hours dancing — it is still crowded at 3:00am.

• **Cats**, *New World Hotel, Makati*. Cats has a music lounge where a live band plays, and KTV rooms. The decor is modern, with neon graffiti on the walls. The dance floor is on the ground floor, with an open ceiling so you can watch the action from above.

• **Mars**, *Arnaiz Avenue corner Makati Avenue*. Crowds start coming in around 1:30 am. Mars serves "rave" and techno music to a (usually) teenage and college crowd.

• **Studebakers**, *Glorietta, Makati*. Multi-level entertainment at a late-night coffee shop on the ground floor, this is one of the few places you can go for a quiet evening to chat with friends. The second floor is a bar where live bands play, usually Latin music, and the dance floor is on the top level. Above it is a small "members only" room darkly tinted.

• **Limits**, *St. Francis Square, Ortigas Center, Pasig*. Set up is like a classier huge warehouse, music here varies; including a lot of trance music and techno — mostly sounds from the UK. Sometimes there are live bands. The crowd is mixed.

Adults Only

Girlie bars are found in clusters around the metropolis, where authorities turn a blind eye. Several are along the Pasay City portion of Roxas Boulevard; along P Burgos Street and Makati Avenue in Makati; and along Quezon Avenue in Quezon City.

Movies

Check the daily newspapers for what is showing in the local theaters; usually half the films showing in a theater complex are in English (mainly from the US) and half are local movies in Tagalog. Not all theaters can be considered clean, and, with the exception of two movie houses, you can bring food — don't be surprised to see someone with a full meal. The movies provide cheap entertainment: in most theaters, a seat will cost 75¢ downstairs and $1.50 upstairs. The theaters are large. Some people come to sleep — in most theaters you can watch the same movie over and over (until closing if you wish), and there is air conditioning.

The theaters in **Harrison Plaza** (*Harrison Street, Pasay*) are relatively decent; those in **Quad** (*Ayala Center, Makati*) are relatively clean; and theaters inside **Galleria** and **MegaMall** (*Ortigas Center*) are clean. **Shangri-La Mall** has one theater that is kept very clean and you are not allowed to bring food inside; it also costs more ($2.50 per person).

Performing Arts

• Various open air performances are held during dry season (late November to March) at the **Luneta** and **Ft. Santiago**, and there are concerts at **Paco Park** (Friday at 5 pm).

• Philippine folk dancing is performed at **Maynila Restaurant**, *Manila Hotel, Tel. 527-0111*, with dinner 7:00pm to 10:00pm Monday through

Saturday; and **Pistahan**, *Philippine Plaza Hotel, Tel. 832-0701*, open 6:00pm to 9:00pm.

• Plays, musicals, concerts — Broadway and local shows are performed at **William J Shaw Theater**, *Shangri-La Mall, Tel. 633-4821*; **Meralco Theater**, *Ortigas Ave., Pasig*; and **Music Museum**, *Greenhills Shopping Center*. As there are no regular schedules, check the newspapers for current information. **PCI Bank Tower**, *Makati Avenue, Makati, Tel. 840-7000 loc. 2258/2360 for details*, hosts concerts ranging from solo flautists and chamber orchestras to plays. The **CCP**, *Roxas Boulevard, Tel. 832-1125*, hosts ballets, concerts, and other performances in its main theater, with smaller performances in the Little Theater, downstairs.

SPORTS & RECREATION

Bowling & Billiards

You can bowl at **MegaMall** and **Robinson's Galleria** (with billiards) in *Ortigas Center, Pasig*; **Bowl-O-Drome** *on C5 in Pasig*; **Greenlanes** (with billiards) at the *Greenhills Shopping Center in San Juan*; **Bowling and Billiards** in *Alimall, Cubao*; and in Makati at **Coronado Lanes** (with billiards), *above the Anson's Arcade along Arnaiz Avenue*, and at **Super Bowl** (with billiards) in the *Makati Cinema Square*.

The prices are more or less the same at all establishments: $2 per game of bowling; 40¢ for shoe rental (bring your own socks, some shoes can be squishy); and $4.60 for one hour of billiards.

Cockfighting

You can watch cockfights (Sabong)on Sundays and holidays. The largest arenas are the **Pasay Cockpit Arena**, *Dolores Street, Pasay City*; the **Elorde Cockpit**, *Santos Avenue, Sucat, Parañaque*; the **La Loma Cockpit**, *68 Calavite, La Loma*; and the **Araneta Coliseum**, *Cubao*.

Football: Rugby and Soccer

Rugby games are sponsored by the **Nomads Sports Club**, *Madrid Street, Merville Park, Parañaque*; you can also watch soccer games there. Only a small community is interested in this sport, and games are played on Saturday afternoons, if enough players show up. There's no entrance fee.

There is no American football.

Gambling

There are a number of casinos, run by Casino Filipino, in hotels in Manila: **Heritage Hotel**, *corner of Roxas Boulevard and EDSA*; **Holiday Inn**, *UN Avenue, Ermita*; **Hotel Sofitel**, *along Roxas Boulevard, in Malate*; and **Philippine Village Hotel**, *near the airport*.

Golf

You can play golf at a few places in the city. We have included the rates for courses open to the public. Courses in Manila include **Intramuros** (greens fees: $15, weekdays, $40 weekends; caddie fees: $5.75); **Wack-Wack** *in Mandaluyong*; **Manila Golf Club** *in Makati*; **Villamor Airbase Golf Club** *next to the South Superhighway in Makati* (greens fees, including caddie fees: $55 weekdays, $62 weekends, there is also a driving range); and **Capitol Hills** *in Quezon City* (greens fees: $15, weekdays, $40 weekends; caddie fees: $7.50 for 18 holes, $5.75 for nine holes).

There are driving ranges at **Power Golf** and **Rod Taylor's**, *both on C5/ E Rodriguez in Quezon City.*

Horse Racing

Races alternate between **San Lazaro Hippodrome**, *2000 Felix Huertas Boulevard, Sta. Cruz, Tel. 711-1251*; and **Santa Ana Park**, *AP Reyes Boulevard, Makati, Tel. 895-3112.* Races are usually on Tuesdays, Wednesdays, and weekends.

Horseback Riding

You can rent a horse and take lessons at **Pook Ligaya Stables**, a small family-run establishment. Facilities include an open bullring and a small jumping area. The place is charming, with a relaxing atmosphere, and is run by a very nice family who truly care about their horses. Cost is $15 per hour and a guide for children is free of charge. Operating hours are 9:00am to 6:00pm, Tuesday through Sunday. The stables are inside the Isadora Hills Subdivision, *Diliman, Quezon City, Tel. 931-5643, 931-5949.* Look for Totti or Linda de Leon.

Ice Skating

In Manila you can go ice-skating at **MegaMall** *in Pasig* and at **SM Southmall** *in Alabang, Muntinlupa*. The rinks are open from 10:00am to 9:00pm Sunday through Thursday, and stay open until 10:00pm on Friday and Saturday. You pay $4.20 for the first two hours, and $2 for each addition hour. A set of eight, 30-minute lessons costs $70 per person in a group of five to 10 people, and $96 for individual lessons.

Martial Arts

Karatedo lessons are given at the **Association for the Advancement of Karatedo (AAK)**. Outlets of AAK are *MegaMall, Tel. 635-6608, 635-6611*; *SM North EDSA, and SM Cubao*. The fees are $20 for registration and $24 per month for one lesson a week or $28 for lesson twice a week.

Taekwondo lessons are available at the *Rizal Memorial Sports Complex, Pasay, Tel. 522-0518.* You must attend in uniform, which will cost $24, and lessons are $28 per month and are three times a week; either Monday,

Wednesday, and Friday from 7:30 pm to 9:30 pm, or Tuesday, Thursday, from 5:30 pm to 7:00pm, and Saturday from 1:00pm to 2:30 pm.

Polo

You can watch this exclusive "game of kings" at the **Manila Polo Club** on Sundays during January to May. To play polo, you will have to be sponsored by a member of the club. Sometimes games are played in Canlubang and in Alabang (Muntinlupa). Regular players include a Malaysian prince who sponsors one of the cups.

Sailing

Sailing lessons are available at the **Manila Yacht Club (MYC)** on *Roxas Boulevard, Tel. 521-4457.* Courses begin in January, and include four hours of lectures and 24 hours of practice time. Classes are run only on Saturdays (Sundays are race days at the club) and cost $80 per person for the series. If you are experienced and would like to crew during a race, there is usually a sign-up list for privately owned yachts looking for extra hands.

The MYC will also accommodate visiting foreign yachts, and can help organize guides and an escort if you will travel through any pirate infested area.

Swimming

All the higher-priced hotels and a few of the moderate ones have swimming pools. If you are not a guest, you are usually allowed to use the pool for a fee ($6 in the moderate hotels, and $12 in the first-class ones). The **Philippine Plaza** has a very nice large pool that curves around a waterfall and a bar.

Tennis

Most high-end hotels in the major cities have tennis courts open to non-guests for a fee. You can also play at the **Rizal Sports Complex** (per hour: $8 for covered courts without lights; $1 more with lights; $6.50 outdoor courts, plus $1 with lights; lessons are $80 for 16 two-hour sessions); at the *Provincial Capitol Compound, Shaw Boulevard, Pasig;* and at the **Pasay City Sports Complex** ($2 per hour no lights; $4 with lights; $4 per hour for a trainer; and $1.20 per hour for a ballboy; all courts are covered) on *FB Harrison Street, Pasay City.*

SHOPPING

Manila has many great buys that come from all over the country — handicrafts made from natural materials, antiques, handwoven fabrics,

---

EXTINCT IS FOREVER!

Remember – purchasing items made from coral will encourage the destruction of reefs. Do not purchase sea turtle shells and products made from other endangered species. This trade will lead to their extinction.

---

and embroidered articles and clothes. If you do not have time to venture all over the country, you may find the goodies here.

When shopping in markets, you should always bargain. Small stores may give a discount if you ask. Some of the larger shops may not, unless you are ordering wholesale quantities, but it is worth asking. Salespeople may stick to you as you browse around.

Handicrafts

• **El Amenecer**, *General Luna Boulevard between Sta. Potenciana and Victoria Streets, Intramuros*, has nice handicrafts from various parts of the country, a good selection of handwoven material, woodcraft and furniture, brass, pottery, shell crafts, and a stock of maps and books.

• **Ricardo Baylosis** and **Tribal Arts**, *Padre Faura Mall, corner Padre Faura and del Pilar Streets, Ermita*, have interesting handicrafts. (You can bargain here.)

• **Terry Baylosis**, **Likha**, and **Via Antica**, *1400s block of Mabini Street, Ermita*, have a selection of handicrafts. You can bargain here.

• **T'Boli Arts and Crafts**, *1362 Mabini Street, Ermita*, has a good collection of Mindanao tribal crafts. You can bargain a bit here.

• **Tesoro's**, *1325 Mabini Street, Ermita*, has handicrafts and very nice embroidered or woven fabrics, *barongs*, and other clothes made with delicate local cloths. Other outlets are at *1016 Arnaiz Avenue, Makati; and in the Shangri-La Mall, Ortigas Center*.

• **SC Vizcarra**, *464 UN Avenue, Ermita*, has various handicrafts. You can bargain here.

• **Balikbayan Handicrafts**, *1010 Arnaiz Avenue, Makati*, has a range of items from wood products including bamboo and wicker; crafts of shell, stone, metal, and pottery; paintings; and embroidery.

• **Tahanan**, *second floor of SM MegaMall, Ortigas Center*, has some expensive and very lovely items for the home – blankets, throw rugs, pottery, trays, frames, tableware, coffee and tea sets, etc.

• **Rose Laed's Kalinga Etnica**, *Panay Avenue, Quezon City*, has some very good things from the Cordillera provinces – wicker tables; wood carvings and furniture; blankets, table runners and other woven products. Prices are good, and you can bargain a bit here.

Most of the large department stores have a section of handicrafts: **Crossings** (*Shangri-La Mall, Ortigas Center*); **Robinson's Department Store** (*Adriatico Street, Ermita; Galleria, Pasig*); **Rustan's** (*Harrison Plaza, Pasay; Ayala Avenue, Makati; Shangri-La Mall, Ortigas Center; Araneta Center, Cubao*); **ShoeMart** (*Harrison Plaza, Pasay; Ayala Center, Makati; SM MegaMall, Ortigas Center; Araneta Center, Cubao; SM City, EDSA, Quezon City*).

All major hotels have shops that stock some nice handicrafts; you will pay a premium for them, but the quality is usually very good.

Markets

If you are adventurous, explore the many markets of Manila. Here you can exert or enhance your bargaining skills. Be aware of your belongings when in and around public markets. Keep wallets in front pockets, bags held in front.

• **Ilalim ng Tulay** and **Quiapo Market**, *under Quezon Bridge, Quiapo*, literally translates as "under the bridge." It has various handicrafts and amulets. Also try the stalls around Quiapo Church.

• **Divisoria**, *just beyond Binondo*, has just about anything and everything, retail and wholesale.

• **Central Market**, *in Santa Cruz by Quezon Avenue*, spills onto the streets with fabrics and clothes.

• **Baclaran**, *just off Roxas Boulevard, beside the Baclaran Church*, has clothes and some handicrafts.

Miscellaneous

Shoes and clothes and accessories are available in many shops, large and small. **D'Paul's** and **King Philip** (*both at 1030 Arnaiz Avenue, Makati*) are among the many tailors who will make men's clothing at short order. If you are willing to wait longer for a better suit, try **Giovanni Sana** *on Arnaiz Avenue*.

Antiques and wood furniture are available on the fourth floor of MegaMall, at the Shangri-La, on the second floor of Glorietta, in the Greenhills Shopping Center, and in Malate.

PRACTICAL INFORMATION

Banks

Banks and other places that will change cash and travelers' checks are listed below. Some of them have branches that may be close to your lodging: call the telephone numbers below to inquire. Banking hours are from 9:00am to 3:00pm Mondays through Fridays. Bring your passport for identification.

• **Bank of America**, *BA Lepanto Building, Paseo de Roxas, Makati, Tel. 892-9057*

- **Bank of the Philippine Islands** (BPI), *BPI Building, Ayala Avenue, Makati, Tel. 813-8823*
- **Citybank NA**, *City Bank Building, Paseo de Roxas, Makati, Tel. 813-9117*
- **Citytrust**, *379 Sen. Gil Puyat (Buendia) Avenue, Makati, Tel. 899-8511*
- **Deutsch Bank**, *26th Floor, Tower One, Ayala Triangle, Ayala Ave., Makati, Tel. 894-6900*
- **HongKong Bank**, *6780 Ayala Avenue, Makati, Tel. 814-5200*
- **MetroBank**, *MetroBank Plaza Building, Sen Gil Puyat (Buendia) Avenue, Makati, Tel. 810-3311*
- **PCIBank**, *PCI Bank Building, corner de la Costa and Makati Avenue, Makati, Tel. 840-7000*
- **Philippine National Bank** (PNB), *Roxas Boulevard, Pasay, Tel. 890-6040*
- **Standard Chartered**, *Bankmer Building, 6756 Ayala Avenue, Makati, Tel. 892-0961.*
- **American Express** office is *6750 Ayala Avenue, Makati, Tel. 818-6731; and 4th Floor Ace Building, corner of Rada and de la Rosa Streets, Legaspi Village, Makati, Tel. 814-4770 to 73*
- **Thomas Cook** has an office at *Skyland Plaza Building, Tel. 816-3701*

Books, Magazines, & Newspapers
The major outlets for travel-oriented literature are Bookmark, National Bookstores, and La Solidaridad. **Bookmark** is a small chain of bookstores, mostly educational, and a good source for books and maps on the Philippines. They have a branch in Makati at the Greenbelt. **National Bookstore** has outlets all over the metropolis and is the largest retail bookstore in the country, with a wide assortment of books and supplies. It is also a good place to get maps and books on the Philippines and other countries. **Powerbooks**, Arnaiz Avenue on the 5th floor of MegaMall, is a small version of a Border's-style bookstore — you can browse while having coffee. **Solidaridad**, P Faura St., between J Bocobo and Mabini in Ermita, has an interesting selection of intellectual books, mostly on the Philippines and Asia. They also have some maps on the Philippines. Try also **El Amanecer**, in Intramuros.

Most bookstores sell magazines and newspapers. You should have no problem getting a newspaper — they are sold at almost every corner on the main streets of Manila, and in hotels. Magazines are harder to come by outside the major hotels and bookstores; you will find them in a few magazine stands inside the malls.

Doctors
If you need a physician, call your embassy for a list of recommendations. It is especially important to consult this list if you need hospitalization, as patient care here often presumes that the patients' families will be

looking out for them. Medical fees are lower here than in the US. You can find good doctors at the major hospitals: **Makati Medical Center** (*Makati*), **Manila Doctors** (*UN Avenue, Ermita*); **Medical City** (*Ortigas Center, Pasig*); **St. Luke's** (*E Rodriguez Boulevard, Quezon City*); and **Cardinal Santos** (*Wilson Street, Mandaluyong*).

Popular with the expatriate community is **Dr. Heinz Varwig**, *Royal Match Building, Ayala Avenue, Makati*. His office hours are Monday to Saturday, from 7:30am to noon. Other doctors are available in his clinic all day.

Embassies & Consulates

Australian, *Paseo de Roxas, Legaspi Village, Makati, Tel. 817-7911*

Austria, *Prince Building, Rada Street, Legaspi Village, Makati, Tel. 817-9191*

Bangladesh, *Paseo de Roxas, between Perea and Gallardo Streets, Makati, 817-5001*

Belgium, *Don Jacinto Building, de la Rosa Street, Legaspi Village, Makati, Tel. 892-6571*

Brunei, *BPI Building, Ayala Avenue, Makati, Tel. 816-2836*

Burma (Myanmar), *DAO 11 Building, Salcedo Street, Legaspi Village, Tel. 817-2373*

Canada, *Allied Bank Building, Ayala Avenue, Makati, Tel. 810-8861*

China, *2018 Roxas Boulevard, Manila, Tel. 525-8586*

Denmark, *2331 Chino Roces (Pasong Tamo) Avenue, Makati, Tel. 843-6926*

European Union, *Salustiana D Ty Building, Paseo de Roxas, Legaspi Village, Makati, Tel. 812-6421*

Finland, *BPI Building, Ayala Avenue, Makati, Tel. 815-1401*

France, *Pacific Star Building, Sen. Gil Puyat (Buendia) Avenue, Makati, Tel. 810-1981*

Germany, *777 Paseo de Roxas, Makati, Tel. 892-4906*

Greece, *Sage House, Herrera Street, Legaspi Village, Makati, Tel. 816-2309*

India, *2190 Paraiso Street, Makati, Tel. 843-0102*

Indonesia, *Adelantado Street, Legaspi Village, Makati, Tel. 892-5061*

Israel, *PS Bank Building, de la Rosa Street, Makati, Tel. 892-5329*

Italy, *Zeta II Building, Salcedo Street, Legaspi Village, Makati, Tel. 892-4531*

Japan, *Roxas Boulevard, Pasay Tel. 895-9050*

Malaysia, *107 Tordesillas Street, Salcedo Village, Makati, Tel. 817-4581*

Mexico, *Adamson Center Building, Alfaro Street, Salcedo Village, Makati, Tel. 892-7323*

Nauru, *Pacific Star Building, Sen Gil Puyat (Buendia) Avenue, Makati, Tel. 818-3580*

Nepal, *Athenaeum Building, Valero Street, Salcedo Village, Makati, Tel. 816-2466*

Netherlands, *Kings Court Building, C. Roces (Pasong Tamo) Avenue, Makati, Tel. 812-5981*

New Zealand, *Gammon Center, Alfaro Street, Salcedo Village, Makati, Tel. 818-0916*

Norway, *69 Paseo de Roxas, Makati, Tel. 893-9866*

Pakistan, *Alexander House, Amorsolo Street, Legaspi Village, Tel. 817-2776*

Saudi Arabia, *First Bank Center, Sen Gil Puyat (Buendia) Avenue, Makati, Tel. 810-2671*

Singapore, *de la Costa Street, Salcedo Village, Makati, Tel. 816-1764*

South Korea, *2 Harvard Road, Makati, Tel. 812-6046*

Spain, *Act Tower, de la Costa Street, Salcedo Village, Makati, Tel. 818-3561*

Switzerland, *Solid Bank Building, Paseo de Roxas, Makati, Tel. 819-0202*

Sweden, *PCI Bank Tower II, Makati Avenue, Tel. 819-1951*

Taiwan, *Pacific Star Building, Sen. Gil Puyat (Buendia) Avenue, Makati, Tel. 816-1920*

Thailand, *M Cristina Building, Rodriguez corner de la Rosa Street, Legaspi Village, Tel. 894-0404*

United Kingdom, *Locsin Building, corner Ayala and Makati Avenues, Makati, Tel. 816-7116*

United States of America, *Roxas Boulevard, Manila, Tel. 521-7116*

Vietnam, *544 Vito Cruz, Pasay, Tel. 524-0364*

Mail

Regular airmail to and from the US will take a week or two to arrive. There are post offices at Liwasang Bonifacio, Intramuros, and Rizal Park near the Manila Hotel; in Makati at the Central Post Office, Sen Gil Puyat (Buendia) Avenue; and at the domestic and international airports. Post Office hours are from 8:00am to 4:00pm, weekdays only. Postal officials inspect incoming and outgoing packages. Do not send money or valuables through the mails.

Several companies offer courier services. International companies include **DHL** (several branches, and will pick up, *Tel. 831-8888*); **Federal Express** (several branches, and will pick up, *Tel. 891-3595*); and **UPS** (Delbros Avenue, Paranaque, will pick up, *Tel. 832-1565*). Several local companies serve points within the country and abroad; most have branches inside malls: **JRS** (will pick up, *Tel. 631-7351*); **LBC** (branches include the domestic airport, *Tel. 832-1414*; and Park Square 2, *Tel. 819-5767*); and **TNT** (will pick up, *Tel. 897-3457*).

Maps

Maps are available at the bookstores and from the Department of Tourism. You can get detailed regional geographical and nautical maps at the **NAMRIA** (formerly the Bureau of Coast and Geodetic Survey) on Barraca Street, San Nicholas and at Fort Bonifacio.

Places of Worship

There are Roman Catholic Churches all over Manila; ask at your hotel for the one nearest to you. Most will have at least one mass in English. The following are churches and temples of other denominations.

- **Beth Yaacov Synagogue**, *Tordesillas Street, Legaspi Village, Makati, Tel. 815-0263*
- **Cathedral of the Holy Trinity** (Anglican & Episcopal), *48 McKinnley Road., Makati, Tel. 817-9440*
- **Church of Jesus Christ of Latter Day Saints**, *Temple Drive, Katipunan, Quezon City, Tel. 634-7421*
- **International Baptist Church**, *Salcedo Street, Makati, Tel. 892-5892*
- **United Methodist Church**, *900 UN Avenue, Manila, Tel. 521-1114*
- **Union Church** (Inter-denominational), *corner Legaspi and Rodriguez Streets, Salcedo Village, Tel. 892-1631*

Telephones

There are many pay phones conveniently located throughout the city, but they do not always work. Local calls require a P2 deposit (approximately 8¢). Most hotels have phones in the rooms; the budget hotels will have a phone in the lobby. Several shops and stands have telephones you may use for 20¢.

Tourist Information

The head office of the **Department Of Tourism**, *DOT Building, Rizal Park, Manila, Tel. 523-8411 (local 146 for tourist information),* has rate and schedule information throughout the country, but it may not be up to date. They also have several nice looking brochures and maps that may come in handy.

The tourist assistance hotline is available 24 hours on Mondays through Saturdays: Tel. *524-1660*, and DOT has an information desk at the International Airport.

Tours & Travel Agencies

We have listed a few reliable agencies that do inbound tours. Most local agencies cater to international tours and do not have much information on local destinations. They also offer only a very limited selection, often catering to the more expensive tastes, or specialize in Boracay packages. Check the daily newspapers for advertisements on package specials to frequented locations.

- **Asiaventure**, *Holiday Inn Manila Pavilion, Ermita, Tel. 523-7007, 526-1212,* is run by a group of expatriates that specialize in several of the less frequented but worthwhile destinations (Pandan Island, Mindoro; General Luna, Siargao; Flower Island, Palawan).

- **Buenavista Travel**, *State Condominium 1, 186 Salcedo Street, Legaspi Village, Makati, Tel. 817-3296, 817-3271, 817-3740* specializes in southern Mindanao and has a branch in Davao.
- **Clique Traveler**, *24 Platinum Street, Camella Homes, Las Piñas, Tel. 806-6274, Fax 802-1588* offers some off-the beaten-track type tours.
- **InterTravel**, *657 San Andres Street, Malate, Tel. 524-0130, 523-2207, Fax 521-6498,* has branches in Cebu and in Pampanga.
- **Morella Travel and Tours**, *Ground Floor Carolina Building, 2106 Madre Ignacia Street, Malate, Tel. 524-0691 to 95, Fax 526-0651.*
- **Rajah Tours**, *3rd Floor Physicians' Tower, 533 UN Avenue, Manila, Tel. 522-0541, Fax 521-1283.*
- **Tribal Holdings**, *2772 Daanhari Street, United Hills, Parañaque, Tel. 823-2725, offers* Boracay and kayak tours (around Boracay, Panay, Guimaras, and Palawan).

Water

To be safe, stick to boiled or bottled water. Most Manila residents drink boiled or bottled water. Restaurants usually serve tap water, but sell bottled water.

12. EXCURSIONS & DAY TRIPS FROM MANILA

This chapter covers a number of trips near Manila that are relatively easy to do. Within a three-hour drive, and even as close as an hour, are a wide range of destinations for day outings:
• tee off at a world-class golf course;
• hike around a volcano island that sits in a crater lake;
• visit towns with colonial churches and ancestral houses;
• head to a beach or scuba dive at one of the country's popular dive destinations;
• climb a dormant volcano, or, in an ultralight, soar over the desolate lahar fields created by **Mount Pinatubo**, take a day or two to climb around it and its canyon-like valleys;
• visit the **former US bases**, which are being transformed into special economic zones with factories, resorts, and a free port;
• collect a variety of souvenirs as you venture from town to town: *balisongs*, more commonly known as butterfly knives; embroidered cloth of *piña* or *jusi*, fine local fabrics; woodcarvings and intricate wood filigree; the list goes on;
• admire the work of national artists in a quaint town where houses also serve as studios and galleries; and,
• if you are around in May, *the* month for fiestas, experience the festivities.

Some destinations offer overnight possibilities. If you plan on spending several days in this area, acquire *Luzon by Car* (the map and/or book), which has more extensive coverage and detailed directions for getting to places mentioned.

BATAAN & ZAMBALES

The **Zambales** mountain range extends from the northern border of Manila Bay to the southern reaches of Lingayen Gulf. Ilocano immigrants

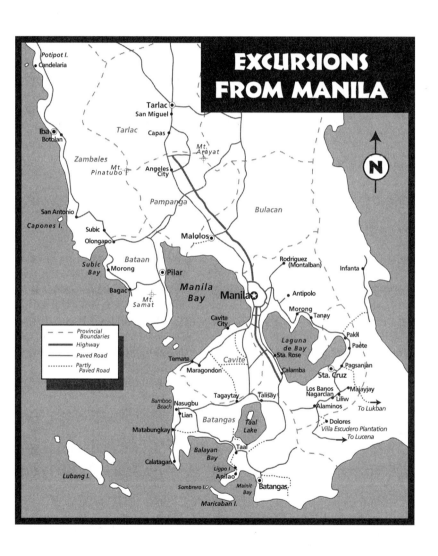

EXCURSIONS FROM MANILA

displaced the earlier inhabitants (the Zambals and Negritoes). During the Spanish era, the forests shrank as great quantities of wood were used for building galleons. Today, the Zambales Mountains and much of Bataan are bare. In the valleys you will find rice and other crops growing; this is seasonal, though, as little irrigation has been installed. During the latter half of dry season, April through May, the area is extremely hot and dry.

This area played an important part in the country's World War Two history. Shortly after the war broke out, most of the combined American and Filipino troops were stationed on **Corregidor** or **Bataan**. The 76,000 soldiers on Bataan surrendered on April 9, 1942. Because the Japanese believed in fighting to the end and considered surrender disgraceful, they assumed their opponents would behave accordingly and did not have the logistics to deal with the captives.

Consequently, the Japanese force-marched them all 184 kilometers to internment facilities in Capas, Tarlac. The **Death March**, which started on April 9, took place during the hottest season and claimed the lives of 7,000 to 10,000 soldiers (including about 2,600 Americans). The famous march is reenacted yearly on April 9 by Boy Scouts. Memorial markers show the way.

ARRIVALS & DEPARTURES

Victory Liner and Saulog have frequent buses to Balanga and Olongapo; trips usually start at 6:00am, with the last trip leaving Manila at 5:00pm — fare is $3-4. Victory continues from Olongapo through Iba to Sta Cruz. From Balanga, buses go to Bagac and Morong. Tricycles and jeeps meet the buses and take passengers to points in between. The road from Manila to Mariveles is in fairly good condition.

Swagman has a bus that runs daily between Subic and the Swagman Narra hotel in Angeles; the fare is $10.

WHERE TO STAY

Baloy Beach in **Olongapo** has a number of simple beach resorts.
ZANZIBAR COTTAGES, *Baloy Beach. Tel. 222-6192. $40-50 per single or double.*

This place has simple air conditioned rooms with private bathrooms and a campground where you can pitch a tent.

SUBIC BAY CASINO & RESORT, *Subic Bay Port. Manila reservations: Tel. 732-9888, Fax 712-8575. $130 per single or double, $242 per suite. Visa, Master Card, American Express, Diners.*

This is a well-run attractive place with friendly staff. All rooms are air conditioned and have cable television. Facilities include a restaurant and tennis courts. Arrangements can be made for golf, horseback riding, fishing, and diving.

SUBIC INTERNATIONAL HOTEL, *Subic Bay Port. Tel. 888-2288, Fax 894-5579. $113 per single, $127 per double, $145 per triple, $160 per suite. Visa, Master Card, American Express, Diners. Manila reservations: Tel. 243-2222, Fax 243-0852.*

All rooms are air conditioned and have cable television and a refrigerator. There is a swimming pool, restaurant, and coffee shop.

BINICTICAN HOUSING, *Subic Bay Port. Tel. 252-4129. $200-295 per house.*

These are former houses of US navy people and families and each can accommodate 8-15 people. All are centrally air conditioned, have at least two bedrooms, two bathrooms, kitchen, and a living room with cable television. Furnishing is not impressive and some houses could use renovation. The cleaning staff are very friendly and helpful.

WHITE ROCK, *Matain, Subic. Tel. 222-2398, 222-2378. Manila reservations: Tel. 811-3088. $50-63 per single or double. Visa, Master Card, American Express, Diners.*

This is a nice hotel with friendly staff. All rooms are air conditioned. Swim at the beach or the pool. Various aquasports equipment are available for rent. Tours are available to Grande Island and around the base. There is a restaurant.

OCEAN VIEW, *Kalaklan, Olongapo. Tel. 222-2309, 222-4021. $50 per single or double.*

This place has simple air conditioned rooms by the beach. There is a restaurant.

CAPONES BEACH RESORT, *along the beach in San Antonio. Manila reservations: Tel. 522-3650, Fax 522-3663. $40-50 per single or double.*

The owners and the atmosphere in this nice place are very friendly. You can choose from simple fan-cooled nipa cottages or air conditioned rooms. All are clean and have private bathrooms. The resort is set in a garden by the beach. Behind, the Zambales mountains provide a nice backdrop. Scuba diving equipment, *banca* rental, and other water sports are available. The owners will also make arrangements for hikes up the mountains and to the waterfalls.

SAND VALLEY BEACH RESORT, *along a dark sand beach in Iba. Manila reservations: Tel. 924-7410. $40 per single or double aircon, $45 per suite, $23 per single or double nonaircon, $25-36 per beach cottage.*

This is a pleasant resort with clean and simple rooms — the best rooms are on the beach. The staff is friendly and the restaurant has good food. Facilities include badminton, volleyball, and billiards. You can also use their aquabikes or rent a *banca*.

WHERE TO EAT

Fast food and other American-influenced fare are available in and around San Fernando and Olongapo. There are a few establishments inside the confines of Subic Bay. **CAPONES**, *along the beach in San Antonio*, has good Filipino and Asian food, continental dishes for the less-adventurous, and well-chilled beer in a native setting. The atmosphere is friendly. **CAPTAIN GREGG'S**, *National Highway, Barretto*, serves good international fare. It is an interesting place where you can read up on information on the wrecks scattered in Subic Bay. Some of the ancient loot from the wrecks are also on display.

MR PUMPERNICKEL'S, *Baloy Beach, Barretto*, specializes in German food and also serves Filipino, Chinese, and American food. **BEACH BOULEVARD CAFE**, *Baloy Beach, Barretto*, offers fastfood and a variety of simple dishes in an airy setting. **SAND VALLEY**, *Iba*, has good food; during dinner there is also a buffet. The restaurant is nice and comfortable, furniture and decor are native.

SEEING THE SIGHTS

Dambanang Kagitingan, or Shrine of Valor, is a park that includes a tall cross atop **Mount Samat**. The shrine is a memorial to those who fought and died in Bataan. There are spectacular views of Manila Bay from Samat. Halfway down the Bataan Peninsula, a road splits from the main route to Mariveles and heads to Bagac and Morong. Mount Samat is about seven and a half kilometers from the road to Bagac. **Bagac** has a few pretty beaches, and you may hire a *banca* to go exploring. In **Morong** there is a long beach with four rustic resorts, an Aeta village (Sitio Kanawa), and a Vietnamese refugee camp.

Subic, formerly a huge US naval base, is the center of Zambales' economic life. The base has been converted to a free port and special economic zone. Federal Express uses Subic as a regional hub, and Thompson/Acer computers is among the resident businesses. Outside the zone are some girlie bars, etc., which once provided "entertainment" for visiting navymen.

Subic Bay offers beaches, many facilities (boating, diving, casino, golf, tennis, horse riding, etc.), a tour of the once restricted base, and walks through the rainforest with men who once trained US military people in jungle survival. A valid picture ID is required for entry.

The coast above Olongapo and Subic has a sprinkling of pretty coves and beaches. There is a good beach with a few small resorts in **San Antonio**, also the take-off point for the **Capones Island**, and a pretty white sand beach in **Botolan**.

Iba, the capital of Zambales, has an impressive **church**. At the **market** next to the church, you can get baskets and fine salt made in Zambales. There is also a simple beach resort.

Potipot Island, off Candelaria, is a little island ringed with white sand; there is snorkeling offshore and small basic cottages for overnights. You may also camp out. Ask at Candelaria for the caretaker of the island and for transport (around $20-25 per *banca*, one way), and bring all your supplies.

North of Candelaria, **Sta Cruz** has a nice beach with a few basic resorts.

PAMPANGA RIVER VALLEY

Two centuries ago, the **Pampanga River** was frequented by galleons coming from Mexico (the country south of the US) to Mexico (the town in Pampanga). Today, what remains is a shallow channel — much of the river's water has been diverted to fish ponds and farms, and lahar from Mount Pinatubo has clogged many tributaries.

Two of Northern Luzon's major roads slice through the valley: (1) the North Expressway, used to get to Baguio, the central mountains, and the Ilocos coast; and (2) the Cagayan Valley Road, which diverges from the expressway and passes along the Pampanga River, over the precipicious Balete (Dalton) Pass, into the Cagayan Valley.

ARRIVALS & DEPARTURES

Bulacan and the Pampanga Valley are served by a number of buses: Baliwag, Five Star, Saulog, Times, Victory, and Viron. Other buses go to the Cagayan Valley: Dangwa (to Banaue), Autobus, Baliwag, Nelbusco, and Victory (to Tuguegarao). Buses to Ilocos and Baguio that pass through Pampanga and Tarlac include Autobus, Fariñas, M de Leon, Times, Rabbit, Rapid and Victory.

WHERE TO STAY & EAT

The hotels mentioned have restaurants. Also try **Barrio Fiesta** and **Café Valenzuela** in Dau, popular stops for Filipino food. In Tarlac are McDonald's, Jollybee, Shakey's and a number of other fast-food places.

HOLIDAY INN RESORT, *Clark Field, Pampanga. Tel. 599-2246, 599-2247, Fax 599-2248. Manila reservations: 818-1506, Fax 812-6859. US reservations: Tel. 800-465-4329. 273 rooms & 100 villas. $105 per single or double, $165 per suite, $220 per villa, $22 per extra person. Visa, Master Card, American Express, Diners.*

This place offers a nice retreat from the city. Rooms are comfortable, bright, air conditioned, and have cable television, coffee and tea maker,

BULACAN'S FOUR FESTIVALS

• *San Miguel de Mayumo*, on May 8, is a very colorful celebration in San Miguel. Residents display folk art decor and there is a religious procession. Local food and confectioneries are sold on the streets.

• *Carabao Festival*, on May 14 in Pulilan, decorated carabao and oxen parade into town, some pulling carts with people, produce, and saints. A few of the animals are made to kneel in front of the church. May 15 is a day of races and games.

• *Fertility Rites*, May 17-19 in Obando, is a festival that combines ancient animist beliefs with Christian overlays. The rites became popular when a couple that had been childless for many years had a baby after dancing before the image of San Pascual. San Pascual then replaced the town's original icon to become the benefactor of the fiesta. Our Lady of Salambao (fishnet) is a statue of Mary that was brought in with a fisherman's catch. She, Sta Clara, and San Pascual are Obando's three patron saints. Their celebration dates were merged and are now one long fiesta where townspeople of all ages perform rhythmic, somewhat suggestive dances in the plaza and everyone has a good time.

• *Fluvial Festival*, first Sunday of July in Bocaue, features the Holy Cross of Wawa, which is paraded down the Bocaue river enthroned on a decorated boat, accompanied by many smaller bancas as hundreds of worshipers holding candles line the riverbanks.

and a hairdryer in the bathroom. Rooms for nonsmokers and people with handicaps are available. Facilities and services include a clinic, swimming pool, rooftop deck with jacuzzi, gym, babysitting services, tours, tennis, and golf. There are also jogging and bike trails. Dine at Mequeni Cafe, for the local Kapampangan or international cuisine; Manyaman, for Filipino dishes; al-fresco at the Pool Bar; or in your room (room service is available 'round the clock).

CLARKTON HOTEL, *620 Don Juico, Clarkton, Angeles City. Tel. 22-267, Fax (cell. phone) 0912-305-0614. $55 per single or double aircon, $15 per single or double nonaircon.*

Facilities include a pool, tennis, and gym; golf can be arranged. There is a restaurant and a bar.

MARLIM MANSION, *MacArthur Highway, Balibago, Angeles City. Tel. 560-2200, Fax 560-2212. 100 rooms. $27 per single, $39 per double, $65 per suite.*

All rooms are air conditioned, carpeted, clean, and have cable television. Facilities include a swimming pool and tennis courts. There is a restaurant and a coffeeshop.

INN ON THE PARK, *San Miguel, Tarlac, Tarlac. Tel. 985-0486, 982-2072 to 74. Manila reservations: Tel. 818-3911. 20 rooms. $75 per single or double. Visa, Master Card, American Express, Diners.*

This is a charming, quiet, small inn. The rooms are comfortable, air conditioned, and have cable television. The atmosphere and the staff are friendly. The restaurant serves good local and continental food. You may play golf on a good course, designed by world renowned Robert Trent Jones, at the Luisita Country Club.

SEEING THE SIGHTS

The capital of Bulacan, **Malolos**, was a political center in the 19th century. **Barasoain Church** was the site of the First Philippine Congress and the place where the first constitution of Philippines was written. There is a small museum, open daily from 8:00am to 5:00pm. Barasoain was the birthplace of Balagtas, one of the country's first poets. His poetry has two levels of meaning — the first used amusing anecdotes to disguise the second level, in which he castigates the abusive Spanish regime.

Further down the road is **Casa Real**, a reconstructed turn-of-the-century house with displays of historical memorabilia and art works, open 8:00am until 5:00pm daily. Other historical and art exhibits are available at **Hiyas ng Bulacan** along the MacArthur Highway, open 8:00am to 5:00pm weekdays.

The area of **Baliwag** is known for its inlaid furniture. You may watch *carabao* ribs cut, soaked in bleach to whiten and soften them, and inserted into the wood. The furniture is then stained and varnished, and the dry varnished is scraped off the bone.

In **San Miguel**, visit the **Biak na Bato National Park** if you like the rugged outdoors. Here Aguinaldo, President of the short-lived first Philippine Republic, was captured by Americans. The park has some beautiful limestone formations by the Baliculing River, and Bahay Paniqui (bat house) Caves. The **Sibul Spring** area, north of San Miguel, has the Madlum Caves to explore. While in San Miguel, try its famous *pastillas de leche*, candies made from sugar and *carabao* milk.

One of the oldest churches in the Philippines is in **Calumpit**, on the border of Bulacan and Pampanga. The church was built over 400 years ago, and tunnels beneath it once led to the river, providing an escape route for the priests and their treasury if threatened with attack.

Pampanga has several beautiful and ornate Spanish churches. **Betis Church** is an outstanding example of the baroque ornate workmanship seen in several churches. The churches in **Arayat** and **Sta Ana** are also impressive.

Mount Arayat, Pampanga's dormant volcano, has a **national park** with fenced swimming pools of spring water and trails that lead to the top of the mountain. You can climb and descend the mountain in one day or camp out on the summit. Guides are available at the entrance of the park. Ask for Ariel; if he is not around, the guard at the entrance can recommend another guide. Settle all prices in advance and tell the guide that he is to stay with you for the whole trip.

On the other side of the expressway, **Angeles City** once housed the US's **Clark Air Force Base**. The city still has a profusion of bars (many run by foreigners), restaurants, fast-food outlets, and handicraft shops. The **Mimosa Country Club**, on the grounds of the former airbase, is a leisure estate with a casino, a 27-hole golf-course, and hotel. North of Angeles, in Mabalacat, the expressway ends and joins the MacArthur Highway. Just beyond Mabalacat, the road has been breached by lahar flows, but is usually passable. During the end of World War Two, **General Douglas MacArthur**'s troops marched down it en route to retake Manila.

Much of Pampanga's northern region has been blanketed by an extensive flow of lahar from **Mount Pinatubo**. *Lahar* is the gritty sand and ash that Pinatubo spewed into the atmosphere when it erupted in 1990. Pinatubo's ash circled the globe many times and intensified sunsets the world over for several years. The thick blanket of lahar that settled on the volcano's slopes will continue to flow down the mountain during the rainy season for many years to come, clogging the rivers, displacing people, overwhelming roads and fields. You must see it: a trip to this area will not be forgotten. Try an ultralight flight up Pinatubo's slopes and down its gullies of lahar. Arrangements are made at Clark Airfield or the local tourism office. Or, walk up the volcano for a close-up experience, through the awesome canyons of lahar to a pretty aquamarine crater lake.

Ask for a guide at barangay **Sta Juliana**, Capas (about $8-10 per day). From here, you continue about 10 kilometers over lahar (by jeepney or 4WD vehicle) to the trail head. Bring all your supplies, and a lot of water. The best time to climb is December-mid February. Do not attempt it when it is raining, and during the summer the heat can be excruciating. As the lahar is unstable, you do this walk at your own risk.

Nueva Ecija, the northern gateway of the Pampanga River Valley, flanks Bulacan's north, Pampanga's northeast, and Tarlac's east. A not-so-frequented tourist destination, there are some sights that adventurers and nature trippers are sure to enjoy: **Minaluñgao National Park**, in Gapan and General Tinio, has an enchanting network of caves to explore. In Rizal, there is a 100-foot water fall. If you continue eastward toward the Pacific Ocean, **Baler**, in Aurora, has some lovely beaches, excellent fishing, and friendly people, but no facilities.

LAGUNA DE BAY

Laguna de Bay is a large inland body of water that was formed when the land between Makati and Marikina rose, isolating it from Manila Bay. It became a freshwater lake supplied by streams from the surrounding mountains. Laguna was once infested by huge crocodiles, and for centuries, the only access to towns around it was by boats that sailed up the Pasig River to ferry passengers and cargo.

Today, the lake has been taken over by fish and duck farmers, and access to towns is provided by a good road that circles the lake. A day trip around the lake will take you through quaint towns and scenic spots.

ARRIVALS & DEPARTURES

The best way to circle the lake in one day is to hire a vehicle. Buses and jeepneys ply various parts of this route, but most stop in Antipolo in the north, or Santa Cruz in the south. Between these points, you will find some buses (BLTB and Tritran) and jeepneys.

Several buses for Antipolo leave from the corner of Aurora Boulevard and EDSA. RRCG King leaves from the corner of EDSA and Shaw Boulevard. Buses for Sta Cruz pick up passengers on the South Superhighway in front of South Supermarket. Jeepneys and occasional buses continue from Sta Cruz to Pagsanjan or Majayjay.

WHERE TO STAY

LAKE ISLAND RESORT, *Binangonan, Rizal. Tel. 531-0446, Fax 531-0653. $81 per person single or double, includes meals.*

This place has nice wooden cottages with air conditioned rooms, a small swimming pool, and conference rooms. In the evenings, the resort is lit by lamps in the trees and along the walks. The restaurant serves mostly Filipino food.

U-UGONG PARK RESORT, *Morong, Rizal. Tel. 653-2422, Fax 653-4573. $17 per single or double.*

Nestled into the mountainside are simple native-style cottages. The resort is in a quiet area and has nice views of Laguna, the Uugong waterfalls, and Morong. There is an interesting art gallery.

LAGOS DEL SOL, *Caliraya. Manila reservations: Tel. 523-8441, Fax 521-5328. $65 per single or double aircon, $30 per single or double nonaircon. Visa, Master Card, American Express, Diners.*

This is a nice resort; the lakeside rooms have good views (rooms 211-220 of the "Banahaw Rooms" on the ground floor, but 216 has a big column in the center). The second floor rooms are bigger and have a view of the driveway. The air conditioned rooms have television and a small fridge. Watersports include jet-skis, kayaks, and windsurfing. Facilities include a swimming pool, jacuzzi, small gym, and game room. There is a restaurant; the omelets and fruit shakes are good, the fresh fish and the steaks are recommended. Be patient — your meal may take a while.

CALIRAYA REC CENTER, *Caliraya. Manila reservations: Tel. 892-7777. $60 per single or double.*

Rooms are simple and air conditioned. There is a pool and a restaurant.

CALIRAYA HILLTOP, *Caliraya. Manila reservations: Tel. 242-5969, Fax 242-5985. $40 per single or double.*

This pleasant place has clean, fan-cooled rooms but needs renovation. There is a restaurant.

PAGSANJAN RAPIDS, *Gen. Tiano Street, Pagsanjan. Manila reservations: Tel. 834-0403, Fax 832-1212. $45-60 per single or double. Visa, Master Card.*

Rooms are air conditioned and simple. The restaurant has a food buffet.

HOTEL LA CORONA, *Pagsanjan, Cellular Tel. 0912-306-9766. $40 per single or double aircon, $18 per single or double nonaircon.*

Rooms are clean and all have a bathroom. There is a swimming pool and a restaurant.

PAGSANJAN GARDEN, *Pagsanjan. Manila reservations: Tel. 812-1984, Fax 812-1164. $20-26 per single or double, $126 for the guest house, $6 per person in the dorm. Visa, Master Card.*

This resort is run by the Philippine Tourism Authority and has simple air conditioned rooms. There is a swimming pool, tennis courts, and a restaurant.

R & R, *Pansol. Tel. 545-2952. $110 per single or double.*

R & R is a spa-type resort by hot springs. It is nice, quiet, and cottages are air conditioned. Aside from the hotspring spa, there is a swimming pool and a gym. The restaurant serves local and continental food, with health food.

CRYSTAL SPRINGS, *Calamba. Manila reservations: Tel. 895-9423. $60 per single or double.*

Rooms are air conditioned and clean. Within the resort are eight natural spring water pools.

WHERE TO EAT

The resorts in Pagsanjan and near Makiling offer dining; in addition, try one of these places:

VIEUX CHALET, *Taktak Road, Anitpolo. Tel. 650-3110.*

Specializes in Swiss cuisine. Recommended is the Matterhorn dish — meat or sometimes seafood, and vegetables that are cooked on a stone slab from the Matterhorn in Switzerland; it is tasty and healthy. The restaurant is a nice, friendly, family-run place. Ask Susan, the owner, for the specialties of the day. You get a good view, very pretty at night, of the sprawling metropolis from here. Hikes around Antipolo can be arranged. **CRESCENT MOON CAFE**, *Antipolo. Tel. 658-3866.*

This is a wonderfully relaxing and casual garden restaurant on the property of Lanel Abueva Fernandez, the lady who makes impressive pottery. The food is very good. You can go fishing in a pond in the garden. **BALAW-BALAW**, *Angono.*

Balaw-Balaw has excellent Filipino food. Try their local specialties — *itik*, deep fried young duck. The restaurant is also an art gallery.

SEEING THE SIGHTS

Rodriguez (Montalban), a bit north of the lake, offers some scenic easy hikes and rock climbing. Start at Wawa Dam and head upriver from there. You will probably need to hire a vehicle to get there, at least from the town of Rodriguez.

Antipolo, closer to Laguna, is frequented by a variety of travelers. Some come to relax and enjoy the views of the metropolis below. Small eateries along the road from Marikina and a family-run Swiss restaurant further up in the hills provide food and good views. You may also hike around the area. Some people come to ask the church icon, Nuestra Señora de la Paz y Buen Viaje (Our Lady of Peace and Good Voyage), for safe passage. And you can come here to get or admire the wonderful pottery of Lanel Abueva Fernandez. Lanel has a small shop that sells some of her impressive wares in her charming house in the Beverly Hills subdivision. You can also visit her pottery shop in town — call ahead, *Tel. 658-3866.* She also has a simple lovely restaurant by her pottery store.

Angono, on the northern fringes of Laguna, is known as an artists' town. You may browse through several artists' home-galleries. The **Blanco Family Museum** shows the works of three generations of the very gifted Blanco family. At Mr. Nemiranda's home-gallery-art-school, you can see various caricatures, paintings, and sculptures. **Balaw-Balaw** is a museum-like gallery and restaurant.

Morong church, 15-20 kilometers east of Angono, took three years to build (completed in 1615) and was funded entirely through donations from the townspeople. Built by Chinese artisans, the church decor has touches of their own culture. Enter the church to see the beautifully done 14 stations of the cross. During the end of the Spanish era, the Katipuneros of the area actively resisted the colonizers. Many rebels were caught and executed beside the church — as you exit through the side door, you can see the bullet holes. **U-Ugong Park Resort** is a simple place with good views and greenery. The resort, owned by an artist, has a nice art gallery.

Continue eastward to the medieval-style 17th century **Baras church**. Nearby **Tanay church** has lovely stations of the cross painted on wood. A road that heads inland northeast from Tanay to Sampaloc takes you to the **Daranak Falls**, where you may swim in the pool at the base of the falls. A small entrance fee pays for the area's maintenance.

Southeast from Tanay, the lakeside road passes through a valley, rises steeply into the mountains and has spectacular views, then ascends to lakeshore communities as it continues around Laguna.

Mabitac church, about 27 kilometers from Tanay, is a solid 18th century structure on top of a hill and overlooks Laguna de Bay and the surrounding flatlands. From here, a road heads into the Sierra Madre Mountains to **Infanta**, where there are nice beaches and great fishing. About three kilometers along this road from Famy, another road leads down to a river where you may hike to the **Siniloan Falls**. This is a lovely area for day or overnight excursions through palms and along rivers. Guides are available at the take-off point to the falls. If you are staying overnight, you will have to bring camping equipment (tent, etc.).

The next town of interest along the route, **Pakil**, is known for its woodcarvings and wood filigree. Finished products are available at **E & R Handicrafts** — you can also watch demonstrations. **San Pedro de Alcantara** is a pretty church that houses the statue of the Virgin of Turumba and over 100 of her costumes. The woodcarvings and the courtyard are interesting. **Danilo Dalena's house-gallery**, diagonally across from the church, displays some of his works and political cartoons. This sleepy town was once famous for its *catalonas* (female shamans). Every Friday preceding Palm Sunday, an ancient *catalon* ritual — the *turumba*, a strange rhythmic dance — is performed by the townspeople. Also during Lent, you can buy cookies shaped like the Virgin Mary.

Paete is famous for its woodcarving and papier mâché. Papier mâché horses, *carabao*, and other figures are made and gaily painted during dry season, and sold at fiestas in many communities. Inside the town's **church** are two remarkable antique paintings.

About eight or nine kilometers after Paete, a road leads uphill to man-made **Lake Caliraya**. Actually a large reservoir, Caliraya was created in 1943 to supply water for a hydroelectric project. This is a lovely and refreshing area for hikers and others seeking a retreat from the city. A few resorts are on its fringes, and you can go windsurfing, swimming, and fishing in the lake. About a kilometer past the road to Caliraya is the town of **Lumban**, known for its superb embroidery. **Deviton-Enduviges Alunan Embroideries** is highly recommended.

In **Pangasinan**, Laguna's most famous town, you can ride a *banca* up the Pagsanjan River through a lovely canyon to the **Magdapio Falls**. At the basin below the falls, you may change to a bamboo raft that takes you under the powerful falls: you will get drenched. You "shoot the rapids" on your trip back down. Rent a life vest and secure non-waterproof belongings in plastic bags. If you go during or just after rainy season, you will not get all the way to the main falls; *bancas* will turn at a smaller one. And, if you go at the end of dry season, the river is low and "shooting the rapids" becomes "carrying the *banca*" — boats and passengers are lifted over rocky areas. Boatmen may complain about it in hopes of getting a fat tip. The Pagsanjan Rapids Hotel is a good place to get a boat; it also has a tasty lunch.

About two and a half kilometers from Pagsanjan town, a road veers off towards the base of Mount Banahaw. The towns of **Majayjay**, **Liliw**, and **Nagcarlan** all have nice churches and scenery. The **bell tower** of Liliw church offers good views of Laguna de Bay. While you are here, try *uraro* biscuits, made from arrowroot. Nagcarlan has a very interesting round-walled **cemetery** with an underground crypt. Rebels against the Spanish regime once met in the crypt. More recently, communist insurgents met here also.

Back along the Bay route, stalls by the road in **Sta Cruz** sell *quesong puti*, a salty white cheese made from *carabao* milk. In **Pila**, a small museum displays Chinese pottery that was unearthed in the area. Ask at the municipio hall, on weekdays from 8:00am-5:00pm, for access.

Los Baños is home to the **International Rice Research Institute** (IRRI), which works on improving rice and disseminating information on its culture worldwide, and the **University of the Philippines**' large campus for forestry, veterinary medicine, animal science, and several other departments. There is an interesting museum and an information office in IRRI; guided tours are available, call *Tel. 845-0563* (Manila) for arrangements.

From the UP campus, an access road leads to a short hike to **hot springs** and to a trail up **Mount Makiling**. You can drive to a good view over the lake from the UP Arts Center.

PLAY TIME

*The Philippines' first theme park, **Enchanted Kingdom**, is in Santa Rosa, Laguna. You can stop in on your way around Laguna de Bay, or take the Enchanted Kingdom Bus. The bus leaves from the Ayala Center in Makati, Thursday and Friday at 10:30am and 12:30pm; and 8:30am, 10:30am, and 12:30pm on the weekend. Fare is $1.50 per person and entrance to the park is $16, unlimited rides. This is best at night – there is very little shade.*

There are several hot spring resorts in Los Baños and **Calamba**, where hot water from volcanic Mount Makiling has been channeled into baths. People come here for cures. The house in which Philippine national hero **José Rizal** was born is in Calamba. Now beautifully restored, it is a **museum** displaying Rizal memorabilia and period pieces. The museum is open daily from 8:00am until 5:00pm and there is a garden with labeled fruit trees and plants.

From Calamba it takes 45 minutes to return to Manila via the South Superhighway.

SOUTHERN POINTS

ARRIVALS & DEPARTURES/SOUTH OF MANILA

Philtranco, BLTB, Columbus, Superlines, Tritran, JB Bicol, and RAM buses serve the route from Manila through to Bicol, passing through Alaminos, San Pablo, Tiaong, Candelaria, Sariaya, Lucena, Pagbilao, Atimonan, and other towns south. Jeepneys connect the highway to other towns.

WHERE TO STAY

HIDDEN VALLEY, *Alaminos. Manila reservations: Tel. 818-4038, Fax 812-1609. $100 per single, $165-185 per double, $180-250 per cottages, $40 per person per tent. Visa, Master Card, American Express, Diners.*

Either stay in air conditioned rooms or cottages or in a tent. The restaurant serves Filipino dishes.

VILLA ESCUDERO, *San Pablo City. Manila reservations: Tel. 523-2944, 523-0392, Fax 521-8698. $72-197 per single, $55-122 per person per double, $44-96 per person per triple, rates include 3 meals. American Express.*

All cottages are native-style, made out of bamboo and coconut lumber with thatched roofs. Rooms are clean, simple, fan-cooled, and have bathrooms.

BATO SPRINGS, *San Cristobal, San Pablo City, Tel. 976.*

This place offers simple cottages and a campsite where you may pitch tents.

WHERE TO EAT

Both **Villa Escudero** and **Hidden Valley** hotels have restaurants. For snacks during merienda time, try the *bibingka* (rice cakes) from stalls along the highway in San Pablo.

TREAT HAUS, *near the Plaza in Sariaya.*
This restaurant has very good home-cooked Filipino and Spanish food. For dessert, try the Food for the Gods; it is excellent here. The atmosphere is casual and friendly.

SEEING THE SIGHTS

In **Alaminos**, Hidden Valley Resort is in a coconut plantation. Relax in the natural-looking pools fed from piped spring water of varying temperatures. The area is attractive, as it has numerous fruit trees and tropical plants. There is also a waterfall to walk to. The $50 entry fee includes lunch (whether or not you want it).

Continue to **San Pablo**, a town with seven picturesque little crater lakes. **Sampaloc Lake**, the most accessible, is behind city hall. **Lake Palakpakin** is beside a provincial road. **Mohicap** and **Calibato** are short walks. You will need to find a guide to hike through the coconuts to get to **Yambao** and **Pandin**. **Bunot** is accessible through the grounds of a now closed resort.

Mount Banahaw, frequented by climbers and worshipers, is a dormant volcano. There are some lovely waterfalls and streams on the mountain's slopes. Short day-hikes will take you to the beautiful **Kristalino Falls**, or further on to **Suplina Falls**. Allow two to three days to climb the mountain. You can start at **Sta Cruz**, **Dolores**, where a rough road continues to Kinabuhayan. Ask the *barangay* captain or Kuya Jose, a religious leader, for a guide. Keep in mind that the locals are more agile than visitors, and discuss the route before setting off. The other route is through Lucban (see below).

The last, very violent eruption of Banahaw was long before anyone living can remember. The mountain has retained its power in a different way — people flock here to worship and meditate on its slopes; some believe Christ walked here and that José Rizal was the reincarnated Christ. Healers, *albularios*, and priestesses live in scattered communities.

Between San Pablo and Tiaong is **Villa Escudero**, a functioning coconut plantation and resort. Amidst the relatively green surroundings you can see demonstrations on the processing and use of coconuts, a cultural show, and the **Escudero Museum**, which has a diverse collection ranging from silver altars to plastic spoons. Ride on a *carabao*-drawn cart while local folk singers serenade you, then eat a tasty Filipino lunch while overlooking the lake. Outside the resort, stands along the highway sell *bibingka* (a tasty rice cake) during *merienda* times.

Back along the route south, past Candelaria, is **Sariaya**. Coconut planters here acquired their wealth from their produce and built ornate, imposing mansions. Although coconuts have ceased to be as profitable as they once were, many of the houses that were not destroyed during the war are still there. The most impressive one is the **Gala house**, on the highway beside the church.

The **Pahiyas Festival**, in honor of **San Isidro Labrador**, the patron saint of Sariaya, Tayabas, Lucban, and Lucena, is on the 15th of May. The festivals of **Lucban** and **Sariaya** are special events worth battling the traffic to attend. Townspeople decorate the routes of the main procession. The folk art decor in Lucban is great. *Pabitin* (chandeliers), made from *kiping* leaves, are placed along house fronts, and millions more *kiping* are worked into creative designs along with coconuts, rice, *palay* (unhulled rice), vegetables, bread, fruits, snacks, candies, table mats, hats, and items related to the family's livelihood. *Kiping* is colored rice flour paste that is pressed onto a leaf and dried.

In Sariaya, although the decor is not as elaborate as that in Lucban, it is still interesting. Houses along the procession route erect large bamboo stems hung with packages of sweets, snacks, games, and other things; house fronts are decorated with fruits; and several have costumed mannequins and children on the roofs. Pandemonium breaks loose in the afternoons when San Isidro ventures forth from the church, high on his palanquin. People lining the procession route, who are supposed to wait until the statue has passed, jump the gun and begin tearing down the decorations and carting them away. Twenty minutes after the procession has passed, residents sweep the debris away, and Sariaya is once again a stately old town.

In Lucban, people spend the morning of the 15th finishing the decor. By noon, the town is transformed into a beautiful lively place thronged with visitors. Near the church plaza, vendors sell food, plants, handicrafts, and local products. The procession starts in the afternoon and is headed by Lucban's century-old old *gigantes* (giant mannequins), which travel along the decorated streets and return to the church.

Lucban is the other departure area for treks up Mount Banahaw. The **Tayabas Mountaineers** can arrange outings on and around the mountain. Call either Jun Redor, *Tel. 219*, or Ronnie Reyes, *Tel. 200 or 201* (the area code is 04278).

Quezon National Park is a good, small park with some foliage and wildlife. Just above the parking lot there is a trail that leads northwest. The hour and a half climb takes you up **Mount Mirador**, and to great views of both sides of Luzon and impressive limestone formations below. The path from the road dips then goes uphill through stones and boulders. Beyond a cave-like passage, the path drops down to the left, then continues through limestones, to some stairs built by Americans in 1930. Climb the stairs and continue on the other side of the hill (the foliage is totally different) and follow the more difficult path to the summit.

On the summit is **Pinagbanderahan**, the flagpole. Here, members of the Katipunan met to plan their moves against the Spanish regime. The view is superb.

After the park, the road continues south. The **Atimonan church** is quite impressive.

CAVITE

The provinces of **Cavite** and Batangas line the coast south of Manila. Many of the country's heroes come from Cavite, which consequently is called the "cradle of the Philippine Republic." Today, its proximity and accessibility make it a popular escape for Manila's residents.

ARRIVALS & DEPARTURES

The easiest way to explore Cavite is by car. Several buses and jeepneys ply the coastal road to Cavite City; some continue to Maragondon. Buses depart from the Baclaran Market for Las Piñas and other points in Cavite. Do not travel the Tagaytay-Naic road at night.

WHERE TO STAY & EAT

CAYLABNE BAY RESORT, *Ternate. Manila reservations: Tel. 813-8519 to 26. 96 rooms. $150 per single, $186 per double, $255-386 per suite. Visa, Master Card, American Express, Diners.*

Rooms inside are nice, Spanish-Mediterranean-style villas on the sprawling landscaped grounds of the resort. All are air conditioned and have cable television. There is a swimming pool, and a variety of water sports. The restaurant serves Filipino and continental dishes

PUERTO AZUL, *Ternate. Manila reservations: Tel. 526-8588. $114 per single, $130 per double, $276-336 per suite. Visa, Master Card, American Express, Diners.*

The golf here is much better than the beach. Rooms are pleasant, comfortable, air conditioned, and have the standard amenities of an up-scale hotel. There is a nice large pool, a restaurant, and bar. A variety of aquasports are available. Staff are friendly and efficient. The resort hosts an annual all-night concert fest during the summer.

SEEING THE SIGHTS

At the **Sarao Jeepney Factory**, many of the Philippines' ubiquitous and unique jeepneys are made. Stop by for an inside look at the manufacturing process.

Continue to the **Las Piñas Church**, a small pretty Spanish-style stone church that houses the **Bamboo Organ**. The organ was built in 1795 by Fray Diego Cera de la Virgin del Carmen. Both the church and the organ were damaged a number of times, and the organ eventually fell into disuse for almost a century. In 1975, it was restored in Germany.

Today, the organ is fully functional. Every February, there is a week-long **Bamboo Organ Festival** where acclaimed local and international musicians are invited to perform in the evenings. You can visit daily from 9:00-11:00am and 2:00-4:00pm, except Sundays. There is usually an organist who can give a demonstration, and the gift shop in the *convento* sells souvenirs and good CDs and tapes of the organ's music.

The **Aguinaldo Shrine** is about nine kilometers down the national highway. Here, on June 12, 1898, General Emilio Aguinaldo declared independence for the short-lived first Philippine Republic. Both his house and its furnishings are remarkable. On the dining room ceiling there is a bas-relief map of the Philippines, with Cavite painted red symbolizing the province's resistance. A marble tomb containing the remains of Aguinaldo is behind the house. The shrine is open daily from 8:00am until 5:00pm.

On a narrow strip of land that protrudes into Manila Bay are **Cavite City** and **Sangley Point**. The city has some interesting old houses, and at Sangley Point are the ruins of **Porta Vaga church**, destroyed in 1647. **San Roque church**, near the ruins, houses Porta Vaga's patron – a 17th century painting of Nuestra Señora de la Soledad. **Fort San Felipe**, built in 1609, served as guardian of Manila Bay and now has an exhibit of Philippine Navy memorabilia.

The coastline of Cavite is lined with several resorts, ranging from up-market with many facilities to simple picnic places.

Maragondon, an old Jesuit town was settled in 1663 by Indonesian Christians and has a nice **old church** that is worth a visit. Notice the intricate carvings on the doors and inside the church. You can get good views from the bell tower. Maragondon figured prominently in Philippine history and historical markers line the roadsides.

TAGAYTAY & TAAL

Tagaytay (in Cavite) and **Taal** (in Batangas) are probably the favorite escape of Manileños of a variety of socio-economic strata. You will find the elite playing golf and relaxing at one of the exclusive clubs in Tagaytay. The area also offers a number of more affordable resorts where the middle class come to enjoy the cooler and fresher air.

The more adventurous will hike around the ridge or continue down it and spend a day walking around the volcano island inside the crater lake of what may once have been the world's largest volcano (estimated at 4,340 meters – 14,000 feet – tall).

ARRIVALS & DEPARTURES

A number of tour operators do excursions to Taal and Tagaytay. Buses, jeepneys, and Tamaraw FXs depart from the Baclaran Market for Tagaytay and other points in Cavite. BLTB buses to Tagaytay depart from the EDSA terminal in Pasay. Although possible via public transport, the Taal circle is best done by private hire.

Easiest access to **Taal Lake** is from the other side: take the South Superhighway to the end, head right toward Lipa City. At Tanauan, a road turns right to Talisay.

From Tagaytay, two roads lead to the lake shore: a rough one (especially during rainy season) from the rotunda to Leynes, and a paved road to Talisay from the road to the People's Park.

WHERE TO STAY

Tagaytay Ridge Area

BANYAN TREE-EVERCREST, *Batulao. Tel. (Manila number with direct access) 712-9293, Fax 712-9299. $153 per single, $211 per double, rate includes 2 rounds of golf. Visa, Master Card, American Express, Diners. Manila reservations: Tel. 243-3151, Fax 49-7268.*

This is Tagaytay's top resort. All rooms are spacious, air conditioned, come with cable television, and have private balconies. There is a restaurant, coffee shop, and a bar. The golf course is excellent and views are great.

CLUB ESTANCIA, *San Jose, Tagaytay. Tel. 413-1133, Fax 413-1047. $97-110 per single or double, $118-143 per suite, $8 per extra bed. Visa, Master Card.*

Rooms are comfortable, air conditioned, carpeted, some have native decor, and some face Taal Lake. Facilities include a swimming pool, sauna, small gym, jacuzzi, tennis, and billiards. There is a restaurant and a bar.

ROYAL PARC APARTELLE, *Silang Crossing, Tagaytay. Tel. 413-1032. Manila reservations: Tel. 805-8122, Fax 805-8123. 26 rooms. $60-70 per single, $78-93 per double. Visa, Master Card.*

This is a nice, quiet compound and all rooms are air conditioned and have cable television. The staff is friendly and the restaurant serves tasty Filipino fare.

TAAL VISTA HOTEL, *Kaybagal, Tagaytay. Tel. 413-1223, Fax 413-1225. Manila reservations: Tel. 817-2710. $103-112 per single or double, $144 per suite. Visa, Master Card, American Express, Diners.*

Some rooms could use a face-lift. All are air conditioned and some have good views of Taal. Facilities include a swimming pool, basketball court, playground, and casino. There is a large restaurant and a bar.

TAGAYTAY PICNIC GROVE, *Tagaytay. Tel. 308-3249. 16 cottages, 14 rooms. $18-50 per single, $23-84 per double, $112 per triple cottage, $9 per person in the dorm.*

All rooms are simple, no air conditioning, and only the cottages have hot water in the bathrooms. This place is large, but popular during weekend days and can get very crowded. There are camping grounds, a skating rink, and a restaurant.

EL CASERON, *Nyogan, Tagaytay. Tel. 308-3249. 6 rooms. $32 per single, $37 per double, $46 per triple, rates include breakfast.*

This is a homey place; rooms are clean and basic. Three rooms have a private bathroom with hot water. The food here is very good and you get a good view of the lake from some of the rooms and from the patio that has nice old iron furniture. The staff are friendly.

TAGAYTAY HILLSIDE INN, *Mendez Crossing, Patutong Malaki, Tagaytay. Manila reservations: Tel. 844-4779, Fax 810-9231. $37 per single or double, $13 per extra bed.*

Simple, clean rooms, some with a view of Taal. Request meals in advance.

Taal Lake-side

GLORIA DE CASTRO'S, *Leynes. Cellular Tel. 0912-310-5071. 3 rooms. $15 per single or double.*

Basic clean rooms and a homey friendly atmosphere. The food is simple — try the grilled fish, fresh from the lake.

RESORTS INTERNATIONAL, *cellular Tel. 097-375-01591. 1 cottage, 2 bedrooms. $23 per single, $30 per double;* **MILO'S PLACE**, *$23-30 per single or double;* **VILLA MARIA**, *$23-30 per single or double*; and **ROSLINA'S PLACE**, *$15 per single or double.*

All are in Talisay and have basic, fan-cooled rooms. Some rooms with private bathrooms.

WHERE TO EAT

GOURMET CAFÉ, *on the road from Silang.*

A very popular place for continental and Italian food. The pesto pasta is pretty good. Service can be slow when the café is full. The atmosphere and decor are pleasant.

SKYLINE GRILL, *on the road from Silang, just before the rotunda.*

Serves tasty local dishes. The bathrooms are clean and service is good.

CAFÉ ADRIATICO, *near the rotunda.*

Offers Spanish-Filipino fare in a cozy atmosphere.

JOSEPHINE'S has very good Filipino food. The restaurant is air conditioned and its glass windows afford a great view of the lake and surrounds. **ANGELINOS** is a casual place for pizza and Italian dishes. **AURELIO'S PRIME RIBS** and **RANCHO DEL ROSARIO** specialize in steak.

MUSHROOMBURGER serves, as the name says, burgers with mushrooms mixed in the meat. Now a chain with several outlets in Manila, this is where it started. **EL CASERON** serves pretty good sizzling dishes (chicken or ribs). Dining is casual, either inside or on the patio with a good view of the lake. The patio furniture is wonderful — nice old wrought iron tables and chairs.

For simple lakeside dining, **GLORIA DE CASTRO'S** has lakeside picnic tables where you can have meals; try the tasty grilled fish, fresh from the lake.

SEEING THE SIGHTS

The best vantage point for viewing **Taal Volcano** is from **Tagaytay**. People flock to Tagaytay for the view, fresh air, picnics, restaurants, casino, pony rides for children, golf, and a few come to hike.

If you are staying at the Evercrest Golf Club and Resort, you can play golf on the scenic championship course, reputed to be one of the best courses in the country. Most of the golf courses here are part of private clubs and you need to be accompanied by a member to play.

Beyond Evercrest, **Mount Batulao** is a destination for trekkers. You may not want to attempt it under the sweltering heat of April-June, as there is not much shade.

Tagaytay sits on the rim of a once massive volcano. Taal exploded, creating a crater lake, and another crater formed within it. Within that crater is another lake that too has a small island inside! The best way to get to the island is through **Leynes**, along the shores of the lake. Mrs. Gloria de Castro, *cellular Tel. 0912-310-5071*, will arrange for a reliable *banca* and guide to take you to the island; she and her husband take very good care of visitors. Several other places also provide *banca* hire. The Volcano Island is also accessible from **Talisay** and other points, but the *banca* ride takes longer.

Plan on leaving Leynes in the morning (before 9:00am): the lake tends to be rough in the afternoons. The newest crater is a 20-minute uphill walk from the shore; it will take an hour longer to reach the old crater and interior lake, where you can swim in its sulfurous waters. Bring a lot of drinking water and start very early if you plan on going to the interior lake. Wear sturdy shoes, it gets dusty and some portions may be slippery. On the island, we usually buy a soft drink or beer to help support the small community on the island.

On the southeast side of Taal Lake is the gracious old town of **Taal City**. Residents once gained their wealth from coffee. As coffee declined as a source of income, so did the fortunes of the townspeople. A few of the ancestral houses that attest to the city's former wealth have been nicely restored. The **Agoncillo Shrine** and **Apacible Museum** are open to visitors from 8:00am to noon and from 1:00 to 5:00pm daily.

Taal Church is unusual: its imposing structure seems like a cross between a government building and a Spanish church. Climb the "bell tower" for a superb vista of the city and Batangas Bay. There may be some good finds in the **market**: embroidered fabric, clothing, accessories, and table linens at reasonable prices; and *balisong*, or fan knives. In nearby *barangay* **Balisong**, a number of road-side stalls sell these knives.

Also on the other side of the lake is a popular destination for local mountain climbing groups — **Mount Maculot**. It is a moderate climb, feasible in a day. Bring gloves as it is very slippery on the way down and you may need to grab onto the vines, branches, and sharp cogon grass for support. From the summit, you'll enjoy magnificent views of Taal and Batangas Bay. Also on the summit, there is an area where the **UP Mountaineers** are replanting trees in hopes of reforesting the area.

ANILAO, BATANGAS CITY, & CALATAGAN

Several areas of Batangas' coastline have nice beaches. The Calatagan Peninsula offers beaches, resorts, and golf. Matabungkay and Lian have beaches. And around Nasugbu, you get sand, sun, and sea at Bamboo (the nicest of this lot), White Sands, and Natipuan beaches.

ARRIVALS & DEPARTURES

The Punta Baluarte resort has a shuttle service. BLTB buses depart from the EDSA, Pasay, station to Nasugbu. From the pier in Nasugbu, a *banca* will take you to the area beaches. If you are headed to Matabungkay, get off at Lian and take a jeepney. One BLTB bus goes daily to Matabungkay and Calatagan.

You can get to Anilao via bus to Batangas City and a jeepney to Anilao. BLTB has frequent trips. You can reach the resorts via *banca*, from the pier in town, or by jeepney to the closer ones.

WHERE TO STAY

Calatagan & Nasugbu

PUNTA BALUARTE, *Calatagan. Manila reservations: Tel. 894-1466, Fax 893-4491. 175 rooms. $102-130 per single or double, $140 per suite. visa, Master Card, American Express, Diners.*

The resort, located on a sprawling estate, has wooden cottages that are air conditioned, dark, and comfortable. The cheaper rooms are further away from the swimming pools and dining area. The beach is not great but there are two pretty and large pools, one fresh water, the other sea water. Aquasports off the beach include hobbie cats and jet-skis. There is a nice golf course. For dining, there is a pleasant pavilion-style open air restaurant that serves seafood, Philippine, and continental dishes.

RESIDENCE INN, *Calatagan. Manila reservations: Tel. 897-3888, Fax 890-6162. 8 cottages. $113-226 per cottage. Visa, master Card, American Express, Diners.*

Rather a unique resort for the area, you stay in a wooden cottage built over the sea. All cottages are air conditioned, have a minibar, loft, and verandah. Facilities include a swimming pool and aquasports. You can fish from your cottage or rent a *banca* and go further out, and you can have your catch grilled. There is a restaurant and a bar.

LAGO DE ORO, *Balibago, Calatagan. Cellular Tel. 0912-301-4325. 16 rooms. $64-70 per single or double.*

This pleasant place has nice, clean, air conditioned rooms. The seaview rooms cost more and the cheaper rooms have a view of the lake. There is a swimming pool, and arrangements to play golf nearby can be made. There is a restaurant and the staff is friendly.

LIAN RESORT, *Lian. Manila reservations: Tel. 890-8131, Fax 896-0929. 16 rooms. $56 per single or double.*

The resort is located on a private beach cove. The rooms are air conditioned, beachfront, with tropical foliage in the back. There is a restaurant and conference rooms.

MUNTING BUHANGIN, *Natipuan, Nasugbu. $120-150 per aircon cottage, $75 per nonaircon cottage, $45 per non-aircon room, $25 per tent.*

There are some interesting nice-looking tree houses. Cottages and rooms are clean. There is no restaurant so you must bring your own food and drinks. The hotel sits above a nice dark-sand beach.

MAYA-MAYA, *Nasugbu. Manila reservations: Tel. 810-6865. $70 per non-aircon cottage, $90 per aircon cottage.*

This resort rents out a few simple rooms. The restaurant has some simple tasty dishes. The dive center offers courses and certification.

WHITE SANDS, *Natipuan, Nasugbu. Manila reservations: Tel. 833-5608. $50-60 per single or double.*

Rooms are simple, fan-cooled, and have private bathrooms. The restaurant serves simple local and western dishes.

Batangas City

ALPA HOTEL, *Batangas City. Tel. 723-1025, 723-0366, 723-1882, Fax 723-0340. $33-44 per single, $34-45 per double, $68-134 per suite.*

All rooms are air conditioned and have cable television. There is a restaurant, bar, and swimming pool.

Anilao

All resorts below are in or near the water at Anilao. We urge you not to spearfish when scuba diving, especially in sanctuaries, and to discourage dive operators from doing this.

EAGLE POINT, *Bagalangit, Mabini. Manila reservations: Tel. 813-3553, Fax 813-3560. $95 per single or double, $175 per suite. Visa, Master Card, American Express, Diners.*

This is the area's most upscale resort. Nice cement and wood cottages with air conditioning and private balconies. Facilities include a good spa, three swimming pools, a variety of aquasports, and a full dive center. The resort seems to be into conservation and rescues sea turtles from the market for rehabilitation and eventual release.

ANILAO SEASPORT, *Manila reservations: Tel. 807-4574, Fax 805-4660. 20 rooms. $58 per single or double, $63 per triple, $82 per "family room" (fits 5), $105 per aircon room. Divers' package: $174 alone or $143 per person in groups of 2 or more, includes room, three meals, 2 tank dives, guide and boat. Visa, Master Card, American Express, US$ and US travelers cheques.*

This pleasant place consists of long thin two-story buildings against a steep hillside. The main area has attractive bamboo dining tables and is along the sea. Most of the rooms are fan-cooled, have good cross-ventilation, native furnishing, and private bathrooms. Aquasports offered are windsurfing, hobie cats, kayaks, and paddle boats. There is a complete dive center (divers must present an international C-certificate) and diving and windsurf instruction are available.

AQUA TROPICAL, *Manila reservations: Tel. 523-1843, Fax 522-2536. 40 rooms. $100 per single or double, meals included. Dive packages are available. Visa, Master Card, American Express, Diners.*

This is an upmarket place. The management and staff are very hospitable. Rooms are clean, air conditioned, have television, and private bathrooms. Aquasports include jet skis and windsurf boards. There dive center offers certification.

CLUB OCELLARIS, *$59 per person, meals included. Dive package: $84 per person, one night, $105 per person, two nights; includes dive master, boat, tanks, meals.*

This dive resort is popular with foreigners. There is a nice bar and dining area, well-kept and furnished with bamboo. Rooms are open, fan cooled, and have private bathrooms. The dive center is complete.

EL PINOY, *11 rooms. $46-50 per person triple occupancy, $50-63 per person double occupancy, $76-107 per single, all meals are included.*

This is a well designed resort with an eclectic collection of Filipiniana used to decorate the place. Rooms are fan-cooled and do not have windows. Service is good. There is a complete dive center that does not allow spearfishing.

ARTHUR'S PLACE, *Cellular Tel. 0912-328-2865, 0912-306-8479. $47 per single, $36 per person double occupancy, $34 per person triple occupancy, all meals included.*

Arthur's is a well-managed place, a favorite for families and divers. There are cottages around an enclosed lawn area, great for kids to play. The food is very good and staff are friendly. The dive center here is professionally run, highly recommended, and Arthur does a good amount of work towards protecting the sanctuaries; he set up buoys near the one in front of the resort.

AQUAVENTURE, *Manila reservations: Tel. 844-1996. 20 rooms. $45 per person, meals included. Visa, Master Card, American Express.*

This is a nice place set up for divers, and gets Japanese groups that dive or are learning. Rooms are bamboo and wood, with bamboo furniture and small but nice tiled modern bathrooms. The dining room area is also mostly bamboo and is quite nice. The dive center is complete and professionally run, but, they have taken groups spearfishing.

DIVE SOLANA, *Cellular Tel. 0912-202-8635. Manila reservations: Tel. 721-2089, Fax 722-5609. 9 rooms. $52 per person double, $48 per person triple, $44 per person quad and up, meals included.*

This is a charming place. Rooms are in very nice, white cottages with nipa roofs. All are clean, fan-cooled, airy, have a bathroom and a porch. The main area has lovely watercolor paintings, and the designer made nice use of wood branches as balustrades. The staff is friendly, the place is well-managed, ambiance is laid-back, and food is great. The dive center is professionally run with Scuba World and is complete and highly recommended.

VISTAMAR, *Manila reservations: Tel. 58-3324, Fax 521-5416. $40-69 per single or double aircon, $30-40 per single or double nonaircon.*

Vistamar is mostly a convention place. It is a large white cement complex. The more expensive air conditioned rooms include a refrigerator. Sports include windsurfing, jet skis, and a glass bottom boat. There is a restaurant and a chapel. Dive equipment and guides are available.

LA LUZ DEL MAR, *Manila reservations: c/o Mr. DBL Lusica, Tel. 823-5878. 4 cottages. $25 for one-room cottage, $42 for two-story cottage.*

This is a simple place with nice, native, bamboo cottages. All rooms have a fan, bathroom, and are furnished with bamboo. The larger cottages have a hammock and nice sea view. There is no restaurant.

DIVE SOUTH MARINA, *Manila reservations: Tel. 812-5888, Fax 892-2465. $15 per person single or double.*

This resort caters to divers, mostly from Japan where they have a tie-up with an agency. Rooms are simple, fan cooled, with native furniture and decor. Bathrooms are common. The restaurant serves Filipino food. The dive center is complete, but they will take people spearfishing.

SEEING THE SIGHTS

Anilao has the best diving on Luzon. It is usually the first destination divers and snorkelers head for. There are a profusion of resorts, most catering to divers, and some that also offer windsurfing and hobie cats. The beaches are not remarkable, mostly rocks. The nearby islands of **Sombrero** and **Maricaban**, and **Ligpo Point** have good sand beaches, with snorkeling off-shore. Other places for snorkeling are **Sepok Point, Layag-Layag, Ligpo Point**, and off **Red Palm Beach** (great, but currents can be strong at times). Always settle *banca* fees in advance.

Most of Anilao's residents have joined with **Haribon Foundation** to successfully set up a number of sanctuaries. Most of the time, the sanctuaries are honored; unfortunately a few resorts do spearfishing tours that include some of the sanctuaries. A number of Philippine armed forces divers frequent the area and are notorious for not observing the sanctuaries either; some leave with souvenir coral along with their kills.

Although most resorts have dive masters, many do not have a resident instructor. Most instructors are based in Manila and come up with groups during the weekends. If you want to take a course, make arrangements in advance to be sure that a qualified instructor is available. An Open Water Diver course will cost from $300-400. Most b*anqueros* know the dive sites and are familiar with divers' needs and safety. The crew of **Lady Susan** are wonderful. Recommended dive operators are mentioned above in *Where to Stay, Anilao*.

Batangas City, the industrial center of Batangas, is the departure point to Puerto Galera, Mindoro.

TOP DIVE SPOTS

• *Cathedral* – *two large mounds with a cross planted in 1983 by President Ramos is the most popular site where fish anticipate divers who come here to feed them. (However, fish may disappear for a while after the sanctuary has been violated by spear fishers – often including men from the armed services of the Philippines.) Night dives are superb.*

• *Sombrero* – *has a shallow wall with good coral growth, and off-shore areas with schools of fish.*

• *Sepok* – *a very pretty area with a wall and coral gardens.*

• *Twin Rocks* – *for nudibranchs, feather stars, and schools of barracuda.*

• *Arthur's* – *corals, clownfish, and goblinfish.*

• *Bonito Island* – *a variety of fish including black tip reef sharks.*

13. LINGAYEN GULF

The **Gulf of Lingayen**, a large inlet of the South China Sea, spans Luzon's west coast from Santiago Island off Pangasinan to San Fernando's Poro Point in La Union. Lingayen Gulf played an important part in **World War Two**. Here, Japanese forces landed on December 22, 1941, and advanced to Manila, and American forces arrived on the 9th of January, 1945, and proceeded to liberate Manila.

Since prehistoric times, the gulf has been a ship's haven during storms. Remains unearthed in the area show extensive contact with Chinese traders. In 1574, after unsuccessful attempts to enter Manila, Chinese corsair Lim Ah Hong and 3,000 followers fleeing from the Ming empire came ashore and settled into the hills. Although the Spanish army went after them and burned their ships, the Spaniards were unable to overpower them. Eventually, Lim Ah Hong's men built some new ships and dug their way out from the siege, creating a new mouth for the Agno River and escaping to sea. The Limahong Channel remains a tribute to their endeavor. Many of Lim Ah Hong's people were unable to travel with the reduced fleet, and joined the local population.

Other people who came to the area to trade included **Igorots** who walked down from the Cordillera to barter gold, honey, and cloth for supplies they needed. The trails they used still exist, now as roads: through Tuba and Sto Tomas, Pangasinan; and the Naguilian trail to Bauang, La Union.

Pangasinan and La Union, the southernmost provinces of the Ilocos region, have coastlines dotted with attractive brown sand beaches, old Spanish churches, caves, and pretty islands, including the famous Hundred Islands.

PANGASINAN

American troops initially chose Lingayen Beach as their landing site in the gulf, and carpet-bombed **Lingayen**, Pangasinan's capital, to flush out the Japanese — who had already left. Plans changed and the troops landed further along the coast on Bonoan Blue Beach, in Dagupan. After the war, Americans rebuilt the capital in southern colonial style.

Other points of interest incude pretty offshore islands, beaches, caves, churches, a museum, and spectacular views from a lighthouse area.

ARRIVALS & DEPARTURES

The most convenient access to Pangasinan is by land, although, there are airports in Angeles and Baguio and you can take a bus from either of these two points. From Manila, the trip to Dagupan takes roughly five hours. Byron, Dagupan, Five Star, Saulog, Victory, and Viron all go to Dagupan; all but Saulog have buses to Lingayen; Byron, Dagupan, Five Star, and Victory have trips to Alaminos; and Dagupan and Five Star go all the way to Bolinao.

To points north, MPCI has minibuses to San Fernando in La Union; trips are frequent and start at 4:30am with the last at 6:00pm. Dagupan and Philippine Rabbit have hourly buses to Baguio.

WHERE TO STAY

SAN FABIAN PTA BEACH RESORT, *Bolasi, San Fabian. Tel. 2052. Manila reservations: Tel. 812-1984, Fax 812-1164. 16 rooms. $21-36 per single, $24-52 per double, $105 per suite, $7 per person dorm or tent. Visa, Master Card, American Express, Diners.*

This is a great place. Some rooms are impressively done with native decor and furniture. Some rooms are spacious. All rooms, except the dorm, are air conditioned, clean, and carpeted. There is a restaurant and camp grounds.

SAN FABIAN RESORT & BEACH CLUB, *Bolasi, San Fabian. Pager: 150-311-511. 15 rooms. $25-69 per single or double.*

This place has simple air conditioned rooms. The cheapest rooms have a common bathroom and the most expensive ones can fit 4-6 people. There is a swimming pool and a restaurant.

SIERRA VISTA BEACH RESORT, *Nabaliw West, San Fabian. Tel. 7532, Fax 7668. 16 rooms. $44 per single, $55 per double.*

Rooms are clean and air conditioned. This is a nice place with a swimming pool, restaurant, and bar.

WINDSURF RESORT, *Alacan, San Fabian. Cellular Tel. 0912-305-5101. 16 rooms. $16 per single or double.*

This pleasant place has nice native-style cottages on a private beach. Rooms have bamboo furniture, are fan-cooled, and have bathrooms. They have windsurfing and the restaurant serves Swiss and Filipino dishes.

DAGUPAN VILLAGE HOTEL, *Lucao District, Dagupan City. Tel. 522-2074. 25 rooms. $30 per single or double.*

Rooms are air conditioned and have television. There is a swimming pool and a restaurant.

LINGAYEN GULF RESORT, *Capitol, Lingayen. Tel. 542-6304. Manila reservations: Tel. 812-1984, Fax 812-1164. 14 rooms, 1 dorm. $30 per single, $40 per double, $130 per suite, $7 per person dorm. Visa, Master Card, American Express, Diners.*

Run by the Philippine Tourism Authority (PTA), this resort is near the Lingayen landing memorial. Rooms are air conditioned, carpeted, and have television. The dorm room is fan-cooled. There are two swimming pools, a restaurant, and a coffee shop.

HUNDRED ISLANDS NATIONAL PARK, *Lucap, Alaminos. Tel. 202-6332. Manila reservations: Tel. 812-1984, Fax 812-1164. **Lucap Point**: 4 rooms, $27-36 per single or double aircon, $18 per single or double nonaircon. **Governor's Island**: 2 cottages, $60 for the large cottage, $15 for the small one. **Children's Island**: 4 rooms, $21-54 per room.*

Only the Lucap Point lodging has air conditioning. There is no electricity on the islands; kerosene and water (to bathe) are provided; bring all your food and drinking water. The large cottage on Governor's can accommodate up to eight people.

LS MARINA 100, *Lucap, Alaminos. Soriano Tel. 655-3643. $26 per single or double aircon, $16 per single or double nonaircon.*

This pleasant place is good value and has nice clean rooms in an A-frame house. It is by the waterfront and there are restaurants nearby.

LAST RESORT, *Lucap, Alaminos. Cellular Tel. 0912-300-8617. 27 rooms. $21 per single or double aircon, $16 per single or double nonaircon, $4 per extra person.*

Last Resort is by the sea and has some nice rooms. There is a restaurant and a souvenir shop. Banca rental arrangements can be made for you.

OCEAN VIEW, *Lucap, Alaminos. Manila reservations: c/o Ms. Rabina Tel. 732-4668. 14 rooms. $25 per single or double aircon, $11.50 per single or double nonaircon, $6 per extra person.*

Rooms are clean and good value. There is a small restaurant.

MAXIME'S BY THE SEA, *Lucap, Alaminos. Cellular Tel. 0912-304-9461. 22 rooms. $25 per single or double aircon, $15 per single or double nonaircon.*

Rooms are small and very basic. There is a restaurant and *banca* rentals can be arranged.

LOURDES CAASI'S, *Patar Beach, Bolinao. 2 cottages. $25 per cottage.*

Lourdes has two beautiful native cottages on a very pretty white coral and sand beach. You will have to bring your own food and drinks. There are plans to add a disco.

WHERE TO EAT

Eating in *Alaminos* is nothing exciting; you can have reasonably good meals at two of the hotels listed above: **MAXIME'S** and **LAST RESORT**.

BANGSAL, *Binmaley*, on the road to Dagupan, has good food at good value.

SIAPNO'S, *Dagupan*, has good seafood; try the *sinigang na sugpo*, a tasty prawn and vegetable sour soup. This restaurant probably has the best seafood in the area ($10-20 per person).

D'ORIGINAL DAWEL, *Dagupan*, serves good, inexpensive seafood in a rustic setting.

For San Fabian, refer to the list of hotels above.

SEEING THE SIGHTS

Bonoan Blue Beach, Dagupan, was the landing site of US liberation forces; a statue on the beach commemorates this event. **Dagupan City** is Pangasinan's bustling business center. There is a busy market.

North of Dagupan, **San Fabian** has an okay beach with a number of simple resorts.

Heading west of Lingayen, **Cabalitian Island**, near Sual, has lovely beaches, but unfortunately has recently been afflicted with a thermal plant.

Next is **Alaminos** and its off-shore islands (see the *Hundred Islands* section below).

Bolinao is a less frequented spot and has a pretty white sand beach. This area, on the northwestern tip of Pangasinan, was once a booming trade center. Some human remains unearthed here date to the 11th and 12th century and have gold face masks, an indication of wealth. The **Bolinao Museum** has a few of the relics; most of the finds are in the National Museum in Manila. Bolinao Museum is open weekdays and Saturday morning.

As you gaze up at the impressive Spanish **Saint James fortress church**, you can quickly see that it was designed to serve as a fort during times of attack. The area has long been visited by many types of ocean-going vessels. The church's façade has remained unaltered since the 17th century and its Aztec-like decor will remind you that the Philippines' links with Spain came through Mexico.

On Saturday mornings, the Plaza fronting the church turns into a **market**, with people selling handicrafts: bags and mats woven from *buri* palm, handbags, shell ornaments, knives, and bamboo cake — a rice cake that is cooked in large bamboo segments and lasts several days.

En route to the **Piedra Point Lighthouse**, you pass lovely small beaches, among them, **Patar Beach**. The lighthouse is a 30-minute tricycle ride from Bolinao. The view from the area is really special. **Dendro Beach** nearby is spectacular, great for swimming and snorkeling, and at the northern end of it, an underground river emerges. Six kilometers inland is a very **pretty waterfall**; get a local guide as it is not easy to find.

Near Bolinao are several interesting islands to explore. If you wish to go **island hopping**, rent a banca from Picocobuan, Bolinao's port. **Cangaluyan**, ringed with a squishy white beach, has good snorkeling. There have been some noteworthy archaeological finds on **Tagaporo** (Dewey). **Silaqui**, with beautiful beaches and good snorkeling and diving, is being used by marine biologists for coral transplant experiments. And **Santiago Island**, off Bolinao, hosted the first Spanish settlement in the area. For safety reasons, the Spanish moved to the mainland in 1609. The west side of Santiago has several good white beaches.

To get further off the beaten track, head to **Umbrella Rocks** at **Sabangan Beach, Agno**. Here, the Balincaguin River exits gently into the sea at a nice dark-sand beach that has several mushroom-shaped lime-stone formations. There is a pretty 18th-century church in Agno.

EXCURSIONS & DAY TRIPS
Hundred Islands

Except during busy holidays, the Hundred Islands is a great escape. Find "your own" little white sand coral islet where you can swim, relax, tan, and snorkel. The **Hundred Islands National Park** is a 20-minute banca ride from barangay Lucap, about two and a half kilometers from Alaminos.

Pay the 50¢ entry fee at the administrators office; this small sum supports having banca traffic and tariffs regulated and reasonable. Before leaving for an island, arrange the pick-up time. Pay for the banca when you return to Lucap. For extensive island hopping, you will have to negotiate prices with the *banqueros*. When seas are rough, the crossing to the islands may be unsafe. Occasionally, conditions render some islands inaccessible while others are easily reached.

Bring sun block, a hat, and other cover ups as it is very easy to get burned. You will also have to bring drinks and food. Not all islands have shade, so if you are sensitive to the sun, ask the boatman to take you to an island with shade.

Some islands have **caves** and areas to explore. If you intend to wander off the beach, bring sneakers or sturdy shoes. Do be careful, there are snakes on several islands. Snorkeling is great off a number of islands, and diving is available: **wreck diving** is the primary interest here. If you intend to dive, make arrangements through **Ocean Deep Diver Training Center**, *Barangay San Francisco, San Fernando, La Union, Tel. 41-4440*; or any of the Manila dive operators listed in Chapter 7, *Sports & Recreation*.

OUR FAVORITE ISLANDS

• **Carias** *has a nice long beach.*

• **Cathedral** *has domed rock formations with a cave inhabited by large fruit bats.*

• **Children's** *has good views and well maintained paths. It is guarded, has bathroom facilities, and overnight camping is permitted.*

• **Clave** *has a pretty little cove and good snorkeling, but not much shade. It is difficult to access during rough seas.*

• **Duque** *(Roque) has a nice beach.*

• **Governor's** *has beaches on both sides of the island, paved steps to a nice panorama of the park, a house for the Governor, and a cottage you may rent.*

• **Kagaw** *(Devil) has the best diving in the area and a good beach with morning shade.*

• **Lopez** *has a nice beach, no shade.*

• **Marcos** *has a nice beach, helipad, and trail that leads to bat-inhabited* **Imelda Cave**.

• **New Scout** *has a small beach and pretty cliffs.*

• **Quezon** *is the largest island. It has a canteen, eating pavilion, concrete walks, decor used by local movie production studios, and good views from the statue of the country's first president, Manuel Quezon.*

• **Quinco** *(Cuenco) is a fun place to explore. It has two small beaches and a cave.*

• **Raganza's** *beach has afternoon shade.*

• **Romulo** *has a good beach with morning shade; during low tide, you can explore its cave.*

• **Scout** *has a nice beach, good snorkeling.*

• **Shell** *has a charming tide pool with many shells. During rough seas, the waves crash between the broken halves of the island and create beautiful cascades down limestone. This is a preserve. It is illegal to take corals or shells away with you. Do not spearfish either.*

PRACTICAL INFORMATION

Banks

PNB, **PCI**, **MetroBank**, **Far East**, and **BPI** all have branches on *AB Fernandez Avenue, Dagupan.* **PCI** has a branch on *Quezon Avenue, Alaminos.*

Film

Photographers can get good supplies at **Fred's**, *Perez Street, Dagupan.*

Mail
The post office is near the PNB in Dagupan.

Tourist Information
The regional office of the DOT is in San Fernando, La Union. **The Pangasinan Tourism Council** has an office in Lingayen, *Tel. 542-6013;* look for BM Roger Law.

LA UNION

La Union was once a favorite excursion place for people spending a holiday in **Baguio**, the summer capital of the Philippines. In the past few years, a number of Bauang's beach resorts have been leased out to Australian managers who cater to low and medium budget tours, often primarily for men. Consequently, the area has lost much of its family atmosphere.

Many beaches line the coast of La Union; most are nice dark sand. The area also has ruins and old churches, historical sites, and museums to visit.

ARRIVALS & DEPARTURES

Like Pangasinan, access is by road. The ride from Manila to San Fernando takes roughly six hours. Autobus, Dagupan, Maria de Leon, Philippine Rabbit, and Times all have frequent trips. All of these companies continue to Vigan, Ilocos Sur, and Maria de Leon goes on to Laoag and Pagudpud, Ilocos Norte.

The hour-long trip from Baguio is served by Philippine Rabbit, Times, and Viron.

WHERE TO STAY

AGOO PLAYA, *Agoo. Cellular Tel. 0912-308-2614. Manila reservations: Tel. 631-2871, Fax 631-2861. 42 rooms. $62-68 per single, $68-73 per double. Visa, Master Card.*

Rooms are simple, air conditioned, and could use renovation. There is a swimming pool and a beach. The restaurant serves very tasty Filipino food and the staff are friendly.

EL CASERON, *Caba. $67 per single or double, $8 per extra person, breakfast included.*

This is a charming turn-of-the-century-style place. Common areas have stone-block walls, capiz shell windows, and antique-looking furnishing. Rooms are comfortable and have a verandah. The staff is friendly.

CABAÑA BEACH RESORT, *Paringao, Bauang. Tel. 412-284, Fax 414-496. 29 rooms. $39-43 per single or double, $6 per extra bed. Visa and Master Card.*

This is an attractive native-style place. The buildings are made of bamboo and timber with nipa roofs. Rooms are clean and air conditioned. Facilities include a curving swimming pool, minigolf, small gym, beauty parlor, water sports for rent, and a dive center. There is a restaurant and a bar.

COCONUT GROVE, *Paringao, Bauang. Tel. 414-276, Fax 415-381. 20 rooms. $30-50 per single or double.*

Rooms are in a white cement building with nipa roofs. All are air conditioned and simply furnished with native decor. Facilities include a swimming pool, lawn bowling, billiards, and a dive center. The restaurant serves Filipino and western dishes.

BALI HAI, *Paringao, Bauang. Tel. 412-504, Fax 415-479. 35 rooms. $43 per single or double aircon, $35-72 per single or double nonaircon. Visa, Master Card.*

The most expensive rooms are not air conditioned because they are large two-room "family" cottages. All rooms are inside native-style nipa cottages. There is a restaurant, swimming pool, and bar.

SUNSET PALMS, *Paringao, Bauang. Tel. 413-708. $15 per single or double.*

This simple place with nice fan-cooled rooms has a swimming pool, tennis, aquasports, and a restaurant.

ACAPULCO, *San Francisco, San Fernando. Tel. 412-696. 36 rooms. $30 per single or double.*

This hotel is located on a nice white sand beach. Rooms are simple and air conditioned. There is a restaurant.

OCEAN DEEP, *San Francisco, San Fernando. Tel. 414-440. 8 rooms. $11.50 per single, $15.50 per double, $19.50 per triple.*

Simple rooms and meals.

LAS VILLAS, *Ili Norte, San Juan. Tel. 412-267. 5 rooms. $23 per single or double, $55 per suite.*

This is a nice-looking Spanish villa-style resort. Rooms are air conditioned. There is a swimming pool, restaurant, and bar.

SUNSET BEACH RESORT, *Montemar, San Juan. Tel. 414-719. 2 rooms. $19 per single or double.*

Rooms are clean, simple, fan-cooled, and have a bathroom. There is a restaurant.

MONA LIZA COTTAGES, *Urbiztondo, San Juan. Tel. 414-892. 6 rooms. $16-18 per single or double.*

This is a simple place, two rooms have private bathrooms, and they serve food.

WHERE TO EAT

Most of the resorts mentioned have restaurants. **AGOO PLAYA**, *Agoo*, has very good Filipino food; and **EL CASERON**, *Caba*, has good home-cooked meals.

DRIFTWOOD, *beside Acapulco in San Francisco, San Fernando*, has good food, great Caesar salad and baked mussels.

For a quick snack, there is an **ice cream house** near the Agoo Cathedral.

SEEING THE SIGHTS

In Agoo there is a lovely **museum**, open Monday-Saturday, and the **Agoo-Damortis National Seashore** is a nice place to walk. You can head inland towards Baguio, along the Marcos Highway, to see the Mount Rushmore-like bust of Ferdinand Marcos. The area was once a park and the limestone monument is weathering so that the past president looks like he has a runny nose.

A long brown-sand beach spans the coast of **Bauang**. There are a number of resorts with bars and restaurants, and some have diving facilities. The beach is safe for swimming except during rough weather. Early in the morning you can watch the fisherfolk drag their nets and bring in the catch. By **Poro Point**, there is a stretch of cream sand beach.

You can dive off Poro Point and see caves, walls, reefs with pretty coral and marine life (including sharks, morays, and barracudas), three World War Two tanks, and World War Two wrecks. A few resorts in Bauang have dive centers, and arrangements can be made through **Ocean Deep Diver Training Center**, *Barangay San Francisco, San Fernando, La Union, Tel. 41-4440*; or any of the Manila dive operators listed in Chapter 7, *Sports & Recreation*.

In **Naguilian**, off the Naguilian road to Baguio, you can sometimes watch basi, a sugarcane based liquor, being made. North of Bauang, a turn-off from the seaward side of the highway leads you to the haunting yet pretty **Pindangan Ruins**. These remains of a small church lie covered in vines beside a small Carmelite monastery.

San Fernando is the capital of La Union. Behind the Capitol Building, perched on a hill, is a museum with displays of Ilocano life, and a loom used for weaving Ilocano cloth.

Behind San Fernando, **Bacsil Ridge** was the site of bloody fighting during World War Two. The Japanese captured the area and dug into the ridge. From here they controlled the entry to the largest port in the north. The Americans recaptured the ridge by coming in from the valleys behind.

Ma-cho Chinese Temple, just north of the capital, is a religious center for the many Chinese residents. Every year, the Virgin of Caysasay makes the seven- or eight-hour journey from Batangas to be worshipped here for a day.

On your way north, you may see pottery displayed along the road in **Tabuc, San Juan**. In Balaoan, a road heads seaward off the main highway to a lovely inlet, **Darigayos Cove**.

In La Union's northernmost town, **Bangar**, you can watch women weave, listen to the rhythmic clinking of the looms' bamboo counter-weights, and buy pretty blankets, runners, and other items quite cheaply ($10 for a nice queen-sized blanket). If you are headed north, turn left on the first small street. Two blocks further on the right side, you will find the weavers in Mrs. de Castro's compound, *39 San Flaviano Street*.

PRACTICAL INFORMATION
Banks

Allied Bank, **BPI**, **MetroBank**, **PNB**, and **PCI** have branches on *Quezon Avenue, San Fernando*. And **PNB** has a branch on the *National Highway, Agoo*.

Tourist Information

The Ilocos Region **DOT** office is in San Fernando. Ask the staff for maps and information.

14. ILOCOS

Ilocos Norte and **Sur** are Luzon's northwest coastal provinces. The area is home to several beautiful and imposing old Spanish churches, a preserved "colonial" city, and pretty beaches. **Vigan**, in Ilocos Sur, has preserved an old-world-ambiance, with ancient houses lining its cobblestone streets.

The early settlers, probably the Dumagats (Negritoes) and Tinguians (of Malay ancestry), were pushed inland by subsequent waves of immigrants. The region gets its name from its next settlers. These people lived along the shores where they set up villages in coves, called *loco* or *looc* in the native dialect. Consequently, the people were named *y-loco*.

In 1574, the Ilocos region, then called Nueva Segovia, stretched from Pangasinan through some towns of the Cagayan Valley and included parts of Northern Luzon's inland provinces. In the mid-18th century, the seat of the northern diocese of Nueva Segovia was moved from Lal-loc, Cagayan to Vigan because the Spaniards found the Ilocanos easier to deal with than the people of the valley.

The Spanish introduced tobacco, and, finding the crop very responsive to the soil and climate, they forbade the farmers to grow anything else and made the farmers sell all the tobacco to the government. As a result of that one-sided deal, the Ilocanos resisted and circumvented the law whenever possible. In the face of determined rebellion in 1881, King Alfonso XII replaced the monopoly.

Ilocanos, known as hard working, pioneering people, have settled and resettled many areas. Immigrant Ilocano populations can be found in many parts of the country.

In Ilocos Norte and Sur, the climate is dry and hot from November through mid-February, and very hot through April. Rainy season starts in May and is heaviest in August and September. The best time to visit is November through January, when the weather is cooler and dry.

ILOCOS NORTE

Long before the arrival of the Spaniards, Filipinos had established trade with the Chinese and Japanese. On February 2, 1818, a royal decree issued by King Ferdinand of Spain proclaimed Ilocos Norte a province. Ilocos Norte is bordered by the South China Sea on its north and west, and to its east are the Cordilleras.

The capital, **Laoag**, is the commercial center and is currently being developed as a major port.

ARRIVALS & DEPARTURES

By Air

Laoag has a small international airport. There are frequent **Philippine Airline** flights from Taiwan, a short plane ride from Laoag. Philippine Airlines also has four flights a week between Manila and Laoag; flying time is 80 minutes.

By Land

From Manila, the trip to Laoag takes about 10 hours. AutoBus, Dagupan, Maria de Leon, Philippine Rabbit, and Times all have daily trips. Maria de Leon continues to Pagudpud, a further 90 minutes.

GETTING AROUND

Ferdinand Marcos, the most illustrious Ilocano of Philippines' recent history, developed a good west coast road system. Many roads were cemented and even small barangay roads were asphalted. These roads, unlike the majority in the country, have withstood time, weathering, and use. Thus, travel on them continues to be pleasant and comfortable.

The most convenient way to tour is by hired vehicle. Most hotels will make hire arrangements, as will the staff at the city tourism office. If your funds are tight, use the jeepneys and minibuses that ply between towns.

WHERE TO STAY

We prefer heading directly to Pagudpud for pleasant lodging amid pretty surroundings; or to stay in Vigan, in Ilocos Sur. There are a few places to stay in Laoag.

FORT ILOCANDIA, *Calayab, Laoag City. Tel. 772-1166 to 70, Fax 772-1411. Manila reservations: Tel. 521-6655, 521-3197. $140 per single, $152 per double, $205 per suite, $20 per extra person. Visa, Master Card, American Express, Diners.*

The hotel is an attractive Spanish-style building. Rooms are dark, air conditioned, have cable television, and could use renovation. Taiwanese tour groups account for most of the guests. Facilities include a business

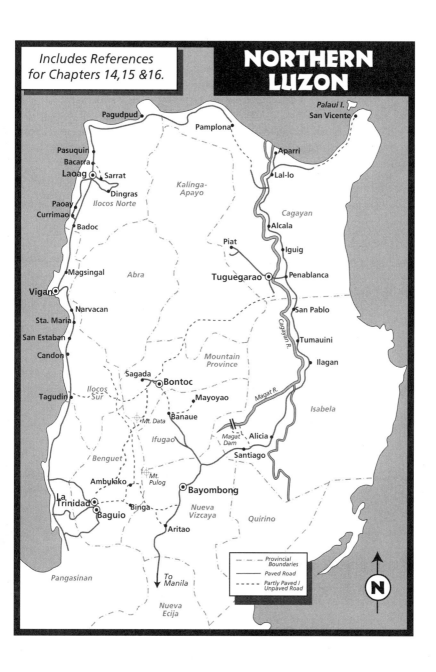

Includes References for Chapters 14,15 &16.

NORTHERN LUZON

center, swimming pool, tennis, shooting range, beauty salon, and a casino. Arrangements for golf and tours are available. Other services include laundry, foreign exchange, and mail. There are Chinese, Filipino, and Japanese restaurants, and for evening entertainment, a club and karaoke bar. Service can be quite slow.

TEXICANO HOTEL, *Rizal Street, Laoag City. Tel. 772-0290. $14-23 per single or $16-25 per double aircon, $5-8 per single or double non aircon, $32-37 per suite.*

This is an old hotel and we suggest that you opt for the more expensive rooms or suites. The restaurant serves tasty Chinese and local food; interesting memorabilia decorate the walls.

PICHAY LODGING, *P Lazaro corner Hernando Street., Laoag City. Tel. 772-1267. $13 per single or double or $16 per triple aircon, $9-10 per nonaircon room.*

Simple clean rooms, and there is a restaurant.

CASA LLANES, *P Lazaro corner V Llanes Street, Laoag City. Tel. 772-1125. 16 rooms. $12 per single or double aircon, $7.60 per single or double nonaircon.*

Rooms are simple and clean, and there is a restaurant.

D'CORRAL BEACH RESORT, *Pias Sur, Currimao. Tel. 772-1133. $18 per single, $27 per double, $55-79 per cottage.*

This place is on a nice beach with simple, native cottages and a restaurant.

WHERE TO EAT

FORT ILOCANDIA, *Calayab.*
Decent food that is nicely presented.

FIESTA ILOCANDIA, *Nolasco Street, Laoag City.*
Serves local cuisine. The restaurant is bright and casual.

CONCORDE, *10 Paco Roman Street, Laoag City.*
Serves local and western dishes. The outside looks like a plane, giving it character.

KIU TIONG HUM, *Texicano Hotel, Rizal Street, Laoag City.*
Good Chinese food and interesting decor.

SEEING THE SIGHTS

Laoag, which means light in Ilocano, has an impressive cathedral and bell tower. The 18th century **Cathedral of St. William** is a squat, solid Italian Renaissance example of earthquake baroque (the term used to describe the architecture used here to create sturdy, quake-resistant church buildings). Its attractive façade has two layers of columns that divide it visually into two storys. The **bell tower**, which is two blocks away from the cathedral, was a later addition. It was built on sandy soil, ignoring biblical warnings against building on sand, and has been sinking constantly since. At present, half the door is below ground level — when the tower was first built, the door was tall enough for a man to ride a horse through it.

The **Ilocos Museum**, in the capitol building, displays some interesting Ilocano items and mannequins that show the lifestyles and dress of tribes from Northern Luzon. The **Tobacco Monopoly Monument**, in the Plaza fronting the provincial capitol building, was erected in 1882 to thank the King of Spain when he abolished the tobacco monopoly.

SHOPPING

The **market** buzzes with activity on Wednesday and Sunday. You will find a good assortment of handicrafts from the coast and mountain areas, *albularios* (herbalists) selling cures for ailments, and garlic (during dry months), which is inexpensive here as it is grown in abundance in the Ilocos region.

EXCURSIONS & DAY TRIPS

You can enjoy a number of half-day trips from the city. Day trips can take you to the beautiful beach of Pagudpud or down south to Vigan in Ilocos Sur.

Rental vehicles can be arranged in Laoag and through the resorts on Pagudpud. Maria de Leon buses continue from Laoag to Pagudpud; the trip takes 90 minutes. Jeepneys and minibuses also ply this route.

Paoay Circle

This circle-trip first takes you to the **Malacañang of the North**, or *Balay ti Amianan* in Ilocano, the northern base of former President Marcos. The extensive manicured grounds are well kept. Beside it is the **Paoay Lake Golf Course**, a scenic 18-hole course that runs along the edge of the lake.

According to legend, the people who once lived here were very materialistic. God warned them to change; when they did not, he punished them by sinking their town. In fact, **Lake Paoay** was created in the 18th century by a cyclone.

South of the lake, the imposing **Paoay church** is one of the few Spanish churches designed by Filipinos. The church architecture shows the influence of the Indonesian Madjapahit Empire whose ties with the Philippines antedate the Spaniards' arrival. If you are here on a Saturday morning, there is a market beside the church where you may find beautiful woven products and a few handicrafts.

From Paoay, a coastal road leads to **Currimao**, a fishing town with a nice beach. There are some nice views if you continue north along the coast from Currimao.

Further south of Currimao, in the town of **Badoc**, is the **Juan Luna Museum**. This is where national artist Juan Luna was born. His house has been restored and furnished with period pieces and reproductions of his paintings. Head back north to complete the circle.

In **Batac**, east of Paoay, is the **Marcos Museum**. At the renovated ancestral home of the former president you can see his memorabilia and his preserved body.

Dingras, 22 kilometers southeast of Laoag, was established in 1598 as an outpost for trade. Here, the Spanish built a truly monumental church, which has been damaged several times by quake and fire. Magnificent in ruins, it must have been truly an awesome sight when whole. Nearby, a smaller church serves the community.

Continue eastward through Solsana where the road returns west to Laoag. In **Sarrat**, the Spanish built their last Ilocos church. **Sta Monica church** has been destroyed twice by earthquake and has recently been restored from massive damage. The impressive *convento* is attached to the church by a very attractive brick stairway. The *convento* once served many purposes, including a basement jail where rebellious natives were held by the Spanish.

North To Pagudpud

North of Laoag, **Bacarra church** is magnificent and has an equally impressive *convento*. The church's **leaning bell tower** was toppled by an earthquake in 1984.

After the town of Pasuquin, a small road turns right off the national highway and heads upward to the **Cape Bojeador Lighthouse**. Climb to the top for a terrific view of the coast and fields below. The lighthouse was built in 1892 and, on a clear day, its light can be seen 14 nautical miles away.

Continue north to a rise where you get a lovely panorama of the pretty **Bangui Valley**. On the far side of the valley is **Pagudpud**. Its **Saud Beach** is one of the world's most beautiful coastlines. Situated in a picturesque cove are miles of fine golden sand fringed by azure water. This is a casual traveler's paradise. You may snorkel off shore, admire pretty sunsets, and relax on the fine sand as the waves break gently on the beach. A few kilometers further north, a road winds through huts and coconut trees to **Mara-Ira**, where you will find another pretty sand beach, but no facilities — bring a packed lunch for a peaceful picnic.

Where to Stay

When this book was published, there was a public phone office in Pagudpud, but no private telephones. You may contact the resorts through the operator; ask to be connected to **Pagudpud**, *Tel. 131-13, 131-14.*

SAUD BEACH RESORT, *Saud Beach, Pagudpud. Manila reservations: Tel. 921-2856. Laoag reservations: Tel. 772-1704. 8 rooms. $64-78 per single or double.*

This place is an attractive white building with a nipa roof. Rooms are air conditioned, clean, and have native furnishing. Rooms sizes vary with cost. The restaurant prepares good fresh seafood and the menu is limited.

VILLA DEL MAR, *Saud Beach, Pagudpud. Manila reservations: Tel. 928-2856, 921-0626. 21 rooms. $40-60 per single or double aircon, $30 per single or double nonaircon, $36 per cottage.*

This is a nice simple place, the first resort on this beach. The owners and staff are friendly and accommodating. Rooms are in a cement building and have bathrooms. The cottage is fan-cooled. The restaurant serves seafood, Filipino, and western dishes.

IVORY BEACH RESORT, *Saud Beach, Pagudpud. $25-30 per single or double.*

This is a simple place and some cottages have private bathrooms.

PRACTICAL INFORMATION FOR LAOAG CITY

Banks

PNB, **PCI Bank**, and **BPI** are on *Rizal Avenue*; **Allied Bank**, and **Far East Bank** are on *Bonifacio Street*; and **MetroBank** is on *Nolasco Street*.

Tourist Information

Assistance and information is available weekdays from:
• the **Ilocos Norte Tourism Council**, *Capitol, Tel. 722-1166 to 70, local Tel. 2029, ask for Mr. Rogelio Bangsil*; or
• the Laoag suboffice of the **DOT**, *Ilocano Heroes Hall, Tel. 772-0467*

ILOCOS SUR

In 1572, Don Juan de Salcedo, grandson of Miguel de Legazpi, arrived in **Vigan**. He named the area Villa Fernandina, after the king's son. Salcedo patterned Vigan after Intramuros, the city created by his grandfather. The Cathedral was built between 1790 and 1800, shortly after the seat of Nueva Segovia was moved to Vigan. Much of the city was constructed by wealthy Chinese merchants and artisans, ancestors of today's aristocracy. Unlike Intramuros, Vigan was relatively unscathed by World War Two.

Anti-Spanish sentiment was strong in the region, and this was expressed through overt and covert activities. The Malong Revolt occurred in 1660-1661; during 1762-1763, Diego Silang was among the many who rose in open and violent revolt. After he was killed, his wife, Gabriella, continued the battle until she was captured and executed. Other revolts occurred in 1807, 1815, and 1898.

Today, people visit Ilocos Sur for a glimpse of the past. Although most of the commerce and influential citizens of the area have moved to Manila, Laoag, and San Fernando, Vigan remains a genteel reminder of the not-always genteel past. Other remainders of the past include a few impressive old Spanish churches.

ARRIVALS & DEPARTURES

The most common way to travel to Ilocos Sur is by land from Manila, although you could fly to Baguio or Laoag and take a bus from those points. Philippine Airlines has daily flights to Baguio and flies four times a week to Laoag.

From Manila, the trip to Vigan takes about eight hours. AutoBus, Dagupan, Maria de Leon, Philippine Rabbit, and Times all have daily trips.

From Baguio, it is a three-hour bus ride to Vigan. Philippine Rabbit, Times, and Viron all serve this route.

GETTING AROUND

If you do not have your own means of transportation, intertown travel is possible by tricycle, jeepney, minibus, and (sometimes) *calesa*.

WHERE TO STAY

Unless otherwise noted, the accommodations below are in Vigan.

VILLA ANGELA HERITAGE, *Quirino Boulevard. Tel. 722-2914, 722-2755, 722-2756. 6 rooms. $40 per single or double aircon, $23 per single or double nonaircon.*

A favorite of many frequent visitors, this is a charming restored mansion. Much of the place is tastefully furnished with antique family relics and memorabilia. Villa Angela is a fine example of an "old-world" wealthy family's residence. Rooms are clean, cozy, and furnished with antiques. Large groups are preferred and meals are served. You will find the staff very hospitable.

RF ANICETO MANSION, *Plaza Burgos. Tel. 722-2383. 11 rooms. $25 per single or double, $29 per triple, $32 per quad.*

A lovely and well-renovated ancestral home. The common area is impressive with antique chandeliers and lamps, and elaborately carved furniture and grandfather clock. Attractive red-brick arches lead you down the dark stone corridor to a red-brick and stone well. A wide, solid-wood stair with balustrade leads you to the cozy air conditioned rooms; some are small, so inspect first. The restaurant serves some very tasty dishes; stick to the local specialties. The staff is friendly.

CORDILLERA INN, *M Crisologo Street. Tel. 722-2526, Fax 722-2840. 23 rooms. $37-41 per single or double aircon, $15 per single or double nonaircon. Manila reservations: 58-2114.*

This is a nice place with dark, clean rooms. Only the aircon rooms have private bathrooms. The staff are friendly and efficient. If you are flying into Laoag, they will make arrangements to pick you up. The restaurant serves good local food.

EL JULIANA, *Quirino Boulevard. Tel. 722-2994. 27 rooms. $30 per single or double.*

Rooms are air conditioned and have private bathrooms. There is a swimming pool and a restaurant.

GRANDPA'S INN, *1 Bonifacio Street. Tel. 722-2118. 19 rooms. $16 per single or double aircon, $10 per single or double nonaircon.*

This pace is cozy and has pleasant clean rooms, all with private bathrooms. The staff are friendly and there is a restaurant.

GORDION, *15 Salcedo Street. Tel. 722-2526. $16 per single or double aircon.*

Rooms are clean, air conditioned, and have private bathrooms. The air conditioned dorm room can accommodate up to 20 people.

VIGAN HOTEL, *Burgos Street. Tel. 722-2588. 7 rooms. $18 per single or double aircon, $12 per single or double nonaircon.*

This is a nice old compound that has a popular restaurant-bar and can be noisy in the evenings. Rooms are simple, dark, and could use renovation. Inspect the rooms and check the bathrooms before chosing.

FERNANDINA HOTEL, *Mabini Street. Tel. 722-2964. $14-18 per single or double aircon.*

This is a nice, friendly place with air conditioned, clean rooms. The more expensive ones have private bathrooms. There is a restaurant.

TEP-PENG COVE, *Tep-Peng, Sinait, north of Vigan. Tel-Fax 722-2526. $33 per single or double aircon, $23-33 per single or double nonaircon. Manila reservations: 58-2114.*

This is a nice place on a beach near Vigan. All rooms have a private bathroom, and the more expensive non-aircon rooms are in simple native-style cottages. Kayaks and jet-skis are available for rent.

ILOCOS MARINA RESORT, *Sabangan, Santiago, south of Vigan. Tel. 742-6136 (c/o the Mayor's office, look for Emie Lou Robañez). 10 rooms. $33 per single or double aircon.*

This a is an attractive place on a great beach. There is a swimming pool and a restaurant.

WHERE TO EAT

In Vigan, most of the hotels have restaurants that serve Ilocano and other Filipino dishes, and some simple western dishes. For a delicious afternoon snack (after 2:00pm) try the *impanada*, a meat or vegetable pastry, from the stalls around Plaza Burgos.

CAFÉ FLORECITA, *RF Aniceto Mansion, Plaza Burgos.*

Serves good Ilocano food. Chinese and American dishes are also available. The ambiance is pleasant as you dine on antique-looking wood tables beneath the brick arches.

COOL SPOT, *Vigan Hotel, Burgos Street.*

A popular place for Ilocano and Filipino food. The restaurant-bar is in a wood and nipa pavilion in the garden on the grounds of the Vigan Inn but separate from the hotel rooms.

MAGNOLIA CAFE, *Plaza Burgos on Florentino Street.*

The cafe serves tasty quick meals and snacks and is air conditioned.

SEEING THE SIGHTS

Vigan is a small town. All sights are within walking distance, and you can probably see all in half a day. Or, you can tour by *calesa* – this is one of the few cities where *calesas* are still used.

The imposing **Vigan Cathedral**, built between 1790 and 1800, has some impressive stained glass windows. The **bell tower**, separated from the church by Burgos Street, stands on **Plaza Burgos**. The nearby **Archbishops Palace** took seven years to build and was completed in 1793. Note its attractive sliding capiz windows and floral decorations. Secured and on display inside are ecclesiastical artifacts and relics.

At the **Ayala Museum** in the Burgos House, you will find an interesting collection of items pertaining to the area's rich history. The dioramas, paintings, artifacts, antiques, and documents are all well-labeled, and the ancient house gives you a real feel for the period. The ground floor contains articles used by the Tinguians, earlier inhabitants of the area. The rest of the first and all of the second story has displays pertinent to the area's history since the Spanish era. Some of the paintings show the gory details of violent incidents. This was the family house of Padre Burgos, one of the three Filipino priests garroted as a warning to natives contemplating action against Spain.

Walk up Quezon Avenue to Liberation Boulevard. Turn left to the **Crisologo Museum**, in the house of Flor Crisologo. The Crisologos are one of Vigan's prominent political families. This museum also exhibits artifacts, documents, and items of the city's past. Most of the items are from the more recent past and give you an interesting insight into Vigan's political scene.

From here, head to Rizal Street where there are two kilns that make **Burnay ware**. This pottery is made from very resilient clay found in the area, fired at a high temperature, and sold throughout the country for water containers, and for aesthetic and other purposes. Once or twice a week, *carabao* come to mix the clay by walking around in it. Chunks of clay are then thrown on foot-powered wheels. At **RG Pottery**, along Rizal Street, the jars are fired in an ancient, almost horizontal kiln that uses heat so inefficiently that several of the pieces collapse, and are then sold inexpensively as unique items. RG Pottery can arrange for shipment of larger purchases to Manila.

Set your own pace and stroll around Vigan to get the feel of the old days. You will see mansions in various stages of construction or in disrepair. Note that the buildings are square: they were designed to serve as warehouses and shops on the ground floor, with the living quarters above. From Plaza Burgos, walk down the cobbled Crisologo Street to see a number of refurbished Spanish-Mexican houses. Enter the **Syquia Mansion** (now **Quirino Museum**) on Quirino Street to see how these houses were furnished during their prime.

SHOPPING

Aside from the Burnay jars, Vigan offers some other good finds. Several **antique shops** on Plaridel, Crisologo, and Bonifacio Streets sell "instant" (newly manufactured) antiques and artifacts, and an occasional really old piece. And for a good assortment of woven and delicate cloth and goods, go to **Hi-Q**, *27 Salcedo Street.*

EXCURSIONS & DAY TRIPS
North Of Vigan

Just northeast of Vigan, **Bantay Church** has a strikingly restored façade that contrasts with the the church's simpler sides. The **bell tower** stands on a mound nearby and commands a good view of the surrounding countryside. *Bantay* means "watch," and this tower is perfectly sited to provide a lookout for intruders from any direction.

Magsingal church, built 1827, is massive and has beautifully carved *retablos*. Above the main *retablo* are two mermaids with suspiciously round bellies; the sculptor's pregnant wife was his model. Beyond the church and striking *convento* are the remains of two previous churches, north of the present structure. Mr. Angel Cortez made a park and **museum** in the ruins of the second church, beside the new one. At the eastern entrance of the park is a stone phallus, believed to be of pre-Hispanic origins, which Mr. Cortez unearthed nearby. The museum once contained much more, but sadly has not been maintained in recent years.

The well-restored second church houses a branch of the **National Museum**. Inside are well arranged and maintained exhibits of Ilocano artifacts with explanatory signs and a collection of pottery and porcelain, a must-see for anyone interested in the area's history and culture. The museum is open daily, 9:00-11:00am and 1:00-5:00pm.

Cabugao church is a massive, low structure.

If you are hungry, you can buy fish and have it grilled for you at Salomague Port, 10 minutes seaward from Cabugao town. It is a pleasant trip inland through bamboo-covered hills and farms.

Pug-os Beach, in Cabugao, is about 30 minutes from Vigan. At this spectacular beach, you may be able to take good photos of fishermen hauling nets into the white sand with green hills beyond. There is a resort at Tep-peng Cove in nearby Sinait (see *Where to Stay*, above).

South Of Vigan

Rancho Beach in Santa was a Japanese landing site during World War Two. **Santa** has a nice little church and some interesting houses.

Further south, prior to the inland road to Abra, is the **Solvec watch tower**.

Just off the highway in **Narvacan**, you may investigate another large Spanish church — its foundations were built over 400 years ago in 1577. Narvacan has a number of interesting old houses, and its church was where Diego Silang held hostages during his revolt against the Spanish government. Both the church and the *convento* are attractive.

The Tinguian tribespeople who were pushed inland still live in **Abra**. As they have had to fight to retain what little land they had, they have learned not to welcome strangers.

Sta Maria church, built in 1769 high on a hill, is massive. It has tiled floors and walls and an attractive façade. As the bell tower was being constructed, the ground beneath it subsided, causing the tower to tilt. If you look carefully, you can see how the builders curved the tower to compensate. Near the church steps, women sometimes sell delicious *bibingka* (rice cakes) in the afternoons. Inland from town, a tricycle can take you to the beautiful **Pinsal Falls**.

The next town, **San Esteban**, has an attractive watch tower; **Atapot Beach**, where American forces landed during World War Two; and the pretty **San Esteban Beach**. Nearby is the lovely deep-water **Santiago Cove**. The area is isolated enough to have been used as a resupply point for guerrillas during the war. The northern side of the cove has a **turreted watch tower**, pretty white beaches, and coral shore lines.

Further south, **Candon church**, built in 1591, has an attractive curvilinear façade. **Darapidap Beach**, three kilometers from the town market, is a long stretch of white-yellow sand — a good place to picnic, swim, or relax. Inland from Candon is the **Tirad Pass**, accessible by jeepney on a very rough road. There, young (22 years old) General Gregorio del Pilar was shot while covering President Emilio Aguinaldo's retreat from American troops.

The southernmost town of Ilocos Sur, **Tagudin**, has an attractive unrestored church and an interesting 19th century sundial. Inland, a rough road goes through the **Besang Pass**, where about 1,500 men lost their lives during the fight to retake this pass from the Japanese during World War Two. The road, which may not be passable during rainy season, continues to the mountain provinces.

PRACTICAL INFORMATION

Banks

Allied Bank, Far East Bank, MetroBank, and PCI all have a branch in Vigan.

Tourist Information

Most of the towns have a tourism office located in the office of the town mayor. The **Ilocos Sur Tourism Council**, *Tel. 722-2740, 722-2746,* is in the Provincial Capitol Building, Vigan, and the **city tourism council**, *Tel. 722-2466,* is in the Vigan Municipal Building.

The regional **DOT** office is in San Fernando, La Union (refer to the Lingayen chapter).

15. THE CORDILLERAS

The central mountains offer you a change of scenery and climate and a whole different cultural experience from Luzon's lowlands. The **Cordillera** region, carved out of Northern Luzon's Cagayan and Ilocos regions, is composed of five provinces — Abra, Benguet, Ifugao, Kalinga-Apayao, and Mountain Province. For reasons of accessibility and safety we have kept our coverage to the central and southern reaches of he Cordilleras: Benguet, Ifugao, and Mountain Province.

Play golf, relax, hike around **Baguio**, the summer capital of the Philippines. This city was built at the turn of the century by Americans and used as an escape from Manila's oppressive summer heat. Go off the beaten track spelunking in the burial caves of **Sagada**, a picturesque mountain town with several interesting limestone formations, waterfalls, and pretty views of terraces. Venture to one of the World's Eighth Wonders: **Banaue's famous rice terraces**, a haven for hikers, trekkers, and photographers who often return to admire the beauty created by nature and by the toil of generations of mountain people.

Witness a *cañao* (festival) and other rituals that antedate the Spanish and American arrival and are still performed today.

CAÑAO

*A **cañao** is a combination of ritual and party. Animal sacrifices are performed to read omens, ask the spirits and gods for assistance, and thank them for favors. Rituals that pertain to each type of cañao are different, but all involve a good deal of eating and drinking. Every November, Baguio's Grand Cañao is held in conjunction with an arts festival.*

Tribes

The Cordillera areas are inhabited by peoples who for centuries have had a separate culture from the lowlanders. Collectively called **Igorots**, they prefer their individual tribal names: Ibaloi, Kankana-ey, Ifugao,

Bontoc, Kalinga, Gaddang, etc. Traditionally, the people lived off the land, earning their living primarily through slash-and-burn farming augmented by panning and mining gold and collecting honey, which they bartered in the lowlands for articles they needed.

When not tending to crops or other chores, women weave strong colorful fabric, traditionally from bark and cotton fibers. Each tribe has its distinguishing pattern. The material is used as blankets, skirts for women, and g-strings for men. Today, most of the mountain people don jeans and shirts, and women often weave cloth from synthetic yarn. You may still see some of the old people wearing the traditional tribal costume, especially during rituals, but only in the most remote areas do women still forgo tops.

You will notice that architecture varies. **Ifugao** houses are grass and wood structures on tall stilts; **Bontoc** houses are close to the ground; and traditional **Sagada** houses are built partly into the ground for protection against the cold. Traditional houses in most areas were small and only accommodated the parents and youngest children. Older children (eight and above) lived in "boarding houses" with others of the same gender. Only a few traditional houses remain near central Sagada. Attractive grass roofs are being replaced by unappealing tin, preferred because it does not catch fire easily. Western-style homes of tin, wood, and stone have replaced most houses of traditional architecture.

All tribes have skilled basket weavers and woodcarvers. Sadly though, as a result of mass production (orders for local souvenirs and items sold in other areas) and western influence (Disney characters and American Indians), most of the carving is monotonously repetitive.

Tribal people treasure their antiques and family heirlooms passed down through generations. They only part with these items in times of dire need, and, when doing so, must perform a ritual to placate the spirits of ancestors. Even though most of the people here are Christian, many still practice their ancient religion, with its pantheon of spirits and numerous rites that are intimately tied to the land and planting.

Before the Spanish arrived, the mountain tribes had distinct cultures and lived in a constant cycle of war, peace, or transitional stages with their neighbors. They were almost always at war with the lowlanders, except when trading. Head taking was considered honorable. Some tribes required a man to prove his prowess to his future wife by presenting a head before marriage was allowed. It was considered a disgrace if a person lost his head. The body was not accorded the usual intricate burial, and relatives of the murdered person had the responsibility for avenging the death, for until this was done, his or her spirit would not rest in peace and would return to its people and make trouble. The by-product was constant warring.

Western Influence

The Spanish attempted to access the mountains, primarily for gold, and well, yes, "to spread the seeds of Christianity." The tribes successfully defended their territory. Until late in the 19th century, any foothold the Spaniards took was eventually recovered. Except for giving the mountain people a new and more dangerous enemy, the Spanish did little to change indigenous culture. Although they claimed to have come to civilize, the Spanish avenged head taking with reciprocal decapitation.

Only when the Americans arrived did outside influences begin to have an impact. The Americans who went into the Cordilleras were rough and ready, willing to live in the tribes' own style, marry mountain girls, raise families, and administer justice in the native way. They built hospitals, schools, trails, and roads. Hence, the Americans were accepted and respected. Eventually, headhunting was officially banned and the incidence of it declined. But you may still see people with tattoos, an indication that they or close family members have completed a head hunt, and the occasional personal vendetta may still result in an offending party having his head separated — elsewhere he might merely have been shot.

Travelers need not be concerned about this in the quiescent areas. Benguet, Ifugao, and Mountain Province are frequently touristed destinations. It is sensible to limit your travel to these areas. Abra and Kalinga-Apayao have been periodic hot-spots and unless you have reliable information that tension has abated in areas you intend to visit, we suggest you give these provinces a miss for now. When traveling in remote areas, be sure to have a companion or guide who is from the area and knows the trails and people.

BAGUIO

Baguio is the best known tourist destination of Benguet, the southernmost province of the Cordillera. Baguio was built at the turn of the century by the Americans. They also constructed the Kennon Road, the first route through which vehicles could access the Cordilleras. The Americans developed Camp John Hay (now Club John Hay) as a place its officials and officers could come for vacation. Baguio became the summer capital, where the government and Manila's elite came to escape the oppressive summer heat of the lowlands. Today, Baguio is a mixture of many life styles, yet some mountain flavor remains.

ARRIVALS & DEPARTURES
By Air

There is usually at least one trip a day from Manila to Baguio and back on **Asian Spirit** and **Philippine Airlines**. The flying time is 50 minutes.

Because of fog conditions, the clouds may roll in as the day progresses, so the flights leave Manila early in the morning and return shortly after landing in Baguio. If, due to weather conditions, the flight cannot land in Baguio, the plane may be rerouted to La Union and passengers are then shuttled to Baguio.

By Land

• **Baguio-Manila**. Several companies ply (fly) the six- or seven-hour trip: Autobus, Dangwa, Philippine Rabbit, Saulog, Times, and Victory all have several daily trips.

• **Baguio-Ilocos Region**. the one-hour trip to San Fernando, La Union is served by Marcita's, Philippine Rabbit, Times, and Viron; to Dagupan, Pangasinan, there are hourly Dagupan and Philippine Rabbit buses; and the three-hour trip to Vigan is served by Philippine Rabbit, Times, and Viron.

• **Baguio-Bontoc-Sagada**. The road trip between Benguet and Mountain Province is a very scenic, and, very rough seven hours. If you go by jeep or bus, you will whiz by the scenery and around corners at amazing speeds. If your funds permit, hire a vehicle for this trip. Pine Tree travels between Bontoc and Baguio, and Dangwa and Lizardo go to Sagada; all have daily early morning trips.

• **Baguio-Banaue**. Dangwa makes this trip once in the morning and once at night via the lowlands. The trip takes 10 hours. The alternative is to take a bus to Bontoc and catch a jeepney from Bontoc to Banaue; the final leg takes about three hours.

ORIENTATION

Three roads provide access from the lowlands. **Kennon** is the oldest and its American builders named points of interest along the way after spots in California's Yosemite National Park — Bridalveil Falls is six kilometers from the beginning, and Colorado Falls is a further two and half kilometers plus a short walk upstream. Along the "zig-zag" portion of the road, a lion's head carved from a huge limestone boulder marks the entrance to Baguio City.

Following one of the regions' oldest foot trails, **Naguilian Road** has been used since time immemorial as access between the mountains and La Union. It is less precipitous than Kennon and is the best route to La Union's beaches and to northern Ilocos.

The newest road, **Marcos Highway**, goes from Agoo in La Union to Baguio. The drive is scenic and takes you past the **Marcos Park**. The visual focal point of the park is the gigantic head of ex-President Ferdinand Marcos; it has long been a controversial monument. Today, the golf course and facilities of the park are overgrown, and weathering has streaked the bust so that the former president has a runny nose.

Average temperature is a comfortable 68°F (20°C). Except during the Easter and Christmas holidays, Baguio is a relaxing place to stroll. During the holidays, the city overflows with lowland visitors and most hotels are booked in advance. As there are numerous places to stay and eat in Baguio, access to food isn't a problem, and public transport is readily available. Bottled water is available at almost all establishments.

GETTING AROUND

Jeepneys and taxis provide transport in and around the city. A number of agencies offer tours: ask for recommendations from your hotel or by the DOT. Additionally, some taxi drivers double as tour guides.

Jeepneys and buses ply deeper into the Cordilleras, unless the road is out due to bad weather and/or landslides. There is at least one daily trip to Sagada and another to Bontoc, and two to Banaue.

Car rental agencies include:
• **A-1**, *Session Road, Tel. 442-8846*
• **Avis**, *Harrison Road, Tel. 442-4018*
• **EMC**, *Session Road*
• **Hertz**, *Session Road, Tel. 442-3045, 442-4601; and John Hay, Tel. 442-7901, 442-7171*
• **Lakbay**, *Harrison Road, Tel. 442-4302*
• **SGS**, *Upper Session Road*
• **Starr**, *37 Harrison Road, Tel. 442-6896*

WHERE TO STAY

Baguio has a wide assortment of places to stay. If your budget allows $100-150 per day for lodging, consider staying at a cottage or room in **Club John Hay**, amid the pines and with access to golf or tennis, children's parks, and a generally quiet environment. If your budget is very tight and you are in transit, you will prefer a simple lodging house. In between are a large number of places ranging from downtown hotels to inns along the roads and in quieter places.

You could probably find a room without reservations at any time except Easter and Christmas, but many Filipinos head for Baguio during Easter through June, so you should call ahead for reservations if you have a specific place or type of accommodation in mind at this time.

The Top End: a Former American Military Country Club
    CLUB JOHN HAY, *in a large semi-wooded area. Tel. 442-7902, Fax, 442-6798. Manila reservations: Tel. 816-7443, Fax 816-7445. 287 rooms in assorted*

facilities. $91 per single or double, $111-220 per cabin. Visa, Master Card, American Express, Diners.

Camp John Hay was an American base used primarily for rest and recreation by soldiers on furlough from other stations. The beautiful, wooded area has numerous facilities, including a respected golf course, driving range, minigolf, tennis courts, skating rink, bowling, hiking trails, and several restaurants.

John Hay is great for families, groups, or for peace and quiet. Many rooms and cabins have fireplaces, which are delightful especially in cold weather. Cabins range from one to four bedrooms, and are priced accordingly. They also have refrigerators, phones, hot water, and cable TV. You may request extra beds, cribs, hair dryers and cutlery. Pony rides are available for children just beyond the gate to Baguio Country Club. Taxis are available at the gates and restaurant areas.

There are plans to build a large hotel complex here. This could change the atmosphere of the area considerably, especially if the builders remove the stands of tall pines to make way for the buildings.

In Town

MOUNT CREST HOTEL, *Legarda corner Urbano Street. Tel. 442-3324, Fax 442-6900. $60-90 per single or double. Visa, Master Card, American Express, Diners.*

This is a very nice, well-managed place. Clean, comfortable rooms come with cable TV and bathrooms. There is a restaurant.

BAGUIO PALACE HOTEL, *Legarda Road. Tel. 442-7734. 28 rooms. $45-75 per single or double.*

Baguio Palace is near Burnham Park, with nice views from the back rooms; rooms are ample size with bathrooms and television. The carpets tend to be musty and the corridors dark. They have a restaurant and easy access to transport.

HOTEL SUPREME, *113 Magsaysay Avenue. Tel. 442-2855. 59 rooms. $35-75 per single or double, $85 per suite. Visa, Master Card.*

Centrally located, the Supreme has comfortable carpeted rooms with telephones, cable TV, refrigerators, and private bathrooms. There is a pool, spa, and restaurant.

NEW BELFRANLT, *General Luna Road. Tel. 442-5014, 442-4298. 33 rooms. $30-75 per single or double. Visa, Master Card.*

Near Saint Louis University, this hotel has carpeted rooms with private bathrooms, and offers massage services.

BAGUIO AMBASSADOR, *25 Abanao Street. Tel. 442-2746, 442-5078. 40 rooms. $16-50 per single or double.*

Rooms in this budget hotel are small and dark, but ceilings are high and bathrooms clean.

ATTIC SWAGMAN INN, *90 Abanao Street. Tel. 442-5139. 20 rooms. $35 per single, $40 per double. Manila reservations: 522-3663.*

Run by an Australian-owned group that gets many single males on tour, this is perhaps not a family place. Rooms are nice and have private bathrooms. The inn will pick you up at the airport (free) and can arrange for transport to other points.

EL CASERON DE LOS PINOS, *Lower P Burgos Street. Tel. 442-6099. Manila reservations: Tel. 61-7631. $30 per single, $43 per double.*

This cozy place has a log-cabin-style interior. Rooms are simple, nice, and clean. There is a restaurant.

BURNHAM HOTEL, *21 Calderon Street. Tel. 442-2331, 442-5117. 17 rooms. $23 per single, $26 per double.*

This budget hotel is good value; all rooms have phones, TV, and private bathrooms.

BADEN POWELL INN, *26 Governor Pack Road. Tel. 442-5836. 51 rooms. $20-34 per single or double, $115 per suite, $5 per person per dorm. Visa, Master Card, American Express, Diners.*

This is a clean, good cozy place; its rooms have private bathrooms. Rooms in the annex (where the suite is) have telephones and a good view of Session Road.

VENY'S INN, *24 Session Road. Tel. 442-2420. 19 rooms. $15-24 per single or double.*

Good for low-budget travelers, rooms are clean, carpeted, and have private bathrooms.

CASA VALLEJO, *Session Road. Tel. 442-3045. 28 rooms. $16-22 per single or double.*

Nice rooms, clean, some have private bathrooms. Restaurant on-site.

PATRIA DE BAGUIO, *Session Road. Tel. 442-5851. 16 rooms. $16-24 per single or double.*

Rooms are nice, clean, and have private bathrooms, high ceilings, and wide windows. There is a restaurant and a bakeshop.

Around Town

HOTEL MONTICELLO, *Mary Heights, off Kennon Road. Tel. 442-6566. 23 rooms. $45-55 per single or double.*

Monticello is a Japanese-style hotel (with ties to Japanese agencies) in a quiet area. Nice rooms with private bathrooms, great views from the balconies of the back rooms, walls are thin. The restaurant serves mostly Japanese food and is a pleasant place to sit.

JADE PENSION, *Marcos Highway near Legarda Road. Tel. 442-2521. 7 rooms. $20 per single or double, $24 per triple.*

This cozy place has comfortable rooms with private bathrooms and a good Chinese restaurant.

EL CIELITO, *North Drive corner Leonard Wood Road. Tel. 442-8743. Manila reservations: Tel. 815-8951. $36 per single, $40 per double. Visa, Master Card.*

This relatively new hotel is in an attractive rose-colored building. The rooms are comfortable, clean, and have private bathrooms. There is a coffee shop and the staff are friendly and helpful.

BAGUIO VACATION HOTEL, *45 Leonard Wood Road, across from the Botanical Gardens. Tel. 442-4545. Manila reservations: Tel. 843-7936. 50 rooms. $46-73 per single, $53-73 per double, $61-73 per triple, $66-73 per quad, $80 per suite. Visa, Master Card, American Express, Diners.*

This hotel is convenient to transport and has a large restaurant. Its rooms have private bathrooms, but are dark and dank.

HOTEL TEPEYAC, *17 Leonard Wood Road, across from the Botanical Gardens. Tel. 442-5167. Manila reservations: Tel. 823-3210. 14 rooms. $35-43 per single or double, $48 per suite.*

This relatively new hotel is similar to a lodge — access to rooms is from a balcony walkway. Rooms are spacious, bathrooms are small. The building is new and cement, and the hotel is in a wooded area. It has a small coffee shop and gift shop, and is convenient to transport.

MUNSAYAC INN, *Leonard Wood Road. Tel. 442-4544. 20 rooms. $25-35 per single or double. Visa, Master Card.*

This converted private home is also the residence of the owners, and is often booked well in advance by repeat customers who know it is a good place and good value. Rooms are comfortable and homey with minibars and private bathrooms. There is cable TV in the common area, great food in the small restaurant, and a good handicrafts shop downstairs. The place is restful and yet accessible to transport. Staff is friendly and helpful.

GILBERTOS, *43 CM Recto. Tel. 442-4367. $24 per single or double, $30 per triple or quad.*

This is a good place for large groups. Some rooms are large and can accommodate up to eight people. Rooms are clean and some have private bathrooms.

PEREDOS, *CM Recto. Tel. 442-5091. $15-30 per single or double.*

This place is in a lovely old house. Room prices vary with size. Bathrooms are shared between rooms. The largest room has a verandah and private bathroom.

WHERE TO EAT

Almost every hotel and lodge has a restaurant, and eating places in Baguio tend to come and go. Mainstream fast foods are readily available, and small restaurants serve an assortment of dishes at reasonable prices. Most meals will cost $4-8.

CAFÉ BY THE RUINS, *Chuntug Street. near City Hall. $6-12.*

This is a wonderful place built into the ruins of an old house and is owned by a group of artists. Tastefully furnished and decorated with bamboo, traditional artwork, and plants, you will find the atmosphere is very laid back and friendly. The food is delicious: dishes vary from regional Cordilleran to European. Try the salmon roe on warm home-made bread, mountain tea, and brewed coffee. They also have a bakery at John Hay. Information on exhibits and performances is posted by the entrance. If you visit during the Baguio arts festival, this is where the action is, and you may have to wait for a seat.

O-MAI-KHAN, *Otek Street, near City Hall.*

Rather plain decor, but the Mongolian barbeque is flavorful.

ROSE BOWL, *21 Harrison Street.*

Serves Chinese, American, and Filipino dishes. The restaurant is simple and casual.

GANZA, *Burnham Park.*

Ganza has some tables where you may sit outside. The food is Filipino and Chinese, and the chicken is recommended.

MARIO'S, *Session Road. $10-20.*

This is the first of what is now a chain with several outlets in Manila. Mario's is still a favorite in Baguio, and some say the food is better here than in the Manila branches. Mario's specializes in steaks and Italian food, but also offers some Asian dishes. The Caesar's salad is superb. The interior is dark and pleasant, and the ambiance is relaxed; some may find it romantic.

DON HENRICO'S, *Session Road.*

This Italian restaurant serves casual pasta and pizza. It is set up like a typical small American-style pizza place.

DAINTY, *Session Road.*

This is a casual place with tasty noodles and other Chinese fast food dishes. It is reputed to have the best coffee in town.

BARRIO FIESTA, *Session Road.*

They serve traditional Filipino fare here in a bright fluorescent setting.

STAR CAFÉ, *Session Road.*

Pretty good Chinese food. Its character is typical of old Baguio restaurants.

MUNSAYAC INN, *129 Leonard Wood Road.*

A small, cozy restaurant with native decor. They serve delicious home-cooked Filipino dishes and fresh vegetables. Try the *pinakbet* (a mixed vegetable dish). Most of the servings are large and the staff is friendly.

MATSUKAZE, *Brent Road.*

This is a small, simple, and friendly place that serves Japanese cuisine.

VILLA LA MAJA, *Outlook Drive.*
A homey place with good Filipino food.
HALFWAY HOUSE, *John Hay.*
Good for Sunday brunch, this is a casual, relaxed place that gets full during the Easter and Christmas holidays.
19th TEE, *John Hay.*
Serves light meals and snacks, American cafeteria-style.
LONE STAR STEAK HOUSE, *John Hay, $8-15.*
Popular for its steaks and barbeque ribs.
NEW BONUAN, *Happy Glen.*
Serves simple home-cooked Filipino fare.
HAKUUN SANSO, *Hotel Monticello, Maryheights.*
This is the place to go for good Japanese food and a nice view.
JADE RESTAURANT, *Marcos Highway corner Legarda Road.*
Jade serves simple tasty Filipino and Chinese dishes.

SEEING THE SIGHTS
City Proper
Baguio offers a variety of things to do, most of it within walking distance of the center. Your first stop should be the **Department of Tourism**, on Governor Pack Road, for information, assistance, and advice.

The city has a number of resident and visiting artists; some are well known internationally. There are usually exhibits at colleges or other places. Artists often meet at **Café by the Ruins**, just downhill from the city hall. The café usually has a schedule of ongoing events.

Near Session Road is **St. Louis University's silver shop**, where you can watch delicate silver filigree work in progress. The shop is closed on Sunday. Enter the nearby **cathedral** to see its attractive interior. A block down General Luna Road, behind the silver shop, local artists sometimes exhibit their works in a room at the **Baguio University**.

Return to Session Road: at the end is the interesting **market**. Turn left to **Burnham Park**, the focus of activities in the city. Here, you may rent boats and row, paddle, or sail in the shallow **Burnham Lake**. Bicycles are for hire in the park. Many children learn how to bicycle here. The "Bicycle Boys" are masters at the art of teaching young children. There is also a good-sized children's playground and a skating rink. Rollerskates can be rented, but not rollerblades.

Around the City
Other points are accessible by taxi and/or jeepney. The **Duntog Foundation**, at the corner of Leonard Wood and Brent roads, makes and sells attractive handmade paper. Further down Leonard Wood is the

Botanical Gardens. The highlight of the park is a "**Japanese Cave**." It was made by the Japanese during the war, and was rumored to contain some of **General Yamashita's treasure** (see sidebar below). Other attractions include a collection of souvenir shops, some native houses, and usually a few Igorots at the park posing for photos and expecting a peso or two for each snap.

YAMASHITA'S TREASURE

*For many years, many groups of treasure hunters have dug in caves, crevices, and even under people's houses (they may buy the lot that the house is on for a generous sum) in search of "**Yamashita's Treasure**." Supposedly, during their retreat at the end of World War Two, the Japanese hid large amounts of gold, gold bars, and other precious items all over the country. Baguio seems to have one of the highest concentrations of possible "treasure sites." A golden Buddha was unearthed here, and President Marcos claimed that his fortune came from discovering part of Yamashita's treasure rather than from his political involvements.*

Just how many hunts have been successful? Nobody knows.

General Yamashita was executed as a war criminal. Yet he is remembered as a true soldier, a top general, and a humanitarian who tried to avert destruction where possible.

At the end of Leonard Wood, on the opposite side of the rotunda (called Pacdal Circle), is **Wright Park**. People come here to stroll or to rent ponies for children. Most ponies are small — adults and large children should not ride the small ones. Rides along the roads and trails can also be arranged, although you will have to contend with traffic.

When you are at Pacdal Circle, the first road right from Leonard Wood takes you past the exclusive **Baguio Country Club** and its golf course to **John Hay**, the former US military camp that was used for recreation and relaxation. The area maintains a golf course, tennis courts, skating, mini-golf, children's playgrounds, restaurants, accommodations, and hiking trails. Sadly, the number of beautiful trees, once found in abundance, has diminished. Stop by the Department of Tourism's excellent **Mountain Provinces Museum**, temporarily located here. It has well-labeled displays of artifacts and clothing, plus photographs of the culture and life in the mountain provinces. The museum displays works by local artists and has a small shop.

Past the Wright Park is **The Mansion**, summer home of the Philippine President. The gates are replicas of those to Buckingham Palace. The grounds are open to visitors when the President is not in Baguio.

Follow the road beyond as it goes upward to the top of the hill, where **Mines View Park** offers a good collection of souvenir shops and views. Nearby, the **Good Shepherd Convent** sells very good peanut brittle and home-made jams. Proceeds go towards the convent's support for unwed mothers.

NIGHTLIFE & ENTERTAINMENT

There are a number of bars and a disco that are lively during the holidays. **Rumors** on Session Road is a pleasant place for jazz and mellow music. **Songs**, next to Patria de Baguio along Session Road, offers jazz and sometimes classical music. **Spirits** on Otek Street is a popular disco inside a lovely old house.

SPORTS & RECREATION

Golf

There is a nice golf course at **John Hay**; its steep hills will keep you in shape. Greens fees are $25 on the weekends and $20 on weekdays. **Baguio Country Club** has a course, but you must be sponsored by a member to play.

Hikes

There are a number of trails around **John Hay**. Get a trail map from the John Hay lodging office. For a longer trek, walk up to **Mount Santo Tomas** — follow the road beside the Green Valley Country Club. The seven- to eight-kilometer walk will take you to the summit for great views of the area. The mountain is mostly limestone and stretches almost to the shores of Lingayen Gulf.

SHOPPING

The **city market** is a must for anyone who goes to Baguio. You can easily spend a couple of hours wandering around its stalls. During peak season, stalls overflow into Burnham Park. The vegetable section offers a feast of greens, other vegetables, and fruits; when in season, the strawberries are very sweet. There is a corridor of beautiful freshly cut flowers and an extensive handicraft section where you may find woven fabric, blankets, knitwear, baskets, *bulol* (granary gods), silver, brass, jewelry, woodcarvings, and jars.

Also available are a variety of readymade goods: clothing (from underwear to coats), shoes, some camping equipment, leather goods, costume jewelry, baked goods, jams, jellies, and, do try the strawberry *pastillas* (milk candies).

Be very careful with your wallet in and around the market!

Near the market, **Banawe Handicrafts** has a selection of woven goods. Most hotels and lodges have souvenir shops. The one in **Munsayac Inn** on Leonard Wood Road is very good and has an extensive selection of wooden products. The salad bowl sets are quite nice, there is an inhouse workshop, and they accept orders. Handmade paper and products are available at the **Duntog Foundation**, at Leonard Wood and the corner of Brent Road. The foundation can also make arrangements to visit the house of Mike Parson, two and a half hours from the city, where you can watch craftspeople work on paper, *sumingashi* marble, boxmaking, and *shifu* and *shikat* weaving. **Mrs. Sabado's factory** on Outlook Drive has modern decorative baskets.

The **Easter School**, on Easter Road behind the Bureau of Plant Industry, is a great place for woven blankets, table runners, and other products.

EXCURSIONS & DAY TRIPS

The **Easter School** on Easter Road is a great place to purchase attractive woven blankets and runners. It is run by the Episcopalian and Philippine Independent churches and has two weaving rooms. You can watch women use the upright looms to produce colorful blankets on the entry floor. Downstairs, the traditional mountain cloth is produced on backstrap looms. The work is very peaceful to watch and listen to.

Downhill from Baguio is **Asin**, a woodcarvers village. You can find a few interesting pieces and see some work in progress. Most of the finished products are in La Trinidad and Baguio markets.

La Trinidad, Benguet's capital, has several points of interest. Inside the pagodas of **Bell Temple** are statues of different saints from many religions. You may also have your fortune read by a priest. Here, Baguio's large Chinese community practices an amalgam of Taoism and Christianity. La Trinidad's **market** is a small version of the one in Baguio. At the ground floor of the **Provincial Capitol Building** there is a good exhibit of photographs pertaining to provincial activities. Across the driveway, the **museum** displays antique articles of clothing and mining information. The museum is open weekdays and there is a small gift shop.

If you have your own car or a rental vehicle, try the lovely picturesque drive to **Ambuklao** and **Binga Dams**. If you are interested in poking about the dams, get prior permission from the National Power Corporation office in Baguio City.

Mount Pulog, the tallest mountain on Luzon, is a favorite climb of mountaineers and trekkers. You need to make arrangements with the **Department of Environment and Natural Resources** (DENR) for guides and permit ($2), *Tel. 442-7315*; ask for Ms. Grace Solano. Budget three to four days and bring hiking and camping gear, food, and water. A park ranger at the entrance to the park on Mount Pulog collects $1 per person, a small fee that goes towards maintenance of the park. An annual climb in March is arranged by the office of the Governor of Benguet Province.

PRACTICAL INFORMATION

Banks

All major local banks have a branch and money withdrawal machines in the city. Along Session Road are **PNB**, **BPI** (Cirrus and Amexco withdrawal machine), **Citytrust**, **DBP**, and **PCI**.

Mail & Post Office

The **Post Office** is at Upper Session Road. For courier services, use **Abiotiz Express**, Session Road; **DHL**, Session Road; **JRS**, Harrison Road; and **Kuehne & Nagel**, Loakan Road.

Tourist Information

At the **Department Of Tourism**, on Governor Pack Road, *Tel. 442-6708*, you can get information about the mountain provinces and travel assistance and advice. The staff is quite helpful.

The Cordilleras Map and *Luzon by Car, the Map* both have a small and detailed city map of Baguio and one of the vicinity. Other helpful maps to look for are *The Baguio Landmark Map* of Bookmark, and the *Baguio Road Guide*.

BANAUE

Banaue's rice terraces, one of the World's 8th Wonders, are indeed both beautiful and amazing. It is said that if the Cordillera's terraces were placed end-to-end, they might stretch around the globe. The Ifugao labored for several centuries prior to the Spanish arrival, carving an extensive area of terraces out of the mountains. The terraces were built with painstaking manual labor. People dug down to bedrock, carried in stones, and constructed walls to make the terraces permanent. When bedrock could not be reached, they buried the solid trunk of the tree fern as the base for the wall. All this was achieved with only rudimentary tools. The Ifugao perfected the art of wall-building and irrigation — the walls and the irrigation system that channels precious water from the highest terraces into lower and lower ones are indeed a product of genius.

Although Banaue's town proper has become a cluster of boxy tin buildings, some of the nearby villages retain their timeless ways. The houses here stand on stilts in village clusters among the terraces and are built of reeds and wood. In the villages, you can see women weaving under the houses and the blacksmith creating jewelry, and (these days) products for tourists also.

Some of Banaue's people have retained their ancient customs. However, having been subjected to Spanish lectures about paganism and lowlanders' scorn, the locals keep their ways to themselves. This adherence to the traditional ways gives Banaue a special atmosphere.

ARRIVALS & DEPARTURES

- **Banaue-Manila**. From Manila, the easiest access route to Banaue is through the Cagayan Valley. Dangwa has daily trips that depart both Manila and Banaue early in the morning. Travel time is nine to ten hours, and the fare is $8. Baliwag, Autobus, and other lines have buses that go through Solano, where jeepneys go to Lagawe and Banaue.
- **Banaue-Bontoc**. The delightful but rough two- or three-hour trip to Banaue passes impressive terracing and a bit of remaining forest. At Talubin, a road exits to Barlig, which is a lovely community amid attractive terraces. Bay-yo, which is 18 kilometers from Bontoc along the road to Banaue, has impressive, fortress-like terrace walls. The road continues to rise to Mt. Polis pass. From here you descend, with a few more rises, to Banaue. Make this trip early in the day, as the road is "being improved" and is in poor condition.
- **Banaue-Baguio**. See Baguio's *Arrivals & Departures*.

GETTING AROUND

Jeepneys are almost always available by the market. There are daily trips to Mayoyao and to Hungduan. To get to the viewpoint, you can hire a jeepney or tricycle. To arrange for renting a jeepney, look for Nick Piog at the Dangwa station, or speak to tricycle and jeepney drivers in front of the market. Rates are fixed by the jeepney drivers' association — establish fares before starting out.

WHERE TO STAY

Banaue has a range of places to stay, from one up-market hotel to several moderate-priced lodges and inns and a few very inexpensive places. All are refreshingly clean, regardless of price. All are family-run (except for the hotel) and have a good family atmosphere. Most are within walking distance of restaurants if they don't have a resident cook; can recommend guides; and have a telephone in the reception area but not in the rooms.

The owners and staff are usually trustworthy, but other visitors may not be, so don't leave your room open or possessions laying about. Bottled water is available at almost all establishments.

You could probably arrive without reservations at any time except Easter, but do telephone ahead if you have specific ideas about where you would like to stay. Telephone service is occasionally problematical. Call at the least busy time, such as early morning. If you can't get through using direct dial (the least expensive method), ask the PLDT operator for assistance.

Just Beyond the Center of Town

BANAUE HOTEL AND YOUTH HOSTEL, *before town, on the main road in from the lowlands. Tel. 386-4037, 386-4088. Manila reservations: Tel. 812-1984, Fax 812-1164. 60 rooms. $63 per single, $70 per double, $120 per suite, $15 per person per dorm. Visa, Master Card, American Express, Diners.*

This is Banaue's only real hotel, with carpeted, good pine-board rooms with private bathroom, aircon, hot water, phone, and balconies overlooking the terraces. There is an ample restaurant with good terrace view; small pool good for a swim after a hot summer hike and invigoratingly cold at other times; cavernous lobby used for cultural performances when there are enough guests; and ample parking. The staff is helpful and good. The dorm is not good value, as other places have less expensive space except occasionally at peak season.

BANAUE VIEW INN, *Banaue. Tel. 386-4078. 11 rooms. $15-20 per single or double, $5 per person per dorm.*

This quiet place is clean and has good rooms, many with a good view. Some rooms have private bathrooms, others are shared. The phone is in the lobby. Run by the progeny of Otley Beyer, the American anthropologist who made Banaue famous, the inn also has a small museum of antiques and artifacts that is a good introduction to the area, ample parking, and is within walking distance to restaurants — then a good uphill pull back to the inn. Popular with consultants, this inn is often booked.

SPRING VILLAGE INN, *Banaue. Tel. 386-4087. 9 rooms. $10-30 per single or double.*

This family-run inn has a large central area. The phone is at the desk in the lobby. All rooms are clean, nice, and homey. The three more expensive rooms have private bath and are in the back. The other rooms face the main road, have a surrounding balcony, and are quiet at night. The two common bathrooms are kept very clean. Walking distance to restaurants.

FAIRVIEW INN, *Banaue, on the main road before town. Tel. 386-4002. 9 rooms. $10-20 per single or double.*

This solid attractive cement house is on the main road in from the lowlands. Bathrooms are shared, with hot water in the showers. Some rooms have good views. There is a balcony to sit on, a few parking spaces in the driveway, laundry is available, and the phone is in the lobby. This inn is walking distance to restaurants. The proprietress is attentive and quite inquisitive.

J&L LODGE, *Banaue, on the main road before town. Tel. 386-4035. 5 rooms, 3 native houses. $5-10 per single or double, $15-20 per native house.*

This attractive house is on the main road in from the lowlands; and has small dark rooms. The bathrooms are common with hot water in the showers. Laundry is available and the phone is in the lobby. There are a few parking spaces in the driveway. This inn is walking distance to restaurants.

TERRACEVILLE INN, *Imbatugan (on the road to the viewpoint beyond town), Banaue. Tel. 386-4069. 8 rooms $10-15 per single or double.*

This attractive house is on the main road in from the lowlands and has small dark rooms with private bathrooms and hot water in the showers. Laundry is available and the phone is in the lobby. There is parking space in the driveway. Meals can be prepared; the inn is a fair walk to restaurants.

In the Town Center

SANAFE LODGE, *Banaue, beside the bus stop and across from the market. Tel. 386-4085. 13 rooms. $10-30 per single or double, $5 per person per dorm.*

Some rooms have good views with private or shared bathrooms. Corridors and stairwells are dark. The restaurant-bar has a terrace with good views. The phone is at the reception desk.

GREENVIEW LODGE, *Banaue, on the road to Mayoyao. Tel. 386-4021. 19 rooms. $10-20 per single or double.*

The assortment of rooms include singles, doubles, and family rooms with private or common bathrooms, and dorm accommodations. Some rooms have good views, and there is an excellent eating place — Las Vegas — downstairs, as well as a gift shop with some interesting items. Telephone service is available at the reception.

STAIRWAY LODGE, *Banaue, on the road to Mayoyao. Tel. 386-4053. 15 rooms. $5-20 per single or double.*

The assortment of rooms includes singles to family rooms and private or common bathrooms, and dorm accommodations. The more expensive rooms have a private bathroom. Some rooms have good views, and there is a restaurant in the lobby area. The owners are friendly and helpful. Telephone service is available at the reception.

HALFWAY LODGE, *Banaue, on the road to Mayoyao. Tel. 386-4082. 21 rooms. $5-20 per single or double.*

The assortment of rooms includes singles to family rooms, and dorm accommodations. The more expensive rooms have a private bathroom. Some rooms have good views, and there is a large restaurant (still being completed) with a terrace view. The owners are friendly and helpful.

Telephone service is available at the reception. There is a curio shop and a small drugstore in the lobby area.

WONDER LODGE, *Banaue, on the road to Mayoyao. 10 rooms. $4 per person.*

The rooms are above the main road and bathrooms are common. The cozy central area is decorated with native artifacts — lots of atmosphere and a friendly, helpful owner. Restaurants are nearby.

COZY NOOK, *Banaue, on the road to Mayoyao. 10 rooms. $5-10 per single or double.*

The rooms are above the main road; bathrooms are common. Restaurants are nearby.

BROOKSIDE, *Banaue, on the road to Mayoyao. 10 rooms $4-5 per person.*

Bathrooms are common, the owner speaks Hebrew(!), and restaurants are nearby.

Bangaan, Batad, & Cambulu

These out-of-the-way places are excellent value, and the food is generally amazingly good in Batad and Bangaan. In Batad, we especially like Simon's, Hillside, and Waterfallview (no food). Supplies carried into Batad and Cambulu (there are no roads) will of course cost more than they do in Banaue — this includes beer, bottled water, etc. You may not find bottled water in Cambulu. Standard rates in Batad and Cambulu are $1-1.25 per person per night.

BANGAAN FAMILY INN, *Bangaan, Banaue, on the road to Mayoyao about 13 km from Banaue center. 9 rooms. $3-5 per person.*

This peaceful spot near the trailhead to Batad has friendly owners and usually good food. Bathrooms are common and floors tend to be wet.

HILLSIDE INN, *Batad, Banaue, overlooking the village. 13 rooms.*

Fabulous views and great food, good clean rooms (plywood walls), but don't leave belongings near open windows beside the balcony. Bathrooms are outside, very basic, and one is open on the side towards the terraces — a loo with a view! Menu includes Israeli food. Very friendly, helpful owners.

SIMON'S INN, *Batad, Banaue, overlooking the village. 13 rooms.*

Fabulous views and great food, good clean rooms (plywood walls) but don't leave belongings near open windows beside the balcony. Bathrooms are outside and are very basic. Menu includes Israeli food. Very friendly, helpful owners.

RITA'S INN, *Batad, Banaue, overlooking the village; 5 rooms.*

Good clean rooms. Bathrooms are outside and very basic. Friendly, helpful owners.

WATERFALLSIDE INN, *Batad, Banaue, overlooking the village. 2 rooms.*

Good clean rooms in a quiet area, beside the trailhead to the waterfall. Walk through terraces to eat at Simon's or Hillside. Outside bathrooms. Friendly, helpful owners, lots of young children — they are curious, so put your things away.

LYDIA'S, *Cambulu, Banaue, village center. 3 rooms.*

Good clean rooms in a family home — the family moves downstairs when they have guests. Good clean outside bathroom and shower room. Friendly, helpful owners, but looking for help. Can provide simple meals. Beer and soft drinks usually available, but no bottled water. If full, the house next door also rents rooms.

WHERE TO EAT

Food in Banaue is simple, good, and inexpensive. Most places will do chop suey with or without various forms of animal protein (eggs, chicken, pork), fried rice with vegetables with animal protein, plus, when available from the market, beef and fish (usually *bangus* or tilapia). For breakfast you can have rice or toast and eggs, fruit in season, and several places serve pancakes, sometimes with pineapple, banana, or other additions.

A restaurant is of course only as good as its cook, and the best cooks in Banaue are probably Alice at **HIDDEN VALLEY**, Percy at **COOLWINDS**, and Leo at **LAS VEGAS**. Hidden Valley is a small new restaurant just above the driveway to the Banaue Hotel. Coolwinds is on the second story of a new cement structure on the road down to town, just before the market. Its balcony provides a good place to watch the proceedings below. Las Vegas is on the street-level floor of Green View Inn, which is just downhill from the market, on the road to Mayoyao; there are good views from the windows.

In addition, several inns have reasonably good eating places, including Halfway, Stairway, and Sanafe, all of which have good views of the rice terraces from their restaurants' windows.

SEEING THE SIGHTS

Aside from the shops, views, and its people, the town proper is not as interesting as its surroundings. One of the first places most visitors flock to is the **viewpoint**, about four kilometers from town proper, an easy hike or quick tricycle or jeep ride. This is a spectacular spot for scenery and photos. Locals come dressed in traditional regalia and pose for photos. Payment is expected per photo taken. Several other viewing spots have developed on the way to "the" viewpoint.

Back in town, just above town proper is **H. Otley Beyer's museum**. Beyer, the anthropologist responsible for making Banaue and the Ifugao culture known, worked, lived, became part of the culture, and died here. His bones are kept behind the Municipal Hall, Ifugao-style — wrapped in a blanket inside a special house. His children maintain artifacts and documents, collected by Beyer, in an interesting museum in the Banaue View Inn. A small entrance fee pays for the upkeep.

NIGHTLIFE & ENTERTAINMENT

When the Banaue Hotel has enough guests, they hold a **cultural performance**. The performers' native costumes and some artifacts are described and demonstrated. Some of their dances, rituals, and songs are portrayed. The whole presentation is good.

In the evenings, some of Banaue's residents gather around a guitar and sing folk, rock, and local songs at **Coolwinds**, **Las Vegas**, and some other spots. Join in and enjoy.

SHOPPING

Banaue town proper has **numerous shops** with woven goods, wood-carvings, bronze and silver figurines and trinkets, and baskets. These are usually significantly cheaper than at shops in Manila and Baguio. Bargain at all places: ask for "the best price."

Market day in Banaue is Saturday. You will see stalls spilling onto the street fronting the market. Although there are some handicrafts, most of the items are ready-to-wear (sweaters, slippers, shoes), kitchen utensils, etc., things that Banaue's residents may need.

The viewpoint (see below) is surrounded by **souvenir shops**, where you can hunt around for woven goods, bronze and silver, baskets, and T-shirts.

You can hike to villages with **bronzesmiths** (Matang-lag), **carvers** (Bocos), **weavers** (Tam-an). Along the way, you may watch the work in progress and accumulate more handicrafts.

EXCURSIONS & DAY TRIPS
Short Hikes

Banaue is a hiker's paradise where you may walk for minutes, hours, or days. It does present problems for people who are afraid of heights — much of the hiking is along terrace edges. Take a guide as it is fairly easy to get lost. The children here are eager to offer their services for as high a fee as they think they can get — ask at your hotel what a fair rate should be. Before setting off, agree upon the rate with your guide. Consider wearing long pants to protect against cuts and scrapes from sharp grass, branches, and, if you do slip, from rocks.

If you are an adventurous hiker, you could try the trail between town and the **viewpoint**. This requires scrambling around and balancing atop some steep terrace walls. Views along the way are impressive.

Steep steps lead from behind the Banaue Hotel to **Tam-an**, where some of the villagers produce weavings and handicrafts. You can continue through Tam-an, along an ancient irrigation channel, across the terraces, to Poitan. It is less interesting but easier to take the kilometer-and-a-half walk along the road through town, then the cemented trail down to the village.

Poitan is a village of weavers and carvers. It has a special stone that is revered and kept in an area where the villagers gather for rituals. A nearby **waterfall** is regarded as a spiritual place. A rock formation part of the way up it looks like a rice god from certain angles.

On the other side of the Mayoyao road from Poitan are **Bocus** and **Matang-lag**. Bocus, the first village from town proper, has some carvers. A trail from Bocus goes by a **waterfall** to Matang-lag, which is known for its bronzework. You may watch the Abul family make local jewelry (said to bestow good luck and fertility on the wearer), *bulol* (rice gods), and other popular items of bronze through the lost wax process. Several houses have smiths.

LOST WAX PROCESS

This method is an ancient way of making articles of brass, bronze, silver, gold, and other metals. First, a model of each item is made in wax, and the wax is then surrounded by wet clay, which is set to dry. Molten bronze is poured into the mold, through an opening in the clay. The wax melts and runs out (hence is "lost"). The bronze hardens into a unique shape. The mold is broken, the item removed and finished by filing, polishing, and perhaps adding some details.

Eastward Treks

Guihob Natural Pool, four and a half kilometers along the Mayoyao road, is a good place to stop and bathe on the way back from Batad. The pool is just off the road.

Cambulu, a nice native village, is accessed by a trail from Kinakin. Two residents rent rooms to visitors. Sometimes in the evenings, a nearby tree glows with at least a hundred fireflies. From here, a two-to-three-kilometer trail takes you to the amphitheater-like terraces of **Batad**. The village nestles into the foot of steep terraces. You can also get to Batad by taking a jeepney from Banaue town proper to the "junction" or to

Bangaan on the Banaue-Mayoyao road. From the junction, walk up to the "saddle," where the trail descends to Batad — altogether a steep four-kilometer walk, allow two or three hours each way. There are six places to stay overnight.

Beyond Batad, a steep trail leads to a pretty **waterfall**. Wear swimsuits or bring a change of clothes. The trail is very slippery when wet. Proceed slowly and inquire about conditions beforehand.

Two kilometers further along the Mayoyao road is the picturesque village, **Banga-an**. Between March and May there is often a rainbow in the sunset over the terraces from the Banga-an viewpoint. A trail beyond Banga-an leads to Batad.

The trip to **Mayoyao** is lovely: the road dips and climbs among terraces and hills, through forests and villages — a three-hour ride from Banaue. You may do the trip in a day if you hire a vehicle, or stay overnight. The houses here have steeper roofs than those in Banaue, and the whole town is neater and more spread out.

Northwest Treks

In **Hiwang**, four kilometers from town proper, just off the road to Hungduan, a path takes you to Mr. Ordillo's **native house**. The house is extensively decorated with skulls of sacrificed *carabao* and pigs. Beside it is a miniature house containing a **mummified couple**, Mr. Ordillo's grandparents. The couple can be seen through glass walls on three sides of the small house, and Mr. Ordillo can answer questions on Ifugao customs and traditions. A small donation helps maintain the exhibit.

The views along the road to **Hapao** are beautiful. Beyond town there is a **hot spring**. You can also see the terraces in **Hungduan**, which are very pretty and resemble spider webs. This is where General Yamashita surrendered at the end of World War Two.

PRACTICAL INFORMATION

Foreign Exchange

You should change currency before coming to Banaue. The **Banaue Hotel** will exchange currency, but at a disadvantageous rate.

Tourist & Trekking Information

As long as you are prepared for very rustic sanitary facilities, you will enjoy trekking around Banaue. Bring food and bottled water or water purification tablets. Arrange for a guide who knows the area and is liked, as he can accompany you to villages for the nights. We highly recommend Hygie Cayong. He can be contacted at **Coolwinds**, *Tel. 386-4023*. Give advance notice so that all necessary arrangements for a 2-5 day trek can be made. Ask your guide's advice about bringing gifts (matches, candies, vitamins, etc.) for villagers who may host you along the way. Always take your guide's advice should he declare any areas unsafe.

Most hotels have a wonderful map — *The Cordilleras* — that has small area maps as well as hiking trails; the attractive *Luzon by Car, the Map;* and small xerox maps of the area.

Water

Most places in town sell bottled water and other drinks. In the more distant areas, water may need treating, although some places sell bottled water.

BONTOC, MOUNTAIN PROVINCE

Mountain Province is located at the center of the Cordilleras and is inhabited by Bontoc, Kalinga, and Kankana-ey people. An off-the-beaten-track destination, the area's terraces are extensive and as beautiful as – although less-known than – Banaue's.

Many villages observe traditional community patterns. Classic Bontoc houses are of stone and/or grass walls with cogon roofs. Pigs live in holes near or under the owner's house. Although few of these native abodes can be found in town, they are still seen in outlying villages.

Traditionally, only married couples with very young children lived in their one-room houses. Older children lived in housing for unmarried males or females. Separate buildings were provided as granaries. Courtship centered around the girls' dormitories, and marriages were considered only when the gods signified their approval by allowing the girl to become pregnant; however, this tradition disappeared in Bontoc because of missionaries' objections.

Many people in Mountain Province do not like having their photographs taken — respect their wishes. Villagers may expect gifts from visitors. If you plan to stay overnight in a remote village, bring matches, candies, trinkets to give away and food to share. As a precaution, avoid wearing jewelry and expensive watches.

The capital, **Bontoc**, nestles deep within a valley at the junction where two rivers form the mighty Chico. Situated in a valley, Bontoc is hotter and more humid than the highlands — one reason why most travelers head for Sagada.

ARRIVALS & DEPARTURES

Between Bontoc and Sagada, there are at least four daily jeepneys. The fare per person is 80¢. Refer to the *Arrivals & Departures* sections of Baguio and Banaue for schedules of trips to Bontoc.

WHERE TO STAY

Lodging in Bontoc is simple and businessmen are the primary customers.

RIO VISTA INN, *behind the City Hall. 4 rooms. $10-20 per single or double.*

Vista is a nice private home that rents out a few clean rooms — very much a family setting in a quiet area of a fairly busy town. Rooms have either private or shared bathrooms.

PINES HOTEL AND KITCHENETTE, *behind the market in Bontoc. 17 rooms. $15-20 per single or double aircon. $3-4 per person to $10 per single or double nonaircon.*

This central place has an assortment of reasonably clean rooms and a good restaurant downstairs. During summer months, you will need a fan in the room if it isn't air conditioned. Aircon rooms are reasonable, large, and have private bathrooms; the nonaircon rooms have shared bathrooms. The building has been expanded in an ad hoc manner, resulting in some strange arrangements of the corridors. The proprietors are friendly, helpful, and knowledgeable about the area.

VILLAGE INN, *central Bontoc. 8 rooms. $5-10 per single or double.*

This central place is clean and quite nice — good value — and the staff are helpful and friendly. Bathrooms are common.

CHICO TERRACE INN, *on the main road in Bontoc, at the junction of the road leading to the museum. 15 rooms. Under $5 per person.*

This central place is run by religious folk and has numerous business visitors. Rooms are basic and not all have windows. Rooms have either private or common bathrooms. There is a cafeteria for snacks.

MOUNTAIN HOTEL, *central Bontoc, on the road to Baguio. 23 rooms. $2-4 per person.*

This busy little hotel is very convenient to transport, has for many years appeared unfinished, and could be cleaner. Rooms have either private or common bathrooms. It has a small restaurant on the first floor. Staff seem busy or occupied — tourists are not their bread and butter.

BONTOC HOTEL, *central Bontoc. 6 rooms. $2-4 per person.*

Once the town's "premier" hotel, this structure has fallen on hard times and looks rather run down. Bathrooms are common. The lounge area is decorated with old Cordillera photographs.

WHERE TO EAT

The best places to eat in Bontoc are **PINES KITCHENETTE & INN**, **KOYKIE'S BURGER & FASTFOOD**, and **CUSINA IGOROTA**. A meal will cost $1-4, depending on what you order.

Bakeries along the main road sell an assortment of foods that will keep you going — try the *bucchi* (a round doughnut-like snack filled with sweetened mung bean), and other breads with fillings. Some snack items are only P1-2 (4-8¢).

SEEING THE SIGHTS

The **Bontoc Museum** was founded by the Belgian Sister Basil Gékière and houses a well-labeled and attractively displayed collection of authentic artifacts and photos from the mountain tribes. Outside the main building is a collection of traditional Bontoc houses.

A few shops near the market sell an assortment of handicrafts. At the **All Saints Elementary School**, you can watch weavers at work. Across the river, in **Samoki Village**, you can see villagers weave materials and make pat-pots that are fired in burning rice straw.

EXCURSIONS & DAY TRIPS

A two-hour ride northward through lovely terracing takes you to **Sadanga**, near the provincial border between Mountain Province and Kalinga-Apayao, and a nearby hotspring. From the Sadanga junction, an easy 30 minute hike takes you to **Sacasacan**, and 25 minutes further to **Anabel**, across the **Chico River**. Inquire about the peace and order situation before visiting or proceeding north.

To the west are some interesting hikes in the mountains above Bontoc. **Malegkong** village, a three- or four-hour hike from Bontoc, is surrounded by beautiful terraces. And, there are great views of Bontoc from the road to Malegkong. You may have to hire a jeepney to get to Malegkong. A trail leads from Malegkong to Mainit.

Mainit Village, named for its hot springs (*mainit* means hot) that are now surrounded by pig sties, has some gold panning ongoing. You may either take a jeepney or hike (four to five hours) from Bontoc. Trekkers can proceed to Fedlisan and Sagada from Mainit.

SAGADA

Sagada, 600 meters and 18 kilometers above Bontoc, is cool (cold in December and January: evening temperatures can drop to 4°C/40°F) and an almost completely different world than the capital. Sagada is a fairly modern town in terms of its architecture. You will find many new houses of limestone and tin.

Most visitors come here for the climate and fresh mountain air, and to hike out to see the terraces, falls, and villages. The area is riddled with caves and spelunking is one of the main activities. There are many burial caves that contain residents' ancestors — treat the caves and contents with respect, some bone's relative may be beside you.

NO FUNERARY SOUVENIRS, PLEASE!

When caving in this area, do not take any pieces of coffins or their contents as souvenirs!

One of the negative side effects of tourism here is that many visitors have come to "hang out," and have been disrespectful of the local culture. Some confuse "going native" with nudity and public displays of affection, when in fact these acts offend indigenous peoples. Others have expressed disdain for some traditional practices. And, although most people come here to get high on the scenery, some get high on other things. Consequently, ill feelings have occasionally arisen. Nevertheless, Sagada is a very popular destination. Once you get out of the town proper, people are very friendly and curious.

The months of January through March are dry here; expect showers at other times.

ARRIVALS & DEPARTURES

You can travel to Sagada through Baguio or Banaue. We prefer the route from Banaue, as travel time over rough roads is much shorter (two to three hours, compared to Baguio's seven or eight). Both routes are wonderfully scenic.

Coming from Banaue, you may rent a jeepney ($55 one-way, $70 roundtrip), or take a jeepney to Bontoc ($2) where you change to another jeepney (50¢) bound for Sagada. Dangwa and Lizardo bus companies have daily bus trips between Baguio and Sagada, leaving in the early morning.

WHERE TO STAY

You will find that lodging in Sagada is simple, clean, and inexpensive. Rates in general are $3 per person per day in early 1997. During the drier months of the year (March through May or June), water may be scarce.

During **peak tourist season** (Easter and Christmas), all lodging may be booked or taken. Booking can be a problem as there were still no telephones in Sagada at the time of publication. You could write or send a telegram to the lodging of your choice, ask them to hold rooms for you, and hope that the letter arrives and is heeded. If all normal lodging is full, Sagada's hospital will rent spare beds to travelers, and the school will allow you to use space, as they are not in session at these times.

All lodging that we inspected in Sagada was clean. Bathrooms are either shared (between two rooms) or common.

COUNTRY INN, *central Sagada. 9 rooms. $3 per person.*

This nice old building is beside the town plaza, which becomes a market place on Saturday mornings. Rooms are fairly spacious, but not quiet if there is a large group. It is managed by the son of the photographer, Eduardo Masferré, and his wife. The small restaurant is near the large fireplace, and they serve good food.

GANDUYAN INN, *central Sagada. $3 per person.*

The owners are friendly, helpful, and maintain clean, cozy rooms, and a pleasant atmosphere.

GREENHOUSE INN, *near central Sagada. 5 rooms. $3 per person.*

This is a nice, central place, with restaurants nearby. It is homey and has a nice atmosphere, good people.

MAPIYAAW, *the first inn on the road into Sagada. 28 rooms. $3 per person.*

This peaceful place is a 4-story building of tin and pine wood nestled in a limestone outcropping that is on the ancestral land of the Solang family, who are the owners. Also in the outcropping is the traditional family house and a burial cave. Management changes every couple of years or so, still within the Solang clan.

The second and third floors have fireplaces, making the place very cozy when it is cold outside. There are good views from all the rooms. Some rooms have a shared bathroom, but most use common bathrooms.

Given advance notice, they can usually do a good, simple meal. Meals are served in an attractive central area on the second floor. Mapiya-aw is about a 20-minute walk from town — bring a flashlight if walking after dark. Parking here is ample and safe.

MASFERRÉ'S INN, *in central Sagada. 7 rooms. $3 per person.*

This central place, once called "Julia's," has long been a meeting place for travelers. Some rooms have good views, others have no windows. The cafe serves good, simple meals. The proprietress is the widow of Eduardo Masferré, and you can see some of his marvelous photographs on the walls.

OLAHBINAN, *near central Sagada, on the road to Ambasing. 5 rooms. Prices vary with what they think they can get.*

This large new building is central, but occasionally has water problems.

ROCKY VALLEY INN, *on the road into Sagada. 8 rooms. $3 per person.*

An absolutely spectacular limestone formation was dynamited by its owners, who then built this inn out of the rubble. It is a 10-minute walk from town.

SAGADA GUEST HOUSE, *near central Sagada, on the Besao road. 15 rooms. $3 per person.*

This central place has good rooms, a cozy atmosphere, and serves good meals.

ST JOSEPH'S RESTHOUSE, *central Sagada. 29 rooms. $3 per person.*
This central place is run by nuns of the Episcopalian church and was Sagada's first lodging establishment. Its assorted rooms in three buildings run from private, small, and quiet to large dorm-types and possibly noisy. Rooms and beds are simple but good. The central dining area in one of the buildings is a good place to meet other travelers and exchange information, as the long tables almost preclude "privacy" and facilitate interaction.

WHERE TO EAT

Eating in Sagada is a pleasant experience, but you usually have to book meals in advance. This can be problematical if you arrive in the evening and there are many other visitors. Most inns will provide simple, tasty meals, given some notice.

For the best dining in Sagada, try **THE LOG CABIN** for delicious western-style food in a (US) western-style building with lots of atmosphere. Great lasagna — everything we ordered was super. We did order a couple of hours in advance. Prices vary around $2-4 per meal.

COUNTRY CAFE and **MASFERRÉ INN** both have set or short menus that provide good, filling meals for about $2-3 per meal. They also have good cakes for those with a sweet tooth.

More local flavor is available at the **SHAMROCK CAFE**, between Masferre Inn and the town hall. Here, in a relaxed setting, you can have fried rice (red or white) with vegetables and, if you wish with chicken, pork, tuna, and/or egg, a filling meal for less than $1. Try also **CAFE BILIG**, behind the town hall, on the path to the church.

SEEING THE SIGHTS

The small and unobtrusive **Ganduyan Museum** has a collection of antique baskets and artifacts that Christina Aben has collected. The museum is beside the family's inn, and is sometimes closed — do visit if it is open and ask Christina regarding items you would like to know more about. Ganduyan was formerly the name of Sagada.

Sagada's Episcopal **St. Mary's church**, built in the early 1900s, is a pleasing structure with some nice stained-glass windows. The original church was badly damaged during World War Two, and the original bell, dating from 1921, sits outside the church.

Echo Valley, beyond the church and cemetery, has beautiful views of limestones with some cliff burials visible. It is a nice place to sit — listen to your echo if you wish. A path leads to the valley floor.

Along the road to Bontoc, the **Sagada Weaving Shop** is a great place to buy the beautifully woven Bontoc cloth. Backpacks are a very popular product and are often out of stock.

Also check out **Eduardo Masferré's Studio**, at the corner of the roads to Banga-an and Bontoc. Revered as the father of Philippine photography (see sidebar below), the late Masferré spent over 50 years documenting mountain life with his keen eyes and camera.

EDUARDO MASFERRÉ'S TIMELESS IMAGES

Eduardo Masferré was the son of a Spaniard who came with the military, married a local woman, and stayed. The older Masferré was an unusual man.

When drafted into the military, he was lucky enough to get a low number that would have allowed him to stay in Europe. He traded it for a high number and came to the Philippines. Not content with the cavalry in the lowlands, he switched to the infantry and went to the Cordillera, where many Spaniards lost their heads. When the Americans came, Masferré had started a coffee farm that failed due to blight. He changed his religion to become an employee of the new Episcopalian church in Sagada. His wife, given the Christian name Mercedes, helped him run the family businesses and raised the children.

Eduardo was the second son. He and his elder brother were sent to Spain for education when they were very young. However, the older brother died there, and Eduardo was brought home, never to leave his Cordilleras again except for a rare trip to Manila.

As a young man, Eduardo taught himself photography and even built his first enlarger from directions in a magazine – it was solar powered because there was no electricity in the area at that time. Eduardo supported himself working at the mission and then taking portraits, and hiked into surrounding areas to take photographs. After he married, he continued photography with his wife's encouragement, but had to reactivate the family farm to support his growing family.

During the 1980s and 1990s, his work gained international acclaim, and was exhibited in Japan, Denmark, Switzerland, and (by invitation) at Les Rencontres Internationale de la Photographie, the world's most prestigious photographic festival. A collection of his images has been exhibited at the Smithsonian's National Museum of Natural History (Washington, DC), has toured to other American museums, and is kept in the Smithsonian's photographic archives where the prints are preserved under very good conditions.

You may see some of his original images at his studio (when it is open), Masferré Inn, and the Bontoc Museum.

SHOPPING

Your best buys here are the **Bontoc cloth** and products of the material, available at the Sagada Weaving Shop, and **handmade paper**. The Stephens have a house near the school, where Pamela makes lovely handmade paper. If you meet her and she is making paper at the time, she may show you how she does it. Sometimes Christina Aben has some beautiful antique and reproduction baskets for sale; check at the Ganduyan Inn to see if she is around.

EXCURSIONS & DAY TRIPS
Hikes & Caves

There are dozens of hikes in and around Sagada. Many places sell maps and the Stephens' guide, which show the trails. A number of paths close to town criss-cross and you may have to ask for directions. For assistance with finding a guide, ask at your inn or from the Sagada Environmental Guides Association at the municipal hall building.

There is a good and easy one- to two-hour walk through the **farmers' gardens** near town. You will see one or two traditional houses and several *dap-ays*, and go through terraces that grow rice or vegetables, depending on the season. The scenery is lovely. *Dap-ays*, which are paved with stone and often have stones around the perimeter, are traditional gathering places for men and centers for performing rituals.

Past Sagada Weaving, a path takes you to **Matangkib Cave** and **Latang Underground River**, 10 minutes from town center. There are some pretty sparkling formations inside the cave. If you intend to explore the underground river, bring torches and a guide.

Also close to Sagada, a 35-minute walk through terraces takes you to **Bokong Falls**. It is a nice place to swim (wear a swimsuit or clothes) and relax.

Other caves to explore are:
- **Lumiang**, a 30-minute walk past Ambasing, with many burials
- **Sumaging**, where your guide can point out unusual limestone formations, including Pregnant Woman and *Dap-ay* (this cave is for properly equipped spelunkers) and an ice-cold pool at the bottom
- **Loko-ong** (Crystal Cave) was once very beautiful, but sadly tourists have in the past left with "souvenirs," so residents have closed the cave to prevent further defacing
- **Balangagan**, past Crystal Cave, has stalactites and stalagmites
- **Sugong**, a small cave along a cement path then a trail, 15 minutes from the Ambasing Road

Just beyond the Mapiya-aw Pension, a two and a half-kilometer walk takes you to the communications tower for a breathtaking view of the **Kiltepan Terraces**.

Fedilisan, an interesting village, is either a three-hour walk from Sagada or a jeepney ride to Banga-an and a 45-minute hike downhill. The **Fedilisan (Bomok-od) Falls**, 45 minutes further, offer a refreshing dip in the pool where water cascades down from above. A taller waterfall is further downstream — don't swim in this one, it is not safe.

If you are interested in the ancient ways, take a jeepney to Agawa, Besao, then a 40-minute walk to **Gueday**, where the rocks of the *dap-ay* are specially arranged. In past times, they were used to tell when planting should begin. The walk is lovely and you pass coffins placed high into precipitous rock faces. In April, you may see Gueday men mill sugarcane using manual presses.

PRACTICAL INFORMATION

You will not be able to change money here: do so in Manila or Baguio. You are supposed to register at the Mayor's office when you arrive. We have never done so and nor do most people. Gary and Pamela Stephens have made an informative guide booklet about Sagadal; it is available in most inns and restaurants. Drink only water that has been bottled or boiled.

BETWEEN SAGADA & BAGUIO

The drive from **Baguio** to **Bontoc** or **Sagada** is a very scenic and rough seven-hour bounce. There are spectacular views of terracing and mountain life along the way. If you take public transport you will find yourself whizzing by these scenes and around corners at amazing speed, so it is well worth the money to hire a vehicle if you can afford to do so.

Alab is a pretty village where you may sometimes see panning in the river. A three-hour climb takes you to Ganga, above the village and past burial caves to **petroglyphs** that have not been deciphered. You will need a knowledgeable guide.

Further south, **Balili**, known for jewelry making, is a short hike into the mountains.

One-third of the way from Sagada to Baguio, the **Mt. Data Lodge** nestles in the few pines remaining from a once extensive forest. It is a nice place to stop for a break to stretch your legs, a good lunch, or for an evening rest.

WHERE TO STAY & EAT

MOUNT DATA LODGE, *off the Halsema "highway" in Bauko, between Baguio and Bontoc, just over the border from Benguet. Manila reservations: Tel. 812-1984, Fax 812-1164. 22 rooms. $40 per single, $55 per double.*

This little-used lodge is a great peaceful place built of pine and among a few trees, on a once-forested mountain. Rooms are comfortable, carpeted, and have private bathrooms. The restaurant is spacious and well decorated with antique photographs that should be better preserved, and the food is good — try the chicken *adobo*.

There are several walks in the vicinity, through farms and the remaining bit of forest. Cultural performances are given when there are enough guests — it is interesting to compare the dances and rituals of the Bontoc of this area with those presented by the Ifugao at the Banaue Hotel. Management is friendly and helpful.

16. CAGAYAN VALLEY

The **Cagayan Valley** is an off-the-beaten-track destination. If you're adventurous, the area offers an array of interesting sites and activities: historic and scenic spots, hiking, swimming, fishing, churches of religious and architectural appeal, beautiful caves, and the **Palanan rainforest**. If you need the comforts of first-class amenities, you had better skip this area.

Provinces of the Cagayan Valley include Nueva Vizcaya, Quirino, Isabela, and Cagayan. The valley's **Cagayan River**, also known as the Rio Grande de Cagayan, is the Philippines' longest and mightiest water-course. Streams from the Balete (Dalton) Pass; Luzon's central mountain ranges: Cordillera Centrale and Caraballo Sur; and the Sierra Madre converge with other streams and rivers forming an impressive expanse of water that eventually flows into the Babuyan Channel at the north of Luzon.

TUGUEGARAO

The capital of Cagayan Province, **Tuguegarao**, bustles with commerce and students who come from all over the valley to attend colleges. Tuguegarao is accessible by both air and land, and has the most developed tourist facilities in the area.

ARRIVALS & DEPARTURES

By Air

The daily Philippine Airlines flight from Manila to Tuguegarao takes 65 minutes.

By Land

The trip to Tuguegarao takes 10-12 hours. Autobus, Baliwag, Columbus, and Victory have at least one daily trip, and continue to Aparri. Several minibuses and jeepneys ply the Tuguegarao-Aparri route; travel time is two hours.

THE BALETE (DALTON) PASS

The **Balete (Dalton) Pass** is a rugged piece of terrain where a spur of the Caraballo Sur reaches out and joins the Sierra Madre. The major watercourses of the Pampanga and Cagayan valleys trace part of their origins here. This pass long prevented commerce and contact between the people of the two valleys. As a result, different cultures and dialects developed.

Strategically important as the only access between two huge valleys, the Balete Pass was the scene of bloody fighting towards the end of World War Two. American and Filipino soldiers were determined to dislodge the Japanese troops who were trying to hold their positions. As a result, the blood of almost 10,000 soldiers mingled with the soil and, for a while, the river ran red. Today, white markers commemorating the sacrifices on both sides stand near the road's highest point. From this point there are good views of both valleys.

The next fatal event, about 45 years later, was a devastatingly intense earthquake (7.7 on the Richter scale) that collapsed buildings (including schools and hospitals), destroyed roads, and skinned the topsoil off the hills. Thousands of people were killed or injured. Driving north from San José to Santa Fé you can still see the evidence of the massive landslides that closed the road for 5-6 months and filled the Digdig River. Today, the upper level of the river is several meters higher than before, and you can still see evidence of the massive scars left when vast areas of topsoil was shaken off the hills.

GETTING AROUND

Minibuses, jeepneys, and tricylces provide intertown transport. If you are planning on seeing a number of points, consider renting a jeepney for the day (about $40-60).

WHERE TO STAY

HOTEL LORITA, Rizal Street. Tel. 844-1390. 25 rooms. $28-41 per single or double, $41-50 per suite.

Rooms are fair, simple, and air conditioned. There is a restaurant.

HOTEL ROMA, Luna Street. Tel. 844-1057, 446-1728, 30 rooms. $13 per single $23-30 per double aircon, $32 per suite, $9 per single or double non-aircon.

The Roma has a newer building; simple, clean rooms; and a restaurant.

CASA LUDIVINA, Maharlika Highway. Tel. 844-1739. $13 per single or double aircon, $8 per single or double non-aircon.

Simple and homey; clean rooms with private bathrooms; restaurant.

GEORGIE'S INN, *Aguinaldo Street. Tel. 844-1434. 23 rooms. $10 per single or $13 per double aircon, $7 per single or $8 per double non-aircon.*
Georgie's is a simple place with good clean rooms and a restaurant.
HOTEL DEL FINO, *Gonzaga Street. Tel. 844-1952, 844-1953. 54 rooms. $10 per single, $12 per double, $16 per suite.*
The suites are nice, and all rooms are air conditioned and sort of clean. There is an ice cream house and a restaurant.
HOTEL LEONOR, *Rizal Street. Tel. 844-1806, 844-1627. $12 per single or double aircon, $8 per single or double non-aircon.*
This place has simple clean rooms with private bathrooms, and a restaurant.
CALLAO CAVES RESORT, *Callao, Peñablanca. Tel. 844-1087, 844-1801; $18-27 per single or double cottage, $4 per person per dorm.*
Ideally located for hiking, caving, and swimming, some of the cottages here may be in better condition than others; inspect first. Food will have to be prearranged or brought along. At the end of the driveway is a small store where you can order simple meals.

WHERE TO EAT

You can get simple lunches and snacks from a **canteen** at the capital site. For restaurants, try:
LA PAMPANGUEÑA, *Bonifacio Street.*
Serves good native food: *kare-kare, batsoy,* and *sinigang* are the specialties.
THE BULAKEÑA, *Gonzaga Street.*
Serves good Filipino fare.
MARILYN'S has been recommended for local food.
MYROSE, *Hotel del Fino, Gonzaga Street.* and **HAI TIN**, *Gonzaga Street.*
Both restaurants pecialize in Chinese cuisine.

SEEING THE SIGHTS

Tuguegarao's imposing **St. Peter's Cathedral** has an interesting façade with three-dimensional columns and a pediment that curves gently rather than the usual straight lines. Adjacent to the cathedral are some **ruins**. From here, walk five blocks south down Rizal Street to the remains of the **Old Horno** (kiln) by the river. During the Spanish era, bricks were formed and baked at the Old Horno, then sent to nearby towns to build houses and churches.
The provincial capital is seven kilometers south of the city center along the highway. This is where you'll find the **Cagayan Provincial Museum**, with a collection of Spanish-era artifacts, archaeological finds that include fossils of elephants that once roamed the area, and a display

about the indigenous people of the Cagayan Valley. The small museum shop sells baskets and other handicrafts made by the valley's minorities; the baskets made by the Aetas are especially attractive.

Opposite the Provincial Museum, the **National Museum** displays some of the geological and archaeological remains from the valley. The exhibit is well arranged so that it explains the region's history. Pygmy elephants, rhinoceros, and other now extinct flora and fauna inhabited the Cagayan Valley a million years ago.

EXCURSIONS & DAY TRIPS
Callao Caves, Peñablanca

Along the highway, just south of the capital site, a road heads eastward to **Peñablanca** and the **Callao Caves**. If you do not have private transport, take a jeep to Callao at Don Domingo in Tuguegarao. Fare is 30¢ (P8) per person.

The caves are named after the beautiful *kalaw*, or hornbill, which once inhabited the area. The Spanish Hispanized the spelling to callao, but the original pronunciation remained. The *kalaw*s' habitat was encroached upon by people who came to farm and cut the forests; sadly, you will no longer find them in the area.

You can follow the road to the cave's entrance, or, from the simple resort, take a *banca* (40¢ per person) across the river and then climb 200-250 stairs to the spectacular caves. Even though some formations have been destroyed, the caves remain a beautiful sight. Stroll through the seven chambers, and ask the caretaker to turn on the lights in the first chamber so you may see how lovely the cave is.

If you take a banca upriver, past Mororan, there is an idyllic place where water showers into the river from an underground stream in the cliff above. On a small white beach, relax and watch the sunset and, at dusk, see the bats stream out of the cave above.

Further upstream, fishermen dig trenches to create traps for ipon, the tiny fish fry that make their way upstream. Tiny dams, constructed by the fishermen, channel the fish into banana trunk tubes. Try *ipon* or *mori*, tiny hatchlings caught in the Cagayan River and fried in an omelet. Both delicacies are seasonal.

Within Callao and Peñablanca are at least 11 other caves, and more in Solana. Some have yielded very ancient remains. Spelunkers and those with exploratory urges should contact the **Sierra Madre Outdoor Club**, *Tel. 844-1560*, for guides and information.

TEDDY ROOSEVELT OFF THE BEATEN TRACK

When Teddy Roosevelt was in the Philippines, he visited the Callao Caves. He arrived on horseback and scaled the steep hillside clinging to roots and vines to get to the mouth of the cave. This was quite an achievement – Roosevelt suffered from physical infirmities his whole life.

South of Tuguegarao

If you are driving up from Manila, we have listed a few points to visit enroute. If you are flying in to Tuguegarao, these sights are accessible by bus, minibus, or jeepney. If you have adequate funds, consider renting a jeepney. Points of interest are listed from south to north.

Bayombong is the capital of Nueva Vizcaya. Negritoes come from the hills every year to celebrate the town's fiesta, which occurs during the first week of August. Reenacting the welcome originally accorded the patron saint, they dance in front of the church and around houses. A few kilometers further north, the highway splits and the left spur heads into Ifugao Province and its fabled rice terraces.

From Nueva Vizcaya, the highway takes you to the province of Isabela. At **Santiago**, a road heads westward, 26 kilometers to the Magat River. The immense **Magat Dam** provides water for farms and some electricity. From here, there are fantastic views. Back along the highway, two towns later, **Alicia's** pretty church is an example of typical old Spanish architecture and is worth a stop.

Ten kilometers above **Ilagan**, the capital of Isabela, a road turns east to the **Fuyot Springs National Park** and **Sta Victoria Caves**. The park has over a dozen caves, and lots of mosquitoes — it is a malaria area — make sure you've taken the proper medication, cover up well, and apply plenty of bug spray. The land was donated to the government in hopes that the caves and springs would be preserved. However, the lone keeper cannot keep squatters, *kaingeros* (slash-and-burn farmers), and illegal loggers from eating away at the more remote areas. To make arrangements to get to the caves, contact Mr. Arturo Ansa (whose father gave Fuyot to the government); he lives near Sta Victoria. If you can not find him, then ask the DENR officer in charge of the park to accompany you to the caves or arrange for a guide.

The **Palanan Rain Forest** is eastward by the coast of Isabela. This is one of the Philippines' few remaining rainforests, and it hosts numerous unknown species of flora and fauna. Research has been conducted here by international and local organizations concerned with rainforest preservation. It is a paradise for adventurers and researchers. The area is not easily accessible. To fly in from Cauayan, contact Mr. Jess T. Limbo of **Northern Air Services**, *Cauayan Airport, Cauayan, Isabela, Tel. 634-5517, Fax 634-5450, or in Manila at Tel. 362-2894.* The flight takes one hour and costs $80 per person. The other alternatives are by *banca* from Sta Ana, Cagayan or hiking in from Ilagan, Isabela.

The long, cemented road between Ilagan and Tuguegarao winds gently through farms and over rivers. Tobacco grown in the Cagayan Valley is used for cigars. When mature, it is picked and hung to dry, but not smoked in kilns, as is Philippine Virginia tobacco of the western Ilocos provinces.

Thirty kilometers north of Ilagan, along the long cemented road, is **Tumauini**. Its unique 18th century **Church of St. Matthias the Apostle** is a must see. One of the most beautiful churches in the country, it was built of brick to compensate for the region's lack of good stone. The round bell tower has wedding-cake-like decor around its exterior. The church and its extensive plaza walls repeat and accentuate the motif. Look closely to see how ordinary bricks were transformed into detailed works of art. The raised designs were baked into the bricks before building started, a feat that requires much forethought.

The ruins of **San Pablo** are further north along the road to Tuguegarao. Over three decades ago, a cyclone destroyed the church. Because the community is not large enough to warrant complete repair, the ruins have been partly covered by tin sheets to provide the parishioners with a place to worship. The remnants of the once large and elegant church show that it may have rivaled the beauty of Tumauini's. It is probable that San Pablo's church antedates Tumauni's, as the bricks of San Pablo are not as highly fired as those used in Tumauni. Climb the bell tower for great pictures and views across the valley and farms below.

Excursions North

Most of the people in the towns between Tuguegarao and Aparri are of **Ilocano**, **Ytawes**, and **Ybannag** ethnic origins. For centuries, these people lived side-by-side but in separate communities, each group retaining a different dialect. The Ybannag originally lived in the Cagayan Valley lowlands. Their name derives from Bannag, the Cagayan River's pre-Spanish name, and *y* means "of or from" in Ilocano. The Ytawes, a subgroup of the Ybannag, came from the hilly areas of southern Cagayan.

When the Spanish arrived, they encouraged Ilocanos to immigrate to Cagayan because they were considered more cooperative than the natives. The Ilocanos named areas they settled after towns they left. Most town centers are inhabited by Ybannag and Ytawes. The Ilocanos settled in the surrounding areas, and some Ilocano mayors have rebuilt the town hall outside the center, in predominantly Ilocano *barangays*.

Northwest from Tuguegarao, in the pretty little **church** of Piat, is the statue of **Our Lady of Piat**. Thousands of visitors visit her annually in hopes of benefiting from the miraculous powers attributed to the icon. She came from Acapulco via Macao, arrived in Lal-lo in 1604, and was evacuated to Piat. Shortly after she came, the warlike Ytawes people became peaceful, a feat she is credited with. Across the Chico River is another pretty town, **Tuao**.

Iguig (an Ytawid word pronounced "hig-ig") has an attractive **church** that was built between 1765 and 1787. The church has unusual flying buttresses that protect it from soil erosion. On a hill right beside the church are larger-than-life-size stations of the cross. Walk with them over the hill to the last moving sculpture of Christ on Mary's lap with the vast river, valley, and mountains as its backdrop.

Continue northward to the Ilocano town of **Alcala**. Its church is large and attractive. Just before the town proper, stop at the "Milk Candy" sign on the right side. Try the delicious *pastillas* made from *carabao* milk.

Before you reach Gattaran, a road turns right to the **Mapaso Hot Springs**. From the springs, a long hike (feasible only during dry season because of river crossings) takes you to **Tanlagan Falls**. Both water sources flow into the Dumon River, a tributary of the mighty Cagayan.

Sixteen kilometers north from Gattaran, you arrive in **Lal-lo**, the first seat of the northern diocese of Nueva Segovia. The parish dates from 1595 and the church, of a later construction, was the first built in the Cagayan Valley. Ruins of an old fort now lie in grass and weeds on private property nearby.

Continue northward to **Camalniugan**, where the church's unremarkable bell tower houses the oldest European bell in the Orient. The **Sta Maria bell** was forged in 1595.

Beyond town, a road leads right for a 90-minute ride to **San Vicente**, the northernmost tip of eastern Luzon. The road by-passes Buguey, where the Spanish first landed in Cagayan, and continues through Sta Teresita and Mision. The Cagayan River may once have had its mouth in Mision, later shifting westward to its current riverbed. San Vicente is known as the "sailfish capital" of the Philippines — a popular place for game fishermen, who maintain a dorm-like guest house. You may be able to stay at the guest house when there is no fishing tournament.

Palaui Island was once a volcano where lava flowed and twisted dramatically down to the coast. Small pretty sand or pebble beaches and interesting rock formations dot the island's coast. Snorkeling off shore is pretty good, and a walk up a hill will take you to the **Cape Engaño lighthouse** for great views of the sea and nearby **Dos Hermanas Islands**. Below is a beautiful white sand beach set against azure waters, a great place to climb down to and relax. Palaui is inhabited by Dumagats and mainlanders who come to fish and may stay several days in huts by the shore.

To get to the island, *bancas* may be arranged from San Vicente. Lodging is available at the **PALAUI ISLAND RESTHOUSE**; arrangements can be made through Mr. Terry Collado, *Tel. (Manila) 69-2965* or at the DOT in Tuguegarao, *Tel. 844-1621*.

Aparri is situated at the end of the mighty Cagayan, where the river finally joins the sea. Here, you can hear the winds that come howling in across the **Babuyan Channel**. Even in good weather, large waves push onto the wide, sloping beach — the power of the sea and the river are awesome, and the roofs of houses are tied down with bamboo poles.

While you are in Aparri, notice the unusual space capsule-looking four-wheeled pedicycles. There are a few basic places to stay in Aparri.

The top of Luzon is truly a beautiful and remote place. Buses journey from Tuguegarao on the east to Laoag on the west. It is a wonderfully scenic route across flat paddy lands and wide rivers, over mountains, and along cliffs where the Cordilleras plummet into the sea. There is an impressive old church in **Pamplona**; sadly, though, it is deteriorating from lack of funds. Continuing westward, you cross over into the province of Ilocos Norte.

PRACTICAL INFORMATION

Banks

Perhaps the best place to change money in Tuguegarao is at the **PNB**, along Bonifacio Street. Along the same street are **Allied**, **Equitable**, **Far East**, and **MetroBank**. **PCI Bank** has a branch on Luna Street. PNB and MetroBank also have a branch in Aparri.

Tourist Information

The regional **DOT** office, second floor of the Supermarket building on Bonifacio Street, *Tel. 844-1621*, is a good place to get information, advice, and arrangements for guides and transportation. The staff are helpful and friendly. Also try the **Provincial Tourism Council**, capital site, *Tel. 844-1039, 844-1010*; ask for Mrs. Wilma Guzman.

If you are an avid spelunker, contact the **Sierra Madre Outdoor Club**, c/o Mr. Mario Kanapi on Bonifacio Street, *Tel. 844-1560*.

17. BICOL

Bicol's best known attraction, **Mount Mayon**, is almost a perfect cone that soars gracefully to 2,462 meters above **Legazpi City**. Among Bicol's lesser-known attractions are several other volcanoes, some good beaches, and great handicrafts.

The **Bicol** region comprises Luzon's southernmost provinces: Albay, Camarines Norte and Sur, and Sorsogon, plus the island provinces of Catanduanes, Masbate, Romblon, and Tablas. This chapter treats Bicol's provinces on Luzon from north to south: first Camarines Norte and Sur, then Albay, and last, Sorsogon. Catanduanes is included in Chapter 17, *Islands Around Luzon*.

Bicol has a number of other volcanoes, most notably mounts Isarog, Asog, Masaraga, and Bulusan. Mayon and Bulusan are active, and Masaraga's latent energy powers the **Tiwi Geothermal Project**. The region also offers some lovely, remote beaches, hiking, surfing, and excellent diving. If you are looking for handicrafts, the Bicolanos are well known for their artistry with abaca and other fibers.

THE LEGEND OF MOUNT MAYON

Long ago, a maiden named **Magayon** *(which means "beautiful"), was being courted by many suitors. She fell in love with a Tagalog named* **Ulap** *and her father agreed to the marriage.* **Pagtuga**, *one of her Bicolano admirers, could not accept rejection and kidnapped Magayon's father, threatening to kill him. To save her father, Magayon consented to marry Pagtuga. Ulap appeared at the wedding ceremony and slew his rival, but a fight ensued and Magayon and Ulap were killed.*

Magayon's father buried the two lovers together. Their grave shook and grew into Mount Mayon. When Mayon quakes, it is said that Pagtuga is trying to retrieve his wedding presents. And when the top is blanketed with clouds, it is said that the Ulap and Magayon are kissing.

CAMARINES NORTE & SUR

There are a few good beaches in the **Camarines**. **Naga** is renowned for its annual fluvial festival in September, when over 10,000 people come to watch **Our Lady of Peñafrancia** floated down the Naga River.

ARRIVALS & DEPARTURES

By Air

Asian Spirit and Philippine Airlines each have two weekly flights to Daet. Flying time is 50 minutes to an hour. Philippine Airlines has two daily flights to Naga.

By Land

BLTB, Columbus, JB Bicol Express, Philtranco, RAM Transit, and Superlines all have a few daily trips to Legazpi and stop in Daet (about seven hours from Manila), Naga (about nine hours), and Iriga (about ten hours).

WHERE TO STAY & EAT

APUAO GRANDE, *Apuao Grande Island, off Mercedes, Camarines Norte. Manila reservations: Tel. 524-5816. $35 per single, $50 per double.*

Newly reopened, the resort has nice native-style cottages that are clean, fan-cooled, and have private bathrooms. Facilities include fishing, golf, and a few aquasports. The restaurant serves seafood, local, and continental dishes.

GRAND IMPERIAL HOTEL, *Burgos Street, Naga. Tel. 214-193, 211-965. $30 per single or double, $60 per suite.*

Suites have TV and a refrigerator. All rooms are air conditioned and have private bathrooms. There is a restaurant and a coffee shop.

CROWN HOTEL, *Burgos Street, Naga. Tel. 212-585. $20-30 per single or double aircon, $8 per single or double non-aircon.*

The air conditioned "suite" rooms are nice, all rooms have private bathrooms. The restaurant is the best in town. Staff is friendly.

PEÑAFRANCIA RESORT, *San Jose, between Naga and Iriga on the east coast.*

There are some nice spacious cottages (inspect first) with tiled bathrooms and a restaurant.

IBALON HOTEL, *San Francisco Street, Iriga. Tel. 353, 352. $20 per single, $30 per double.*

This is a pleasant hotel with a restaurant and friendly staff.

SEEING THE SIGHTS

Camarines Norte

Daet is the capital of Camarines Norte. Its visitors are mostly businesspeople. **Bagasbas Beach**, four and a half kilometers from Daet, is a dark sand surfing beach. From November-February, the *amihan* (onshore wind) offers surfers some good waves.

Apuao Grande Island, in San Miguel Bay just off Mercedes, has a very nice beach and a resort.

Camarines Sur

Camarines Sur's twin hubs are Naga, the business center, and Iriga, its quiet, pretty capital.

Naga City is the province's business center and facilities are geared accordingly. Its main attraction is the pretty **Peñafrancia church**, which once housed **Our Lady of Peñafrancia**. The icon is now housed in the city's new basilica. Miraculous cures have been attributed to the statue, which first arrived via Macao during the 17th century. A **fluvial parade** in her honor is held each year. During the third week of September, over 10,000 people gather to watch her tended down the Naga River by boats with all-male crews.

Pasacao Beach, less than an hour's drive from Naga, has golden-beige sand. You may be able to buy fish to roast on the beach. Very primitive overnight facilities are available. Nearby **Daruanak Island** you'll find a good place to snorkel. **Refugio Island's** white sand beaches are about an hour away by *banca*.

Mount Isarog, southeast from Naga, is an extinct volcano with a number of pretty waterfalls on its slopes. A good four-hour hike takes you to the striking **Panigwasan Falls**.

On the coast around the volcano is the long, dark sand **Partido Beach**, in Sabang, San José. There are simple resorts on the beach. If you are looking for white sand and snorkeling, take a *banca* to **Rosa** or **Aguirangay Island**.

Bonbon's attractive **church**, about 30 minutes from Naga, is flanked by a curiously leaning bell tower.

Iriga is the province's postcard pretty capital. The town nestles around the spacious city plaza with Iriga's white church in the center. The small **museum** in the Ibalon Hotel displays interesting artifacts and documents that antedate the arrival of the Spanish. Almost nothing is known of the area's ancient beliefs, as the Spanish destroyed everything they found that was associated with pagans and that could not be incorporated into Roman Catholicism. However, Attorney Reyes of the Ibalon discovered one of the few surviving documents detailing local myths. There is a great view of **Mount Asog** from behind the Ibalon.

Buhi town is beside a small crater lake that was once home to the world's smallest freshwater fish, called *tabios* or *sinarapan*. The fish no longer inhabit the lake but are found in smaller lakes. If you want to see them, head for smaller **Lake Danao**; *sinarapan* are cultivated in it and other small lakes nearby. You will need to get a guide from *barangay* Makangay, near Danao town.

LEGAZPI CITY & ALBAY PROVINCE

Albay province is home to **Mayon Volcano**. Although its once perfect conic symmetry has been knocked slightly akilter by recent eruptions, Mayon remains one of the most beautiful volcanoes in the world — a captivating, powerful presence. The last eruption was in February 1992.

You can fill several days with activities exploring Albay, always in view of Mayon. Check with the DOT office for information and assistance, especially if you are interested in climbing the volcanoes and caving.

Legazpi, Albay's capital, was built on mangrove swamps that once fringed its excellent deepwater port. The Spanish arrived in 1567 and introduced Christianity. They grouped Albay, Sorsogon, the Catanduanes, and much of Camarines Sur into a single political entity called Partido de Ibalon. During the Spanish era, Legazpi was raided several times by Muslim and Dutch pirates. And, during the Spanish-American War and World War Two, the city was the scene of much bloody fighting.

ARRIVALS & DEPARTURES
By Air

Philippine Airlines has two daily flights from Manila (65 minutes), four flights a week from Cebu, and two a week from Virac, Catanduanes.

Tricycles and jeepneys meet each incoming flight and go to Legazpi's center, and some hotels provide airport shuttle service.

By Land

The 14-hour trip between Manila and Legazpi is served by BLTB, Columbus, JB Bicol Express, Philtranco, RAM Transit, and Superlines.

GETTING AROUND

Getting around the city may be done by public transport, but it is far simpler to rent your own vehicle. Points in the Camarines and Sorsogon may be visited from Legazpi — refer to those sections, and ask the DOT or your hotel to assist with arrangements.

A constant flow of jeepneys ply the route from Legazpi to Daraga. Tricycles are available at Daraga market for short trips. Jeepneys frequently leave Legazpi for Tabaco, where you change for Tiwi or Ligao.

You can ask the driver to let you off at your intended stops on the way around the volcano. You should start early if you are going by public transport. Jeepneys and tricycles go from Camalig to Hoyophoyopan, but it is best to take a jeepney.

Buses depart frequently for Iriga and Naga. To go to Iriga, you may have to get off at Nabua and switch to a jeepney.

WHERE TO STAY

HOTEL LA TRINIDAD, *Rizal Street. Tel. 22-951 to 955. Manila reservations: Tel. 523-8054, Fax 521-1309. $31-40 per single, $36-40 per double, $62 per suite. Visa, Master Card, American Express, Diners.*

This is the most up-market hotel in Legazpi. Rooms are carpeted, air conditioned, and have private bathrooms and cable TV. Services include airport shuttle, car rental, and tours. There is a swimming pool, restaurant, coffee shop, and bar.

HOTEL VICTORIA, *Rizal Street. Tel. 22-101 to 104. $31-41 per single, $36-41 per double, $6 per extra person.*

Centrally located, this hotel has carpeted, air conditioned rooms with private bathrooms and cable TV. They offer free airport shuttle, and tours can be arranged. There is a restaurant with piano music in the evenings.

HOTEL CASABLANCA, *Peñaranda Street. Tel. 23-130, 23-131. $30 per single, $35 per double. Visa, Master Card.*

This pleasant hotel has very clean air conditioned rooms with private bathroom and cable TV. Some rooms have a good view. There is a restaurant and a disco. The staff is friendly.

LEGAZPI PLAZA, *Lapu Lapu Street. Tel. 23-344, 23-345. Manila reservations: Tel. 58-2144. $26-32 per single or double aircon, $15 per single or double non-aircon. Visa, American Express.*

This is a nice simple place, rooms have private bathrooms, and there is a restaurant.

TANCHULING, *Imperial Subdivision, Jasmin Street. Tel. 22-788, 23-494. $20 per single or double aircon, $10 per single or double non-aircon.*

Rooms are very clean and spacious. Aircon rooms have private bathrooms, and the non-aircon rooms have a very nice common bathroom. There is a restaurant.

EXECUTIVE TOURIST INN, *Lapu Lapu Street, Tel. 23-533. $15 per single or double aircon, $8 per single or double non-aircon.*

Rooms are simple, clean, nice, and have private bathrooms. There is a restaurant.

WHERE TO EAT

In Legazpi but you will find tasty Filipino and Chinese dishes. Local dishes to try include *laing*, a spicy mixture of shrimp and pork rolled in *gabi* (taro) leaves and stewed in coconut milk; and the Bicol Express, ground beef tartare with chili peppers — guaranteed to clean out any cobwebs you may have in your mouth.

SALO-SALO and **FAMILY RESTAURANT**, *both on Peñaranda Street.*
Both are simple places for Filipino food. Try especially the clams and seafood, also the fried chicken.

PEKINGHOUSE RESTAURANT, *Peñaranda Street.*
Serves good Chinese and Filipino fare.

FOUR SEASONS, *Rizal Street.*
A good place for Chinese food.

MIKE'S OAKROOMS, *Peñaranda Street.*
Good, inexpensive meals but can get stuffy in summer.

MY BROTHER'S PLACE, *Rizal Street.*
This is a simple folksy place for beer and music.

SA BAY BAY, *along the Beach just before the city proper.*
A good place for seafood and Spanish dishes.

SEEING THE SIGHTS

Legazpi is a nice city to stroll about. At the junction of Quezon and Rizal Streets, a **monument** commemorates the American forces' defeat of Filipino freedom fighters in 1900. **San Rafael Church**, on the corner of Peñaranda and Aguinaldo Streets, has a massive altar made of a 10-ton lava block. The City Hall Annex Building houses the **Legazpi City Museum**, which has a collection of photographs, documents, and artifacts that depict the city's history.

Browse through the city's **market** and many small handicraft shops, all great fun for bargain hunters.

EXCURSIONS & DAY TRIPS

Excursions include a circle around **Mayon**, a visit to Sorsogon's **Rizal Beach** and circling **Bulusan Volcano**. If you are headed to Mayon Volcano by car, consider taking time to see some sights of the Camarines provinces.

Allow anywhere from half a day to several days to explore Mayon's many attractions. You may visit ancient churches, swim at a coral islet, dive, watch scissors and knives forged, traverse recent lava flows, hike to falls, visit the volcanology station on Mayon's slopes, walk through caves, and see the ruins of a community buried by Mayon's 1814 eruption. Mayon is a great volcano to photograph, but it is often shrouded in clouds except during March, April, and May.

We have arranged the points starting at Legazpi and progressing northeast to Tiwi, then back-tracking and going inland.

Sto Domingo has a picturesque twin-towered church that was made from lava blocks. Off **Buhatan**, a simple fishing village eight kilometers from Sto Domingo, there is a **galleon wreck**. From Bacacay, you may hire a *banca* to visit the **Batan Islands** (note: not to be confused with the islands off the top of Luzon, which have the same name). Bacacay's town tourism office will help make arrangements to see the islands' rapidly disappearing wilderness and explore the **Minarosa Cave** in Villahermosa.

Rapu Rapu Island reportedly has some good diving. There are no dive operations, so you will have to provide your own equipment. Rapu Rapu town is charming, right on the water, has tricycles for transportation, and the people are friendly. A four-hour ferry ride from Legazpi City's pier takes you to Rapu Rapu; ferries leave around noon and the fare is $1.10 per person.

From **Tabaco** you may head inland and around Mayon, or take side trips to **Tiwi Geothermal Springs** or any of the area's several **waterfalls**. Tabaco's port serves passengers and cargo between the mainland and the islands of San Miguel, Cagraray, Batan, Rapu Rapu, and Catanduanes. To get to **Vera Falls**, head to *barangay* Bantayan, which is 20 minutes from Tabaco. A three- to four-hour hike from Bantayan takes you to one of the many cascades of the Malinao Mountain Range. Behind the falls is a cave. **Palele Falls** are accessed through *barangay* Labnig — ask the *barangay* captain in Labnig for a guide. An hour's hike through seven rivers and streams and an abaca plantation takes you to the secluded spot where a stream plummets 80 feet to a pool below. The falls resemble a lacy ribbon.

In **Malinao**, see the **church**'s interesting façade: St. Anne holding baby Mary, riding a cow, chasing pirates. St. Anne was credited with saving Malinao from a pirate attack.

From **Tiwi**, you can take a *banca* to **Coral Island**, a white sand strip with good snorkeling but no vegetation or shade. Near the black sand beach of **Putsan**, in Tiwi, you may see **pottery** being made. To see the **Tiwi Geothermal Plant**, make arrangements through the DOT in Legazpi.

The **Mayon Rest House and Convention Center** and the **Volcanology Station** are at the end of an access road about a third of the way up Mayon's slopes. On a clear day, you get spectacular views of the Volcano above and the bay below. There is a display about volcanism in the Volcanology Station, and you can watch the seismograph and tilt meter operating.

Hoyophoyopan Caves, about 10 kilometers southeast of Camalig, have yielded 4,000-year-old remains. During World War Two, the caves first served as a refuge from Japanese atrocities and then from American bombs. "Hoyophoyopan" means "blow, blow" in the Bicol dialect. At the entrance of the cave, you can hear the wind whistling "hoyop, hoyop." If you are interested in caving, contact Mr. Fred Nieva. He is the owner and caretaker of the caves and heads a spelunking society. He will take you on a leisurely 30 minute stroll through the cave and tell of the caves' history. Serious spelunkers will want to contact him in advance to make arrangements to explore **Calabidongan Caves**. This takes a whole day, and be prepared to get wet in the underground river.

The remains excavated from Hoyophoyopan can be viewed in **Camalig church**. The bell tower served as a lookout post during World War Two.

Cagsawa Church was built in 1587, burned in 1636, and rebuilt in 1724. In 1814, Mount Mayon erupted with great violence, and pelted **Cagsawa** with hot boulders. Over 1,000 residents who took refuge in the church were buried alive in cinders and lava. Its **ruins** are a poignant reminder of the 1814 tragedy. The grounds are now a lovely park, from which the traditional photo of Mayon behind the Cagsawa bell tower is taken. The survivors of the eruption moved to **Daraga** and built a very attractive church. There are many little handicraft shops along the road in Daraga.

Southeast of Legazpi, in Manito, is **Ilogan Beach**, a long stretch of white corral sands with diving and fishing offshore. **Balubagon Boiling Lake** is near the seashore in Manito. Here you can see geysers through the sand and corral rocks.

SPORTS & RECREATION
Caving
You can explore **Hoyophoyopan** and **Calabidongan** caves near Legazpi. Contact Mr. Fred Nieva, head of Albay's Spelunking Society, through the DOT.

Diving & Snorkeling
You can snorkel off Apuao Grande in Camarines Norte, Rosa and Aguirangay Islands in Camarines Sur, and Coral Island off Tiwi in Albay.

There are no facilities for diving. You will have to bring your own equipment, and perhaps make arrangements with one of the dive shops in Manila. There is diving off Rapu Rapu Island near Legazpi and Ilogan Beach in Manito, Albay.

Surfing
Surfers frequent Bagasbas Beach near Daet, Camarines Sur, from November through February.

Volcano Climbing
To climb Mayon, allow three or four days, and you must be in top shape. Contact Albay's DOT in Legazpi in advance, *Tel. 455-057*, and

request for their assistance in making arrangements with Eduardo Arnaldo or Ricardo Diy for guides, porters, and equipment.

Mayon is a live volcano and is monitored; inquire about any current activity before climbing.

PRACTICAL INFORMATION

Banks

PNB and the **Central Bank** are along Rizal Street in Legazpi.

Tourist Information

The **DOT office**, *Albay Freedom Park, Tel. 44-492, 44-026, Fax 455-050*, the **Albay Tourism Development Council**, *Governor's Office, Provincial Capitol, Tel. 44-411, 44-451, Fax 455-057*, and the **Legazpi City Tourism Council**, *City Hall*, can help with arrangements for caving, shorter hikes, trips to the offshore islands, and transportation, as well as suggest itineraries. The City Tourism Council has a helpful map of Legazpi City.

SORSOGON

Sorsogon's landscape has been compared to that of Hawaii, with precipitous volcanic peaks, green valleys, and pretty beaches. This province does not get many tourists. The **Sorsogon Provincial Tourism Council**, *in Fernando's Hotel, Tel. 211-1537, 211-1357*, is well staffed and very helpful. Contact them for information and they will also make arrangements for guided tours.

ARRIVALS & DEPARTURES

From Manila, Columbus, JB Bicol, and Philtranco have trips that continue from Legazpi City to Sorsogon. Several other buses depart frequently from Legazpi to Sorsogon City. The trip takes 90 minutes. JV Liner goes through to Gubat. Take a tricycle or jeepney to Rizal Beach from Gubat.

GETTING AROUND

Jeepneys ply the route around the volcano. Buses continue from Sorsogon City through to Matnog, where some await the ferry and continue the journey in Samar. Roads to Rizal Beach and to Matnog are very good, but the road around Bulusan Volcano is sometimes only negotiable by jeepney or similar sturdy vehicle.

WHERE TO STAY & EAT

As Sorsogon is a less-frequented tourist destination, facilities are limited. Fernando's Hotel and the Rizal Beach Resort are the best places to stay. The owners are involved with promoting the area's tourism and are helpful and informative.

FERNANDO'S HOTEL, *Pareja Street, Sorsogon City. Tel. 211-1573, Fax 211-1357. $30 per single or double.*

This very pleasant place has nice, clean, air conditioned rooms with private bathrooms and friendly staff. It is well managed and has a restaurant and a coffee shop.

RIZAL BEACH RESORT, *Gubat, Sorsogon. Tel. 211-1056. $20 per single or double aircon, $12 per single or double non-aircon, $6 per person per dorm.*

This place is on a nice beach. Rooms are simple, clean, and have private bathrooms. There is a restaurant.

MATEO HOT & COLD SPRINGS RESORT, *San Benon, Monbon, Irosin. $15-20 per single or double.*

The resort has simple, native-style cottages with fans, private bathrooms, and basic furnishing. Some cottages have a kitchenette and there is a restaurant.

SEEING THE SIGHTS

Before entering Sorsogon Province, as you go through **Bascaran**, **Albay**, the road may be lined with anahaw fans drying in the sun. Small ones are used as fans and large ones serve as shades. All may be used for decor.

Gubat's spectacular **Rizal Beach** has miles of golden sand in a large cove. Swim near the resort area as some portions near the center of the cove are unsafe due to the undertow. You can spend a leisurely day here enjoying the sun and sand, and looking around for shells.

A trip around **Bulusan Volcano** takes you through a remote area of hot springs, forest, picturesque coastlines, and a crater lake. South along the highway, in Irosin, are **the San Mateo Hot Springs**. Here you may bathe in healing waters of varying temperatures and stroll along the resort's forested walks. The nearby **Bulusan Volcano Observatory** monitors the volcano and has a good display of illustrations that explain volcanic activity. If you want to climb Mount Bulusan, contact the Sorsogon Tourism Council for assistance. It's a live volcano, so inquire about current activity before climbing.

Other hot springs in the area of Irosin include the **Masacrot Hot Spring** where, for a small entry fee, you may bathe, and the **Mapasao Hot Springs**, noted for its beautiful scenery. There are also several springs that flow beside the road.

After Masacrot, a road turns into **Bulusan's crater lake**. This pretty emerald-green lake nestles under steep walls lined with tropical growth.

You can walk around the lake's edge and picnic in sheds (available for rent). Bring insect repellent.

Bulusan town, after the lake, is very pretty — its houses are draped in a profusion of shrubs and flowering plants. From Bulusan, the road heads through Barcelona to Rizal Beach, and passes spectacular coastal views. The church in **Barcelona** is quaint, attractive, and has the twin bell towers characteristic of the area.

If you venture southward from Irosin, you will find remote, lovely beaches around **Sta Magdalena** and **Matnog**. From Matnog, ferries depart to Samar. Beyond the pier is the very pretty **Tiklin Island**. Although it is privately owned, the caretaker sometimes allows people to camp on the island.

In **Sta Magdalena**, five kilometers off the main highway, is a very pretty beach, great for swimming and picnics.

18. ISLANDS OFF LUZON

Luzon is surrounded by numerous islands and islets. In this chapter, we cover four of the larger islands, which together consist of five provinces. Perhaps the most developed, in terms of tourist facilities, is **Puerto Galera**, in Mindoro Oriental on Mindoro. All the islands offer spectacular scenery and activities that include hiking, diving, relaxing on a beautiful beach, visiting tribes, and more.

At the northernmost part of the Philippines lie the **Batanes Islands**. A veritable paradise for travelers who want off-the-beaten-track destinations. You can enjoy the spectacular scenery of the distinctively beautiful and unique islands; people who are peaceful and friendly in a reserved, unobtrusive way; and the interesting architecture devised to withstand gale-force winds.

Mindoro is a popular destination for many expats, city folk, and tourists, as it is not far from Manila but is a different world of precipitous mountains, primitive tribes, and nice beaches with dive spots nearby.

Marinduque, just east of Mindoro, is a small heart-shaped island known best for its **Moriones Festival**: Easter-time performances based on the story of Longinus, a Roman Centurion — his conversion to Christianity, and subsequent beheading. Participants wear colorful costumes and masks resembling Roman gladiators. Mountain climbers can also enjoy scaling the forested **Mount Malindig**.

The less-traveled island province of **Catanduanes** flanks the southeastern side of Luzon. Known to surfers for the waves at **Mystic Beach** (locally known as Puraran), this charming island has picturesque coves with fine cream sand beaches, waterfalls, churches, warm people, and a small version of a geological oddity found elsewhere in the country — the **Chocolate Hills**.

BATANES

The **Batanes** are the Philippine's northernmost islands. They are beautifully unique. Flanked by the Pacific Ocean on the east and the South China Sea on the west, the islands are lashed by gale-force winds six months of the year. Buildings have been structured accordingly — the residents live in low dwellings with massively thick walls. Even the people here look strong, and must be to survive.

Most of the time, the people live on root crops, goats, and pork. Seas are calm enough to permit fishing only during the short summer — March through June — and two weeks of Indian summer in late fall. During the Indian summer, flocks of birds migrating south for the winter stop in the Batanes for a brief respite, then continue on their journey. In recent years, cattle production and a few hardy crops have been introduced. Much of the year, everything must move in and out by air, as seas are too violent to allow shipping. There is no market and householders arrange for their needs by negotiating directly with fishermen, farmers, and butchers.

The islands' original inhabitants were probably a mixture of Malay plus Chinese and Japanese. They spoke a language that was a combination of several Philippine dialects: Tagalog, Ilocano, Pangasinan, and Ibannag from Cagayan. Y'Ami is the Batanes' northernmost island. It is only 50 miles south of Lanyu, the southernmost island of Taiwan. The people on Lanyu may have originally come from the Batanes.

When the Spanish missionaries arrived in 1686, they found the people illiterate, oppressed by the climate, and hungry for a new religion. After several tries at accommodating the islanders' wishes and adapting to climatic exigencies, the Spanish finally established a permanent settlement in 1855. Until then, the people had lived in grass and cane houses. The Spanish taught them to build solid houses of mortar and stone. The buildings you see today combine the two architectures into a westernized native house. And the boats used by the Ivatanes resemble European wooden dories more than Eastern craft.

It is difficult to single out the islands' most striking assets: the people, neat little white-walled houses, clean villages with no trash nor the odor of the animals that are everywhere, or spectacular scenery. The Batanes is a peaceful place: it is safe to camp anywhere, and the residents are honest. People are almost always ready to say "Good morning," "Hello," or "Good afternoon," in response to a greeting.

Basco, the capital, has about 12 hours of electricity daily. Residents often say they meet the planes at the airport just to have something to do, even if they don't know anybody arriving or leaving. There is a tennis court, and many residences have nightly video showings for a small fee.

The people of the Batanes are called Ivatans; in the local language this means "place where boats are cast ashore."

Climate

From July through December the Batanes are bleak and inhospitable. Rains and cold winds often continue through February. But from March through June the islands transform into a veritable paradise for travelers who like places way off-the-beaten-track. There are two weeks of good weather in late October.

ARRIVALS & DEPARTURES

During the summer months, Philippine Airlines flies to Basco three days a week. The flight takes two hours and forty minutes.

GETTING AROUND

A few jeepneys travel to Uyugan and sometimes Itbud. The most convenient way to see Batan Island is to hire a vehicle (about $60): try Liling Astudillo, Felipe Amboy, or Engineer Abad. Public transport does not reach the beautiful interior. If you have lots of time, prefer to conserve money, and are a good walker, set out on foot or do a combination of jeepney and walking.

Basco Development Corp. can also provide guides. If you are interested in **bird watching**, contact Tony Fidel.

WHERE TO STAY & EAT

Lodging is available in **Basco**. Places are basic and bathrooms are common. In Ivana, there is a campsite where you may pitch tents and on Sabtang Island there are dorm rooms in the Fishery School. The Philippine Tourism Authority has plans to complete the construction of a simple resort in Basco. A few small shops in town sell the basic necessities, plus junk food. Food shortages in the Batanes are not uncommon. Bring snacks and any other needed items.

MAMA LILY'S, *$14 per person, including meals.*
Cean rooms in a family home. The food is very good. Liling Astudillo, Mama Lily's daughter, can arrange transport and guides.

IRAYA LODGE, *$12 per person.*
A nice place that serves meals.

IVATAN LODGE, *$8 per person.*
Run by the provincial government and serves food.

ST DOMINIC COLLEGE, *$5 per person.*
Dorm rooms.

Pronounce "e" as "uh" and "j" as "h" (like "j" is pronounced in Spanish).

Dios Mamajes – *pronounced "dee-os mama-huhs," Thank You*
Dios Mavidin – *Goodbye, said by the person departing.*
Dios Machivan – *Goodbye, said by the person staying behind.*
Avayat – *west*
Valugan – *east*

SEEING THE SIGHTS

Basco, the capital, is a pretty community of attractive, solid buildings and somewhat resembles the wind-swept isles off England. There are no industries and few souvenirs to buy. Many visitors purchase a *so-ot* (the grass headdress Ivatan women use to protect their head, shoulders, and back from rain, wind, and sun). You can ask Liling (see *Where to Stay,* Mama Lily's above) to help you acquire a *so-ot* and you may find some interesting baskets in town or along the Mahatao road. The capitol building has a few small outlets selling handicrafts.

Basco's lovely **church** stands in the center of town and looks towards the harbor and bay below. The first stone church was built in 1787-96, but was destroyed by a typhoon. The front and north wall of the original church are used by the current one. The back and south walls have been constructed within the ruins, a thrifty and sensible adaptation.

The spacious **plaza** fronts the capitol building. Behind Basco are hills with fields and pastures. Steep volcanic Mt. Iraya provides a back-drop.

EXCURSIONS & DAY TRIPS

Walks can range from a few minutes in and about town to days spent exploring around the south of the island, a good 30 kilometer hike.

Past the cemetery, up **Naidi Hills**, are three abandoned prewar telecommunication houses and great views. They say that the rocks are home to the spirits of Basco's ancestors who once lived on highland plateaus and gathered piles of rocks for self defense. If there are spirits, they are as peaceful as their descendants.

Espicoco Beach, a few hundred meters along the south road, is a pretty beach fringed by coconut trees. This is the closest place for a swim.

A pleasant three-kilometer walk east from Basco takes you by picturesque farms, farm houses, and dory-builders to a tremendous pebble beach at **San Joaquin**. Powerful waves from the Pacific Ocean crash ashore with such intensity that receding waves move the rocks and cause a thunderous roll. Listening to the power of the sea is truly an invigorating experience.

For a more swimmable pebble beach, head three kilometers north from Basco to **Chadpidan Beach**. Along the way are beautiful views of **Mount Iraya** and its steep foothills. Bring a hat, as there is almost no shade.

Island Circle

About four jeepneys a day go from Basco to **Uyugan** and back. On Sundays and "plane days" (when PAL flies in), jeepneys may go as far as Itbud. The drive around the coastline is breathtaking. Whether you do this trip by jeepney, on foot, or a combination, bring several rolls of film. Each village has clusters of attractive houses. The China Sea coastline, from Maijin point in the south through to Basco, has lots of pretty beaches with sandy shores and coral coasts good for snorkelers.

Proceed to **Mahatao**, a picturesque village. During fiestas, as many as 75 cattle are slaughtered to feed revelers, and bullfights are held for amusement. Just above Mavatui Point, south of Mahatao, is **White Beach**, one of the prettiest beaches here.

From Mahatao, head eastward and take a left at the fork to **Diojo**, a spectacular pebble beach. At the village to the right of the wharf, you can get water and, occasionally, fish. The right fork takes you on an 8-10 kilometer walk past fabulous views and through steep pastures where ponies and cattle run free — remember to close and latch all gates after you. You can camp out at the old **Loran Station**, where the high road meets the coastal road. If there is no water, then continue to **Itbud** or backtrack one kilometer to **Imnajbu**.

As you follow the road between Itbud and Uyugan, you will pass **Vanishing Barrio**, ruins of houses deserted in the mid-1950s after a tidal wave wiped out the village.

Continue around the southern tip to **Ivana**. The church was built in 1785 and made smaller in 1844 because the community's population decreased. There are also many solid old houses, with heavy windows and doors, and six century-old bridges to admire. From Ivana, boats ply the 35-minute passage to Sabtang Island.

Sabtang

Sabtang is a great island for trekking. You can spend your time hiking to the different villages and up the hills for wonderful views of the entire area and the sea. A circle of the island is either a brisk day excursion or a two-day walk; you may also hire a motorcycle.

Sabtang's stone and thatched houses are grayer and look older than those on Batan. Do investigate the *idjangs*. These pre-Hispanic fortresses were once used by the inhabitants as defensive positions from which they threw rocks down upon enemies below.

One ferry leaves daily, early in the morning, from Ivana. If you do not catch it, then you may rent a *falowa* (the local round-bottom boat). Do the crossing as early as possible; the Ivana channel can get quite rough, even in good weather. You will get wet, especially as you clamber aboard the ferry. To catch the ferry, you should board an Ivana-bound jeepney that leaves Basco between 4:30-5:00am.

There are no formal lodging places on Sabtang. You may stay at the **Fishery School**, which has nice dorm rooms. Bring a sleeping bag, supplies, water, and food. Contact Mr. Valerio Cabildo, schoolmaster, for information and lodging in Sumnanga. Bring gifts to exchange for meals if no charge is made.

Itbayat

Itbayat is the largest island of the Batanes' islands. It is four hours from Basco by boat, and crossing should only be attempted in the best of weather.

CATANDUANES

The peaceful **Catanduanes** islands are ideal for vacationers seeking relaxation or adventure. Best known for surfing, the main island has much more to offer: great sandy beaches, waterfalls, lagoons, churches, hospitable people, and a small version of the **Chocolate Hills**.

Historians claim that "Catanduanes" stems from *Katandungan*, Malay for a place of refuge in times of danger – for centuries the island has been refuge during stormy seas for ships plying the Pacific Ocean. Others contend that an ancient legend traces the province's name to *tandu*, a common click beetle that was found throughout the island.

What is known about Catanduanes' history comes from church chronicles and word of mouth. Much information on the island's past was lost during Moro pirate attacks. It is believed that early immigrants that came during the 13th century were from Borneo, China, and Malaysia. First contact with the Spanish was in 1573, when Juan de Salcedo arrived in pursuit of Moro pirates. Then, in 1576, the galleon *Espiritu Santo* sank off Batalay, Bato, en route to Manila from Acapulco. Among the survivors were Friar Diego de Herrera and Agustinian missionaries. Friar Herrera was buried alive for attempting to Christianize the inhabitants. Eventually, the missionaries succeeded and today the majority of the islanders are Roman Catholic.

The first Christian cross erected on the island marks Friar Herrera's grave, and there are many chapels and old stone churches around the island. Its churches are shorter than many on the mainland, structured for an area hit hard by typhoons, but are just as impressive.

ARRIVALS & DEPARTURES

By Air

Two carriers fly between Manila and Virac. Asian Spirit has a daily trip that takes 80 minutes and Philippine Airlines has a daily 50-minute flight.

By Sea

From Tabaco, Albay, a daily ferry takes four hours to reach Virac. Fare is $5 per person. (If you are coming from Manila, take a BLTB, JB Bicol, or Philtranco bus to Tabaco.)

GETTING AROUND

Catanduanes is for travelers who are accustomed to being off-the-beaten-track. The most convenient way to get around is by renting a jeepney or motorcycle. Although most points are covered on regular jeepney routes, the trips may be infrequent. If you are fit, you may do portions on foot. Catanduanes is a nice place to walk – clean air and roads, nice scenery, friendly people; but it can get quite hot.

Because the province is often hit, and hard, by typhoons, some of the main roads are repeatedly under repair. The people make do with what they have, and set up temporary systems – when we were last there, the main bridge was out, and people and cargo (including several motorcycles) were ferried in small, very thin, *bancas* that were rowed across the muddy river. Everyone works together, the strong sense of community (which crosses social borders) adds to the Catanduanes' charm.

Before traveling north of Virac, inquire about the roads and travel time from the office of the engineer in the Capitol Building, *Tel. 811-1690.*

WHERE TO STAY

Lodging in Catanduanes is simple, and outside **Virac** is very basic. You may have to flush the toilets *tabo-tabo* style – using a *tabo* (container) to pour water into the bowl until it flushes. Most staff are friendly and helpful.

City Proper

CATANDUANES HOTEL, *San Jose Street, city proper. $12-18 per single or double.*

Rooms are simple and fan cooled. The more expensive ones have private bathrooms. There is a restaurant.

SANDY'S (BLOSSOM'S) PENSION, *by the pier. $8-14 per single or double.*

This is a friendly place with simple, clean, fan-cooled rooms with either private or common bathrooms. The restaurant has good food and the staff are friendly.

Resorts Nearby

BOSDAK BEACH RESORT, *Bosdak Beach, Magnesia del Sur, near city proper. $80 per single or double aircon, $35 per single or double non-aircon.*

This is the nicest resort here. Air conditioned rooms are in a small building beside the main pavilion (where reception and the restaurant are). The cottages, of white cement walls and thatched roofs, are on the hillside and are quite nice. The inside is spacious, and can comfortably fit up to four single beds. Cottages and rooms have private bathrooms. The restaurant serves seafood and Filipino dishes; the sizzling squid is excellent. Staff are friendly and amusing. Bosdak is a good beach for swimming and there is diving offshore.

MONTE CIELO MAR, *San Andres. $30 per single, $35 per double.*

This resort was not finished when we went. The cottages are very attractive and native-style. Some are by the beach and all have private bathrooms. The main pavilion is on a small hill, and has a nice view. The resort is on a pretty golden sand beach. There is a restaurant.

DOLLY'S BEACH RESORT, *just outside the city proper. $38 per single or double aircon, $30 per single or double non-aircon.*

Located on a dark-sand beach, this is a pleasant and friendly place with simple, clean rooms and cottages, all with private bathrooms. The staff are friendly and meals are served.

PENSION DE PAZ, *barangay Francia, Virac, Tel. 811-1680. $30 per single or double aircon, $20 per single or double non-aircon, $10 per person per dorm.*

Simple clean rooms with private bathrooms on a dark sand beach. There is a coffee shop.

Puraran (Mystic)

SORIA'S, *Puraran. $8 per person.*

Formerly "Puting Baybay Resort," Soria's is the only operational place on this lovely beach, which is known for its surf. All the other places were destroyed during a typhoon in 1995. Soria's used to include nice cottages on the beach — these, too, were destroyed by the typhoon, leaving simple, clean, fan-cooled rooms inside a main hillside cottage. Bathrooms are common. Cecilia prepares good meals for her guests. This is a great place if you are looking for peace and quiet.

WHERE TO EAT

Food in Catanduanes is simply prepared and very good, especially the seafood. The lapu-lapu and blue marlin are usually very fresh. Most resorts and lodges have a restaurant or serve meals. In Puraran, **Soria's** has a small restaurant (two tables), where Cecilia is happy to prepare a simple, tasty meal.

TRELLIS GARDEN CAFE, *Rizal Street.*

Opens at 4:00 pm, and serves good seafood and Filipino dishes. Simple pasta dishes are available The lapu-lapu is good. They also have brewed coffee, made from beans grown on Catanduanes.

CHICKEN HOUSE, *Rizal Street.*

Serves local fried chicken.

FAMILY STEAK HOUSE, *Rizal Street.*

Features flavorful local steak, tough but tasty.

SANDY'S, *by the pier.*

Open for all meals. The food is simple, tasty, and cheap (under $4 per person).

CAFE DE PAUL, *A Surtida Street.*

Serves Filipino, Chinese, and seafood dishes; try the sizzling blue marlin.

BOSDAK, *Bosdak Beach, Magnesia del Sur.*

Serves seafood and Filipino dishes with a few western dishes available. The sizzling squid is delicious and very tender.

SEEING THE SIGHTS

Virac is the small, peaceful, and very clean capital of Catanduanes. Like the rest of the islands, the people are friendly and helpful. Interesting sights around the city proper are accessible by jeepney, tricycle, or on foot.

The **Chocolate Hills**, in *barangay* Sto Domingo, is a smaller version of Bohol's geological oddity.

All around Virac are several pretty **beaches**, all fringed with aquamarine water:

- **Twin Rocks** in Igang, eight kilometers from Virac, has a picture-pretty rock formation on a nice beach. If you access the beach via the resort and are not staying there, you may be charged a fee, even though beaches are classified as public property.
- **Bosdak** in Magnesia del Sur, 12 kilometers away, has a nice beach for swimming, a good resort, and diving off-shore.
- **Batag** in Batag, is in a picturesque little cream sand cove with a limestone arch on its left. Mr. Co, who has property nearby, is happy to make arrangements for divers (see below). A coral reef nearby is good for diving. *Batag* means banana in the local dialect.

· **Mamangal** and **Balite**, neighboring coves in Balite, both have powdery golden sand and are the safest for children — the waters are usually very calm.

Antipolo, which you pass en route to Igang, has an attractive **old stone church**. Further west, in *barangay* Lictin, are the **Luyang Caves**. The cave system is a very long network with outlets in the Santo Domingo River and one in Magnesia. The entrance is cemented to facilitate some investigation, but if you intend to do serious spelunking, get a guide and have proper gear. The caves are also the tomb of countless Catandunganons who were massacred by Moro pirates in the 17th century.

East of Virac are three small waterfalls: **Maribina** in *barangay* Cabugao, **Balongbong** in *barangay* Sipi, and **Solong** in San Miguel, just north of Bato.

SPORTS & RECREATION
Hiking
Isla 911 is a local NGO that specializes in disaster relief (remember, the island is frequently ravaged by typhoons). In their free time, most of the members double as tourism promoters. They are an enjoyable and active group that can help make arrangements for hikes, spelunking, and mountain biking. Contact Bobby Deinla, Joseph Quinto, and Napol Co (c/o Napol Co., *Tel. 811-1628*) or through the **Department of Trade and Industry**, *Tel. 811-1506*.

Scuba Diving
There are no dive centers in Catanduanes, but a handful of its residents dive. Mr. Napal Co is a diver and is happy to make arrangements. Contact him in advance, *Tel. 811-1628*. He has five tanks and a compressor ($4 per refill). Not much exploration has been done here, but a few sights have been found:
· off **Batag Beach**, where Mr. Co has pretty beach house, there is a coral reef;
· off **Bosdak Beach**;
· at the **Agojo Marine Sanctuary**, in **Yocti** in San Andres; and
· off **Soboc Beach** in northeast Catanduanes.
Banca rental is $20 for half a day.

SHOPPING
Market days are Wednesday, Saturday, and Sunday. Native handicrafts are limited to abaca baskets and the local version of a *bolo,* which you'll find at the market. Souvenir T-shirts are available in town at the small department stores.

EXCURSIONS & DAY TRIPS

East Coast

Head east from Virac and cross the **Bato River** to the pretty, centuries-old **Bato Church**. Although short, its massive stone walls give it a powerful presence. If the bridge across the river is still out, you will be rowed across the river for P5 (20¢) per person or $2 per motorcycle. From Bato, a jeepney takes you to **Baras**. The trip takes about an hour and fare is 80¢ per person. Baras also has an old church, as well as waterfalls in nearby *barangay* Macutal.

En route to Baras, you may want to take a detour to **Batalay**, where the island's first religious marker, **Shrine of the Holy Cross**, rests on the site where Friar Diego de Herrera was buried alive.

If you continue north from Baras, you will get to **Puraran** (known as **Mystic** in surfing circuits). Puraran has a very pretty cove of fine cream sand and emerald water. Offshore, the waves can rise to 20 feet high, great for surfing. As of 1997, there was only one simple place to stay. It is a peaceful place, great for relaxing and getting away from "civilization." If the road from Baras is still not passable by jeepney, you can go by motorcycle (which you can rent in Virac for $15 a day) or rent a *banca* from the beach fronting Baras. The *banqueros* charge $25-50; do bargain.

Further north is another nice beach in **Dororian**. Continue to **Gigmoto** where you may take a refreshing dip in the pool at the bottom of the pretty **Nahulugan Falls**. Also in Gigmoto is the **Little Mindanao Virgin Forest**. This coastal route, from Puraran to Gigmoto, is a nice scenic hike or bouncy motorcycle ride.

Viga is probably most easily accessed through the inland road from Virac. Its **Saod Falls** plummet powerfully 100 meters. **Soboc Point**, east of Viga has a spectacular view of the Pacific Ocean. The **beach** below is surrounded by beautiful **lagoons**, and there is diving nearby. North of Viga are the **Paday Falls** in Bagamanoc, and small **Panay Island** is accessible by *banca* from Tambongan ($20-32 per *banca*).

West Coast

The **Maqueda Channel**, which flanks the west coast of Catanduanes, is well known for its very good deep sea fishing. Marlin abound in the channel. Head north along the coast to **Caramoran**. Its **Church of St John the Baptist** is the oldest church in Catanduanes. Nearby **Toytoy** is yet another pretty beach.

Continue to **Pandan** for the small but pretty **Paruway Falls**, and head to the northernmost point of the island to panoramic **Hiyop Point** for great views.

PRACTICAL INFORMATION

Change all your currency before arriving in Virac. There is a **post office** in town. For **tourist information** and assistance, contact Joy at the Department of Trade and Industry, *Tel. 811-1506,* or Bobby Deinla of **Isla 911,** *Tel. 811-1628.*

MARINDUQUE

This small heart-shaped island off the southwest coast of Luzon's Quezon Province is famous for its Easter week **Moriones Festival**. If you come for the festivities, book well in advance — most hotels, private homes, and all forms of transportation are full. Every year, returning residents, their friends and relatives, and tourists come to see the unique and imaginative reenactment of a Roman centurion's conversion to Christianity and his subsequent beheading. Performances last several days, affording enough time to visit the island's more constant attractions: its beaches, islands, and mountains. Or you can come at another time. When the island reverts to its relaxed pace, you will not run into many other tourists and will have Marinduque's sights to yourself.

Marinduque's original settlers were Mangyan and Malay people. Evidence from Sung Dynasty pottery dates contact with Chinese traders to between 920 and 1289, and remains of a junk, over 500 years old, rest on the ocean floor off the Tres Reyes Islands.

Spanish settlers, lead by Martin de Goiti and Juan de Salcedo, sailed up Marinduque's coast in 1571, and promptly claimed the island for Spain. The Spanish had trouble pronouncing *"Malandic,"* the island's original name, and changed it to Marinduque. *Malindic* means sloping.

A legend holds that the island is named for two lovers from Quezon, Princess Marin and Garduke, a poet (in Tagalog, the "e" is pronounced like Spanish "eh"). Marin's father, King Batumbacal (literally, "iron-stone"), opposed their relationship and ordered the poet slain. The two sailed out to sea and drowned together. Marinduque Island grew from the spot where the couple commited suicide.

ARRIVALS & DEPARTURES

By Air

Philippine Airlines has a daily early morning flight from Manila; flying time is 35 minutes. The airport is four kilometers north of Gasan. As most lodging is in Boac (12 kilometers north from the airport), take a jeepney or tricycle from the airport to Boac.

Given advance notice, some hotels will pick you up.

By Sea

To/From **Lucena, Quezon**, there are two or three trips daily aboard a catamaran that takes two hours, and the fare is $4 per person. There is also a ferry that takes four hours. To get to Lucena from Manila, take a BLTB bus; travel time is three hours.

To/From **Pinmalayan, Mindoro**, there is a *banca* daily; the trip takes three to four hours and costs $2 per person.

GETTING AROUND

The nicest way to see the island is to take a trip around it. To do the trip in one day, you need to hire a vehicle. If time is not a problem and you don't mind very simple accommodations, take public transport and break the trip in Torrijos. An alternative is to hike inland from Boac and emerge along the coast. For information, ask Marinduque's **Tourism Coordinator**, *c/o the Provincial Capitol, Boac, Tel. 332-1520.*

Jeepneys ply the route from Boac to Gasan and Buenavista every hour. There are daily trips between Gasan and Torrijos. Jeepneys go from Torrijos to Sta Cruz every hour. From Sta Cruz to Mogpog and Boac, there are jeepneys every half hour. In Boac, jeepneys wait near the market for passengers. Note: jeepneys operate only during daylight hours.

WHERE TO STAY

Accommodations vary: one up-market resort on a private island; a few nice seaside places, simpler cottages by the sea, and lodging houses.

Elefante Island

FANTASY ELEPHANT, *Elefante Island, off southern Marinduque. Manila reservations: Tel. 522-0101. $100-160 per single $130-190 per double, $240 per suite. Packages available: $100 per person, inclusive of meals, golf fees, transfers, $100 per couple, inclusive of breakfast and transfers. Visa, Master Card, American Express, Diners.*

Rooms are air conditioned and have the standard amenities of upscale hotels, though the standard rooms are small. Facilities include a swimming pool, tennis, golf, jacuzzi and spa, and various aquasports including diving. There is a restaurant, a bar, and a disco. The beach is well below the main resort, which is situated on a hill above. Good views.

Gasan & Buenavista

SUNSET GARDEN, *Gasan. Tel. 795-745. 10 cottages. $15 per single or double.*

This place has nice cottages. Each cottage has a double bed, ceiling fan, and common bathroom. The restaurant specializes in German-Austrian food and there is a live band every Saturday.

SUSANNA HOTSPRING, *Malbog, near Buenavista. Tel. 332-1997. $22 per single or double.*

Simple clean assorted rooms by great hot and cold springs. Arrange meals in advance.

Boac

BOAC HOTEL, *Nepomuceno Street. Tel. 332-1121. $25 per single or $30 per double aircon, $8-18 per single or double non-aircon.*

This recently renovated hotel has an attractive exterior. The aircon rooms and higher-priced non-aircon rooms have private bathrooms. The lower priced rooms have common bathrooms. There is a restaurant and a coffee shop-deli.

SUSANNA HOTEL, *Magsaysay Street. Tel. 332-1997. $20 per single or double aircon, $10-14 per single or double non-aircon.*

Rooms are small but clean, and partitions are plywood (thin). The aircon and higher priced non-aircon rooms have private bathrooms; the lower priced non-aircon rooms have common bathrooms. There is a restaurant.

CELY'S PLACE, *10 de Oktubre Street. Tel. 332-1519. $8 per person.*

This place has basic, clean, fan-cooled rooms with common bathrooms. There is a restaurant.

Around Boac

MARINDUQUE MARINE, *Balaring. $18 per single or double.*

This pleasant place has nice native sawali cottages. Rooms are fan-cooled, clean, and have private bathrooms. You can rent windsurfs and there is a dive center, restaurant-coffee shop, and bar. The staff is friendly.

AURORA'S BEACH HOUSE, *Balaring. $14 per single or double.*

Duplex cottages of cement and sawali. Bathrooms are private.

AUSSIE-POM GUESTHOUSE, *Balaring. $4-8 per single or double.*

Simple rooms with common bathrooms. There is a restaurant and guests may use the kitchen. Snorkeling gear is available.

SEAVIEW, *Cawit, Tel. 332-2840. 10 cottages. $6-12 per single or double.*

This place has nice, clean rooms with private bathrooms, good value. Home-cooked meals are provided for guests.

PYRAMID RESORT, *Caganhao. $4 per person.*

Simple, nice place, rooms are fan-cooled and have common bathrooms. Meals may be arranged.

CASSADRA BEACH RESORT, *Caganhao. 8 rooms. $6-10 per single or double.*

This is a nice place. The higher-priced rooms are cottages with private bathrooms, and the lower-priced rooms are with a common bathroom. Meals are provided for guests.

Sta Cruz

STA CRUZ HOTEL, *town proper. Tel. 321-1260. $38 per single or double.*

The hotel has air conditioned carpeted and non-carpeted rooms with private bathrooms, a coffee shop, and a disco.

JOVILLE'S RESORT, *Matalaba. $12 per single or double.*

This place has simple, nice, fan-cooled, spacious cement cottages with private bathrooms.

WHERE TO EAT

A few places do simple, tasty meals. Most hotels and resorts have a restaurant or provide meals for guests. In Gasan, **AMIGO'S** has local fare. And in Torrijos there are sometimes **barbeque stands** by White Beach.

KUSINA SA PLAZA, *Meralco Street., fronting Boac's Plaza.*

This is a local favorite serving good Filipino food.

BODEGA, *Del Mundo Street, Boac.*

Actually a beerhouse, Bodega serves meals as well.

SEEING THE SIGHTS

Boac, on the west coast, is Marinduque's capital. The original settlement was called *biak* (split) because it occupied both sides of the Boac River. The **cathedral** is massive, beautifully restored, and sits high on a hill. There are good views from the bell tower.

The **Marinduque Museum** has interesting displays, including some pieces found in the ancient junk that is submerged in the waters off the Tres Reyes Islands. Several shops in town sell *nito* baskets, decorative wooden birds, and, during Easter, Moriones helmets and T-shirts.

Moriones Festival

The **Moriones Festival** was first introduced in 1870 by **Father Dionisio Santiago**, a Mexican priest. To show the power of Christian faith, he dramatized the simple biblical passage about the Roman Centurion who ended Christ's suffering on the cross. The myth of **Longinus**, the centurion, and the week-long Moriones Festival is Father Santiago's unique creation.

The story, as narrated by Father Santiago, centers round Longinus, a one-eyed soldier. Out of pity, Longinus pierced Christ's side to end his painful suffering. Blood spurted from Christ's wound into the centurion's blind eye, and sight was restored to the eye. Longinus immediately converted to Christianity and stood watch over Christ's body. For this treasonous act, he was condemned to death. A chase ensued and three times Longinus escaped the centurions' clutches. Ultimately he was recaptured and beheaded.

SCHEDULE OF MORIONES ACTIVITIES

Use this schedule as a general guide, but expect changes.

• **On Palm Sunday:** *an early morning procession of gaily decorated palms is followed by the blessing of the palms.*

• **Holy Monday through Black Saturday:** *Moriones roam the towns of Boac, Gasan, and Mogpog.*

• **Holy Wednesday and Good Friday:** *a procession of religious statues in their carrozas (silver- and tin-plated carriages) at 5:00pm.*

• **Maudy Thursday:** *the religious reenactment of Christ's washing of the apostles' feet takes place at 4:00pm in the Boac Cathedral. At 8:00pm, the* **Sinakulo** *(passion play) is reenacted by the riverbed in Boac. It lasts several hours.*

• **Good Friday:** *starting from the riverbed in Boac, the* **Way of the Cross** *(Via Crucis), reenacting Christ's last journey, finishes at the cemetery, where Christ is placed upon the cross. In Boac, it is not a real crucifixion. There sometimes are actual brief crucifixions in Mogpog at around noon. Throughout the morning, flagellants congregate in the Mogpog town cemetery. Participants maintain amazingly good spirits as they beat their backs and draw blood from tiny razor cuts made to accommodate the process (sometimes to the beat of rock tunes from their hand-held radios). This phase ends when they go to the riverbed to "wash away their sins," and the blood from their arms and backs.*

During the **Santo Entierro** *procession, all the santos are paraded forth. They proceed from the Boac cathedral at 5:00pm, wind through the town, and return to the cathedral.*

• **The night of Black Saturday:** *the* **Moriones parade** *in Boac at about 7:00pm. A vigil mass is held in the cathedral at 8:30, and the scripted version of the beheading of Longinus takes place at 10:00pm at the riverbed. To accommodate the schedules of vacationers, the beheading is sometimes repeated at around 10 am on Easter Sunday morning.*

• **Easter Sunday:** *at 4:00am, the* **Salubong** *takes place in all towns. Communities act out the resurrection of Christ and the meeting of Mary and Christ. In Gasan, an angel (a child) is lowered from an arch, removes Mary's veil of mourning, and the choir sings the Alleluia. The original version of the* **Pugutan** *(beheading of Longinus) and the events leading up to it, take place in Mogpog at 8:00am, followed by festivities through out the morning.*

During the festival, the chase is free-for-all fun. Longinus and other centurions donning masks chase willing children and ad lib what ever comes to mind.

Moriones is a Spanish-Mexican word for helmet. You will see participants wearing colorful costumes and traditional masks that have helmets and faces with Caucasian features and beards. Some masks are very imaginative variations.

The festival's popularity spread nationwide and inevitably became commercialized. Masks are often sold after the festivities, and some are made purely to be sold along with Marinduque's traditional handicrafts and other festival souvenirs: T-shirts, hats, etc.

Other events that you can enjoy include pageants and traditional religious observances. Many reenactments are scheduled at hours convenient for visitors. Everything is great fun. Most visitors stay in Boac, but for the more authentic proceedings, head to **Mogpog** where they have retained a traditional, close-knit community feeling.

EXCURSIONS & DAY TRIPS

If you are a photography buff, consider this itinerary — head north from Boac in the morning and visit Mogpog, Sta Cruz, and Torrijos. Go to Buenavista and Gasan on the west coast in the afternoon. You will need half a day to see the Padayao Falls, *barangay* Bocboc just outside Mogpog.

In Gasan, stop by UNI Store, in front of the town hall. UNI sells **decorative birds** and **baskets**. You may watch the birds being painted.

Southwest of Gasan are the **Tres Reyes Islands**, where the remains of an ancient Chinese junk (over 500 year old) have been found. Most of the contents have been removed. A few of the items are in the museum in Boac. **Melchor**, one of the islands, has good diving, snorkeling, and swimming. Contact Marinduque Marine for diving.

Beyond **Buenavista**, a dirt road heads right. Cross the river on foot to visit the **Malbog Hot Springs**, where springs flow naturally from an attractive pool. The springs are relaxing and therapeutic. A resort is about 500 meters away.

The inland road to Torrijos climbs **Mount Malindig**'s northern slopes. At 1,157 meters, it is Marinduque's tallest mountain and is popular for trekkers and mountain climbers. Contact Marinduque's Tourism Coordinator for arrangements, *Tel. 332-1520*. The zig-zag route takes you through forested land then descends through great views of the valley and **Marlanga Bay**.

Torrijos, named after a revolutionary general, has the lovely **White Beach**. From the beach's white sands, you get fabulous views towards Mount Malidig and great swimming. There are a few rustic native cottages. You will need to bring your own bedding, and food is available in the market. You may also ask the mayor for assistance with lodging.

Northeast of Torrijos is **Talisay Cave**, in Bonliw, interesting for children.

Further north, **Salomangue Island** lies offshore. There is a very beautiful beach and a simple resort. Arrangement can be made through Willie Red of Joville's Resort in Sta Cruz.

The town of **Sta Cruz** is the hub of Marcopper Mining. In 1996, the company was responsible for a major tailings leak that killed the aquatic life of Marinduque's main river. The company has been ordered to clean up. Massive **Sta Cruz church**, built in 1714, has walls that are one and a half to two meters thick and a restored façade.

Polo and **Maniwaya islands**, of the Sta Cruz Islands, have nice beaches and good snorkeling. There are no facilities, so you will have to bring camping gear. You will have to hire a *banca* from Bitik to do the trip. Fisherman leave from Bitik at 7:00 am, but they live on the island.

After Sta Cruz, the road winds through hilly countryside to **Mogpog**. Along the way, you can stop to visit the **Bathala Caves**. The Mendoza family, who live at the trailhead to the caves, can guide you there. Interesting caves are **Simbahan**, **Snake**, **Cemetery**, and **Sekreto**.

On the northwest tip of Marinduque there are good views of **San Andres Point**. There is good diving around the point.

Mogpog town gets its name from "*mag-aapog*" meaning lime-maker, possibly in reference to a lime kiln the Spanish found when they arrived. Mogpog is where the Moriones festival started, and its reenactments are still considered most authentic.

If you have spare time, the **Padayao Falls** in *barangay* Bocboc, outside Mogpog are a nice half-day trip. Jeepney trips between Mogpog and Bocboc may be infrequent: consider hiring a jeepney in Mogpog. From Bocboc there is a 12-minute walk up-river. Cross the stream twice and bear left along an obscure path; stay close to the stream. You may swim in the pool of the falls.

PRACTICAL INFORMATION

The **Tourism Council** is very helpful and can suggest various itineraries: day trips, island hopping and diving, spelunking, and mountain climbing. Contact Marinduque's **Tourism Coordinator**, *c/o the Provincial Capitol, Boac, Tel. 332-1520.*

MINDORO

Mindoro is a favorite weekend destination for many of Manila's expat residents. It is not far from the metropolis, it's easily accessible, and is a different world: precipitous mountains, primitive tribes, great beaches, and diving. A rugged central mountain range divides the island into two provinces — Mindoro Oriental on the east, and Occidental Mindoro on the west. The highest peak is Mount Halcon (2,505 meters) in the north, followed by Mount Baco (2,488 meters) in the south.

Mindoro's name comes from *mina de oro*, Spanish for gold mine. Although no commercially viable deposits have been found, panners eke a living from streams. The economy is based on fish, rice, coconut, some cattle, and marble quarrying. As an industry, tourism is only major in **Puerto Galera** in Mindoro Oriental.

Most of today's visitors come to Puerto Galera to enjoy the beaches, reefs, and other recreational activities. Few head to the mountains to visit the tribes and the forest habitat of the reclusive *tamaraw* (small water buffalo-like animal) and Philippine Eagle. Sadly, their habitat is being encroached upon at an alarming rate.

Puerto Galera is accessible at any time of the year (except of course during major typhoons). Visit San José and Mamburao during dry season or you may find yourself stranded for a few days until the weather clears.

The Tribes

As is the case throughout most of the country (and many other parts of the world), the first settlers have successively been pushed inland by waves of more aggressive immigrants. The government has set aside reservation areas. However, the allotted spaces seldom suffice for the tribes to maintain their traditional ways. And, as the lowlanders' population continues to swell, the pressure on tribal land increases.

Mangyan is the term given to the descendants of Mindoro's original inhabitants. Alangan, Buid, Iraya, Hanunoo, Tagaydan, and Tatagnon peoples are all Mangyan. The Mangyan are an artistic people, known especially for their weavings — making belts, bags, purses, and baskets from *nito*, bamboo, *buri*, and other forest plants. More recently, they are making bead necklaces and other ornaments.

The **Hanunoo** are known for their rich musical and poetry heritage. They compose and play music on the *git-git*, a small violin-like instrument with strings made of human hair. They etch poems on bamboo tubes in an Indic script language that is different from what they use in every day life.

The Mangyan were once a friendly and hospitable people. Now, many will vanish at the sight of strangers. This is understandable. Through the years, outsiders have come to take their land and ridicule their culture.

If you do visit the tribes, respect their way of life, always request permission if you want to take their photographs, and bring gifts (matches, canned food, vitamins, medicine, etc.) in exchange for their genuine hospitality.

PUERTO GALERA

The coast of **Puerto Galera** is fringed by several beautiful little white sand beaches, some with reefs teeming with diverse marine life. Its fine deepwater port has served for many centuries as a haven for ships escaping stormy seas.

When the Spanish first arrived, they found Chinese traders bartering porcelain, silk, and jewelry, and, took the goods by force. As a result, Spanish missionaries and, later, the Americans who followed in their stead, were met with resistance from the islanders.

As news of the area's spectacular beaches spread, Puerto's citizens built little huts. Many foreigners stayed, some married local girls and built resorts. Today Puerto is a major destination, especially for low-budget and free-living travelers that come for sun, sand, and other diversions. Puerto's reefs were declared a marine sanctuary in 1974 and a number of dive shops and resorts help enforce a stringent ban on damaging or taking any of the marine life.

Around Puerto, you will find numerous beaches crowded with huts, restaurants, discos, and various aquasports outlets. The town center has many restaurants and inns, and a thriving T-shirt and flour-sack clothing industry.

Visit the small museum beside the church. It houses Chinese porcelain that was unearthed in nearby Bayanan. Ask at the church school, the *convento*, or the house behind for permission to see the collection, and leave a small donation to help with the museum's upkeep.

ARRIVALS & DEPARTURES

By Bus & Ferry

The most hassle-free and direct route to Puerto is via a private bus from the **Centrepoint** (formerly Sundowner) **Hotel** in Ermita (see Chapter 10, *Manila*), which has a tie-up with **Si-Kat Ferry**; call *Tel. 521-3344* for reservations. Cost is $12 per person. From Batangas Port, the Si-Kat ferry takes an hour and 30 minutes.

In addition, there are early morning Tritran, JAM, Batangas Express, or BLTB buses to the pier in Batangas, where you board one of the three ferries that leave at about 11:30 and 12:30. Stay on deck for spectacular views as you come into Puerto. Prices vary: $1.60 for ordinary and $2.40 for air conditioned travel. Travel time is about three hours. Inexpensive seats are quickly filled by locals, and others are reserved by touts who will try to get you to stay at a place they recommend. If you do not have a reservation, the touts may come in handy.

Returning ferries leave Puerto at 7:30, 8:00, and 9:00am. From April-May, when the seas are usually calm, there is sometimes an afternoon trip.

Manila-bound buses wait for the ferries to arrive. Be aware of your belongings at all times on the ferry and on the bus.

By Banca

Another alternative is to rent a *banca* from Batangas or Bauan. This costs around $35 and the *banca* operator must negotiate clearance with the Coast Guard – do not pay anything until you are certain that the Coast Guard will grant clearance.

GETTING AROUND

The port where the ferries dock is in Puerto Galera town. Some resorts provide transport. Jeepneys service the west coast as far as White Beach, occasionally one kilometer further, and ply the route to Sabang from where you walk to Small and Big La Laguna. They fill up very fast. Jeepney service is frequent during daylight.

You may also take a *banca* to most resorts. Fees are set by an association and depend on your destination – $6 per *banca* to Big La Laguna, or $4 per person if shared. You may have to bargain down to the standard association rate.

WHERE TO STAY

Most resorts are simple and cater to the low budget tourists, but there are a few more upscale places. Choose your area and inspect the rooms before settling in. Most places have package deals (two nights, including transport from Manila, transfers from Batangas, and breakfast). Some places also have seasonal rates: peak season (most expensive) is during Christmas through New Years, Chinese New Years, and Easter Week; high season is December-May; and off season is June-November (cheapest). Prices can vary as much as $25.

COCO BEACH ISLAND RESORT, *Coco Beach. Cellular Tel. 0912-304-7017, Fax 305-0476. Manila reservations: Tel. 521-5958, Fax 813-2286. $50-90 per single or double.*

Lovely native cottages are set in an equally lovely surrounding. All rooms are fan-cooled and have private bathrooms. Coco is on a quiet golden-sand beach that is rocky offshore. Facilities include a swimming pool, tennis, watersports, and complete dive center. The restaurant faces the beach and has good food.

TANAWIN LODGE, *Palangan. Cellular Tel. 090-306-6588. Manila reservations: Tel. 521-5958. $70-82 per person per single, $45-57 per person per double, $28-40 per person per triple, rates include breakfast, transport from Manila, and transfers. Visa, Master Card.*

Tanawin is above Varadero Bay and commands a great view of the area. It is a very nice place with attractive stone and wood cottages with nipa roofs. The interiors are tastefully furnished with native decor. All rooms are fan-cooled and have private bathrooms. Facilities include a pretty swimming pool. Diving and *banca* rentals can be arranged. The restaurant serves local and German food, and there is a bar.

CARLO'S PARADISE, *Small La Laguna. Cellular Tel. 0912-301-0717. Manila reservations: Tel. 521-2751. $41-64 per single or double aircon, $15-50 per single or double non-aircon.*

Room types vary from cottages to rooms and apartments (rooms that have kitchenettes and can fit up to four people). Bathrooms are private. There is a restaurant.

LA LAGUNA BEACH CLUB, *Big La Laguna. Cellular Tel. 0912-306-5622. Manila reservations: Tel. 521-2371, Fax 521-2393. 30 rooms. $51-65 per single or double aircon, $38-52 per single or double non-aircon. Visa, Master Card, American Express, Diners.*

The fanciest resort on La Laguna. All rooms have private bathrooms. Facilities include a swimming pool, a dive center, and aquasports. There is a restaurant and a floating bar.

ENCENADA BEACH RESORT, *Balete Beach. Cellular Tel. 0912-301-2989, Fax 305-5678. Manila reservations: Tel. 522-4105, Fax 522-4152. $30-45 per single or double. Visa, Master Card, American Express.*

This nice place is on a pretty beach. Its attractive native cottages have clean, fan-cooled rooms with private bathrooms. Aquasports and diving are available, tours can be arranged, and there is a restaurant.

EL GALLEON, *Small La Laguna. Cellular Tel. 0912-305-7087. $20-35 per single or double.*

Rooms are simple, clean, fan-cooled, and have private bathrooms. There is a complete dive center and a restaurant.

TERRACES GARDEN RESORT, *Sabang Beach. Cellular Tel. 0912-308-0136. $20-35 per single or double.*

This place has a great view. Rooms are fan-cooled and have private bathrooms. There is a restaurant.

CORAL COVE, *Sinandigan. Cellular Tel. 097-371-0892. $15-25 per single or double.*

Located on a secluded, private beach, Coral Cove has attractive concrete and sawali rooms that are fan-cooled and have private bathrooms. The resort also runs yacht trips to El Nido and Coron in Palawan, and to Boracay. There is a complete dive center, water sports, and a restaurant.

CATHY'S INN, *Boquete Beach. $15-20 per single or double.*

This is a friendly place with clean, fan-cooled cottages that have private bathrooms.

TAMARAW BEACH, *Aninuan Beach. Cellular Tel. 0912-306-6388. $15-25.*

This place is nice and on a good, uncrowded, sandy beach. Rooms are clean, fan-cooled, and have private bathrooms. There is a restaurant.

CAPT'N GREGG'S, *Sabang Beach. $10-20 per single or double.*

This place caters to divers and has fan-cooled rooms with private bathrooms, a complete dive center, and a good restaurant. Capt'n Gregg's has a case of relics recovered from junks claimed by offshore reefs.

WHERE TO EAT

As many foreign nationals have settled down here, you will find a variety of cuisines. It is sensible to ask around when you arrive — a normally good place may be in a slump if the cook is off, and places come and go with amazing rapidity.

PIER PUB PIZZA, *at the end of the harbor front.*
A casual, friendly place with good seafood pizza.

HARBOR POINT, *midway along the harbor front.*
They offer tasty wiener schnitzel and the best french fries in Puerto.

EL CANONERO, *by the wharf.*
Serves both European and Filipino fare.

MARGARITA'S, *by the pier along the main road.*
Local and western meals.

PALABOK, *near the pier along the main road.*
Serves Filipino food.

CHINA MOON, *near Rizal Street, on the road to Balete Beach.*
Features a variety of international dishes.

BAHAY PILIPINO, *where P. Conception meets Rizal Street.*
A popular place with a Filipino and international menu.

MAIRITCH BAKERY, *P. Conception Street near Rizal Street.*
A great place to pick up some fresh rolls and breads for a light breakfast.

CAPT'N GREGG'S, *Sabang.*
Specializes in European food and has some interesting relics collected from the offshore wrecks.

GIGI'S, *Sabang.*
Local and western fare.

NIGHTLIFE & ENTERTAINMENT

Puerto Galera has an active night scene, with discos and bars (including two floating bars). Most of the places are concentrated along Sabang Beach. The floating bars, **Calypso** and **Yap-Yum**, are in Sabang.

SPORTS & RECREATION

Diving

The reefs around Puerto Galera have abundant and colorful marine life. The area is a marine sanctuary – it is illegal to collect any form of marine life or to spearfish here. The residents take an active role in enforcing this, and expect you to respect the sanctuary.

There are numerous dive spots in the area. Go with a reliable guide from one of the dive centers. **Escarceo** has the reputation of being the prettiest area. Its marine life is abundant and it has several unique rock formations. A guide is necessary as currents can be unpredictable.

Recommended dive operations include:
• **Asia Divers**, *Small La Laguna, Coco Beach, and Sabang, Cellular Tel. 0912-305-0652, Manila contact: c/o Swagman Travel, Tel. 522-3650*
• **Capt'n Gregg's**, *Sabang, Manila contact: Capt'n Gregg's Nautical Bar, 1313 del Pilar Street, Ermita, Tel. 522-0248*
• **Cocktail Divers**, *Sabang, and Balete Beach, Manila contact: Tel. 551-5555*
• **Galleon Diving**, *Small La Laguna, cellular Tel. 0912-305-7087, Manila contact: Tel. 673-4849*
• **South Sea Divers**, *Sabang*

EXCURSIONS & DAY TRIPS

Puerto has a variety of beaches to offer. Westward, the beaches are sandy, good for swimming but not snorkeling. **White Beach** is very popular and crowded. The sea floor drops a few meters from shore, and may get too deep for young children and people who do not know how to swim. A number of simple resorts line the beach. As you continue west, the beaches are quieter. **Tamaraw** has some nice cottages. **Aninuan** has a few simple resorts, as does **Talipanan**, the farthest west of this lot.

The beaches along the coast of the peninsula that juts northeast of town proper are mostly rocky and offer good snorkeling with some good dive spots just off shore. On the tip of the peninsula are:
• **Sabang**, the most crowded, which has much of the nightlife, several dive operators, and a path that leads east to **Escarceo Point** for a lighthouse and great views (especially sunset);
• **Small La Laguna**, relatively quiet, most people come here for snorkeling and diving;
• **Big La Laguna**, crowded – resorts are packed together, but the reef just off-shore has great snorkeling; and
• **Coco Beach**, pretty, private, and peaceful.

The islands in **Boquete Bay** have a number of resorts and good beaches. **Boquete Beach** on **Paniquian** (actually attached to the mainland) has strong currents. **Haligi Beach**, on the other side of Paniquian, has good snorkeling, as does **Long Beach** on **Medio Island**, at the mouth of the Bay. Farther away, **Verde Island** has good snorkeling and several dive spots that range from easy to difficult (very strong currents).

South of the town center are **Balete**, **Hundora**, **Tabinay**, and **Dulangan beaches**. The seas can get rough. Leisurely walks along the coastal roads give you many fabulous views of the azure waters and white beaches, sometimes with boats, all framed by coconut trees.

When you tire of the beach scene, you can make arrangements to visit the **Mangyan**. There are two reservations: one at **Baclayan**, the other at **Talipanan**. It is about a two-hour walk to either settlement. Near Baclayan is the deep and narrow **Python Cave**.

You may also want to take a 90-minute to two-hour walk uphill to the **Ponderosa Golf Club**. Follow a foot trail from behind White Beach. It joins the jeep track that forks off the coastal road. There are great views along the trail, and you can get an excellent meal at the club.

The **Tamaraw Falls** are further in from the Calapan road, and you need a guide ($12-15). En route to Calapan, you may see gold panning and marble quarrying at **Dulangan**.

PRACTICAL INFORMATION
Banks
Although you can change money and travelers checks at the rural bank in town, you will get a better rate in Manila.

Mail
The post office is by the church.

SAN JOSÉ
San José, Mindoro's largest town, is mainly business-oriented. It is a good departure point if you intend to visit Mangyan settlements. San José does not have a tourism organization, and some locals who come in to contact with travelers have asked high prices for their services.

ARRIVALS & DEPARTURES
By Air
Two companies provide service between Manila and San José: Asian Spirit has a daily flight that takes 70 minutes, and Philippine Airlines has a daily 55-minute flight.

By Sea
A ferry departs the Batangas City port early each morning; the voyage takes 10 hours.

GETTING AROUND

The only way to get around is by tricycle (which go off service at 7:00pm) or jeepney. As this is not a tourism-oriented place, to get around conveniently you may have to rent a jeepney.

To get to Apo Island, take a take a jeep to Sablayan, and hire a *banca* ($100) for the day. There is no regular boat service.

WHERE TO STAY

Lodging in town is fairly simple, most places cater to local traveling business people. A nearby beach resort caters to divers.

MINA DE ORO, *Ilin Island off San José. Manila reservations: Tel. 812-4665. $45-60 per single, $55-70 per double, $15 per extra bed. Visa, Master Card.*

This place has pleasant, clean rooms in attractive native cottages along a pretty cream sand beach. The staff is friendly and the restaurant serves native and fresh seafood dishes. There is a complete and professionally run dive center.

BIG NEWK, *near the municipio, San José. $15-25 per single or double.*

This simple place has clean, airy, air conditioned rooms and private bathrooms. The staff are very helpful.

SIKATUNA BEACH RESORT, *San José. $15-25 per single or double aircon, $5-10 per single or double non-aircon.*

Small rooms and a restaurant on a beach.

WHERE TO EAT

You can have simple, inexpensive, and tasty meals in San José. At the **market**, several stalls serve small meals with rice for about 60¢-$1. In the evenings, a number of **turo-turo stands** open in the plaza. Dishes run from 50¢ for vegetables to 70¢ for meat, and the *lumpia* is very good and costs 30¢. Nearby, a few **barbeque stalls** sell chicken, pork, and other meats on a stick.

EXCURSIONS & DAY TRIPS

From San José you can hike into the beautiful mountains and visit the **Mangyan**. You will need a guide. Do try to contact Mr. Vic Victorino, in Manila, *Tel. 711-4507*. He can organize very nice excursions into the mountains, to visit the pretty waterfall on **Mount Tanisan**, then hike down to his **ranch** for the evening (or several more) and visits to the Mangyan who live near his property.

Remember to bring gifts (candy, matches, vitamins, etc.) to share. You can also visit the tribes from town, but they may not always be around when you get there. **Bato Ili**, along the road, is the most accessible settlement. A small store occasionally sells some Mangyan articles.

Another settlement can be visited by taking a jeepney to **Paklolo**, where you walk about 20 minutes to the start of the **Mangyan Reservation**. Here you may visit the Nalwak tribes. Most Mangyan are nomadic, so time and patience is needed if you wish to enjoy those who still live the old way. If you intend to spend some time here, take anti-malarial medicine.

You may also visit **Mount Igit**, exclusive habitat of the *tamaraw*. Although these animals are normaly reclusive, they will charge if cornered. Sadly, this species is facing extinction as its forest habitat is being destroyed. The government has started a breeding station, but the herd is small and often very hard to find.

San José is also the departure point for **Apo Island and Reef**, which lies between Mindoro Occidental and Busuanga Island in Palawan (this is not the Apo Island near Dumaguete), and for **Pandan Island**, both popular with divers. There is a nice resort on Pandan (see the Mamburao section below for details).

MAMBURAO

Mamburao is Mindoro Occidental's quiet capital, and sits on a long stretch of beach. Like San José, it is an-off-the-beaten-track destination. Resorts are simple but quite friendly. The town is small and its economy is almost completely based on agriculture.

ARRIVALS & DEPARTURES

Philippine Airlines has two weekly flights, and Pacific Air has flights scheduled seasonally. At the airstrip, vendors meet the morning flights with grapes, fish, shrimps, and live crabs to sell to departing passengers.

If there are no flights, you can take a bus from Manila to Batangas City, then a two-hour ferry ride to Abra de Ilog, and then an hour jeepney ride to Mamburao.

GETTING AROUND

Resorts will arrange for your transport to and from the airport, and for visits to the **Mangyan Reservation**.

WHERE TO STAY & EAT

MAMBURAO BEACH RESORT, *Barangay Fatima. Manila reservations: Tel. 819-0285, Fax 819-0282, 819-0286. $40-50 per single or double.*

This place has lovely native cottages along a light gray sand beach. All rooms are fan-cooled and have private bathrooms. Watersports, diving, and boating are available and there is a restaurant. Bring baby oil to deter the sand fleas.

LA DOLCE VITA, *Barangay Fatima. Manila reservations: Tel. 650-3110. $60 per person inclusive of meals.*

This is a very nice, homey, quiet, place, good for families. Clean, airy, fan-cooled rooms with private bathrooms are in pleasant native-style cottages. Various watersports are available. They also offer tours to the Mangyan and island hopping to Pandan. The food is superb.

TRAVELERS LODGE, *town proper. $15 per single or double aircon, $5-10 per single or double non-aircon.*

This very simple place has helpful staff. The low-priced non-aircon rooms have common bathrooms; all other rooms have private bathrooms. There is a restaurant.

SEEING THE SIGHTS

To get to the **Mangyan Reservation**, take a jeepney to the Pagbahan River and follow the road up its southern side to a small *barangay*. From here, a three- to four-kilometer walk takes you to the reservation.

Four kilometers north of Mamburao is **Tayamaan Beach**, in a very pretty white sand cove. It is a lovely place to rest beneath the coconut trees, and swim. **Crocodile Hill** marks the southern end of the cove and a long pier is at the northern end.

Pandan Island, west of Sablayan (access through San José or a two-hour *banca* ride from Mamburao) has good diving and a very nice resort: **PANDAN ISLAND RESORT**, *North Pandan Island, $35 per person, inclusive of meals and transfers; packages are available and rates decrease as number of people (in the same group) increases.* Situated on a pretty beach and island, this place has attractive native cottages that are fan-cooled and have private bathrooms. Facilities include a complete dive center and windsurfing. There is a restaurant and bar.

19. PALAWAN

Often called the Philippines' last frontier, the main island of **Palawan** is long and narrow and is surrounded by numerous smaller islands and islets. All together, Palawan has about a quarter of the islands in the Philippines. Palawan offers travelers many beautiful beaches, islands that are still delightfully unspoiled, and her remaining forests and reefs (logging and dynamite fishing, which have taken quite a toll, are now held somewhat in check). And, in the **Sulu Sea**, east of Palawan is one of the best diving spots in the world – **Tubbataha**. You will find a wide range of accommodations in Palawan – from very expensive and exclusive resorts to cheap, simple huts and lodges.

Palawan's (and Mindoro's) flora and fauna are more similar to Bornean life than to that found on other Philippine islands. Many species, including the first human inhabitants, came to the country over a land bridge that connected Borneo, Palawan, Mindoro, and Luzon during the ice ages. By the time the ice melted, several species had immigrated to Palawan but had not continued to Luzon.

Among the unique species are the rare fish-eating Palawan eagle, scaly anteater, giant turtles, Palawan peacock pheasant, Palawan bear cat, mouse deer (*chevrotain*), imperial nutmeg dove, siete colores (seven colors) dove, Tabon bird, several orchids and numerous butterflies. Although butterfly collecting is permitted, you may not take other animals off the island.

History

Palawan gets its name from Chinese traders who frequented the area over 1,000 years ago. They named the island *Pa-lao-yu*, meaning "land of beautiful safe harbor," in recognition of the many save havens for seafaring vessels during bad weather.

Southern Palawan has yielded the earliest human remains excavated in the Philippines. The remains date back some 22,000 years, but other evidence suggests that human habitation here may date back to over 50,000 years.

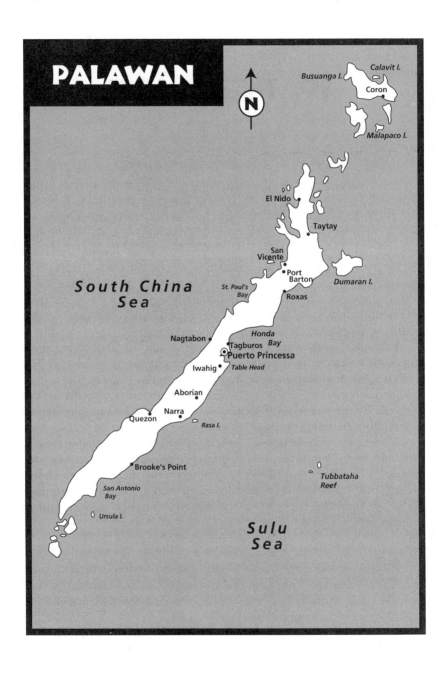

Palawan's tribes may be descendants of the original settlers that came via ice-age land bridges, and later on boats. The next recorded immigrants were Indonesian settlers from the Madjapahit Empire, who came in the 13th century. Today, their progeny — the Tausugs, Jama-mapun, and Molbog — inhabit the southern coastal areas.

When the Spanish first arrived, Palawan was ruled from Jolo by Borneo. Spanish settlers first occupied northern Palawan, then worked their way south. In the 18th century, the Sultan of Borneo gave up central Palawan. Shortly after, the Spanish moved their capital from Taytay to Puerto Princessa.

For many years, Palawan remained sparsely populated compared to other Philippine Islands. However, it then received some spillover from Luzon's and the Visayas' overpopulation. As a result of this influx and the lack of understanding (and sometimes concern) many immigrants have about the environment, Palawan's delicate ecology and the lifeways of its indigenous people are severely threatened.

The Tribes

Successive waves of Muslim, Visayan, Tagalog, and Ilocano settlers have pushed Palawan's native peoples inland. There is even a group of Igorots (inhabitants of Luzon's mountain provinces) that has been residing on the island for years.

The **Batak** are Negritos — small, dark, kinky-haired people. They sleep in treetops or in hearths to keep mosquitoes away. Traditionally, the men wear g-strings and women don only skirts. The Batak are found in several areas north of Puerto Princessa.

The **Tagbuana** are brown-skinned, slender, and have straight hair. The women may wear brightly colored clothes and ornamentation. The Tagbuana believe that fairies, called *diwata*, are responsible for their lives. Traditionally, marriage is arranged when children are 12. During courtship, the man must place a banana stalk by the woman's doorstep. Only if the stalk stays healthy will the marriage be pursued. Polyandry is common; women with several husbands are considered to be in demand, hence worthy of high dowries. The Tagbuana are found in the northern and central areas.

Both the Tagbuana and the Batak have a written language which, like that of the Mangyan of Mindoro, consists of over a dozen gracefully curved letters that are inscribed on bamboo tubes.

The **Pala'wan** are a brown, straight-haired people. The **Kanuys** (of Brooke's Point) and the **Tao't Bato** (of the Rizal area) are said to be subgroups of the Pala'wan. To restrict outside negative influence, the Tao't Bato are supposed to be off limits to visitors. The Pala'wan are found in the southern area.

ALTERNATE ADVENTURES ON PALAWAN

If you are adventurous and want to try something different, here are two great ways to see the more remote islands, beaches, caves, and lagoons:

*• **Live-Aboard Cruise:** You leave from Puerto Princessa and cruise the coast to remote islands and islets aboard a motorized yacht. There is a minimum of five days, and six passengers. Cost is $50 per person per day and includes all meals. Contact Mark Bratschi, PO Box 107, 5300 Puerto Princessa; or via Fax at "21st Century, Puerto Princessa," Tel. 804-0331 (Manila). This tour has received high praise and a number of returning guests.*

*• **Sea Canoe:** Tour around the far northern islands of Palawan on a one- or two-person canoe. Book either in Manila through Blue Horizon Travel in the Shangri-La Manila Hotel, Ayala Ave., Tel. 813-8888, or contact through e-mail: sea.canoe@phuket.com.*

PUERTO PRINCESSA

Puerto Princessa, often shortened to Puerto (like Puerto Galera in Mindoro), is a laid-back and spread-out town. It is mainly an intermediary destination, where you rest, eat, and prepare for trips further afield. Puerto is a wonderful place to stroll around — Mayor Hagedorn has done a terrific job of cleaning up: littering, including dropping cigarette butts, is fineable — the damage is $20! It is a picturesque town, and if you do stay a while, its surroundings have much to offer.

ARRIVALS & DEPARTURES

By Air

Air Philippines and Philippine Airlines each have a daily flight between Manila and Puerto Princessa. Philippine Airlines also flies twice a week between Cebu and Puerto, and twice a week between Iloilo and Puerto.

By Sea

• **Puerto Princessa-Manila**. The voyage takes 20-23 hours, *WGA SuperFerry* has two trips a week. Cost is $18-108.

• **Puerto Princessa-Iloilo**. This is an interesting and long trip; there are usually three voyages a month. The *Milagrosa* departs Iloilo City on days ending in 6. It first stops in Cuyo, and then proceeds to Puerto. The first leg takes 14 hours and the second, 12 hours. Fare is $14 per person for the whole journey. The *MV Andrew* does the same route, its schedule is not definite, and fare is $16 including meals.

GETTING AROUND

The most convenient way to get around outside of Puerto Princessa is by hiring a vehicle. This is quite expensive. Current hire rates are available at the City Tourism Office and the Provincial Tourism Office in Puerto; they can also recommend reliable drivers and vehicles. Public transport is available, often packed, sometimes plagued with mechanical problems, and departure times vary.

Within the capital, tricycles ply the main roads for P2 (8¢) per kilometer, and they will drop you at your resort.

ORIENTATION

Outside of Puerto Princessa, the roads are not paved and transport is by buses and jeepneys that are usually heavily laden. Roads are dusty, and at the end of a long journey, travelers are often covered with "Palawan Powder," a term coined by the locals. From July-August, heavy rains and flooding render roads impassable, and seas are quite rough.

June-November is usually rainy; some showers continue into February. Rains usually last from June through November, with showers continuing as late as February.

WHERE TO STAY

City Proper

ASIA WORLD RESORT, *barangay San Miguel. Tel. 433-2111, 433-2122, 433-2022. Manila reservations: Tel. 242-6546, Fax 241-3950. 109 rooms. $100-115 per single, $110-125 per double, $245-730 per suite. Visa, Master Card, American Express, Diners.*

This is Puerto's top-of-the-line hotel. All rooms are pleasant and have the typical amenities found in first-class hotels. Facilities include a swimming pool, good restaurants (see *Where to Eat* below), and a disco.

PUERTO AIRPORT HOTEL, *442 Rizal Avenue. Tel. 433-2177. 26 rooms. $20 per single, $25 per double, $50 per suite.*

All rooms are air conditioned and have private bathrooms. The suites have a television and a refrigerator. They have a swimming pool, restaurant, airport shuttle, and tour services.

EMERALD HOTEL, *Malvar Street. Tel. 433-2263, 433-2611. 50 rooms. $20 per single, $27 per double, $36 per suite.*

This is a nice place with good service. All rooms are air conditioned and have private bathrooms. The suite rooms have a television. The Emerald has a swimming pool, laundry and tour services, and a restaurant.

DOUBLE L HILLSIDE, *Sandiwa, Tiniguiban Tel. 433-2416. $26 per single or double aircon, $53 per suite, $16 per single or double non-aircon. Manila reservations: Tel. 356-270, c/o Susan.*

All rooms have private bathrooms and are clean. Services include laundry, postal, tours, airline reservations, airport or pier transfers, and photo developing. At the restaurant, you may eat in an air conditioned room or open air.

BADJAO INN, *Rizal Avenue. Tel. 433-2180, 433-2380. 26 rooms. $19-26 per single or $21-28 per double aircon, $9 per single or $12 per double non-aircon.*

This nice and friendly place has clean rooms, all have private bathrooms; a restaurant; a bar; and facilities include mail, laundry, airline booking, and tours. The staff are very helpful.

CASA LINDA, *Trinidad Road. Tel. 433-2606. 8 rooms. $21 per single or $25 per double aircon, $13 per single or $17 per double non-aircon.*

This nice place has clean rooms with private bathrooms. The staff are very helpful. Services offered include mail, tours, and laundry. There is a restaurant and a bar. You may also stay at Casa Linda's simple beach resort on Nagtabon.

BAVARIA PENSION, *Junction 1, San Miguel. Tel. 433-2388. 2 rooms. $25 per single or double. Visa, Master Card, American Express.*

Rooms are air conditioned and have private bathrooms. There is a restaurant and bar, and tour and laundry services are available.

TRATTORIA TERRACE, *Rizal Street. Tel. 433-2719. $18 per single or double aircon, $32 per suite, $8-10 per single or $12-14 per double non-aircon.*

The suite rooms are the only rooms with TV, minibar, and private bathrooms. The aircon rooms have a shared bathroom between rooms, and the lower priced non-aircon rooms have common bathrooms. There is a restaurant, and tour arrangements are available.

YAYEN'S PENSION, *294 Manalo Ext. Tel. 433-2261. 19 rooms. $15 per single or double aircon, $4-8 per single or $6-10 per double non-aircon.*

Rooms are clean and monthly rent is available. The aircon rooms and the higher priced non-aircon have private bathrooms. The lower priced non-aircon rooms have common bathrooms. There is a restaurant, and laundry service is available.

ABELADO'S PENSION, *62-D Manga Street. Tel. 433-2049. 6 rooms. $7-10 per single, $8-12 per double.*

All rooms are nice, clean, and fan-cooled. The higher-priced rooms have a private bathroom, the lower priced ones have common bathrooms. Some of the rooms are spacious, so inspect first. The owners and staff is friendly and helpful. There is no restaurant, but home-cooked meals can be provided.

DUCHESS PENSION, *107 Valencia Street. Tel. 433-2263. 25 rooms. $4-10 per single, $6-12 per double.*

This pretty place has small, clean, fan-cooled rooms with private or common bathrooms. There is a restaurant, and tour and laundry services are offered. You may also make arrangements to stay at their beach resort which has pretty good cottages. Cecile and Joe, the owners, are helpful and informative about Palawan.

Nearby Beach Resorts
MEARA MARINA, *Honda Bay. Tel. 433-2575. $20-30 per single or double.*

Rooms are fan-cooled and have either private or common bathrooms. There is a restaurant, a complete dive center, and windsurfing, sailing, and water skiing are available.

STARFISH SANDBAR, *Honda Bay. Tel. 433-2740. $20-25 per single or double.*

This place has simple, clean, roomy cottages with private bathrooms. Diving and snorkeling are available. Meals are available from a canteen.

ISLA DE NAGUSUAN, *Honda Bay. $15 per single or double.*

Cottages are spacious and can comfortably accommodate four people. Bathrooms are common. There is a restaurant.

GEORG PLACE, *Nagtabon Beach. $7-17 per single or double.*

This place has fan-cooled, clean, native-style cottages. Bathrooms are private or common. There is a restaurant and laundry service is available.

WHERE TO EAT

You won't go hungry in Puerto Princessa. The local food is usually very good, and the city offers a variety of international cuisines. There are a number of fastfood establishments in Puerto, and beyond town there are *turo-turo* restaurants along the road in the larger towns.

ASIAWORLD RESORT HOTEL, *barangay San Miguel. Tel. 433-2111.*

There are several restaurants at this resort: Japanese, two Chinese, Filipino, and Western.

KA LUI, *369 Rizal Avenue.*

This is a unique restaurant and a great place for local culinary delights. A casual place, made of nipa and bamboo, you leave your shoes outside and enter barefoot. The chairs are comfortable, made of abaca sand sacks, and the motif is Filipino, complete with native baskets and jars. Louie, the owner, was a financial analyst in a Manila bank who fell in love with Palawan, and the rest is history. The food is very good. Specialties are seafood and vegetable dishes. Another attraction is the group of children and adults who create beautiful music from local instruments: bamboo flutes, bamboo harp, maracas made with flame-tree seeds, and other uniquely Palawan instruments. The service is personal and Louie is a great conversationalist.

CAFÉ PUERTO, *Rizal Avenue.*

Serves delicious international meals — ask Andrew, the English chef and owner, what he recommends.

KAMAYAN, *Rizal Avenue.*

Serves very tasty native fare. You can eat on the terrace or in a tree house.

THE HAGEDORNS OF PUERTO

*Kamayan is owned by the **Hagerdorns**. For many years Ellen Hagedorn ran the province's tourism effort while her husband and his buddies hung around Kamayan and other places drinking. Then Edward Hagedorn ran for mayor of Puerto and won. To everybody's surprise, he changed his ways, cleaned up Puerto, enforced laws, became an ardent environmentalist, and even took on powerful and dangerous politicians and loggers successfully.*

In 1996, Ellen retired from tourism, while her husband is still mayor. If you think this is the stuff legends are made of, you are right, and the local movie "Hagedorn" is helping to perpetuate an amazing story.

ZUM KLEINEN ANKER, *Rizal Avenue.*

Come here for German and Filipino food and cold beer.

SWISS BISTRO, *Rizal Avenue.*

The Swiss Bistro has good European dishes, steak, and pleasant music.

TRATTORIA TERRACE, *Rizal Avenue.*

Serves tasty steaks and has a decent selection of pasta.

BISRTO VALENCIA, *Valencia Street.*

Specializes in European meals.

EDWIN'S, *Valencia Street.*

Edwin's whips up tasty Chinese and native dishes.

DUCHESS PENSION, *Valencia Street.*

This restaurant makes good snacks and great fruit shakes. Meals are available but you must order in advance.

PHO VIETNAMESE, *Valencia Street.*

Specializes in Vietnamese cuisine.

BAVARIA, *National Highway.*

Serves good German fare.

PHO DAC BIET, *behind the airport.*

Serves simple, tasty, inexpensive Vietnamese dishes and fresh French-style bread.

SEEING THE SIGHTS

Take a leisurely stroll along the waterfront where there are a number of picturesque houses on stilts over the water.

Walk to the old City Hall Building on Valencia Street, where the **Palawan Museum** has an excellent display on Palawan, its people, history, and life ways. Archaeological artifacts and fossils are displayed as they would appear in situ.

The **Palawan State College museum** is in Tiniguiban, five kilometers south of town. On display are archaeological finds, artifacts, and butterfly and shell collections, all well labeled. The museum is open weekdays and the campus is very pretty. To get there, take a tricycle, and have it wait for you or you may have to walk back to town.

SPORTS & RECREATION

Diving

One of the best diving spots in the world — **Tubbataha Reef** — is east of Palawan in the Sulu Sea. Palawan also offers divers a variety, from week-long live-aboards to numerous spots around islands.

A number of great dive spots are sprinkled around Puerto Princessa, the northern reaches of mainland Palawan, and the northernmost islands. The best time for diving is October-June. But be aware that from October-November most beaches have sand fleas, so when you are resting on the sand, cover yourself with a generous amount of oil (or Avon's Skin-So-Soft oil or lotion).

Most of the diving off Puerto Princessa is enjoyable and fairly easy. **Tablehead Reef** has a good variety of invertebrates and fish.

Just off Club Paradise, on Busuanga, **Classroom Reef** is an easy and interesting dive. There are several other spots in the area, including a Japanese World War Two wreck that is now home to coral and other marine animals. Spots around El Nido have interesting rock formations and abundant marine life. At **Punk Rock** (locally called Pacanayas), by Matinloc Island, you may see turtles and sometimes whale sharks, Bryde's whales, and mantas.

Tubbataha is very remote and is accessible by live-aboard dive cruises. Refer to the chapter on *Sports & Recreation* for a schedule and list of live-aboard dive operators. And we strongly suggest that you get a copy of *Dive Versions – Dive Log & Maps* on Tubbataha the Sulu Sea by Hutchinson & Ventura. It is informative and very helpful for divers who have never been to the Sulu Sea region before. It is available on most dive boats; you may also send an e-mail to: *gdh@hkstar.com*.

At Tubbataha and around the Sulu Sea you will be diving around small tropical Pacific atolls with reefs that plummet from the shallows and are densely populated with a variety of life.

Several resorts have a dive center. Recommended dive operators in the area include:

- **Island Divers** (contact Norman Songco). *371 Rizal Avenue, Puerto Princessa*
- **Asia Divers**, *Coron, Manila contact: 1133 Guerrero Street, Ermita, Tel. 522-3650, Fax 522-3663*

SHOPPING

Palawan basketry is extremely attractive. The weaving is close-knit and designs are simple and beautiful. If you are looking for souvenirs, visit **Kamantian**, **Russell's Native Crafts**, *Rizal Avenue, towards the airport*; **Makawili's**, *Public Market*; and **Karla's Etnicraft**, *Garcellano Building, Rizal Avenue*. Several lodging places have small shops.

EXCURSIONS & DAY TRIPS

Nearby Islands

The islands in **Honda Bay** have some wonderful beaches. You can spend a whole day, or half, snorkeling and cruising the islands. **Snake Island** is a long strip of white sand with a fishing village and mangrove area. You may find some lovely shells on the beach. Snorkeling is great. There are no facilities so you will have to bring food and drinks. Between **Cowrie** and **Pandan Islands** is a coral reef. **Starfish Island** is a sandbar — no vegetation. And other islands you can hop to include **Meara** and **Bat**, where large fruit bats emerge in the evening. There is lodging on Meara and Starfish.

To get there, hire a tricycle to **Tagburos** and arrange for your pick up time. You may also take a jeepney headed for Sta Lourdes, get off at the large Caltex tank, and walk seaward. *Banca* rentals run from $10 for a round-trip to nearby islands to $25 to the further off ones, Island hopping tours and diving tours start at $20. Do not go if the seas are rough, and the wharf at Tagburos is a mercury slag heap — do not eat the fish caught in the area.

Nagtabon Beach on the west side of Palawan is lovely. Its stretch of white sand is fringed by azure waters. The beach has been known to have sand fleas, so coat yourself with baby oil, or Avon's Skin-So-Soft oil, through which they do not bite. There is an occasional jeep that goes to Nagtabon. The cost is $1 per person. From Nagtabon town, an hour's walk takes you to the beach. You may also rent a jeepney for around $44.

St. Paul's Underground River

Palawan's best known attraction gets hundreds of visitors yearly. The river, over eight kilometers long, exits from a cave of stalactites, stalagmites, and other interesting rock formations into a beautiful pool near the beach in the well-kept **St. Paul's National Park**. When you arrive by sea from Baheli or Sabang, you land at a cove where trees drape over a beautiful white beach. Through the trees is the mouth of the underground river. Stop along the way to read the signboard about the park and river.

Transfer to a small *banca* and continue upriver for three kilometers. You need powerful flashes for photography. Proceed through several huge domed areas and past some interesting formations to a turn in the river beyond which the *banca* cannot go. Explorers have gone 8.2 kilometers into the cave, partly through knee-deep guano, without finding its end. The entrance fee ($4 for Filipinos, $6 for foreigners) includes the *banca* ride and helps pay for maintenance of the park.

The routes to St. Paul's are scenic trips. One way is to take a jeepney to Baheli. The 90-minute ride crosses mountains and has great views of Honda Bay. From Baheli, board a *banca* for a spectacular three-hour trip to the cave. Rental is $55. Consider bringing lunch, cover-ups, and a powerful flashlight. This route is often feasible from February through June. The trip starts as you float down the river into Ulugan Bay. An hour later you emerge from the bay into the ocean. Only here will you know if the sea is calm enough to permit the full voyage. Should the *banquero* decide the journey is unsafe, settle for snorkeling at Sta Rita Island. When the seas are calm, you proceed north along spectacular cliffs, past pretty waterfalls and beaches.

The more frequented route is to continue from Baheli to **Sabang** by jeep, an hour further. The road is often not passable during rainy season. From Sabang it is a 30-minute *banca* ride to St. Paul's — $12 per *banca* — or a pleasant two-hour walk over the "monkey trail," an elevated walkway in the trees, to the cave.

Other alternatives are (1) a *banca* to Tag Nipa, and hike from there to where the river goes underground; (2) a two and a half-hour *banca* hire from Port Barton ($70); or (3) trekkers could hike over from Tanabag, which takes three to four days.

Accommodations in Sabang are simple, inexpensive, and range from dorm-style (about $3/person) to cottages with bath. Near Sabang are a **lovely waterfall** (30-minute hike) and **Penrat Cave**. You may also tent or use a room at St. Paul's for a maximum of three nights. Bring all supplies and food.

South of Puerto Princessa

The **Crocodile Farming Institute** in **Irawan** is about 30 minutes from Puerto. Here you may see crocodiles that are being bred for conservation purposes.

The **Iwahig Penal Colony** was established in 1904 and is the largest free institution of its kind in the world. When prisoners first arrive, they are incarcerated for several months, during which they are chained and are made to do hard labor. They are then integrated into the community of 5,000 convicts and their families who lead a fairly normal life. The colony is completely self supporting, and **handicrafts** are made by inmates who want to earn a little extra.

Handicrafts produced include fairly good-sized knives and beautifully inlaid sheaths, woven basketry, walking sticks, etc. It is sometimes possible to buy delicious wild honey at the camp. Prisoners are quite amiable, often ask for cigarettes, so it might not hurt to have an extra pack on hand.

Many inmates choose to stay, even after they have served their sentences, and are given a small homestead to farm.

The most convenient way to get to Iwahig and back is to hire a tricycle or jeepney. A few jeepneys leave the market in the early morning for Iwahig, and may return in the afternoon; schedules and frequencies are uncertain.

PRACTICAL INFORMATION
Health

As a safety precaution, take preventive medication for malaria (start a couple of weeks before your visit), especially if you intend to stay a while and do some treks. Most travelers who stay in Puerto Princessa explore other places during the day, or if they spend a night out of Puerto it is on the beach and are not bothered, as the malarial mosquito is a beast of the dusk. However, the forests are inhabited by malarial mosquitoes. Antimalarials are essential if there is any chance that you will spend a night outside Puerto in or by the forests.

If you get sick in Palawan, head for Puerto Princessa immediately and get medical attention. **Dr. John Mendoza** is a wonderful physician; there are probably other good ones.

Mail

The **Post Office** is on Burgos St. Courier and cargo services include **Delbros** (*Salcedo Building, Rizal Avenue*), **DHL** (*Olorga Building., Rizal Avenue*), **LBC** (*Garcellano Building., Rizal Avenue*), **JRS** (*Garcellano Building, Rizal Avenue*), and **Pambato Forwarder** (*Manalo Street*).

Money

Several major Philippine Banks have branches in Puerto Princessa. Outside of the city, there are no authorized currency exchange services.

Change travelers checks and foreign currency at the **PNB** on *Rizal Avenue* (probably the best exchange rate), or **MetroBank**, *Rizal Ave*nue

Travel Assistance

This is a very tourist-friendly city. The support services are wonderfully and competently staffed. Information and recommendations for guides and hired vehicles are available from Cora Timones, Tourism Officer of the **City Tourism Office**, *Olorga Building, Rizal Avenue, Tel. 433-2983*, and her staff at the airport; or Milagros Navarro of the **Provincial Tourism Office**, *Capitol Building, Tel. 433-2968*.

Many establishments are happy to help visitors out. Nancy San Juan of Karla's can recommend reliable guides. Joe and Cecile of the Duchess Pension, *Tel. 433-2263*, are a fund of information and offer a bay tour as they have a boat in Honda Bay. Their inn is popular with many lower budget travelers. It is a great spot for getting up-to-date information on out-of-town places, as well as finding others to share a ride. They also have delicious fruit shakes.

SOUTHERN PALAWAN

Southern Palawan is for the more off-the-beaten-track travelers. Accommodation is generally simple. Its most noted point is the **Tabon Cave Complex**, now a museum reservation, which consists of over 200 caves. The earliest human remains found in the Philippines were unearthed at Tabon.

ARRIVALS & DEPARTURES

Access to Quezon is by very expensive hire ($150 round trip, three to four hours each way) or you can go by public transport that is usually very crowded: Puerta Royale, Mic Mac, Charing, and Princess buses or by jeepneys, for about $2 per person, taking four to five hours.

WHERE TO STAY & EAT

Lodging in and around **Quezon** includes camping at the National Museum, for which you must make prior arrangements. There are basic in-town places and beach resorts. There are several places to eat near the market in Quezon: **THE ISLANDER** is a favorite.

TABON VILLAGE, *Quezon. 10 rooms. $4-10 per single, $7-14 per double.* This pretty place has simple, clean, fan-cooled rooms. Bathrooms are private or common. The restaurant is good and cheap, and there is a bar. Theo, the Belgian owner, has a number of good tours, including boating and hiking through a mangrove swamp, up the Tumarbon River, to a pretty waterfall. Tabon Village also has property with basic cottages on

Sidanao Island (near the Tabon caves) and Malapakun Island (an hour *banca* ride from Quezon).

SEEING THE SIGHTS

Before you get to Quezon (the main town of southern Palawan), there is a Tagbanua reservation 10 kilometers from Aborlan.

The town of Quezon offers a beautiful waterfront, offshore islands with white sand beaches, and a branch of the National Museum. On display in the museum are some of the finds from the Tabon Caves, geological specimens collected from the area, some stuffed animals, and a good collection of native peoples' handicrafts. There is a small shop with lovely ethnic products from the Pala'wan and colorful mats by the Jamamapun. Vivian Brown, the museum's vivacious curator, has a wealth of information on the caves and area tribes.

The Tabon Caves, first excavated by Dr. Robert Fox and staff from the National Museum, are scattered on a 134-hectare reservation. Thirty-three sites have been extensively explored and are guarded against damage. The area was inhabited over 50,000 years ago, and perhaps was an ideal location during rainy season. Tool and bone remains demonstrate that the people who lived here were food gatherers, and ate small animals as well as vegetables. Tabon was probably abandoned 9,000 years ago, before land bridges submerged and when the seashore was still 35 kilometers away. Nearby Guri Cave, occupied between 8,000 and 4,000 years ago, yielded evidence of coast-dwelling people with a more advanced civilization.

It is easiest if you make arrangements to see the caves through the city tourism office in Puerto Princessa. You may also inquire at the museum, or go on your own. Guides are available at the west entrance of the Tabon Caves. Museum guides are free.

A 20-minute boat ride from Quezon takes you to the caves. The Coast Guard station at the wharf can help find boats for hire. Round-trip prices are $15-24 per *banca* (depending on the size) or $1.50 per person for more than 20 passengers. You disembark on a beach at the mouth of the first cave where you climb cement stairs to Tabon Cave, beautiful views all the way. In this cave, the dig has been left as it was completed so you can see the sites' locations. Continue to Diwata Cave, where inhabitants buried some of their dead and held religious rites.

On the opposite side of the mainland from Quezon, and a bit north, is Narra. The town has several basic lodges, restaurants, and resorts. Of interest are the nearby Malinao Hot Springs for some nice pictures, a six-kilometer walk into the mountains to Estrella Waterfall, and the pretty Rasa Island.

Further south is **Brooke's Point**, where an interesting watchtower was erected by the Englishman, Sir James Brooke. There are a few basic resorts in the area.

Offshore is **Ursula Island**, the nesting place for thousands of birds that return from the mainland in the evenings, around 4:00pm. You need permission from the Maritime Police Station in Rio Tuba for access to the island. Past Rio Tuba, the far southern areas have historically been risky to travel through.

NORTHERN PALAWAN

Port Barton and **El Nido** areas are the most popular spots on Palawan's northern mainland. There are several nice spots in between, and the northernmost islands of Palawan are special enough for travelers to spend hours by land and boat to get to, although there are flights. The area has pristine white beaches, mangrove forests, waterfalls, caves, and impressive limestone formations to enjoy.

ARRIVALS & DEPARTURES

Port Barton

Port Barton is fairly easily accessed by land from Puerto. Take a jeepney or bus to Roxas, then change to a ride for Port Barton. Royale Express has a bus that leaves Puerto at 8:00am and another one at midnight, fare is $2.50 per person. A jeepney to Roxas is $2.50 per person or $110 (round-trip) to rent. Occasionally, jeepneys go all the way to Port Barton, $3.50 per person, or rent one for $110 (round-trip).

Taytay

From Puerto Princessa, the trip to Taytay takes six to seven hours. Royale Express has daily departures at 8:00pm and midnight, fare is $4 per person. Jeepneys ply the route infrequently, $4 per person, or you can rent one for $160, round trip, plus $20 overnight (if you have the driver wait.)

El Nido

The easiest way to get to El Nido is by air from Manila. A. Soriano Aviation has daily flights to El Nido. You may also charter a flight from Puerto Princessa, this of course is expensive. Or hire a *banca* from Sabang ($250), Taytay ($58 per *banca* or $6 per person), or Abongan (look for Lando, $60).

A bus leaves Puerto at midnight and goes to El Nido; it is a long and rough trip, $7 per person, and travel time is 10 hours.

Coron

From Manila, both Air Ads and Pacific Air have a daily flight. A few boats go from the mainland:

• **From Taytay**: departure every Wednesday and Saturday, $16 per person, travel time is nine hours;
• **From El Nido**: departure every Tuesday and Saturday, $26 per person, travel time is 10 hours; and
• **From Puerto**: $24 per person, travel time is 32 hours.

We give these scheduled departure times as a general guide; remember that most things in the Philippines are fluid, and schedules change frequently. Trips will be canceled during rough seas.

WHERE TO STAY & EAT

Roxas

COCO LOCO ISLAND RESORT, *off Roxas. 39 cottages. $10-20 per cottage.*

This well-liked and well-managed place has nice, clean, native cottages. Bathrooms are private or common. Activities include squash, ping-pong, billiards, water skiing, river trips, and island hopping. Boat transfers from the mainland are available, and there is a restaurant. The service and staff are very good.

Taytay

CLUB NOAH ISABELLE, *Apulit Island. Manila reservations: Tel. 818-2623, 810-7241. 30 cottages. $190-210 per single or double. Visa, Master Card, American Express, Diners.*

This place has nice, native-style air conditioned cottages, some are on stilts over the water. There are watersports and kayaks for rent, tours are offered, and there is a restaurant. The staff are well trained and hospitable; they are also share-holders of the resort, giving them a sense of ownership and responsibility.

FLOWER ISLAND, *Flower Island. Manila reservations: c/o Asiaventure at Holiday Inn, Tel. 526-1212. $45 per person per day, inclusive of meals.*

This is a lovely place, not really known, so you get privacy, peace, and quiet. The service is good, and the owners are a French couple. Meals are super. You may go fishing or boating around the area.

El Nido

EL NIDO RESORTS, *Miniloc Island, Pangalusian Island, Lagen Island. Manila reservations: Tel. 810-3611, Fax 810-3620. $190-240 per single, $160-210 per person per double, inclusive of meals and transfers. Visa, Master Card, American Express, Diners.*

The El Nido Resort chain has establishments on three islands and plans for a fourth are under way. All the facilities are shared and you may hop around all three. Pangalusian has the reputation for being the "most romantic," and it is nice for couples. You may feel out of place if you go on your own; Miniloc is for the more active. The resort staff actively promote conservation of the surrounding area, and have a turtle-raising project in an effort to help the species survive. The food is good at all three resorts. All the cottages are attractive, simple, and native-style. All are air conditioned and have private bathrooms.

There are many activities, and all are included in the room rates (except a full diving course): hiking, windsurfing, kayaking, island hopping, snorkeling, and diving. The staff is very friendly but can sometimes be absent-minded. If you are using a boat, alone, make it wait for you!

MARINA DEL NIDO, *Malapacao Island. Manila reservations: Tel. 59-5154, Fax 831-9816. $90-120 per person, meals included.*

This is a pleasant place, all rooms are air conditioned and comfortable. Sailing charters are available.

MALAPACAO ISLAND RETREAT, *Malapacao Island. Manila reservations: Tel. 828-5330. $35-50 per person.*

This nice nature resort prides itself on its harmony with nature. There is no electricity. Lights and other equipment are powered by solar panels. Cottages are delightful, native, simple, airy, and clean. Meals are home made, most ingredients are grown on the property, the fresh, whole grain bread is superb. The staff is friendly, the proprietress is chatty. The resort is in a cove that is frequented by sea turtles. Snorkeling gear and boating are available.

Coron

CLUB PARADISE, *Dimakya Island. Manila reservations: Tel. 816-6871, Fax 818-2894. $45-90 per person. Visa, Master Card, American Express, Diners.*

Rates decrease as your group (in the same room) increases. Rooms are nice, simple, clean, and have private bathrooms. The resort was tastefully designed. The staff is friendly and food is good. Activities include diving and various watersports. There is a swimming pool.

HACIENDA RESORT, *Manila reservations: Tel. 721-5343. $65 per person, all meals and island hopping included.*

This is a homey place, rooms are in a very pretty hacienda-style house. Each room is uniquely and tastefully furnished, designed and orchestrated by the owners, a great couple. Bathrooms are common. Meals are good; you will not go hungry here. During the day, you will be taken around the beaches, rivers, mangroves, etc. If you dive, arrangements can be made for you to join a group from a nearby resort.

BAYSIDE DIVERS LODGE, *6 rooms. $40 per person, meals included.*
This is a simple place, obviously geared to divers, with pleasant, clean rooms. Bathrooms are common. Do not expect a fancy meal, but the food is great, and the french bread fresh. Island hopping and diving are offered.

KOKOS NUSS, *13 cottages. Manila reservations: Tel. 922-9750. $15-35 per person, meals included.*
This friendly place is geared to divers. Cottages are simple, native-style, and clean. Bathrooms are private or common. The restaurant is in the garden, and food is tasty. They have a complete dive center, and offer island hopping and exploring by motorcycles or trekking. The staff is friendly.

EXCURSIONS & DAY TRIPS

If you are interested in visiting the **Batak**, make prior arrangements at the City Tourism or at Duchess Pension in Puerto Princessa. You may sometimes find a knowledgeable guide in Roxas City. There are a few very basic lodges in town, but if you are going to stay in the area, continue to **Coco Loco**, a simple resort on an offshore island.

Port Barton and the nearby islands have lovely white sand beaches. There are several resorts in the area. There are a number of small but pretty waterfalls in the forests near Port Barton. **San Vicente**, a bit north of Port Barton, also has a beautiful beach and **Little Baguio waterfalls**, which are surrounded by lush scenery.

Taytay, north of Roxas, was the original Spanish capital of Palawan. Today it is a quiet town with a 300-year-old church and **Puerto de Sta Isabel** (Taytay Fort). Construction of the fort started in 1667 and took 71 years. Walk around the interesting ruins of the fort and its chapel. **Taytay Bay** has several pretty islands with good beaches. Some of the islands have resorts; Flower Island and its resort are great. Access to Taytay is through Roxas, but the road between may not be passable during rainy season.

El Nido is home to towering mountain cliffs and **Bacuit Bay**, which has massive limestone rocks and beautiful islands scattered in its waters. The mountain cliffs are home to the *balinsasayaw*, the swift bird that produces edible birds' nest.

Among its special islands are:
• **Miniloc**, with three beautiful lagoons and a turtle-raising project run by the up-market resort on the island;
• **Pangalusian**, a captivating island with limestone cliffs that plummet into the sea, pretty lagoons, caves, and like most of Palawan, great beaches. Short hikes to the top of the mountains treat you to the unique flora and fauna and a terrific view of the bay and its islands. Pangalusian is also a marine reserve and has an up-market resort.

- **Lagen** has a rich forest, interesting limestone formations, and an up-market resort.
- **Malapacao**, with caves and off-shore coral, is a breeding ground for sea turtles. It has a unique resort that is seriously into conservation.
- **Matinloc** possesses a lovely beach, good for swimming, a "hidden beach," rich tropical foliage, and crystal clear waters.
- **Cadlao** has an incredibly high peak, higher than the Christ's Figure in Rio de Janeiro and the Tokyo Tower, and has a pretty lagoon enclosed in lush vegetation.
- **Dilumacad, Entalula, Kalmung, Pinaglugaban**, and **Tapiutan** are good for snorkeling. Entalula has a wonderful beach and Pinaglugaban has a cave with sparkling rock formation.

The far northern islands of Palawan, although hard to reach, have become special places to many travelers. Their remoteness is part of their charm and many remain pristine.

Busuanga is the main and largest island in this group. It and the surrounding islands have a number of white sand beaches, mangrove swamps, waterfalls, and caves to explore. This is where Sea Canoe has its wonderful tours.

At **Calauit Island Wildlife Sanctuary**, you can see African wild animals and rare Philippine animals roaming around. **Calauit Island** is just north of Busuanga. To get there, you need to take a *banca*, but it is best to make arrangements in advance, through your resort, as you may not be met by the sanctuary's jeep and will spend quite some time waiting, often under sweltering sun. The jeep hire to see the sanctuary is about $20.

Coron, on the southeastern part of Busuanga Island, is renowned for its fine basketry, delicious wild honey, and pearls. Visit the pretty **Maquinit Hot Springs**, where you bathe in warm sulfuric waters, then swim in the ocean nearby. Accommodations range from simple to upscale, including the homey Hacienda Resort.

DISTANT ISLANDS

Even more remote is the **Cuyo Islands** group, the far northeasternmost islands of Palawan. The **diving** and **snorkeling** are great, but for most places (except the posh resort) you will have to bring all your equipment. **Cuyo**, on Cuyo Island, has a lovely 300-year-old church inside a massive fort. **Pamalican Island** has a beautiful white sand beach, nearby reefs, and an exclusive resort. Simple accommodation and home-stays are available on other islands. **Cagayancillo**, south of Cuyo, has two caves and an old Spanish fort. South of Cagayancillo is **Cavili Island**, which houses a bird sanctuary.

If you are planning on exploring the more rustic side of Cuyo (excluding Pamalican) then drop by the Municipal Mayor's Office in Cuyo for assistance and recommendations. Interisland transport services do not exist, so you will have to rent a *banca*; prices start at $50 for the day. Inquire at the Mayor's office.

ARRIVALS & DEPARTURES

It is not easy getting to the Cuyo Islands, unless you are staying at Amanpulo on Pamalican Island.

By Air

From June through October, A Soriano Air has a flight except on Tuesday or Saturday. From November through May, flights are daily flight except on Wednesday.

Pacific Air sometimes has flights from Puerto Princessa to Cuyo Island.

By Sea

From Puerto Princessa, the *MV Milagrosa* has a trip to Cuyo that departs three times a month, on the 7, 17, and 27, from Puerto. After Cuyo it continues on to Iloilo City. Travel time between Puerto and Cuyo is 12 hours, and fare is $10 per person. The *MV Andrew* plies the same route (no definite schedule), takes 16 hours, costs $15 per person and includes meals.

From Manila, the *MV Asuncion* has a weekly voyage that departs Manila on Saturday. Travel time is 24 hours, and fare is $15, including meals.

WHERE TO STAY & EAT

Except on Pamalican Island, the accommodations are rustic. Homestays may be arranged ahead of time through the City or Provincial Tourism Offices in Puerto. Another alternative is to bring your own tent. Mrs. Espelita Villon rents out rooms in her house on Cuyo for $7 a day.

AMANPULO, *Pamalican Island, Cuyo. Manila reservations: Tel. 532-4044. 40 cottages. $300-610 per cottage. Visa, Master Card, American Express, Diners.*

"*Amanpulo*" means peaceful island, and not only is it peaceful, but breathtakingly beautiful. It is a private island you may visit only if you are staying at the resort. The island is fringed with fine white sand, aquamarine water, and a coral reef that abounds with life. The beaches are indescribably beautiful.

The cottages, called *casitas*, are well spaced, affording guests privacy. All casitas are attractively designed and are the same size. Prices vary with season, and casitas 39 & 40 are the most expensive as they are on "their private beach." All have air conditioning, cable TV, laser disc players, are lavishly and tastefully furnished, and have nice views. The casitas are spacious, have king-sized beds, and a large bathroom and dressing area. Each casita is provided with a personal motorized cart so you can tour the island on your own time and pace.

The architecture of the main areas gives the resort an expensive yet refreshingly airy feel. The attention given to details is obvious. Aside from its beautiful swimming pool, facilities and services include tennis, a library with a good selection of Filipiniana and international material, small art gallery, jogging and walking paths, and massage services (in the privacy of your casita). Aquasports are ample: sailing (hobie cats, lasers, windsurfs), rowing, fishing, snorkeling, and diving. The dive center is complete and courses are offered from introductory to advanced levels. An open water course costs $480, boat fees not included.

The air conditioned restaurant overlooks the swimming pool and has good views of the sea and Pamalican. The more informal Beach Club serves light meals and lunch. The Lobby Bar, open all day, affords you views of the pool, adjacent islands, and in the evenings, the stars. You may also dine in the privacy of your casita.

As one expects from an exclusive resort, service and staff are first-rate. This is a well-managed resort, you get top-of-the-line facilities, views, and service, for top dollars.

TABUNAN BEACH, *Tabunan Beach, Cuyo Island. 3 cottages. $6 per single or double.*

A simple place with native cottages on a nice beach. Bathrooms are common and meals are provided upon request.

20. PANAY

Panay Island is in the northwest area of the Visayas and contains the provinces of Aklan, Antique, Capiz, Guimaras, and Iloilo. The outstanding features of the area are the fabled fine white sand beach of Boracay and the raucous Ati-Atihan festival of Kalibo in the north; the inspiring churches and Iloilo City in Iloilo; and the less frequented beaches on Guimaras Island.

Panay is bordered by the Sulu Sea on the west, the Sibuyan Sea on the north, the Visayan Sea on the northeast, and the Panay Gulf on the south. Panay is relatively dry from November to April, and rainy the rest of the year.

ROXAS CITY

Roxas City is the peaceful capital of Capiz Province. Fishponds and shrimp hatcheries abound and are major industries of the area.

Although Roxas serves primarily as a junction on the road between Iloilo and Boracay, it has an 11-kilometer-long beach and several offshore islands to investigate.

ARRIVALS & DEPARTURES
By Air
Philippine Airlines is the only carrier that serves Roxas City. Daily flights from Manila take 50 minutes.

By Land
- **Roxas-Iloilo City**. The trip takes three hours and costs $2 on an air conditioned bus. Ceres Liner and 76 Express have several trips a day, usually departing at 30-minute intervals starting at 5:00am, with the last trip at 5:30.
- **Roxas-Kalibo**. The two-hour trip costs $1.50 and is serviced by Ceres Liner, 76 Express, Obuyes Liner, and GM's Liner.

By Sea

The voyage from Manila takes at least 22 hours. Negros Navigation ($12-40) has two weekly trips and WGA SuperFerry ($16-62) has one trip a week.

GETTING AROUND

Roxas is not a frequently touristed destination. Ask the staff at your hotel for advice on arranging transport (land and sea).

WHERE TO STAY

Accommodation in town is very simple and inexpensive (under $15 for airconditioning, under $8 for non-airconditioned rooms).

VILLA PATRIA, *Baybay Beach, Roxas City. Tel. 210-180. 21 rooms. $21-36 per single, $27-36 per double, $36 per cottage.*

The villa has nice air conditioned rooms with private bath, and its restaurant serves local and continental dishes.

MARCS, *Baybay Beach, Roxas City. Tel. 210-491, 211-103. 7 aircon rooms, 12 non-aircon rooms. $19.25 per single or double aircon, $11-14 per single or double non-aircon.*

Marc's has air conditioned or fan-cooled rooms with private bath, bowling, volleyball, and a beach-side restaurant that serves Filipino and continental fare.

SEASIDE FAMILY INN, *Baybay, Roxas City. Tel. 211-340. 6 aircon rooms, 1 non-aircon room. $15 per single or $21 per double aircon, $11.50 per single or double non-aircon.*

There is a restaurant and disco.

ALTA COSTA, *Baybay, Roxas City, Tel. 210-344. 1 aircon room, 2 non-aircon rooms. $15.50 per single or double aircon, $10 per single or double non-aircon.*

This inn has billiards and a restaurant that serves seafood, local, and continental dishes, and Mongolian grill on Saturday.

WHERE TO EAT

All the hotels and inns serve meals and snacks. **ALTA COSTA** has good seafood and **MARCS** is also popular. Several places along Baybay Beach serve beer, barbeque, and snacks; great at sunset.

SEEING THE SIGHTS

Roxas City **market** is clean, expansive, and an interesting place to wander around. **Baybay Beach** is inhabited by sand fleas — coat your skin with baby oil or Avon's Skin-So-Soft to keep them away.

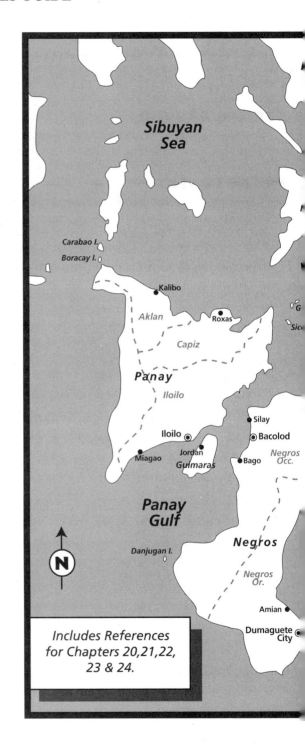

Includes References
for Chapters 20,21,22,
23 & 24.

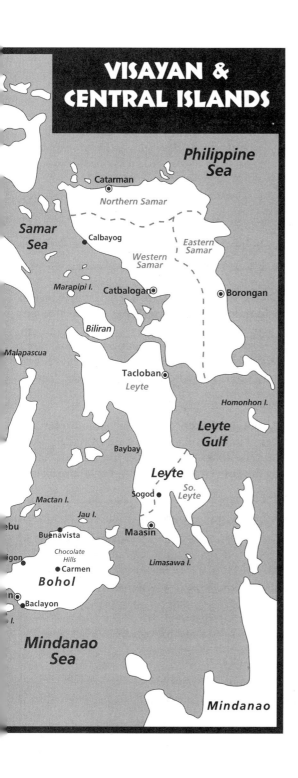

VISAYAN &
CENTRAL ISLANDS

Philippine Sea

Catarman

Northern Samar

Samar Sea

Calbayog

Eastern Samar

Western Samar

Marapipi I. Catbalogan

Borongan

Biliran

Malapascua

Tacloban

Leyte

Homonhon I.

Leyte Gulf

Baybay

Leyte

Sogod

So. Leyte

Mactan I.

Jau I.

ebu

Buenavista

Maasin

igon

Chocolate Hills

Carmen

Limasawa I.

Bohol

n

Baclayon

I.

Mindanao Sea

Mindanao

A few islands are nearby. **Mantalinga Island** has some snorkeling and shallow diving, as do the **Mabaay** and **Tuad** islands, west of Culasi Point. **Olotayan Island** has nice white beaches where you can also snorkel just offshore.

Pan-ay town, seven and a half kilometers from Roxas City, has a huge, massive church. Inside the three-meter thick walls are beautiful retablos. The bell tower has eight bells, and one, at 10.4 tons, is the largest bell in the Philippines. This bell was cast in 1878 from 70 sacks of coins donated by the townspeople.

Pre-Spanish rituals and a number of mystical beliefs are still followed here. A businessman must have the local spiritist perform the appropriate ceremonies before starting a new endeavor — without the rituals, workers would believe the project will fail. Spirits are taken very seriously here.

KALIBO

Kalibo is the capital and oldest town of Aklan, the oldest province in the Philippines. Aklan was founded in 1213 by settlers from Borneo and included what is now the province of Capiz.

Generally an unprepossessing place, Kalibo is mainly a jump-off point for Boracay. However, the city is transformed during the third week of January, when the locals and a myriad of visitors participate in the famous **Ati-Atihan festival** and Kalibo bursts forth into an incredible party lasting Friday through Sunday.

The small **Museo it Akean**, on the corner of Martelino Street and Burgos Street, has a number of antiques that were unearthed in the area and art works on display. For **local handicrafts**, try J-Land Native Products (Mabini Street at the corner of Martyrs Street) or Roxas and Kalipayan Handicrafts.

ATI-ATIHAN FESTIVAL

The festival focuses on the legend of Panay's purchase by Bornean Datus from the Negritoes (Aetas). People perform a multitude of colorful riotous reenactments of the Negritoes swapping their land for trinkets and gold. Like all festivals in the Philippines, many activities are centered around the church.

Costumes vary from the artistic to the outrageous. People blacken their faces to resemble the Negritoes, who come to partake in the fun that is had in their name. Everyone joins the processions and partying. Nobody knows how much alcohol is imbibed. All lodging fills to overflowing, and other visitors sleep on the beach or on offshore boats.

Many other areas have copied Kalibo's raucous festival, but in a more ordered way: it isn't quite the same.

ARRIVALS & DEPARTURES

By Air

There are daily trips from Manila via **Air Philippines** and **PAL** to Kalibo. The flight takes 50 minutes. The small airport is a few kilometers from town proper. To get into town, you may rent a tricycle for 40¢, but you may be asked for $2. Reconfirm your return flight as soon as you arrive. If you are coming for the festival, you must book your flight several months ahead.

By Land

• **Kalibo-Roxas City-Iloilo City.** Refer to *Arrivals & Departures* of Roxas City. The trip between Iloilo City and Kalibo takes approximately four and a half hours.

• **Kalibo-Caticlan.** Southwest Tours and 7101 Island Tours have air conditioned coasters that ply this route daily. Cost is $6 per person and the schedules are dependent on flight schedules.

WHERE TO STAY

Accommodations and transport for Ati-Atihan are booked months in advance. Many visitors camp on the beach. Lodging here is simple. Prices have been known to triple at Ati-Atihan time.

HIBISCUS GARDEN CLUB, *Andagao, Kalibo. 2 aircon rooms, 4 non-aircon rooms. $28 per single or double aircon, $9.60 per single or $17 per double non-aircon.*

This establishment has clean and simple rooms and is a 10-minute tricycle ride from downtown. Facilities include a swimming pool, restaurant, and bar.

CASA ALBA & CASA FELICIDAD, *Arch. Reyes Street. Tel. 2676. 15 rooms $32 per single or double, $42 in the suite.*

Basic air conditioned rooms with private bathrooms. There is a restaurant.

GLOWMOON, *S. Martelino Street. Tel. 3193, 3247, 3264. 6 aircon rooms, 9 non-aircon rooms. $25-40 per single or double aircon, $10 per single or $14 per double non-aircon.*

Rooms are simple and there is a restaurant, drugstore, and small shop.

LITTLE GLOWMOON, *F. Quimpo Street. Tel. 3280. 7 rooms. $20 per single or double aircon, $16 per single or double non-aircon.*

Must be relatives or same owner as the Glowmoon; rooms are simple and you may have cable TV for $4 extra.

WHERE TO EAT

Most inns serve meals. **CAFÉ AU LAIT** *on Martyrs Street* does a good fruit shake and mushroom sandwich, and decent schnitzel.

BORACAY

Boracay's fabled beaches, with white sand granules as fine as icing sugar, attract scores of tourists every year. What first made Boracay famous was its pristine beauty. Although it has changed, losing much of its natural charm and environment, the white sand and azure waters continue to sparkle and draw people from all over the world.

White Beach, a three and a half kilometer stretch of fine white sand, is a densely touristed area. You will find most of the resorts, restaurants, bars, and shops here. Vendors certified by the local tourist association walk the beach with an assortment of shell jewelry, supplies, and food. Certified masseuses also roam the beach; you will see many people having a relaxing massage on the sand. A massage costs around $6 and Merlita Flores, #48, comes highly recommended. The masseuses use coconut oil: tell them ahead of time if you do not want it.

If you are planning to visit during December-January, or during the Lenten Season (March or April), book at least two months advance.

ARRIVALS & DEPARTURES

By Air

Access is via Air Philippines and PAL to Kalibo (50 minutes), then a two-hour partly bumpy ride overland takes you to Caticlan (see *Arrivals & Departures* of Kalibo).

AirAds and Pacific Air (90 minutes) and Asian Spirit (60 minutes) fly directly to Caticlan. The runway is short and the terminal is a nipa hut.

If you arrive on a packaged tour, an agent will be waiting for you (with a sign, or you may have a sticker to wear, which came with your ticket and voucher) and will take you to your lodging. If you are not on a package, then immediately board one of the tricycles (40¢-80¢ per person) that head to the dock. From here, take a short *banca* ride to Boracay ($1 per person). Tricycles await passengers on the other side. The day before you leave, book the Boracay-Caticlan *banca* to make sure you get to the airport on time.

By Sea

Trips from Manila directly to Boracay Island are infrequently scheduled. WGA SuperFerry ($18-80) may have a trip during Holy Week (March or April).

GETTING AROUND

White Beach is the highly concentrated tourist area of Boracay, where all the shops and most of the lodging and restaurants are; everything is within walking distance (a leisurely 30 minute stroll is enough to cover this area). You will have no problems finding a tricycle during the day — they are all over the touristed areas of the main road. During the late evenings, tricycles are harder to come by — after a night's revelry, plan on walking back to your lodging, with a group of people. Tricycle drivers charge around 30¢-40¢ per destination along White Beach.

To take a trip around the island or for beach and cove hopping, hire a tricycle (about $6 an hour); rent a motorcycle ($6-12 an hour, $30-57 a day); or rent a bicycle ($2 per hour, $12 per day); all rates are negotiable. Once you are away from the White Beach area, tricycles are harder to come by.

For island hopping, diving, snorkeling, or exploring by sea, you can rent a *banca* almost anywhere along White Beach, or make arrangements through your resort. *Banca* rentals are about $20 for three to four hours for 10 people; sailing *bancas* are $4 an hour, a bit more with a "driver." Flagged "taxi" *bancas* ferry people from one spot to the next very inexpensively.

WHERE TO STAY

There are numerous establishments on the island, and many of them crowd densely along **White Sand Beach**. Facilities range from up-market resorts with very nice cottages and private bath and air conditioning to very rustic. Prices vary seasonally: they "peak" in mid-December to the first week of January, Chinese New Year, and Easter, and are lowest June to October 31. If you are not going on a package deal, then contact the resorts yourself — you will get a lower rate because they will deduct the travel agency commission from the published rate. Reservations are a must during Easter Week (March or April) and from mid-December through early January.

Most people prefer staying toward the north end of White Sand — the beach is wider and whiter.

There are a number of decent budget resorts (under $35): **BAN'S**, *Balabag, Tel. 288-3156*, **CASA PILAR**, *Manggayad, Tel. 288-3202*, **LA ISLA BONITA**, *Manggayad, Tel. 288-3501*, **NOEL'S PLACE**, *Bulabog Road, Balabag, Tel. 288-3169*, **A ROCK**, *Ambulong*, and **LAUGHING WATER** *Diniwid Beach*. These places have simple and clean rooms, but no hot water in the bathrooms.

Other Beaches

CLUB PANOLY, *Punta-Bunga Beach, north of White Beach. Tel. 288-3011. Manila reservations: Tel. 536-0682 to 86, Fax 525-5396. 55 rooms. $132-143 per single, $133-154 per double, $16.50 per extra bed. Visa, Master Card, American Express, Diners. Beachfront.*

Rooms are tastefully decorated and spacious. The deluxe rooms have cable TV and a balcony. Panoly is on a pretty stretch of beach that has a bit more privacy than White Beach. Facilities include a swimming pool, tennis, beach volleyball, basketball, recreation room and sauna. Watersports equipment includes windsurfing, paddleboats, scuba and snorkeling gear, and canoeing. The restaurant specializes in seafood, and the coffee shop serves continental fare. Evening entertainment is provided at the karaoke bar or the Sampaguita Bar.

SUNDANCE, *Diniwid Beach, just north of White Beach. Manila reservations: Tel. 890-9032, Fax 897-2659. 7 rooms. $100-120 per single or double, $240 per suite. E-mail: Sundance@mailhost.net. Beachfront.*

This place offers a quieter and more private atmosphere in a small and pretty cream sand cove. Located on the hillside just above the beach, there are great views from the café-bar-restaurant and from all the rooms. The rooms are pleasant, very clean, air conditioned, and all have a balcony that faces the sea. The food is good and the staff is very friendly.

BORACAY BEACH AND YACHT CLUB, *Cagban Beach, Manoc-Manoc, south of White Beach. Manila reservations: Tel. 831-8140. 10 rooms. $72 per single, $100 per double, $24 per extra bed. Visa, Master Card, American Express. Beachfront.*

Located on a nice private white sand beach, this establishment offers pleasant and roomy native cottages. The rooms, with native furnishings, are fully air conditioned, clean, and may fit up to four beds. Transfers to and from Caticlan are included in the room rates.

White Beach — North

FRIDAYS, *Pinaungon. Tel. (dial Manila for direct connection) 815-2027. Manila reservations: Tel. 892-7443, 819-0282. 40 rooms. $168-180 per single, $200-204 per double, $24 per extra person. Visa, Master Card, American Express, Diners. Beachfront.*

The most up-scale establishment on White Beach, Friday's is ideally located on the widest stretch of powdery white sand. The cottages are duplex style, and each room has a small porch with a hammock. The rooms are comfortable, tastefully decorated, air conditioned, and have television. Rooms closer to the beach cost more. The restaurant-bar is large, and the food and service are very good.

PEARL OF THE PACIFIC II, *Cagban. Tel. 288-3220. Manila reservations: Tel. 924-4880, Fax 924-4882. 33 rooms. $84-168 per single or double, $240-456 per suite, $18 per extra bed. Visa, Master Card, American Express, Diners. Beachfront suites.*

The cottages could use renovation, but the suites are wonderful. The suites are located on White Sand beach, and all the rooms have a seaward view, probably the best on this beach. Each suite is two levels, the beds and bathroom on the top level, and a few steps down takes you to the living room (where two people can sleep on the sofas) and balcony. The cottages are on the other side of the main road. The staff in the restaurant are delightful. Discounts are given if you book directly through the Manila office.

SEA WIND, *Cagban. Tel. 288-3091, Fax 288-3425. 24 rooms. $115-150 per single or double (breakfast included). $20 per extra bed. Visa, Master Card. Beachfront.*

This is a very charming resort. The rooms are spacious, air conditioned, and the decor is styled after the province for which the room is named. Some rooms have cable television and a small refrigerator. The pretty restaurant is underneath a canopy-like nipa roof, tables are wrought iron and glass, and the chairs are wrought iron and abaca. The staff is friendly.

WILLY'S PLACE, *Cagban. Tel. 288-3151, Fax 288-3016. 16 rooms. $115-135 per single or double, $15 per extra bed. Visa, Master Card. Beachfront.*

The staff and service are superb here. The rooms are simple and comfortable, and have cable television and a minibar. Breakfast is included in the room rates, and they serve excellent fruit shakes.

COCOMANGAS, *Balabag. Tel. 288-3409. 13 rooms. $65-110 per single or double aircon, $48-55 per single or double non-aircon. Visa, Master Card, American Express. (8% is added for credit or charge cards.) Main road.*

The rooms are simple and clean; most people that stay here enjoy nightlife (Cocomangas has the most popular bar on Boracay, so do not expect to sleep early). The staff are friendly. The restaurant serves both local and continental food, and has very good pizza.

BORACAY PLAZA, *Cagban. Tel. 288-3702. 8 aircon, 10 non-aircon. $80 per single or double aircon, $40 per single or double non-aircon. Beachfront.*

The rooms are simple and clean. The air conditioned rooms are bright, and have hot water. The fan-cooled rooms are small and tastefully decorated with native materials; there is no hot water in the bathrooms. The staff and management are very friendly and can help arrange for *bancas*, motorcycles, etc.

VIP LINGAU, *Cagban. Tel. 288-3150. 10 rooms. $63 per single or double aircon, $30-44 per single or double non-aircon. 50% discount May-October 31. Beachfront.*

This is a simple resort, with friendly and helpful staff. All rooms are clean and simple. The "VIP rooms" have a balcony with a hammock. The restaurant serves Filipino and European dishes, and good pizza.

JONY'S PLACE, *Balabag. Tel. 288-3119. 7 rooms. $65-80 per single or double aircon, $40 per single or double non-aircon. Main road.*

Nestled into a nice and simple landscaped garden are tastefully done bamboo cottages with nipa roofs. The air conditioned rooms have hot water. The restaurant specializes in Mexican dishes.

White Beach – Center

SANDCASTLES, *Balabag. Tel. 288-3207, Fax 288-3449. Manila reservations: Tel. 823-2725. 20 rooms. $100-210.87 per single or double, $20 per extra bed. American Express. Beachfront.*

The rooms vary with size and price; some can accommodate three to four people comfortably. The most interesting room is the "Fan-Villa" on the second floor – three of its sides have no walls, making the room very airy and refreshing (during December-February you do not need air conditioning), and the motif is safari. Other rooms available are either a bungalow (with an attic where one more person can fit) or those inside the native wood cottages. The restaurant specializes in Thai food, and the staff is nice.

LORENZO MAIN, *Manggayad. Tel. 288-3806. Manila reservations: Tel. 928-0719, Fax 926-1726, e-mail: boracay@mnl.sequel.net. 34 rooms. $108-144 single or double aircon, $52-74 per single or double non-aircon, $20 per extra bed. Visa, Master Card, American Express, Diners. Main road.*

This pleasant resort is near the beach in a landscaped garden. The rooms are inside wooden cottages with nipa roofing and are clean and nicely decorated with native furnishings. Facilities include two swimming pools, a game room, and a disco with karaoke rooms. The restaurant serves local and continental dishes.

MILA'S, *Balabag. Tel. 288-3536, Fax 288-3637. 24 rooms. $90 per single, $110 per double. Beachfront.*

The comfortable and clean air conditioned rooms are in a Spanish-villa styled complex. The restaurant specializes in Spanish cuisine.

BORACAY HIDEAWAY, *Balabag. Tel. 288-3363, 288-3335. 15 rooms. $100 per single or double, $10 per extra bed. Beachfront.*

This is a nice family-oriented resort. All rooms are air conditioned and have hot water and a small porch. The rooms are simple and spacious. This place is family-run and well-managed.

ISLANDS GARDEN, *Bulabog Road, Balabag. Tel. 288-3161. Manila reservations: Tel. 522-2685. 17 rooms. $60 per single or double aircon, $28-40 per single or double non-aircon, $15 per extra bed. Inland.*

This very quiet resort is an alternative to beachfront accommodations. A short walk inland off the main road takes you to this complex of nice native cottages. All rooms have a small porch where a hammock hangs. There are billiard and ping-pong tables in the recreation area. The staff are friendly and helpful. The restaurant serves pasta and pancit dishes.

NIGI-NIGI NU-NOOS, *Manggayad. Tel. 288-3101. Manila reservations: Tel. 521-5053, c/o Margie. 22 rooms. $35 per single, $50 per double. Beachfront.*

This resort has interesting cone-shaped bamboo cottages. The rooms are simply furnished using native materials and are clean. For breakfast and dinner, tables are set up on the beach. In the main building, there is a restaurant, bar, movie room, and a souvenir shop. Good management and staff.

White Beach — South

LORENZO GRAND VILLA, *Manoc-Manoc. Manila reservations: Tel. 928-0719, Fax 926-1726. E-mail: boracay@mnl.sequel.net. 20 rooms. $114-160 per single or double. $20 per extra bed. Visa, Master Card, American Express, Diners. Cliffside.*

Although this place is not on a beach, it is on a cliff and commands spectacular views of the passage between Boracay and Panay. All rooms are spacious, air conditioned, and comfortable. There is a swimming pool, gift shop, karaoke bar, and restaurant.

LORENZO SOUTH, *Angol, Manoc-Manoc. Tel. 288-3810. Manila reservations: 928-0719, Fax 926-1726, e-mail: boracay@mnl.sequel.net. 24 rooms. $114-150 per single or double, $122-160 per suite. $20 extra bed. Visa, Master Card, American Express, Diners. Beachfront.*

This resort is on a secluded beachfront near some very good snorkeling. All rooms have a balcony with a panoramic ocean view. The rooms are air conditioned and have television. The suite has a jacuzzi.

TITAY'S SOUTH, *Angol, Manoc-Manoc. Tel. 288-3407. 22 rooms. $100 per single or double aircon, $50 per single or double non-aircon, $15 per extra bed. Beachfront.*

Titay's has simple clean rooms with hot water. The restaurant has pretty good seafood and Filipino dishes.

WHERE TO EAT

A melange of food is available in Boracay. Seafoods are best. You may select from an array of cuisines, as many foreigners came as tourists, decided to settle here, and set up restaurants. A meal in most places will cost $4-10. Fresh fruit shakes are available in many places — **WILLY'S PLACE**, *Balabag,* has excellent shakes.

Most resorts have simple restaurants. The finer dining places are in the expensive resorts but even there dress is casual.

FRIDAYS', *Balabag*.

Has a cultural show twice a week in the evenings, and very good food ($10-20 a meal) — especially the *leche flan*.

CAFÉ COCOMANGAS, *Balabag*.

Pizza.

JONI'S, *Balabag*.

A popular place for Tex-Mex food.

EL TORO, *Mangyad*.

Specializes in Spanish food.

SANDCASTLES, *Mangyad*.

Serves Thai cuisine.

BAZURA, *Mangyad*.

Tasty barbeque.

CHEZ DE PARIS, *Mangyad*.

Owned by a Frenchman, the food is quite good.

The **BRITISH TEA ROOM**, *inland off the main road in Mangyad*.

A nice place for afternoon tea; tucked into a field, it is an alternative to beachfront hangouts.

SEVERO DE BORACAY, *Angol*.

Superb Italian fare.

JOLLY SAILOR, *Angol*.

Tasty meals.

TITAY'S THEATER GARDEN, *Angol*.

Good seafood and Filipino fare, with cultural shows in the evenings.

The **ENGLISH BAKERY & TEA ROOM** has fresh European breads and pastries, with outlets in Balabag, Mangyad, and Angol.

ASIAN VILLAGE, *Club Panoly Resort, Punta-Bunga Beach*.

Probably the most up-market dining on Boracay; the seafood is pretty good. Expect to spend $10-25 per meal.

SEEING THE SIGHTS

There are several other nice beaches, though none as extensive as White Beach, where you may find a bit more privacy. Just north is **Diniwid**, a nice beach in a small cove, and further is **Punta-Bunga** where there is an up-market resort. **Puka Shell**, further north, is a very nice panoramic beach that faces **Carabao Island**. The hawkers on the beach claim to have genuine pearls — if they are real then they should not melt when you hold a flame up to them.

On the northeast coast, at Ilig-Iligan, there are **bat caves**, home to large fruit bats which are considered a delicacy, and the **Kar-Tir Shell Museum**. The bats are becoming scarce because they are eaten.

There are pretty and quiet beaches in the island's southern coves. You may also set off to one of the nearby islands: **Small (Laurel) Island** and **Crocodile Island** off the southwest tip of Boracay. Small Island has a nice beach and a haunted house to explore.

NIGHTLIFE & ENTERTAINMENT

Boracay's nightlife is another attraction. **Moondogs** is a very popular bar. If you are daring, try the infamous shooters: 15 shots of a mix of various liquors, and, if you are still conscious, your name is added to the plaque of your country. Other bars include **Barracuda, Bazura, Beach Comber, Mango Ray's, Starlight**, and **Kontiki**. People dance at many of the bars and there are discos at **Inso's** in Lorenzo Main and at **El Capitan** in Club Panoly. You may listen to folk music in the **Guitar Bar & Restaurant**.

SHOPPING

Aside from the many vendors that scope the beaches, there is a wide selection of souvenirs at the **Talipapa Flea Market** and at several smaller stores on the main road; always bargain. The **Boracay Shopping Center** by the Tourist Center has wine, snacks, imported sunscreens and oils, toiletries, basic medicine, silver jewelry, and beach clothes; prices are fixed.

SPORTS & RECREATION

Kayaking

Adventure tours that include kayaking, are run well by **Tribal Holdings**, *c/o Sand Castles, White Beach, Balabag, Tel. 288-3207, Fax 288-3449; or in Manila at Tel. 823-2725.* Day tours cost $40 per person (minimum of two) and overnight costs $100-200 per person (minimum of four), depending on the destination.

Scuba Diving

Thanks to the efforts of Boracay's diving industry, reef protection has allowed many areas to recover. There are a few dive sites just offshore, but you need to take a *banca* to a number of better ones. Soft corals, small fish, shellfish, starfish, and sea urchins are common. Larger fish (shark, barracuda, tuna, etc.), rays, and turtles are further offshore. Be aware that the currents in the channel between Boracay Island and mainland Panay can be very strong.

Several dive operations line White Beach. **Beach Life**, *Tel. 288-3401*, **Boracay Scuba Diving School**, *Tel. 288-3327*, **Calypso**, *Tel. 288-3206*, **Inter Island, Lapu Lapu**, *Tel. 288-3302*, and **Victory**, *c/o the Jolly Sailor, Tel. 288-3209,* are among the recommended operators.

Snorkeling

Snorkeling is good at **Lapuz-Lapuz, Ilig-Iligan, Crocodile Island, Small (Laurel) Island**, and **Yapak**. If you did not bring gear, you may rent it from any of the dive shops.

Windsurfing

Windsurfing is available in several places. **Green Yard Seasport Center** and **Richie's Mistral** in Mangayad rent and give lessons. Rental costs around $10 and hour, and lessons may run around $40 for three sessions, including the board.

An annual international windsurf competition is usually held in January or February.

PRACTICAL INFORMATION

Banks

A number of banks and money changers are along the main road. Banking hours are Monday through Friday, from 9:00am until 3:00pm. Money changers stay open later, and operate on the weekends.

Clinic

A Rock Restaurant has a clinic, and on the main road in Balabag is the **Boracay Medical Clinic & Drugstore** and the **Boracay Emergency Hospital**.

Mail

A small post office is in Balabag.

Safety

Many low-budget travelers hang out, hang loose, and hang around until their funds run low. A number have come to benefit from the tourist traffic and have often offended locals. As a result, peace and order problems have surfaced periodically. Do not bring valuables.

Sand Flea Warning

Niknik (sand fleas) abound during rainy season (June-November). Apply a generous coat of baby oil or Avon's Skin-So-Soft, through which they cannot bite. *Niknik* are very small and they lay eggs in your skin — you will not see or feel anything for several days, until small very itchy bumps appear; don't scratch!

Tourist Assistance

Most of the resorts sell maps of Boracay. At the **Tourist Center**, along White Beach in Mangayad, near boat station 2, you can get information and reconfirm local and international tickets. There is a **DOT office** at the Oro Beach Resort, Mangayad.

The **Jolly Sailor Bar & Restaurant** has safe deposit boxes, and is a good place to get information, assistance, and help with sending communications and visa extensions.

Water

You should only drink bottled water, as the water is not potable. All resorts, restaurants, and stores sell bottled water.

ILOILO

Iloilo is an ideal destination for a relaxing and varied vacation: enjoy the city sights and handicrafts, visit the fabulous churches and the delightful scenery along the south coast, or head northward to one of the beaches and linger for several days.

This is a charming city with a relaxed pace, clean and gracious hotels, delectable seafood, and imposing churches and ancestral houses. The province celebrates a number of interesting festivals: **Dinagyang**, on the fourth week of January, is the best known; **Paraw Regatta**, usually the last Sunday of February; **Pasungay**, the second Saturday of January; and **Carabao Carroza Races** on May 1.

History

Among the early migrants to Iloilo were 10 Bornean *datus* fleeing the repression of the Sri Vishayan (or Swirijaya) Empire. In the early 13th century, the datus bartered gold for the coastal and lowland areas, which they bought from Marikudo, a native chief. Among these areas was Irong-Irong, meaning nose-like. If you look at a map you will see that Iloilo City is on the wide mouth of the Iloilo River, which juts out snout-like into the Guimaras Strait.

In 1566, the Spaniards, lead by Juan Miguel de Legazpi, arrived in Iloilo and found thriving towns that had enjoyed relative peace and prosperity for about 300 years. Legazpi established a settlement and proclaimed a governor in Otong (now Oton). The capital was moved south to Arevalo in 1581. Because of repeated raids by Moro pirates, the Dutch, and English, in 1667 the capital was moved to Irong-Irong, where the river mouth provided better protection.

The economy of Iloilo grew rapidly. By 1855, Iloilo was the center of commerce and trade in the Visayas, the second most important city in the country (Manila being the first).

Under the Americans, Iloilo gained more prominence in the nation's politics, industry, and agriculture. The infrastructure — roads, extensive railway lines, airport, and irrigation — was good. Fishing and sugar industries flourished. Progress was hindered during World War Two as the Ilongos challenged the Japanese forces. The postwar recovery was slow but sure.

Today you can see the genteel and cultured Ilongo history mirrored in the ancestral mansions, pleasant dialect, artistic crafts, clean and well-managed hotels, and superb cuisine.

ARRIVALS & DEPARTURES

By Air

The flight between Manila and Iloilo takes one hour, and the route is served by Air Philippines (daily), Cebu Pacific (twice daily), and Philippine Airlines (five times daily). Philippine Airlines also has a daily trip between Cebu and Iloilo that takes 30 minutes.

Iloilo's airport is in the Mandurriao district, about seven kilometers from the center of the city. The easiest way to get to town is by taxi (PU), costing $3-4.

By Sea

From the wharf in Iloilo city proper, boats ply various interisland routes.

• **Iloilo-Manila**. The voyage takes 18-21 hours and is served by Negros Navigation with trips departing Manila every day except Thursday ($12-60); Sulpicio Lines with trips from Manila on Tuesday and Saturday ($13-60); and WGA SuperFerry leaving Manila every day except Sunday ($20-76).

• **Iloilo-Cebu**. The trip from Cebu takes 12-13 hours and is served by Sulpicio Lines ($5-20), leaving Cebu on Wednesday, and by TransAsia ($10-16), departing Cebu on Tuesday, Thursday, and Sunday.

• **Iloilo-Bacolod**. The three daily ferry trips are a delightful experience. Sit on the upper deck for better views, and, aboard the afternoon ferry on good days, a nice sunset.

• **Iloilo-Palawan (Cuyo & Puerto Princessa)**. This route is served by Milagrosa J Shipping. The trip to Cuyo takes 14 hours and departs Iloilo on the 6th, 16th, and 26th of every month. The Cuyo-Puerto Princessa leg takes another 12 hours, and departs Cuyo on the 7th, 17th, and 27th. The return trips depart Puerto Princessa on the 11th, 21st, and 30th. The fare is: Iloilo-Cuyo, $6; Cuyo-Puerto Princessa, $10; Iloilo-Puerto Princessa, $15, or $20 including snacks and a bed. The MV Andrew does the same route, its schedule is not definite, and fare is $16 including meals.

By Land

Buses to other points on Panay leave from the Tanza bus terminal, at Rizal corner of Ledesma Street. See *Arrivals & Departures* of Kalibo.

ORIENTATION

Iloilo City spans several districts: the city proper is northeast, La Paz and Jaro are west of the center, Mandurriao is southwest, Molo is south, and Arevalo is furthest south.

GETTING AROUND

Hiring cars and taking public transport in Iloilo is pleasant; most of the drivers are friendly. The cheapest way to get around is by jeepney, at P1-2.50 (5-10¢) per ride. The people of Iloilo are friendly and helpful; ask at your embarkation point which jeepney to take to your destination, and inform the jeepney driver of your destination so he can let you know when to alight.

Taxis (PUs) cruise the streets, and rental cars wait at the airport and at the larger hotels. Arrange the price in advance. Among the car rental companies in Iloilo are **Avis**, *Hotel del Rio, Tel. 271-171*; **Taruc Locsin & Sons**, *Tel. 78-779, 78-865, 73-705*; **Bobby Uy**, *Tel. 76-169, 74-811*; **Sarabia Manor Hotel**, contact Luz Lubareto, *Tel. 271-021, 74-676*; **Regine's Car Rental**, *Tel. 81-181*; and **Gelyn Hormillosa**, *Tel. 70-373, 73-336*. Rates range from $8-12 per hour and $40-120 per day.

WHERE TO STAY

Iloilo City Proper

AMIGO TERRACES HOTEL, *Iznart corner Delgado Street. Tel. 74-811 to 13. 97 rooms. $36 per single, $40 per double, $61-120 per suite, $4 per extra person. Visa, Master Card, American Express.*

Rooms are clean, air conditioned, and have cable TV. Facilities include a swimming pool, foreign exchange, and a souvenir shop. There is a restaurant, pastry shop, bar, and disco.

HOTEL DEL RIO, *MH del Pilar Street. Tel. 271-171, Fax 70-736. 57 rooms. $36 per single or double, $40-78 per suite, $5.50 per extra person. Visa, Master Card, American Express, Diners.*

Situated by a pretty river, this hotel is well managed, has clean rooms and friendly service. All rooms are air conditioned and have cable TV. Facilities include a swimming pool, travel agency, rent-a-car, barber shop, and souvenir shop. Services offered include secretarial, laundry, mail, and arrangements for golf. You may dine at Café del Prado, for a continental breakfast buffet; Igman-an, which specializes in charcoal broiled seafood and native dishes; Golden Salakot, for continental dishes; and Owari, a Japanese restaurant.

SARABIA MANOR, *General Luna Street. Tel. 271-021. 88 rooms. $34-60 per single, $40-60 per double, $93-185 per suite. Visa, Master Card, American Express.*

All rooms are carpeted, air conditioned, and have cable TV, and suite rooms have a refrigerator. Facilities include a large swimming pool, newsstand and souvenir shop, and beauty parlor. Services offered are secretarial, laundry, and tour arrangements.

RESIDENCE HOTEL, *44 General Luna Street. Tel. 81-091 to 93, Fax 72-454. 30 rooms. $24-30 per single or double, $57 per suite, $8 per extra person. Visa, Master Card, American Express, Diners.*

This cute boutique hotel has a cozy atmosphere. Rooms are clean, comfortable, air conditioned, and have cable TV. The restaurant specializes in grilled seafood and there is a bar.

HOTEL MADIA-AS, *Aldeguer Street. Tel. 72-756. 43 rooms. $18 per single, $22.50-30 per double. Visa and Master Card*

Rooms are large, bright, clean, and air conditioned.

THE CASTLE HOTEL, *Bonifacio Drive. Tel. 81-021 to 23. 25 aircon and 3 non-aircon rooms. $17 per single or $20-35 per double aircon, $10.50 per single or double non-aircon, $4 per extra bed. Visa, Master Card, Diners.*

The higher priced rooms have cable TV, or for an extra $2.50 one is added to rooms without. Rooms are simple and clean and the restaurant serves inexpensive ($2-4) local and Chinese dishes. There is karaoke and live music in the evenings.

PENSION CASA PLAZA, *Gen Luna Street. Tel. 73-461, Fax 72-543. 14 rooms. Rates include breakfast, $24.50 per single, $30-42 per double, $6 per extra person. Visa and Diners.*

All rooms are carpeted, air conditioned, and clean. The coffee shop serves continental and local dishes; average meal cost is $3.50.

CHITO'S ILOILO PENN, *180 de Leon corner Jalandoni Street. Tel. 76-415, 76-135, Fax 81-186. 23 rooms. $25 per single or double, $3.25 per extra person. Visa and Master Card.*

Rooms are clean and air conditioned. There is a pool, and arrangements for transportation and car-rental can be made at the front desk. The restaurant serves tasty seafood and Filipino dishes. The staff is friendly.

JARO PENSION HOUSE, *36A DB Ledesma Street. Tel. 320-2863. 8 aircon and 7 non-aircon rooms. $16.50 per single or $21 per double aircon, $4 per extra person.*

Rooms are simple; meals are provided in the common dining area.

RIVER QUEEN, *Bonifacio Drive. Tel. 76-667, Fax 270-176. 26 aircon and 16 non-aircon rooms. $16 per single or $20 per double aircon, $8.25 per single or $11.20 per double non-aircon, $2.50 per extra person. Visa and Diners.*

This friendly establishment has simple rooms. Its restaurant serves Filipino, Chinese, and Continental food and has a live band in the evenings.

FAMILY PENSION HOUSE, *General Luna Street. Tel. 270-070. 27 rooms. $12.70 per aircon room, $8.70 per non-aircon, $6 per extra person. Visa and Master Card.*

Rooms are simple and clean.

Beach Resorts

VILLA ROSA BY THE SEA, *Calaparan Villa, Iloilo City. Tel. 76-953, Fax 79-127. Manila reservations: Tel. 894-3586, 894-3765, Fax 894-3708. $16 per single or double, $4 per extra person. Visa and Diners.*

The resort has 18 cottages with clean air conditioned rooms, a pool, and a restaurant that serves seafood and local dishes.

SOL Y MAR, *Kilometer 21, Tigbauan. Cellular Tel. 0912-520-2106. $24 per single or double, $4 per extra person.*

The rooms are very simple and are fan-cooled. The resort caters mostly to day visitors. The restaurant serves barbequed seafood and chicken. Facilities include a playground for children and bareback pony rides for small kids.

SBS IYANG, *Concepcion. Tel. 71-994. Cellular Tel. 0520-0399. 14 rooms. $8 per single, $12 per double.*

Accommodation is simple and meals are provided upon request. *Bancas* are available for fishing, island hopping, and scuba diving. The resort can arrange for guides if you wish to go trekking. There is a small floating cottage where you can have a meal, drink, or relax.

SHAMROCK, *Guimbal. Cellular Tel. 0912-520-0501. Manila reservations: Tel. 818-8076, 818-4262, Fax 817-0161. 7 rooms. $18-32 per single or double, maximum per room 4 adults, $2 per extra person.*

A simple, friendly resort, facilities include a swimming pool and aquasports (jetski, seadoo, and boat). The restaurant serves continental dishes.

WHERE TO EAT

We've always had good meals in Iloilo, especially the seafood. The Ilongos say it's because they like to eat well. Try the local specialties: *Pancit Molo* (meatballs wrapped in noodles and cooked as a soup) and *La Paz Batchoy* (tripe). Try also *biscocho, barquillos,* and other biscuits. Most of the lodging establishments have restaurants. **Casa Plaza** has a very nice coffee shop, and the food in **Amigo Terraces** is good.

In general, a meal will cost around $3-6.

IGMAN-AN, *Hotel del Rio.*

Outstanding blue marlin, prawns, smoked *bangus*, and soup-of-the day.

OCEAN CITY, *across the river from Del Rio.*
This open air restaurant has good seafood.
REGENT GARDEN, *second floor, Amigo Terraces Hotel.*
Tasty Chinese cuisine.
TAVERN, *Delgado Street.*
American, Spanish, and Italian fare and a friendly atmosphere.
TRY ME, *Delgado Street.*
This is an ice cream chain with seven other outlets. Short orders are also available.
FATIMA GARDEN, *Delgado Street.*
Serves good Filipino food.
ANG KAMALIG, *Delgado corner Valeria Street.*
Specializes in local Ilongo dishes.
PAYAG-PAYAG, *off MH del Pilar, the road to Mandurriao.*
This simple restaurant prepares fish very well.

For Chinese food, try **REGENT GARDEN**, *second floor Amigo Terraces Hotel*; **SUMMER HOUSE**, **MANSION HOUSE**, **JAMES**, and **KONG KEE**, *are all along JM Basa Street.*
SILVER SPOON, *Bonifacio Drive.*
Come here for "finer-dining" in Iloilo, featuring European dishes.

In Jaro District, try **JOEY'S DINER & CHICKEN HAUS**, *Lopez Jaena corner Rizal Street, Jaro* for tasty fried chicken; **GRANDMA'S**, *Amigo Plaza, La Paz,* for home-style meals; and **BREAKTHROUGH**, *E Lopez Street,* for tasty seafood. And do stop by **BISCOCHO HAUS**, *8 Lopez Jaena Street,* where you can pick up *biscocho* and other home-baked goodies.

Along the beach in Villa, Arevalo District, are a number of restaurants for seafood, barbeque, and oysters: **SEASIDE** has tables on the beach; the oysters, barbeque chicken, vegetables, and garlic fried rice are very good; **BREAKTHROUGH** has a variety of tasty seafood dishes; also try **VILLA ROSAL**, and **TATOY'S**, *further southward along the beach,* for great native food in a native setting.

SEEING THE SIGHTS

In the city proper stop by **Museo Iloilo**. You will find a well-labeled interesting collection that includes artifacts, prehistoric fossil finds, pottery from sunken ships, secondary and primary burial jars, photos of the more recent past, a loom on which the delicate *sinamay* (*jusi* and/or *piña* fabrics) is woven and an exhibit of recent creations of local artists. There is also a good collection of *santos* and religious articles

Jaro, the district west of the city proper, has several ancestral homes. Also see the attractive **Jaro Cathedral**. Across the street from the cathedral is the attractive bell tower, which was partly destroyed during the earthquake of 1948.

South of the city proper is **Molo District**, once a community for Chinese immigrants. It is said that the district acquired its name from a Chinese settler who saw Moro pirates and shouted "Molo, Molo." Visit the striking **Gothic-Renaissance church** (dating from about the late 1800s). The interior and exterior design is ornate, the five retablos even more so. Fronting the church is the ancestral house of Timoteo Consing. And, just around the corner, is the century-old **Panaderia de Molo**, where delicious biscuits are still made today. At the **Asilo de Molo Orphanage**, on Avancena Street, young girls are taught intricate embroidery and spend hours making religious and other embroidered articles. You can watch them create delicate designs and flowers — some of them appear at first glance to be paintings.

Further south is **Villa Beach**, a nearby getaway. It is popular with the people of Iloilo who come to swim and enjoy the great food at the many seaside restaurants. There are a few places with simple cottages for overnight stays.

SHOPPING

In Jaro, if you like biscuits, stop by **Biscocho Haus** on Lopez Jaena and sample the *biscocho* (hard toasted buttered bread with sugar), *barquillos* (wafers rolled into round tubes, great with ice cream), and other delicacies. Also visit the **Jesena and Dellota antique collections**. Mrs. Dellota is chatty and knowledgeable about the antiques she sells. She also has a simple cottage on Guimaras Island that she rents out to visitors.

In La Paz, at the **CM Bamboocraft**, out-of-school youths create artistic religious and bamboo pieces. At the **PAGPA display center**, at the Department of Trade on JM Basa Street, in Iloilo City Proper, you can see and buy local handicrafts including wood, shell, and embroidered items.

In Molo District, aside from the Asilo de Molo (see *Seeing The Sights*, above), you can find some woodcraft that includes bracelets, bags, and other wares at **Rodson Woodcraft** on Timawa Avenue.

Arevalo, the flower district of Iloilo, has a **Sinamay Dealer** on Osmeña Street. Here you can buy the delicate *sinamay* fabric, embroidered clothes, linens, and other articles.

EXCURSIONS & DAY TRIPS
South from Iloilo

The southeastern coastal towns are home to some of the Philippines' most striking Spanish churches, plus a number of good swimming beaches with rustic accommodations.

The façade of the **Tigbauan church** is exquisite — decorations around the main door look like delicate filigree work carved in stone. A marker to the right of the church commemorates the first Philippine Jesuit school for boys, established in 1592. One kilometer south of Tigbauan is a marker for the **American liberation** of Panay from the Japanese in 1945.

Near the simple solid stone **Guimbal church** are the **ruins** of a seaside watch tower, once used to spot incoming pirates. A road inland from Guimbal leads to the **huge church ruins** in Leon.

Panay's most interesting church is in **Miagao**, 11 kilometers further south. Carved into the unique sandstone façade is a Philippinized Christian scene of St. Christopher, with the Christ child on his shoulders, planting a coconut tree amid native foliage. The botanical motif resembles ancient Aztec art. The church is flanked by massive bell towers; each are different and were built by different friars. The church was built over 200 years ago and is now on UNESCO's World Heritage List.

Nadsadan Falls are a pleasant 60- to 90-minute walk. To get there, head for Igbaras, eight kilometers inland from Miagao, then another four kilometers by road from the town to the point where you begin the walk. The last part requires negotiating boulders. Find a guide in town and check with the Mayor's office before going. The falls are like a veil that runs 50 feet down a rock face into a deep pool where you may swim.

San Joaquin church was built in 1869 from white coral. The façade depicts the 1859 defeat of the Moors in the Battle of Tetuan, Spain. San Joaquin's **coral cemetery**, built in 1892, has a remarkable hexagonal chapel.

There is **scuba diving** at Cataan Cove, 20 minutes from San Joaquin along the road to Anini-y. It is best December through April, and can be difficult at other times. Call Anton Lee, *Tel. 75-956*, for information and assistance.

North of Iloilo

The north also has a number of interesting 19th century churches. You may see them by jeepney or PU in about half a day.

The unfinished Byzantine **Pavia church** is long and low. The holes in the warm red brick exterior walls were made by bullets aimed by guerrillas at the Japanese troops that were inside during World War Two. The interior of the church is very pleasant and has a peaceful aura.

Santa Barbara church has a large *convento* and a nice interior court. From the church, General Martin Delgado launched the 1989 Visayan Revolution. Nearby, the well-kept **Iloilo Golf and Country Club**, started in 1907 by 10 Britons and Americans, has 37 holes. Guests are welcome to play; green fees are $25 and caddie fees are $15.

There is an **attractive cemetery** and a solid neoclassical church in Cabatuan.

You can get some good photographs at **Janiuay's century-old church ruins,** beside the current church. The original bells of the first church are still used. Along the way to Mina, there is a cemetery with three impressive stairways and a pretty Gothic chapel. The cemetery in Pototan has a Mexican cross in the center.

Further north in Dingle is a yellow sandstone **church** that has a massive and pleasing façade. While at Dingle, you may visit the **Moroboro Springs**, a series of swimming pools fed by the springs.

And, on the return to Iloilo City, stop by **Barotac Nuevo**'s church. The architecture is a mix of Roman, Ionic, and Doric influences. **Mount Salihid,** just outside Barotac Nuevo, attracts devotees during Holy Week; there are also caves which you may explore. You may also stop by the **San Juan Falls,** a series of waterfalls and pools — the water descends a total of 100 feet. The falls are in a lush valley approximately six kilometers from Sara and are accessible by road.

PRACTICAL INFORMATION
Banking

You should have no problems changing US dollars in Iloilo City. Most of the major local banks have branches: **BPI**, **Far East**, and **PCI Bank** on Iznart Street; **MetroBank**, Delgado St., and **PNB**, General Luna Street corner Valeria Street. Banking hours are weekdays from 9:00am-3:00pm.

Tourist Information

The **DOT**, Bonifacio Drive, *Tel. 270-245*, is helpful and informative. Stop in for information and assistance — especially if you are interested in visiting any of the antique collections, as this may require assistance for arranging entry. There is also a desk at the airport; both offices are closed during weekends.

GUIMARAS

Guimaras Province, the largest offshore island near Iloilo, has a number of nice beaches and several resorts on small islands around its fringes. The island, totaling 60,465 hectares, lies southeast of Iloilo City.

The island's name is attributed to two legends. One is that the name is derived from *paghimud-us*, meaning struggle for survival — Guimaras was once inhabited by Negritoes who fled there from Panay and then struggled to survive. The other traces the name from a forbidden affair between Guima and Aras, who left the island to flee their parents' wrath and opposition to the union and died in the sea.

. The island abounds with prolific mango trees, and is renowned for its very sweet golden fruit. Guimaras is home of the National Mango Research and Development Center, dedicated to studying the breeding and maintenance of the fruit. The **Manggohan sa Guimaras Festival**, on May 21-22, coincides with the celebration of the day that Guimaras was proclaimed a province in 1992. Festivities include parades, contests, and exhibits featuring mangoes and mango-related industries.

ARRIVALS & DEPARTURES

Boats cross hourly from the port in Iloilo to Jordan. Jeepneys go from Jordan to Nueva Valencia in the mornings. Tricycles serve the route to Buenavista.

The **Buenavista wharf**, 20 minutes by *banca* from Iloilo, was built in 1903 by General MacArthur and the US Corps of Engineers when they where in Guimaras.

WHERE TO STAY

Guimaras is not fully set for tourists, so it is best to have your resort make the arrangements for transportation (water and land).

NAGARAO, *Nagarao Island, Guimaras. 18 cottages. Iloilo reservations: Tel. (033) 78-613, Fax 71-094. $90 per person single occupancy, $80 per person double occupancy, all meals included.*

The pleasant exteriors of the native cottages are stone, wood, and nipa, and the interiors are simple, clean, and tastefully furnished using bamboo and other local materials. Each cottage has a small porch with a view of the sea. Rooms are fan-cooled.

Enjoy your meal feasting on a seafood buffet, and your coconut juice cannot get any fresher as it will be served to you straight from the tree. You may swim at the nice small beach or in the round swimming pool. Other facilities include tennis, table tennis, and water sports, with equipment for snorkeling, sailing, and surfing. The resort also organizes various tours.

ISLA NABUROT, *Naburot Island, Guimaras. 6 cottages. $80 per person, all meals included.*

The cottages are very simple, made of bamboo and nipa. There is no electricity on the island, but the plumbing works fine (strong flushing toilets). There are some great antiques inside the rooms. The owners promote a very homey atmosphere, the food is very good — meals are home-cooked with dishes including the catch of the day and other fresh seafood. There are *bancas* for exploring nearby points. This is a charming "get back to nature" resort. Behind the resort, a trail leads to a bench over looking the sea, and is a great place to watch the sunset.

COSTA AGUADA, *Inampulugan Island, Guimaras; access is better via Bacolod, Negros Occidental. Manila reservations: Tel. 890-5333; Bacolod reservations: Tel. (034) 28-665, Fax 24-858. $60-80 per cottage.*
The resort has nice spacious native cottages. Facilities include a swimming pool, tennis, basketball, and a small playground. The pavilion restaurant serves fresh seafood and local dishes. Rooms are fan-cooled. The resort is designed as an eco-tourism project and features a zoo, jungle trek, mangrove forest, and turtle farm.

SEEING THE SIGHTS

From Buenavista there is a nice walk to **Daliran Cave** where water from several springs collects inside and forms a pond, There are also limestone formations. **Tinadtaran Target Range** and **Camp Jossman**, in Buenavista, are remnants from the US occupation. This was the headquarters of General Douglas MacArthur when he was here on his first assignment to the country as a second lieutenant.

A pleasant 30 minute walk from Jordan takes you to **Balsan Bukid** (Holy Mountain) for a great view of Iloilo. During Holy Week, the crucifixion of Christ is reenacted on this hill. Also during Holy Week, **Ang Pagtaltal sa Guimaras**, a passion play, takes place in Jordan on Good Friday.

Nueva Valencia has a number of nice beaches nearby. A 45 minute walk from town will take you to **Alibuhod Bay**'s nice beach, good for swimming. At **Igang Point** there is a marine research center – inquire from the DOT in Iloilo or Bacolod if you wish to visit. You may also snorkel or dive off the sandy beaches. **Tiniguiban Island**, nearby, has a white sand beach and dive spots off Fiona's Reef. During high tide, red shrimp surface from their holes; these shrimp are a protected species.

EXCURSIONS & DAY TRIPS

Islets Off Guimaras

The islands surrounding Guimaras provide nice beaches where you can get away from it all. And, if you enjoy adventure, consider island hopping – bring plenty of bottled water, a sleeping bag, insect repellent, etc., as some islands have no facilities.

• **Siete Pecados** (Seven Sins) is a group of islands north of Guimaras. The impressive summer estate of the Lopez family, built 1910, is on Roca Encantada.

• **Naburot Island**, off western Guimaras, is an escape – very private, with nice white sand beach, and abundant marine life. It is 2.5 hectares, and has a charming resort (see *Where to Stay* above). It takes 30-45 minutes by boat from Iloilo.

- **Taklong Island**, a 24-hectare white sand and coral reef island, is off southern Guimaras. The island is a nature reserve and has the first Visayan Marine Park and Bird Sanctuary. To visit, make arrangements through the DOT or the University of the Philippines, Visayas.
- **Nagarao Island**, southeast of Guimaras, has a coral and sand beach, and some corals nearby. It takes two hours to get to Nagarao from Iloilo — two boat rides with a jeepney ride in between.
- **Inampalugan Island**, off southeastern Guimaras, is usually accessed from Bacolod. There are some nice walks to a jungle, mangrove forest, and turtle farm (see *Where to Stay* above).

PANAY'S NORTHEASTERN ISLANDS

There are several very pretty islands off northeastern Panay. The area is best for adventurers — there is no formal lodging except on Balbagon Island.

Sicogon Island has a nice cream sand beach and **Mount Upao** (300 meters). Upao is a nice hike with birdwatching. Behind Buaya Beach, you may see some brown monkeys that visit.

Balbagon Island has a four-kilometer stretch of cream sand, blue waters, and corals nearby.

Gigantes Sur and Norte are two islands with several caves. **Pawikan** (Turtle) **Cave**, on Gigantes Sur, is the most frequented cave and has a turtle-shaped mouth in the middle (you may have to cliff-hang to get to the turtle). You may also see grey monkeys hanging on roots from the top of the antechamber. Other caves to explore are Elephant and Tinihagan.

The **Cabugao Islands** are just south of the Gigantes and have a small cave and nice fine-sand beaches.

WHERE TO STAY & EAT

On Gigantes and Pan de Azucar Islands, you can find lodging with villagers.

CORAL BAY RESORT, *Balbagon Island, northern Iloilo. Manila reservations: Tel. 890-8131, 890-8593, 896-2547, Fax 896-0929. 80 rooms. $100 per person, meals and boat transfers included. Visa, Master Card.*

The semi-Spanish-style resort is behind a lovely golden-cream sand beach. All rooms are air conditioned and are comfortable. The restaurant has continental and seafood dishes. Facilities include a simple business center; tennis, volleyball, and basketball courts; driving range; playground; and various aquasports. The ride from Iloilo takes about 40 minutes by boat.

21. NEGROS

BACOLOD, NEGROS OCCIDENTAL

Bacolod and the surrounding areas have something for almost everybody: hiking on the lush slopes of **Mount Canlaon**, lovely beaches and offshore islands to escape to, quality handicrafts and antiques to admire and collect, mansions and churches to browse through, antique trains for locomotive buffs, and great local cuisine to feast on. If you visit during the third week of October, you will be treated to **Masskara**, Bacolod's Mardi Gras-like festival (see Chapter 7, *Basic Information,* "Fiestas").

The area has many families whose wealth was generated from sugar plantations. Cane grew green and tall on the plantations, was harvested manually, and transported to the mills on steam locomotives. These "iron dinosaurs" can be seen plying the same routes; to economize they have been converted to wood burners. During the late 19th century, many people spent their time on a huge estate, golfing at one of the three courses in the area, gambling at the casino or at cockpits, giving or attending parties, and traveling abroad.

Bacolod is a relatively new city and was built on income from farming the rich soil of Mount Canlaon. About four decades ago, sugar prices plummeted below most sugar centrals' production costs, business had to diversify, and the elite trimmed their budgets. Mansions and monuments remain as evidence of the hey-days of sugar industry. Bacolod's wide and straight streets, built to accommodate the limos and sports cars of the elite, also attest to the sugar wealth.

ORIENTATION

The capital of **Negros Occidental**, gateway to the Philippines' sugarlands, Bacolod sprawls gracefully over 16,000 hectares, including Bago City to the south and Silay to the north. The best time of the year to visit is November-June.

ARRIVALS & DEPARTURES

By Air

Cebu Pacific has a daily flight from Manila. Philippine Airlines has four daily flights to Bacolod from Manila and a daily flight from Cebu. Flying time from Manila is one hour; from Cebu an hour and 15 minutes.

The airport is just five kilometers south of downtown. It's cheapest to take a jeepney: walk to the road and flag down any of the jeepneys. They all stop at the city plaza. Perhaps the easiest way is a taxi-PU; the trip may cost $2-4, settle on the price beforehand.

By Sea

If you're going to **Iloilo**, take the ferry; see *Arrivals & Departures* of Iloilo in the previous chapter.

• **Bacolod-Manila**. The voyage from Manila takes 24 hours, **Negros Navigation** has a trip departing Manila every day except Sundays. The fare is $12-50.

By Land

• **Bacolod-Cebu**. There are five daily trips between Cebu and Bacolod. Ceres Liner serves this route and takes six to eight hours. After a ferry trip between Cebu and Negros islands, the buses continue from San Carlos City to Bacolod. The entire trip costs around $6 per person.

• **Bacolod-Dumaguete**. The seven morning trips start at 3:00am and the last trip is at 11:45am. The trip takes seven hours via San Carlos. A seat aboard a Ceres Liner "express bus" costs $4.

GETTING AROUND

You should have no problem with transport in Bacolod. Jeepneys ply all main routes, and are 10¢ (P2.50) a ride. Ask anyone which ones to take and where to alight for your destination. Another option is to hire a taxi (PU) or rental car for the day. If you are hiring a taxi for just one ride, the minimum flag-down fare is 50¢ (P12.50); settle the price of the trip before heading off.

Car rental companies include **Avis**, *Bacolod Convention Plaza Hotel, Tel. 83-55*; **Far-Go**, *Venus Street, Tel. 433-0718*; and **Parmon**, *Narra-Hilado Street, Tel. 22-531*.

WHERE TO STAY

City Hotels – Expensive

L'FISHER HOTEL, *Lacson corner 14th Street. Tel. 82-731 to 39, Fax 433-0951. Manila reservations: Tel. 892-2119, Fax 892-3328. 96 rooms. $75-87 per single, $87-113 per double, $140-210 per suite. Visa, Master Card, American Express, Diners.*

All rooms are air conditioned and have cable television and a minibar. The suite rooms have a bathtub. Services and facilities include a swimming pool, safety deposit box, parlor and barber shop, massage, and a gift shop. Café Marinero is a 24-hour coffee shop, Don Ricardo is the "finer dining" place for lunch and dinner, and there is a cocktail lounge.

BACOLOD CONVENTION PLAZA HOTEL, *Magsaysay Avenue. Tel. 83-551 to 59, Fax 83-392. Manila reservations: Tel. 892-9184, 892-9152, Fax 893-3293. 112 rooms. $84 per single, $108 per double, $125-160 per suite. Visa, Master Card, American Express, Diners.*

The Spanish-style building gives this place the nicest exterior of the higher-priced hotels in the city. All the rooms are air conditioned, clean, and have cable television. The staff is friendly and helpful. Services and facilities include a small business center, swimming pool, tennis, and a clinic. Dine at Four Seasons for Chinese cuisine, Tapas Lobby Café for continental and local fare, Coco Cabana Poolside Grill for seafood and other dishes, or have a snack and drinks at the Pantalan Cocktail Lounge.

Moderate

GOLDENFIELD GARDEN HOTEL, *Goldenfield Complex. Tel. 433-3111, Fax 433-1234. 94 rooms. $46 per single or double, $93-105 per suite. Visa, Master Card, American Express, Diners.*

This pyramidal hotel is conveniently located in the city's main entertainment complex (restaurants, casino, bars, bowling, etc.). All rooms are air conditioned, clean, and have cable television. The staff is friendly. There is a swimming pool and a billiard room. Restaurants include the Lobby Café and, for good Japanese food, Nagoya.

SUGARLAND HOTEL, *Araneta Street, Singcang. Tel. 22-462 to 63, Fax 28-367. 120 rooms. $40 per single or double, $55-62 per suite. Visa, Master Card, Diners.*

All rooms are air conditioned, clean, and have cable television. The service is friendly and the hotel offers shuttle service to the airport and dry cleaning. There is a coffee shop and the Volare disco.

BACOLOD PAVILION, *Reclamation Area. Tel. 82-626 to 28. 21 rooms. $35 per single, $45 per double (called "suite"), $6 per extra person. Visa, Master Card, Diners.*

Overall, a nice place; the rooms are clean, air conditioned, and have cable television. There is also a swimming pool and service is friendly. The restaurant serves seafood and local dishes.

Budget

SEA BREEZE HOTEL, *San Juan corner Gonzaga Street. Tel. 245-7175, Fax 81-231. Manila reservations: Tel. 521-0773, Fax 521-9166. 45 rooms. $27-*

35 per single, $31-35 per double, $46-55 per suite, $6 per extra person. Visa, Master Card, Diners.

This was the first hotel in Bacolod. It was built during the booming sugar trade years in 1940 as a pension and was rebuilt into a hotel in 1963. It is a charming place with a warm ambiance and friendly staff. All rooms are air conditioned, clean, and have television. It has one of the best restaurants in the city. The disco is open weekends only.

BASCON HOTEL, *Gonzaga Street corner Locsin Street. Tel. 23-141, Fax 433-1393. 34 rooms. $23-32 per single, $27-36 per double, $4 per extra person. Visa, Master Card, American Express, Diners.*

All rooms are air conditioned; the lower priced rooms are not carpeted. The staff is friendly and helpful. The coffee shop serves local and continental dishes.

BACOLOD PENSION PLAZA, *Cuadra corner Gatuslao Street. Tel. 27-076 to 79, Fax 433-2213. 60 rooms. $29-37 per single or double, $4 per extra bed. Visa, Master Card, American Express, Diners.*

All rooms are air conditioned and have television. The restaurant serves Filipino and Chinese cuisine. The staff is helpful and the pension is conveniently located in front of the city plaza.

KINGS LODGE, *Gatuslao corner San Sebastian Street. Tel. 28-686, Fax 433-0576. 45 rooms. $18 per single, $21 per double, $41 per suite, $4 per extra person. Visa and Master Card.*

Simple, clean, air conditioned rooms and friendly staff.

PALM INN, *Locsin corner San Sebastian Street. Tel. 433-0543 to 45, Fax 433-3438. 17 rooms. $26 per single or double, $4 per extra person. Visa and Diners.*

Rooms are simple, clean, and air conditioned. The staff is friendly and there is a small gym, and a coffee shop that serves Filipino and American fare.

G & J HORIZON PENSION, *Hernaez corner Locsin Street. Tel. 433-3101 to 03. 12 rooms. $24-36 per single, $31-36 per double, $51 per suite. Visa.*

Rooms are nice and clean, all are air conditioned and have television. The staff is friendly and helpful, the coffee shop serves local cuisine.

CASA DE AMIGO, *Libertad Street. Tel. 26-029. 3 aircon rooms and 5 non-aircon rooms. $14 per single or $17 per double aircon, $6 per single or $8 per double non-aircon.*

This charming place is in a pre-war house that has been renovated. The rooms are clean and staff are friendly. There is a restaurant.

PENSION PHOENIX, *Rosario corner Mabini Street. Tel. 28-930, 20-483, 433-0298. 10 aircon rooms, 34 nonaircon rooms. $11 per single or 16 per double aircon, $6.50 per single or $9 per double non-aircon, $4 per person in dorm room.*

Simple short order meals are available.

FAMILY PENSION, *123 Lacson Street. Tel. 81-211. 8 aircon, 6 non-aircon rooms. $11 per single or double aircon, $7.50 per single or double non-aircon, $4 per extra person.*
All rooms have a private bathroom.

Beach Resorts

Note: for details on **Costa Aguada Resort**, *Guimaras Island*, see the previous chapter on Panay. There are a few simple beach resorts in Negros Occidental:
JARA BEACH RESORT, *Bago City. Tel. 22-054, 22-056. $20 per single or double. Diners.*
Jara is on a dark beach and has a pool. The restaurant serves seafood and local dishes.
LAKAWON ISLAND RESORT, *Cadiz City, Tel. c/o Casa de Amigo II, Tel. 433-0808, 433-0810. 6 rooms. $25 per single or double.*
Cottages are simple and clean, packages are available that include transportation (land and sea) and all meals. There is a *banca* available for rent.

WHERE TO EAT

Bacolod has many restaurants, with most offering Negrense cuisine, and is known for its very tasty *"Manok inasal,"* also called "Bacolod chicken." This is barbequed chicken with a unique marinade — try it.
SEAFOOD MARKET, *Goldenfield Complex, Araneta Street, Singcang.*
Serves tasty fresh seafood. Also in the Goldenfield Complex try **OLD WEST STEAK HOUSE** for great local beef and **CARLO** for good Italian fare.
The restaurant of **SUGARLAND HOTEL**, *Araneta Street, Singcang*, has great gambas. And nearby **TING-TING'S** is a cozy, native-style beer garden, a good place for budget travelers looking for tasty seafood and other native dishes.
ANG SINUGBA, *Mabini corner San Sebastian Street. Visa, Master Card, American Express, Diners.*
Come here for good seafood and Filipino dishes.
KRISTINE'S, *20 Lacson Street; Visa, Master Card, American Express.*
Serves very tasty local steak.
MANOKAN COUNTRY, *Reclamation Area.*
Sample their *manok inasal* in a row of stalls where you can have an early evening dinner of barbequed chicken and a beer in a relaxed friendly atmosphere.
The Japanese restaurant at the **SEA BREEZE HOTEL**, *San Juan corner Gonzaga Street*, has good misono.

ABBOY'S KAMALIG, *Burgos Street beside the YMCA.*
Delectable local dishes and a comfortable ambiance. The blue marlin steak and pork chops are highly recommended.

For Chinese cuisine, **APOLLO**, **HOLIDAY** and **UNITED HOUSE**, *all on Hilado Street*, have good food.

BOB'S BIG BOY DRIVE INN, *BS Aquino (North) Drive*, has good quick Filipino meals and snacks. And for other fast food places try **SNACK PLAZA** (*Gatuslao Street, one each at the corner of Cuadra Street, the corner of Ballesteros Street, and on Lacson Street*); for burgers, **CHINKY'S** (*Araneta corner Rosario Street*), **JOLLIBEE** (*Gatuslao corner Cuadra Street*), and **MCDONALD'S** (*Lacson corner 6th Street*); for pizza, **SHAKEY'S**; and foodcourts in **Gaisano's** and **Iris**.

Out of town, the **VICMICO COUNTRY CLUB**, *Victorias,* sometimes has lobster from March to May.

SEEING THE SIGHTS

The many outlets, rich with products tied to Bacolod and Negros, will please both shoppers and non-shoppers. If you are interested in arts and antiques, visit the DOT (see *Practical Information* below) for a list of collections that are open for public viewing. For a list of places to shop, see *Shopping* section below

San Sebastian Cathedral was built in 1876 using 45,179 pieces of coral and stone — the 8,287 stones for raising the walls were held together with lime that came from quarries on Guimaras. Two interesting old bells, from a smaller church predating the cathedral, still hang by the church. On some Sundays in the spacious plaza fronting the church, there are cultural performances, lectures, and other activities.

North from the cathedral on Gatuslao Street are the **Fort San Juan ruins**. Here, 33 friars were incarcerated after the 1898 revolution against Spain and were later expelled from Negros.

The imposing **Ramos ancestral house**, two blocks east down Burgos street from the cathedral, was occupied briefly by General Tagaiishi Kone of the Japanese Imperial army. The **Luzuriaga family mausoleum**, six to eight blocks further, stands in the centerstrip where North Drive splits to accommodate the structure.

Along Narra Avenue is an interesting **Chinese temple**.

Yulo Park is an impressive ancestral home built during the early 1900s by the sea. This was the "social hub" of the city before World War Two. It is located by the reclamation area, at the end of Hernaez Street.

The **Santa Clara Chapel**, in the Santa Clara Subdivision, is a remarkable work of art made with native craftsmanship and materials. The wood and capiz shell chapel has intricate shell mosaics of saints. The mural behind the altar is composed of 95,000 pieces of shell and took 60 men

100 work-days to complete. The project was supervised by Mrs. Leticia Ledesma, the owner and designer of **Artwares**, a shop where you can see beautifully sculpted religious works.

NIGHTLIFE & ENTERTAINMENT

Bacolod has several bars, discos, and singalong bars. At the **Goldenfield Complex** there is a **Casino** (open daily from noon to 5:00am; men may wear sports shirts, but with collars; shorts and thongs are not allowed), **Quorum Disco**, and the **Hot Spot Bar**. Nearby is **Ting-Ting's**, a popular beer garden.

SHOPPING

Bacolod City's **central market** has many stalls selling local **handicrafts** — baskets, shell and wood products, jewelry, etc., and should be your first shopping stop. **Bacolod Shellcraft**, in the Airport Area, sells a range of souvenirs made of wood and shell. **VS Heirlooms Pacifica**, 22 Lizares Avenue, *Tel. 24-963*, has handcrafted crochet items including Christmas decor and dolls. **NDS Ceramics**, on Gatuslao Street, has some nice ceramics. **Anaware Ceramics**, Gardenville Subdivision, has a number of ceramic items, among them jars, vases, frames, figurines.

At the **Negros Showroom**, at Lacson Street in front of the Philippine National Bank, you will find just about all types of Negros' handicrafts and other products. Also on Lacson Street are **Dorca's** and **Reeds and Weeds**, which sell very nice baskets and other crafts; and for antiques try **PSST Antiques** or **Casa Grande Antiques**, for a good collection of *santos*, furniture, pottery, etc.

East of downtown, **Samodal**, 2nd Road, Block 6-Lot 8, Czarina Heights, *Tel. 22-876*, has remarkable shaved wood products and other items. And just north of the center, **Nature's Gift**, Santa Clara Subdivision, *Tel. 81-134*, in the home of Sonia Sarroza, has products from the House of Negros — a project that helps the poor earn income through handicraft production. If you wish to visit the factory, Sonia can make arrangements. Also in Santa Clara, **Woven Fancies**, *Tel. 27-683*, has bags of woven abaca with leather.

You can also get **inexpensive pottery** from stands along the roadside, south in Pohonocoy and north, just before Silay City. In Silay City: **Silay Paper Craft**, Dr. J. Locsin Street, *Tel. 51-989*, sells handmade paper products; and **Unlimited Possiblitites**, Dr. J. Locsin Street, *Tel. 51-989*, has various items including boxes, frames, desk accessories, and Christmas decor.

Department stores in Bacolod City include China Rose, Gaisano, Lopue's, Robinson's, and Servandos where you may get standard articles.

SPORTS & RECREATION
Bird Watching
See section on Mount Canlaon below.

Bowling
There are bowling alleys at **Super Bowling Lanes**, *Goldenfield Complex, Tel. 28-652; $5 for 14 games*; **Top's Bowling**, *10th Street, Tel. 23-013; $3.75 for 14 games*; and out of town at **Sta Fe Resort** and **VICMICO**.

Golf
Visiting golfers are welcome at **Negros Golf & Country Club**, Barangay Bata, *Tel. 28-257*, greens fees are $22.50 per person, a caddy is $6, and club rentals are $14 per set; **Bacolod Golf & Country Club** on the road to Murcia, greens fees are $22.50 on the weekday, 26.50/weekend, a caddy is $6; and **Vicmico Golf & Country Club** in Victorias Milling's land, greens fees are $10 and a caddy is $5. All courses have 18 holes.

Mountain Biking
A great way to tour the countryside while exercising, biking can be challenging, especially around the mountainous areas of Negros. Contact Mr. Mayo Monteza of the **Negros Outdoor Club**, *Tel. 21-839*.

Mountain Climbing
See section on Mount Canlaon below.

Scuba Diving
The waters of the South China Sea, especially around **Danjugan Island**, have dive spots. Contact the **Negros Divers Club**, c/o Edwin Gatia of the DOT in Bacolod.

Sky Diving
If you are looking for an adrenaline rush, contact the **Cyclone Skydiving Club**, c/o Edwin Gatia.

Spelunking
Ubong Cave, in **Hinobaan**, is a system of passages that are easy to explore. Hinobaan, 200 kilometers south of Bacolod, is the last southern town of Negros Occidental. Travel time is six hours; buses leave from Bacolod every 45 minutes starting at 3:00am with the last trip at 12:15pm. You may also hike to the **Alabanan Falls** — get a guide in *barangay* San Rafael; the falls are a three-kilometer hike from there.

Around **Calatrava**, there are four caves: **Bagacay** in Sitio Bagacay, **Tigbon** in Sitio Magpayao, and **Daan Lungsod** in Sitio Castellano have been explored and are fairly easy. **Penocutan**, in Sitio Cabacungan, has not been explored, its entrance faces seaward, and it is said to have large snakes inside. Take a bus from Bacolod to Calatrava, a three hour ride. From here, you take a tricycle to the area of Bagacay or Penocutan then an additional easy hour-walk.

Kabankalan has two caves to explore. According to legend, the native chieftain, Datu Sumakling, lived at **Pating Cave** until his wife died and was changed into a banana stalk. The roof of the cave is quite high. **Hagdanan Caves** are named after the natural formation of stone stairs that lead to the water below. Kabankalan is a 3.5-hour bus ride from Bacolod, and has two very simple lodging places.

Tennis

Bacolod has five tennis courts, at **Bacolod Convention Plaza Hotel**, *Tel. 83-551, $5 per hour*; **Negros Occidental Tennis Association**, *Gatuslao Street, Tel. 21-234, $2 per hour*; **Montevista Tennis Association**, *Montevista, Tel. 28-137, $1 per hour*) **Sta Fe Resort**, *Tel. 29-467, $3.50 per hour*; and **VICMICO Country Club**, *Victorias, $8 per hour*.

EXCURSIONS & DAY TRIPS
Inland Activities

A few kilometers from the city at **Santa Fe Resort** there is a small zoo with birds, a hawk, three monkeys, and a crocodile, all in apparent good health.

Mambucal Resort, 660 meters above sea level, is a nice outdoors place. There are sulfurous hot springs and cool mountain springs; you can bathe in either. This place is also a convenient base for hikes on Mount Canlaon. You can stay and eat at the resort; book in advance for rooms and meals. There are some nice rooms with bath in the main building and camping is permitted. Other facilities are run down and the grounds need cleaning up (this is not a problem for those whose interests focus on the mountain and not the resort). Mambucal is 30 kilometers east of Bacolod City.

Mount Canlaon

This 2,465-meter-high volcano offers lush valleys and meadows, and mountain streams that cascade down a succession of seven falls. Over 90 species of birds may be seen at **Mount Canlaon National Park**.

To climb Mount Canlaon, contact the **Negros Mountaineering Club** for assistance and guides. Do not go off on your own as this is a live volcano and it killed several climbers in 1996. The club can be contacted through DOT's Edwin Gatia, an avid mountaineer, *Tel. 29-021, 433-1862*.

The whole climb should take four days. The trek, through rainforest and dwarf forest, and by some small lakes will take you to a beautiful view of Canlaon's main crater. From there, descend and spend the night on a nearby beach.

The North Coast

The **Lacson House** in Talisay, seven kilometers north of the city, is a fine example of mid-1800s architecture — its terrace is Chinese influenced on the inside and Spanish-style on the outside; there is a chapel inside, and the window panes have etched glass from Belgium. It was also the short-lived seat of the Cantonal Government of the Republic of Negros (1898-1899).

Pretty **Silay City**, eight kilometers further north, has several old mansions; two are now museums:

• **Balay Negrense** is owned by Victor Gaston, the son of Frenchman Yves Germaine Leopolde Gaston. The elder was a pioneer in Negros' sugar industry. The museum is a showcase of post-Spanish era lifestyle and local art and culture.

• The **Isabel-Jalandoni Museum**, an ancestral house built from select wood that came from Mindoro, has ceilings that are said to have been carefully measured and molded in Hamburg, Germany.

Also in Silay City is the **Hofileña Ancestral House**, home of artist Ramon Hofileña. He has an impressive collection of rare antiques, art, and paintings including works of national artists Juan, Rizal, and Hidalgo. Ramon also gives art tours, and can be contacted through the DOT.

VICMICO (Victorias Milling Corporation), 20 kilometers further north, offers tours of the sugar mill. You may see locomotives deliver raw cane to the factory. The estate has 365 kilometers of railroad track and steam engines that date back to 1924-1928 and have been converted from gas- to wood-burning to economize on fuel. Tours are offered Tuesday-Friday, from 9:00am to noon and 2:30pm until 4:30pm. VICMICO's **Church of Saint Joseph** is very striking and houses a mural of a colorful Christ and saints donning native Philippine garb. The company, partly owned by the employees, has a restaurant and an 18-hole golf course.

The unique **Chapel of Cartwheels** is just north in Hacienda Rosalia, Manapla. The chapel, constructed with local farm implements, has a Filipino Christ crucified on a cartwheel.

Lakawon Island has pretty white sand beaches. It is off the coast of Cadiz Viejo, 20 kilometers further north, about two hours by bus from Bacolod. There is a resort with a simple cottage and camp grounds. Arrangements can be made in Bacolod through Casa de Amigo Pension, *Tel. 26-029.*

The municipality of Escalante, about 100 kilometers north of Bacolod City, has a number of interesting points: **Isla Puti**, a two-hectare white sand bar 15 minutes by *banca* from town; **ruins of the church** of St. Francis de Assisi; and **Bantayan Island** (refer to the chapter on Cebu) for nice beaches and diving.

Points South

Around Bago City, 16 kilometers south of Bacolod, are **Buenos Aires**, a premier resort during the late 1920s where President Quezon hid from the Japanese prior to joining General MacArthur en route to Australia; the nearly 100 foot **Kipot Twin Falls**; and Jara Beach Resort — good seafood, simple rooms, and an artificial beachfront area.

Just before the city is the **Bago Bridge** which played a vital role in the American liberation of Negros. Early on the 23rd of March, 1945, American forces foiled the plan of the Japanese troops to destroy the bridge in hopes of making access to Bacolod more difficult for the Americans. The bridge was saved, but Private First Class Theodore Vinther was killed heroically in action. The **Vinther Monument**, a shrine for him and thousands of others who sacrificed to free the Philippines, stands on the southern side of Bacolod's City Plaza.

The impressive **Montilla House** is 31 kilometers south of Bacolod City, in *barangay* Ubay, Pulupandan. This is a beautifully preserved century-old ancestral house, restored and furnished with century-old pieces including furniture from Vienna, Soong and Ming porcelain, Chinese chests, over a hundred *santos*, and photographs and portraits of the Montilla family. You must make arrangements to visit through the Casa Grande Antique Shop, on Lacson Street in Bacolod. If possible, try to go when Mr. Herbert Montilla Tomkins is there so he can show you around.

The **Central Azucarera de la Carlota** has a long network of tracks including fantastic bridges. Steam locomotives that date back to the 1920s, use the network to haul cane to the mills. Check with the DOT for visits. If you are interested in locomotives, the DOT has an eight-hour train tour.

Danjugan Island

This 42-hectare island is a newly started wildlife sanctuary 175 kilometers south of Bacolod. Danjugan is fringed with reefs, coral and white sand beaches, and mangrove forests. Residents of the island include several **endangered species**, among them the white breasted sea eagle, gray-headed fishing eagles, hawksbill turtle, green-winged ground dove, and black-naped oriole. The sanctuary was made possible through a grant from the World Wide Land Conservation Trust.

Danjugan Island is private; you must make arrangements to visit ahead of time through the **Philippine Reef & Rainforest Conservation Foundation Inc.**, *Bacolod, Tel. 81-935, Fax 25-007*. If you are interested in helping the program, "green shares" are available for $40.

PRACTICAL INFORMATION

Banks

A number of banks along Araneta and Lacson streets change dollars. **PNB** (Lacson Street corner North Capitol Road) changes most currencies as well as travelers checks. Banking hours are weekdays from 9:00am-3:00pm.

Tour & Tourist Information

The DOT office is wonderful; its staff is very informative and helpful. The DOT has a number of good set tours: a five-day steam locomotive experience; four-day Canlaon climb, eight-hour sugar mill and city tour, eight-hour Mambucal tour, three-day island hopping tour, and the World War Two memorial tour through the Patag Valley (which also has the Negros spotted deer and cool waterfalls). Itineraries can be arranged to suit your tastes and schedule. Art tours are run by Ramon Hofileña and usually include the extensive and very impressive art collection at his home in Silay City, the pop-art chapel at Victorias, and other points of interest — contact him in advance through the DOT.

Stop by the office where you may also pick up more information and maps. The DOT is closed on weekends; contact them in advance for weekend activities. Write or call Edwin V Gatia, **DOT**, *City Public Plaza Building, Bacolod City, Tel. 29-021.*

DUMAGUETE, NEGROS ORIENTAL

Dumaguete, the charming provincial capital of **Negros Oriental**, is one of the few cities where you can experience genuine hospitality and a slow, relaxed pace — a Philippine lifestyle generally unaffected by tourism. At Dumaguete's heart is **Silliman University** and its marine laboratory, which attracts professors and students from around the world. The academic influence permeates Dumaguete: neighborhoods have small sanctuaries initiated by residents and people are often well-educated.

Relax into the provincial Visayan pace and you will enjoy your stay as you swim, snorkel, or dive off one of the lovely beaches nearby; or go on a dolphin watching cruise. Landward, tour the quaint towns, hunt for handicrafts, play golf or tennis, or hike into the hills and birdwatch.

ARRIVALS & DEPARTURES

By Air

There is a daily 70-minute Philippine Airline flight from Manila. Philippine Airline also has a flight from Cebu on Tuesday, Thursday, and Saturday; it takes 40 minutes.

The airport is north of the city proper; larger resorts will pick you up. Ask around before hiring a tricycle and settle the price beforehand; it should be about 25¢ or P5 per person to the city center, although it may sometimes cost $40¢-60¢.

By Sea

The voyage from Manila takes 23-28 hours. Sulpicio Lines ($10-50) goes once a week and WGA SuperFerry has two trips a week ($20-96).

From Cebu, the trip takes six to eight hours. Cokaliong ($5-20) departs from Cebu every day except Wednesday and Friday; George & Peter ($5-20) has daily trips; and Sulpicio Lines ($5-20) departs Cebu every Monday at midnight.

By Land

The trip to **Bacolod** takes six to eight hours and is serviced by Ceres Liner, which has several morning trips.

From **Cebu**, several buses ply the Santander City route ($1.50 per person). A ferry crosses to Amlan ($2 per person), north of Dumaguete, and from there a jeepney will take you to Dumaguete or Bais. The ferries do not cross when the tides are strong. Another route is by bus from Cebu City to Toledo ($2.50 per person), where a high-speed ferry crosses hourly to San Carlos ($2 per person), and from there a bus takes you to Dumaguete.

GETTING AROUND

The city is small and everything is within walking distance. People are friendly and the streets are relatively clean. Walking around is an enjoyable way to get the feel of Dumaguete. Tricycles are the most common means of transport within and to points near the city.

If you want to hire a private vehicle, inquire at your lodging or ask around for Doming Rubio.

WHERE TO STAY

Beach Resorts

SOUTH SEA RESORT HOTEL, *Bantayan, 2 km north from downtown. Tel. 225-0481. $38-91 per single or $44-102 per double aircon, $29-38 per single or $34-40 per double non-aircon.*

This is a lovely resort, and the open air pavilion restaurant is a nice place to sit, relax, and watch the local fishermen in the sea. Some cottages have a screened porch. All rooms are clean, and the higher priced aircon rooms have television and a refrigerator. There is also a swimming pool.

PANORAMA, *Sibulan, 6 km north from the city. Tel. 225-0704. $26 per room.*

You get a nice view across the Tañon Strait from this resort. It is a homey place run by a Swiss fellow; rooms are fan-cooled and clean. There is a restaurant.

DIVE SIBULAN, *Sibulan. Tel. 225-1421. $25 per room.*

Also with a nice view, rooms are clean, simple, and pleasant. The resort caters to divers and has a very good dive center.

STA MONICA RESORT, *Banilad, 4 km south of the city. $33-41 per aircon room, $28-33 per non-aircon room.*

Facilities include diving and various watersports. This establishment does not mind making arrangements for spearfishing with scuba diving, which should not be allowed.

EL ORIENTE, *Mangnao, 3 km south of the city. $26 per aircon room, $13 per non-aircon room.*

Rooms are simple.

City Hotels

HABITAT, *Hibbard Avenue. $32-41 per single or $36-51 per double aircon, $18-25 per non-aircon room.*

This is a pleasant hotel with clean rooms. Some of the air conditioned rooms have a small balcony.

OK PENSION HOUSE, *Sta Rosa Street. $30 per room.*

Rooms are simple, nice, clean, and air conditioned. The staff is friendly and there is a restaurant.

INSULAR FLINTLOCK, *55 Silliman Avenue. $27 per aircon room, $20 per nonaircon room.*

This is a simple place with clean rooms and friendly staff. The interior is much better than the outside. There is a restaurant.

HOTEL EL ORIENTE, *Real Street. $21-31 per single or $24-39 per double aircon, $12 per nonaircon room.*

The air conditioned rooms are larger, pleasant, and clean. The higher priced rooms have a television and a fridge. There is a restaurant.

CASA LONA, *Real Street. $28 per aircon room, $8 per non-aircon room.*
Rooms are very simple but spacious and clean.

AL MAR HOTEL, *Rizal Boulevard corner San Juan Street. Tel. 225-2576. $13-21 per aircon room, $8-13 per non-aircon room.*

Room sizes vary: some are quite small, others are large. There is a good restaurant.

OPENA'S, *18 Katuda Street. $20 per aircon room, $13 per non-aircon room.*

Rooms in the back are less noisy. The restaurant is good.

PLAZA INN 1, *50 Dr. V Locsin Street;* **PLAZA INN ROYAL SALUTE**, *Alfonso XII Street. $23 per aircon room, $17 per non-aircon.*

Both establishments have pleasant clean rooms. Plaza Inn 1 has a restaurant.

WHERE TO EAT

South Sea, **Yuishin**, and **Sta Monica** resorts and most of the lodges serve meals. You can have an inexpensive evening feast of **barbeque** by the docks, and along Quezon Boulevard you'll find a number of places for a snack or a drink. Silliman University's **cafeteria** has inexpensive dishes. And for fresh baked local breads stop by **Rosalie's & Jo's Bakeries**, on Alfonso Street near San Juan Street

OPENA'S, *along Katuda Street.*

Serves reasonably priced good food.

SINUGBA, *corner of San Juan Street and the Boulevard.*

Features grilled seafood.

KAMAY KAINAN, *San Juan Street by Sta Catalina Street.*

Serves seafood and folk music.

Try **CHIN LUN**, *along Rizal Boulevard between San Jose Street and Dr. V Locsin Street.*

Good Chinese cuisine.

KAMAGONG, *Maria Cristina Street near Dr. V Locsin Street.*

This restaurant serves local specialties.

SEEING THE SIGHTS

Dumaguete is a wonderful place to walk around. People are friendly and the streets are relatively clean. Stroll along Lo-oc Road and Rizal Boulevard, near the pier, where you can also sit, enjoy the company of the locals, and collect information. There are also stalls selling drinks and snacks.

Silliman University, just west of the pier, has a small and interesting **anthropology museum** displaying prehistoric finds including burial remains, Chinese pottery and porcelain, Philippine tribal relics and artifacts, and implements used by the sorcerers of Siquijor. Some of the students help to pay their tuition by selling artifacts at the museum shop. Also on campus, the **Luce Auditorium** sometimes has evening entertainment; current engagements are usually posted at the entrance to the University or inquire at the student affairs office.

Between the city and the airport is the **Silliman University Marine Laboratory and Farm**, *Tel. 225-4808.* The lab is engaged in several projects geared at promoting marine conservation. Its ongoing conservation program combines marine biology and sociology to encourage reef conservation and community awareness and development on Apo Island and on Bohol's Pamilacan and Balicasag islands. Before visiting any of the island reserves, it is best to get permission. The marine lab has a crocodile propagation program in conjunction with the **World Wildlife Fund**, and one for giant clams. Seaward from the marine lab, you may swim at **Silliman Beach** (dark sand).

Downtown, on the east side of Rizal Park, vendors sell orchids and other flowers and plants. On the west side of the park is the **Saint Catherine Cathedral**. Continue through to Katada Street, the other side of the church, to the **public market**. The wet market offers fresh seafood, most of which is delivered in the early morning. The dry market displays handicrafts and various items (see *Shopping* section below for more details).

On the other side of the Bianca River near the sea is a **Chinese Bell Tower**, and further south is the port for boats to Siquijor Island. Inland are the Ceres Liner terminal and the city cockpit.

SHOPPING

The **public market** is pleasantly clean. Its wet market has freshly caught tuna, beautiful jack fish, crabs, lobsters, and sometimes curacha — a delicious sort of crab-lobster-like shellfish. You can also enjoy fruits in season such as mangoes, papaya, jackfruit, and kalamansi; vegetables, corn, and seaweed — *latu* and *gulaman* (both are delicious). Snack on tasty *budbud* or *suman* (sweetened sticky rice that is wrapped and cooked in banana leaves). In the dry market area, you will find a variety of handicrafts and other items: beautiful *banig* (hand woven mats that are great for sunbathing and picnicking), baskets, hammocks, hats, clothing and tools.

Vintola's, at 92 Real Street north of the Market, carries samples of products made in their factory in Motong: impressive boxes, jewelry, and furniture made from shell, stone, *carabao* horn, brass, and coral. As we've mentioned in other chapters, purchasing coral products will encourage further reef destruction.

SPORTS & RECREATION
Dolphin Watching

You can rent a boat or *banca* and go **dolphin watching** in Bais City — the dolphins are accustomed to the sound of the boats used by the Mayor's office, so contact the office in advance (ask for Rowena of Tourism, *Tel. 541-5161*). Boat rentals cost $100-250; the largest boat has conference facilities. April to September are the best months for dolphin watching.

Golf

Golf is available at the **San Antonio golf course**, north of Sibulan on the San Antonio Road. The **Pamplona Plantation Golf & Country Club**, 30 minutes from Dumaguete City at the foot of Cuernos de Negros (Mt. Talinis), has an 18-hole course.

Scuba Diving

Reliable dive operators in Dumaguete include **International Diving Center**, Canmating Road, Sibulan, *Tel. 225-1421*. It is run by Bernard Jackenroll and is highly recommended. Jackenroll is among the few operators who does not run spearfishing tours. **Scuba Ventures Philippines**, behind South Sea Resort, Dumaguete, *Tel. 225-2381*, also respects sanctuaries, as does the **Silliman University Marine Lab**, Silliman Beach, Bantayan, *Tel. 225-4808*.

Costs vary: $85 for two dives with a dive master, $400 for a three-day dive trip to $900 for seven days, and an open water course runs around $350-400.

Around Dumaguete are some nice dives. Among the reef inhabitants are small fish, nudibranchs, starfish, and (occasionally) sea horses.

Nearby **Apo Island** is the best dive spot here — you can see a variety of fish and beautiful coral. Apo is a **marine sanctuary** managed by Silliman University, and is one of the few successful ones in the country. Currents can sometimes be strong.

North of the city, at **Calongcalong Point** you may see some rays, soft corals, and sponges. Off **Sibulan** is an underwater mountain with coral. And far north, between Tampi and Amlan, are **Polo 1 & 2**, sunken islands where you may see table corals, soldierfish, and an assortment of reef dwellers.

Siquijor Island has a few dive spots; unfortunately the area is not protected and has suffered from abuse. The most interesting area is off the west side at **Tongo Point** and **Talingting**. Soft corals, fluorescent anemones and clownfish, and small reef fish are among the dwellers.

Tennis

You can play tennis at **Proxivilla tennis courts** by the Provincial Capitol Building, two courts in **Rizal Park**, or on the two courts of **Silliman campus**.

EXCURSIONS & DAY TRIPS

Inland from Dumaguete

Valencia is seven kilometers west of Dumaguete in the foothills of Cuernos de Negros (Mt. Talinis). Its houses are mantled in beautiful plants, some of which are for sale. Stop by the **market** for a snack of *budbud* or banana-Q (banana coated in sugar then barbequed), and thick hot chocolate. Continue four kilometers further to **Camp Lookout** for a great view of Dumaguete, Siquijor, and Cebu. Above Valencia is the **Philippine Japanese Amity Shrine**.

North of Dumaguete

You can visit the **Twin Lakes** after a pleasant 15-kilometer hike through forests. The trail to the crater lakes, Danao and Balinsasayao, is just south of San Jose, 14 kilometers north of Dumaguete. Take a bus to San Jose, where a jeepney or tricycle can drop you by the trailhead. There is also a route to the lakes from the San Antonio golf course. Inquire about the peace and order situation from the provincial tourism office before proceeding, and take a guide.

Tampi, north of San Jose, has several places that make *buri* furniture and has a terminal for ferries headed to and from Cebu. **Amlan** also has several establishments that make *buri* furniture.

Bais City, 45 kilometers north of Dumaguete, is where you go for **dolphin watching** tours (see *Sports & Recreation* above). Nearby is a seven-kilometer white sand beach with snorkeling and diving at a coral reef offshore. Bais Bay has a bird sanctuary and a mangrove forest on a small island. Ask at the tourism department in the mayor's office in Bais for permission and arrangements to go to the island.

If you want to stay overnight, try **DEWEY ISLAND HILLTOP HOTEL**, *cellular Tel. (092) 515-1899, $30 per single or double*, on a peninsula connected to the city. Rooms are air conditioned. In town there are five places with very simple rooms.

South from Dumaguete

As you head north, notice the signs along the road just beyond Dumaguete: "Welcome to Nicaragua," and "New York, home of the hoot boys."

Dauin, 16 kilometers from Dumaguete, has a nice beach and a market on Saturday. 11 kilometers further is **Malapatay**, known for its seaside market on Wednesdays: people come from all over to buy, sell, and gossip. Select your fish, have it cooked, and eat it with *pusa* (rice attractively wrapped in banana leaf for added flavor). You may also try *tuba*, a slightly fermented coconut liquor. There are picnic tables by the pretty beach where you can hire *bancas* to visit nearby Apo Island.

The quaint fishing town of **Zamboanguita** is another five kilometers south. There is a small zoo and park run by the Lamplighters, a religious sect. The park has native animals, a stuffed white monkey (reputed to be seen only on Siquijor), and the favorite sayings of Father Tropa, the founder of the sect. **Salawaki Beach Resort** has a nice beach with overnight facilities. Just south is **Siyt**, a good beach for swimming and snorkeling.

The **Siaton Bird Sanctuary**, 50 kilometers from Dumaguete, was created by Silliman University and is lovely.

Apo Island

This marine sanctuary is a lovely day trip with good swimming, snorkeling, and diving. The friendly residents ask for a small donation to help with the maintenance of the marine sanctuary and reserve. You can rent picnic tables, and residents sell fresh fish, which they will roast for you on the beach. Bring your own water and drinks. You can also watch some women weaving beautiful mats out of pandan leaves.

To get to Apo Island, hire a *banca* from Malapatay ($20-40). Kan-Upi resort will arrange for pickup and transfer from the airport for around $45 for 1-4 people.

For lodgings, try the **KAN-UPI COVE BEACH RESORT**, *Manila reservations: Tel. 831-7836; 6 cottages; $25 per cottage*, a friendly place with simple and clean cottages with private bath. Meals usually consist of the catch of the day and chicken.

Sumilon

This island, at the tip of Cebu, was once a good marine preserve developed by Silliman University. Sadly, a political struggle between two provinces ensued and some greedy fishermen and unscrupulous dive operators have benefited. The beaches are still lovely; however the snorkeling and diving are not what they used to be.

Siquijor

Once called *Isla del Fuego* (Fire Island) by the Spaniards, mysterious **Siquijor** is known for its mysticism and *mangkukulam* — healers or sorcerers who cure illnesses and cast spells. Each *mangkukulam* has his or her own technique; many sell *anting-anting* — amulets intended to give you special powers or protect you from harm. The towns of San Juan and San Antonio are reputed to be the best places to find *mangkukulam*. You may have an evil spell cast upon someone for a small fee (a man in Zamboanguita can reverse a curse cast upon you, for a small fee). Many people take pride in having supernatural powers, and during Holy Week perform rituals that combine Christianity and practices they believe enhance their mystical powers.

The pretty coastal town of **San Juan** has a freshwater pool and spring that run into the sea, and an old Spanish watchtower that is an easy climb up a hill from town.

Siquijor is the largest town, and the only one with a hospital. VCR tapes provide the town's primary entertainment, a small fee is charged if you want to watch. Go to the market for a great cup of thick and rich hot chocolate and for rice cake.

To get here, a public ferry runs twice a day from Dumaguete ($2.50); private hire can be expensive ($50-100). The crossing is dangerous in bad weather. The Coco Grove resort will pick you up from the airport in Dumaguete.

The best way to tour Siquijor is by tricycle hire from San Juan, Siquijor, or Larena. The trip around the island takes a full day. It is also best to have your lodging arrange for a tricycle.

For lodgings, you can stay at **COCO GROVE**, *Manila reservations: Tel. 831-7836; 15 cottages; $25 for non-aircon cottage, $32 for aircon cottage*. The hotel has nice, simple cottages (same friendly atmosphere as their sister resort on Apo) with private bath. In addition, the hospital in Siquijor town rents beds in the staff quarters for $4 per night.

PRACTICAL INFORMATION

You can get maps and more information on the city and province from the **provincial tourism office** in the Provincial Capitol Building, a lovely structure with beautiful grounds, and the **city tourism office** at City Hall.

22. CEBU

The island of **Cebu** is roughly 200 kilometers long and its maximum width is 40 kilometers. Most of the terrain is hilly and there are several good beaches on its shores and peripheral islands. The climate is too arid to produce much rice; the main crops here are corn, coconuts, grapes, mangoes, sugar, and tobacco. The island's main industries include mining copper, coal, and cement, and building ships. Around the coast, the main industry of many villages is fishing. Cebu is known for its fine handicrafts, most notably rattan and *buri* furniture, porcelain, guitars, and costume jewelry.

History

Prior to Spanish colonization, Cebu was a major trading port. The first Chinese traders and settlers arrived around 900 AD. Chinese junks came with silk and porcelain and left with honey, gold, and wood, and with spices that came mainly from the Moluccas. Trade flourished until the coming of the Spaniards, who imposed trade restrictions that resulted in the decline of Cebu's importance as a port.

On April 8, 1521, **Ferdinand Magellan** arrived in Sugbo – the island's pre-Spanish name. As recorded by Pigafetta, Magellan's chronicler, natives lived in stilt houses made of bamboo, wood, and nipa, and men were extensively tattooed while women were adorned with gold jewelry, donned silk cloth, and had color on their lips.

Magellan befriended Rajah Humabon and baptized him, his queen, and many of their followers. However, Mactan Island was not as welcoming – Magellan and many of his men were slain by Rajah Lapu-Lapu and his clan. As a result, colonization of Cebu was deferred until Miguel Lopez de Legazpi and Fray Andres de Urdaneta arrived in February 1565. They found an image of the Sto Niño, which may have been left by Magellan. The image is currently enshrined in the Basilica Minore.

Until Manila was proclaimed the capital of Spain's new colony on June 24, 1571, Cebu served as the capital. The Galleon Trade between

Acapulco, Cebu, and Manila started in 1600, but, Cebu lost its rights to the galleon trade in 1604. Not until the 19th century, when many restrictions were lifted, did Cebu again become a thriving city.

CEBU CITY

Cebu City is the Philippines' second busiest metropolis and is the center of activities in the Visayas. Many people come to Cebu for its well-managed hotels, the beach resorts on Mactan, several historical sights, and the more recent developments of sprawling malls that rival Manila's.

ARRIVALS & DEPARTURES

By Air

The airport, on **Mactan Island**, is relatively new and one of the nicest and cleanest in the country. It is also the country's second busiest international terminal: Cathay Pacific Airlines from Hong Kong; Continental Airlines from Guam; Silk Airlines from Singapore; Malaysian Airlines from Singapore and Malaysia; and Philippine Airlines from Hong Kong, Taiwan, Australia, and Japan land here.

From Manila, Cebu Pacific has three 90 minute flights daily, Grand Air has three 70 minute flights, and Philippine Airlines has six 70 minute flights.

The domestic terminal serves as a hub to other points in the Visayas and Mindanao. Cebu Pacific has a daily flight to Davao. Philippine Airlines flies daily to Bacolod, Iloilo, Davao, and General Santos; five times a week to Butuan; four times a week to Kalibo, Tacloban, Dipolog, and Surigao; and three times a week to Dumaguete, Tagbilaran, and Cagayan de Oro.

Getting to the city from the airport is pretty much hassle-free. There are a number of chauffeur-driven car rental desks inside the terminal; rate sheets are posted at the desks: take a copy for reference. Pay at the desk ($6-8 to resorts along coastal Mactan and $10-12 to Cebu City). If you like the driver, do tip him. A bus can drop passengers downtown by the Park Place Hotel at Fuente Osmeña ($2 per person).

By Sea

The trip between Cebu and Manila takes 21-22 hours. Sulpicio Lines has four trips a week ($16-68), and WGA SuperFerry has a daily trip ($22-110).

Cebu's port is a major hub for interisland voyages. Some companies have high speed catamarans and other vessels that have reduced travel time considerably, making traveling to points further south cheaper without sacrificing much time or comfort.

• **Cebu-Bohol**: the quickest carriers are WaterJet, with daily trips departing Cebu 4:30am; travel time of 1.5 hours, and fare at $8-16 per person; and the SuperCat with trips departing Cebu at 5:00am and 11:00am daily, fare is $6 per person. Palacio Lines has trips three times a week that take four hours; and TransAsia has daily trips departing Cebu at 7:30pm. The trip takes three hours, fare is $4-11 per person. WGA SuperFerry has one weekly trip that takes three hours and costs $10-20.

• **Cebu Dumaguete**: SuperCat trips take two hours, cost $4, and daily Cebu departures are at 5:45am and 3:00pm; Cokaliong has five trips a week that take six hours; George & Peter have daily trips that depart Cebu at 10:00pm and take eight hours; Sulpicio has two weekly trips that take six hours; on all three, the fares are $5-20.

• **Cebu-Iloilo**: The trip takes roughly 12-13 hours; Sulpicio has one voyage a week, fare is $5-20. TransAsia has three weekly trips, the fare is $10-16.

• **Cebu-Leyte (Baybay)**: The one hour and 45-minute trip on WaterJet departs Cebu Monday, Wednesday, and Friday in the evenings; the fare is $8-16.

• **Cebu-Leyte (Maasin)**: SuperCat has daily two-hour trips that depart Cebu at 9:00am and 1:30pm, fare is $4. Cokaliong makes the crossing twice a week, in six to seven hours, fare is $5-20; Escaño once a week; Georgia once a week; and TransAsia twice a week, fare is $10-20.

• **Cebu-Leyte (Ormoc)**: SuperCat has six daily trips, travel time is two hours, and fare is $4. WaterJet departs Cebu Tuesday, Thursday, Saturday, and Sunday, the trips takes two hours and fare is $8-16. WGA SuperFerry has daily trips that take six hours, fare is $12-40.

• **Cebu-Leyte (Tacloban)**: K&T Line takes 12 hours, and has three weekly trips. WGA SuperFerry has three weekly trips, travel time is 10 hours. The fares are $12-40.

• **Cebu-Siquijor**: George & Peter have two weekly trips that take 10 hours. Palacio has trips five times a week, travel time is seven to nine hours.

• **Cebu-Cagayan de Oro**: The quickest carrier is WaterJet: travel time is four hours and 30 minutes, fare is $8-16, departure from Cebu is 10:45am daily. Sulpicio has three trips a week, travel time is 12 hours, and fare is $10-30. TransAsia has daily trips, departing Cebu at 7:00pm, travel time is 10 hours, and fare is $10-40. WGA SuperFerry has three trips a week, travel time is nine hours, and fare is $12-40.

• **Cebu-Camiguin**: Cokaliong has a trip every Wednesday at 6:00pm, travel time is 14 hours, and fare is $5-20. Georgia has a trip every Wednesday at 7:00pm, travel time is 13 hours.

• **Cebu-Dapitan**: Cokaliong three trips a week, travel time is 16 hours and fare is $5-20. George & Peter has a daily trip, travel time is 12 hours.

- **Cebu-Davao**: The trips takes 25 hours. Sulpicio has a trip once a week and fare is $10-40; WGA SuperFerry schedules trips seasonally.
- **Cebu-Surigao**: the WaterJet has trips on Tuesday, Thursday, Saturday, and Sunday, departure from Cebu is 8:45am, travel time is three hours and 30 minutes, and the fare is $8-16. Cokaliong has daily trips, travel time is 10 hours, and the fare is $5-20. TransAsia has three trips a week, travel time is 11 hours and the fare is $5-20.

By Land

It is possible to get to Dumaguete from Cebu City by a combination of bus and ferry. Several buses run between Cebu and Santander City ($1.50 per person). From Santander, a ferry crosses to Amlan ($2 per person), north of Dumaguete, and from there a jeepney will take you to Dumaguete or Bais. The ferries do not cross when the tides are strong. Another route is by bus from Cebu City to Toledo ($2.50 per person), where a high-speed ferry crosses hourly to San Carlos ($2 per person) and from there a bus takes you to Dumaguete.

GETTING AROUND

Cebu's points of interest are rather spread out. You may see them in comfort by hiring an air conditioned car or taxi (fix all rates in advance) or do a combination walking-jeepney tour (see *Seeing The Sights* below).

Car rental agencies/taxis include:
- **Dollar Rent-A-Car**, *36 Osmeña Boulevard, Tel. 254-7425, 254-8255, 254-8256*
- **Guani Rent-A-Car**, *San Jose Ext., Tel. 253-5463, 253-5465, 253-5367*
- **Hertz Rent-A-Car**, *Escario Street, Tel. 254-5004, 254-5006*
- **Metro Rent-A-Car**, *North Reclamation Area, Tel. 92-176, 96-245*

Additionally, Pio Lagulay has a private hire car (unmarked taxi) and is friendly. He usually waits around the port. His rates (hourly and daily) are cheaper than the rent-a-car companies. Try contacting him through his daughter, Mary Jane Lagulay in the evenings from 5:00-11:00, *Tel. 255-0366, 255-0365.* You may also reserve a taxi (one trip, by the hour, or by the day) through **Holiday Taxi**, *Tel. 25-4811 to 15*; Mang Jose, number 66, is very nice.

WHERE TO STAY

Cebu City Proper – Expensive

CEBU PLAZA HOTEL, *Nivel Hills, Lahug. Tel. 231-1231 to 59, Fax 231-2071. Manila reservations: Tel. 634-7505 to 08, Fax 634-7509. US reservations: 1-800-44-UTELL. 385 rooms. $110-150 per single, $140-198 per double, $224-437 per single or double "Presidents Club" floors, $377-1,192 per suite, $30 per extra person. Visa, Master Card, American Express, Diners.*

The Plaza is superbly managed and staffed — you are made to feel at home in the city's top hotel — and commands wonderful views, especially at night, of the city, so request a city-view room. The rooms on the regular floors are a mix of European and native styles. The furniture is wood and nicely varnished bamboo, and all rooms have the usual amenities you expect from a first-class hotel (carpeting, air conditioning, cable TV, minibar, etc.). If you are staying at the "Presidents Club," you can enjoy the 24-hour butler service, business center, complementary breakfast, and 6:00pm cocktails. The spacious rooms have been elegantly decorated. The furnishing is European and the solid dark wood door with faint light brown streaks is very striking.

Facilities include two swimming pools, two tennis courts, a shooting range, minigolf, sauna, salon, and business center. The hotel also offers car rental, travel and tour arrangements, and massage. You will not be disappointed with the food — the Lantaw offers delectable seafood and Asian dishes and Café Tartanilla's buffet has a wide variety of dishes. For evening entertainment, the popular Pards Restaurant and Bar has tasty food, and the Bai Disco and Raquets Karaoke Bar are equally popular.

CEBU MIDTOWN HOTEL, *Osmeña Boulevard. Tel. 253-9711 to 40, Fax 253-9765. 200 rooms. $114-126 per single, $126-139 per double, $211-423 per suite, $29 per extra person. Visa, Master Card, American Express, Diners.*

The hotel is located above the three floors of Robinson's Department Store. Rooms are carpeted, air conditioned, have cable TV, and a minibar. Facilities and services include a fitness center with gym, swimming pool, jacuzzi, sauna, and massage rooms; a business center; baby sitters; car rental; laundry; and airport shuttle. There is a restaurant.

MONTEBELLO VILLA, *Banilad. Tel. 231-3681 to 89, Fax 231-4455. 142 rooms. $60-129 per single, $72-129 per double, $142-433 per suite. Visa, Master Card, American Express, Diners.*

The hotel's pretty old Spanish-style building is nestled into lush landscape. Montebello's exterior is quite charming; the rooms could use renovation. Rooms are air conditioned and have cable TV. The hallways are decorated with some nice paintings by Cebuano artists. The pool area is in the extensive garden that also has an orchid garden and bird houses, a nice oasis in a bustling city.

Other facilities include a small business center, tennis courts, putting green, and bowling alley. The restaurant has good food and serves seafood, local, and continental dishes. Nearby is a mall with several movie theaters.

Moderate

PARK PLACE HOTEL, *Fuente Osmeña. Tel. 253-1131 to 49, Fax 253-0118, 253-0119. Manila reservations: Tel. 634-7505 to 08, Fax 634-7509. US* *reservations: Tel. 1-800/44-UTELL. 115 rooms. $47 per studio, $74-99 per single or double, $126 per suite. Visa, Master Card, American Express, Diners.*

Conveniently located at the center of Cebu's commercial and shopping district, the Park Place offers good rooms for good value. The service is quite good, all rooms are comfortable, air conditioned, come with cable TV, and a minibar. Request for a room facing Fuente Osmeña; the windows in those rooms are nice and big (some rooms do not have a window). Facilities and services include airport shuttle, business services, car rental, foreign exchange, laundry and dry cleaning, salon, gift shop and massage. There is a restaurant that has local and continental fare.

CENTREPOINT HOTEL CEBU, *Plaridel Street corner Osmeña Boulevard. Tel. 254-7111, 253-1831, Fax 253-0695. 145 rooms. $59-85 per single or double, $105 per suite, $15 per extra bed. Visa, Master Card, American Express, Diners.*

All rooms are air conditioned, have cable TV, and a minibar. The staff is friendly and helpful. Facilities include a swimming pool, business center, souvenir shop, parlor and barber, laundry, car rental, and foreign exchange. There are also baby-sitting and mail services. The restaurant serves seafood and local dishes and there is a disco.

CEBU GRAND HOTEL, *Cebu Capitol Commercial Complex, N. Escario Street. Tel. 254-6331, 254-6339, Fax 254-6363. 85 rooms. $45-65 per single or double, $124-141 per suite, $16 per extra bed. Visa, Master Card, American Express, Diners.*

The lobby is small and pleasant. Rooms are simple, comfortable, air conditioned, and have cable TV. The suites are spacious. Views from the rooms are either of the city or the mountain. The staff is friendly and facilities include a business center, small gym, swimming pool, barber shop and beauty parlor, and gift shop. The restaurant is open from 6:00am until midnight and serves continental food. Across the parking lot from the hotel is the Cebu office of the nice up-scale Badian Island Resort.

HARBOR VIEW, *MJ Cuenco Avenue. Tel. 254-3338, Fax 253-0485. 127 rooms. $67-94 per single or double, $107 per suite, $15 per extra bed. Visa and Master Card.*

The outside is not remarkable, but the rooms are spacious, nice, and clean. All rooms are well-maintained, carpeted, air conditioned, and have cable TV. A nice small pool nestles into the lawn. The hotel offers secretarial and massage services. There's a good Chinese restaurant.

STREET MORITZ, *just off Gorordo Avenue. Tel. 231-1148, 231-2408. 20 rooms. $56-67 per single or double, $88 for the suite. Visa and Master Card.*

This is a charming, villa-style hotel. The rooms are a bit dark but are very spacious and have a living room area with cable TV. Rooms have air conditioning and are carpeted. The restaurant has European and local dishes and there is a nice pub.

WEST GORORDO HOTEL, *110 Gorordo Avenue. Tel. 231-4347 to 49, Fax 231-1158. 20 rooms. $44-57 per single or double, $106 per suite, $10.50 per extra bed. Visa, Master Card, American Express, Diners.*

This is a clean, comfortable, charming, friendly place. All rooms are air conditioned, cozy, nicely furnished, spacious, bright, and have cable TV; some rooms have a small balcony. Facilities include a business center; a fitness center with a gym, spa, and sauna; and a library. Laundry service is available. The Family Choice restaurant has very good Chinese cuisine.

DYNASTY TOURIST INN, *Don Filemon Sotto and Jasmin Street. Tel. 253-7598, Fax 253-5655. 37 rooms. $42-55 per single or double, $6 per extra bed. Visa and Master Card.*

Rooms are cozy, simply furnished, spacious, bright, air conditioned, and have cable TV. The deluxe rooms have one double bed, "executive" rooms have two single beds, and "family" rooms have three single beds. The cream corridors are refreshing, well-lit, and have nice potted plants. This place is popular with Chinese-Filipino business people. The coffee shop serves Chinese cuisine.

ADERAN APARTELLE, *Salinas Drive, Lahug. Tel. 231-4858, Fax 231-3397. 30 rooms. $41-46 per single or double, $58-72 per suite. Visa and Master Card.*

All rooms are simply furnished, carpeted, air conditioned, clean, and have cable TV. All bathrooms have tubs. The coffee shop is beside the swimming pool. The staff is friendly.

Inexpensive

ANACLETUS TOURIST INN, *Sanson Rd., Lahug. Tel. 231-4910, 231-4921, Fax 231-4922. 17 rooms. $33-35 per single or double, $38-65 per suite. Visa and Master Card.*

Same management as Aderan Apartelle. Rooms are small but homey and simply furnished. All are air conditioned and have cable TV. There is a small swimming pool and a restaurant-bar-karaoke. Car rental service and airport/seaport shuttle are available. The staff is friendly.

D'VILLA HOTEL, *St Michael's Village Road off Archbishop Reyes Street, Banilad. Tel. 231-4871, Fax 90-350. 18 rooms. $29 per single, $33 per double, $37 per triple.*

This place is in a nice quiet area, near the Cebu Country Club and golf course. All rooms are air conditioned, clean, and comfortable. There is a coffee shop in the hotel and two good restaurants nearby.

TONROS APARTELLE, *Gorordo Avenue near corner of N. Escario Street. Tel. 315-201, 315-202, 75-407, Fax 310-520. 32 rooms. $29 per single or double.*

Good value: you get a kitchenette and cable TV in spacious, bright, clean, air conditioned rooms.

CEBU CENTURY, *Colon corner Pelaez Street. Tel. 255-1341 to 47, 255-1652, Fax 255-1600. E-mail: kenneth@gsilink.com. 99 rooms. $14 per single, $16-26 per double, $35 per suite.*

This is a good-value budget hotel. All rooms are spacious, air conditioned, clean, and simple. The more expensive ones have cable TV. Services offered include car rental, tours, plane and boat ticketing, postal, and massage. There is a restaurant.

KUKUK'S NEST, *157 Gorordo Avenue Tel. 231-5180. $19 per aircon room, common bathroom; $26 per aircon room, private bathroom; $9.50-16.50 per nonaircon room.*

A charming cozy place with character and simple clean rooms. The most expensive room has cable TV. The owners, Bambi and Raimund, are fun people and very accommodating and helpful. They divide their time between Kukuk's Nest in the city and the one in Moalboal.

The restaurant is unique: local materials were used for the decor, and it resembles a tropical-jungle setting. The food is very good, and the white wine chilled perfectly. See *Where to Eat.*

If you are interested in *Lapunti Arnis de Abanico*, a form of Arnis named for the graceful fan movements of the Arnis stick, Bambi and Raimund can help you make arrangements for lessons. Ondo, the grand master of this martial art, comes to the Kukuk's Nest for demonstrations on Saturdays.

JOVEL PENSION, *24 Kuytengsu Road corner Jones Avenue. Tel. 254-9950. 10 rooms. $16 per single or $19 per double aircon, $10.50 per single or $ 12.60 per double non-aircon, $3 per extra bed.*

A very hospitable place with clean rooms. Private bathrooms are available only in the air conditioned rooms. For an small fee, cable TV is available in the rooms.

C'EST LA VIE, *13 Juana Osmeña Street. Tel. 253-5266. 14 rooms. $14 per single or $17 per double aircon, $8.50 per nonaircon room.*

A simple homey place with clean rooms, all with private bathrooms, and satisfied guests. The staff is friendly and there is a coffee shop.

Mactan Island – Very Expensive

SHANGRI-LA'S MACTAN ISLAND RESORT, *Punta Engaño Rd., Lapu-Lapu City. Tel. 231-0288, Fax 231-1688. Manila reservations: Tel. 813-8888. US reservations: Tel. 1-800/942-5050. 547 rooms. $224-430 per single ($290 for ocean view), $245-450 per double ($310 for ocean view), $390-1,126 per suite, $40 per extra bed. Visa, Master Card, American Express, Diners.*

Mactan's top of the line resort is indeed luxurious. The lobby is very pretty and airy. You are greeted warmly at the reception then whisked away to the comfort of your well-appointed and tastefully designed room. All rooms have a private balcony and complete amenities.

"Bayview" rooms overlook the Bay of Cebu; "oceanview" rooms overlook the beautiful pool and gardens and the ocean, and cost more because of the view. The "terrace" rooms have a large terrace, perfect for private sunbathing. The staff is warm and friendly. The many places to dine here include the Pool Bar where you can feast on fresh seafood, which you grill or have grilled right by your table; the Cowrie Cove, for more delectable seafood, overlooking the ocean; Asiatica for a selection of Asian cuisines; Shang Palace for good Chinese dishes; the Garden Patio, for buffet and continental fare; and the Lobby Lounge for snacks while listening to the piano.

The pool is impressive. Other facilities include a business center, complete gym, an extensive aquasport center that has parasailing, and a very good scuba center.

Expensive

WATERFRONT HOTEL & CASINO, *right across from the airport. Tel. 340-4888, Fax 340-5862. Manila reservations: Tel. 634-6477, Fax 634-6476. 367 rooms. $158-290 per single or double, $462-2,376 per suite, $50 per extra person. Visa, Master Card, American Express, Diners.*

The hotel and its rooms are spacious and luxurious. All rooms are furnished with very nice locally made furniture and have a coffee and tea maker as well as all the regular amenities of first-class hotel rooms. The paintings that you see around the hotel are done by Cebuano artists. The views from the rooms are either the airport or the city, and 11 rooms overlook the small and pretty pool area.

Facilities include a complete business center, swimming pool, and a large casino that attracts people from all over Asia. Dine at either Tin Gow Palace, a Chinese restaurant (the head chef is Cantonese); Kanchiku, for Japanese food prepared by Japanese chefs; Cafe Uno for buffet and continental fare; Verandah Cafe, the charming poolside coffee shop beneath Spanish-style arches; and, in the casino, the Café Fortuna (a coffee shop) and Del Sol (for fine dining).

WHITE SANDS, *Maribago. Tel. 340-5960, Fax 340-5969, 254-3801. 15 rooms. $139-252 per single, $167-279 per double, $528 for the suite, $13 per extra bed, $33 per extra person. Visa, Master Card, American Express, Diners.*

This charming resort retains a turn-of-the-century ambiance. Wood and capiz shell windows and decorative dividers give the lobby its antique flare. The guest rooms are equally as pretty and are furnished in the same style as the lobby. All rooms are spacious, air conditioned, and have cable TV and a balcony. Within the sprawling landscaped garden is the swimming pool; a few steps down and you're at the beach. Dine at the Buena Vista Bar overlooking the beach, or at Doña Estrella for finer dining. The resort is very well managed and the staff is friendly.

MARIBAGO BLUEWATER, *Maribago. Tel. 253-1620. Manila reservations: Tel. 522-1532. 62 rooms. $132-145 per single, $145-158 per double, $237.60 for the "Royal Bungalow" suite. Visa, Master Card, American Express, Diners.*

After passing through the nice rattan furnished reception area, you cross a pond with starfish and a baby shark on one side and tropical fish on the other, and get to a fountain with the resort's signature seven dolphins.

The "Garden Wing" rooms are cheaper than those in the "Beach Wing." All rooms are spacious, pleasantly decorated, and equipped with air conditioning, minibar, and cable TV. There are two curved pools. Aquasports include jetskiing, water skiing, windsurfing, and more. The resort also has a shooting gallery, gym, sauna and whirlpool, billiards, badminton, volleyball, and tennis. Meals are served at Sunset Cove (fresh seafood), Palmera Restaurant (indoor air conditioned dining), and Allegro Café (open 24 hours).

Moderate

EGI BY THE SEA, *Maribago. Tel. 253-7341, cellular Tel. 0912-501-4181. Manila reservations: Tel. 890-8131, Fax 896-0929. $49 per "family studio," $142 per suite, $14 per additional person over a party of four. Visa, Master Card, American Express, Diners.*

For alternative lodging, EGI is a condo-tel. The "studios" can comfortably accommodate four people: each has two double beds, a patio overlooking the pool and beach, and air conditioning. The suites have queen beds, sofa, dining area, kitchenette, air conditioning, and cable TV. You can get good home-cooked meals at the restaurant; main courses are under $4.

HADSAN, *Maribago. Tel. 70-247. $41-56 per room.*

Rooms are air conditioned. You may swim in the pool or off the resort's nice stretch of cream sand beach. It is a popular place for day visitors, entrance is only 40¢.

Budget

CLUB KONTIKI, *Maribago. Tel. 340-0292, 340-0310, Fax 340-0294, 340-0306. 24 rooms. $23-37 per single, $25-40 per double, $42-45 per suite. Visa and Master Card.*

This good and friendly resort caters to divers. It is small, peaceful, and secluded, located on a cliffside. All rooms are very clean, cozy, and are fan-cooled. Kontiki is very well managed and the staff are delightful. Feast on fresh seafood and other delicious dishes at the cliff-top restaurant.

The dive center offers PADI, NAUI, CMAS, SSI courses, and the instructors have a good reputation.

KALINGAW, *Marigondon. Tel. 253-0265. $25-40 per room.*
Another resort that caters to divers and has a professionally-run dive operation. Rooms are simple and clean.
HOTEL CESARIO, *Pusok, Lapu-Lapu City. Tel. 340-0211 to 16, Fax 340-0615. 55 rooms. $23-70 per single or double, $75 per suite.*
The cheaper rooms are in the older annex building, and room prices vary with size. All rooms are clean, air conditioned, carpeted, and have cable TV. There is a restaurant
HR TOURIST INN, *Pusok, Lapu-Lapu City. Tel. 340-0048, 340-1702, Fax 340-0158. 37 rooms. $25-35 per single or double aircon, $17 per single or $21 per double non-aircon, $6 per extra bed.*
Located near the bridge between Mactan and Cebu, this place has simple rooms and friendly service. The restaurant is beside the swimming pool.

WHERE TO EAT

There is a bewildering profusion of places to refuel in Cebu City. A meal should cost around $4-10 in most places except when noted (expensive or really cheap).
For quick lunches, snacks, and informal evening meals, try **Food Street**, the short-order places along Jones Avenue near Fuente Osmeña, and **Lechon Manok**, along Mango Avenue. Prices vary from stall to stall, but you can eat cheaply (under $4) and well. For a variety of fast food, there are **food courts** in the malls (Ayala Center, Gaisano, Robinson's, SM, etc.). And, as in almost all cities nationwide, you will find McDonald's and Jollybee for burgers, and Pizza Hut and Shakey's for pizza.

North
PATIO ISABEL, *Old Banilad Road, near the Country Club and Gaisano Country Mall.*
This is the place to go for turn-of-the-century ambiance and Filipino cuisine.
GINZA, *Old Banilad Road, next to Patio Isabel.*
Very good Japanese food, some Korean dishes, and friendly staff. Expensive.
VIENNA KAFEEHAUS, *Banilad Road corner Fortuna Street.*
This is a charming café, with good sandwiches and strong coffee.

Just North of the Center
LANTAW, *Cebu Plaza Hotel, Nivel Hills, Lahug. Visa, Master Card, American Express, Diners.*
Very good seafood and finer dining. The ambiance is pleasantly native and service is good. Expensive.

TALK OF THE TOWN, *406 Gorordo Avenue, Lahug.*

This is a Chinese restaurant with pretty good Szechuan Cuisine. Other specialties include Shanghai and Peking dishes.

KUKUK'S NEST GARDEN RESTAURANT, *157 Gorordo Avenue.*

Specializes in German fare and has excellent burgers. And your white wine or beer is perfectly chilled. The ambiance is great, as you sit in a "tropical jungle." Service is great and the owners are very friendly and are a good source of information on Moalboal. The restaurant also has weekly or monthly specials that range from wine-tasting to celebrations such as OktoberfeStreet

FAMILY CHOICE, *110 Gorordo Avenue.*

This is a popular place, especially on Sundays, for Chinese food.

ROYAL CONCOURSE, *Gorordo Avenue near Arch. Reyes.*

A popular, bright, large, and air conditioned *turo-turo* style place with a wide selection of local food. The barbequed chicken is tasty and the crowd is a mix of social classes.

STREET MORITZ, *just off Gorordo Avenue.*

Serves some tasty European and local dishes in a pub-type atmosphere.

ALAVAR, *Gorordo Avenue.*

This originally from Zamboanga City; come for fresh seafood, especially blue marlin from Mindanao, and crab.

EUROPA DELICATESSEN, *QC Pavilion, Gorordo Avenue.*

This deli has good sausages and good strong coffee.

GOLDEN COWRIE, *Salinas Drive corner La Guardia Street, Lahug.*

Excellent seafood in a nice, casual, open-air setting; try the clams.

CARUSO, *Escario corner Kamagong Street.*

Serves Italian cuisine and has a pleasant ambiance.

CRAB HOUSE, *Arch. Reyes corner Bauhinia Drive. Visa, Master Card.*

Serves a variety of great crab dishes as well as seafood and other local food.

GRAND MAJESTIC, *Arch. Reyes.*

A very large Chinese restaurant, one of the best in the city.

DAVID'S, *36 Arch. Reyes Avenue across from Ayala Center.*

Fine European and Mediterranean cuisine, and serves choice cuts of prime US beef and succulent Cornish hen. Expensive.

Center City

ARANO'S BAR & RESTAURANT, *B Rodriguez Street.*

Serves Spanish food and has a pleasant atmosphere and friendly service.

GREAT HAN PALACE, *Osmeña Boulevard.*

Good Chinese food; some dishes are inexpensive.

LARIEN, *Fuente Osmeña by the rotunda.*

This is a must if you like barbeque — it is excellent and very cheap — a very casual, no frills place.

CHIKA-AN SA CEBU, *Century Plaza complex, Juana Osmeña Street.*

Tasty char-broiled dishes, including fresh seafood.

MIKADO, *General Maxilom Avenue.*

Good sushi and Japanese dishes.

SWISS RESTAURANT, *General Maxilom.*

Serves pretty good Swiss (naturally!) food in a relaxed and friendly ambiance.

CAFE BADEN-BADEN, *121 Raintree Mall, 524 Gen. Maxilom Avenue.*

This is a nice coffee shop that also serves western dishes.

KIMCHI, *Gen. Maxilom before Gorordo Avenue.*

Tasty, almost authentic, Korean fare.

EUROPA DELICATESSEN, *F Ramos Street.*

Good sausages and a good cup of strong coffee.

CAFÉ ADRIATICO, *F Ramos Street.*

Offers European and some westernized local dishes. The ambiance is pleasant, decor is old Spain. It is also a popular place for evening snacks and drinks.

EDDIE'S LOG CABIN, *MC Briones Street, near Fort San Pedro.*

This is the city's oldest restaurant. Eddie's serves Western and Filipino dishes; steaks and salads are recommended. The daily specials are quite cheap.

VIENNA KAFEEHAUS, *SM City, North Reclamation Area.*

A charming café — good sandwiches and strong coffee.

Mactan

At the Lapu-Lapu Monument, there is a **fish market** where you can get very cheap and very fresh seafood and have it cooked for you. It is a good deal if you do not mind eating by the road.

TIN GOW, *Waterfront Hotel, beside the airport.*

Serves good Cantonese cuisine (prepared by Cantonese chefs). The restaurant is large, has private rooms, and service is polite. Expensive-Very Expensive.

MACTAN SEAFOOD RESTAURANT, *just before the Lapu-Lapu monument.*

A casual and friendly open-air place that serves very fresh and inexpensive seafood.

COWRIE COVE, *Shangri-La's Mactan Island Resort. Very Expensive.*

This place has a good seafood buffet. The ambiance is pleasant, you dine in an open-air pavilion-style restaurant that overlooks the ocean.

For a more casual atmosphere, grill your own meal (or, if you prefer, have it grilled for you) on a small grill set up by your table at the **POOLSIDE GRILL**. Select from seafood and meat, and you have the option of having the staff grill it for you. Service is excellent and friendly. Very Expensive.

TALK OF THE TOWN, *EGI City, Maribago*.

A casual Chinese restaurant, specializing in seafood, Szechuan, Shanghai, and Peking dishes.

SEEING THE SIGHTS

City Tour

This tour can be completed in one day by hired car, or in a leisurely manner by foot and jeepney — start at 8:00am, plan for lunch at Fuente Osmeña and a relaxing sunset at the Cebu Plaza or perhaps dinner at the Golden Cowrie, and continue the next day.

Start at **Fort San Pedro**, a lovely historical area run by the National Museum. Construction began in 1565 but was not completed until 1738. The fort was first used to repel Moro pirates and has served various other purposes: stronghold for Filipino revolutionaries; defense post and barracks for the US army; a prison camp during the Japanese occupation; a city zoo; and today, as a small park. The small entry fee of 60¢ (P15) helps pay for its maintenance. Once at the edge of the waterfront, reclamation has moved the fort inland. Flanking the Fort are statues of Legazpi, at the front, and Pigafetta, on the side.

Beside the Fort is **Plaza Independencia**. The offices of the **DOT** are across the street from the Plaza. Walk up Magellan Street to a gazebo housing the fragments of the cross that Magellan and Fray Pedro Valderrama left. On the ceiling is an impressive mural of the first mass. Around the gazebo, women sell candles. For a small fee they will dance in front of the cross with the candles lit, wishing luck on anyone you want to help.

The **Basilica Minore del Santo Niño**, dating from 1740, is across the street. Inside is the image of the Sto Niño thought to have been left by Magellan and recovered 44 years later by Fray Urdaneta. There are usually lines of people waiting their turn to file past the statue; lines are longest on Friday. Small shops sell religious memorabilia. The Basilica is closed daily from noon to 2:00pm.

On the other side of the Basilica, head west towards Burgos Street where you take a left to the **Cebu Metropolitan Cathedral**; it is closed for lunch from noon til 3:00pm.

The next stop is **Casa Gorordo Museum and Art Gallery**. To get there, continue along Burgos Street for three and a half blocks where the road forks. Take the right fork, and look for a century-old house with a tiled roof. Take the second right after the house, Lopez Jaena Street. You will find the museum at the end of the first block on the left. This former residence of Bishop Gorordo has been restored by the Aboitiz, a prominent family in Cebu. In a lovely setting, the museum houses historic and cultural relics of old Cebu, photos, and contemporary art and paintings. The museum hours are Monday through Saturday, 9:00am until 5:00pm. Entrance is 60¢ and includes a good guided tour that is a must if you are interested in Cebu's cultural heritage.

Backtrack to Burgos Street and walk up Colon to the corner of Juan Luna Street, where you can catch a Lahug-Carbon jeepney, headed to Lahug. Get off just before the rotunda, where the **Osmeña** house has MacArthur and Osmeña memorabilia on display. Osmeña was the first Philippine President after World War Two.

For a great, inexpensive lunch, try the barbeque at **Larien** at the corner of Fuente Osmeña and the north leg of Osmeña Boulevard.

Next are the Chinese temples: **Phu San** (Buddhist), a **Taoist Temple**, and the **Cebu Heavenly Temple of Charity** (Taoist). The Taoist temples, both attractive, are open to the public. To get there, head over to Gorordo Avenue and continue to Beverly Hills, where wealthy Cebuanos (many of them Chinese) live. Climb the steps of the Taoist temple to the highest shrine, where people visit to pray and seek, through priest intercessors, answers to problems and questions — ask a temple official if you wish answers to some pressing questions.

Continue up Gorordo for **great views** and a sunset drink or meal at the Cebu Plaza Hotel. The views are especially impressive at night. This hotel is a major landmark — it stands out and appears to be facing you from most points in the city and parts of Mactan.

To visit the **University of San Carlos Museum**, head back to Gorordo Avenue and catch a jeepney headed to the Carbon Market (4B, 4C, 17B, or 17C). Get off at the USC's main campus, between P. del Rosario and Sanciangco Street. The museum is through the first door on the right of the right corridor. It houses a well-labeled collection of religious carvings, ethnic artifacts, preserved botanical and zoological specimens, and archaeological finds. Museum hours are weekdays, from 8:00am until noon, then 1:30 until 5:30; and on Saturday mornings.

Points Nearby

If you are interested in seeing **butterfly wing mosaics**, take a #9 jeepney from Colon or Carbon. See *South Coast Excursions* for more details on Professor Jumalon's museum.

The **Chapel of the Last Supper**, in Mandaue, is a nicely restored church. Inside are life-size figures of Christ and the Apostles at the last supper. Take a jeepney with a Manadaue-Oanao sign and tell the driver to let you off at the chapel.

Mactan Island

Among the main attractions in Mactan are its beaches, beach and dive resorts, guitar factories (see *Shopping*), and the elegant and exclusive **Shangri-La**. To get to Mactan inexpensively, take a Cebu-Opun or Cebu-Lapu-Lapu jeepney. From the terminal just beyond the bridge in Mactan you can hire a tricycle or taxi.

The handsome bronze **Lapu-Lapu Monument** stands in a stunning spot, looking out to sea from the place where Magellan was slain by Lapu-Lapu. Several small shops flank the shore nearby, and a small fish market offers the freshest fish in Cebu – select your meal and have them grill it for you.

Mactan's eastern shore it dotted with a range of beach resorts, a number of which cater to divers and most have instructors. If you are visiting for the day, Hadson Beach Resort has the lowest entrance fee – 40¢; the high-end resorts may charge up to $12.

From the beaches, you can hire a *banca* ($20) to visit **Olango Island**, a bird sanctuary nearby. It is easiest to get a *banca* near the Kontiki Dive Resort.

If you like to gamble, there is a large **casino** at the Waterfront Hotel at the Mactan airport.

NIGHTLIFE & ENTERTAINMENT

Outside of Manila, Cebu city has the liveliest nightlife. Chose from loud discos, karaoke, casinos, bars, and pleasant sing-a-long and piano bars. For discos: **Bai**, Cebu Plaza Hotel and **Balls**, General Maxilom Avenue are very popular.

For the bar scene, try **Charlie's**, F Ramos Street, for excellent martinis, easy-listening music, and good meals; **Prince William's Pub**, N. Escario Street, and **Street Moritz**, off Gorordo Avenue, for a European pub atmosphere; **Kukuk's Nest**, Gorordo Avenue, for a good selection of wine and a charming open-air tropical setting; **Slabadu**, General Maxilom Avenue, for jazz music; **Café Adriatico**, F. Ramos Street, for café-bar atmosphere and a selection of coffee-liqueur concoctions; and **Cassanova**, Don Mariano Pi., for a gay bar.

Tops, on Busay Hill, is a very popular destination. Tops is 15 kilometers from the center and offers a great panorama of the lights from the city, Mactan Island, and ships in the ocean and bay. Sunset and after dark are good times to come. The atmosphere is very casual: sit on the ridge and admire the vista as you drink a beer; drinks and beer are available at the stalls. The bathrooms, however, leave something to be desired.

On Mactan Island, most resorts have a casual bar. There is a relaxing **piano lounge**, and a **disco** at the Shangri-La; and a large casino at the Waterfront Hotel.

SPORTS & RECREATION

Casino Gambling

Try your luck at **Casino Filipino** at Nivel Hills, **Satellite Casino** at the Cebu Plaza Hotel, the **Waterfront Hotel** beside the airport, and a floating casino aboard the *Delta Philippine Dream* at the Cebu Yacht Club.

Golf

Cebu Country Club, Banilad, *Tel. 74-901, 74-905, 74-813*, has 18 holes on a relatively flat course. Greens fees on the weekdays are $70, and on the weekends are $120; caddy fees are $8; a set of golf clubs is $15 per day.

Club Filipino, Danao, has 18 holes.

Kan-Irag, Busay Hills, *Tel. 253-3453*, is an 18-hole course located high in the mountains. Greens fees on the weekdays are $30, and on the weekends are $40; caddy fees are $6; a set of golf clubs is $20 per day.

Cebu Green Island, Badian Island, *Tel. 95-935*, is part of a Japanese-owned resort and has 18 holes. Entrance is $5 per person; greens fees are $60; caddy fees are $8; a set of golf clubs is $15 per day.

Martial Arts-Arnis

See Kukuk's Nest in *Where to Stay* above.

Parasailing

If you like to soar above the water, you can go parasailing in the Hilutungan Channel off Mactan Island. The **Advance Marine Sports**, at Shangri-La's Mactan Island Resort, *Tel. 231-5060, Fax 231-5061*, offers parasailing daily; make reservations a day in advance. The company, run by Americans, is licensed by the International Parasail Boating Association and by the US Coast Guard. Cost per flight for guests (single or tandem) is $50, and because of limited space on the accompanying boat, observers are charged $19.

Scuba Diving

Cebu's diving industry is quite developed. Efforts to conserve marine life are seen in the many anchor buoys that have been installed, and many dive sites have substantial coral while others show good signs of recovering. Small reef fish are abundant, and you may also see dolphins, whale sharks, pilot whales, and mantas.

Frequented sites near the city include **Fish Feeding off Tambuli**, right off the beach resort; **Marigondon Cave**, inhabited by a variety of small reef fish, including a school of flashlight fish that make your night diving truly a treat; **Loco** has small reef fish, nudibranchs, and soft coral; there is a cave (at 95 feet) at **Liloan**; and the **Wall of Death** just west of Liloan Point is only for advanced divers — currents are very strong.

On the west coast of Cebu, the most popular area for diving is around **Moalboal**, where most resorts cater to divers. You will find areas just off **Panagsama Beach** full of life. **Pescador Island**, near Badian, has great day and night dives — the reef, caverns, and tunnels house larger fish and sea snakes, and you may also see whale sharks, hammerheads, and mantas.

If you go north, make arrangements for diving around **Sogod** through the Alegre Beach Resort; **Capitancillo Island**, northeast of Tabogon, has a large, gradually sloping reef; and there is diving off **Bantayan Island** and **Malapascua Island**.

Most of the upscale resorts have an in-house diving center. Good dive operators include:
- **Badian Island Beach Hotel**, *Badian Island, Tel. 253-6452, Fax 253-3385*
- **Club Kontiki**, *Angan Building, Pusok, Lapu-Lapu City, Tel. 86-555, 40-0292, 40-0310, Fax 40-0294*
- **Diving Safaris Inc.**, *Lower Lo-oc, Sanander, Tel. 19-601, Fax 21-6993*
- **Fun & Sun Travel**, *2nd Floor Krizia Building, Gorordo Ave., Tel. 31-4620, Fax 31-4715,* (also operates the dive center at the Alegre Beach Resort in Sogod)
- **Kukuk's Nest**, *Moalboal, Tel. 231-5180, cellular 0917-320-0726*
- **Ocean Safari**, *Moalboal, c/o Nelson Abenido*
- **Saavedra's**, *Moalboal, c/o Hans Boetgen, cellular Tel. 0918-770-781 or 0912, 501-9034, Fax 340-0306*
- **Scotties Dive Center**, *Shangri-La's Mactan Island Resort, Tel. 231-5060, Fax 231-5061*
- **Seaquest**, *PO Box 558, Cebu City, Tel. 84-708, 210-2650*

Good dive shops include:
- **Aquaventure**, *Unit 2, Mercedes Commercial Center, A. Cortes Avenue, Mandaue, Tel. 84-565*
- **Cebu South Sea Dive**, *Manros Plaza, General Maxiliom Avenue, Tel. 21-4798, 21-4761*
- **Liquid Assets**, *Cebu Grand Hotel Complex, N. Escario Street, Tel. 22-5359, Fax 31-4980*
- **Scuba World**, *QC Pavilion, Gorordo Avenue, Lahug*

Tennis
The **Cebu Plaza Hotel** has tennis courts where non-guests can play.

Other courts in the city are at **Casino Español**, V Ranudo Street, *Tel. 78-254*; **Cebu Tennis Club**, Banilad, *Tel. 95-529*; **Super Courts Pelotadium**, Juan Osmeña Street, *Tel. 92-116*; and **VECO Tennis Club**, Banilad, *Tel. 75-446*.

SHOPPING

Cebu offers shoppers a profusion of shell jewelry, basketry, rattan, arts, handicrafts, almost anything Philippine you desire.

The best way to shop is on your own — no guides, drivers, or tours. Many places give tour guides and drivers a percentage of sales; you may be able to get this percentage "discounted" from your purchases if you are "unaccompanied."

Ferimar (just below Cebu Plaza), **Gaisano's**, **Robinson's**, **Rustan's**, **ShoeMart**, **Tesoro's**, and a number of shops inside the **Ayala Center** carry a range of quality handicrafts. Knowing the maximum reasonable prices in these places will come in handy when you bargain elsewhere.

Carbon Market is an interesting place bustling with activity, crammed with stalls of handicrafts, fruits, vegetables, meat, fish, flowers, and more. Hold your belongings close — it is also happy hunting ground for thieves.

For Philippine and Chinese antiques and paintings by local artists, visit **Arthaus**, downtown, off Archbishop Reyes Street. **Col Roska**, Pelaez Ext., also sells antiques.

Good places for reasonably priced shell items are **Irfel Trade**, Citicenter, Junquiera Street, *Tel. 52-807, 90-467*; **Jewel of the Sea**, STC Campus, General Maxilom Avenue, *Tel. 78-431*, where proceeds support Saint Teresa's orphanage; and **Cebu Marbel Supply & Shellcraft**, at the intersection to Mactan on A. Cortes Avenue, where you can watch shell jewelry being made.

Lucky Tableware in Mandaue has a shop (open Monday-Thursday) selling beautiful Chinese porcelain, you may also visit the factory behind the shop. To get there by public transport, take a jeep marked "Carbon-Consolacion," (#24), get off at Cubacub, and from there take a tricycle.

Mactan has a number of factories that offer good prices and the opportunity to see how **guitars** are made: try the shops in Abuno and in Maribago.

THE SLAUGHTER OF MARINE TURTLES IS ILLEGAL
Do not encourage poachers by purchasing turtle shell products: such purchases help threaten marine turtles with extinction.

EXCURSIONS & DAY TRIPS
SOUTH COAST EXCURSIONS

Beaches, diving, and quaint towns with interesting churches and houses are among the points of interest south of the city. Bring a packed lunch if you are going for the day.

During the 17th century, wealthy *mestizo* families began buying sugarland and building beautiful homes and churches in the countryside. **El Pardo** is the first pretty church southward.

In Basak, **Professor Julian Jumalon's museum**, off Tres de Abril Street in Basak, *Tel. 91-029*, displays impressive lepido-mosaic artworks by the professor. He creates "alive" works of art by laying bits of damaged butterfly wings, collected from all over the world, over his oil paintings. The museum is in his home, nestled among lush foliage, and is open Monday through Saturday from 8:00am to 6:00pm.

Continue along Tres de Abril through the town of **Talisay**, where the interesting **Tabunok Market** spills out into the road.

Naga church has a nice exterior.

Head further south to **Carcar** to see the pretty quasi-baroque **church**, completed in 1876. Impressive Spanish buildings, once ancestral mansions, line the plaza. Ask around for directions to an *ampao* (puffed-rice sweet) factory.

There is an impressive **church** in the charming town of **Argao**. Enter to see the handcarved pews made from heavy wood and the beautiful retablos. Also in Argao are a Spanish fort and the fine cream sand Mahayahay Beach.

Further south is **Dalaguete**, which has a nice beach. Most of Cebu's vegetables are grown in the mountains behind the town.

In **Oslob**, there is an old Spanish watch tower. Santander, on Cebu's southern tip, is where you can catch a ferry to Amlan and a jeepney to Bais for **dolphin watching** (see the previous chapter, Dumaguete section). You will pass great views and churches as you continue around the tip to Bato, the ferry departure point to Dumaguete.

Moalboal

Many vacationers head to **Panagsama Beach**, three kilometers from the quaint town of **Moalboal** on the west coast of Cebu. Panagsama is popular with low-budget travelers and divers. Most of its resorts are simple, have a friendly atmosphere, and cater to divers. It has good inexpensive restaurants, nightspots, and clothing made from flour sacks. Panagsama's atmosphere, its movable discos, Sunday *sabong* (cockfights), and local brews, give the area great color. The town has a market, church, school, cockpit, and tennis court.

Beyond the neighboring town of **Badian** are the **Kawasan Falls**, where you can swim in the cool pool at the base of the 12-meter falls. To get there, cross the bridge in Matutinao just past Badian. The trail to the falls starts at the church. It is a 30-minute hike to the first waterfall and another 15 minutes to the second one. There is a small entry fee at the falls.

Scuba diving is very good around this area. Among the diving destinations are **Badian Island**, which also has a well-run up-market resort; **Pescador Island**, also good for snorkeling; **White Beach**; and around **Santa Rosa** for good drift diving, turtles, and stingrays. (See *Sports & Recreation* above for a list of dive operators.)

Kukuk's Nest (also has a pension in Cebu City) offers **mountain biking tours** to the waterfalls, and **dive trips**. An open water coarse costs $250 and includes equipment, boat rental, and license.

If you are around on a Thursday, rent a vehicle, or if you came or are leaving with a private hire, stop in the central mountains where the **Mantalongon market** offers handicrafts, produce, and local color.

To get to the Moalboal area, take a taxi or jeepney to the south bus terminal, then take an Abines (ABC), Autobus, Cetrasco, Philippine Eagle, SM Liner, or Villanueva bus to Carcar, then across the mountains. Some buses may, upon request, go to the beach. ABC has a daily round trip of the southern part of the island. The night before you leave, check departure times and ask your resort to arrange for a tricycle to take you to the bus. By private hire, Moalboal is 90 kilometers and takes two and a half to three hours. Some resorts can arrange transport for you if given advance notice.

For lodgings on Panagsama Beach, try any of the following:

MOALBOAL REEF CLUB, *Panagsama Beach, $55-83 per single or double aircon, $21-28 per single or double non-aircon.*

The Reef Club has some comfortable air conditioned rooms. Most of the rooms have a private bathroom; the cheapest non-aircon ones do not. There is a restaurant and a dive center.

SAAVEDRA DIVE RESORT, *Panagsama Beach. Cellular Tel. 0918-770-7818, 0912, 501-9034, Fax (Cebu) 340-0306. $40-57 per bungalow.*

Simple, nice, clean bungalows, each with air conditioning, private bathroom, and a balcony. Saavedra is well-run; the owners and staff are friendly. The dive center is very professional and highly recommended, and offers a range of activities including dive safaris. There is a restaurant.

SUMISID LODGE, *Panagsama Beach. Tel. (c/o Aquarius Water Sports) 84-708, 82-781, Fax 460-592, price includes full board and two dives: $60 per person.*

Simple, well-kept rooms with private bathrooms. The dive center is professional and highly recommended.

KUKUK'S NEST, *Panagsama Beach. Tel. 231-5180, cellular 0917-320-0726. $22 per single or double aircon, $14 per single or double nonaircon.*

This is a simple homey resort with clean rooms. Its owners, Bambi and Raimund are delightful and a good source of information on the area. They divide their time between the resort and its counterpart in Cebu City and arrange for their guests' transport between the two. Bambi is a dive master and runs dive tours and Raimund takes biking tours to the falls. Meals are very good; you may select from fresh seafood, local and continental fare, and German sausages.

Other simple, inexpensive lodging places include **Cora's**, **Eve's Kiosk & Ocean Safari Lodge**, **Norma's**, **Pacita's Nipa Hut**, and **Pacifico's**. Rooms are fan-cooled, and cost around $15.

For lodgings on Badian Island, try any of the following:

BADIAN ISLAND BEACH HOTEL, *Badian Island. Tel. 253-6452, Fax 253-3385. 50 cottages. $69 per person per triple, $86-119 per person per double, $142-150 per single, group discounts and packages are available. Visa, Master Card, American Express, Diners.*

The pretty, native-styled bungalows are divided into two rooms with spacious private balconies. The interior is tastefully decorated with local furnishing and the windows are wood with capiz shells. Facilities include a fully-equipped scuba diving center and an 18-hole golf course nearby. Use of sailboats and windsurfs, and various excursions are included in the room rates.

This is an attractive resort. Tropical flowers enhance the sprawling garden, there are two nice beaches, and in the late afternoons you can enjoy vibrant sunsets. Colorful *calesas* provide transport between the cream sand beach in the lagoon and the beach that runs along the coral reef. The pavilion-style restaurant serves fresh seafood daily and has a selection of local and European dishes on the menu. For evening drinks, there is a charming bamboo bar. Entertainment includes some local folk singing and beach or pool-side parties. The resort is managed by a German, and the ambiance and staff are delightful and very friendly.

CEBU GREEN ISLAND, *Lambug, Badian Island. Tel. 73-980. $80-120 per single or double $250 per suite. Visa, Master Card.*

This resort caters to Japanese travelers. Included in the hotel complex is an 18-hole golf course, a swimming pool, and aquasports. Arrangements for scuba diving are available. The restaurant serves continental fare.

LAMBUG BEACH RESORT, *Lambug, Badian Island. $20-40 per single or double.*

The resort has simple, pleasant cottages by a nice cream sand beach, a restaurant, diving, and water skiing. The resort is run by an American and the staff is friendly and efficient.

NORTH COAST EXCURSIONS

Northern Cebu also provides the traveler with natural pretty beaches, islands, and diving.

Sogod

Sogod is a very pretty area, two hours from Cebu City. Primarily a fishing town, it is home to a very nice and well designed up-market resort adjacent to coves fringed with fine cream sand and aquamarine water. Arrangements for day trips can be made through the Cebu Plaza Hotel. There are several interesting places to hike to nearby. The resort has arranged a number of tours, including lunch, transportation, and guides to **Bagatayam Falls**, a 10-minute drive and an hour walk along a river; **Labangon Caves**, an hour drive north to Ilihan plus an hour hike through sugarcane plantations and small rivers; **Libaong Hills**, an hour and 30 minute hike from Ilihan — good for bird watching; and **Mainit Springs**, a 30 minute drive south to Catmon and two-hour hike following a river through rice fields to the hot springs for a warm dip.

Nearby **Capitancillo Island**, a 30 minute boat ride from Sogod, is a small coral island with an old light house. The island was named after Captain Cillo of the US navy; his vessel ran aground here during World War Two. The island offers three good dive spots and is excellent for snorkeling.

Arrangements for transport can be made at the Cebu Plaza Hotel or take a north-bound bus and get off in Sogod.

For lodgings in Sogod, try:

ALEGRE BEACH RESORT, *Calumboyan, Sogod. Tel. 254-9800, 254-9811, 254-9844, Fax 254-9833. Manila reservations: Tel. 634-7505 to 08, Fax 634-7509. US reservations: Tel. 1-800/44-UTELL. 40 rooms. $240 per single or double. Visa, Master Card, American Express, Diners.*

This lovely resort, perched above white sand beach coves, commands nice views, and has 20 cabanas set among lush tropical foliage. Each cabana is divided into two spacious rooms with entrances through private verandahs. Fitted with pretty native rattan furniture, solid wood flooring, and a large marble bathroom with separate bathtub and shower, the rooms have with cable TV, minibar, brewed coffee and tea maker, and a safe.

The free-shape pool is attractive, large, and fringed by a stone perimeter with a few palms. Adjacent is the Pavilion Restaurant and Lounge Bar, offering dining al fresco or air conditioned. You may select from the buffet or the menu of local and international dishes. Other facilities and services include a tennis court, library, game room, mountain bikes, a well-trained masseuse, and manicurists.

Aquasports include jetskiing, windsurfing, island hopping, snorkeling, scuba diving, and dolphin watching. The dive center is complete and very well managed and staffed. Service is wonderfully warm and attentive. All the employees are very friendly. The resort is a perfect escape: it is very peaceful, offers a range of interesting activities, and affords complete privacy too. The adjacent coves have fine sand fringed by azure water, and you can relax on one of the hammocks hanging from the palms.

CLUB PACIFIC, *Sogod. Tel. 79-147, 21-2291, Fax 31-4621. $100 per cottage.*

This was the first resort in the area and has nice cottages with clean air conditioned rooms, tennis courts, hobbie cats, windsurfs, water skiing, and diving. The restaurant serves seafood and continental dishes.

Malapascua Island

The island has a number of very nice beaches ideal for swimming and snorkeling.

Malapascua can be reached by a four-hour trip on **D'Rough Riders** bus line from the Cebu City to Daanbantayan, at the northern tip of Cebu, then a one-hour *banca* ride to the island ($11.50-20.00 per *banca*). The public *banca* makes only one trip a day, leaves at 5:45am, and costs $2.70 per person.

Lodging is simple. The resorts provide meals, but you can also try **LA ISLA BONITA RESTAURANT**, owned by a German, for seafood and European dishes; **GING-GING'S FLOWER GARDEN**, a nice simple restaurant with tasty local fare; **SALLY'S EATERY**; and for good breakfast and home-made bread, **TOMMY DESAMPARADOS**.

COCOBANA, *10 rooms, $28 per room from December-April, $20 per room from May-November, $8 per tent.*

Cocobana is probably the most developed. It is owned by a Swiss fellow; unfortunately, when he is out of the country, the staff has a reputation of slacking off and jacking up the prices. The resort has equipment for windsurfing and snorkeling.

MONTERUBIO, *4 rooms, $16 per room.*

This small place has simple, clean rooms.

MONTELUNA, *4 duplex cottages, $14 per room.*

Nice clean rooms, water comes from a private deep well.

Another resort, unnamed at the start of 1997, has two rooms, each with a private bath, and the restaurant is two meters from the cottages.

Bantayan Island

The island is known for its tasty fresh crab and prawns; great sandy beaches that slope gradually, making it possible to walk far into the ocean; and a few nice dive spots.

Ferries go directly from Cebu City to Bantayan Island. Palacio Lines has trips departing Cebu at 9:00pm on Tuesday, Thursday, and Saturday. The voyage takes eight hours and costs $4 per person in "economy," $6 per person in "tourist," and $8 for a private cabin. Return trips leave Bantayan Wednesday, Friday, and Sunday. Sto Niño Lines leaves Cebu City on Monday and Friday at 7:00am, arriving in Bantayan at 9:00pm. Fare per person is $4 in "regular" and $6 in "aircon." Return trips are Saturday and Tuesday.

An alternative route is by a three-hour bus ride from the city to Hagnaya Wharf in San Remegio, followed by a one-hour ferry trip to Bantayan. Boats leave at two-hour intervals starting at 7:00am with the last trip at 9:00pm; return trips start at 6:00am, with the last trip at 8:00pm; fare is $1.60 per person. From Cebu City, Autobus has trips at 5:00, 6:00, and 7:00am, then again at 12:00, 1:00, and 2:00pm; return trips leave at 7:00am and 1:00pm. Fare is $2.50 per person.

For lodgings in Bantayan Island, consider:

KOTA BEACH RESORT, *Tel. 254-2726, 35 rooms. $40-50 per aircon cottage, $20 per standard room.*

This resort has a restaurant and a dive center with certified instructors.

We have heard good reports about **SANTA FE BEACH RESORT**, *Tel. 253-1339, 26 rooms, $35-65 per aircon room, $20 per non-aircon cottage.*

PRACTICAL INFORMATION

Banks & Money Changers

You should have no problems finding a place to change most foreign currency in Cebu. Near City Hall are **Bank of the Philippine Islands**, **PNB**, and **Standard Chartered Bank**. **Equitable Bank**, Juan Luna Street, also gives cash advances on Visa or Master Cards. **PCI Bank** is on Gorordo Avenue.

To change Amex travellers cheques or get an advance on your card, the **American Express Office**, 2nd Floor, PCI Bank Bldg. by the US Consulate, Gorordo Avenue is open weekdays from 8:30am to 4:00pm, and on Saturdays from 8:30am to 11:00am. **Thomas Cook** has an office at the ground floor Metro Bank Plaza, Osmeña Boulevard.

Some of the large department stores change money.

Consulates
• **Consulate of the United Sates of American**, *3rd floor PCI Building, Gorordo Avenue, Tel. 231-1261*
• **Honorary Consul of Austria**, *Escario Street, Tel. 231-0605, 231-4030*
• **Honorary Consul of Belgium**, *Benedicto & Sons Building, Plaridel Street, Tel. 31-5331 to 63*

- **Honorary Consul of Chile**, *Aboitiz & Co. Building, Banilad, Tel. 231-2580, 231-0633*
- **Honorary Consul of Denmark**, *Unit 3, 6th floor MetroBank Plaza, Osmeña Boulevard, Tel. 253-3122, Fax 253-0773*
- **Honorary Consul of Great Britain**, *35 Paseo Eulalia, Maria Luisa State Park, Banilad, Tel. 234-6182*
- **Honorary Consul of Netherlands**, *Mataphil Compound, Tipolo, Mandaue, Tel. 82-291*
- **Honorary Consul of Norway**, *Aboitiz & Co. Building, Banilad, Tel. 90-464*
- **Honorary Consul General of Turkey**, *103 Plaridel Street, Tel. 95-533, 95-440*
- **Honorary Consul of Spain**, *476-6 Molave Street, Lahug, Tel. 231-1329*
- **Honorary Consul of Sweden**, *Visayan Electric Co., General Maxilom Avenue, Tel. 254-2842*
- **Honorary Consul of Thailand**, *Eastern Shipping Lines Building, MJ Cuenco Avenue, Tel. 93-013*

Post Office
The city's **main post office** is on Quezon Boulevard, near the pier.

Tourist Information & Maps
The **DOT**, GMC Plaza Building, Legaspi Street near Plaza Indeoendencia, *Tel. 254-2811*, is staffed with helpful and friendly personnel. Ask for Mr. Rafael Mercurio, a wealth of information on Cebu and Bacolod. The DOT has maps and information and can recommend tour agencies that offer packages such as city, Mactan Island, industrial, and evening tours. The DOT also has a clean bathroom. *The 24-hour emergency tourist assistance number is 254-1136.* The DOT has a desk at the international arrival area of the airport — look for Bebut Estillore, he is very helpful and a great person.

The **Cebu City Tourism Commission** is in City Hall.

For dive tours, see the Philippine Commission on Sports Scuba Diving, in the Philippine Tourism Authority office (Beside the DOT).

Some hotels may provide maps.

Travel Agencies
- **Eagle Wings Travel and Tours**, *Basement 1, Ayala Center, Tel. 315-711*
- **Fun & Sun Travel & Tours**, *2nd floor Krizia Building, Gorordo Avenue, Tel. 31-4620, Fax 31-4715* (for "dive safaris")
- **Intas Travel & Tours**, *ground floor, Shangri-La's Mactan Island Resort, Tel. 310-288 local 8901 to 03*
- **Rajah Tours**, *Suite no. 3 Astron Gestus Building., Gorordo Avenue, Tel. 31-2461 to 63, Fax 31-0852*

23. BOHOL

The **Chocolate Hills** are the best publicized attraction in **Bohol**, but the island's beaches and reefs, people, handicrafts, towns, and churches entice you to linger. The oldest stone church in the Philippines stands in **Baclayon** and there are many other interesting churches, three to four centuries old, on Bohol. The architecture of the churches is a blend of European, Mexican, and Moorish influence. They have ornately carved *retablos* and double façades, and a spacious and airy feeling. Many of the churches have beautifully painted ceilings. Bohol is also home to the rare tarsier and flying lemur, and many species of butterflies.

The capital of Bohol, **Tagbilaran**, is a quiet city with a range of hotels and lodges, a market, several handicraft shops, and numerous small restaurants. When you make your plans for traveling to Bohol, remember that the Philippines is a very fluid place and you could arrive to discover that everything is at a standstill due to a fiesta. Join in the festivities. The Boholanos will be delighted and it will be an experience for you to treasure. Bohol's best-known fiestas occur during May to July, especially **Tagbilaran City Day**, May 1, in honor of its patron, Saint Joseph the worker.

History

Bohol's contact with other civilizations antedates the Spanish "discovery" of the Philippines. Finds from the Anda Peninsula show that among the early settlers were people who used gold jewelry, death masks, and heavy wooden coffins, and who "beautified" their women by flattening and shaping their skulls.

Data also shows that Chinese traders frequented Bohol before the 5th century. Boholanos profited as middle-men: they took Chinese wares as far as the Moluccas and returned with spices, honey, and trinkets they used for bartering.

Before the Spanish came to Bohol, the main population center may have been on stilts between Panglao Island and the mainland. Legend says that the town was razed by Portuguese sailors who abducted one of the

TARSIERS, FLYING LEMURS, & BUTTERFLIES

Tarsiers are primitive primates that probably came from the root stock that eventually evolved into monkeys, apes, and men. These shy little nocturnal creatures with long tails, large round eyes, and fuzzy bodies are threatened with extinction due to the destruction of their forest habitat and poaching. It is extremely difficult to keep tarsiers alive in captivity.

If you are offered a caged tarsier (along with a story that it was born and raised in captivity), do think twice – although you may want to purchase it to set it free, keep in mind that, though you may save one tarsier, you are supporting this illegal trade, and, many more will be caught. Please do not buy the stuffed tarsiers either!

Flying lemurs, members of a family of gliding mammals, are roughly the same size as a house cat. They are not lemurs (primates) nor can they fly; but, the generous flap of skin between their legs and tail allows them to glide between tree branches. Like the tarsier, their principal enemy is man, who destroys their natural habitat and hunts them for food.

Bohol's forests teem with colorful butterflies from November through May, attracting many people from Japan and points beyond who net and preserve specimens. As butterflies hatch, mate, lay their eggs, and die within a few days (some within hours), a modest amount of butterfly hunting probably will not affect the survival of the species.

queens. As a result, Sultan Sikatuna and his people moved to Bool, which is just outside Tagbilaran City. Other sultans moved their people to Dapitan and other areas in Mindanao.

Legazpi's arrival in Bohol was peaceful, unlike most other places. Impressed with the economic possibilities trade would bring and by Sultan Sikatuna's friendliness, he signed a peace treaty with the sultan. Legazpi spread Christianity and initiated church building.

The peace treaty lasted 45 years. Just before Sikatuna died, he chose to be baptized. Feeling betrayed, many Muslims turned on Sikatuna's people and frequently raided Bohol.

Boholanos converted to Roman Catholicism but refused to acquiesce to friar abuses. In 1744, Dagohoy lead a successful revolt. For 85 years, Bohol remained an independent island within Spain's colony. The island's importance as a trading center declined. And although Bohol was eventually retaken by Spain, the Boholanos have never been easily suppressed: American colonizers often had problems that were exacerbated by violent retaliation, and the Boholanos did not accept Japanese rule. They moved their government away from Japanese control, printed their own money, and supplied local and allied forces with produce.

Since the end of the war, Bohol has remained a peaceful province. When the Spanish friars were ejected, Boholanos retained their farms and, as a result, a wealthy landed class never evolved. There are few extremely rich or very poor people in Bohol.

TAGBILARAN

The capital of Bohol, **Tagbilaran**, is a good base for great area hiking, scuba diving, and fun shopping. There are a number of nice resorts in and around town. Nearby **Panglao Island** has some nice beaches.

ARRIVALS & DEPARTURES

By Air

There are daily flights between Manila and Tagbilaran, and three flights a week between Cebu and Tagbilaran. Philippine Airlines is the only company serving these routes.

The airport is your typical small provincial airport. It is on the northern fringes of the city, and a tricycle will cost around 40¢ to town and around $5-8 to Panglao Island. Upon request, most resorts and hotels will pick you up.

By Sea

• **Bohol-Manila**. Two companies have a weekly trip: Sulpicio Lines ($15-60) and WGA SuperFerry ($21-58); the voyage takes 30 hours.
• **Bohol-Cebu**. WaterJet has daily 1.5-hour trips departing Cebu 4:30am, fare $8-16 per person. SuperCat has 1.5-hour trips departing Cebu at 5:00am and 11:00am daily, fare is $6 per person. Palacio Lines has trips three times a week that take four hours. TransAsia has daily trips departing Cebu at 7:30pm, the trip takes three hours, fare is $4-11 per person. WGA SuperFerry has one weekly trip that takes three hours, fare is $10-20.
• **Bohol-Mindanao**. Sulpicio Lines has a weekly trip to Dapitan and one to Iligan; the fare to both is $10-40.

GETTING AROUND

Public transportation serves all towns in Bohol. You should make arrangements in advance with your hotel for private transport. The Laos of Gie Garden and Momo Beach Resort are willing to arrange almost anything for guests, so long as adequate notice has been given and their schedules permit.

Two bridges connect Bohol and Panglao Islands. Tricycles and jeepneys will take you to Panglao and back. Negotiate the price beforehand. From Tagbilaran to points along the northeast coast or the southeast, you may hire a vehicle or go by public transport.

You can also make arrangements for renting a car with a driver from **Mantours,** *Ideal Cinema Building, CP Garcia Avenue, Tel. 411-4023, Fax 411-3592.*

WHERE TO STAY
Tagbilaran

BOHOL HOTEL LA ROCA, *Graham Avenue. Tel. 411-3179, 411-3796, Fax 411-3009. Manila reservations: Tel. 634-2029. 25 rooms. $22 per single, $25-34 per double, $39-50 per suite. Visa, Master Card.*

All rooms are air conditioned, have cable TV, and a bathroom. Facilities include a swimming pool, business center, and souvenir shop. La Roca has a restaurant and will make arrangements for island tours.

GIE GARDEN HOTEL, *18 MH del Pilar Street corner CP Garcia Avenue. Tel. 411-3182, 411-2031. Manila reservations: Tel. 50-9522, 59-2217. 20 rooms. $16 per single, $22 per double. Visa, Master Card, American Express, Diners.*

This is a pleasant well-run hotel with dark, homey, and clean rooms. All rooms are air conditioned, carpeted, and have bathrooms. The restaurant is on the second floor and serves good Chinese and Filipino dishes. Services offered include airport transfers, laundry, island tours, river safari, and diving.

CORLANDIA RESORT, *45 Graham Avenue. Tel. 411-3445. 14 rooms. $16 per single or $26 per double aircon, $11.50-21 per single or double non-aircon.*

Cottages vary in size: the largest is fan cooled and can take six people. All cottages have a bathroom. The resort is by the sea, you can swim off the beach, and there is a restaurant.

ISLAND LEISURE INN, *Ilaw International Center, Barangay Bool. Tel. 411-2482. 20 rooms. $10.50-15 per single, $13-20 per double.*

Rooms are simple, air conditioned, each has a bathroom. The nice looking long restaurant specializes in seafood and local dishes. There is a basketball court.

CASA JUANA, *2nd Floor JJ's Foodstream, CP Garcia Avenue. Tel. 411-3306. 10 rooms. $11.50 per single, $21 per double.*

All rooms are simple, air conditioned, and have a private bathroom. There is a restaurant and bar on the ground floor.

TAMBLOT PENSION HOUSE 1, *30 Tamblot Street. Tel. 411-2253, 411-3180. 6 rooms. $16 per single or double aircon, $7 per single or double non-aircon.*

Air conditioned rooms have a bathroom, fan-cooled rooms share a common bathroom. Rooms are simple and clean.

Panglao Island – North
TAMBLOT PENSION HOUSE 2, *Totulan, Dauis. Tel. 411-3180. 3 rooms. $20 per single or double, $46 for the chalet.*
The chalet is fully furnished, has two bedrooms, a kitchen, television, and a patio that faces the sea.

Panglao Island – West Coast
MOMO BEACH RESORT, *Bilisan. Tel. 411-3182. $60 per single or double cottage, all meals included. Visa, Master Card, American Express, Diners. Manila reservations: Tel. 59-2217.*
This place is well-managed and has lovely cottages nestled into the vegetation beside the beach. Meals are fresh seafood and local dishes, food is good. The staff are delightful, and can make arrangements for various tours.
PALM ISLAND RESORT, *Doljo. Tel. 411-3162. 12 rooms. $7.50 per single, $14 per double.*
Simple beachside fan-cooled cottages, each with their own bathroom. The restaurant serves seafood. Sports include billiards, volleyball, and table tennis. Palm Island is on a pretty stretch of white sand beach.

Balicasag Island
BALICASAG ISLAND DIVE RESORT, *Tel. 411-3369. Manila reservations: Tel. 812-1984, Fax 812-1164. 20 rooms. $42 per single, $50 per double. Visa, Master Card, American Express, Diners.*
This establishment is managed by the Philippine Tourism Authority. Each room is inside a simple native bamboo cottage, and is fan-cooled. There is diving and snorkeling off the island and the resort has a dive center.

East Coast
BOHOL BEACH CLUB, *Bolod. Tel. (via Cebu, code: 032) 231-4020. Cebu reservations: Tel. 254-0640. Manila reservations: Tel. 522-2301, Fax 522-2304. 49 rooms. $60-114 per single, $66-120 per double, $180 per suite, $11 per extra person. Visa, Master Card, American Express, Diners.*
Located on a lovely beach, this is Panglao Island's most up-scale resort. All rooms are air conditioned. Facilities include a swimming pool, giftshop, various table games, tennis, and scuba diving. There is a restaurant and bar.
ALONA KEW WHITE, *Alona Beach, Tawala. Tel. 411-4686, Fax 411-2471. 22 rooms. $32-57 per single or $34-63 per double aircon cottage, $22 per single or $25 per double non-aircon room.*
Some of the rooms are spacious and have a balcony. The restaurant is attractive, native-style, and serves seafood and local dishes. Facilities

include billiards, windsurfs, and scuba diving. The resort also rents jeepneys, cars, tricycles, and motorcycles.

BOHOL DIVER'S LODGE, *Alona Beach, Tawala. Tel. 198-8111, 198-8112. 37 rooms. $12-34 per single or double. Cebu reservations: Fax 253-6993.* This is a charming friendly dive resort. Rooms are simple, clean, fan-cooled, and have bathrooms. The restaurant serves seafood, European, and local dishes. The dive center is complete and professionally run. The place is managed by a Frenchman and the staff are friendly. Island hopping tours and motorcycle rental are available.

AQUATICA, *Alona Beach, Tawala. 16 rooms. $25 per single or double.* Rooms are in a nice white building with a nipa-thatched roof. All are fan-cooled and have a private bathroom. There is a restaurant and the bar has karaoke in the evenings.

ALONAVILLE, *Alona Beach, Tawala. 14 rooms, 2 dorms. $18 per single or double, $4 per dorm bed.* All 14 rooms have a private bathroom and are fan-cooled. The rooms are clean and there is a restaurant-bar. The diving facilities are complete and the resort can be crowded.

TGH CASA NOVA, *Alona Beach, Tawala. 10 rooms. $25 per single, $30 per double aircon. $12.50-17 per single $15-20 per double non-aircon.* This nice native-style resort has cottages of bamboo and nipa. All rooms have private bathrooms. There is a restaurant and facilities include a swimming pool, billiards, table tennis, and motorcycle rental. Diving can be arranged at the Bohol Diver's Lodge nearby.

PLAYA BLANCA, *Alona Beach, Tawala. 9 rooms. $9-12.50 per single or double.* This simple resort has rooms inside native-styled cottages. All rooms have a private bathroom. There is a restaurant and a swimming pool.

CRYSTAL COVE VILLAS, *EA Lim Drive, Tawala. Tel. 411-3179, Fax 411-3009. Manila reservations: Tel. 634-2029. 10 suites. $29 per single, $37 per double, $50 per triple, $64 per quad. Visa and Master Card.* The pleasant white structure is on a cliff and overlooks the sea. All suites are air conditioned and have a sun deck facing the sea. There is a kidney-shaped swimming pool and a restaurant-bar.

WHERE TO EAT

Most resorts and hotels have a restaurant or provide meals. The **GIE GARDEN HOTEL** has tasty dishes and specializes in Chinese food. For lunch or snacks, try the **GARDEN CAFE** at the cathedral grounds. It is run by and for the benefit of the deaf. In and about the market, a number of small places serve light meals and snacks, among them, **HORIZON RESTAURANT**, with an extensive menu. You'll also find a number of other restaurants along **Gallares Street**.

ALTURAS, *basement of Alturas Supermarket, B. Inting Street.*
Alturas is mainly a fast food place offering local, Chinese, and "Hawaiian" fare.
JJ'S SEAFOOD VILLAGE, *K of C Drive.*
Good seafood, Chinese, and local dishes.
BQ GARDEN, *Carlos P Garcia Avenue.*
Specializes in seafood and also has Chinese cuisine.
M-R SEAFOOD, *Tagbilaran Wharf Road.*
Serves native and seafood dishes.
SEABREEZE, *Gallares Street.*
Chinese and Filipino fare: specialties are the chicken and seafood.

SEEING THE SIGHTS

Tagbilaran

The capitol building has been restored to its original design by Rolando Butalid G, a former Governor. Another well-restored structure worth seeing is the **cathedral**.

If you are interested in old Spanish-era houses, there are two near Crossway Bridge. The **300-year-old house** of Tagbilaran's former mayor, José Maria Rocha, has been restored to its original form and is fascinating from the outside and the inside. Also at Crossway is a **market** that bustles with activity early in the mornings, which is also when boats come in. Try the local *puto*. It is a rice cake leavened with fermented *tuba* (coconut alcohol) that gives it a brown color.

The marker commemorating the **blood compact** between Sikatuna and Legazpi is one kilometer south from the city center. Here, the two leaders drew their blood, mixed it with wine, and drank it, sealing the peace pact between their people.

Panglao Island

Panglao Island, popular for its beaches, beach resorts, and dive areas, also has two interesting churches. Several establishments crowd the fringes of **Alona Beach**'s beautiful white sands. The pleasant **Momo Beach** is on the other side.

Dauis church is an ancient structure that has suffered extensive renovation — the façade is poorly done but the two baroque bell towers are interesting examples of the Moorish influence in Bohol's architecture. There is also a well inside the nave. Also in Dauis you may watch the jewelers remodel silver coins into rings and other items.

Hinagdanan Cave in Dauis is easy to visit. In Visayan, *hinagdanan* means laddered; at the cave you descend steps to a cavern with an underground pond. Many children dive into the cave; you probably will not want to join them as the water is not clean.

The **Panglao church** in Panglao town is interesting. What remains from the original church has been incorporated into a grotto. The current church was reconstructed following the old style, using coral blocks and wooden ceiling beams. Behind the church, the **watch tower** affords a pretty view of Balicasag, Gadang, and Puntod Islands.

For **Pamalican Island**, see *Southeast Coast* below.

NIGHTLIFE & ENTERTAINMENT

The few evening diversions include dancing at **Coralandia, Bohol Tropics**, and **BQ Garden**; bowling at **Marbella Leisure Plaza**, off Gallares Street near the sea; and having a few beers at one of the cafés or beer gardens.

SPORTS & RECREATION

Hiking

Bohol offers great hiking. Unfortunately, getting places has become difficult due to deterioration of roads. Camping can be arranged at the boy scout camps — **Magsaysay** in Bilar and **Roxas** in Valencia. Contact the Laos of Gie Garden, *Tel. 411-3182,* or the office of the Governor.

River Safari

A superb way to end your day is a boat trip up the **Loay River** from Loboc to Busay Falls. This safari, started by the Laos of Gie Garden and Momo Beach Resort, begins at **Loboc** where a *banca* takes you on a scenic trip up the Loay River. You may also grab a meal or snack at the floating restaurant that goes upstream. The trip ends at **Busay Falls** for a refreshing dip before you head back downstream into the sunset (depending on the schedule). Make arrangements in advance.

Bohol Beach Club and the **Bohol Divers' Lodge** also offer the Loay River trip.

Scuba Diving

Bohol's steep limestone walls are alive with marine life. Shallower sites host many species; you may see a whale shark. **Panglao Island** has a number of sites around its shores: **Duljo Point**, on the western shore; **Tangnan** and **Napaling**, on the northern coast; **Biking** on the east side; fronting **Alona Beach** and **Arco Point** off Bohol Beach Club, on the southeast; and nearby **Cervera Shoal**.

Other islands with good sites include:

• **Pamalican Island**: a marine sanctuary with shallow caves and marine life that includes sea turtles.
• **Balicasag Island**: a portion of its reef is a successfully protected sanctuary, with impressive corals housing tiny reef fish, morays, and other species.

• **Cabilao Island**: the main attraction is hammerheads, you may also see other sharks and fish

Most of the beach resorts cater to divers. An Open Water course will cost around $300-350, including equipment, lessons, and certification.

On Panglao Island, **Bohol Divers Lodge Sea Explorer**, Alona Beach, Panglao Island, *PO Box 48, Tagbilaran City, Tel. 198-8109, cellular #: 0917-320-1940, Cebu contact: 253-6993, Fax 340-0293*, offers reliable PADI Scuba Diving courses. An Open Water course costs $300, one boat dive is $30, two are $50-70 depending on destination. A 20% discount is given to divers who bring their own equipment. All dives include tanks, weights, transportation, and a guide.

The **Cabilao Island Sea Explorer**, *La Estrella Beach Resort, Loon, Cabilao Island, Cebu contact: Tel. 253-6993, Fax 340-0293*, is also recommended. Rates are about the same as Bohol Diver's Lodge.

SHOPPING

You can buy mats and intricate baskets at the **Agora market** and small shops nearby. At the market, you may encounter some persistent beggars, immigrants from Mindanao (especially Badjao).

Ilaw Community Center, just beyond and behind the blood compact marker, is a community development center funded by the United Nations and some individual countries. Its shop offers **handicrafts** from projects that the center is developing. There is also a canteen and rooms (available when not booked for a conference).

Dauis has a back-yard **jewelry** industry where you can watch old silver coins being remodeled into rings and other items. Quirino Hora **shell dealer** is near the market in Panglao town. You can find inexpensive and very rare shells for sale. Quirino Hora is very candid about the shells he offers.

North of Tagbilaran, Antequera is the distribution center for **exquisite baskets** made from *nito*, bamboo, *sig-id*, and other vines. Sunday is market day, and buyers come as early as 4:00am to purchase what is available and to place orders. By 8:00am, much of the better items are taken. Jeepneys ply the Tagbilaran-Antequera route hourly on Sundays; on other days there may be only three trips. The bus doesn't leave until it is full, and the last trip back may be as early as 3:00pm.

Loboc is where most Boholanos come to get new **carved wood furniture**. At Vigal's furniture shop, just beyond the plaza, you may see workers carving and the finished product, including stunning pieces of molave.

PRACTICAL INFORMATION

Banks & Money Changers

You may change money and travelers checks at the **PNB** along A. Clarin Street near the Plaza. There is a money changer along Carlos P Garcia Avenue between MH del Pilar Street and B. Inting Street.

Mail

The post office is near the Town Hall.

Tours & Tour Agencies

Most hotels and resorts offer tours around Bohol and Panglao. We have enjoyed the tours set up by the Laos of the Gie Garden Hotel and Momo Beach Resort. Three local companies offering tours are **Bohol Travel & Tours**, Ideal Cinema Building, Carlos P Garcia Avenue, *Tel. 411-3840, 411-2948*; **Mantours**, Ideal Cinema Building, Carlos P Garcia Avenue, *Tel. 411-4023, Fax 411-3592*; and **Sun Travel**, DWCT Building, Carlos P Garcia Avenue, *Tel. 411-2476, Fax 411-2645*.

THE NORTHEAST COAST

Between Tagbilaran and Tubigon, the departure point for the ferry to Cebu, the road is fairly good. Beyond Clarin, the road is less traveled and there are many bridges to cross at the northern end of the island where you will pass vast mangrove and nipa swamps. Every town has at least one point of interest, usually centered around the church and/or market. On a clear day along the coast, enjoy the spectacular views across the sea to Cebu.

Barangay **Taloto** has a seminary, and at neighboring **Manga** you can buy fresh fish and have it cooked on the beach. As you continue north, you will cross the winding **Abatan River** three times, and a vast nipa swamp. Nipa swamps have long been community property in Bohol. Anyone may harvest the nipa, and is obliged to leave enough of each plant to ensure adequate regrowth. Behind the imposing **church of Cortes** is a good view of the river mouth and a nipa swamp.

The ride to Antiquera is pleasant. You pass rice fields, foliage, villages, and hills. **Antiquera church** houses a nice palanquin. The outside of the church is not interesting. To get to **Inambacan Falls**, a road that starts about one kilometer from town leads to a river. You cross the river and follow it up stream to the falls and a cave that is fun for equipped advanced spelunkers.

Maribojoc church has lovely *retablos* and beautifully painted ceilings. Beyond Maribojoc, the **Punta Cruz watch tower** offers good views of Tagbilaran Bay and the coast of Panglao. The tower was once used as a look-out for pirates.

Next is **Loon**, Bohol's largest municipality, where fishing is the main industry. The pretty **church**, made of large coral blocks, has twin bell towers. Enter to see the beautifully painted ceilings, impressive *retablos*, tiled floors, and a massive archway that supports the choir loft. A long, wide staircase leads down from the church to town.

Sandigan and **Cabilao islands** are accessible by a combination of boat from Catagbacan and tricycle. Cabilao has a white sand beach, good diving, and a nice simple beach resort.

Calape church is ornate and gothic. The beautifully painted exterior depicts *palay* (unhulled rice) and *lanzones*. The interior is equally interesting, with columns, an ornate *retablo*, and pointed arches that exemplify Moorish influence.

The towns of Calape and Loon have images that many believe to be "miraculous." Loon houses the Lady of Light, and Calape has a miraculous virgin and a miraculous St. Anthony. Worshipers communicate with St. Anthony through an interpreter-spiritist. The images are in *barangays* near the towns; you will need a guide to locate them.

You pass lovely views of the channel and Cebu as you continue to **Tubigon**, an area known for its bananas and red sugar. It is the only place on Bohol that you will see *calesas* being used. Tubigon's old church, in need of maintenance, is large, with massive columns down the nave. Directly seaward from the church, the **wharf** has good views and cafeterias serving delicious *alimasag*, a deep sea crab. From the wharf, boats depart for Cebu; the trip takes two hours.

Off Tubigon is a private island with a white sand beach and a nice friendly resort: **INANURAN BEACH RESORT**, *Inanuran Island, two nautical miles from Tubigon, cellular Tel. 0912-501-9736, 502-4778, 10 rooms, $92 per person all meals included.* The resort has pretty bungalows, each with either a twin or double bed, minibar, bathroom, and private balcony. The restaurant serves French, international, and Filipino cuisines. You will be treated to fresh fruit juices and homemade French bread and pastries. Inanuran is well managed by a Frenchman with friendly staff.

The town of **Clarin** is pretty, there are broad-leafed San Francisco plants along the road and flowering bushes around the houses. The church has an attractive exterior, a central bell tower, and a double façade. Inland from town, a road leads to Carmen and the Chocolate Hills.

There are a number of interesting houses in *barangays* Badiang and Cogon. You may also see villagers weaving *buri* chairs and curtains.

There is an old Spanish church in **Inabanga**, a market, and restaurants — but watch your belongings in this town. Beyond Inabanga, several bridges cross rivers and streams that merge into nipa and mangrove swamps. There is a picturesque little bay by Buenavista, which is a collection of shacks.

The **Jetafe** church is small and interesting. The simple façade and *retablo* are both attractive, and the church has a handsome brown Sto Niño.

Talibon, the town of former president Carlos P Garcia, has an attractive old church with a convent school. You can get a good view of **Jau Island**, known for high-quality buntal hats, from the town. There is a small resort on the island, run by a Canadian-German. The resort has anchorage facilities for yachts.

The road from Talibon is flat, smooth, and straight. In Trinidad, where people from Jau come on Thursdays to do marketing, a road heads inland to Carmen.

THE SOUTHEAST COAST

The southeast coastal road is a long and pretty drive. You may combine this exploration with a visit to the Chocolate Hills (when the road is fixed) or the Loboc River Safari. All three cannot be happily managed in one day, however.

You may notice several mangrove swamps lining Bohol's coast. These areas serve as breeding ground for crabs and fish.

A kilometer before *poblacion* Baclayon, an **underground river** flows into the sea. During low tide, people wash their clothes in the freshwater pool; at high tide the water is salty. **Baclayon church**, built in 1595, is the oldest church in the Philippines. Inside the solid fortress-like structure are beautifully ornate *retablos* that still have a bit of their original gold leaf paint, and attractive *santos*. The convento was a later addition. It houses a small museum containing some interesting religious relics. To enter, ask permission from the priest. If you are here on Wednesday, market day, you will see fish, food, and handicrafts: mainly abaca and *buri* hats, mats, and rope.

Nearby **Pamalican Island** is lovely. Unfortunately, its reefs have suffered from past dynamite fishing. Off the northwest side of the island is a marine sanctuary, which is a good place to dive. To get here you can make arrangements with one of the dive operators on Alona Beach or with your resort or hotel, or rent a *banca* from either Panglao or Tagbilaran. Nita's Nipa Hut has simple cottages and is the only place to stay on the island.

Back on the mainland, further south, enter the **Alburquerque** church to see the beautifully painted ceilings. The church has a central bell tower, and a *convento* that is in need of repair. Wednesday is also market day here.

Clarin Beach is a pretty cove with beige sand and is fringed with houses. **Loay Church**, just after the beach, has a sculpture over the point of the façade. Inside are paintings on the ceiling, an ornate choir loft, and an unappealing canopy over the alter. Although the church is not very large, there are no pillars, which enhances its wonderful spacious and airy feeling. Near the church is the **Clarin House**, a fine example of a well-preserved one- or two-centuries old ancestral home. You need to ask permission from the occupants to enter. The rooms are airy and have wide floorboards, and pictures and mementos of the past.

Just past Loay, the road forks. Inland will take you to Loboc and the Chocolate Hills. The other road continues along the coast to Jagna.

As you pass Lila (its church is quite recent: 1925), the Maguey cactus growing beside the road is pounded, dried, and woven into rope, sacks, and doormats. From here, you have a good view of **Camiguin Island** and its **Mount Hibok-Hibok**. Continue north to **Dimiao** to see a seaside rock known as **MacArthur's hat** and its large church with a double façade and very nice *retablos*.

In front of the **Valencia**'s newish gothic church, statues of José Rizal and the Sacred Heart face each other; the Sacred Heart appears to be giving the free-thinking Rizal a lecture. About three kilometers from the main road is **Roxas Park**, with two natural pools. This is a boy scout camp. On the coast beyond Valencia, people come to swim and wash their clothes at the **Badiang Springs**, where water from under the mountains runs into a pool and over the hillside.

Jagna has a beautiful church with a high choir loft, semicircular façade, and ceilings painted in 1930 by Rey Francia, a Cebuano who painted many ceilings in Bohol. From the town's pier, boats depart for Camiguin, four hours by *banca*, and for Butuan in Mindanao. There are a few restaurants just before the pier; if the food doesn't look fresh, have it reheated or buy fish from the market and have it cooked in a restaurant. If you get the chance, try *calamay*, the town's delicacy made of coconut meat and served in the shell.

Continuing south, just before you get to "kilometer 78," is the pass where Bohol's guerrillas wreaked havoc on American forces in 1901 and the Japanese in 1945.

The **Anda Peninsula**, just beyond Guindulman, is an unspoiled area with impressive beaches and coves. A typhoon in 1984 damaged Anda's pretty church and most of the town's houses. There is one simple resort for overnights, the **Dap-dap Resort**.

On the other side of the peninsula, in **Lamanoc**, is a dig site of the National Museum. To visit, you must make prior arrangements with the National Museum in Manila (see the Manila chapter). The museum office in **Cogtong** displays a molave wood secondary burial coffin decorated with a reptile head motif on the lid, and some other finds. Apparently, the ancient people of Anda also flattened skulls, a practice that existed in other central Visayan islands and northern Mindanao. Anda finds date man's record on Bohol back to 10,000 BC. Next door in the fisheries school is an exhibit of fossils, some shell jewelry and Neolithic and Paleolithic stone tools, and some items of biological interest.

THE CHOCOLATE HILLS

Your first glimpse of this curious creation of nature will be when you fly in. To get a closer look, ask your hotel or resort to make arrangements. You should pack lunch, and the trip will take a day as the roads are in disrepair. Public transport will take more time.

The hills are "chocolate" between February and May, and become green after July, when rain revives the grass cover.

There are many stories about the origin of the Chocolate Hills. One legend tells of two giants that fought here: they threw boulders at each other, and when tired of the contest, left without cleaning up the battlefield. The other legend is of Arogo, a giant who fell in love with a mortal named Aloya. Arogo kidnapped her, but she did not love him and died. Grief-stricken, the giant cried many tears which ran into rivers and eroded the soil, forming the Chocolate Hills.

Scientific explanations include simple weathering of limestone formed beneath the sea and then uplifted; formation of the hills by suboceanic volcanism, then uplift of the seafloor; and a more recent theory, born from observations of similar structures, which maintains that as a massive volcano self-destructed it spewed huge blocks of stone. These were then covered with limestone and later uplifted from the ocean bed.

Whether green or brown, of mythical or scientific origins, the Chocolate Hills are impressive.

ARRIVALS & DEPARTURES

In 1996, the road to **Carmen** was in bad shape. You should inquire about the status before setting out. After it has been fixed it should take two hours to the hills by private vehicle, more by public conveyance. To take public transport from the main road in Tagbilaran, take a bus to the **Chocolate Hills Complex**, which is before Carmen. Ask the driver to let you off on the road to the complex. From there you have a one kilometer walk uphill.

If you pass the Loboc-Carmen route, stop by the Loboc church and furniture maker (see below). A few kilometers inland from Loboc is the Tontonan hydroelectric plant and park. Coming through the town of Bilar, you may hear rice pounding — families in this town demand large quantities of rice in exchange for a daughter's hand in marriage, so young men are kept quite busy.

WHERE TO STAY & EAT

The **CHOCOLATE HILLS COMPLEX** has a restaurant, dorm beds and rooms. They have water problems during dry months.

SEEING THE SIGHTS

Loboc River Safari

A superb way to end a day is to take a boat trip up the Loay River from Loboc to Busay Falls (see *Sports & Recreation* above). Be sure to leave time to investigate **Loboc** town and its church before the river trip.

Other Sights

Loboc church is massive and impressive. Note the faces of a Pope and angels in the upper portion of the exterior relief work; the lower part has been damaged. Enter to see ornate paintings (from 1926 and 1927) that decorate the ceilings and the lovely *retablos*.

Loboc also has a woodcarving and furniture industry; see *Shopping* above.

24. LEYTE & SAMAR

Leyte and **Samar** are the easternmost provinces of the Visayas, and both are less frequented tourist destinations, Samar even less so than Leyte. Seven of the country's national parks are found within Leyte and Samar, and the islands are rich with World War Two history.

Samar and Leyte are separated by the **San Juanico Strait**; Leyte lies south of the strait, Samar to the north.

TACLOBAN, LEYTE

Tacloban, the capital city of Leyte, is a major destination for those with Philippine World War Two ties. At **Red Beach**, just south of Tacloban in Palo, **General Douglas MacArthur** fulfilled his famous promise "I shall return": on October 20, 1944, with 700 ships and 174,000 soldiers, MacArthur landed along the coastline of Leyte. A major part of the city's tourism activities are based on this event. Many veterans and their families, Filipino, American, or Japanese, come to Tacloban to remember and pay their respects.

Prior to the Spanish arrival, Tacloban was a *barangay* of Basey, Samar. At the time, it was known as Kankabatok, meaning that it belonged to Kabatok, its leader and most prominent inhabitant. Tacloban was probably proclaimed a city in 1770; some believe that it was a year earlier. In 1830, Tacloban was made capital of Leyte.

Tacloban's name is derived from *"tarakluban."* During the time of Kabatok, the area was frequented by fisherfolk. A *"taklub"* is a bamboo tray that was used to catch crabs or shrimp, and when fishermen were asked where they were going, the reply would be *"tarakluban"* — the place where they use their *taklub*.

ARRIVALS & DEPARTURES
By Air

Several carriers fly between Tacloban and Manila: Cebu Pacific has a daily flight; Grand Air has flights on Monday, Wednesday, Friday,

Saturday, and Sunday; and Philippine Airlines has three daily flights. Flying time between Manila and Tacloban is 65 minutes. Philippine Airlines has flights to and from Cebu four days a week; flying time is 40 minutes.

Tacloban's airport is 11 kilometers south of the center. Jeepney fare is 80¢-$1 from the airport to town. You may also hire a car ($6). Some hotels offer airport shuttle service; Leyte Park and the MacArthur Park hotels will have you picked up from the airport.

By Sea

From Manila, the trip takes 30 hours. Sulpicio Lines ($13-60) and WGA SuperFerry ($18-58) each have two weekly trips.

• **Tacloban-Cebu**. The voyage aboard K&T Line takes 12 hours, there are three weekly trips; WGA SuperFerry has three weekly trips, travel time is 10 hours and fare is $12-40.

via Baybay: the one and three-quarter hour trip on WaterJet departs Cebu Monday, Wednesday, and Friday in the evenings, fare is $8-16. Baybay is a two and a half-hour bus ride from Tacloban.

via Maasin: the SuperCat has daily two-hour trips that depart Cebu at 9:00am and 1:30pm, fare is $4; Cokaliong's voyage takes 6-7 hours, trips are twice a week, fare is $5-20; Escaño goes once a week; Georgia, once a week; and TransAsia, twice weekly, 6-7 hours, fare is $10-20. Maasin is a three-hour bus ride from Tacloban.

via Ormoc: the SuperCat has six daily trips, travel time is two hours, and fare is $4; the WaterJet departs Cebu Tuesday, Thursday, Saturday, and Sunday, the trip takes two hours, and fare is $8-16; WGA SuperFerry has daily trips that take six hours, fare is $12-40. Ormoc is a three-hour bus ride from Tacloban.

By Land

Philitranco has daily trips from Manila that pass through Bicol. The bus is ferried to Catarman, and passes through Calbayog and Catbalogan, all in Samar. It arrives in Tacloban 28 hours after leaving Manila. From Tacloban, the bus continues southward through to Maasin, where it is ferried across the Surigao Strait to Surigao City.

GETTING AROUND

Jeepneys are the main form of public transport in the city. The top hotels can make arrangements for car hires and tours. There are PUs (taxis) for hire, although they are not as numerous as they are in other cities.

WHERE TO STAY

LEYTE PARK RESORT, *Magsaysay Boulevard. Tel. 325-6000, Fax 325-5587. Manila reservations: Tel. 924-0085. 90 rooms. $86 per single or double, $126 per cottage, $138 per suite. Visa, Master Card, American Express, Diners.*

The Leyte Park has some well-appointed rooms and cottages. All rooms are air conditioned and have a minibar and cable TV. Facilities include two swimming pools and tennis courts. The restaurant has good food, the specialties are seafood and local dishes.

MACARTHUR PARK HOTEL, *Candahug, Palo, just south of the city proper. Tel. 323-3015. Manila reservations: Tel. 812-1984, Fax 812-1164. 43 rooms. $60-69 per single, $69-76 per double, $110 per suite, $14 per extra bed. Visa, Master Card, American Express, Diners.*

The beachfront MacArthur Park has air conditioned rooms with a minibar and cable TV. The hotel is near MacArthur's landing site. Facilities include a swimming pool, and you may rent small sailboats and go fishing. There is a restaurant and a bar. Tours and car rentals can be arranged.

DIO ISLAND RESORT, *San José, approximately 20 minutes from downtown. Tel. 323-2389. 4 aircon, 10 non-aircon rooms. $67 per single or double aircon, $25 per single or double non-aircon*

The native-style air conditioned rooms are spacious and nice. Fronting the resort is a nice stretch of beach. There is a swimming pool, restaurant, and small disco.

ASIA STARS HOTEL, *P. Zamora Street. Tel. 325-3015. $28 per single or double, $50 per suite. Visa, Master Card.*

All rooms are nice, clean, air conditioned, and have cable TV. The staff are friendly and there is a restaurant.

TACLOBAN PLAZA, *J Romualdez Street. Tel. 325-5850. 43 rooms. $16-29 per single, $22-34 per double, $42 per suite.*

All rooms are air conditioned, clean, and have a private bathroom. The cheaper rooms are not carpeted, and the more expensive ones have a bathtub and a refrigerator. There is a small bowling alley (note: rooms directly above it are noisy) and a restaurant.

MANHATTAN INN, *Rizal Avenue. Tel. 321-4170. 49 rooms. $21 per single, $27 per double, $30 per suite.*

The rooms are simple, clean, air conditioned, and have bathrooms. There is a restaurant.

CASA ANSON, *Lopez Jaena Street. Tel. 321-4138. 17 rooms. $17 per single, $25 per double.*

This is a simple place with clean, air conditioned rooms and a restaurant.

For very simple and inexpensive ($5-15) lodging, try **Manobo's Lodge**, *P Zamora Street, Tel. 321-3727;* **Quarter Haus**, *Romualdez Street, Tel.*

325-5362; **Leyte State College House,** *P. Paterno Street, Tel. 321-3175;* **Rosenvil Pension,** *P Burgos Street, Tel. 321-2676;* and **Casa Real Inn,** *Real Street, Tel. 321-2523.*

WHERE TO EAT

LEYTE PARK, *Magsaysay Blvd.*
Excellent grilled seafood and a pleasant native ambiance.
MACARTHUR PARK, *Palo.*
Offers seafood and other native dishes.
DON'S CABIN, *Romualdez Street.*
This is a simple place with good chicken, also known for its pizza and steak.
ROYAL SEAFOODS, *Romualdez Street.*
Serves seafood and Chinese dishes.
MANDAUE FASTFOOD CENTER, *Romualdez Street.*
Offers a variety of quick and inexpensive meals or snacks.
SAVORY STEAK HOUSE, *P Zamora Street.*
Serves local steak, has tasty buttered fried chicken.
CHINATOWN, *P Zamora Street.*
Specializes in Chinese cuisine.
COVESIDE, *Sagkahan.*
Serves seafood and Filipino dishes.
AGUS SHED, *Old Road, Sagkahan.*
Serves native fare and some seafood.
SINUGBA, *San José, 20 minutes from downtown.*
Good and inexpensive grilled seafood.

SEEING THE SIGHTS

World War II Sights

The walk down World War II memory lane begins at MacArthur's landing site, at **Red Beach,** Palo. Here, larger-than-life-size statues depict General MacArthur, President Sergio Osmeña, Carlos P. Romulo, and several other men wading ashore. Also in Palo, a short hike up a 522-foot hill takes you to the memorial of **Hill 522,** more commonly called **Guindhangdan Hill** by the locals. Palo was the first town liberated in 1944, after having been heavily bombarded in order to destroy Japanese garrisons. You can explore several foxholes built by the Japanese. The **Monument of the Filipino Soldier** at the rotunda at Pawing, in Palo, is a tribute to Filipino soldiers who took part in the liberation of Leyte.

At **Hill 120** in Dulag, 34 kilometers south of Tacloban, the first American flag was raised by the US Army Liberation Forces on October 20, 1944. Currently, this site is a well-landscaped tropical garden with benches and tables, and, decent restrooms, and offers views of Leyte Gulf and the surrounding coastal towns.

In Burauen, approximately 17 kilometers west of Dulag, is a **Japanese War Memorial Cemetery**. This is the site of one of the fiercest battles that took place on Leyte during the liberation. You can see remnants of the airfield built by Japanese soldiers, and a pretty flower garden where Japanese visitors offer gifts and prayers for the departed.

The **Battle of Baluarte** took place in **Barugo**, 52 kilometers north of the city. Here, a monument with rifles, helmets, and bayonets marks the site of the historic battle between Filipino guerrilla forces and Japanese troops that took place on August 24, 1944. The battle was highly significant for the Filipinos, whose forces only had one reported casualty compared to only one Japanese survivor. If you are thirsty when you visit, ask around for fresh coconut juice — it will be served to you in the coconut shell.

Carlota Hills in Ormoc City, a three- or four-hour ride from the capital, houses an impressive marker. The **Philippine-Japan Peace Memorial**, which was put up by relatives of Japanese war veterans, commands picturesque views of Ormoc Bay.

Buga-Buga Hills in Villaba, 126 kilometers west of Tacloban, was the stronghold of General Suzuki. Here, a fierce battle claimed the lives of thousands of Japanese and hundreds of American soldiers.

City Sights

The city's significant World War Two sites include the **Price Mansion**, on Romualdez Street, where General MacArthur stayed. On the night of his arrival, MacArthur was narrowly missed by a Japanese bomb. The **Leyte Provincial Capitol**, fronting Plaza Libertad and the University of the Philippines, has murals of the landing of General MacArthur, President Osmeña, and the liberation forces. President Osmeña was billeted at the **Redoña House**, on T. Claudio Street, until the Philippine Commonwealth was reestablished in Manila.

If you are interested in archaeological findings, the **Divine Word University Museum** has some relics from the Sohoton Caves in Samar, a photo exhibit of the landing, and other interesting items. On display are two crania, one flattened (flat-top-skulls were "in vogue" for some Visayan and Mindanao women around the 12th century) and one coated with calcium carbonate, the compound stalagmites and stalactites are made of. Other displays include pieces of Ming and Sung dynasty pottery and porcelain that have been donated by wealthy families; some church accouterments; an exhibit of Mangyan (tribespeople from Mindoro) photos and artifacts; and historical documents and manuscripts.

The **Sto Niño Shrine and Heritage Museum** houses an image of the Santo Niño, said to be miraculous, and other objects collected by Imelda Marcos during the Marcos era. This included an awesome collection of carved ivory and Chinese porcelain. Each of the many rooms of the museum displays a motif representative of a different region or style. The museum is an extravagant showpiece for Filipino architecture and materials — ceilings made of wooden squares give the visual impression of the woven matting the area is well known for. The Imelda cult was strongly reinforced here in Tacloban. Most of Tacloban's tourist points were developed by Imelda Marcos, a native of Leyte.

Beside the shrine is the **Convention Center and Library**. Inside is an extensive library and 82 dioramas of Philippine cultural minorities.

You cannot help but notice the beautiful two-kilometer long **San Juanico Bridge** that snakes its way from the shallows and spans the very deep San Juanico Strait. It is the longest bridge in the Philippines.

Twelve kilometers southwest from Tacloban, the **Palo church** has some impressive *santos* and *retablos*. It's worthwhile checking out while you are visiting MacArthur's landing site.

SHOPPING

The **city market** is a good place for fresh fruit. **Waling-Waling** and other handicraft stores on the corner of Romualdez and Rizal Avenues have very good handicrafts, especially the colorful *banig* (mats), and abaca and bamboo products.

The **NACIDA handicrafts display center** in Palo also sells impressive handmade items. In **Basey**, Samar, you can watch people weave the colorful *banig*.

PRACTICAL INFORMATION

Banks

Most major local banks have a branch in Tacloban. **PNB** has a branch along Romualdez Street, and **Equitable** has a branch at the corner of Gomez Street and Rizal Avenue.

Mail

The post office is along Bonifacio St., near the port area.

Tourist Information

Your hotel or the helpful people at the **DOT**, Magsaysay Boulevard beside the Leyte Park Hotel, *Tel. 321-2048*, are the best sources for information and assistance with transport.

ORMOC, LEYTE

This quiet city has a pleasantly clean market where you can find some inexpensive baskets and other handicrafts.

Ormoc's main feature is **Lake Danao**, 20 kilometers from the city. The lake is part of a national park and offers a 10-kilometer circumferential road and trail, as well as other walks through pretty wild flora. You may sometimes see wild fauna as well. From here, a three-day-hike along the "Leyte Nature Trail" will take you to **Maginhaw National Park**. To stay overnight, you need a permit from the BFD Regional Office in Tacloban; also be sure to inquire about safety.

ARRIVALS & DEPARTURES

By Land

Several buses leave from Tacloban to Ormoc daily. The first trip is at 4:00am and the last is mid-afternoon. The trip takes three hours.

To get to Lake Danao, hire a vehicle or take public transport from Ormoc. One jeepney leaves Ormoc for Ga-as at about 6:00am, and returns immediately. From Ga-as it is about a five-kilometer walk to the lake. Other jeepneys go more frequently to *barangay* Milagro, which is about six kilometers from the lake.

By Sea

See Tacloban's *Arrivals & Departures* above.

WHERE TO STAY & EAT

DON FELIPE, *Bonifacio Street. Tel. 51-2460, 51-2007, Fax 51-2160. $17-34 per single or $19-37 per double aircon, $25-63 per suite, $10 per nonaircon room.*

The hotel is well-appointed and offers a good view of the area. The rooms are clean; price varies with size. The cheaper rooms are in the annex building. There is a restaurant.

PONGOS, *Bonifacio Street. Tel. 51-2481, 51-2482, 51-2211. $20 per single or double aircon, $25 per suite, $14 per non-aircon room.*

Rooms are simple and have private bathrooms. The restaurant has good food.

PONGOS LODGE, *c/o Pongos Hotel.*

Basic rooms for under $5.

LIMASAWA ISLAND

The first recorded mass in the Philippines was held on Limasawa in 1521. A cross in *barangay* Magallanes marks the site where the first mass took place. Limasawa has charming white sand beaches, mountains, and lagoons. Nearby **Panaon Island** has some areas good for diving and snorkeling.

ARRIVALS & DEPARTURES

The island is off the southern tip of Leyte. From Tacloban, it is a four-hour bus ride to Maasin plus a three-hour boat ride. From Cebu, Maasin is two hours by SuperCat; see Tacloban's *Arrivals & Departures*.

WHERE TO STAY

At press-time, there was only one place to stay offering two air conditioned studios. Make arrangements by writing the Limasawa municipal office at: Limasawa Municipal Office, Limasawa Island, Leyte.

BILIRAN & MARIPIPI ISLANDS

These islands north of Leyte offer beaches and extinct volcanoes for climbing. To climb **Biliran Volcano**, take a jeep to Caibiran and then get a guide to the camp. The summit is a one-hour-hike from camp. From Biliran, a 10-kilometer *banca* ride takes you to Maripipi. The smaller island has a 1,000-meter volcano and a very nice white beach with clear water in **Napo Cove**.

ARRIVALS & DEPARTURES

From **Tacloban**, buses leave from the wharf area to Naval and Almeria. The trip takes five hours, there are usually two buses that leave between 4:00 and 5:00am, then again between noon and 3:00pm. Another bus goes to Caibiran, leaving between 9:00 and 11:00am.

From **Ormoc**, buses leave Ormoc City's bus station daily between 4:30 and 5:30am; the trip takes two to two and a half hours.

WHERE TO STAY

There are two very basic places to stay on Biliran: **AGTA BEACH RESORT**, *Almeria, $18 per aircon room, $10 per non-aircon room*, has a pleasant restaurant and friendly staff; and **ROSEVIC**, *Vicentillo Street, Naval, $15 per aircon room, $10 per non-aircon room*.

SAMAR

The island of **Samar** is divided into three provinces: Northern Samar, Eastern Samar, and Samar. The province closest to Leyte is Samar. Being a relatively little known tourist destination, most accommodations are rather basic, and transportation is by bus or jeepney, unless you rent a car from Tacloban, which can be costly.

Access to the **Sohoton National Park** from Tacloban is fairly easy. Transport can be arranged by your hotel; consider renting a jeepney or car for the day so that you can come and go as you please. Jeepney fare is 80¢, and *banca* rental is $20-30.

ARRIVALS & DEPARTURES

By Air

Philippine Airlines has flights from Manila to Catarman every day except Saturday, and to Calbayog five days a week.

By Sea

Sulpicio Lines and WGA SuperFerry ply between Catbalogan and Manila once a week; the trips take 23 hours; and fare, on both, is $16-60.

From Matnog on the tip of Sorsogon, a number of ferries cross daily to Allen, Samar. The voyage takes an hour and a half.

By Land

Philitranco has daily trips from Manila to Leyte, passing through Samar from Allen to Catarman, Calbayog, and Catbalogan, then on to Tacloban in Leyte. Philippine Eagle also has trips between the four cities, and small buses serve routes between the cities (i.e., Catarman-Calbayog; Calbayog-Catbalogan, etc.). Jeepneys serve these and more remote routes.

SEEING THE SIGHTS

Sohoton National Park

The **Sohoton Natural Bridge National Park** is one excellent reason for naturalists and spelunkers to visit the area. The best time to visit is from March through early August; during rainy season the rivers may be too swift to navigate.

The park has numerous caves. Sohoton and Panhulugan caves are accessible by a *banca* ride and a short walk. **Panhulugan Cave**, near some cliffs, was used by guerrillas that fought the Spanish and later the Americans. From the cave area, rebels threw logs and stones down on enemies coming up the river, then disappeared quickly and could not be found by the colonial troops. The cave has numerous chambers and several very interesting formations. Park Officers can point out formations to you. Some have signs indicating their similarities to other things: a flow area looks like the Banaue rice terraces, a horizontal ribbon-like formation is compared to the Great Wall of China going past the Chocolate Hills of Bohol; there is a group of elephants, organ pipes, etc.

Sohoton Cave is a long tunnel near the Sohoton River, upstream from Panhulugan Cave. From Sohoton Cave, an hour's climb takes you to the **Sohoton Natural Bridge**. This entire park abounds with flora and fauna; although there has been some poaching, the efforts of the park personnel minimize it. Archaeologists have unearthed from the caves remains that include tools and items of the early inhabitants and Ming and Sung pottery and porcelain. Some of the finds are on display at the Divine Word University Museum in Tacloban.

A few hundred meters from the junction of the Sohoton River, the Basey River emerges from the mountainside. It is a nice place to swim, the waters are said to be pure and sweet.

To visit the national park, make arrangements ahead of time through the DOT office in Tacloban, *Tel. 321-2048*. Word will be sent, via the Bureau of Forest head office in Tacloban to the Park's officers, who will then arrange for a boat and an experienced guide to meet you when you arrive in Basey. *Banca* rentals cost $25. If you enjoyed your guide, show your appreciation with a tip.

Other sites of Samar are less frequented. The **Gubingob Caves** are in Calbiga, north of Basey. And Calbayog, "the city of waterfalls," is surrounded by several waterfalls. **Bangon Falls**, seven tiers of cascading water, is the most impressive. The area also has springs, the **Guinogo-an Cave**, and beaches in **Lo-ok** and **Bagacay**. These beaches are not frequented by tourists, and are typical of south sea tropical beaches – cream sand, blue water, and coconuts. You may stay at simple cottages on Lo-ok. As the area is not a frequented tourist destination, contact Linda Calesa of the **Calbayog Tourism Council**, *Tel. 201 (area code 5741)*.

From here, if you continue on a bus along the coastal highway, there are very pretty views between Calbayog and Allen, in Northern Samar.

Northern Samar

Catarman is the capital of Northern Samar. The tourism office, *Tel. 554-0206 (*call via the local long-distance operator) at the capitol site, is where you get information and assistance. Ask for Frumens Lagrimas, who can help make arrangements to tour the area and the surrounding islands. The city's festival, **Embajada**, is held on January 22. Activities are centered on a reenactment of the area's history. Groups stage the fight between the Spaniards and the natives during the quest to convert the natives to Christianity.

The **Balicuatro Islands**, north of Rosario, are reputed to have good diving. Unfortunately, there are no facilities and you will have to bring all your equipment, including tanks.

Dalupiri Island, southwest of Allen, is a great place to get away from urban life and noise. The one place to stay here is the **FLYING DOG RESORT**, *Manila reservations: Fax 521-5075*. The resort's native-style cottages are nestled between the tall coconut trees that line the shore.

Torches light the paths in the evening, and aside from guests, the only sounds heard are from the birds and insects. Rates are based on the number of people and include all meals and transfers from Allen.

West of Dalupiri is **Capul Island**. The island offers secluded beaches, World War Two memorabilia, an old Spanish church, and a watchtower. The 18th-century stone church and belfry stand on the site of the original wood and nipa church built in 1606. You can also see the stone watchtower, constructed in 1768 to warn of pirates. From the lighthouse built by the US army, you get a panoramic view of the San Bernardino Strait, and of Mayon Volcano on a clear day. The island also has two Japanese tunnels and two large caves with impressive stalactite and stalagmite formations.

Eastern Samar

More adventurous travelers will enjoy the history, beaches, snorkeling, diving, surfing, hiking, caves, and falls this province has to offer.

Very simple accommodations are available in Borongan and Guiuan. The **Eastern Samar Tourism Council** will help make arrangements and provide information and advice, *Tel. 830-0297 or 461-2155.*

From **Borongan**, the capital, a one-hour *banca* ride takes you to the **Lologayong Falls**. You may also go spelunking through the **Suhutan Cave** nearby.

Leyte Gulf, at the southern tip of Samar and east of Leyte, was the site of one of the biggest naval battles between the Allied Forces and the Japanese — **The Battle of Leyte Gulf**. Guiuan, on the southern tip of Samar, once housed **Navy 3149 Base**. The base was constructed for the final attack on Japan (Subic and Clark were bombed out of commission). A good runway and other structures from the base remain. Also in Guiuan is the 16th century **Church of the Immaculate Conception**. The original structure, carved altars and doors, and *santos* are still intact.

Off the shores from **Sulangan Beach**, 22 kilometers from Guiuan, the rare **golden cowrie** may be found. Sulangan is a long stretch of cream sand fringed with blue water.

Magellan's conquistadors landed on **Homonhon Island** on March 16, 1521. This completed the initial phase of the first recorded circumnavigation of the globe, and initiated the spread of Christianity in Asia. The island is a two-hour *banca* ride from Guiuan ($100 per *banca*, large enough for 25 people).

25. NORTHERN MINDANAO

Mindanao, the Philippines' second largest island, is a meeting place of many people from many cultural backgrounds. An adventurer's paradise, it is home to **Mt. Apo**, the tallest peak in the country (see Chapter 25, *Davao*, for more details); spectacular beaches (do you prefer your sand the consistency and color of sugar? or how about a shade of pink?); exotic fruits; a variety of wildlife, on land and under water; warm smiles; and much more.

The original tribal inhabitants, of Malay extraction, either were converted by more aggressive later immigrants, or moved successively deeper and deeper into the forests and mountains. The Muslim influence first came in the 14th century from Malaysia through the southern islands of Tawi-Tawi, Jolo, and Basilan. For many years, the Sultanate of Sulu ruled much of the Philippines and Borneo. By the 16th century, the Spaniards and a few Portuguese were attempting, with little success, to convert Mindanao Muslims to Christianity.

Because Mindanao was less densely populated than the Philippines' more northern islands, settlers were encouraged to go south. They found land that was untitled, and registered it as their own. The original inhabitants felt the land was theirs by rights of inheritance and/or Koranic law. The scene was set for many bitter wars and lasting enmity.

Although considered a Muslim island, most areas of Mindanao, especially around the coasts, have predominantly non-Muslim populations. Tribal and Muslim inhabitants feel justifiably bitter about their loss of lands, while Christians feel they and their forebears laid legitimate claim to the property. There is no easy solution to the problem.

Several groups feel the law will not work for them and have united to defend their people or claim power for themselves. Davao, General Santos, Zamboanga, Cagayan de Oro, Iligan, Butuan, Surigao, all major

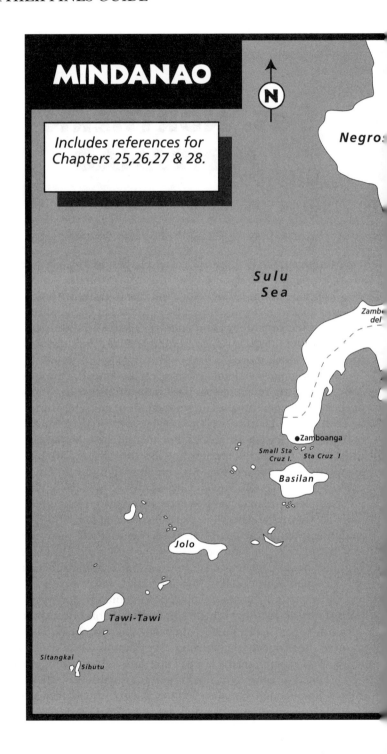

MINDANAO

N

Includes references for
Chapters 25,26,27 & 28.

Negros

Sulu
Sea

Zamb
del

●Zamboanga
Small Sta
Cruz I.   Sta Cruz I

Basilan

Jolo

Tawi-Tawi

Sitangkai
Sibutu

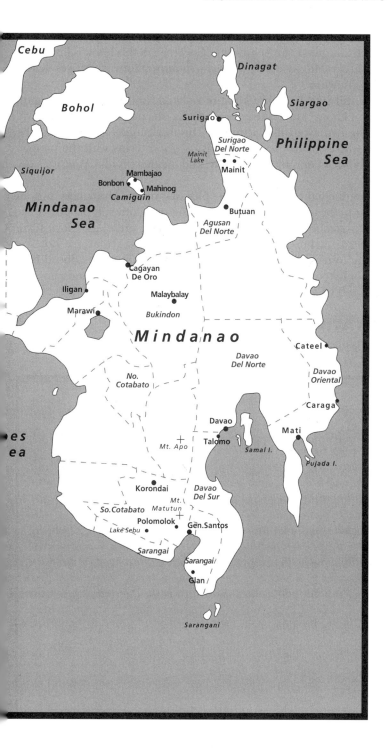

Cebu

Bohol

Dinagat

Siargao

Surigao

*Surigao
Del Norte*

**Philippine
Sea**

*Mainit
Lake*

Mainit

Siquijor

Mambajao

Bonbon   Mahinog

Camiguin

**Mindanao
Sea**

Butuan

*Agusan
Del Norte*

Cagayan
De Oro

Iligan

Malaybalay

Marawi

Bukindon

M i n d a n a o

Cateel

*Davao
Del Norte*

*Davao
Oriental*

*No.
Cotabato*

Caraga

Davao

Mati

Mt. Apo

Talomo

Samal I.

Pujada I.

Korondai

*Davao
Del Sur*

*Mt.
Matutun*

So.Cotabato

Polomolok

Gen.Santos

Lake Sebu

Sarangai

Sarangai

Glan

Sarangani

es
e a

population centers, are usually quite safe, as are the touristed areas (Camiguin, Siargao, Lake Sebu, etc.). Coverage in this book is limited to areas that are usually safe for travelers — inquire at tourism offices before venturing elsewhere.

There still remain a sprinkling of isolated "hot-spots" in the region (portions of Lanao, and less frequented areas deep in central Mindanao). It is also best to avoid the vicinity of Diwalwal unless accompanied by someone who is from the area and is on good terms with the people. Diwalwal is a gold mining community, and life there is like America's old wild west.

It is precisely the mixture of peoples that makes Mindanao such an interesting place to visit. The people, some of whom still proudly wear their tribal costumes, are fascinating. In most areas, the locals are genuinely warm, hospitable, and curious. In places that are not frequented by tourists, once a visitor has been properly introduced by a friend, people too are hospitable and warm. Although the landscape has been stripped of much of its fabled forests, it is still lovely.

ORIENTATION

This southernmost region of the Philippines is as diverse geographically as it is culturally. Towards the center of the main island it is

BIMP-EAGA

Once called the Philippines' back door, Mindanao is a booming area and a gateway to one of the world's fastest growing economic regions: the **East ASEAN Growth Area** *which is made up of Brunei Darusalam; the the Northern Sulu Sea area and east and west Kalimantan of Indonesia; Sabah, Sarawak, and Labuan of Malaysia; and Mindanao and Palawan of the Philippines. Some people believe that these areas were united before the Spanish colonial era.*

Officially formed in March 1994, this mouthful is more commonly referred to as EAGA (pronounced ee-ahga) or **BIMP-EAGA***. As with most unions, the aim is to strengthen economic cooperation among the members. Representatives from each area compose a work group. Within each work group, one country – the most advanced in a particular sector – is selected as the lead, and each work group is devoting immediate attention to sharing and developing the following:*

- *air linkage, with Brunei being the most advanced in this field*
- *sea linkage, with Indonesia leading*
- *tourism, with Malaysia as the leader*
- *fishing, with the Philippines leading*

mountainous, and relatively more lush than the lowlands, Luzon, and the Visayas. Mindanao's Mt. Apo (aptly called, as *Apo* means "grandfather") rises to 2,945 meters, and is the country's loftiest summit. As the mountains gradually slope towards the shorelines, farms, and plantations dot the landscape. Along the coastlines you'll find beaches with dark, pink, or cream sand, with consistencies ranging from course to fine. Under water, divers are treated to a variety of terrain and marine life; and although there is evidence of dynamiting, spear fishing, and overfishing, recent protection is encouraging new growth in some areas.

Mindanao is blessed with a favorable climate free of strong typhoons — it has much of the nation's agriculture-based industries. The southeast region is virtually typhoon-free and enjoys good weather year-round.

Tourism and tourist assistance facilities in some areas are well-developed and well-managed, but in others are less so. Most cities and major towns have a city tourism council, which is usually located in the office of the Governor or Mayor.

Visayan and Tagalog are the prominent languages spoken, especially in the major cities. If you listen carefully, you hear a different intonation or pronunciation in the way people speak those dialects (in the same way that Mexicans, Argentineans, and Bolivians accent their Spanish differently). Chavacano, a "corrupted" version of Spanish, with unconjugated verbs, is spoken in southern Zamboanga. Many other dialects are used in the region. In the cities and frequented tourist areas, most people speak good English. Even in the more remote areas, you will run into locals who can understand English.

Bugs & Leeches

Hikers venturing into the mountains and forests don't have to worry about dangerous wildlife (only the occasional drunk human, who is usually more annoying than harmful but should nevertheless be avoided). We have been told that there are leeches on Mt. Apo (we have not encountered any when we went); as a precaution, you should bring shirts with long sleeves, long pants (leggings, jogging pants, jeans), and rubber bands that you will use to block the sleeve and pant-leg entry ways.

In the mountains or at the beaches it is always handy to have insect repellent, especially in the evenings. We recommend Cutters, Off, and Avon's Skin-So-Soft, purportedly what the GIs used to combat mosquitoes.

Land

Much of rural Mindanao is used for farming, and land is cheap. As Mindanao is developing rapidly, the price of land in the cities is escalating. Some landowners increase their prices every week; a process sure to raise reasonable doubts among prospective investors. There are still some great deals on land on some of the islands, beachfront too.

Communications

There will be no problem getting to a phone in any of the cities. Most hotels have fax machines, Davao has an Internet cafe if you must check your e-mail while on vacation, and several places (most notably PT&T) send and receive telegrams. Local cellular phone coverage is available in the cities. Mail is generally slow and not always reliable. Siargao does not have phone lines yet, but one line connects the city hall of Siargao's General Luna to Surigao City. Visitors may use the line during office hours.

MINDANAO'S SPORTING LIFE

Trekking

*Mindanao has several mountains that are frequented by experienced mountaineers and avid trekkers. You should be physically fit if you are planning on scaling any of the mountains, as they are several hours' bus ride away from a major city with medical facilities. **Mount Kitanglad**, in Bukidnon Province, and **Mt. Hibok-Hibok** on Camiguin Island, are recommended climbs in the northern Mindanao.*

Kayaking

*One of the two places in the Philippines equipped with kayaks is **Siargao Island** (the other being Palawan). A French couple organize island-hopping and kayak trips around the area; a favorite is kayaking through the breathtaking **Suhoton Caves** into a blue lagoon surrounded by lush greenery.*

Fishing

*Mindanao has some great spots for deep-sea fishing, especially the Pacific Ocean area of **Surigao del Norte**. Unless you have a buddy in Manila with a yacht, your only bet is to charter a boat in Manila, which is very expensive.*

Tribes

*If you wish to visit the **Bukidnon** or **Manobo tribespeople**, make advance arrangements with Ella Baroso of the **Bukidnon Tourism Office**, Tel. (088841) 3272.*

Souvenirs

You can find great deals on souvenirs even in the cities. When not in a department store, you *must* bargain. Mindanao has some wonderful ethnic fabrics and brass work, although be forewarned that most "tribal antiques" are probably good remakes.

Weather

Mindanao is generally pleasant year round. Humidity is generally lower than on Luzon and in the Visayas. Expect a short period of rain, usually in the late afternoons. **Camiguin** is driest from April to June. **Surigao del Norte** has pronounced rainfall from November to January. **Zamboanga del Sur** is drier from November through April.

The mean temperature is 26.8°C or 80°F; and, as expected, at higher elevations (Mt. Apo, Lake Sebu, etc.) temperatures are lower.

CAGAYAN DE ORO

Industry-oriented **Cagayan de Oro**, the most developed city in northern Mindanao, covers a large and varied landscape. The downtown area bustles with shoppers and traffic, the harbor is filled with shipping activity, and a few industries hug the coastline, but much of the city consists of grassed flatlands and forested canyons. Upland, just into Bukidnon, is the vast **Del Monte plantation. Macahambus Cave and Gorge**, **Huluga Cave**, and **Catanico Falls**, are within city limits.

Among the earlier inhabitants of the area were the Bukidnon and Manobo. The Muslims, who arrived in the 16th century, pushed the tribes inland from the Cagayan de Oro River valley. The Muslims fiercely resisted the 18th century Spanish coming, but in turn were pushed inland by the influx of Christian immigrants from the Visayas and Luzon. The Christians successfully, although temporarily, defeated US forces in battle at Macahambus Cave in 1901. The cave remains one of the prettier and more interesting sites the city has to offer.

ARRIVALS & DEPARTURES

By Air

Cagayan de Oro's **Lumbia Airport** is small; its arrival and departure areas are open air, and clean. The porters are not as pushy as they tend to be in other places. The airport is located 10 kilometers west of the city center. The easiest way to get your hotel, or to the bus stations, is by a PU-taxi, which will cost under $6. (PU is short for public utility, an official class of vehicle.)

The flight from Manila takes roughly one hour and 20-40 minutes. From Manila, Cebu Pacific has daily morning flights, Grand Air has morning flights on all days except Tuesday and Thursday, and Philippine Airlines has three daily flights. Philippine Airlines also has flights (a) from Cebu on Monday, Wednesday, and Saturday; flight time is 35 minutes; (b) from Davao on Monday, Wednesday, and Saturday; the flight takes 35 minutes; and (c) from Cotobato on Tuesday, Thursday, and Saturday; the plane is small and takes 40 minutes.

By Sea

The **Macabalan Wharf** is three kilometers north of the city center. From Macabalan, WGA SuperFerry departs Manila for the 30-hour trip to Cagayan de Oro every day except Monday and Saturday. Unless you are on a tight budget, we recommend opting for the flight.

If you are going to/from Cebu, there are several options by sea. WaterJet has a daily trip ($20 for tourist or $26 for business class; for tickets purchased five days in advance, $12 for tourist or $17 for business class). The trip takes four hours and 30 minutes, and departs from Cebu at 10:45am, returning in the afternoon. WGA SuperFerry has trips three times a week ($10-$40) that take nine hours. Trans Asia plies the route daily ($10-$40), departing Cebu in the late afternoon, and takes 10 hours.

Getting to the city center by taxi from Macabalan should not cost more than $2.

By Land

The central bus terminal is next to (seems more like part of) the Agora Market. If you are there early in the morning or in the evening, be very careful, especially if you are female and traveling without male companions. Most bus trips start at 6:00am and run until 5:00pm; however, the long routes to Zamboanga and Davao also have night trips, similar to the "red eye" flights, but with no discounts on the fare.

To Camiguin. The trip can be done by bus (two hours) or PU vehicle (one hour, 30 minutes). Bachellor, Ceres, and Tomauis bus lines leave every 30 minutes and stop in Balingoan; the fare is $1.50. As Balingoan is not a final destination, you will not see a bus sign for it; look for buses that say to Butuan, and ask the bus drivers or conductors. At the bus depot in Balingoan, take a tricycle, for no more than 10¢ (P2.50) per person to the pier. Several air conditioned Tamaraw FX taxis wait at the Agora Market for passengers to Balingoan, and make for a more comfortable and direct ride than the bus. Fare is P50 (under $2) per person. The quickest and by far most expensive route to Balingoan is by taxi, which you can hire from your hotel or at the airport. If you are in a rush to meet the ferry (the ferries usually run a bit late) or to catch the last ferry to Camiguin (at 4:00pm), you may opt for renting a taxi. This will cost you from $30-

45; settle on the rate before you leave, and remember that bargaining does not hurt. The taxi driver may ask to be paid before you arrive at the wharf; this is so that he doesn't have to pay a fee (probably unofficial) to the "wharf officials." Some taxis wait around for ferries to dock, so they can get a passenger on the return trip; the fare for the return trip is much cheaper, and can be up to half off.

To Bukidnon. This scenic trip takes an hour to the Del Monte Plantation and roughly two hours to the capital, ($1.50 for non-aircon, $3 for aircon buses). Bachellor, Ceres, Rural Mindanao Transit (RMT), and Tomauis have several daily trips.

To Butuan. The rather uninteresting trip takes four hours, and you arrive at a busy depot that is dusty and full of very pushy porters; if you are carrying a lot and are changing buses (to Surigao), then a porter can come in useful. Do not pay over $1, unless you really have a lot of heavy baggage, and settle on the price before your bag gets carried, or you may get a taste of an attitude and some local swear words. Bachellor and Ceres lines go to Butuan.

To Surigao. Only a few buses continue to Surigao after stopping in Butuan. Bachellor is the only bus line that runs between Surigao and Butuan, so it is easier to get on a Bachellor bus to begin with. Look for any bus going to Butuan, then change to a bus that has a sign indicating it goes to Surigao. The trip between Butuan and Surigao cities takes two hours, the buses are not air conditioned, and they charge $1.75 per passenger. The trip is scenic, especially when you near Mainit Lake, a 17,000-hectare body of water that lies between the provinces of Agusan del Norte and Surigao del Norte.

To Iligan. RMT and Bachellor, sister companies, ply the two-hour Cagayan de Oro-Iligan route several times a day ($1.75 non-aircon, $3 aircon).

To Davao. The scenic trip takes seven to eight hours, and bits of the road are rough. Both Bachellor and Ceres serve this route; the trip costs $10 via Butuan and $6 via Bukidnon. The Bukidnon route is rougher and buses are not air conditioned.

To Zamboanga. This 10-hour trip, partly on rough roads, is served by Bachellor, Ceres, and RMT ($6). Several buses leave daily, from 4:30am to 7:00am.

ORIENTATION

The city has pleasant weather most of the year, with rains from June to October. Unlike parts of Luzon and the Visayas, the area has not yet been hit badly by a typhoon. As expected in most cities, streets tend to get dusty as the day progresses. It is easy to catch a taxi or jeep as there are no regulations against stopping anywhere. The taxi drivers are generally

NORTHERN MINDANAO

Cagayan de Oro serves as a jump-off point for excursions in and about northern Mindanao, especially to Camiguin Island, Bukidnon, Iligan, and Marawi City.

Most of Mindanao is historically restive, and you cannot be sure until you arrive which of the remote areas are calm and which are not at any particular time. It is best not to travel into the remote areas of Lanao. While in Cagayan de Oro, check with the Regional Tourism Office in the Pelaez Sports Center before venturing into remote areas, and with the City Tourism Office in the basement of the building behind City Hall before visiting the more rural city areas.

very friendly and curious; the usual questions you will encounter are: Where do you come from? What are you doing here? Feel free to ask them questions too; they like it.

Most of the service-oriented people (the hotel staff, drivers, restaurant staff, etc.) are very helpful and friendly. However, walking around on the streets, we felt that people were staring, not in a friendly curious way, but in a not too warm look that seemed to say: "What are you doing here?" The amicable curator of the shell museum warns against walking around alone, especially if you are female.

GETTING AROUND TOWN

Most hotels either have rental car services or can arrange to rent a car for you. Car rental agencies include **Triple C** at the VIP, *Tel. 728-856*, Lauremar, *Tel. 735-411*, and the main office, *Tel. 727-136*; **Nissan Limousine Service** (priciest for out-of-town trips), available 24 hours a day at the Pryce Hotel, *Tel. 725-776*, Dynasty Court, *Tel. 725-934*, and at the Jacutin Building, *Tel. 727-928*; and **House of Travel Inc**, *Tel. 726-891*. All agencies rent cars with drivers, Triple C will rent cars with out drivers. Rates are generally the same and will run from $20 for three hours; $35 to Del Monte; $50 to Balingoan, Malaybalay, or Iligan; and $250 to $310 to Davao (all rates quoted are for one way and include a driver).

There are also several private taxi services that work in a group or under one person. You will usually find them waiting outside the downtown hotels, and their rates are cheaper and you can bargain — we paid $28 for a one-way trip to Balingoan.

To get around downtown, jeepneys are relatively safe during the daytime and are much cheaper than taxis (10¢ to 40¢). Don't take them alone at night or get on one without any passengers. Although you can use jeepneys to visit the outskirts, for your return trip you may be waiting on the side of the road for a long time before one flies by. To go to the Macahambus Gorge, a jeepney ride costs 40¢. A taxi will cost $5 but you can make arrangements to be picked up at a specified time.

WHERE TO STAY

Most hotels are located downtown. The exceptions are the priciest hotel and the beach resorts. The rates mentioned below include tax and service charge. Hotel staff are generally courteous, efficient, and helpful with arranging transportation. Most places offer discounts for groups and long-term stays.

Better Hotels

PRYCE PLAZA, *Carmen Hill. Tel. 722-791 to 93, Fax 722-687. Manila reservations: Tel. 818-3421. $100-125 per single, $115-143 per double, $161-185 per suite, $13 extra bed. Visa, Master Card, American Express, Diners.*

Located on a hill, under 10 minutes from downtown, this is Cagayan de Oro's top hotel. It has a great view of the city and Macajalar Bay. Rooms have the expected air conditioning, cable TV, and carpets. The rooms are nicely decorated, with burgundy and cream being the predominant colors. Beds are comfortable and firm. Bathrooms are done in marble, are spacious, and have bathtubs. Most of the standard rooms face the driveway; the superior and deluxe rooms face the city and overlook the pool, which gives you a nice view, especially at night. The deluxe rooms also have a balcony.

Service is very good, the pool is small but long enough to do laps, and there are three restaurants and a music lounge. Car rental service is available at the front desk.

Moderate Hotels

VIP HOTEL, *Don Apolinar Velez (or A. Velez) Street. Tel. 726-080, 726-552. $25-36 per single, $30-45 per double, $54-107 per suite. Visa, Master Card, American Express.*

Right smack in downtown on the main street, this is one of the oldest hotels, and is slowly undergoing renovation. The new rooms are much nicer and although they cost slightly more, request one. All rooms are air conditioned and carpeted; furnishing is simple, there is cable TV, and some bathrooms have tubs. The hotel has many faithful clients, mostly businessmen, as it is well-managed and the bellmen are very attentive and look out for the safety of guests. Fax services are provided, and there is a car rental desk and a travel agency on the ground floor.

SOUTHWINDS, *Captain Vicente Roa Ext. Tel. 727-623, 724-803. 31 rooms. $26-33 per single or double, $43 suite. Visa, Master Card, American Express.*

One of the newer hotels in the city, this small place has very nice, clean, and spacious rooms for the price. The staff is very friendly and seem eager to please guests. All rooms are air conditioned and have cable TV; "executive" rooms and the suite have a mini-bar. Although the furnishings in the rooms are simple, it is refreshingly done, and all rooms are bright.

There is a coffee shop and bar, function rooms, and services offered include fax, photo copying, computer, laundry, and car rental. The reception will also assist in booking/reconfirming tickets for both airline and shipping companies.

HOTEL CONCHITA, *Yacapin Ext. corner Guillermo Street. Tel. 728-361, 727-899, 718-122, Fax 727-962, 727-355. 62 rooms. $20-37 per single, $25-47 per double, $70 in suites, $8 per extra adult. Visa, Master Card, Diners.*

Conveniently located near the Cogon Market, all rooms are centrally air conditioned, carpeted, and have cable TV. Rooms are plainly furnished and small, yet bright and comfortable. The suites (three) are spacious and do not seem to be occupied often. There are two restaurants: one specializes in Chinese food, the other is a rooftop grill. This hotel seems to be frequented by Chinese businessmen. There is a small business center and secretarial services can be arranged. The hotel has function rooms and a ballroom. Other services available include laundry, car rental, and a battery charger for Motorola cellular phones.

DELUXE HOTEL, *Capt. Vicente Roa. Tel. 726-527. 40 rooms. $23-28 per single, $28-34 per double, $40-63 per suite. Visa and Master Card.*

Also near the Cogon Market, this hotel, not as deluxe as its name, could use renovation. I recommend the "deluxe" rooms: for $5 more you get a bathtub, a larger room, and fresher air than in the area with the "standard" rooms. Rooms are small but clean. The hotel's Silver Court Chinese restaurant is popular with the city folk.

DYNASTY COURT HOTEL, *corner of Tiano and Hayes Street. Tel. 727-908, 726-876, 724-516, Fax 727-825. 96 rooms. $36-48 per single, $43-66 per double, $80-101 per suite, $9 per extra person, $9 extra bed. Visa, Master Card.*

The largest hotel in the center, the Dynasty has nice rooms that are more spacious than most other hotels in town. Although the corridors are dimly lit, lighting in the rooms is adequate. All rooms are air conditioned, and have pretty paintings on the walls. Services offered include mail and laundry. Its Chinese restaurant is very good, and a favorite with the local Chinese Filipino community.

GRAND CITY HOTEL, *A Velez Street. Tel. 723-551, Fax 723-658. 47 rooms. $29-43 per single or double.*

Centrally located, this small hotel has a nice lobby of marble and granite, with wood trimmings. The staff is attentive and efficient. Rooms are small but clean, and the headboards on some of the double beds are a unique fan shape. All rooms are air conditioned and have cable TV. The restaurant specializes in seafood; the hotel also has a bar, function rooms, and a ballroom.

CASA CRYSTALLA, *T Chaves corner Pabayo Street. Tel. 726-600, 722-465, Fax 722-480. $21-38 per single, $25-38 per double. Visa, Master Card.*

All rooms in this simple hotel are air conditioned and have cable TV. The rooms are very clean but quite small and tend to be on the dim side. The bellboy is attentive and courteous; however, on my last visit the receptionist was chit-chatting on the phone while I was left waiting for her to finish her conversation. Mom's Corner, the coffee shop, is popular with university students. Lunch and dinner cost $2-3, and breakfast, $2.50-3.50. There is also a conference room, and services offered include laundry and reconfirming/booking plane tickets.

VACATION HOTEL DE ORO, *Ramon Chavez Street. Tel. 723-263, 723-241, Fax 727-715. 46 rooms. $41 per single, $50 per double, $70 for suites. Visa, Master Card, American Express.*

This hotel is undergoing a needed renovation. All rooms are air conditioned, have cable TV, minibar, and are carpeted. Although the rooms are a bit dark, the furniture is nice and is of ethnic Mindanao designs. The staff is courteous, there is a pool and jacuzzi, and services offered include a business center, laundry, car rental, and airline information. There is a 24-hour coffee shop (good iced tea; a bar; and ballroom dancing is offered on Sundays to Tuesdays in the music lounge.

Budget Hotels

LAMAR INN, *JR Borja Street near VIP Hotel. Tel. 723-474. $20-25 per single or double.*

This budget hotel is a sister establishment of the VIP, and as expected it is well-managed with friendly and efficient staff. All rooms have air conditioning and are carpeted.

GOODNEWS TRAVELLERS INN, *Capt. Vicente Roa. Tel. 728-244 to 48, Fax 728-255. $17 per single, $23 per double, $28 per triple, $36 per "family" (4 people).*

This small hotel is conveniently located near the Cogon Market. Rooms are small, clean, and all are air conditioned and have cable TV. The coffee shop serves mostly fastfood, and there is an in-house travel agency.

WEST SIDE TOURIST INN, *Serina Street. Tel. 723-185, 727-786. 16 rooms. $17-19 per single or double, $32 per suite.*

When you walk in, you will be greeted by the friendly and cheerful staff. The inn is right across the bridge from City Hall. All rooms are simple and very clean, air conditioned, and have cable TV. Its restaurant, Cipriano's, serves western and local fare, and on Thursday nights has ballroom dancing.

MEGA PENSION HOUSE, *MegaHomes subdivision. Tel. 724-815, 724-831. 44 rooms. $14 per single or double, $30 per "family" (four people).*

This place is highly recommended for budget travelers. It is cheap, clean, safe, and the staff is friendly.

Beach Resorts

LAUREMAR BEACH HOTEL, *Opol. Tel. 735-411, Fax 726-441. 37 rooms. $43 per single or double, $105 per suite. Visa, Master Card.*

One of the few hotels on the outskirts of the city, it is a 15-minute car ride to downtown. This attractive, three-story resort, U-shaped with white-washed walls, looks like a typical beach hotel. The atmosphere here is more relaxed. The small but simple open-air lobby with wicker sofas exudes a homey feeling. The rooms are very nice, and all have air conditioning and have a view of the pool area.

The three suites are tastefully decorated with native wood furniture, a divider separates the bedroom from the livingroom-bar where a basket of fresh fruit awaits guests, and glass sliding doors open up to a small balcony. The suites are air conditioned, and have televisions and marble bathrooms with tubs. The regular rooms are also decorated with local furniture, are air conditioned, have televisions, and marble bathrooms with showers. There are two restaurants: Mama Iyay's, which looks into the pool area, serves Asian and local fare; and the Surfside Deck offers grilled food.

HARBOR LIGHTS, *Old Road, Gusa, 5 minutes northeast from downtown. Tel. 724-878, 726-022, 732-771. 31 rooms. $41 per single or double, $72 per suite.*

This pretty place is a two-story L-shaped white building and has magenta bougainvillea vines winding up the posts and grills to the second floor. The entrance leads to the small reception area and a mini courtyard garden with tropical plants and flowers. The rooms are nice, very clean, and furnished with white rattan. All rooms are air conditioned and face the pool, lawn, and harbor. The suites are larger, and have a living room area and a bathtub. The restaurant serves seafood and Filipino cuisine.

CHA-LI BEACH RESORT, *Cugman Old Provincial Road. Tel. 722-301, 732-929, Fax 732-840. 30 rooms, 16 cottages, and expanding. $34-39 per single or double, $34-44 per cottage. Visa, Master Card.*

Approximately 12 minutes from the center of Cagayan de Oro, Cha-Li is a simple resort that includes in its regular clients multinationals that book foreign consultants who are in town on projects here, and large local companies using the resort for seminars. The cottages are cute, made of stone and bamboo with nipa roofs. Rooms are simple and large as they can fit up to 10 beds (tight), five comfortably. All rooms are fully air conditioned and have cable TV.

Amenities include a swimming pool, a court that can be used for basketball or tennis, and function rooms. The resort also offers fax, transportation, and laundry services. The restaurant specializes in seafood and native fare. Bert, the manager, is a friendly guy and does a good job of taking care of the place. The staff is a bit shy, but friendly and efficient.

WHERE TO EAT

The city has many restaurants, and as long as you are not expecting fancy gourmet food you will not be disappointed. Fruit stands on the corner of Abejuela and Rizal and a block from the VIP on A Velez can provide between-meal nourishment. For breakfast, try tasty little white *puto* (rice cake), available in the vegetable section of Cogon Market in the mornings until about 10 o'clock. Chicken seems to be a specialty of the area, and if you are looking for a tasty quick meal, the city has many places for *lechon manok* (roasted chicken) — **King Roy's** and **Coron Coron** are popular and the chicken is succulent. The more adventurous can try the countless barbeque stands found on the sidewalks.

There are several other fast food-type places that serve your standard local burgers made of beef or pork, as well as fried chicken and pizza. **Gaisano**, **Oro Rama**, **Plaza Fair**, and **Lim Ket Kai** all have food courts where you can take your pick of various fast food.

Hotel restaurants generally serve continental (western) and Filipino fare. Stick to main dishes, as sandwiches tend to be light on the fillings and heavy on the mayo.

Service in most establishments comes with a smile, which is not what you usually encounter on the streets. Expect to spend $2.50-$6 for a full meal in Cagayan de Oro. Drinks and soft drinks will cost around 60¢, and bottled water, 75¢.

Downtown

PATIO RESTAURANT, *A Velez Street in the VIP Hotel.*

Tasty food; as in most places, the local food is recommended. This casual restaurant and coffee shop seems to be popular with the local politicians. The staff is friendly.

THE GRILL, *Corrales corner Yakapin Street.*

Serves fish, chicken, pork, or beef; obviously, grilled is the specialty, though you can order other local dishes.

SUGBAHAN, *R Chavez corner Corrales Street.*

Serves good local food; grilled specialties include fresh seafood.

TIA NANANGS, *R Chavez corner Corrales Street.*

Good Filipino food in a homey setting.

CONSUELOS, *Corrales Street across from Sugbahan.*

A popular dining place with the local city people; considered one of the finer dining places. Steaks are the specialty.

FIESTA DE ORO, *beside the De Luxe Hotel.*

A native-style restaurant specializing in *ihaw-ihaw* (barbeque).

PAOLO'S, *A Velez corner Gaerlan Street.*

Another finer dining place, specializes in Italian food, but also serves sashimi, which tastes better than the pastas. Dim yet charming inside, what we liked about the restaurant is the nice decor, which gives the ambiance of a dark Italian place. The service is very good.

DYNASTY COURT, *in the Dynasty Court Hotel.*

Good Chinese food and courteous service.

GRAND CAPRICE, *across from Lim Ket Kai center.*

Another place to go for good Chinese cuisine. This very large restaurant is popular for banquets.

SILVER COURT, *in the De Luxe Hotel.*

Another large Chinese restaurant, this place is popular with the locals.

City Fringes

CAFE CAGAYAN, *in the Pryce Hotel on the way to the airport.*

This place has one of the best iced teas we have had traveling around the country; although the tea is pre-sweetened the sugar is not overdone. The specialty is steak (imported from the US). The food and service are very good, and, as it is in the most upscale hotel, it is pricier ($8-$12 for a full meal).

SURFSIDE DECK, *in Lauremar Resort, Opol.*

On top of a boardwalk spanning the hotel's beachfront, this is a great place for a late afternoon fruit shake and snack (french fries are soft yet crisp on the outside) where you can occasionally watch a fisherman dragging his net in the shallows. The specialty is grilled food, and the staff is friendly.

CHA-LI, HARBOR LIGHTS, and **BULAKEÑA BY THE BAY,** *all near each other in Cugman,* are by the sea and specialize in seafood and Filipino cuisine. All are popular for locals who like to bring dates for a change of scenery.

SEEING THE SIGHTS

Xavier University's **Museo de Oro** is an important stop for visitors who are interested in the city's past. The museum displays include exhibits of prehistoric archaeological finds, Spanish-era historical relics, and artifacts of and ethnological information about current Mindanao tribes, mainly the local Bukidnon and Manobo, but also the Maranao, T'Boli, and Mandaya. Among the finds exhibited are artifacts excavated from the **Huluga Cave**. Located eight kilometers south of the city, this cave yielded evidence of a settlement that dates back to between 400 BC and 200 AD. As the cave and dig site have been completely excavated, there is not much else to see at Huluga Cave.

Xavier University has good archives pertinent to the above fields. For more in-depth information than the museum displays, contact Fr. Demetrio, Museum Curator, or Joy Enriquez, a professor at the University, who is often at the museum. The museum is open weekdays, 8:00am-noon, 1:00-5:00pm; special arrangements can be made for weekends.

Macahambus Cave is 14 kilometers southeast of the city, about 30 minutes by road. You may hire a taxi ($6) or take a Talacag jeepney from Carmen market and tell the driver you want to get off at Macahambus (40¢ per person). The jeepneys leave at 1-2 hour intervals. Bring a powerful flashlight.

The cave is of aesthetic rather than archaeological interest. A short walk through it brings you to a spectacular view of the Cagayan River hundreds of feet below. Walk carefully; the floor is slippery.

Continue uphill on the road past the cave, and turn right on a flagstone path. Walk through the houses to the gorge. Descend steep iron steps, 50 meters down to a river that flows through the gorge and gurgles out through a cave. Eons ago, the underground river's roof collapsed, creating this massive hole now filled with lush vegetation. One tall tree pokes its way through the top of a gorge.

Several **beach resorts** are within five to 15 minutes of the city. Unfortunately, Cagayan de Oro's shoreline is not impressive, as the water can be murky at times due to silt washed in from the Cagayan River. The resorts, however, do provide a refreshing change of scenery from the city, you get a nice view looking into the bay, and fresh sea breeze. Lauremar in Opol is a nice place for afternoon drinks, snacks, or a seaside dinner. You may also see fishermen dragging nets in the shallow waters. In Cugman, there are Cha-Li, Harbor Lights, and Bulakeña by the Bay; all specialize in seafood.

Other things to do in Cagayan de Oro city proper include strolling around **Gaston Park**, which fronts San Agustin Cathedral, and if you are interested in **shells**, see the **Shell Museum** in the City Library on A Velez Street at the Pelaez Sport Center. The Museum houses the extensive and well kept collection of Delicia Sontillana. If the door is closed, ask for Nelson Jabulin, the museum's friendly caretaker, at the entrance to the library.

NIGHTLIFE & ENTERTAINMENT

Cagayan de Oro does not seem like a city with too many night owls, but, there are a few nice places. The two popular discos are **Gonzi**, across from the Dynasty Court Hotel, and **Colors**, across from the Philtown Hotel.

Near the Lim Ket Kai center is the **Jazz Club**, a small but nice place for live music that ranges from jazz to rock, and you better like it loud. If you feel like singing, next door is the **Pyramid Karaoke Bar**. For a more relaxing scene, the VIP Hotel's cozy **Piano Bar** has a very talented pianist. The Pryce Plaza Hotel also has a music lounge.

SHOPPING

Shopping in the city is limited to a few wood, coconut, and brass handicrafts. The **Cogon Market** is an interesting place to poke around. There are several handicraft and brass shops. Watch your things here, and on jeepneys. There is also a **brass shop** on Panaca Street near the VIP Hotel. Try also **Tribal Craft** on Pabayo Street, and the **AIM Foundation** on Saco Street in Macasandig, for souvenirs. The city's malls also have limited souvenir items.

Near the port area, **Paras Ceramics** sells ceramic ware, some of which is quite nice and you can order items that you see in the display or in their albums. The problem is transporting the ceramics, as the sales staff do not offer to arrange freight for you. Give it a miss unless you really must have a set of dishes.

EXCURSIONS & DAY TRIPS

Bukidnon

The **Bukidnon** (people of the forest) inhabit the eastern Lanao area, number about 50,000, and are known to be fierce and independent. The **Manobo**, who inhabit part of the highlands of Bukidnon and Agusan, have a rich artistic tradition and are respected for their prowess as warriors. They live in village settlements on reservations.

Both these tribes frequently find it necessary to actively resist efforts to take over their lands. Hence, you should contact the Tourism Office in Bukidnon in advance of planned visits, and let them prepare your trip, transportation, and guides. You could also go to Malaybalay, Bukidnon, and stay overnight, taking the chance that you may proceed to the Manobo settlement 10 kilometers away; get a local guide.

Although the Americans were originally repulsed in northern Mindanao, they quickly established themselves and realized the value of the land. Today, the vast **Del Monte Plantation**, with its American-style agriculture and buildings, rests just over the border in Bukidnon. The cannery is at **Bugo**, seven kilometers east of the city. You can visit the cannery and venture up to the plantation to see vast fruit fields, play 18 holes of golf, eat a good lunch (the specialty is steak from cows fed on pineapple), and shop at the souvenir shop.

En route to Del Monte, you can take a side trip to **Catanico Falls**. Water cascades over boulders into a pool where you may swim. The falls are 20 minutes from the city by road, then a 45-minute walk.

The last major fork in the road before Camp Philips leads through Bukidnon. You may continue to **Malaybalay**, the pretty capital, and stay overnight. Sometimes Manobo people come into town to sell honey they have collected from the forests.

To get to Camp Philips, hire a car ($40-55 per roundtrip) or take a Bachelor, Ceres, or Tomauis bus to Camp Philips ($3), and try to find transport from there to the club.

Mt. Kitanglad National Park in Impasugong has over a dozen mountain peaks, and is host to several rare birds. Mt. Kitanglad, over 9,000 feet, is a challenge for climbers. Contact **PENRO** (Philippines Environment and Natural Resource Office) in Malaybalay for arrangements, *Tel. 2705*, or Rani Vidal of the Kitanglad Mountaineers, *Tel. 2550*.

If you are in the region around the first weekend of September, make a trip to Malaybalay to see the **Kaamulan Festival**. On Saturday morning, the tribes, adorned in their native dress, perform traditional dances.

In **Baungon** there is a **canopy walk** through a tropical forest. It is closer to Cagayan de Oro than Malaybalay. Interested parties should contact the mayor's office in Baungon. To call the mayor's office in Baungon, dial the domestic long-distance operator (109) and asked to be connected to the mayor's office in Baungon, Bukidnon. To write, address the letter to Office of the Mayor, City Hall, Baungon, Bukdinon.

Iligan & Marawi City

In **Iligan**, visit the few Maranao shops (prices higher than Marawi) and many waterfalls. **Maria Cristina Falls** is interesting but is not as full as it was prior to the hydroelectric project. There are several other smaller falls in the vicinity. You may swim at the foot of **Tinago Falls**' cascading water; the **Residence Inn** overlooks the falls.

September 23-29 is the colorful festival in honor of the city's warrior patron saint **San Miguel**. The fiesta is similar to the Sinulog in Cebu, with street performances of ritual dances and reenactments of the fights that occurred at the start of Christianization by the Spaniards. Also presented is *Yawa-yawa*, a play depicting Lucifer's unsuccessful revolt.

Marawi City, capital of Lanao del Norte, is frequently a political hot spot. To visit, take public transport from 9:00am-noon and 2:00-5:00pm only (unless things really cool down). If you really want to stay overnight, stay at the **MARAWI RESORT HOTEL** on the grounds of Mindanao State University (MSU) – if you are on a stringent budget, you may be out of luck. Be very careful about your goings and comings. Foreign men should not to sit down next to local women on the buses. Ask permission before taking photographs of people.

In Marawi, the **Aga Kahn Museum**, at the **Mindanao State University** (MSU), has good exhibits of cultural items from Maranao and other Mindanao Muslim tribes. Brass shops line Marawi's wide central road and you may also buy things at Dansalan College's art shop. The market is fascinating. There is an excellent view of picturesque **Lake Lanao** from the site of the old city hall. Don't swim in the lake, or you risk a nasty schistosomiasis (liver fluke) infection.

The quickest way to get to Iligan is by bus (see Cagayan de Oro's *Arrivals & Departures*). Sulpicio Lines goes once a week from Manila to Iligan; the trip takes over 24 hours, with the final port in Dipolog City, Zamboanga del Norte. Price ranges from $24 for a bunk in a common cabin, or a private cabin for $80.

To continue on to Marawi, take a jeepney or taxi from Iligan for a 45-minute ride to MSU. Jeepneys will have a sign indicating "Iligan MSU" the last trip from Marawi to Iligan is at 4:00pm.

For lodgings in Iligan, consider one of the following hotels:

RESIDENCE INN TINAGO, *Buruan, Iligan. Manila reservations: Tel. 897-3888, Fax 890-6162. $20-50 per single or double with private bathrooms, $15 per single or double with a shared bathroom. Visa, Master Card.*

This resort offers a view overlooking the Tinago Falls. Upon request they will also light up the falls at night (ten minutes only or they will wipe out the resort's power supply). There is also a mini-zoo that includes a lion. The restaurant serves good food. Facilities, aside from the zoo, include a small pool next to the falls, detracting a bit from the natural scenery.

ILIGAN VILLAGE HOTEL, *Pala-o, Iligan. Tel. 21-752. $22-35 per single or double, $55 per suite.*

The hotel has air conditioned rooms with bathrooms, fish ponds, a garden, and a restaurant that specializes in seafood.

MARIA CRISTINA HOTEL, *Aguinaldo corner Mabini Street. Tel. 20-645. 420-25 per single or double, $50 per suite.*

The best downtown hotel, Maria Cristina is frequented by business-men and is well-managed. The restaurant is good.

MC TOURIST INN, *Tibanga Highway, Iligan. Tel. 5194. $15 per single or double aircon, $6 per single, $10 per double non-aircon.*

This simple lodge, slightly out of town, has rooms with private bathrooms.

PRACTICAL INFORMATION
Banks

There are several banks in the city, you can find a number of them along A Velez Street, including **PNB** and **PCI Bank**. Near the Cogon Market is **Interbank**, on Borja Street. **Equitable Bank** has a branch on Borja and Tiano Brothers. Banking hours are Mondays through Fridays, from 9:00am to 4:00pm.

Maps

Probably the best map and information on the city and its surroundings is available at the **City Tourism Office**, located in City Hall. They also have an outlet called the **Oro Tourism Center**, which is on A Velez Street between Abejuela and Chavez Streets.

There is a **Department of Tourism Office** and a **Philippine Tourism Authority Office** at the Pelaez Sport Center. These two government offices seem to be in competition with each other. Extracting accurate information can at times be a bit tedious, and any wrong information may be blamed on the "other side," as "a person from their office must have been in ours and that was who you talked to...." Who knows why the government has three different organizations concerned with tourism nationwide? The city tourism offices are under the direct auspices of the mayors, and are not a nationwide government organization.

Post Office

The post office is two blocks from City Hall on T Chavez Street. Several courier services (international DHL and UPS, and local JRS and LBC) offer express mail nationally and to a few international destinations.

CAMIGUIN ISLAND

Small, pretty **Camiguin Island**, with friendly peaceful people, lies off the eastern end of Macajar Bay. Its current inhabitants are almost wholly of Visayan and Chinese origin. Their way of life revolves around the land, its coconuts, and fishing. Known for producing what many consider the sweetest *lanzones* in the country, the island celebrates the **Lanzones Festival**, two days of exhibits and parades during harvest time, which usually falls at the end of September.

Camiguin is a volcanic island, and in 1871 an eruption submerged its old capital, Bonbon. In 1951, **Mt. Hibok-Hibok** erupted, asphyxiating 2,000 inhabitants. The volcano has been quiescent since then. Volcanic activity is monitored by a Comvol (Commission of Volcanology) station on a mound between Mts. Hibok-Hibok and Timpo-ong.

The island's shores consist mainly of pebble and dark sand beaches between rocks and lava flow areas. There is white sand on White Island, a sand bar; on Magsaysay (Mantigue) Island; and along a small stretch in Kabila. Inland, springs and rivers tumble down Camiguin's volcanic slopes, producing two impressive falls and many lesser ones.

Camiguin is well-liked by the more active tourists; the main activities are hiking to these natural phenomena and soaking up the peaceful aura. Children everywhere call out, "Hi friend!" to visitors, and then, if you respond, ask, "What's your name?" Even the police go around unarmed, a rarity in the Philippines.

ARRIVALS & DEPARTURES

By Air

To come in by air, you will have to charter a plane: there are no scheduled commuter airlines. The airport's runway is still under construction, and perhaps once it is done you will be able to fly in from Cebu.

By Land

For transport to Balingoan, the departure pier for Camiguin, refer to Cagayan de Oro's *Arrivals & Departures* section above.

By Sea

From Balingoan, it takes an hour and 30 minutes to arrive on Camiguin, at Benoni. The ferry is scheduled usually on the hour starting at 7:00am; with the last trip at 3:00pm. The return trips are from 6:00am until 4:00pm. Two companies (two ferries each) serve the route; when one ferry is under repair, the intervals are an hour and a half. Arrive early and be prepared to wait. There is a small restaurant where you can get a cup of instant coffee and snacks. In calm weather, you can rent a *banca* to take you from Balingoan to Benoni. Ferry passage is about $1.15, *banca* hire $20-$32.

Camiguin is also accessible via sea from Cebu. The trip takes 13 to 14 hours. Both Cokaliong and Georgia lines have a trip once a week, on Wednesdays ($5-$20 per person).

Upon arriving at the Benoni Wharf, "multicab" drivers will pounce on you, offering their services to take you to your destination. Multicabs are the island's main form of transportation: they are large motorized tricycles. Most resorts are in the Mambajao area. The trip will cost 60¢ per person, or $6 for the whole multicab.

ORIENTATION

Pear-shaped Camiguin Province lies southeast of Bohol and north of Cagayan de Oro City and Misamis Oriental. Its climate is cooler than most sea-level places; the daytime temperature averages about 27°C or 80°F. Rainy season is from June to December, while dry season usually starts in March and lasts two or three months.

GETTING AROUND

Multicabs frequently ply the Benoni-Mambajao route (60¢ or P15 per person, $4 or P100 for the whole vehicle), and can be rented to circle the island for $32. Motorcycles are rented for $15 per day; several resorts can make arrangements for you. Look for Edgar, "the basketball player," a former professional basketball player who now resides on the island. He is a wealth of information and very helpful. His house is near Paradiso.

WHERE TO STAY

If you must have all the amenities of a first class resort, then Camiguin is not for you. The easier-going tourists will be quite pleased with the simple facilities available at most of the resorts. All are clean and staffed with friendly people eager to practice their English and make new friends. Some will offer to guide on their breaks, or days off, or to recommend a guide.

Most of the resorts are along the shoreline of Mambajao, and a few inns are in the town proper. There are a few other places on the other parts of the island.

Mambajao Resorts

CAMIGUIN BEACH CLUB, *Yumbing, Mambajao. Tel. 879-028. 6 rooms. $43 per single, $57 per double, $11.50 extra bed.*

This small but charming resort is a one-story white building with nipa roofing, and is one of the better hotels in terms of facilities. All rooms are air conditioned, have cable TV, and a minibar. The small pool is ringed with stones, and you can sit at the adjacent bar that faces the shoreline and has a view of White Island. The rooms are clean and the staff is friendly and helpful, as with most places on Camiguin. The specialty of the small poolside restaurant is grilled food.

PARAS BEACH RESORT, *Yumbing, Mambajao. Tel. 879-008. Cagayan de Oro reservations: Tel. 722-161, Fax 724-173. Manila reservations: Tel. 361-3646. 8 rooms, 3 cottages. $42 per single or double, $64-105 in cottages. Visa, Master Card, American Express.*

The other top hotel of Camiguin, this resort is an interesting mixture of styles, probably a result of two expansions. The rooms are in a cream-colored cement building, simple wood furniture inside with *amaca* (woven bamboo) ceiling. The first set of cottages (two) are cream with nipa roofing. Each cottage has two rooms, four beds in each room. The last structure is a circular cottage, with walls of tinted glass that have sliding doors. One of the rooms in this cottage has double-sized bunk beds; the other part of the cottage is a suite.

The staff is very friendly and does a good job of maintaining the place. All rooms have air conditioning and cable television. Facilities include a restaurant-bar specializing in American food. There is a small business center, and a function room with basic audio-visual equipment. For recreation, a swimming pool, billiards, and a few board games are available. The resort also rents scuba equipment.

BAHAY BAKASYUNAN, *Balbagon, Mambajao. Tel. 871-057, 870-027. 6 rooms. $40 per single or double, $7.50 per extra bed.*

The native-style rooms are tastefully done with rattan beds and *amaca* covering the ceiling and walls. All rooms are air conditioned and bathrooms have hot water. The resort provides free transfers to and from the Benoni Wharf. They also offer scuba tours and lessons through the Alibuag Dive Tours; equipment and boat rental is also available. There is cable television in the restaurant, and laundry service is offered. Island tours are also offered, using their air conditioned van, for $120 per whole day or $60 per half day.

CAVES BEACH RESORT, *Agoho, Mambajao. Tel. 879-040, Fax 870-077. 8 cottages, 10 rooms. $11.50 per cottage, $6 per room.*

One of the bigger resorts on the island, Caves is on a large beachfront property. The cottages are nestled between coconut trees. The main building is between the cottages and the beach, and houses the restaurant, rooms, and an in-house dive center: Bubbles Dive Center. The owner, Mr. Gallardo involves himself with tourism and promoting the island. He also owns three other lodging establishments (Treehouse, White Beach Resort, and Casa Grande). He and his wife, both nice people, divide their time between their hardware store in town and all the establishments.

Mosquito nets are provided in all rooms and cottages; you can ask for electric fans. The cottages have private bathrooms, while the rooms have common ones. The staff are wonderful, and Marilyn (a staff member) enjoys showing people around her charming island. When she isn't working, she will guide people around for $12-15 per group.

JASMINE BY THE SEA, *Agoho, Mambajao. Tel. 879-015. $10-11.50 per cottage, $2 per extra person.*

This simple resort seems popular with foreigners. Because of uncertainties concerning the lease on the property (by Thomas, a friendly Swiss fellow), maintenance has slipped and the place could use renovation; nevertheless, it has a number of returning customers. Rooms are simple, and have bathrooms. The 15 dogs living on the property howl at unpredictable times. The restaurant specializes in Swiss cuisine.

MORNING GLORY COTTAGE, *Agoho, Mambajao. Tel. 879-017. 5 cottages. $10 per cottage, $2 per extra person.*
This place has fan-cooled rooms in simple cottages that are a bit run-down, but kept clean, on a quiet property.

CAMIGUIN SEASIDE LODGE, *Agoho, Mambajao. Tel. 879-031. 16 cottages. $11 per cottage, $3-4 per person in the dorm.*
This simple resort has an oval beachfront restaurant with a view of White Island. The cottages have fans, mosquito nets, and private bathrooms, but no hot water. Each dorm room has either a private bathroom ($4) or shared one ($3). The lodge has a jeepney and *banca* available for rent. The restaurant serves Filipino food.

PAYAG VILLAGE HUTS, *Agoho, Mambajao. Tel. 879-024. 4 cottages. $11.50 per cottage.*
These simple and nice cottages are on a well-kept lawn, a short walk from the beach in a quiet area. All cottages have fans, mosquito nets, and private bathrooms, but no hot water.

TREEHOUSE BEACH COTTAGE, *Tapon, Mambajao. Tel. 879-040, Fax 870-077. 1 tree house. $11.50.*
This small but nice cottage is built part way up a tree, and is a popular place to stay for foreigners. As there is only one treehouse, it is best to book in advance. Meals are provided at the restaurant in Caves Resort.

TIA'S COTTAGES, *Mambajao, beside the airport. Tel. 871-045. 15 cottages, 3 dorms. $10 per cottage, $3 per person in the dorm.*
Owned by Mrs. Tia, this resort is simple, charming, and well maintained. Mrs. Tia is a wonderful and helpful person, and divides most of her time between her resort and pension. The native wood and nipa cottages have bougainvillea vines covering roofs and linking the cottages together. Each cottage has a small porch. The rooms are small but clean, and all have electric fans, mosquito nets, and bathrooms. The restaurant serves tasty native and seafood dishes.

MAMBAJAO BEACH RESORT, *Balbagon, Mambajao. Tel. 871-059, 870-069. 6 cottages, 2 duplexes. $13.50 per cottage, $10.50 per duplex, $4 per extra person.*
All cottages have ceiling fans, private bathroom, cable TV, and a nice small porch. Each duplex can accommodate up to six people, and has a fan and private bathroom.

ARDENT HOT SPRINGS, *Tagdo, Mambajao, right beside the hot springs. Tel. 879-048. 3 cottages and 5 dorm rooms. $18.50 per cottage, $4.50 per person in the dorm. Cagayan de Oro reservations: Tel. 727-432. Manila reservations: Tel. 812-1984, Fax 812-1164.*
This resort, not by the beach, is nestled into the trees and plants at the base of Mt. Hibok-Hibok. The cottages are nice looking on the outside, a mix of stone, cement, and wood, with nipa roofing. Pathways through

the manicured lawn lead to the cottages. All cottage rooms have electric fans and bathrooms. The dorms have common bathrooms. Meals are $3.20-4.00 for set breakfast; lunch and dinner are á la carte and run around $4-6 for a complete meal.

PARADISO, *Agoho, Mambajao – nestled into a hill. Tel. 879-037 ask for Annie. 1 cottage, 1 room. $20 per cottage but the rate includes a motorbike! The room is $10.50.*

This place goes by the name of the best restaurant on the island (same owners), and is a five-minute walk from the restaurant. The cottage is simply furnished, has hard beds, bathroom, and a kitchenette. The room is in the house of the owners and can accommodate four people.

Mambajao Inns

TIA'S PENSION HOUSE, *Mambajao Poblacion. Tel. 870-010. $4 per person.*

Mrs. Tia's pension is a small building in town. The rooms are clean and have electric fans. The bathrooms are common, separate for males and females. Meals are $2 for breakfast and $3 for lunch or dinner.

CASA GRANDE, *across from the Provincial Plaza, Mambajao Poblacion. Tel. 879-040, Fax 870-077. 5 rooms, $40 per single or double.*

This beautiful old house has been converted into a nice looking inn. All rooms are spacious, with wooden floors, air conditioning, and bathrooms with hot water. The entrance is through sliding doors of wrought iron; a wide staircase takes you upstairs to the rooms, lounge area, restaurant and kitchen. The house is very airy, as its huge windows are usually left open.

Resorts Out of Mambajao

WHITE BEACH RESORT, *Kabila between Kanta-an and Cabu-an. Tel. 879-040, Fax 870-077. 1 cottage. $11.50.*

This is the place to go if you are looking for total privacy. It is beside a small but pretty stretch of fine white sand beach two kilometers from the main road. The cottage is simple with native decor, has its own bathroom; however, at night you use lanterns as there is no electricity yet. There are plans to install electricity, perhaps part of the charm is the lack of it.

MYCHELLIN BEACH COTTAGES, *San Roque, Mahinog. Tel. 874-005. $11.20 per cottage, $2 per extra person.*

This simple resort faces Magsaysay (Mantigue) Island, the other island with white sand. Meals are provided.

SRJ BALHON, *Catarman. Tel. 877-000, ask for Racquel. 2 cottages and 3 rooms. $13.50 per cottage, $3 per person in a room.*

Located about an hour from the Benoni Wharf, this resort is near the Santo Niño Cold Springs and Tuwasan Falls, in a very quiet area with a rocky beachfront. The owner says that there are corals nearby and good diving. The cottages and rooms have electric fans, and the ceilings and walls are decorated with *amaca*. The restaurant, which is below the rooms, serves good Filipino food, with some Chinese dishes.

WHERE TO EAT

All resorts have their own simple restaurants. There are only a few other places outside the resorts. At the **pier** there is a fast food place where you can get a snack while waiting for the ferry to come. You can also buy barbequed fish at the **Mambajao market**.

Resort restaurants generally serve simple meals; it is best to have their specialties. Paras Beach Resort specializes in American fare, for Swiss food try Jasmine by the Sea, and Caves Resort does grilled or fried fish. Expect to spend $2.50-$6.00 for a full meal. Drinks and soft drinks will cost around 60¢, and bottled water 75¢.

PARADISO, *on the main road between Caves and Jasmine Resorts.*

This is a wonderful surprise — you will be treated to great pasta. The flavorful tomato-based sauce is made with just the right amount of herbs, spices, and garlic. The seafood is also quite tasty. This restaurant is run by Collin, who is from the United States, and his wife Annie, who comes from Cagayan de Oro. They also serve fresh fruit shakes, and another plus is the friendly staff.

J&A FISHPEN, *Benoni.*

Serves local fare. The tables are on a pier that extends into the water of a small lagoon.

SRJ RESTAURANT, *Catarman.*

SRJ is a family-owned and -managed, homey, native-style restaurant that serves Filipino food and a few Chinese dishes.

SEEING THE SIGHTS

There are several gracious old buildings to admire in **Mambajao** — Camiguin's postcard-pretty capital. It has an impressive volcano as backdrop. You can tour the entire island, including a few stops to enjoy some sights and take photos, easily in one day on a multicab.

White sand aficionados can check out **White Island**, a beautiful half-moon stretch of sand, perhaps 300 meters long. It is a 10 minute ride from Kuguita, Mambajao. The ideal time to go would be early in the morning, or after 3:00pm, as there is no shade on the sandbar. *Banca* rental to and from the island will cost $8. **Magsaysay (Mantigue) Island** off Hubangon, Mahinog, has a white sand beach, but is rocky under the water. Nearby corrals provide snorkeling. Access is also by *banca* for $8. **Kabila**, south of

Benoni Wharf, near Guinsiliban, between *barangays* Kanta-an and Cabu-an, has a nice white sand beach.

For an easy hike, check out **Mt. Vulcan Daan**, 13 kilometers west of Mambajao. This volcano last erupted over a century ago, and has 14 stations of the cross that wind up a walkway. The last station is carved out of a volcanic rock.

If you intend to climb **Mt. Hibok-Hibok**, plan on at least two days, and a guide is essential. You should probably stay overnight at the Comvol station or Ardent Hot Springs. The ascent takes about six hours if you are in good shape.

Katibawasan Falls punctuate a very beautiful, powerful stream which plummets 40 meters into a cool pool. The falls are about four and a half kilometers from Mambajao, on the slopes of Mt. Timpo-ong. Bring lunch and have a relaxing picnic.

There is a resort located by a stream that has been dammed where the **Ardent Hot Springs** bubble up, providing 36°C (96.8°F) mineral water to soak in. The entrance fee is 60¢, and you can rent picnic tables for $1.20.

At **Naasag** are coastal hot springs where you may soak in hot fresh water at low tide and warm brackish water at medium tide. Find out when low tide is expected before heading for Naasag or for **Bonbon**, where the **sunken church** and **cemetery** (casualties of the 1871 eruption) are visible only when the waters are very low. On land, just before reaching Bonbon, are the ruins of the **old Spanish church**.

Further along, on Camiguin's western slopes, you may hike from Catarman to the less-developed **Tuasan Falls**. The falls are shorter than Katibawasan, but the water cascading down is more and powerful. Also visit the **Sto Niño** cold springs' swimming pools and relax under the trees. **Pamunglo**, another cold spring, is outside Sagay. In the town hall in Catarman are centuries old artifacts dating back to the Ching and Ming dynasties of China.

You will need to arrange transport to these places, as public transport is frequently not available on the western side of the island. Consider hiring a multicab or a motorcycle for the day. If you go around the island, stop in **Guinsiliban** to see the 300-year-old watchtower.

Because there is frequent transport from Mambajao to Benoni, sights on the eastern side are more accessible. The **Benoni (Tanguines) Lagoon**, man-made, is situated in a picturesque setting. You need a guide with local knowledge and a good flashlight to find the cave in **Magting**. At the cave, believed to be millions of years old, archaeologists found ancient human skeletons and primitive utensils.

NIGHTLIFE & ENTERTAINMENT

There really is not much nightlife here, as most people are resting after an active day exploring the island. Tourists do go to **Paradiso** for drinks and music in the evening. Other popular night spots where tourists and locals like to hang out are the **Ardent Hot Springs** and the **Benoni Lagoon**. Wear a swimsuit or bring extra clothes if you intend to take a dip.

PRACTICAL INFORMATION

Money

Change all money you think is necessary before arriving in Camiguin.

Maps & Tourist Information

For assistance and information see the **Camiguin Tourism Office**, Capitol Hills, Mambajao, *Tel. 871-097, 871-014*. Catalino Chan, the Provincial Tourism Officer, is very friendly and helpful. The office also has a decent map and brochure of Camiguin. Also see Mrs. Tia of Tia's Lodging House, and Edgar, near Paradiso (he rents motorcycles and is known as the "basketball player.") Marilyn in Caves Beach Resort is happy to guide people up Mt. Hibok-Hibok, and to other points on the island.

The people in Camiguin are very friendly and most are glad to act as guides for a fee. There is no fixed rate, but fees are around $12 for one to two people, and $5.75 for each additional person (rates for three or more are negotiable).

SURIGAO CITY

The clean and peaceful capital of Surigao del Norte, at the northeast tip of Mindanao, faces the Pacific Ocean. **Surigao** and much of its surroundings are not frequented by tourists. While the area is relatively safe, it is not readily accessible.

As a tourist destination, there are various activities: island hopping, spelunking, cruising through mangroves, and relaxing on one of the nice beaches. Its **Maradjao Karadjao Festival**, in honor of its patron saint, San Nicolas de Tolentino, is impressive. The ideal time to travel to this area is around the time of the fiesta, which falls on September 9-10. For this event, the whole city comes together, proud and full of life. The highlights are the various presentations of *Bonok-bonok*, a dance performed as a thanksgiving ritual. The festivities begin with a parade through the streets, with performances in front of the Mayor's house. Competing groups are rated by a panel of judges. The parade ends with final performances in the athletic field. The winning group competes in Cebu's Sinulog Festival (in January), and Surigao's entries frequently win top honors in the Sinulog.

The city has pleasant weather most of the year, with seasonal rains from July to September. It does not get severe typhoons as frequently as other parts of the Philippines.

ARRIVALS & DEPARTURES

By Air

Surigao City's small airport is served by Philippine Airlines. Flights are from Manila on Tuesday, Thursday, Saturday; and from Cebu on Monday, Wednesday, Friday, and Sunday. The flight from Manila takes roughly two hours, and from Cebu it takes 45 minutes. If you arrive by air, reconfirm your flight at the airport upon arrival. Tricycles will take you into town for 40¢.

By Sea

The wharf is a two-minute tricycle ride from the town center, and is inundated by tricycle drivers when boats arrive, so you won't have problems finding a ride.

Surigao-Manila. This trip takes 26-30 hours. Sulpicio Lines has two trips a week as does WGA SuperFerry.

Surigao-Cebu. The quickest way is via the WaterJet, which has trips Tuesday, Thursday, Saturday, and Sunday. The WaterJet leaves Cebu at 8:30am and takes three and a half hours ($20 for tourist and $26 business class; for tickets purchased 5 days advanced $12 for tourist and $17 business class). The return trip leaves Surigao between 12:00 and 1:00pm. Cokaliong has daily trips taking ten hours ($5-20). The boat leaves Cebu in the morning and returns in the evening.

Surigao-Siargao. Ferries (large *bancas*) for the three-to-four hour trip to Siargao leave the wharf early every morning, with the last trip no later than 9:00am, as the crossing tends to get rough later in the day. The return trips depart at more or less the same times.

By Land

The Bachelor terminal is on Borromeo, the street that leads to the town plaza and to the wharf. Refer to Cagayan de Oro's *Arrivals & Departures* section.

Philtranco, the only bus line that covers parts of Luzon, Visayas, and Mindanao, takes a ferry from southern Leyte to Surigao City, then heads down to Davao.

GETTING AROUND

The only way to get around town, if you do not own a vehicle, is by tricycle. As these vehicles are all over the place, you should not have any problems hailing one. The city is quite small and most destinations are within walking distance. If you take a tricycle, do not pay over 10¢ (P2.50), unless you have a lot of luggage (a surf board perhaps); then add an extra 10¢. The tricycle drivers, seeing that you are an outsider, will try and charge you more.

WHERE TO STAY

In town, facilities are limited, although construction of a "better" hotel is under way. This hotel will probably be run by the city government, which is pretty good.

TAVERN HOTEL, *Borromeo Street, Tel. 87-300. $10-20 per single or double.*

This landmark may be the city's oldest hotel (and looks it too). It has air conditioned rooms and rooms with fans.

FAIRVIEW HOTEL, *near the athletic field, on the way in to town center. $10-15 per single or double.*

Rooms come with fan or air conditioning.

MAHARLIKA COMPLEX, *about 10 minutes from the City. 6 room. $15-35 per single or double.*

Nice rooms, simple and clean, with a good view of Surigao Strait. Each room is air conditioned and has a bathroom.

Cheaper dorm-style rooms are available at **DEXTER**, **GARCIA**, and **LITANG**, *$5-10 per single or double*, and bathrooms are common.

WHERE TO EAT

There are about as many eating places as lodging facilities, and you can get a good meal in town. There is a fast food place across the street from the plaza. You can get sandwiches, and hot dishes that taste good enough and cost under $2. They also have ice cream. This fast food place is actually the entrance to a small grocery, where you can buy chips, bottled water, and most things you expect to see in a mom and pop grocer.

CHERRY BLOSSOMS on San Nicolas Street is a canteen-type place, and you can stop in at **SWEET RAIZA** (Narciso Street near Rizal Street) or **DELICIOUS BAKEHOUSE** (Borromeo Street) for tasty local breads and sweets. The most "upscale" dining is at the **TAVERN**, Borromeo Street, where the restaurant area is large and casual, and the food is good. The Tavern also has a grill that doubles as a beer garden at night, and the barbeque is very good; on the not-so-good side are the bathrooms.

SEEING THE SIGHTS

Island hopping can be arranged through the City Tourism Office. The office has a number of good itineraries, and if you have a large group, prices are low as you will split the cost of renting a *banca*. Among the trips that they offer are **Sagisi Beach**, a three-kilometer stretch of white sand on **Bayagnan Island**, pretty three-kilometer **Buenavista Cave** on **Hikdop Island**, and **Suyang Cave** on **Dinagat Island**. *Banca* rental will cost $58 for the day and seats 10 people plus the *banquero*.

At the **Maharlika Complex**, a 15-minute ride from downtown, you can get a good panoramic view of the **Surigao Strait**, location of the historic World War Two Battle of Surigao Strait. The strait is infamous as a graveyard for many ocean-going vessels, including several Japanese warships sunk during the battle.

EXCURSIONS & DAY TRIPS
Mainit Lake

Mainit is a 17,000-hectare body of water that spans parts of Agusan del Norte and Surigao del Norte provinces. As there are no facilities, it is a place to go to photograph and enjoy the scenery. If you visit during summer, its shorelines are speckled with purple water hyacinth flowers and wild ducks paddling around. The best way to get to the lake is to hire a tricycle for the day, and ask at the city tourism in Surigao for a guide. Also in Mainit is the **Togonan Waterfalls**, a small but pretty waterfall amidst lush vegetation.

Butuan

The capital of Agusan del Norte, **Butuan** may be the site of the oldest human settlement in the Philippines and the country's first Catholic mass. Next to the town hall is an interesting **museum** that displays ancient human bones, pottery, and a *balanghai* (similar to a large *banca*) believed to be pre-11th century. The grounds of the museum is the site of the first mass here.

The DOT head office for the Caraga region (provinces of Agusan del Norte and Sur, Surigao del Norte and Sur) is in the City Hall compound in Butuan. Contact the office in advance for help with arrangements and information on the more remote areas. In Agusan del Sur, if you don't mind getting wet (there is almost no dry season), a **day-long marsh cruise**

BARANGAY
*These large outriggered craft were once used for interisland travel. They could carry several dozen people, and probably brought immigrants – possibly in small clans. The political subdivision below the municipality-level, the **barangay**, is named after these vessels.*

down the Agusan River to lush wetlands full of life and some wooden houseboats of the Manobos can be arranged through the **DOT**, *Tel. 92-712*; ask for Zeny Pallugna; she is adventurous and enjoys showing people around.

Bachelor is the only bus line that runs between Surigao and Butuan. The trip takes two hours, and costs $1.75; buses are not air conditioned. Butuan is a key transportation point – the main stop of buses plying the Davao-Cagayan de Oro route, and buses headed for Surigao City. It is also a port for ships to the southern Visayas.

PRACTICAL INFORMATION

Banks

There are several banks in the city. **PNB**, **BPI**, and **Far East Bank**, are all on Rizal Street. **Allied Bank**, **RCBC**, and **PCI Bank** are on San Nicholas Street and **MetroBank** has a branch on Borromeo St. Banking hours are Mondays through Fridays, from 9:00am to 4:00pm.

Post Office

The post office is on Rizal Street near the Grandstand. Courier services include **JRS**, **Haribon Express**, and **LBC**, and they all offer fax services.

Tourist Assistance

Cherla Tibay and the staff at the **City Tourism Office** in Luneta Park, *Tel. 87-228,* provide great information and help for getting around the city and its sights. They also have island-hopping packages ($20 per person with a minimum of 10, the price is higher for lower numbers), including *banca*, accommodations on an island, and meals.

SIARGAO/GENERAL LUNA

Siargao and much of **Surigao del Norte** are one of the country's best kept secrets. The islands offer much more than the powerful waves that have made **"Cloud Nine"** (Tuason Point) of General Luna, Siargao, infamous in the international surfing community. This area is, without a doubt, one of our most favorite destinations in the Philippines.

Imagine fine white sand beaches that are among the best in the world; breathtaking caves with limestone formations and lagoons; lush mangrove and tropical forests teeming with a variety of wildlife – crocodiles, tarsiers, and various tropical birds; and genuinely warm people. Sounds like paradise? Well, that's what you'll find here, and more ... note: the crocodiles are seldom seen and we have not heard of them attacking anyone.

Siargao, at the northeastern tip of Mindanao, faces the **Philippine Deep**. Siargao is flanked by the **Pacific Ocean** on its east, to its west is the **Surigao Strait**, and the islands of Bucas Grande and La Januza lay to the south. The main towns of Siargao are Dapa, General Luna, Pilar, San Isidro, Santa Monica, and Del Carmen.

General Luna is the best base, with several simple, nice beach resorts, and a pension house. A more high-end resort is set to open mid-1997. Most of the tourists here are surfers; others come for the serenity and beauty of the place, nature tripping, island hopping, and kayaking.

You are likely to run into the current mayor, Jaime Rusillon. He has a wealth of information on the area and a big heart full of compassion for General Luna and its people. Mayor Rusillon and the City Council are responsible for much of the public tourist facilities. They and the people of General Luna are justifiably proud of Siargao.

THE PHILIPPINE DEEP

This abyss, where the ocean floor plummets about 10,500 meters, is the world's second deepest chasm. It has formed where two plates of the earth's crust meet and push together. One plate is subducting – folding – under the other, which sometimes causes earthquakes. This submarine depression is also called the **Philippine Trench** *and the* **Mindanao Trench** *(or Deep).*

ARRIVALS & DEPARTURES

Passenger boats operate between the wharf of Surigao City and Siargao daily, but only in the morning. Ferries (large *bancas*) for the three-to-four hour trip to Siargao leave early every morning, with the latest trip no later than 9:00am. There may be a General Luna Tourist Assistance Office at the pier (the office is presently under construction, and the completion date is uncertain). Sometimes, only one or two ferries go, so make arrangements the afternoon before you leave for Surigao, and plan to be at the wharf early: the first ferry may leave at 7:00am, or earlier if it is full. Fare is $1.60 per person, *banca* rental is $120 (small, for 20 people) or $160 (large, for 40 people)

Sit on top, not inside the cabin, for fresh air (fumes from the engine tend to make the cabin air stale); be prepared to get a bit wet, and wear a hat and sunblock if you are sensitive to sun. Another reason to sit on top is the lovely scenery, which makes the trip seem short as you pass islands that are red (from nickel) and lush green from vegetation, with emerald and deep blue waters, and forests of mangroves. You pass through the **Surigao Strait** (notorious as a graveyard for boats, including a World War

Two Japanese war vessel), where the Pacific Ocean meets the Philippine Sea. Here, you will see several whirlpools that gain momentum during a full moon and typhoons (boats won't usually cross then).

The ferries usually land at **Dapa**, the closest port to Surigao. If you are lucky, there may be a ferry going directly to **General Luna**. Upon landing in Dapa, take a jeepney headed to General Luna; it will cost around 80¢. You will be dropped off at City Hall. Ask around for directions to your resort and for help getting a tricycle. Look for Rico, as he is usually around City Hall and enjoys showing off his home town to visitors. If he is not busy, he is a great guide, and can arrange for *banca* rentals.

ORIENTATION

The landscape varies. Shorelines may have powdery sand, coral reefs, or pretty mangrove forests. The marine life is diverse, but there are not yet any facilities for diving. Dolphins and whales have been sighted in the area. Inland, there are several small mountains (or large hills), still pretty much covered with a good amount of vegetation: this is where the tarsiers live.

The weather is good year round. Rains usually occur from July to October, and even then, they come briefly and in the afternoon or evening. Humidity is relatively low, and the average temperature is around 26°C (78.8°F). This is another area that does not get severe typhoons as frequently as other parts of the Philippines. The last time it was hit by a bad typhoon, which did rip many towns apart, was over 10 years ago.

GETTING AROUND

The only way to get around town is by tricycle. Jeeps mainly serve the routes between towns. You will not see tricycles all over the place (which is a pleasant change), but you should not have any problems making arrangements for one through your resort. A ride around town should cost from 20¢ (P5) within town proper to 50¢ (P15) to Tuason Point.

WHERE TO STAY

There are a few simple beach resorts along General Luna's main beach and at Tuason Point, and there is a very nice pension in town. Facilities are limited, but you will be pleased with some of the resorts. Phone lines have not been set up yet; to make reservations you will have to call through the **town hall**, *Tel. 96-591* (in 1997, the area code was the same as Surigao City's). Basic places to stay ($3 per person) include BRC Resort, Jade Star, and Tourist Guest House. The more up-market resort will open in mid-1997.

SIARGAO PENSION HOUSE, *center of General Luna, on the main road. Tel. 87268-204-1283 (this is a satellite phone, so wherever you are, dial the country's international prefix and then this number, e.g. in the US dial 011, then 87...), Fax 87268-204-1284. 4 rooms. $20 per person, all meals included.*

This is a charming pension, run by a French couple — Nicolas and Florence Rambeau. Each room is named after one of the nearby islands. Pictures of guests are posted along the staircase that leads up to the rooms on the second floor. The clean rooms are small but can accommodate two people comfortably; they are cozy, and the decor is tastefully done with a beach theme. You do feel at the beach here. Bathrooms are common and are kept clean; hot water is available for showers.

The Rambeaus are a nice couple with a serious demeanor, and run the pension very well. The staff is friendly. You will not be disappointed with the food here. Florence arranges the daily meals, which may include excellent crêpes for breakfast. If you are interested in kayaking, this is where you go. Priority is of course given to in-house guests.

TUASON POINT RESORT, *Tuason Point, General Luna. 10 cottages. $11.50-30 per single or double, $4 per extra person.*

This resort is operated by two surfers, David Motby and Kevin Davison. The property faces Cloud Nine, and has very nice looking cottages. Their base is cement, walls are a woven combination of a dark and light wood, the roofs are nipa. The cottages fit two people comfortably, are airy inside, clean, and furnishing is native. The six front cottages have private bathrooms. There is a common bathroom structure with separate toilets and showers for the back four cottages. Two of the front cottages have a loft where two more people can fit. Fans and mosquito nets are provided.

The restaurant is in the main pavilion, where people hang out to watch the surf or surfers, or come to relax after surfing and have a cold beer. The menu consists of a variety of dishes, western and local, with some other Asian fare. The food is good, the company amusing.

SURF CAMP & GREEN ROOM, *Tuason Point, Catangnan, General Luna. 9 cottages and 6 rooms. $11.50-23.00 per single or double.*

These neighboring resorts are managed together. Surf Camp was started by Larry Hinton; Kevin is in charge of the Green Room. Most of the cottages are A-frames designed by Larry himself. Larry said he built them this way so that the walls serve as support against the wind, which comes from any direction. The walls are of wood, but with nipa covering some. The A-frames are cozy inside, and all have their own fan, shower, and flush toilets. Aside from the A-frames, there are three square cottages, and a long house with rooms and common bathrooms.

There is a cozy restaurant/bar at Surf Camp, and an adjoining room with two billiard tables. There is a television where Larry can show a documentary that he has made about Siargao and its surf. Larry also has a resident kite, who has made the area his territory and comes in to be fed daily.

At the edge of the property, over the sea, is a cute gazebo. It is very peaceful here — a perfect place to sit, relax, and enjoy the end of the day and admire the view. Surfboards can be rented for $8 a day, and lessons can be arranged; rates are negotiable.

MAITE'S BEACH CAMP, *along the beach west of General Luna town center. 8 cottages. $3 per person.*

This is a very basic resort with seven small cottages for two people and one big cottage with 10 beds. Furnishing consists of beds and a table. Fans can be requested and mosquito nets are provided. Separated by a wall and curtain is a narrow room that serves as the toilet and shower area, both of which are worked manually, *tabo-tabo* style: a large drum of water is left there, and you use the small pail to shower, and to pour water into the toilet to flush it.

Meals are provided in the restaurant. The food is simple but tasty. The staff will do your laundry for a small fee, and although the female staff may not seem too welcoming at first (probably shy), they warm up and are friendly. Overall, this is a good place for people on a tight budget.

SIARGAO PACIFIC, *Malinao, General Luna. For telephone, see Siargao Pension House. 8 cottages. $57-96 per person, meals included.*

Although this place has not officially opened yet, we were shown around the resort during its construction. Siargao Pacific will cater to the upmarket tourists, and it will be beautiful. It is set facing the beach at Malinao, which is a gorgeous stretch of fine white sand. At the back of the resort, a wooden walkway leads through a mangrove forest to a pagoda over the lake where guests will dock as they arrive (if they come during high tide). The cottages were constructed around the coconut trees, none of which were felled. The design of the cottages is unique, as it is a combination of styles from Thailand, Indonesia, and the Philippines.

The lower price range cottages will have fans, while the higher priced cottages will be air conditioned. There are two resident hornbills, which roam freely. One is very friendly and loves fruit. In the back of the resort is a nursery for tropical plants and flowers.

WHERE TO EAT

Most resorts have small restaurants that prepare meals for guests; and you should plan on having at least one meal a day in your resort.

MARIDYL'S sari-sari store and restaurant, *on the main road north of City Hall*, has good meals, *turo-turo* style. At **MEL & RHAT DISCO HOUSE**, *across from City Hall*, they serve terrific barbeque chicken, juicy and tender, the sauce unique and excellent.

The **PIRATE'S ANCHORAGE BAR & RESTAURANT**, behind the Municipal School, is a popular late afternoon or evening hangout and is a perfect place for a well chilled beer or fruit shake, and a snack — the fries are very good. The owner, Pete "the Pirate," as he is fondly called by many, is actively into preserving the beauty of the island and educating the people on the environment, especially through school. His wife is from General Luna and they have a handful of beautiful kids.

For drinks and snacks in the vicinity of Cloud Nine, try **TUASON PT. RESORT** and **SURF CAMP**, which has billiard tables. If Larry is around, he may show you a short documentary on Siargao and surfing. Surf Camp has a nice gazebo jutting out into the water, perfect for relaxing.

SEEING THE SIGHTS

In *barangay* **Malinao**, the opposite side from the city proper, is a beautiful stretch of fine white sand: ideal for walking barefoot or swimming in the clean azure waters. Inland, across the road, is a path to one of Siargao's many mangrove forests; another option for access is by *banca* through a river that ends around the bend from the beach.

Tuason Point (Cloud Nine) is the place to go to catch the surf on good days, especially when there is or has just been a typhoon in the eastern Visayas. Even if you don't surf, Tuason Point is worth a visit — watch a few surfers and soak up the ambiance and panoramic views.

EXCURSIONS & DAY TRIPS

Tours

For tours around Siargao, and to neighboring islands, most resorts can help with arrangements. Hopping to the closest islands will cost $8 to rent a small motorized *banca* for three hours. Pete "the Pirate" of the **Pirate's Anchorage Bar and Restaurant** has organized very good tours around the island, for $15 per person (with a minimum of eight and maximum of 15 people), inclusive of jeepney, guides, snacks, and drinks.

The Rambeaus of **Siargao Pension** also have package tours to the outer islands, including to the Suhoton Caves on Bucas Grande. They also rent kayaks.

Island Hopping Near General Luna

• **Guyam** is a frequently photographed little island of white sand with a few coconut trees on its center. There are reefs nearby, but a long stretch of sand into the water allows for swimming without the need for protection on your feet. You can swim to General Luna in about 30 minutes.

• **Dako** has a picture pretty, long stretch of fine white sand fringed by azure water. Its a good place to swim, and coconut trees and a hut provide shade.

• **Pansukyan** is a sand bar with fine sand and small shells, also a nice place to swim.

Visiting Islands Further Off

• **La Januza** has a nice beach and some mangroves. The trip there will take 45 minutes to an hour.

• **Caob** has a lake on its east side with a nice little native village nearby. There is a very pretty lagoon on the west side. The island is near Del Carmen, which is northwest of General Luna. Travel time will be approximately an hour.

• **Bucas Grande** is the home of the very beautiful **Suhoton Cave**. As you pass through the cave (by *banca* or kayak), admire the limestone formation, and on the other side you will be treated to a breathtaking blue lagoon, surrounded with lush vegetation. The trip is a two-hour *banca* ride from General Luna.

SPORTS & RECREATION

Surfing

Popular and world-renown in the surfing circuits, **Cloud Nine** is a five-minute tricycle ride from the town center. Its waves are among the world's most powerful and dangerous to surf; the sand is nothing special as the surrounding area is mostly reefs.

Surf lessons are available at any of the resorts. At the end of September, Cloud Nine hosts an **annual international surfing competition** that attracts amateur and professional surfers.

Kayaking

The Rambeaus of **Siargao Pension** and **Siargao Pacific** arrange island-hopping tours that include kayaks. The cost of renting a kayak is included in their island-hopping tours ($40 including meals); to rent a kayak costs $10 an hour and priority is given to in-house guests.

There are several places to kayak: through mangroves, around and to nearby islands, and the favorite is taking a *banca* to **Bucas Grande Island**, then kayaking through **Suhoton Cave** into the lagoon.

Fishing

The Pacific Ocean is a good area for deep sea fishing, as there are large tuna and marlin. Unless you have your own fishing yacht or have a friend with one, you will have to charter a boat.

Try **International Golden Horizon Cruise and Travel**, *Manila Tel. 525-5698, Fax 524-1571*, or **Excello Aquatic Charters International**, *Manila Tel. 785-225.*

HELPFUL HINTS FOR SIARGAO

Phone lines have not been set up yet, and calls must be placed at the City Hall during office hours only, and on the weekends only if someone is around. If you need to make an urgent call, it should be no problem to find the operator or someone in the Mayor's office who can make the call, as the people here are very friendly, accommodating, and helpful.

*You cannot change **money** here, so estimate the amount you will need beforehand.*

26. DAVAO -
SOUTHERN MINDANAO

The **Davao** region of southern Mindanao spans three provinces:
Davao, Davao del Sur, and Davao Oriental. This area's treats include
pretty islands, fruit and souvenir markets, museums, shrines, plantations,
an array of palate-pleasing cuisines, golf courses, and at the **Eagle
Breeding Station** on Mt. Apo's foot hills, you may be fortunate enough
to see one of the few remaining **Philippine eagles**. Here people continue
to try and save this magnificent bird, although it is probably doomed to
extinction by man's relentless encroachment into its natural habitat.

Davao gets its name from "daba-daba," meaning fire and referring to
the ritual drum beats and fires lit along the riverbanks, and to the tribal
wars that were once part of the area's active past. Among the first settlers
of the Davao area were the ancestors of today's tribespeople – the Bagobo
(Mt. Apo); Guiangas (Davao); Manobo, B'Laan, Calaganes, and Tagacaoili/
T'Boli (all from Davao del Sur); and Mandaya (Davao Oriental). Sama
people occupied the offshore islands. Aetas lived among the valleys,
coasts, and hills. The coast dwellers were moved inland when the
aggressive Maguindanaos arrived from Cotabato, Zamboaga, and Jolo.

The first people to bring Christianity to the area were the Portuguese
(late 15th-early 16th century). The Spanish arrived in the 16th century,
and did not gain control of the once predominantly Muslim area until the
mid-19th century. Davao's resistance ended with the slaying of the leader
Datu Bago in 1847. Davao's earlier residents were then displaced by
Christian settlers from the Visayas and Luzon.

ORIENTATION

This southernmost region of the Philippines is as diverse geographically as it is culturally. The center of the main island is more mountainous
and relatively more vegetated than the lowlands and much of Luzon and
the Visayas. **Mt. Apo** is aptly called as *apo* means "grandfather." The

mountain rises to 2,945 meters, and is located in southern Mindanao. As the mountains gradually slope towards the shorelines, farms, and plantations dot the landscape. Along the coastlines you'll find beaches with dark, pink, or cream sand, with consistency ranging from coarse to fine. Under water, divers are treated to a variety of terrain and marine life; and although there is evidence of dynamite fishing, spear fishing, and over-fishing, recent protection is encouraging new growth.

During the monsoon, rains occur mostly at night. There are no typhoons. Davao is an amenable place to visit year-round.

Tourism and tourist assistance facilities in some areas are well-developed and well-managed, but in others are less so. Most cities and major towns have a city tourism council, which is usually located in the office of the Governor or Mayor.

DAVAO CITY

Pretty islands, fruit and souvenier markets, museums, shrines, orchid plantations, an array of delicious food, and friendly people: could you ask for more in one city?

Davao is the prettiest southern metropolis, and its attractions range from islands in the bay to markets, museums, religious shrines, orchid and fruit plantations, golf, and mountain climbing. There is a good variety of resorts, hotels, lodges, and restaurants.

Davao City is one of the world's largest cities in land area: it spreads over 942 square miles (244,000 hectares); New York City covers only 369 square miles.

ARRIVALS & DEPARTURES

By Air

Davao's airport is 12 kilometers north of downtown. Landing at this airport is scenic, the view switches (several times) between land and sea. The arrival and departure area is a two-story open air building. The terminal and the bathrooms are kept clean.

When you get to the small room that is used as a baggage claim area, be prepared for pushy porters. It is easier to give them your claim tag and let them rummage for your bags than to do it yourself, and their fee is 75¢ (P20), a bit more if you have a lot of baggage.

Getting to downtown is easiest by taxi and will cost $6. You can also go by tricycle (25¢) or wait for a jeepney (30¢ per person).

The flight from Manila takes roughly one hour and 35-50 minutes. From Manila, Air Philippines has daily morning flights, Cebu Pacific has flights three times a day, Grand Air has two flights a day, and Philippine Airlines has three daily flights. Cebu Pacific and Philippine Airlines also

---

DAVAO FINDS & FAVORITES

- *Kinilaw "raw" fish marinated in vinegar and spices*
- *Claude's Bistro de Ville (see where to eat)*
- *The leche flan (custard) in Cecile's Snack Inn (see where to eat)*
- *Casa Leticia (see where to stay)*
- *Eagle Breeding Station (see day tips and excursions)*
- *Mount Apo (see Excursions below)*
- *Pujada Island, especially when you see a school of dolphins (see daytips and excursions)*

---

have daily flights from Cebu; flying time is roughly 55 minutes. Corporate Air's Mindanao Express has flights twice a day between Davao and General Santos City.

There are also international flights from Manado in Indonesia and from Malaysia.

By Sea

The trip from Manila takes 43-60 hours. Negros Navigation ($20-100) has a trip once a week; Sulpicio Lines ($25-100) has a trip once a week; and WGA SuperFerry ($38-130) has two trips a week. The trip from Cebu takes 25 hours; Sulpicio Lines ($10-50) goes once a week.

By Land

The central bus terminal is five minutes from downtown. Although it is usually busy, and there is a small market beside the area where buses wait, we did not see any porters; if there are any, they are not pushy like they are in many places.

To General Santos City. The trip can be done by bus (three hours) or PU vehicle. Yellow Bus Lines and STM Express cost $3 one-way on an air conditioned bus, and $1.75 on a regular bus. There is slightly more space on the "Mabuhay Class" buses of Yellow Bus Lines — there are only four seats in a row (two seats per aisle); the other buses seat five per row.

To Northern Mindanao. The scenic trip takes seven-to-eight hours to Cagayan de Oro, and bits of the road are rough. Bachellor and Ceres serve this route. The trip costs $10 via Butuan, and $6 via Bukidnon. The Bukidnon route is rougher and buses are not air conditioned.

GETTING AROUND TOWN

Because Davao City's land area is extensive, attractions are well spread out. Jeepneys ply main routes. Taxis are available, and hire cars may be found in front of the Apo View and Insular hotels. Fare from the Insular Century Hotel to the city center is P3.50 (15¢) by jeepney, $5 by taxi, and $10 by hire car. Several tour companies offer city and country-side tours, see *Practical Information*, "Tour & Travel Agencies" below, for a list of knowledgeable and reliable agencies.

Car rental agencies and taxis include:
• **Holiday Taxi**, *Tel. 221-2493, 221-2494, 221-9666*
• **Safeway Taxi**, *Tel. 221-7341, 221-7220*
• **Guani**, *Tel. 221-5000 to 02*
• **Avis**, *Tel. 234-2336, 234-2337, 234-3050*
• **Nissan**, *Tel. 221-8604 to 06*

WHERE TO STAY

Davao has an assortment of accommodations: a few nice pensions, several good moderate priced hotels, four upmarket hotels, and several beach resorts, including one with first-class amenities.

Better Hotels

INSULAR CENTURY HOTEL, *Kilometer 7, Lanang. Tel. 234-3050, Fax 62-959 Manila reservations. Tel. 526-4483, Fax 526-4484. 153 rooms. $103-141 per single, $123-161 per double, $207-483 per suite. Visa, Master Card, American Express, Diners.*

Definitely a landmark and a destination in itself, this is mainland Mindanao's top hotel. The hotel is spaciously laid out on an eight-hectare property, and its native decor gives it an elegant Mindanao feel. The large manicured lawn between the hotel and the beach has two interestingly sculpted plants: one is a *vinta* and the other is a horse and *calesa*.

The main difference between the standard, superior, and deluxe rooms is the size (deluxe being most expensive and largest). The standard rooms do not have a pool view, and are darker. All rooms come with cable TV, minibar, and are air conditioned. The rooms are typical of hotels in this price range: beds with a heavy bedspread and matching curtains, carpet, plush chairs, and marble bathrooms.

The presidential suite, however, has unique charm. This beautiful room is really three rooms combined. All are tastefully decorated with Asian artifacts and antiques. The bedroom has a solid wood and bamboo king-sized poster bed. A sliding door opens up to a porch, facing the lawn and pool, with a brass table and bamboo lounge chairs. Baskets with *tinalak* and a capiz tissue box give the marble tiled bathroom a native flare. Wooden chests with capiz inlays decorate the cozy living room. Amenities included in the suite are a television and CD player inside an antique wooden cabinet, fax, and kitchen.

The hotel's service is very good; the staff seem eager to please all their guests. The pool is part of the main lawn: it is small, but with enough area to do laps. You also have a selection for dining: coffee shop or restaurant indoors, and a poolside bar or La Parilla for grilled seafood outside.

DURIAN HOTEL, *JP Laurel Avenue. Tel. 221-8216, Fax 221-1835. 137 rooms. $65 per single, $74-85 per double, $103 per suite. Visa, Master Card, American Express, Diners.*

Do not worry, the hotel does not smell like its namesake – the exotic fruit. A new building of 12 floors has been added behind the original structure of five stories. The rooms are a lot bigger than those in most of the other hotels here. All rooms are carpeted, and come with a minibar and cable television. The swimming pool is in the roof-garden, on the top floor. Other facilities include a small gym, business center, souvenier shop, jazz bar, and disco. There is a grand piano, played sometimes, in the coffee shop, which serves Filipino and western cuisine. You will find the staff efficient and friendly.

APO VIEW HOTEL, *J Camus Street. Tel. 221-2281, Fax 221-0748. Manila reservations: Tel. 893-1288, Fax 894-1223. 108 rooms. $55-77 per single, $65-87 per double, $96-192 per suite. Visa, Master Card, American Express.*

The Apo View, which once had the best view of Mount Apo (hence the name) and much of the city, has been dwarfed by recent construction in Davao. You can still get a pretty good view from the Top of the Apo, its coffee shop on the top floor.

The rooms in the new wing are nice; some are very red (colors of the carpet and curtains). Framed and hanging on the wall is an attractive western (probably Italian) silk scarf. All rooms are air conditioned and have cable TV.

The lobby is pleasant, the furnishing is mostly native, except for the Chinese-style marble floor, and there is a very nice painting of an Indo-Malay tribe. The interior architecture of the hotel gives you the feeling that its designer was partial to mazes: it is easy to get lost. Among the facilities are a pool, barber shop, business center, several function rooms, and a travel agency. The hotel also has a bar and disco, and its restaurant specializes in fresh grilled seafood, which is excellent. Service in the hotel varies, but the room cleaning staff is very pleasant.

GRAND MEN SENG HOTEL, *Magallanes corner Anda Street. Tel. 221-2431, Fax 221-5889. 70 rooms. $57.50-71 per single, $69-82 per double, $100 per triple, $134 per suite, $19 per extra bed, $11.50 per extra person. Visa, Master Card, American Express.*

Grand is what you feel when you enter the hotel: marble floors, red carpets, and a high ceiling in the lobby. All the rooms are on the top two floors of this white three-story building. Function rooms take up most of the first floor. The swimming pool is on the second floor, and there is a good unobscured view of Mount Apo.

The rooms are very spacious, and carpeting in the rooms is either green or red. There are also "rooms for asthmatics" (wooden tiles and no carpet), available upon request. The marble tiled bathrooms are large and have bathtubs. The suites can accommodate 10 people, with room left to move around. In each suite you will find a good sized sofa, large bedroom, ample closet space, and an elegant burgundy bathroom. All the rooms are air conditioned and have cable TV, minibar, daily newspaper, and complementary shoeshine service.

Moderate Hotels

CASA LETICIA, *J Camus Street, Tel. 224-0501, Fax 221-3585. E-mail address: casalet@interasia.com.ph. 41 rooms. $35-53 per single, $51-65 per double, $85-135 per suite. Visa, Master Card, American Express, Diners.*

This charming hotel is in an attractive Spanish-style dusty rose-colored building, and is one of our favorites. The friendly staff is very efficient, and the hotel is well-managed and family run. The rooms are very clean, and all are painted a light pastel green. The studios, the cheapest of the single rooms, are narrow but long. All other rooms have sufficient space and are very comfortable. In the bathrooms you will find a note on tips for water conservation, which is impressive for the Philippines, as you usually see this only in the five-star hotels. Ask for a room facing J Camus Street for a better view, and adjoining rooms are available upon request. All rooms are air conditioned and have cable TV. The suites include a hairdryer, refrigerator, and an extension phone in the bathroom. Daily newspapers are provided in all rooms.

Facilities include business center services, safe deposit boxes, and function rooms. The lobby coffee shop specializes in local cuisine, has some western dishes, and is open 24 hours a day. On the sixth floor is the popular bar, Toto's.

Included among the regular guests of this hotel are people working with the US Agency for International Development (AID). The staff is honest and guests who are going out of the city for a few days have left their baggage with the staff to watch. Everyone here, from the manager to the reception, concierge, bellboys, guards, waiters, and room staff, is hospitable, and this makes you feel almost at home.

HOTEL MAGUINDANAO, *86 CM Recto Street. Tel. 78-401 to 05. 56 rooms. $42 per single $51-62 per double, $113 per suite. Visa, Master Card.*

This was one of the first hotels in the city, and it has recently been renovated. The centerpiece hanging on the wall in the lobby is wonderful — concrete and brass molded into scenes depicting different stages of Philippine history. The standard rooms are average size and are simply furnished and clean. The deluxe rooms are spacious and have a unique canopy sofa made of bamboo that can also serve as another bed. Some rooms are of a native motif while others are more western. The staff is very friendly. Continental and local food is served in the Rajah Café.

HOTEL GALLERIA, *Gov Duterte Street. Tel. 221-2480, 221-2657, 221-2693, Fax 221-8162. 43 rooms. $35 per single, $50-54 double, $65-110 per suite, $11.50 per extra adult, $13 per extra bed. Visa, Master Card, Diners.*

Galleria is in a nice three-story white and green building with wrought iron balcony fences. This hotel is reminiscent of small hotels in Europe. There is no elevator: a winding wooden staircase takes you to the upper floors. Request a pool view: the street does not provide interesting scenery. The pool is located centrally in the patio; it is cute and small, with a fountain running into it. Bougainvillea and small palms are arranged around the sides of the patio. Two wrought iron tables are set up around on one side, where you can have a snack. A winding iron staircase takes you from the upper floors directly to the patio.

The rooms are small if you are accustomed to American-size hotels, but are the standard size here. Rooms are furnished simply and kept clean, and have cable TV. A complementary basket of fruit comes with all rooms. Staff are friendly. There is a small restaurant, and the hotel offers rent-a-car and mailing services.

VILLA MARGARITA, *JP Laurel Avenue. Tel. 221-5674, 224-2712, Fax 62-968. 32 rooms. $35-46 per single, $38-55 per double, $60-70 per suite. Visa, Master Card, American Express, Diners.*

This pretty two-story Spanish-style villa has a charming exterior and reception area. The tastefully decorated reception area has native and antique decor displayed on the wall. Rooms are the standard size, nice, and clean; all come with cable TV. The stairwell leading to the second floor is a bit dim. There is a small pool, and a poolside cafe area where grilled food is served. The restaurant serves food from various Southeast Asian countries, and the café provides western and Filipino fare.

TOWER INN, *Elpidio Quirino Avenue. Tel. 221-1099, Fax 221-8034. 38 rooms. $34-41 per single, $46-76 per double, $75-88 per suite, $10 per extra bed. Visa, Master Card, American Express.*

This cute grey marble building has some rooms with a small balcony and potted plants. It is a busy hotel and seems to be frequented by business managers. The suite rooms have a small cute porch that is covered, and a table and chair for relaxing outside (the view is not anything special). The regular rooms are the standard size for the area; color combinations are a bit odd. All rooms are clean and come with cable TV. The hotel also has a free shuttle service to the airport. Facilities include a small business center, rent-a-car, and laundry services.

HOTEL MARIO, *Magallanes Street. Tel. 224-0659 to 63, Fax 224-0663. 27 rooms. $33-40 per single $42-55 per double, $76-84 per suite. Visa, Master Card.*

All rooms in this simple hotel are air conditioned and have cable TV. The rooms are clean and designed for the serious business traveler — dark subdued serious colors and wood furniture. Check the room before taking it — if recently fumigated, it may need to be aired out. The bathroom is small compared to the size of the rooms (big rooms compared to others in this price range). Rooms facing the street tend to be noisy, it's on a busy street. The staff are very delightful. The owner, Mr. Mario Cleto, a well-known columnist, provides a wealth of stories and information.

Budget Hotels & Pensions

ELLE'S PENSION, *Mt. Apo corner General Luna Street. Tel. 221-8499, Fax 221-2637. 25 rooms. $20-24 per single, $28-34 per double, $39-45 per "family" (four people). Visa, Master Card.*

This is a very white inn, outside and in. The building is well lit, including inside the rooms. All rooms are clean, simple, air conditioned, and have cable TV. The bathrooms are small, which is generally the case in the budget hotels.

MIRAGE PENSION INN, *Daisy Alley, off Quirino Avenue. Tel. 221-2707, Fax 224-1490. $11.50-20 per single, $17-27 per double, $4 per extra bed.*

This nice villa-style building is in a quiet area and has small, bright, and clean rooms. The bathrooms are also small and there is no shower curtain to separate the bathing area from the sink and toilet. The cheaper rooms have fans, while the more expensive ones are air conditioned ($8 difference).

PARK SQUARE INN, *Sandawa Plaza Quimpo Boulevard. Tel. 298-0258, 298-0259. $16-21 per single, $20-24 per double, $27 per triple.*

This small hotel is blue and white on the inside and outside. Rooms are small, clean, simply furnished, and all are air conditioned. There is a Coffee Shop and bakery on the ground floor, and *Karinderya*, a great place for *turo-turo* (canteen style) fastfood, is across the street.

LAROUS PENSION HOUSE, *Ilustre Street. Tel. 74-822. $13-28 per single or double aircon, $7-11 per single or double no-naircon.*

Rooms are generally clean and bare. Women who are 5'6" and above should see the bathrooms before choosing a room — in the interior-facing rooms, the window by the shower is a bit too low for comfort.

ALJEM'S INN, *Tel. 221-3060, Fax 221-3059,* and **THE MANOR PENSION**, *Tel. 221-2511.*

Both places are on the same side of A Pichon Street, and charge $24 per single $28-34 per double. Rooms in both places are clean and small, and hallways are on the dark side.

Beach Resorts

PEARL FARM BEACH RESORT, *Samal Island. Tel. 221-9970. Manila reservations: Tel. 526-1555. $191-219 per single, $202-251 per double, $362 per suite, $612-721 per villa. Visa, Master Card, American Express, Diners.*

This former pearl farm has been transformed into a resort with a unique blend of western and ethnic styles. The beach is nothing to rave about, but the resort more than makes up for it. The resort was designed by one of the country's top architects – Bobby Mañosa – who incorporated the pool into the landscape: it appears to flow into the South China Sea.

Beside the pool, a waterfall flows into a pond, home to turtles and starfish. The dining room, behind the pool, resembles a ski chalet, but is made with bamboo. And by the beach, an old watch tower has been converted into the Parola Bar, a nice place to have a drink as the sun sets. Landward, the resort is encased in lush flora and tall coconut trees.

The Samal suites and cottages, built over the water, take their design from the stilt houses of the Sama tribe found around the Sulu Islands. As you walk out onto the verandah of your cottage, imbibe the spectacular view of the sea, the marine life right below you, and Isla Malipano in front. The interiors are decorated with tribal handicrafts and materials with ethnic designs, and the furniture is mostly bamboo.

The Mandaya cottages, more expensive rooms, are on the other side of the resort. Built beside the shore, these attractive cottages are more spacious than the other rooms (price varies with space).

Isla Malipano is a small island right in front of the Pearl Farm, and is part of the resort. The beach on the island is better than that of the main area. This is where the Luxury Villas are located. These spacious cabins have three or four bedrooms, ideal for a group of people seeking privacy.

The resort also has a complete dive center where you could take an intensive course and be certified in three days. The cost will be $400, including equipment, boat rental, and certification. There are also jet skis for rent at $100 per hour.

PARADISE ISLAND RESORT, *Samal Island. Tel. 234-1229, 233-0251, Fax 234-2926. $55 per single or double aircon, $29 per single or double non-aircon, $4 per extra bed, $4 per extra person.*

The resort's simple beach cottages are behind the coconut trees that line the nice beach. All cottages have a private toilet and shower room, and a small porch to lounge around on. On weekends during the day, the resort is full of people, and will not be quiet; nights and weekdays, the area is peaceful. The restaurant serves Chinese, Filipino, and American food.

ISLA CRISTINA, *Talicud Island. Tel. 221-2653, 221-2495, Fax 221-5958. 10 cottages. $46 per single or double, $11.50 per extra bed.*

The cottages are on a grassy lawn behind the coconut trees that line the nice white sand beach (natural sand, not taken from elsewhere). The cottages are simple and nicely decorated with a native motif. The attractive headboards of the bed are fan shaped. There is a small living room area with a sofa and bamboo tables. All cottages have electric fans and private bathrooms. The restaurant serves local food, and has a buffet lunch for $7.

ISLA RETA, *Talicud Island. Tel. 77-134, 74-092. 5 cottages, 4 rooms. $15 per single or double, $20 per cottage, $4 per extra bed.*

The facilities in this resort are very simple, but nice and clean. The quality of the beach here is better than those on Samal (and the sand is not "imported"). The cottages have one double bed and a bathroom. The four rooms share a shower and toilet. The food is mainly Filipino, and the menu is limited, but if you have something simple in mind they will be happy to make it for you, provided the ingredients are available; try the grilled fish, it's fresh and tasty. The rice is good too. There are some caves to explore nearby.

BUENAVISTA ISLAND, *Small Ligid Island. Tel. 297-1432. Manila reservations: c/o Buenavista Travel Tel. 817-3296, 817-3271. Rates are for the entire island: $400 for 1-5 people to $1,125 for a group of 21-25.*

Imagine having your own private island with a very nice white sand beach fringed with azure water and corals nearby, and good diving! The owners have a house on the island, but are rarely there. Two small but very pretty wooden cottages are on one side of the island. Each cottage has one large room, with a bed in the center that is built into the floor (the top of the mattress is floor level). As you lie on the bed you can enjoy the panoramic sea view — the entire wall is a sliding glass door. The bathroom is spacious and has a marble bath. The swimming pool blends into the landscaping of the lawn area. Flowering bushes line the walkways that lead you around the island, passing by bushes that have been sculpted into diving dolphins, to a gazebo that hangs over the sea. The rate includes roundtrip transfers by yacht.

MARINA AZUL RESORT HOTEL, *Times Beach, Matina, Davao City. Tel. 298-0263, Fax 64-052. $51-90 per single or double, $144-165 per suite. Visa, Master Card, American Express.*

The rooms in this resort are called suite rooms. They are large rooms with a porch or balcony, and are nicely decorated using local materials and furniture. A woven cloth with a tribal design is framed and hung on the wall. Room prices vary with size; the largest, the Presidential Suite, can accommodate eight people comfortably. At the center of the resort is a good sized pool, with restaurants beside it, and a deck that serves as a grill and a bar. The food is tasty and service is good. The resort is managed well and staffed by friendly and efficient people.

WHERE TO EAT

You will not go hungry here or be disappointed with Davao's food: there are many good places to eat. For fast food, try the Davao-based **CHICKIES & PATTIES** and **YUMMY CHICKEN & BURGER**; **JOLLYBEE** and **MCDONALDS**; foodcourts in the malls (if you like *shawarma*, similar to a pita sandwich – the best one is at a stall in the University Mall); and several street-side food stalls usually serving barbecue.

You can also feast on fresh fruit at the stalls in the **Madrazo Fruit Market** (see the *Shopping* section for more details).

Downtown

CLAUDE'S LE CAFÉ DE VILLE, *29 Rizal Street, downtown.*

We highly recommend this place. Probably the only gourmet restaurant here, it is one of the most upscale places (jeans or nice shorts and a shirt suffice). The French food is great. Although expensive for Davao restaurants, a scrumptious meal with a glass of perfectly chilled white wine, dessert, and coffee will cost you $16. The chicken breast, slowly cooked in red wine, is succulent.

Through a picture window between the kitchen and dining area, you will see Claude, the owner, and yes, a Frenchman, cooking alongside the other chefs, all in white hats. When Claude is not busy, he chats with the guests and inquires about the food — he sincerely wants to know. He and his wife, who is from Davao and the reason he remained here after being General Manager of the Insular for some time, add to the friendly and charming atmosphere of the place.

KUYA EDS, *Apichon Street across from the Grand Men Seng.*

This native restaurant is very popular with local business people. As you walk upstairs to the air conditioned restaurant, you will be greeted by two pretty parrots inside a wooden bird cage. Although spacious, Kuya Eds is packed for lunch; come early for its $4.50 buffet, which comes with very good *leche flan* (cream custard), fresh fruits, and an assortment of other desserts.

Other places to go for native cuisine are **KUSINA DABAW**, *with outlets on Legaspi Street, Anda Street, Santa Ana Avenue, and Monteverde Avenue*; **MANG AMBO**, *J Camus, one block from Casa Leticia,* a very casual place that is popular for its *inihaw ni palikpik* (barbecue tuna and marlin fins); and **COCONUT GROVE** *on Anda Street*, a cute 24-hour stall that serves grilled food.

ZUGBA, *Apo View Hotel (pricey at $20 per person).*

Come here for great fresh seafood. You can have succulent grilled fresh seafood in a casual native setting. You chose from the seafood laid out on a table. The *sashimi* is also good. Also in the hotel is **TOP OF THE APO**, your typical hotel coffee shop, but it commands a great view of Davao. This is a nice place to go for the view, evenings and during the day. There are several lovely wall hangings of woven cloths from the Maranaw. It is better to come for coffee and dessert (inquire what flavors of ice cream are available before you have your heart set on one or two).

FIESTA DABAW, *Tionco corner Arellano Street, between E Quirino Avenue and F Torres Street.*

You can have a tasty local meal ($4 per person) of pretty good *sugba* (grilled) and *turo-turo* (cafeteria style) here. The restaurant has native decor, including colorful mats woven in Zamboanga. You can sit in the small air conditioned room, where many of Davao's doctors prefer to lunch, or outside in the fan-cooled open air setting.

The city's good Chinese restaurants, are all near each other on *Magsaysay Avenue.* Try **CHINA ROYAL**, a typical Chinese restaurant with large round tables, the food is excellent especially the fresh steamed fish; also try **DAVAO FAMOUS, SHANGHAI**, and **TAI HUAT CLAY POT HOUSE**. Near Casa Leticia is **DENCIA'S**, *35 Pelayo Street*, where you can get a whole meal for about $2.

Popular places for *merienda* (a snack) are **CECILE'S SNACK INN** (*Anda Street*) — try their great flan; **MOTHER BAKER** (*Gov. Duterte Street*) for good homemade chocolate mousse cake; and the **MERCO** outlets (*Quirino corner Mt. Apo Street, Bolton corner Rizal Street, and Guerrero Street*), probably the closest thing you will come to a diner here, all are open late.

Santa Ana Wharf

For a real treat in a native setting, try the restaurants near the Muslim village south of Sta Ana Wharf. The pioneer restaurant of its kind, **LUZ KINILAW**, *Salmonan, Quezon Boulevard,* is still one of the best. Choose from *kinilaw* (marinated raw tuna), barbequed *bariles pangga at buntot* (tuna jaw and tail), and barbequed *pusit* (squid). Arrive early to sit by the window overlooking the river and Muslim village beyond.

KANAWAY, in *Magsaysay Park, Quezon Boulevard*, also excellent, offers the same delicacies plus very good *lechon kawali* (sliced roast pig served in a special sauce). Bathroom facilities in these places are not always clean; bring some paper napkins (from the table) or tissue.

Bajada – Just North of Downtown

HARANA I and **II**, and **SARUNGBANGGI**, *F Torres Street (between JP Laurel Avenue and E Jacinto).*

These restaurants, all in one complex, are known for good Filipino food and grilled seafood. The restaurants are popular with visitors and locals. You have your choice of dining area — open-air or air conditioned — and can order from either of the three menus. We suggest ordering the sashimi (it is fresh) and at least one grilled seafood. The restaurants are furnished with native materials, and the bathrooms are clean. If you have kids, this is a great place to dine: there is a big lawn with a playground; at night bring repellent.

Next door is **BISTRO ROSARIO**, a popular place for steaks and western fare. The restaurant has a nice ambiance and the building was formerly an ancestral house, or has been designed to appear like one.

ALAVAR'S, *JP Laurel Street, near Victoria Plaza.*

A pioneer restaurant specializing in seafood; the original Alavar is in Zamboanga City. You can get good seafood dishes; crab seems to be the most popular. Inside, the restaurant is small and dark; the place is clean and food is good.

Insular Village Area

LA PARILLA, *Insular Century Hotel.*

Great grilled seafood. The charming restaurant is in the pretty garden of the hotel. Ambiance is casual, and service is good. The food is perfectly grilled, not overdone; the meat is juicy and tender.

HAGAR'S PLACE, *Blucor Building, Insular Village 1, R Castillo Street, very near the Insular.*

This is the place to go if you have a craving for Austrian Sausages and other heavy European dishes. Servings are large and the sausages are good. It is also near the airport, and it's a popular place for meals before flights or when waiting for someone to arrive.

BLUE POST, *near Insular Village 2, R Castillo Street.*

This is a great place for exotic food: you must be adventurous — try bull testicles, *sisig* (cheeks and ears of a pig, minced and spicy, served on a sizzling plate) with pig brains (in most places *sisig* does not include the brains); snake; and the list goes on. A popular evening place, people come here to hang out and play billiards.

Bangkal – Just South of Downtown

KARINDERYA, *Sandawa Plaza Quimpo Boulevard, Bangkal.*

This is a great place for cheap and tasty fast food *turo-turo* style (a meal for five with drinks was $11). Try the *laing* (taro cooked Bicol-style in coconut with spices, it is good and slightly spicy), and the *adobong kangkong* (a spinach-like vegetable cooked in soy sauce, vinegar, and pepper with a strong garlic flavor). The restaurant is in a large pavilion (open air with many electric fans) and has a large television. The volume is high so sit accordingly. The bathrooms were surprisingly clean, but may not be stocked with toilet paper.

MOLAVE II, *MacArthur Highway, Matina.*

If you like fried chicken, you must try this place. They have a unique "secret family recipe" for crispy "greaseless" fried chicken. The chicken is a lot less greasy than any other fried chicken we have tried; it is also very tasty and juicy. There is an outlet downtown on P Reyes Street, but we like this one because it is in an ancestral house, and, with the nice paintings on the wall, has much more character.

SEEING THE SIGHTS

You can take a leisurely walk around the city. Enjoy the people, parks, food, and handicrafts. Stroll to **Rizal** and **Osmeña parks**, in front of City Hall, and the **San Pedro Cathedral**. This curious structure attempts to combine Moorish design and Roman Catholicism — a gesture of reconciliation in an area where Christians and Muslims are often at odds.

Stroll or take a jeepney to the spacious and green **Magsaysay Park**, also the site of the DOT offices. Next door is the **Sta Ana Wharf**. Just south of the park is a wooden foot bridge that crosses the river to the **Muslim Fishing Village**. The small toll supports bridge maintenance. You can see picturesque views of mosque spires rising through the dense shanty area.

Further south along the road are several simple restaurants serving *kinilaw* (tuna sashimi), barbequed *bariles pangga at buntot* (tuna jaw and tail), and *pusit* (squid). Try Kanaway and Luz Kinilaw.

Along Cabaguio Avenue are two temples. Davao has a large Chinese community, and 1% of Davao's population is Buddhist. In the **Taoist Temple**, there are saints representing many religions. If you wish to have your fortune told, look for Mrs. Alvarez, the priestess. **Lon Wa Buddhist Temple** is further along. The structure appears to have been transplanted from China. Inside, a large golden Buddha sits atop a slab of Italian marble.

Outskirts of the City

Davao Century Insular Hotel is one of the city's major attractions. Its relaxing gardens spread over four of its eight hectares, and include shrubs sculpted into animal forms: a *carabao* with its yoke, a horse and *calesa*, squirrel, birds, and a fisherman with his *banca*. You can see men climb the coconut trees to remove the *tuba* (sap that is fermented into alcohol).

A small Mandaya settlement, the **Dabaw Etnica**, is just over a bridge behind the main hotel building. In a small house you can watch Mandaya women preparing the abaca fiber, tying, dyeing, and weaving it into the colorful *dagmay* fabric they use for clothing, blankets, and many other purposes. Intricate designs are embroidered on pieces of cloth that will be sewn into blouses. You can buy bags, bracelets, household goods, abaca cloth, and other items. By providing alternative income, Dabaw Etnica is aimed at helping the Mandaya adjust to their greatly reduced tribal lands.

From the Insular's wharf, you can get boats for Samal, Talicud, and Ligid islands.

Take a short walk from the Insular to the **Dabaw Museum**, a project of a local women's club. When you enter Insular Village 1, take your first right, then first left; the museum is on the right side. Well documented displays include photos, tribal artifacts, and costumes. A few high-priced handicrafts are available. The museum is open Mondays to Saturdays, from 9:00am to 5:00pm (the $1 entrance fee goes towards maintenance).

NIGHTLIFE & ENTERTAINMENT

Davao City's nightlife is the most alive of all Mindanao cities. Popular night spots include **Toto's**, in Casa Leticia, a simple version of Hard Rock – the service and finger food are good; **Pop's**, Ilustre Street; **Penec Bar**, Apo View Hotel; and **Blue Post**, R Castillo Street, north of downtown, which also has billiard tables.

The popular dance club is **Spam's**, Apo View Hotel. If you like karaoke (sing-along), check out **Shogun KTV Bar and Restaurant**, Villa Abrille Street, and **Music Hall KTV Lounge**, Victoria Plaza.

SPORTS & RECREATION

Fishing

There is supposed to be some decent game fishing for marlin and tuna around Cape San Agustin. Fishing tours are offered by **Island Tour Transport Services**, Ong Building, Bolton Street, *Tel. 224-2435, 224-1883*. There is a minimum of three people and cost is $195 per person; this includes boat rental, your food, and bait.

Golf

Davao's three golf courses are all within the city. **Apo Golf and Country Club** is a very scenic course. Aside from an 18-hole championship course ($48 green and caddie fee), there is a clubhouse with a restaurant, swimming pool, and pelota courts. The **Lanang Golf and Country Club** has 18 holes laid out in a plantation setting ($25 greens and caddie fee), and a club house with restaurants and tennis courts. And the **New Davao City Golf Club** is a nine-hole course ($15 greens and caddie fee).

Scuba Diving

Most of the interesting dive spots are in Davao Gulf around Samal, Talicud, and Ligid islands. You will find patches of coral with colorful inhabitants. Although there are signs of the abusive fishing of the past, protection has encouraged recent growth. Dive sites include **House Reef**, where fish feeding has been developed; **two wrecks**, one at 75 feet, the other at 140 feet (openings are wide and the wrecks are home to many critters); several small reefs; caves; and areas with larger fish such as sharks, tuna, barracudas, and snappers.

Warning: off the south of Samal Island currents can be strong. There is a dive center at the Century Insular Hotel and another at the Pearl Farm Resort. Trips can also be arranged through **Scuba Davao**, c/o Fishpenn Davao, Anda Street, *Tel. 62-812.*

There is also some nice diving around Pujada Island in Davao Oriental, but there are no facilities and you will have to bring all your gear.

Trekking

There are two scheduled annual climbs to **Mt. Apo** organized by the local mountaineers in conjunction with the regional DOT in Davao. These climbs are usually crowded, so if you are looking forward to peace and quiet, climb at another time. On Samal Island, you can climb **Mt. Puting Bato** (usually a two-day trek) and explore the **Malipano Cave**. Before going you should inquire about getting a reliable guide from the **DOT**, *Tel. 221-0070.*

SHOPPING

The **Aldevinco Shopping Center**, on CM Recto, is a shopper's paradise: antiques (few are genuine), excavated pottery and porcelain, handicrafts, artifacts from Mindanao's varied tribes, a profusion of Indonesian batik, traditional Muslim brass items such as betel nut boxes, tribal weavings, T'Boli bronze figurines, bags made from *banig* (woven pandan leaves), clothing, costume jewelry, etc. Use your bargaining skills here: get as much as 50% off the Muslim brass, and 25% off some other items. **Lakambini Crafts**, across the street, has more handicrafts.

You can get a visual and gastronomic feast of fruits at the **Madrazo Fruit Center**, two blocks from Aldevinco. It's the opportunity to savor a number of exotic fruits very cheaply when in season, including the tasty but very smelly durian (not allowed in your hotel, nor on the plane!), and the delicious and not so odorous *marang*. Other fruits you can sample are mangosteen, rambutan, lanzones, avocado, chico, banana, pineapple, mango, orange, pomelo, santol, guava, and so much more. A meal or two a day from purchases at Madrazo would be good for your palate and wallet.

At **Nieva's Arts & Crafts**, enroute to the Insular, you may watch artists hand paint designs on wood for jewelry, desk sets, boxes, etc., and some pottery. They have a small display room where you can buy a few items. And at **Dabaw Etnica**, at the Century Insular Hotel grounds, you can buy pieces of cloth embroidered with intricate designs, bags, bracelets, household goods, abaca cloth, and other items all made by the Mandaya.

EXCURSIONS & DAY TRIPS

Offshore Islands

You can find a few pretty white sand beaches on the nearby islands. **Samal Island**, the largest, has a number of resorts. Local trekkers frequent Mt. Puting Bato, and the Malipano cave. If shell vendors approach with corals, shells, and dead turtles, let them know you do not support the imminent extinction of the sea turtle nor reef destruction.

There are a number of places where you can go for the day. At the **Paradise Island Resort** you will find a nice white sand beach lined with shady talisay trees. Facilities include beach chairs, a bar, and protective flotation around the swimming area. You may rent *bancas* to paddle around, mahjong sets, and cards. Entry is $1.20 per person. **Coral Reef Beach Resort** also has a nice beach, three rustic cottages with common bath, and a house to rent. They serve barbeque lunches on the weekends; on other days you need to order food a day in advance. Smaller resorts include **Samal Beach Park** and **Palm Hill**.

Tickets to Coral Reef and Paradise are available at the Insular, at $5 for the day, including transport and entry fee. You may also board a boat to Samal Island from the Insular's wharf for an 85¢ "wharf maintenance fee" each way. It is less expensive to take the *bancas* from the Sasa Wharf: transport is 20¢ per person, or $4 to rent a *banca* one way.

Also on Samal is the Exclusive **Pearl Farm Beach Resort**. To go for the day, you have to make arrangements through the Insular Hotel, at least one day in advance. The cost is $25 per person, and includes lunch. There is also a large high-end resort being put up by a group of Malaysians.

Talicud Island is just south of Samal Island. It has prettier beaches and three simple resorts. **Isla Reta** (85¢ entry per person, $2-4 for a picnic table), **Babusanta** (85¢ per hut), and **Isla Cristina** ($4 per person, including use of picnic table). There is some good snorkeling and diving around Talicud. A number of migrating birds pass through the area, so bring binoculars. There is also a cave near Isla Reta; you should bring proper shoes if you intend to go exploring. Both Isla Reta and Cristina have simple cottages if you want to stay overnight.

North of Samal Island are **Big** and **Small Ligid Islands**, both privately owned. There is not much to see on the big island. Small Ligid is quite pretty, fringed with a cream-sand beach and emerald green waters, and can be rented (the entire island and its facilities!) for the day or overnight: see the *Where to Stay* section.

On the Coast & Inland

Times Beach is crammed with picnic sheds and barbeque stands. Even though the water is murky with silt from the nearby mouth of the Davao River, locals still flock here on the weekend.

Gap Farming Resort has orchards full of fruit trees and orchids, a pool, a cave the Japanese used during World War Two, cottages amid pastoral surroundings, and large cement sculptures of animals (including one of a carabao relieving itself). The Gap farm is about 10 minutes from downtown.

A little further from the Gap Farm is the **Crocodile Park**. You can see crocodiles, from hatchlings to an 18-footer, and other exotic animals: snapping turtles, iguanas (bayaw*aks*), and civet cats (the entry fee is 60¢ per person).

If you are interested in religious markers, visit the **Shrine of the Infant Jesus of Prague**. It is five minutes from the Gap Farm. An open air chapel with a replica of the Prague icon and of Our Lady of Fatima is on a nearby promontory. People come to pray. You can enjoy a nice view of Davao City, the bay, its islands, and the farmlands and mountain behind: a nice, peaceful place for liesurely strolls. A nearby **Japanese Shrine** honors those who died during the war.

To see thousands of orchids growing and blossoming in terraces, go to the **Yuhico Greenhills Orchid Farms**.

Return to the coast to visit **Talomo Beach**, where invading Japanese landed in 1942, then American troops in 1944. Several carcasses of sunken vessels lie offshore.

Two resorts popular with the locals are **Caroland Resort** and **Villa Victoria**. Caroland, at Bago Iñigo Farms, has picnicking, pony rides, a pond stocked with big carp that come up for bits of bread, fishing, and a flock of wild ducks. Fruit trees and orchids provide shade. Villa Victoria Beach Resort has clusters of cottages (for day or overnight), a large children's playground, a Chinese restaurant, and a waterfront area for swimming backed by grassy areas shaded by coconut trees.

If you like orchids, the **Derling Orchid Farm** is a great stop. You can see hundreds of rows of many different species; some are for sale.

At the **Mt. Apo Science Foundation** in Eden, Bayabas, Toril, at the base of Apo, you can get great views and the weather is a cool 62 to 70°F. The foundation's research on agriculture and woodlands is supported by the Asia Foundation and the University of Mindanao.

A must is the **Philippine Eagle Nature Center** in Malagos. Here you can see beautiful Philippine Eagles in captivity. The crew hopes to further their breeding and perhaps prevent extinction of the species; so far there have been two successful births in captivity. Wander around to look at other birds and animals of the region. A short film on the Center and the succeful births is shown in a room beside the souvenier shop — a portion of the items for sale goes towards the Center, as does the $1 entrance fee. To get there, you can hire a vehicle ($20-22.50 round trip) or take a jeepney, with a sign that reads Davao City-Calinan, from CM Recto, A Pichon Street, or the Bankerohan Market (50¢ per person one way), then a tricycle to Malagos.

Just before you get to the Eagle Center you will see the **Malagos Garden**. Walk around the large, manicured orchard containing over 20 species of orchids. Some of the orchids are propogated in the **Puentespina Orchid & Tropical Plant** (in Agdao) and replanted in their original habitats by mountaineers. There is also a simple restaurant where you can grab a meal (the flies are shooed away by the waiters using sticks with tassels of plastic rope); the food was tasty when we were there. The restaurant has a nice water color painting of an orchid. The entrance fee is 60¢.

Further north, in **Ipol**, you can do a few good short hikes through a misty forest. Ipol is at higher elevation, and temperatures can drop to 10 degrees Celsius (50°F). A short trek takes you to a cave (bring adequate lighting) with a small spring. In the cave, you will see a small waterfall, stactites, and stalagmites. Another short, pleasant trek will take you to a 20-foot waterfall. To get to Ipol, hire a jeepney ($12 each way); you can make arrangements in Malagos.

If you want to stay overnight, **ISLAND IN THE SKY**, at the starting point to the cave, has a charming private cabin (*call Oliver at Casa Leticia Tel. 224-0501 for arrangements*); and **SEAGULL IN THE SKY**, with basic rooms ($16 a night for a room with four beds) a bit further up the road.

PRACTICAL INFORMATION

Banks

You will find several banks in the city, a number of them along CM Recto Street: **PNB**, **PCI Bank**, **Equitable**, **CityTrust**, **Allied Bank**, and **BPI** (which also has machines for Cirrus cards). **MetroBank** has a branch on Santa Ana. Banking hours are Mondays through Fridays, from 9:00am to 3:00pm.

Post Office

The **post office** is five blocks away from City Hall on A Pichon Street. You can also avail of courier services (DHL and UPS, and local companies:

JRS, LBC, and TNT), which offer express mail locally and to a few international destinations.

Tourist Assistance

This is one of the areas with a well-run **Department of Tourism**, *Tel. 221-0070, Fax 221-6798,* where you can get maps, brochures, and information. The office is conveniently located in Magsaysay Park. The staff are very nice and informative, and can suggest various tours. Mountain climbers should contact Frank Villaraiz. See Mt. Apo below.

Information is also available at the **City Tourism Office**, at the City Hall, *Tel. 78-074.*

Tour and travel agencies include;

· **Buenavista Travel**, *Tel. 297-1432, Fax 298-0193*
· **Morning Star Mindanao**, *Tel. 221-6307, 221-1346, Fax 221-1271*
· **Island Tour Transport Service**, *Tel. 224-2435, 224-1883*
· **Danfil Express Inc.**, *Tel. 234-3050*

MOUNT APO

Apo (meaning grandfather), the Philippines' highest mountain (2,945 meters), is an enjoyable climb year round. There are no recorded eruptions from this dormant volcano. Unfortunately, the forests that once hugged its slopes are being cut down, the land converted to farms and well sites for an extensive geothermal project, and the habitat of the **Philippine Eagle** is fast disappearing. Despite the denudation, it is still a mountain well worth visiting.

Early April is the best time for climbing Apo — cloud cover is minimal and rainfall is less than during August to December. Allow at least four days, five are better, for the climb. To arrange for guides and provisions in advance, contact the DOT Davao (inquire from Frank Villaraiz *Tel. 221-0070, Fax 221-6798*). Experienced climbers can find porters (they too know the way) in Lake Agco, Kidapawen, 110 kilometers from Davao City. Bring a tent, etc. for the porters before starting out. A good rope could be helpful. Guides will cost $155 per guide for the trek, and porters are $6-8 a day.

Before beginning the ascent, you must register at the Municipal Building of Kidapawen. Then proceed by jeepney ($1.50 per person), approximately an hour an a half, to Lake Agco, at 1,200 meters. The lake is fed by several springs of varied temperatures and there is a cabin by the shores where climbers may spend the night. If you arrive at Agco by noon, continue to **Mainit** to camp for the night, crossing the Marbel River at least nine times along the way. Mainit has a small campsite beside a hot spring. Your second day will be climbing to **Lake Venado** (also known as

Maluno), where you will camp for the night on the shores. Venado is a beautiful shallow lake at 2,400 meters.

The next day, you have a three-hour hike to the summit, through rocks, moss, and dwarf trees to the rim. You should stay for at least one or two hours to enjoy the top, its several peaks, and varied views; peer into the sulfurous crater, and out across the land. Return to Lake Venado, or to the hot springs to soak a sore body. On the last day, finish the descent and return to Davao.

Several other routes are feasible for the more experienced climber.

ARRIVALS & DEPARTURES

If you are in a group of 10 or more, you should consider renting a jeepney so that you are not dependent on bus schedules. The rentals cost $40 to Kidapawen, where you must register, and another $32 to Lake Agco. To get to Kidapawen by bus, go to the Ma-a station early in the morning for the trip ($2.50 per person). Don't forget to arrange for your transport out.

DEALING WITH BUGS

Hikers venturing into the mountains and forests do not have to worry about dangerous wildlife. We have been told that there are leeches on Mt. Apo during rainy season, but we have not encountered any. Bring a long-sleeve shirt, long pants (leggings, jogging pants, jeans), and rubber bands to block entries through sleeve and pant-legs.

DAVAO ORIENTAL

Davao Oriental is not frequented by tourists but is a province that has much to offer. Here you can go off-the-beaten-track to one of Mindanao's most beautiful and powerful waterfalls, or hide at one of the secluded islands fringed with powdery cream sand and aquamarine waters.

ARRIVALS & DEPARTURES

Mati, the capital, is a scenic three-hour ride by car or Bachelor Express bus ($5) from Davao City on good roads. There is a small airport used only by private or chartered flights.

Caraga is at least eight hours by rough road from Mati. You can go by bus, but the trips are infrequent. The most convenient way would be renting a car in Davao. The roads from Caraga to Cateel are also rough.

WHERE TO STAY

The only places to stay in **Cateel** and **Caraga** are homestays arranged through the Governor's office in Mati. Otherwise, stay in this nice hotel in **Mati**:

MATI MENZI MANSION, *Mati, Davao Oriental. Tel. via operator-assisted 109 to Provincial Governor's Office, Mati. $23 per single or double.*

Rooms are available on the grounds of the plantation in a charming Spanish style villa. The rooms could use a renovation, but are clean. The pool is small and very clean. Meals are served in the "restaurant," which is actually five large tables. The menu is not extensive: the regular meals are tasty — but the sandwiches are loaded with mayonnaise and not much else, and compared to the price of a meal are expensive! We paid $15 for a meal (three dishes and rice) for six people, and a tiny mayo sandwich, with a hint of chicken, was 75¢.

SEEING THE SIGHTS

If you are staying overnight in Mati, the capital, the first thing you should do is check in at the **Menzi Mati Mansion**. This is on the grounds of the **Menzi Plantation**, just outside town proper. The vast plantation, once owned by the Menzi family, is now a cooperative. The grounds cover 250 hectares of gently rolling hills with mango, pomelo, citrus, and *casoy* (cashew) trees. The landscape, along with the white steel silo and barn (or storage area), resembles the Amish Country in Pennsylvania, except it is fringed with coconut trees. When you walk around, you will notice the sweet scents of the *casoy* trees.

In town and on a hill is the **capitol**. From here, you can get a great view of the area, and information for tourists and arrangements for going to the Aliwagwag Falls in Cateel.

While you are in Mati, check out the **sea turtle** and **mangrove nursery** at the DENR's (Department of Environment and Natural Resources) reserve in *sitio* Guang-guang, *barangay* Dahican. You can walk through the mangrove forest to the turtle nursery to see hatchlings and fully grown sea turtles. If you do not want to get wet, visit during low tide. The caretaker's tower commands a great view, and there are soft drinks for sale. Walking through the mangrove, you see tiny crabs with one bright yellow pincher as big as their bodies.

Dahican Beach is a long pretty cove of cream sand to stroll on. On one side, the beach is bordered by tall coconut trees, on the other by clean blue waters to swim in. The best time to go is March to May; other times of the year, when the wind is strong, the beach is littered with dried coconuts and leaves. You can also check out **Mayo Bay Beach**, a five-minute ride from the town proper. This is a small day resort that has two freshwater lagoons beside the Pacific Ocean. You can swim in the lagoons or the sea; there is a 20¢ entrance fee per person, and picnic tables rent for 60¢.

A 30 minute banca ride from the pier will take you to the pretty **Pujada Island**. Pujada has a fine cream-sand beach, mangroves on one side, aquamarine-emerald green waters, and nearby reefs where you can scuba dive. If you are here from January to May, you will see many migratory birds. Some of the inhabitants of Pujada Bay include sharks, occasionally the rare sea cow, and (if you are lucky) a school of dolphins may swim by your *banca* en route to the island. Although it is a private island, you can come for the day or camp overnight (bring all supplies); arrangements can be made through calling *Tel. 224-0023 (c/o Akasya Ventures)* in Davao City. There is a sandbar nearby called **Oak Island**. Located at the mouth of the bay, Oak Island is in the open sea and the waters tend to be rough — strong swimmers only. You can find small shells on the sandbar.

If you are interested in visiting the **Mandaya** people, they live in the mountains around **Caraga** (87 kilometers from Mati). The fair complexions of the Mandaya are attributed to admixture from early Portugese settlers. The **San Salvador church** in Caraga, considered one of the oldest in Mindanao, was built in the 17th century. Its bells were brought from Spain in 1802, and it has antique *santos* and ancient archives. Two places offer basic accomodations in Caraga.

Three hours north (73 kilometers) from Caraga are the breathtaking **Aliwagwag Falls** in Cateel. Aliwagwag, a series of 84 cascading waterfalls, may be the Philippines' tallest waterfall, at about 344 meters high and 20 meters wide. The beauty of the falls and area make the bouncy trip worth the effort. Since the area is well off the beaten track, make arrangements ahead of time through the DOT in Davao, or the Provincial Governor's Office in Mati (via the local long distance operator – dial 109 in Manila and Davao).

27. GENERAL SANTOS AREA - SOUTHERN MINDANAO

Seaward of **General Santos City**, you have come to the tuna and blue marlin capital of the Philippines, and towards the mountains is where you will find the gentle T'Boli people. You can hike through a tropical forest to a waterfall, visit tribes by a pretty lake, relax on a powder-fine white sand beach, dive in an area not many have been to, get unbelievable deals on tribal handicrafts (and you thought Davao was cheap), and feast on fish as fresh as you can get it short of catching and cooking it yourself.

This area was host to numerous tribal groups whose cultures antedate the Arab coming and who, until recently, lived in symbiosis with the forests they inhabited. The first recorded immigrants here were the Arabs. At the turn of the 15th century, Sariph Kabungsuan, who proclaimed himself Sultan of Mindanao, arrived with his people to spread Islam. The first Christian settlers came during the American period, in 1914. Then, the land was sparsely inhabited by Muslims, B'laans, Manobos, T'Bolis, Tagabilis, and other groups all coexisting peacefully. From the 1920s onward, Filipinos from Luzon and the Visayas resettled here. Many tribes were pushed northward. The population grew, and in 1968 the province was divided into two — **North Cotobato** and **South Cotobato**. In 1992, another province, **Sarangani**, was created out of most of what was formerly coastal South Cotobato.

This area is also referred to as **SOCSARGEN**: SOC for South Cotobato; SAR for Sarangani; and GEN for General Santos City.

GENERAL SANTOS CITY
(Dadiangas, GenSan)

The original name of this city was **Dadiangas**, but it was renamed in honor of a Filipino hero. The new name is often abbreviated to "**GenSan**."

The city is a mélange of religions, cultures, and times. You can watch the fishermen hauling in their catch, then look around and see the spire of the Muslim mosque. Look to the right side of the bay (if you are facing the water), and you will see the hi-tech fish port, built with much funding from the Japanese. If you come by air, you land at one of the best airports in the country — construction overseen (and funded by) the US Agency for International Development. Walk up to the plaza, which has been laid out as a typical Spanish town. And on Sunday, most of the people you see will be headed to or coming from Roman Catholic mass.

One of the main attractions of the city (and area) are the people. They are very friendly and hospitable; here, the smiles are always warm and genuine. The city has pleasant weather most of the year, and has not been hit by a severe typhoon, at least not in this century.

ARRIVALS & DEPARTURES

By Air

The **General Santos City** airport is served by Philippine Airlines from Manila on Tuesday, Thursday, Friday, and Saturday, and daily from Cebu. The flight from Manila takes roughly an hour and a half, as does the flight from Cebu. Mindanao Express of Corporate Air flies twice a day between Davao and General Santos; the flight takes 30 minutes.

When you land, watch the surroundings: the airport must be the most scenic in the country. The airport is higher than the city, and you get a great view of the Sarangani Bay on one side and the elegant Mount Matutum on the other. This is also one of the nicest airports in the country, and probably has the best runway (as of 1997).

By Sea

To or from **Manila**, this trip is a long haul: it takes 42-52 hours. Sulpicio Lines and Negros Navigation have one voyage a week ($20-100); and WGA SuperFerry has two trips a week ($38 to $135)

By Land

The Yellow Bus Lines and the STM Express bus terminals are on the National Highway, across from each other. These two companies ply/fly between Davao and GenSan. The trip takes three hours by bus, slightly less by car (the buses travel at high speeds between stops). Your trip will be smooth as the "highway" is in good condition. The fare is $3 each way for an airconditioned bus, and $1.75 for a regular bus. The "Mabuhay Class" buses of Yellow Bus Lines have only four seats in a row (two seats per aisle); the other buses seat five per row.

GETTING AROUND TOWN

The only way to get around town, if you do not own or rent a vehicle, is by walking or by tricycle or jeepney. As they are all over the place, you should not have any problems hailing one down. Most places are within walking distance.

WHERE TO STAY

In-town facilities are geared to traveling business people who do not mind if the hotel they are staying in is not five-star. You will not be getting anything fancy, but most places are clean, and have efficient and friendly staff.

ANCHOR HOTEL 2, *Cagampang Extension. Tel. 552-4660, 552-4552, Fax 552-4575. $30-32 per single, $34-36 per double, $60 per suite, $7 per extra person.*

All rooms are fully airconditioned, and have cable TV and a minibar. Ask for a room that is facing Cagampang Street; the rooms on the opposite side are a bit dim and your view is a cement wall. The small coffee shop is open from 6:00am until midnight. The restaurant is open for lunch and dinner and serves Filipino and western food.

SYDNEY HOTEL, *corner of Pioneer and Pedatum Street. Tel. 552-5479 to 81, Fax 552-5478. $33 per single, $41 per double, $58-66 per suite. Visa, Master Card, American Express.*

Ask to be on the higher floors (fourth and fifth) so that you can get a view of Mount Matutum or the Sarangani Bay. One of the newer hotels in town, the rooms are slightly larger than the average. All rooms are in hues of brown. The bathroom in the standard room is small, and the toilet and the shower are on the same side of the curtain. All rooms are clean, air conditioned, and have cable TV. The hallways are on the dark side. The staff are very nice and efficient. Services offered are an airport shuttle, business center, car rental, foreign exchange, laundry, and dry cleaning.

PHELA GRANDE HOTEL, *Magsaysay Avenue. Tel. 552-2950, 552-4220, 522-4230. $26-32 per single, $34-41 per double, $55-64 per suite.*

Some of the rooms in the newer wing are nice, and cost $7 more than those in the older area. All rooms are air conditioned and have cable TV. Facilities include a tour and travel agency and car rental.

SANSU HOTEL, *Pioneer Avenue. Tel. 552-2422, 552-7218 to 21. $15 per single, $19-27 per double.*

This simple hotel is good value for budget travelers. It is clean and managed well, with friendly and efficient staff. Rooms are air conditioned and have cable television. Facilities include a coffee shop and restaurant, car rental, and small business center. The city's tourism association is located here.

WHERE TO EAT

General Santos is a much smaller city than Davao and not as busy, but you will be very pleased with the seafood here. Since this is the major landing port for large fish, your seafood will be literally just out of the sea. You can have grilled blue marlin or tuna steaks at rock bottom prices. Other seafood is inexpensive as well. If you are fond of sashimi, this is a great place for it – it is even sold in stalls at the market.

LOLA SISAY'S, *J Catolico Sr. Avenue.*

The large restaurant has a high ceiling. A very native feeling is what you get here: the entire ceiling and walls are covered with *amaca* (woven bamboo), and the table and chairs are also made of bamboo: looks great, but the seats are hard. On the far right side of the place is a small stage, behind which two beautiful T'Boli weavings hang on the wall. The bathrooms look iffy, but are surprisingly clean, with toilet paper too. The food is great: you can tell the freshness in both the taste and the consistency of the fish. You should order most of the seafood grilled (so you can savor the freshness). You also get to chose your seafood, which is in a glass case, just as you walk through the entrance. A meal for eight people was $46, including soft drinks and beer.

FIESTA SA BARRIO, *J Catolico Sr. Avenue.*

Yes, this is the other place for excellent grilled seafood. They also have an assortment of Filipino dishes that are good too. The decor here is native. The restrooms are clean. Price is the same as Lola Sisay's.

CASA LUISA, *also on J Catolico Sr. Avenue.*

Another place for Filipino food. You can also get some Chinese and Spanish dishes here.

If you are looking for Chinese food, go to **DRAGON PALACE,** *J Catolico Sr. Avenue at the Civic Center*; or the popular **NEW CALPIN RESTAURANT,** *45 P Acharon Boulevard.* And, if you want Japanese food, **NI-MOSHO-BE RESTAURANT AND SUSHI BAR** is on *J Catolico Sr. Avenue.*

For western fare, the **COTTON BOWL GRILL AND STEAK HOUSE,** *Pioneer Avenue,* is very popular. There are a few fast food places. By the Gaisano Mall, try **JOLLYBEE** for burgers and sweet and spicy wings, and very clean bathrooms; and **AVC DIMSUM.** If you come late in the evening, about sevenish, they may be out of several dishes; bathrooms are not great. You can get fried chicken at **SUNBURST,** *on Pendatun Avenue.*

The canteen-style **JO-ANN'S,** *P Acharon Boulevard,* is an institution here, one of the first bakeshop/canteens, and now has a few outlets around the city. The place is named after the owners' two children – Jo and Ann – and you can get a quick, cheap and tasty meal here ($3 including drinks). The *pancit* (stir-fried noodles) and the butter fried chicken were very good. For dessert, have *halo-halo* (a mixture of sweet beans, coconut and other preserves, and fruit topped off with ice, milk, and a serving of *leche flan*). The one here is unique, as it has a predominant cantaloupe flavor and a very generous serving of flan. The bathrooms, in the back of the restaurant, are not great.

SEEING THE SIGHTS

You have to be an early bird so you can walk down to the **Lion's Beach Landing** (also the world's largest fresh fish market) to watch the boatmen lugging in their catch. Each day, over 50 *bancas* set off into the sea. Their tools remain the most rudimentary – a hook, strong nylon line, and bare hands. The trip takes four days to get to the prime fishing grounds, four days for fishing, and another four to return.

Early in the morning, the *bancas* arrive in GenSan. The fish are carried (one by one) on the heads of men who go back and forth between the boats. As soon as a fish is put down on one of the tables, it is immediately graded and sold, the higher grades going to the highest bidders (usually the Japanese). Most of the fish are exported to Japan, Taiwan, Manila, and Davao; the lowest grades (which are still good) are found in the market. More hi-tech facilities are at the **Fish Port Complex** in **Tambler**. Just the other side of the road from the "fish market" is the **city's market**; here you will find what was not sold for export or to the local restaurants, and an assortment of other goods ranging from handicrafts and fresh produce to modern clothes and packaged snacks.

As GenSan is chiefly industrial, most of the interesting sights are outside of the city.

NIGHTLIFE & ENTERTAINMENT

This city sleeps early. Nightlife is limited to a **piano bar** with a great view on the rooftop of the Sydney Hotel, and a **disco** in the Phela Grande Hotel.

SPORTS & RECREATION

Fishing

As the tuna and marlin capital of the country, fishing is one of GenSan's major source of income. However, fishing facilities are not geared towards the tourist. If you want to fish, try to make arrangements through the Chamber of Commerce or through the other tourist assistance offices (all listed in Practical Information below); or to charter a yacht from elsewhere (refer to Chapter 8, *Sports and Recreation*).

Scuba Diving

See the section on Sarangani below.

SHOPPING

The **DTI Trade House**, along M Roxas Street, fronting the city's plaza, displays local native handicrafts from different villages of the region. Here you can find rattan and bamboo furniture, batik accessories and decor, t'nalak and other woven cloths, shellcraft, and an assortment of other products. The **Garden Club**, across from the DTI Trade House, sells bonsai, ornamental plants, and tropical flowers.

You can find film or souvenir t-shirts in the **Gaisano Department Store** at the **Gaisano Mall**, along J Catolico and the National Highway.

PRACTICAL INFORMATION

Banks

There are several banks in the city. **MetroBank**, **BA Savings Bank**, and **BPI**, are on Santiago Boulevard. **Far East Bank**, **RCBC**, **PCI Bank**, and another branch of MetroBank are on Pioneer Avenue. **Solid Bank** and **Allied Bank** are on P Acharon Boulevard. Banking hours are Mondays through Fridays, from 9:00am to 3:00pm.

Post Office

The **post office** is in the plaza, next to City Hall. Courier services include JRS, Haribon Express, and LBC, and the hotels have fax services.

Tourist & Business Information

The bubbly Flor de la Cruz of the **GenSan Chamber of Commerce**, Rivera Building, Cagompang Street Extension 1, across from Anchor Hotel 2, *Tel. 522-6914,* can help arrange trips to her native Lake Sebu. She can also help you rent a jeep, and get permission for you to visit the expansive **Dole Plantation**. If you are interested in doing business here, the Chamber of Commerce is the place to get most of the information and help you need. The Chamber also has great maps of the city.

The **General Santos City Tourism Association**, second floor of Hotel Sansu, Pioneer Avenue, *Tel. 552-7218 to 21*, has information on SOCSARGEN and a map of the city. They can also help you with guides.

The **City Tourism Office** is in City Hall, at the Plaza. Look for Mr. Thumby Cadorna.

SARANGANI

This recently created (1992) province flanks General Santos City on the east and west. You can find 230 kilometers of powdery white sand beaches and coves here, but there are no developed facilities (as of 1997) and the sand is so fine that, if you are wading near a bed of seaweed, it feels like you are walking on mud.

In **Gumasa, Glan**, 20 minutes from GenSan by car, you will find over one kilometer of fine sand to walk, and picnic huts for rent (60¢) in a pretty cove. This is a relaxing place to have a snack or lunch. You can bring your own food, or if you are lucky, and it's still available, the catch of the day can be grilled for you. Stick to fish: the octopus can be very chewy. We were not so lucky: arriving late, we attempted to eat the octopus which we then christened "Spartans" *adobo* (after a popular brand of slippers and rubber shoes). If you take the path through the shrubs, you will find more scenic coves with nice beaches and views.

Sarangani Island has breathtaking white sand beaches, blue lagoons, and lush tropical forests. There are no facilities yet.

ARRIVALS & DEPARTURES
Gumasa, Glan, & Sarangani Island

The easiest way to get here is to rent a jeepney from GenSan ($30 a day). You can also take a jeepney ($1-2), but there are no regular schedules. Sarangani Island is a four-hour boat ride from GenSan or an hour and a half by road, then an additional 30 minutes by *banca*.

SPORTS & RECREATION
Scuba Diving

Divers will want to contact the **Sarangani Divers**; ask for Mike Kingery, who is a dive instructor, or his son Steve, a dive master from Los Angeles, at 7 Atis Street in Marin Village, behind Greenfield Motors on the Highway, *Tel. 552-5420 and 552-5421*. They take divers on to the reefs just off their beach property in Glan. Full equipment rental and a guided tour around the on-shore reefs will run about $57 per person; offshore will cost around $75 per person (including boat rental). There are some good dive spots off the reefs in the Sarangani Bay, an area few divers have explored.

GenSan Reef Divers is the other operating dive center; look for Raymond Haw, *Tel. 552-5189*.

DOLE PLANTATION, POLOMOLOK

There are a number of reasons for you to visit Polomolok: to see the expansive **Dole Plantation** at the foot of pretty **Mt. Matutum**, play golf on a scenic course, try the "special" steak from cows that have been fed pineapple, and relax in the cool climate of the area. Because it is a private compound (owned by Dole), you will need permission to enter. Contact the GenSan Chamber of Commerce, *Tel. 522-6914*, for arrangements to tour or to stay overnight at Dole. No public transportation goes all the way in, so your best bet is to rent a car.

WHERE TO STAY

CLUB KALSANGI, *Dole Plantation, $30 per single, $47 per double, $134 per four-bedroom house.*

Dole rents out a number of rooms and cottages, usually for groups, but they will accept individuals if space is available. Other facilities include a 25-meter swimming pool and tennis courts. The rooms are large and the bathrooms are slightly smaller than the rooms. The rooms are similar to cabins that you find in the US — stone walls, thick hard wood, and cozy.

LAKE SEBU

The **T'Boli** have an artistically rich cultural tradition that dates back more than two millennia. Most people know the T'Boli from their beautiful **t'nalak cloth**, which you will no doubt see at almost every souvenir shop in the country. The T'Boli also forge useful and attractive brass-bronze ware, and compose mysterious yet peaceful music with a wide array of instruments: bamboo tubes, wooden guitar-like instruments, mouth harps, bronze gongs, drums, etc. Balladeers, they sing of their lives and legends, and dance is an important part of their festivities.

The t'nalak cloth is made from abaca fiber that is tie-dyed black and rust using natural plant coloring. After the dye sets, they laboriously weave the fibers on backstrap looms into one of the loveliest natural cloths you will ever see. The T'Boli are also bronze smiths. They use the lost wax process, which makes every piece unique; they forge bells for their costumes, chain links for jewelry and for their horses, bits for their horses' bridles, and attractive sculptures of their lifestyle.

Despite all their artistic genius, the T'Boli have remained economically naive. Also because they are a reclusive and gentle people, they have lost precious ancestral lands to creditors, politicians, and an assortment of sharp operators. Most lands abutting **Lake Sebu** are owned by lowland migrants. The government has attempted to prevent the T'Boli from losing all their lands, and you can no longer purchase land in the area. However, people with "legal" titles prior to the proclamation are allowed to keep their land.

Now closed, the **Santa Cruz Mission** once operated in Lake Sebu for over 25 years, helping the T'Boli become economically self-sufficient once again, maintain their traditions, and retain pride in their heritage. Unfortunately, greedy outsiders were able to terminate the admirable work of the mission. Its buildings remain, and although in need of restoration, they are hauntingly pretty.

Even though many T'Boli are Christian, they still worship the spirits that they believe control almost every aspect of their lives. Affluent men have several wives; ancient rituals are still practiced.

If you go on a Saturday, market day, you can see the colorfully dressed T'Boli who come in from the hills to sell produce and wares. The handicrafts that you will see for sale (in the market on Saturday or in the roadside stores everyday) are much cheaper than you will find them anywhere else in the country (they are made here). We recently bought a beautiful bronze T'Boli horse for a mere $6; elsewhere it would sell for $12 and up.

The area is also a great place to **hike**. Lake Sebu's waters exit in a small river, then thunder down seven falls and irrigate lowland crops. **Siluton** (also known as Hikong Bente, or Number One), is the highest and strongest of all. Siluton is a delightful and easy three-kilometer walk through lush vegetation (pay 20¢ for path maintenance).

At the lake, you can also arrange to rent a *banca* ($8 for the whole boat) and cruise slowly around the area. On the other side you will see a number of small eagles and other birds.

ARRIVALS & DEPARTURES

To get to **Lake Sebu** from GenSan, a Yellow Bus Line or STM bus to **Koronadal** (still referred to by its former name: **Marbel**) will cost $2 for an air conditioned bus, $1 regular; then a jeepney to Surallah and Lake Sebu ($1.50 per person). The trip to Marbel from GenSan takes an hour and a half, and from Marbel to the lake is another hour and a half.

If you are waiting for the bus in Marbel, try the tasty fruit shakes at the **Breeze Restaurant**.

WHERE TO STAY & EAT

There are several simple lodges on the banks of Lake Sebu. Food for visitors, except freshwater fish from the lake, is brought in.

ESTARES BEACH RESORT AND PENSION HOUSE, *contact through PT-T (public calling office in Lake Sebu 885-4439). $11.50 per single, $15 per double, $9 per cottage.*

The lodging is very basic, although it is probably one of the best places to stay here. The rooms have private bathrooms, and the cottages, called *kubos*, have a private toilet but common showers. All the rooms and *kubos* are clean. You can also eat in the restaurant where music is played loudly, or peacefully in one of the tables in a cottage over the lake. The specialty is fresh tilapia, the fish that abound in the lake. They also rent boats.

Other places to stay include **ARTACHO GUEST HOUSE**, which has simple rooms (*also call through the PT-T office*), and the **DOT RESTHOUSE**, but you have to contact them well in advance (two weeks minimum) so that they can bring in all the food and supplies; *call the DOT in Manila Tel. 523-8411, or Davao Tel. 221-6955*. The resthouse is on a hill that overlooks the lake.

28. ZAMBOANGA - SOUTHERN MINDANAO

Zamboanga is a popular destination for Filipino and foreign travelers. It has a good assortment of acceptable accommodations and restaurants, a superb beach, good diving, a bazaar-like market, weavers, antique and curio shops, walking, a golf course, tennis courts, etc., all awaiting your pleasure.

Located in the southernmost region of the Philippines, the provinces of Zamboanga are found in southwest Mindanao. The weather in Zamboanga del Norte and del Sur is pleasant year round, and the area is rarely hit by typhoons. The average temperature is 27.6°C (80.6°F). Humidity is high in the southernmost islands.

ZAMBOANGA DEL NORTE

When you come to **Zamboanga del Norte**, you will most likely be heading to one of the nice beaches, or going scuba diving. While you are there, you can also visit a number of historical and cultural sights, or go on a scenic short hike along a well-foliated trail.

Zamboanga del Norte is located on the western edge of Mindanao; it occupies the northwestern rim of the Zamboanga Peninsula. You will enjoy the climate here; it is pleasant and has no pronounced rainy or dry season.

ARRIVALS & DEPARTURES
By Air

The **Dipolog Airport** is two kilometers from the city proper. Philippine Airlines has flights from Manila on Monday, Tuesday, Thursday, Friday, and Saturday; and from Cebu on Tuesday, Friday, Saturday, and Sunday.

The **Tourism Display and Information Center** is in the airport. You should stop in and pick up a map and any other information. They also can help facilitate tours for you. A tricycle to downtown Dipolog is 40¢ (for the whole tricycle).

By Sea

The trip from Manila by boat will take you approximately 30 hours. Sulpicio Lines ($18-80) and WGA SuperFerry ($20-97) each have one trip a week.

GETTING AROUND

Jeeps and tricycles are the most common form of transportation.

WHERE TO STAY & EAT

Outside of the hotels and pensions, you will find a few simple places to eat in town; most are canteen style.

Beach Resort

DAKAK PARK AND BEACH RESORT, *Dapitan Bay. Tel. 220-058, 220-052, 220-036, 220-020, Fax 218-000. Manila contact: Tel. 844-5971. 120 rooms. $105-175 per single, $122-300 per double, $600 per suite. Visa, Master Card, American Express.*

This is the top-of-the-line hotel in Zamboanga, and it is expansive enough to be considered a park. It's in a private cove. You will enjoy this resort if you like to feel secluded from the rest of the world (provided you're not there at the same time as a large tour group). One of the highlights is arriving — you are picked up at the airport, then shuttled, by an air conditioned vehicle, to Dapitan, where you will board a large *banca* for a 20-minute scenic cruise to the resort. Just when you think you have left civilization, the resort peeks through the trees as you near the shore.

The grounds are lush with tropical plants and flowers. You can go on a decent walk around the entire property. All the rooms are in cozy native-style duplex cottages with a porch. The cottages are made of bamboo with a nipa roof and capiz shell windows. All rooms are air conditioned and have a television. The beds are firm and comfortable, and all are clean. Some members of the staff (particularly the cleaning people and the waiters) are nice. You can have meals and short orders at the restaurant near the reception. During the evenings, your meals will be served buffet style on the basketball court, which is converted into a charming luau setting; stick to the seafood, it is good.

There is a very good and well-staffed dive center at the resort. (For more information see the Scuba Diving later in this chapter.)

Moderate Hotels
The other places to stay are hotels and simple pensions in Dipolog.
TOP PLAZA HOTEL, *corner Echavez Street and Quezon Avenue. Tel. 415-5777, 415-5888, 415-2218, Fax 415-2371. $35-50 per single or double.*
This is the top hotel in town. The four-story hotel has clean rooms with air conditioning and cable television. The restaurant specializes in Chinese food, and it is good. The staff are friendly and efficient.
CL INN, *Rizal Avenue. Tel. 415-3215, 415-3216. $20-34 per single or double.*
The rooms are spacious and clean, simply furnished but comfortable, and all have air conditioning and television.

Budget Hotels
You can find a few budget hotels in town. Those listed have clean rooms with fans or air conditioning, and range in price from $12 to $30.
• **CASA JOSE PENSION HOUSE**, *A Bonifacio Street. Tel. 415-4240*
• **GONZALES INN**, *Quezon Avenue. Tel. 415-3729*
• **HOTEL AROCHA**, *Quezon Avenue, Tel. 415-2656*
• **HOTEL ELIZABETH**, *P Garcia Street. Tel. 415-3227*
• **RAMOS HOTEL**, *Rizal Avenue, Tel. 415-3504*
• **RANILLO PENSION HOUSE**, *Andres Bonifacio Street. Tel. 415-3536*

SEEING THE SIGHTS
Dipolog, the capital of Zamboanga del Norte, is a nice small city to walk around. The avenues are clean, and at **Magsaysay Park** you can feast on a plethora of fruits that vendors are selling. Climb the **1001 steps** to **Linabo Peak** to enjoy the great view of Dipolog and Dapitan. If you are interested in historical religious markers, visit the **Cathedral**, built in the late 1800s. Its altar was designed by the National Hero, Dr. José Rizal.
In **Dapitan**, just north of Dipolog City, is the **Rizal Park** on the site to which Rizal was exiled from 1892-1896. You can take a leisurely stroll around the 10-hectare park, which is shaded by large trees, and explore the reservoir, aqueduct, and other structures.
If you like the beach, you can spend the day in Dapitan Bay at the **Dakak Beach Resort** ($15 entrance, $20 to rent a jeep for the round trip), or take a 45-minute *banca* ride ($30 per *banca* rental for the day) to **Aliguay Island** for nice white sand and good corals for snorkeling and diving. **Buton Beach** near Dapitan also has a white sand.
If you are interested in World War Two markers, visit the **Filipino-Japanese Memorial Park**. It was constructed in memory of the soldiers who died fighting here during the war. Located in *Barangay* Dicayas, it is a 15-minute jeep ride from downtown Dipolog.

SPORTS & RECREATION
Hiking

Enjoy hiking around **Maria Uray Mountain**, a short three-hour hike near Dapitan. You walk among narra, ironwood (*kamagong*), mahogany, and a variety of fruit trees. When you are at the airport, arrange for a reliable guide from the tourist information desk.

Scuba Diving

Aliguay Island and **Silinog Island** offer good diving with nice corals, and you may even see a ray near Aliguay. A number of nearby reefs have a lot of marine activity, larger fish (including white tip sharks), and rays.

Dakak Resort (see Where to Stay above) has a very good and complete **dive center** owned and managed by Cesar, a veteran diver who you will most likely see there. The dive masters and instructors are highly recommended. The cost for two dives will be around $40 a person. If you are staying at the resort or in the area for several days, you can take a course for $350-400; they have specials (20 percent off) from time to time.

Live-aboard Cruises

The *Svetlana* has trips from April to May that go to the Sulu Sea; and from July to October around the Visayas. The approximate cost is $140-200 per person per day.

ZAMBOANGA CITY

Zamboanga City is a delightful place to shop, watch weavers, island hop (make sure you get to the pink sand beach), and, if you like golf, that too. If you have seen travel brochures of the city, you may expect to see *vintas* (boats) with brightly colored sails — unfortunately, these sails are saved for special occasions and plain white sails are what you will normally see.

The city's name is derived from Jambangan, the name given by the early settlers, the Subanon; it means land of flowers. Later the city was called Samboangan, meaning anchorage, by the Badjao and Sama; to this day they still call it by that name.

Records show that the Chinese established trade with the Subanon, Sama, Tausug, and Badjao as early as the 13th century. Spanish influence came later, in 1593, when a small mission was established in Recodo (then known as La Caldera). However, the Spanish did not mark their founding of the city until 1635, when Jesuit **Father Melchor de Vera** laid the cornerstone of **Fort Pilar**, in the same year that **Legazpi** and **Fray Urdaneta** arrived.

During the Spanish rule, people immigrated to Zamboanga from Luzon and the Visayas. Others came from Basilan and Sulu to escape political problems at home. A dialect unique to Zamboanga, **Chavacano**, is a mixture of unconjugated Spanish and native words, evolved since the first contacts between the Spanish and the Filipino ethnic groups. Until the American regime, Zamboanga was the seat of the Catholic church for all of Mindanao. It became Mindanao's capital during the American period. The City Hall was built in 1907 to house American military governors, including **John (Blackjack) Pershing**.

Today, 80% of Zamboanga's population is Christian. Of the remaining 20%, most are Muslim. Although the city is predominantly Christian in character, the Muslim influence predominates in the markets and some villages.

CHAVACANO LINGO

Good Morning, Afternoon, Evening: Buenas Dias, Tardes, Noches
How are you?: Que tal?
I am fine: Buenamente
Thank you: Gracias
Where are we (you) going?: Onde kita (tu) anda?
How much is this?: Cuanto este?
Do you have?: Tiene be ustedes?
Near, Far: Cerca, Lejos
Can I ask a question?: Puede pregunta?
What is this?: Cosa este?
What is your name?: Cosa de tuyo numbre?
Let's go there: Anda kita allia
Come here: Vene qui
I do not know: No sabe yo

Tribes

Five ethnic groups are found in and around Zamboanga:

- **Badjao** or **Tau-laut** people are either sea nomads and live on house-boats, coming to shore only to be buried, or are found living near the water or in stilt houses over the sea.
- **Subanon** were among the earliest settlers here. They occupied much of the peninsula centuries ago and are now thinly spread through parts of Zamboanga provinces to Misamis Occidental. "Subanon" means "upriver" or "upstream" and referred to the areas they inhabited. They currently live in small family farming units.

• **Sama** (commonly called Samal) people live around the coastal regions of Jolo, Tawi-Tawi, and Zamboanga. A peaceful, sociable people, they live in dense settlements of stilt houses over the water's edge or in houseboats. Fishing and diving for pearls and shells is their main livelihood.

• **Tausug** is the largest ethnic group in this area. They tend to be more aggressive and wealthier than the other minorities. The Tausug are mostly farmers and fishermen.

• **Yakan** people are farmers and they weave and wear beautiful clothing. The Yakan inhabit the uplands of Basilan. There is a small Christianized Yakan settlement on the outskirts of Zamboanga City.

ARRIVALS & DEPARTURES

By Air

The **Zamboanga Airport** has a great little terminal building — open, airy, and attractively done. If you are waiting for a connecting flight, you can get a good snack at J's Pad. From Manila, the flight takes an hour and 30 minutes. Air Philippines has a daily flight, and Philippine Airlines flies twice a day. Philippines Airlines also has a daily flight from Cebu that takes 55 minutes on a 737 or an hour and 30 minutes on a Fokker 50, and flights from Davao on Monday, Wednesday, and Saturday.

The airport is two kilometers from downtown. To get to the city center, you can take a jeep (10¢), tricycle (80¢, but they may charge up to $1.50), or taxi ($2.50-4.00).

By Sea

The voyage from Manila is a long haul (at least 32 hours). Sulpicio Lines ($25-80) and WGA SuperFerry ($25-116) each have two trips a week. From General Santos City, the trip aboard Sulpicio ($10-40) takes 11 hours, and on WGA ($12-40) it takes 15 hours to Zamboanga.

By Land

Bachellor, Ceres, and RMT (all $6 per person) run between Zamboanga City and Cagayan de Oro. The trip takes 10 hours and part of the way is on rough roads. The buses leave daily from 4:30am to 7:00am.

GETTING AROUND TOWN

You can get around easily by tricycle, jeepney, or taxi. Have your hotel recommend a tricycle driver or guide they know, especially in the evening. Always settle the rate in advance, arrange for round trips, and pay when you're through.

When headed to points outside the city, ask your hotel to recommend a travel agent or use one of the guides with a car for hire outside the

Lantaka (ask the hotel staff or DOT office, inside the Lantaka, first about their reliability).

WHERE TO STAY
Best Hotel in Town
GARDEN ORCHID, *Gov. Camins Avenue, near the airport. Tel. 991-0031 to 34, Fax 991-0035. 85 rooms. $66-78 per single, $78-90 per double, $180 per suite, $18 per extra bed. Visa, Master Card, American Express.*

This is the top hotel in Zamboanga City. Tropical flowers and plants surround the premises, and inside facilities exude comfort. All rooms are attractively decorated, fully air conditioned, and have cable TV. The facilities include a salon for men and women, a tennis court, a small gym with a sauna, and a 50-meter swimming pool. Services include laundry, business center, foreign exchange, mail, tours, and car rental.

Food facilities include a coffee shop; Garden Deck for roof-top dining and grilled specialties (very good); The Baron, for European cuisine; and Hanazono, for good Japanese food. Evening entertainment is provided at the Lobby Bar, and dancing in Ground Zero.

Moderate Hotels
LANTAKA HOTEL BY THE SEA, *NS Valderrosa Street, downtown. Tel. 991-2033. $37 per single, $46 per double, $93 per suite. Visa, Master Card, American Express.*

Although not as glamorous as the top hotel in town, the Lantaka, one of the oldest here, has a loyal following. It is conveniently located downtown, the staff is wonderful, and the rooms are cozy. All rooms are very clean, air conditioned, and have cable TV. The staff will do their most to make you feel at home, and will also look out for you (recommend reliable guides, taxis, etc.). The restaurant specializes in local fare and seafood.

Zamboanga's very good DOT office is the best place for tourist information and is in the hotel. There are several places to shop nearby.

ARGAMEL HOTEL, *Governor Camins Avenue, downtown. Tel. 991-2023. $18 per single, $22 per double, $30 per suite.*

This simple hotel is conveniently located downtown and the staff is very friendly. All rooms are big, air conditioned, and have cable TV. There is a restaurant.

PLATINUM 21, *34 Barcelona Street, downtown. Tel. 991-2514, Fax 991-2709. $21-25 per single or double, $5.75 per extra person. Visa, Master Card, American Express.*

Platinum is good value: clean, simple, nice rooms, all with air conditioning and cable TV. The staff is friendly and efficient. There is a coffee shop, and mail and laundry services.

HOTEL PRECIOSA, *Mayor Jaldon Street, just outside downtown. Tel. 991-2020. $21 per single or double, $35 per triple.*

All rooms are air conditioned, clean, and have cable TV. The suite rooms are for three people and have a small refrigerator.

NEW ASTORIA HOTEL, *Mayor Jaldon Street, just outside downtown. Tel. 991-2510. $25 per single, $32-40 per double, $46 per suite. Visa, Master Card, American Express.*

All rooms have air conditioning and cable TV. The restaurant has good Chinese and Filipino food.

ZAMBOANGA HERMOSA, *Mayor Jaldon Street, just outside downtown. Tel. 991-2042. $18 per single, $22.50 per double.*

The hotel is well-maintained. Rooms are nice, and have air conditioning and cable TV. The restaurant specializes in local cuisine.

MARCIAN GARDEN HOTEL, *Governor Camins Avenue, near the airport. Tel. 991-2519. $21-25 per single or double, $33 per suite. Visa, Master Card.*

All rooms are fully air conditioned, have cable TV, and are clean and simple. The staff is efficient, and the restaurant has local and western dishes.

Budget

PARADISE HOTEL, *P Reyes Street, downtown. Tel. 991-202; and* **PARADISE PENSION**, *Barcelona Street, downtown. Tel. 991-1054. $13 per single, $15-19 per double.*

These well-run budget hotels have one owner. They are conveniently located. The rooms are clean and air conditioned, the staff is friendly, the hotels are popular with foreigners, and there is a simple restaurant.

ATILANO'S PENSION HOUSE, *off Climaco Street, on the way to the airport. Tel. 991-4225. $15-19 per single or double.*

The air conditioned rooms are comfortable and big. There is a simple, family-run restaurant; the food is good.

WHERE TO EAT

You will enjoy the food here. Most restaurants specialize in seafood, but, if you are a meat lover, you'll be pleased too.

Downtown

LANTAKA, *in the Lantaka Hotel.*

Specializes in seafood. Treat yourself to an evening meal in this torch-lit restaurant by the water. Even if it is not on the menu, try the seafood platter, and order it in advance.

SUNBURST FRIED CHICKEN, *Corcuera Street.*

Use your hands to eat their tasty fried chicken.

SUNFLOWER, *three outlets downtown.*
All have Filipino dishes, including goat meat, in a casual setting.

Near Downtown
ALAVAR'S, *Don Alfaro Street near the Alta Mall.*
Zamboanga is where this popular seafood chain's first restaurant built its fame. The seafood is very good. The extensive menu also has Chinese and Filipino dishes.
ABALONE, *Mayor Jaldon Street, just outside the center.*
Specializes in seafood and is well recommended.
LOTUS, *New Astoria Hotel.*
Many say this is the best Chinese restaurant in the city.
D' CHIMANG CUSINA CHAVACANO, *Tugbungan, near Alta Mall.*
Seafood and local dishes. Try the barbecue, it's good.

Outside Downtown
PALMERAS, *Climaco Avenue, north of town center, before Pasonanca Park.*
Palmeras has charming decor. Try the house chicken, spareribs, arroz a la marinera, or arroz a la bilao.
ALDEA PASONACA RESTAURANT, *at Pasonanca Park.*
This restaurant is inside a former railway car. The Filipino food is very good; also try the paella and sizzling tenderloin – both very tasty. There is a playground for children.
ANTONIO'S, *Pasonanca Park.*
The place for a steak. The quials' egg soup is also good.
COUNTRY CHICKEN & MANO-MANO, *Pasonanca Park.*
Serves chicken and native dishes. The food is tasty and you use your hands.
VIENNA KAFFEHAUS, *on San José Road, west of the town center.*
This place will satisfy your craving for German and Austrian dishes. The food is good, and they also have seafood.
GARDEN DECK, *Garden Orchid Hotel, near the airport.*
Good grilled seafood. It is a nice place to have a meal, open air, on the roof of the hotel. The **HANAZONO** is the hotel's Japanese restaurant, the food is good – great sashimi and hot spicy tuna.
If you are at the airport, **J'S PAD** has tasty snacks, a good place for breakfast if you are waiting for the flight to Tawi-Tawi.

SEEING THE SIGHTS
In the city, stroll down RT Lim Boulevard to watch the fishing boats (*bisligs* and *basnigs*) come in from the deep sea, and take great sunset photos.
Just east of the center is **Fort Pilar**, built in 1635 by Fray Melchor de Vera. Abandoned in 1663, it was rebuilt in 1718 to fend off attacks from

Muslims, Dutch, British, and Portuguese. The Americans converted the fort into barracks. Today it is a historical shrine on the outside and houses the **Marine Life Museum** inside. The museum, aimed at promoting the conservation of Zamboanga's marine environment, has an underwater life diorama, artifacts, and other exhibits. It is open Sundays to Fridays from 9:00am to noon, and from 2:00pm until 5:00pm. You can get a good view of the Muslim settlement and the waterfront if you climb the ramparts. You can read the history of the fort on a bronze plaque at the eastern end.

Beyond the fort is **Rio Hondo**, a Muslim village. At the edge of the river you can get a nice view, or, to go to the mosque, cross the bridge. Expect a number of children looking for handouts: candy or whatever. Badjao, Sama, and Tausug are residents of this village. If you wish to enter the mosque, remove your shoes first.

North of downtown is **Pasonanca Park**, a 15-minute jeepney ride from City Hall. You can walk about the gardens, where you will find a freshwater swimming pool cleansed by flowing spring water, and a cute tree house (you may get permission from the mayor to stay for a night, but it is open all day for viewing). From Pasonanca, you can walk or drive to another park, **Abong Abong**. Started by the colorful late Mayor Cesar Climaco, it is in the lower end of the city's watershed area. You will find facilities for camping, lots of area to hike, lovely views, and a park dedicated to two assassinated modern heroes — Ninoy Aquino and Climaco (whose grave is here).

For a more ethnic flavor, investigate the **Yakan Village**, seven kilometers from the city. The people here came from Basilan and are now Christian. You will be welcomed by a man playing a xylophone-like instrument, and can watch women weave unique, intricate cloth with colorful geometric designs; you can buy the beautiful cloth. Just beyond the village is **Yellow Beach**, where the US forces landed on March 10 to 12, 1945.

You can wander over to **Caragasan Beach**, a nice pebble and sand area with shades for day use. It is about 10 kilometers from the city, near the **Muslim University**, and is bordered by a typical **Muslim fishing village**. One kilometer away you will find **Recodo**, the site of the first Spanish mission. Today it bustles with boat building and repairing activities.

The **San Ramon Penal Colony** is a self-contained economic unit where prisoners often choose to remain even after their sentence is served. Their families can come and live with them. The colony is 20 kilometers west of Zamboanga.

NIGHTLIFE & ENTERTAINMENT

There are a few places to go for late afternoon and evening entertainment. Beer and snacks are available in the evenings at **Café Bianca**, inside Platinum 21. At **Village Restaurant**, on Governor Camins Road near the airport, try the *papait*, a goat meat dish. **Montemar**, at Hotel Perlita, and the **Garden Deck** (Garden Orchid Hotel) are nice places to have a drink while watching the sunset.

If you want to go dancing, there is **Ground Zero**, inside the Garden Orchid Hotel.

SHOPPING

The most accessible shopping area is **Valderrosa Street**, between Lantaka and City Hall. A few shops here sell ethnic artifacts. Other shops are scattered throughout the city. If you are looking for **shells** and shellcrafts, go to the San José Road and locate **Rocan**, **Zamboanga Shell House**, **Shell World**, and **San Luis** shops.

ZAMBOANGA SHOPPING TIPS

• *Pearls. You will find pearl and gem vendors all over town and around the market. Most of the items offered are imitation. Real pearls aren't damaged by flame: ask if you may test a pearl you like by holding a lighter or match to it. If the vendor declines, the pearl is probably plastic.*

• *General Safety. As in most markets in the country, be very careful with your bag and wallet.*

• *Bargain, Bargain, Bargain!*

At the **City Market** you will find a large fish and vegetable area which is fascinating and presents great opportunities for the photographer. Mats are also sold here – as soon as you show interest you will be surrounded by women unfolding dozens of them. Some stalls in the **flea market** area sell brass wares, antiques, shells, Indonesian batik, *malong* (large pieces of decorative material sewn in a circle, in which the wearers wrap themselves), weavings from Basilan and Jolo, etc.

Smuggling through the Philippines' wide open southern door has never been successfully controlled by the government. In an attempt to limit and legitimize some of this "trade," barter trade outlets were created. You can find some good buys, usually of interest to Philippine residents. **Alta Mall** has the same items as other barter trade outlets.

Zamboanga's **waterfront**, the city's most important economic district, is a very interesting area. You will find the Badjao just outside the

Lantaka Hotel, selling mats and shells from their boats. Initial prices tend to be very high. Some of the boat children will ask to dive for coins.

When you are at the Penal Colony, check out the nearby handicraft store.

SPORTS & RECREATION
Golf
Zamboanga has the oldest golf course in the country; it was built in 1910. The **Zamboanga Golf and Beach Park** is in Upper Calarian, seven and a half kilometers from downtown. This is an 18-hole championship course with mango and acacia trees on the periphery. It is one of the most scenic in the country. Greens fees are $20.

Scuba Diving
There are some nice colorful sites for diving off the Santa Cruz islands, and further south. **Coral Divers**, in Pasonanca, *Tel. (cellular) 0912-740-3462,* rents equipment and has a certified dive master.

EXCURSIONS & DAY TRIPS
Taluksangay, a village 19 kilometers east of Zamboanga, is a very pretty drive. You will pass through farms (decorated with flowers) and a boat building industry. Originally settled over a century ago by a few families, Taluksangay now has over 800 Badjao, Sama, and Maguindanao people. The mosque is very pretty, and you can stroll along the catwalks where women weave mats and children play in the water. The women and children of this village tend to be very pushy, almost insisting that you buy all their mats, and children beg persistently and delight in peering up the catwalks under visitors' skirts — wear slacks.

You should take a trip to the beautiful pink sand beaches of the **Santa Cruz islands**, which are a 25-minute boat ride from Lantaka or from the Golf and Beach Park. (The cost is about $10 per round trip; don't pay until you return; tip if you enjoyed the boatmen.) Shaped like a spear-head, **Great Santa Cruz** has a long stretch of pink sand, with shades, assorted gem vendors, a few masks and snorkels for rent, drinks, and no food. There is an interesting ancient burial ground north along the beach where the Badjao boat people come to rest on land only after death. Their grave markers are decorated with replicas of figures in boats.

On **Small Santa Cruz** you will find a stretch of pink sand beach, a white sand bar, and diving nearby.

PRACTICAL INFORMATION

Banks

All of the major Philippine banks have a branch in the city. Banking hours are Mondays through Fridays, from 9:00am to 4:00pm.

Mail

The post office is on Corcuera Street. The city also has courier companies.

Tourist Assistance

The **Regional DOT Office**, conveniently located in the Lantaka Hotel; *Tel. 991-0218, 991-2033*, is one of the best you will find in the country. It is staffed with competent and friendly people.

THE SOUTHERN ISLANDS

As you travel further south, you will be going further away from the already tenuous arm of the law. Before you go, ask about the safety of the area you intend to visit. When you get there, ask again, and arrange for a guide who knows the area and is known there. The **DOT** office at the Lantaka Hotel in Zamboanga City is a good place to start before you venture south.

BASILAN

Basilan Island is 27 kilometers from Zamboanga; again, check with the regional DOT at the Lantaka Hotel in Zamboanga City on the safety situation before going — there have been kidnappings and ambushes. When you arrive in Basilan, go to the city hall, where the tourism people in the Mayor's office will help with information for places you wish to visit. You should also ask for assistance with transportation, and settle the price before starting out.

In Isabela, look at the **Kuam Purnah Mosque** by the waterfront and shop at the **Claretcraft Handicrafts Display Center** beside Santa Isabel Cathedral. There is a relief map of the islands in the town plaza.

ARRIVALS & DEPARTURES

It will take you an hour and 30 minutes to get to **Isabela**, the capital of Basilan, from Zamboanga City. Four trips leave Zamboanga and Isabela daily, at 7:00am, 10:00am, 1:00pm, and 4:00pm. The trip costs $1.20 per person "first class" or $1.70 in an aircon room in the boats that have them.

WHERE TO STAY & EAT

There is only one basic hotel in Isabela, the **BASILAN HOTEL**, but it is no problem to return to Zamboanga for the night. A pension house is under construction, and there are several simple restaurants in town.

SEEING THE SIGHTS

You can take an interesting and well-done guided tour of the rubber plant and of the palm oil processing area of **Menzi Plantation**, only a five-minute ride from the city hall.

Get on a boat to take a peek at the **Sama Village** on the other side. The people are friendly, and wave and smile back at you as you wave. Children will dive into the swift current for coins that you throw to them. This ride alone is worth the trip to Basilan.

On the other side of Malamaui Island from the Sama Village, is the very pretty **White Beach**. The easiest way to get there is to hire a *banca* for the trip around Malamaui Island ($20). From the port of Isabela, there is a *banca* to Malamaui Island (30¢). At the **Water Farm** on the island, you can see how lobsters are raised.

Sumagdang Beach is closer to Isabela, and has a very picturesque white sand shore. Under the water, the surface is corally.

Tuesdays and Sundays are interesting days at **Lamitan**, as the Yakan bring their goods to market, dressed in their colorful tribal costumes. Lamitan is an hour by bus from Isabela, or you can take one of the three daily ferry from Zamboanga; the ferries leaves Zamboanga at 7:30 am, 1:00pm, and at 3:30pm. There are no lodging facilities in Lamitan. The food at **Nalamar** is good.

JOLO

Jolo is beautiful, but it is a traditional problem area. We suggest that you skip this island until the situation cools down considerably. Kidnapping for ransom is an occasional occurrence.

Jolo is inhabited by **Tausug** people. There are a number of beautiful white sandy beaches and several mosques on the island — **Tulay Mosque** is one of the prettiest in the country. The tomb of Sulu's first Muslim leader is on **Bud Datu**, just under two kilometers from town; there are some nice views on the hill. The market abounds with handicrafts, weaving, and fruits, and tax-free goods from surrounding countries are available at a **barter trade zone**.

TAWI-TAWI

Tawi-Tawi is a beautiful and remote province. There are no direct flights from Manila or Cebu; you will either have to take an early morning flight to Zamboanga, to catch the morning flight to Tawi-Tawi, or stay one night in Zamboanga. You will not regret the time and effort you put in to get there. If you are an active person, you will be enamored with these islands – island hop, trek, imbibe the wonderful views and the culture, mingle with the friendly islanders on Bongao, Sanga-Sanga, and other islands.

Tawi-Tawi's climate is very humid.

ARRIVALS & DEPARTURES
By Air
Your plane will touch down on the island of **Sanga-Sanga**, which is north of Bongao Island. Tawi-Tawi's the capital is Bongao. Philippine Airlines has trips Monday, Wednesday, Thursday, Friday, and Sunday that leave Zamboanga early in the morning. The trip takes one hour on a Fokker. To get to Bongao, take a jeepney (35¢ per person) or a tricycle (60¢ per tricycle); the trip takes 30-45 minutes.

By Sea
Both SKT Shipping Lines and Sampaguita Shipping have trips from Zamboanga to Bongao (via Jolo and Siasi). The long trip will take you 30-36 hours (including 9-14 hours of port time), and the boats are not for the fastidious. As Jolo is a frequent hot spot, we strongly suggest that you play it safe and fly directly from Zamboanga City to Tawi-Tawi.

WHERE TO STAY & EAT
The capital has a few places to stay, including a homestay. You can make reservations by telegram through Philippine RCPI and PT-T stations. Most of the lodging places have restaurants.

BEACHSIDE INN, *Barangay Suwangkagang. 5 rooms. $19 per single, $21-27.50 per double, $7.70 per extra person.*

Expecting the accommodations to be off-the-beaten-track, we were pleasantly surprised. The rooms were neat and clean, some with private bathrooms and air conditioners. The restaurant specializes in Filipino, Chinese, and seafood. The food is good, and people are helpful. From here you can take pleasant morning and evening strolls along the road, beside the sea.

RACHEL'S PENSION, *Lamion. 4 rooms. $15 per single or double. Manila contact c/o Mrs. Swelin Laurenti, Tel. 921-7423.*

All rooms are clean and air conditioned. You can get meals at their fast food restaurant: "You're Special Snack House."

KASULUTAN HOTEL, *Barangay Simandagit. 7 rooms. $13 per person in aircon room, $5.75 per person in fan room.*

Each room has three beds; four of the rooms are air conditioned. The restaurant specializes in local and seafood dishes. Facilities include a basketball and volleyball court.

STONEHILLS HOTEL, *Barangay Nalil. 4 cottages, 13 rooms, 3 dorm rooms. $10 per person in aircon, $5.75 in fan room. Manila contact c/o Faith Tiu, Tel. 522-4797, 522-4912.*

Four rooms are air conditioned, and each room has five beds. The large restaurant serves "any food" — if you have a request that's not on the menu, they will try and make it for you.

SOUTHERN INN, *Datu Halun Street, Bongao town proper. 10 rooms. $10 per person.*

All rooms here are fan-cooled, and there is no restaurant.

The Mayor of Bongao's office organizes homestays. Accommodations vary from air conditioned rooms to "bedspace" (sharing a room). **TAHA** (Tawi-Tawi Homestay Association), *c/o office of the Mayor, Municipal Government Center; in Zamboanga contact c/o Jocelyn Mendoza, DOT, Lantaka Hotel, Tel. 991-0218, 991-2033, Fax 991-0217.* Make arrangements at least one week in advance, and in-town tours can be arranged as well.

SEEING THE SIGHTS

On your way in from the airport, beside the bridge between Sanga-Sanga and Bongao, you will notice the attractive mosque in a village where boat building is the main industry. While on **Sanga-Sanga Island**, be sure to see the **Sama village**. There are picturesque catwalks between houses on stilts. In the houses you will see some villagers weaving beautiful mats from dyed pandan leaves. The people that live here are **Laut Sama**.

Bongao is Tawi-Tawi's capital. Its **market** is interesting, and you can get some really nice photographs at the pier. The capitol building, on a hill behind the town, looks like a mosque. You can get spectacular views from there.

If you like hiking, then the holy mountain **Bud (Mount) Bongao** (314 meters) is a great place to exercise while you climb through rain forest. You should allow four hours to go back and forth together. The views at the top are lovely. The forest on the mountain is inhabited by many **rhesus macaques**, who expect climbers to bring bananas and other food for them. Make sure you bring water for yourself, and bananas or something to share with the monkeys, who accept the food then run away. Near the top are the graves of two of the first Arab missionaries here. The graves are frequented by pilgrims; to enter you must be barefoot, and women must wear *malong* (a circular wrap). You should have some coins with you to toss onto the grave as a sign of respect. It is said that you may have three wishes granted. Those who can not enter may stand outside and toss three coins onto the canopy.

From Bongao port you can visit some of the beautiful surrounding islands. **Simunul**, south of Bongao, is the site of the first mosque in the Philippines (about 1380). The present mosque is attractive and houses the original four pillars of the first mosque. Behind this mosque is the grave of the leader of the original seven Muslim missionaries to the country. **Sangay Siapo Island**, between Bongao and Simunul, is a long narrow strip of land with no water, very shallow offshore waters good for snorkeling, and a lovely white sand beach.

PRACTICAL INFORMATION

The people on Bongao, Sanga-Sanga, and the southern islands are generally friendly and hospitable. When going to a religious shrine or marker, be respectful and remove shoes before entering a mosque.

Tours & Tourist Assistance

For all inquiries and assistance on getting around to the sights, island hopping, tours, a guide, go to the **Bongao Tourism Council**, at the Bongao Municipal Government Center; you will be in good hands.

THE FAR SOUTH

Sitangkai, which is built over a reef, is quite spectacular. It is the southernmost municipality in the Philippines. Much of the community lives in houses built on stilts over the reef that is part of the Tumindao atoll. The people make a living from the wealth of sea life in the atoll: gathering sea urchins, crabs, and diving for pearls. Processed crab meat is frozen and flown to Zamboanga.

Transport in Sitangkay, "The Philippines' Venice," is by boat through the canals or on foot along elevated walkways beside the canals or between the houses. When the tide is out, the boats can not move easily along the canals and most commerce stops until the tide returns.

Shopping includes batik and other items that come in from the sea.

ARRIVALS & DEPARTURES

The regular ferry to Sitangkai takes four hours ($1-2 per person). You may also rent a speed boat (approximately $40). When you arrive in Sitangkay, *bancas* ferry you into town, where you walk above the water through the town and shops, most of which are on stilts over the reef.

WHERE TO STAY

Because there is no formal lodging, you'll need to contact the mayor's office or ask around for home-stays. Hadji Musa Malabong is a tour guide and accepts lodgers.

INDEX

THINGS CHANGE!

Phone numbers, prices, addresses, quality of food, etc, all change. If you come across any new information, we'd appreciate hearing from you. No item is too small! Drop us an e-mail note at: Jopenroad@aol.com, or write us at:

Philippines Guide
Open Road Publishing, P.O. Box 284,
Cold Spring Harbor, NY 11724